MEMOIRS OF THE WESTMINSTER DIVINES

MEMOIRS OF THE WESTMINSTER DIVINES

James Reid

THE BANNER OF TRUTH TRUST

THE BANNER OF TRUTH TRUST
3 Murrayfield Road, Edinburgh EH12 6EL
PO Box 621, Carlisle, Pennsylvania 17013, USA

★

First published 1811
First Banner of Truth edition 1982
ISBN 0 85151 357 3

★

Printed and bound in Great Britain at
The Camelot Press Ltd, Southampton

MEMOIRS

OF THE

LIVES AND WRITINGS

OF THOSE

Eminent Divines,

WHO CONVENED IN

THE FAMOUS

ASSEMBLY AT WESTMINSTER,

IN THE

SEVENTEENTH CENTURY.

BY JAMES REID,
MINISTER OF THE GOSPEL.

"The righteous shall be in everlasting remembrance," PSALM cxii. 6.

VOL. I.

PAISLEY:

PRINTED BY STEPHEN AND ANDREW YOUNG,
High Street.

1811.

PREFACE.

BIOGRAPHY is highly useful and important. It hath been very generally esteemed: and it is commonly allowed to be, both a very pleasant and profitable method of conveying instruction unto the human mind. But here, I shall willingly borrow, from some celebrated writers, and gratefully acknowledge the debt. Montesquieu said, "What histories can be found, that please and instruct like the lives of Plutarch?" And Plutarch himself hath observed, "I live entirely upon history, and while I contemplate the pictures it presents to my view, my mind enjoys a rich repast from the representation of great and virtuous characters." Another celebrated writer says, "Among the smaller histories, *biography*, or the memoirs of the lives of great and good men, has a high rank in my esteem, as worthy of the perusal of every person who devotes himself to the study of *divinity*. Therein we frequently find our holy religion reduced to practice, and many parts of christianity shining with a transcendent and examplary light. We learn there how deeply sensible great and good men have been of the ruins of human nature by the first apostacy from God; and how they have toiled and laboured, and turned themselves on all sides, to seek recovery in vain, till they have found the gospel of Christ an all-sufficient relief. We are there furnished with effectual and unanswerable evidences that the religion of Jesus with all its self-denials, virtues, and devotions, is a very practicable thing, since it has been carried to such a degree of honour by some wise and holy men. We have been there assured, that the pleasures and satisfactions of the christian life, in its present practice and its future hopes, are not the mere raptures of fancy and enthusiasm, when some of the strictest professors of reason have added the sanction of their testimony. In short, the *lives* or *memoirs* of persons of piety, well written, have been of infinite and unspeakable advantage to the disciples and professors of christianity, and have given us admirable instances and rules how to resist every temptation of a soothing or a frowning world, how to practise important and difficult duties, how to love God above all, and to love our neighbours as ourselves, to live by the faith of the Son of God, and to die in the same faith, in sure and certain hope of a resurrection to eternal life."[a] Another observes, that "the lives of good men should be often in the hands of students of divinity. All men are interested in biographical works. These come home to our own heart and bosom. These shew what men are and have been, and what we may be through grace. Faithful biographical sketches are mighty excitements to the love and practice of religion, and the lives of faithful diligent ministers are of great use in the church."[b] From them we may readily learn how to conquer every habit that would obstruct us in the work of the Lord, how to redeem time, and to win souls to Christ. And, by their inviting example, warmly urging imitation, we may learn to be sincerely active, and resolutely passive, for Christ, and for his cause.

The design of this publication is not to "lavish encomiums on the exploits of ambitious tyrants, and bloody wide-wasting conquerors;" but to hold up to the reader's admiration, and imitation, eminently learned and religious characters, glowing with that christian zeal which is *according to knowledge*, and indefatigably diligent, in propagating the spiritual kingdom of our Lord Jesus Christ. Such amiable characters are much more entitled to the remembrance of mankind, than many of those great names which stand very high on the roll of fame,

a Watts' Improvement of the Mind, part i. chap. xx. sect. 14.
b Christian Magazine, vol. v. p. 250.

and have obtained a place among the admired writers. It is justly observed, that "historians and poets have sometimes exerted the whole force of their genius, in order to throw a lustre on the most detestable characters, and to varnish, with false colouring, the most destructive passions; while men of genuine worth have passed uncelebrated, and those labours, which tend to civilize and bless mankind, have shared but a small portion of their envied praise. Hereby they have done much injury. It is high time for them to act on a different system."[a] The life of that *great* monster of ambition and of human depravity, Alexander, has been written by many historians, or rather most fulsome panegyrists, who would have been much better employed in burying his memory in everlasting oblivion; except so far as they serve to shew what terrible and cruel scourges to the human race such dreadful ravagers of the world have been.[b] It is, therefore, high time, indeed, for the professors of christianity, the followers of *The Prince of Peace*, to act on a very different system, from those above-mentioned; and to exhibit faithful portraitures of those who have been eminently distinguished, in their generation, by their learning, their disinterested benevolence to their fellow-creatures, their laudable exertions in the cause of truth, and their piety toward God. Such persons, in any station, are justly entitled to respectful notice. And, as we always ought to esteem very highly the image and grace of God in persons of any nation or station, whether *Jews or Gentiles, bond or free, male or female;* so much respect is due both to the characters and memories of those who possess these: for *the righteous shall be in everlasting remembrance.* Agreeably to this remark, much respect, undoubtedly, must be due unto both the characters and memories of faithful, able, and pious, ministers of the gospel of Christ. Such *are ambassadors for Christ*, assiduously employed, in God's name, and in Christ's stead, to entreat and beseech sinners of the human race, to *be*

a Monthly Review enlarged, vol. v. p. 342.
b See Monthly Review, vol. xiv. p. 435.

reconciled unto God, 2 Cor. v. 20. And, certainly, some tribute is due to the memories of these servants of the living God, who have been indefatigably diligent, faithful and zealous, in *serving him with their spirit in the gospel of his Son.*

Among such respectable characters, the divines who assembled at Westminster, in the seventeenth century, may be justly ranked. Their names are truly illustrious, and worthy of being enrolled among the most celebrated characters of their age, or of their country. Their exemplary lives, and religious experiences, are most excellent mirrors of instruction, which may be highly beneficial to all succeeding generations. They willingly spent an active life, in propagating the gospel of Jesus Christ, and in diffusing profitable and religious knowledge among mankind: and it may very justly be said of them, that they were really *eyes to the blind.* Whatever their hand could write, whatever their tongue could speak, whatever their head could devise, was most solemnly dedicated to the service of God, and to the cause of truth. They did much for the benefit of posterity, when corruption was deeply rooted, and had widely extended it's baneful influence. They flourished, during the time of our Reformation, and were very active in promoting it.

It is justly observed, that, "the rise and progress of the Reformation, in the different countries of Europe, must ever be regarded as presenting one of the most important and striking objects that hath occurred in the revolutions of the human mind, and in the history of the world." [a] And the period of Reformation shines with peculiar lustre in the British annals; and our reforming ancestors ought to be gratefully remembered. All who wish well to society will highly honour their memories; and cheerfully pay their tribute of respect unto them, *after they have served their own generation by the will of God, are fallen asleep, and are gathered unto their fathers.* We happily enjoy the precious fruits of that great

a Universal Magazine, vol. lxxxv. p. 293.

and providential *national deliverance*, the Reformation, though we are but little thankful for them. Nor have we religiously regarded, as we ought, the wonderful operation of the Lord's hand, in seasonably raising up the honoured instruments of this glorious work. And, we have not sufficiently valued either the memorials of the lives, or of the writings of our illustrious reformers. It is high time for us to amend, and to learn from others. Memoirs of the lives of heathen philosophers, of the notable statesmen and warriors of antiquity, have been very highly valued. Plutarch's lives of the famous Greeks and Romans have been so highly esteemed by the learned, and accounted a treasure of such utility and importance, that some have affirmed, "if it were proposed to destroy all the literary works of the Pagan world, except one, Plutarch's lives should be preserved as the most pleasing, instructive and useful." And certainly the lives of our illustrious reformers are not less worthy of esteem. And their writings may be accounted the best wealth, which they could leave behind them at their death, for the benefit of posterity. They contain useful truths; serving to inform the understanding, and to affect the heart and the life. And if they fail to reform, and to be beneficial to this age and country, they may, perhaps, operate upon succeeding generations, and the inhabitants of other countries, and extend their influence to the remotest posterity, under the blessing of God. Other writers, no doubt, have, in later times, advanced beyond them in some things; but they have at least cleared the road, and much facilitated the progress of their successors. And modern improvements are often little more than a revival of the learning of former times, with some alterations, especially in the composition of the English language.

As the particular design of this publication is to give some view of the lives and writings of those eminent divines, who met in the famous Assembly at Westminster; the bright, learned, and pious, constellation, which adorned that very active period of the Reformation, it may probably be expected, that some account should be given of that Assembly, and of the period of the Reformation, in this preface. Supposing that this may be the expectation of some, the following remarks are offered, concerning the occasion and nature of this truly venerable Assembly, and the times, as a key to these memoirs. When King James, the VI. of Scotland, ascended the English throne, upon the union of the two crowns, in the year 1603, he keenly aimed at arbitrary power, and the establishment of episcopacy in his dominions. He distinguished the bishops with very peculiar marks of his favour, extended their power, increased their prerogative, and publicly adopted and inculcated the following maxim; *No Bishop, no King*. He was now a most zealous defender of episcopal government, though he had oftener than once expressed himself against it in the strongest terms. King James died, in the year 1625. His son and successor Charles the I. was confirmed by education, in every speculative tenet which his father had adopted, and had fully imbibed his father's principles. He keenly and resolutely followed the steps of his father, and viewed episcopacy as congenial to monarchy. He used every effort, to extend the royal prerogative, and raise the power of the crown above the authority of the law, to bring all the churches in *Great Britain and Ireland*, under the jurisdiction of bishops, and to suppress the opinions and institutions that were peculiar to Calvinism. William Laud, bishop of London, who was afterward raised, in the year 1633, to the see of Canterbury, was chiefly intrusted by the king with the execution of this arduous plan.[a]

King Charles made a journey to Scotland, his native kingdom, in the year 1633, attended by the court, in order to hold a parliament there, and to receive his crown. The coronation was performed by the archbishop of St Andrew's, but this, though very splendid, was rendered less impressive by the introduction of an altar, and of unaccustomed rites, which the people view-

a Laing's Hisory of Scotland, vol. i. books 1. & 2. Mosheim's Eccles. Hist. vol. v. cent. xvii. sect. ii. part ii. chap. ii. xix. xx.

ed with abhorrence, and were not able to distinguish from the Romish mass. These innovations were ascribed to Laud, whose ascendency over the king began to be perceptible, and his imprudent interference in ecclesiastical affairs was highly offensive to the Scottish nation. It was observed at the coronation, that this haughty prelate displaced the archbishop of Glasgow with the most indecent violence from the king's side, because that moderate prelate scrupled to officiate in the embroidered habits prescribed for his order.[a] The earl of Clarendon, the famous English historian on the king's side, readily allows, that when king Charles made this journey to Scotland, to be crowned there, he carried with him the resolution of propagating episcopacy in that kingdom, and of bringing the church of Scotland to a conformity with the church of England, in all things. For that end, Laud, who was then bishop of London, attended the king in his journey, which, as he was dean of the chapel, he was not obliged to do, and no doubt would have been excused from, if that design had not been in view; to accomplish which he was no less solicitous than the king himself, nor the king the less solicitous for his advice. He preached in the royal chapel at Edinburgh, which scarcely any English man had ever done before in the king's presence, and principally upon the benefit of conformity, and the reverend ceremonies of the church.[b] An episcopal see was erected at Edinburgh, the metropolis of the kingdom, with a diocese extending over ancient Lothian, from the Forth to Berwick; the fairest church in the town was appointed to be the cathedral, and a competent revenue was settled upon the bishop, out of the lands purchased by the king himself, from the duke of Lennox, who sold these much the cheaper, that they might be consecrated to that end.[c]

a Laing's Hist. B. ii. 1633.

b Clarendon's Hist. vol. i. B. i. p. 81 & 82.

N. B. I have generally used Clarendon's History of the Rebellion and Civil Wars in England, Oxford, 1712, in 6 vols. though I have also consulted the folio edition, and sometimes refer to it.

c Laing's Hist. vol. i. B. ii. p. 104. Clarendon, vol. i. B. i. p. 86.

The Scots generally thought, that they had too many bishops before, and this increase of the number was not very agreeable to them. The king returned to England about the end of August, in the year 1633, according to Clarendon. Immediately after his return, he heard the report of archbishop Abbot's death: and, without delay, he conferred that high dignity on his favourite, Laud, who now succeeded Abbot in the see of Canterbury. This business was very quickly dispatched; for we are told, that about a month after the death of the good and grave archbishop Abbot, Laud was completely invested with that high dignity, and settled in his palace at Lambeth. And, by this accession of power, he was now enabled to maintain ecclesiastical discipline with greater rigour, and to aggravate the general discontent in the nation.[a] A respectable historian applies to Laud, what was said of Boniface, "He entered like a fox, he reigned like a lion, and he died like a dog."[b] Juxon, a particular favourite of Laud, was, by his influence, made bishop of London.[c] And, upon the death of the earl of Portland, the archbishop was made one of the commissioners of the treasury, and had interest enough to engage the king to make bishop Juxon high treasurer, one of the highest offices of the crown. The greatest of the nobility, who were in the chiefest employments, expected that this great and beneficial office would be conferred upon one of them: but all were much astonished, when, suddenly, the staff was put into the hands of the bishop of London, a man so little known, that his name was scarcely heard of in the kingdom, who had been, within two years before, but a private chaplain to the king, and the president of a poor college in Oxford. This unexpected promotion gave very great and general offence. The puritans, also, were much dissatisfied with Juxon; and had sufficient reason.[d]

The king continued to raise the bishops to secular

a Clarendon, vol. i. p. 89. Hume's Hist. vol. vi. chap. lii. 1633.
b Stevenson, vol. i. p. 115.
c Clarendon, vol. i. B. i. p. 91.
d Clarendon, vol. i. p. 98 & 99. and Hume, as above.

offices. Upon the death of the earl of Kinnoul, chancellor of Scotland, Spottiswood, archbishop of St Andrew's, was made chancellor, who was ambitious in his old age to unite the first office of the state with that of the church. The great seal had never before been entrusted to an ecclesiastic since the Reformation. The lord treasurer's office, the next in dignity, was solicited by Maxwell, bishop of Ross. Of fourteen prelates, nine were already introduced into the privy council, where their numbers often preponderated, and their intolerable insolence oftentimes provoked disgust. Their pride was immoderate, and their presumption excessive. They readily procured a warrant from the infatuated and despotical monarch to establish subordinate courts of commission; and with six assistants whom they chose to associate with themselves, to exercise in each diocese the inquisitorial powers of the high commission. Greatly elated with their sudden and high exaltation, and presuming on the patient acquiescence of the nation in their lofty measures, they vainly imagined that there was no undertaking beyond their strength; but they reckoned without their host. To such men, the compilation of a liturgy and of canons was entrusted.[a]

Laud excited the king to order the framing of a liturgy or prayer-book for the use of the church of Scotland in her worship, and a book of canons for her government and discipline, and to impose these by royal and episcopal authority, without consent of parliament or of general assembly.[b] And the Scottish bishops were enjoined to prepare them, and trasmit them to Laud, who, with Juxon and Wren, revised and corrected them; and being approved and confirmed by the king, he issued his proclamation for the due observation of them within his kingdom of Scotland.[c] The canons, the more concise production, were first compiled. And they were con-

a Clarendon, vol. i. page 87, 103, 104, 105, 106, 107. Laing. vol. i. B. ii. 1636. Burnet's Hist. of his own times, vol. i. p. 32.

b Stevenson, vol. i. p. 131.

c Clarendon, as above.

firmed by the royal supremacy, which was itself inversely confirmed, and extended by the canons to a full power over the church; requiring that national, or general assemblies should be called *only* by the king's authority; —that none should receive the sacrament but upon their knees; that the clergy should not even conceive an extemporary prayer, but be bound to pray *only* by the form which was prescribed in the liturgy; and that no man should teach a public school, nor in a private house, without a license first obtained from the archbishop of the province, or the bishop of the diocese. And the consecration and power of the prelates were strongly secured from challenge, by the awful penalty of excommunication, much aggravated by confiscation and outlawry, it's civil effects.

Sessions and presbyteries were indirectly suppressed, under the description of irregular conventicles: and their powers were wantonly transferred to the tribunal of the bishops; lay-elders were dismissed from the church, and the whole beautiful structure of presbyterian jurisdiction was at once demolished. A font was ordered to be placed in the entrance, and an altar in the chancel, of the church; the one, in the opinion of the presbyterians, for consecrated water, the other for the idolatrous oblation of the host. And their suspicions were strongly confirmed by several superstitious injunctions; that the remains of the elements, as if actually transubstantiated, should be consumed in the church by the poorer communicants; that ordination, like a real sacrament, should be restricted to four seasons of the year; that the penitent's confessions, a sure sign of auricular confession, should be concealed by the clergy. And the last canon enjoined, that no person should be received into holy orders, suffered to preach, or administer the sacraments, without first subscribing these canons. The liturgy was transcribed from that of the English, with some alterations, which approached nearer to the Romish missal. The consecration of the elements was a prayer expressive of the real presence, and their elevation from the altar of an actual oblation. Thanks were given for departed saints, of whom the calender received a large addition appropriated to Scotland; the cross was enjoined in baptism, and the ring in marriage, while the baptismal water was changed and consecrated twice a-month, and retained for future ministration in the font.[a] Laud was excessively superstitious; and he executed the plans of his royal master, with great rigour. He revived many rites and ceremonies, which were very strongly marked with the turpitude of superstition, that takes the place of religion, and had been very justly abrogated on that account. And he gave many and very plain intimations, that he viewed the Romish church, with all her errors, as purer, and preferable upon the whole, to those protestant churches that were not subject to the jurisdiction of bishops. Laud, by his sentiments, and by his violent measures, drew an odium on the king, on himself, and on the episcopal order in general.[b]

A report was soon spread, that the new liturgy was a translation of the mass, which the prelates had conspired with Laud to establish: and it was generally believed that the church was already undermined, and that the religion of the nation was about to be subverted. The alarm was speedily communicated to all ranks. And the manner in which the liturgy was imposed, by the regal and episcopal power, or rather tyranny, gave great offence. The advice of the privy council; the approbation of the aged and experienced prelates, and the consent of the General Assembly, were alike disregarded. Spottiswood remonstrated, but was obliged to co-operate, and the privy council were forcibly driven to concur in the design. A proclamation had been issued for a general conformity to the liturgy at Easter; but affairs were so badly concerted, that the publication of the service was delayed until the day had elapsed. Upon this, a charge was directed to the clergy, to purchase two copies for each parish; but the council still delayed to en-

a Clarendon, B. ii. vol. i. Laing, vol. i. B. ii. 1636, & 1637. Baillie's Letters, vol. i. p. 1.

b Mosheim's Eccles. Hist. vol. v. cent. xvii. sect. ii. part ii. chap. ii. xx.

force the observance of the charge. The Scottish liturgy was arraigned as worse than the English, and not less impure than the mass itself. But the prelates, who had conspired with Laud and the king to establish it, warmly urged an implicit conformity to it, and threatened the contumacious with the severe penalties of the ecclesiastical censures with which the canons were sanctioned; depravation, outlawry, and the confiscation of their estates. It was about the month of July, in the year 1637, that the liturgy was published, and appointed to be read in all the churches.[a] When an order for the immediate observance of it was obtained from court, without the concurrence or knowledge of the privy council, this was intimated from the pulpit on the sabbath day immediately preceding it's introduction in Edinburgh. The people were greatly agitated by discourses and pamphlets against the liturgy, during that whole week, without any satisfactory recommendation of it: and the whole city was filled with complaints.[b] On sabbath, the 23d of July, the dean of Edinburgh prepared to officiate in St Gile's church, and the bishop of Argyle in the Grayfriars: and to increase the solemnity, each was attended by judges, prelates, a part of the council, and a large concourse of people, much excited by the novelty of the spectacle. The congregation continued quiet until the service began, when an aged woman, impelled by the ardour of her zeal, suddenly arose, and exclaimed aloud, "Villain! dost thou say the mass at my lug!" The greatest confusion instantaneously commenced: and the service was at once interrupted. From the examination of those who were apprehended, there is no appearance that this commotion originated from any secret instigation, or preconcerted design. The bishops keenly urged the service, throughout the rest of Scotland, but were generally unsuccessful, except at St Andrew's, and in the cathedrals of Brechin, Dumblain, and Ross.[c]

a Baillie's Letters, vol. i. lett. ii. Clarendon's Hist. vol. i. B. ii. p. 108. Laing's Hist. vol. i. B. ii. 1637.

b Baillie's Letters, as above.

c Laing, as above.

The former charge, to purchase or receive the liturgy, was executed by the chancellor against the celebrated Mr Henderson, and other nonconforming ecclesiastics, and pointedly directed by the archbishop of Glasgow against all the presbyteries within his diocese. Mr Henderson supplicated the council to suspend the charge, as the new service was not yet authorised by an assembly of the church, nor confirmed by the parliament. Similar petitions, from the presbyteries of Irvine and Glasgow, were warmly recommended by letters from the nobility, and the personal application of many private gentlemen. Mr Baillie says, "All the council were most earnest to satisfy the country, in holding off the yoke of that black book." But their representations were wantonly disregarded or suspected, by an infatuated monarch, who was inflexible in his pursuit of conformity.[a] Affairs now assumed a very serious aspect. The king severely reprehended the lenity of the council on this occasion; and peremptorily enjoined the immediate observance of the ritual. The numbers of the supplicants, who were against the liturgy, daily increased. Supplications were presented from two hundred parishes; and the recalling, or prohibition of the liturgy, would have dissipated every alarm, and removed every complaint, at this time. But two very injudicious proclamations were most inconsiderately issued, enjoining the supplicants to depart from Edinburgh; transferring the seat of government and of justice to Linlithgow; and suspending the consideration of ecclesaistical affairs. These proclamations gave great offence: and a formal accusation was prepared against the prelates, as the authors of a liturgy wherein the seeds of superstition and of idolatry were sown; and of canons whereby the constitution of the church was inverted. This was subscribed by the nobility, the gentry, the clergy, afterward by all ranks, and almost by every corporation in the kingdom.[b] As the late tumults were ascribed to the confluence of the supplicants, they appointed a few as representatives of the rest, in order to prosecute

a Baillie, vol. i. lett. ii. Bishop Guthrie's Memoirs, p. 24, 25. Laing. See Memoirs of Mr Henderson's Life.

b Baillie, vol. i. lett. iv. and Laing, as above.

their complaint against the prelates, and to await the result of their applications to the king. The council, not instructed by Charles, and fearing fresh commotions, acquiesced in the proposal, and a new order was instantly established. A proportion of the nobility was first appointed; and two of the gentry from each county, from each presbytery and borough, one or more of the ministers and burgesses were selected as commissioners for their respective orders. This was the institution of the justly celebrated Tables. The commissioners convened separately in the parliament house, and sat around tables, from which the association obtained the name. Rapin says, The Tables were composed of the most able persons in Scotland.[a] And, they were every where obeyed, with the utmost regularity. Order and union were consolidated by this famous institution.

The supplicants were soon prohibited to assemble, by a proclamation from the king, under the penalties of treason, when they were asking nothing but the preservation of their religious liberties. An alarm was quickly communicated to the whole body of supplicants: and now their grievances must either be perpetuated by a tame submission, or the means of redress preserved by their spirited opposition to the unreasonable edict. And, when the proclamation was announced by heralds, a protest was taken by the lords Hume and Lindsay against it's authority, and, with due solemnity, published and affixed to the market-cross of Stirling, whither the council and courts of justice were removed, Feb. 1638. The Tables now warmly recommended judicious and solemn measures, to cement the union of the supplicants; the renewal of their memorable national covenant, which may be traced to the beginning of the Reformation, when the nobility, or lords of the congregation, by their bond or covenant, first undertook the protection of the infant church, with preparatory fasting and prayer.[b] They readily recollected, that their venerable ancestors had repeatedly bound

a Rapin's Hist. of England, vol. ii. B. xix. 1638. p. 305.
b See Knox's Hist. Reform. in Scotland.

themselves, in times of great danger, by a solemn covenant, to continue in the true protestant religion, and to support each other in that common cause, against all their enemies; and they gratefully followed the example. This famous covenant contained a general profession of the true christian faith and religion of the reformed churches; and a most minute renounciation of popery, including all that is contrary to sound doctrine and the power of godliness. And, it was wisely adapted to the innovations and corruptions which had been particularly mentioned in their late supplications, complaints, and protestations, and to the circumstances in which the covenanters were then placed, and herein it was very different from what was called the king's covenant, afterward enjoined. And, the defence of religion was particularly qualified by the conditional support of the king. It was sworn with the greatest alacrity and solemnity, and subcribed by persons of all ranks, both in the years 1638 and 1639; and approved by the General Assembly of the church of Scotland.[a] This solemn engagement was judiciously and successfully opposed to the king's illegal measures, which were subversive of the constitutional and religious rights of the nation. And, though every application of the covenanters was disdainfully rejected at court; and their petitions were contumeliously returned unopened; yet *their labour was not in vain in the Lord.* By that most famous assembly at Glasgow, toward the end of the year 1638, episcopacy, the high-commission, the articles of Perth, the canons, and the liturgy, were at once completely abolished, and solemnly declared to be unlawful: and presbyteries were restored to their original rights. And thus the whole baseless fabric, which James and Charles had reared with much care and policy, was levelled with the ground.[b]

It ought also to be observed here, that the puritans suffered exceedingly in England, during Laud's severe

a See The National Covenant, and Laing's Hist. vol. i. B. ii. 1638.

b For a more particular account of this famous assembly, and what followed in the most active period of the reformation, See Mr Henderson's Life.

administration. He loaded them with injuries and vexations, and aimed at nothing less than their total extinction. He was much enraged by their nonconformity and faithfulness. And, Arminianism, the harbinger of popery, greatly prevailed, and was much countenanced, while he was high in place. Clarendon says, that Laud had eminently opposed Calvin's doctrine all his life, before the name of Arminius was noticed, or his opinions heard of.[a] And, Laud wrote a small treatise in support of the Arminian doctrines; in the year 1625. And, by his great credit with the duke of Buckingham, he prevailed to have Arminian and anti-puritanical chaplains placed about the king. Upon this, the Arminian doctrines were promoted by the warmest encouragements, and daily gained ground under the protection of the court.[b] And, such as have aimed at arbitrary power, have uniformly considered popery as the most convenient prop for despotism; and Arminianism as most conducive to the firm erection of this prop. And here, "the superinduction of popish ceremonies, was to clear the way for that of popish Arminianism: which two streams, when united in their course, were to have emptied themselves into the dead sea of arbitrary power. Or, such was the plan of that goodly pillar, which was to be erected, as a trophy, on the grave of departed liberty: Arminianism was to have been the base; popery the shaft; and tyranny the capital that should terminate the whole." [c]

Error now raged like the pestilence, and immorality and corruption overflowed the land like a flood. And as an unlimited power was exercised by the crown, the state, at the same time, groaned under an intolerable burden of oppression. The king very plainly intimated, both in his speeches and in his deportment, that he considered parliaments as chiefly designed to supply him with money, and in case of refusal, that he could proceed

a Clarendon's Hist. vol. i. B. i. p. 93.

b Mosheim's Eccles. Hist. vol. v. cent. xvii. sect. ii. part. ii. chap. ii. xx. Lond. edit. 1790.

c Toplady's Historic Proof, vol. i. sect. ii. foot-note: and vol. ii. sect. xx.

without their assistance. Accordingly, he dissolved several parliaments, because they did not readily grant the sums which he demanded. And, by their long intermission, many very unwarrantable things were practised. And, upon their dissolution, the king attempted compulsory loans, or taxations imposed by his own arbitrary power, disguised under the name of *benevolences;* and the non-compliers were imprisoned: a striking violation of the liberty of the subject. And such numbers were thrown into prison, that the council-table now had almost as much work to provide prisons as to supply the king's necessities. And, that the ecclesiastics might contribute their share to the support of the monarch's arbitrary claims, sermons were preached by Sibthorpe and Munwaring, in favour of the general loan: and the court industriously spread them over the kingdom. Passive obedience was there warmly recommended in its full extent, the whole authority of the state was represented as belonging to the king *alone*, and all limitations of law and of a constitution were disdainfully rejected as seditious and impious. And the consent of the parliament was not accounted necessary for raising aids and subsidies. A commission was openly granted, to compound with the Roman catholics, and to agree for dispensing with the penal laws enacted against them, which was highly offensive to the king's protestant subjects. Complaints universally prevailed, that the people were reduced to slavery. The rights and liberties of the whole nation were most wantonly invaded. And all mankind were greatly astonished, when in such awful circumstances, the infatuated Charles, baffled in every attempt against the Austrian dominions, and much embroiled with his own subjects, most inconsiderately entered into a war with France.[a] The king's privy council became by degrees an absolute court, which considered itself above the laws. The court of star-chamber extended its power; and it was matter of complaint, that it encroached upon the jurisdiction of the other courts;

a Clarendon, vol. i. B. i. Hume's Hist. of England, vol. vi. chap. 50. Rapin's Hist. of England, B. xix.

imposing heavy fines and inflicting severe punishments, beyond the usual course of justice, upon those who pretended to dispute the royal prerogative. As Thucydides said of the Athenians, these courts "held for honourable, that which pleased, and for just, that which profited."[a] And the very arbitrary court of high-commission, which had assigned to it the defence of the ecclesiastical establishment, completely seconded the council and star-chamber, and under the excuse of preventing schism, greatly oppressed, as puritans, those who refused submission to an entirely despotic power.[b] And the authority of parliament being shaken off by dissolution, arbitrary power reigned absolutely without it, for eleven years. After this long intermission of parliaments, and after the king had tried many irregular methods of taxation, and amid his most pressing necessities, he summoned an English parliament to assemble in April, 1640. He designed that they should not have a long session, nor enter immediately upon grievances, and, therefore, he at once made application for large supplies of money, to carry on war against the Scots, whom many in the house regarded as their best friends, and firmest allies. The house of commons entered immediately upon grievances, according to the ancient practice of parliament, and the king hastily dissolved this parliament, as he formerly had done, which gave great and general offence.[c] He was now obliged to have recourse to other expedients, being disappointed of parliamentary subsidies. And, being unsuccessful in his unreasonable war with his Scottish subjects, he was reduced to extreme distress. The Scottish army gained a complete victory over the English, at Newburn upon Tyne, on the 28th Aug. 1640. To prevent the advance of the victorious army upon him, the king agreed to a treaty of peace, which was begun at Rippon, and afterward transferred to London. The causes of disgust, which had been long multiplied, were now come to full maturity, and threatened the British dominions with some dreadful convulsion. A

a Clarendon, as above, p. 68.
b Rapin, as above.
c Clarendon, vol. 1. B. ii. Hume, vol. vi. chap. liii.

parliament was generally and anxiously desired. When the despotic king, could not stem the overflowing torrent, he was obliged at last to yield to it. And the people being greatly and generally discontented, a parliament was called, denominated the long parliament, which met, Nov. 3d, 1640, and, from the situation of public affairs, could not be abruptly dissolved, and which was to execute every thing which was left unfinished by former parliaments. On the election of the commons, the most pious and patriotic members were returned to parliament. Dr Welwood affirms, that no age ever produced greater men than those who sat in this parliament.[a] The house of commons was full, and the members numerous, from the commencement of the meeting. And, greatly animated with a warm regard for liberty, those generous patriots viewed with regret the evils which prevailed, under the unlimited power which had been long exercised by the crown. A Pym, and a Hambden, were illustrious names in the cause of liberty. An examinaton of grievances, was the first object that engrossed their attention. And, in all they did, for some years, they closely pursued legal and constitutional measures. They mercifully relieved many prisoners, who were confined by the arbitrary courts above-mentioned, and some of them most cruelly handled, especially Mr Prynne, and Dr Leighton.[b] The star-chamber, high-commission, and other arbitrary courts, were suppressed or regulated; monopolies, ship-money, and other illegal exactions abolished; triennial parliaments were enacted to be held, and a bill passed for the continuance of this parliament, which could not be dissolved without the consent of both houses.

The Scottish commissioners were sent to London to conclude the treaty of pacification, where they were received with great veneration and esteem, and heartily concurred with the English parliament in promoting the work of reformation. Antholine's church was assigned them for their worship, when their chaplains, the eminent divines who

a Rapin. See their character by Clarendon, vol. i. B. iii. Neal's Hist. Purit. vol. ii. chap. vii. Vicar's England's Parliamentary Chronicle. p. 25.

b See Neal's Hist. as above.

attended them, preached. The celebrated Mr Henderson also took his turn here, who was one of the commissioners of the treaty in all matters relating to religion.[a] They greatly encouraged the petitions of the English, to abolish episcopacy root and branch. And their zeal was particularly conspicuous in the treaty, where they strongly urged as the firm basis of a permanent concord, an unity of religion, and uniformity of church government in both kingdoms, warmly recommending the presbyterian form.[b]

Some necessary concessions were now made in favour of the liberty of the subject; but after a very arbitrary reign of fifteen years, the concessions extorted from Charles were justly deemed insincere, and the constitution without proper security, unless the power by which it was invaded were circumscribed, and the repetition of grievances effectually prevented. And the king completely discovered himself, by a most imprudent and fatal step, which speedily produced the most dismal consequences. He preferred an impeachment of high treason, on Jan. 3d, 1642, against lord Kimbolton, and five members of the house of commons, Pym, Hambden, Hollis, Haslerig, and Strode, for conspiring against the king, and the parliament. Their persons were first demanded by a sergeant at arms; but the commons sent a message to the king, "that the members should be forthcoming as soon as a legal charge should be preferred against them" Next day, the king went in person to the house, attended by his guard and retinue, and claimed the accused members from the commons; but they had retired from the house before the king's arrival. He proceeded further to expose his dignity to the contempt of the city, by the same vain requisition at guildhall. He departed without receiving that applause which he expected. And, in passing through the streets, he heard the cry, *Privilege of Parliament! Privilege of Parliament!* resounding from all quarters. One of the populace, drawing near his coach, called out, *To your tents*,

a Clarendon, vol. i. p. 189.
b Laing, vol. i. p. 185.

O Israel![a] Breach of privilege resounded every where. And, the king, entirely disappointed in his design, retired from Whitehall, to which he never returned till a captive. Mr Hume says "The whole world stood amazed at this important accusation, so suddenly entered upon, without concert, deliberation, or reflection."[b] And the severe blow, which the king levelled at those illustrious patriots, recoiled upon himself. And the oppressive policy of this arbitrary reign, terminated in a violent rupture between the king and the parliament, which was followed with a most affecting civil war. Both the aggressor, and the defender, made an appeal to the sword.

Upon the king leaving the parliament, they were obliged either to go home, and leave all affairs in the hands of the king and his party, or to act by themselves, as the guardians of the people, in this very critical time. They ventured to stand forth in their own defence, and to perform such acts of sovereignty, as were necessary to prevent the arbitrary court from trampling upon the liberties and religion of their country. Error, corruption, and confusion, generally prevailed. The faithful ministers of the gospel of Christ, were silenced, imprisoned, and banished, by the imperious bishops, and arbitrary courts above-mentioned, as may be seen in the following memoirs. And there were very different opinions, concerning the doctrine, worship, discipline, and government of the church.

In this dismal state of affairs, the illustrious patriots of this memorable parliament resolved to call an assembly of judicious, learned, and pious, divines, for consultation, and the settlement of the affairs of the church, agreeably to the oracles of God: and that they might enjoy the benefit of the administrations of those divines, at this critical time. Accordingly, this famous assembly was not a convention agreeably to the diocesan government; nor was it called by the votes of ministers, in the presbyterian form; but by the parliament in extraordinary cir-

a Clarendon, vol. ii. B. iv. p. 356—361. Vicar's Parliamentary Chron. p. 65, 66.

b Hume's Hist. vol. vi. chap. lv. 1642.

cumstances, when extraordinary things may be done. They resolved at the commencement of their meeting to remove the grievances of the church as well as those of the state, and for this purpose to address the king to call an assembly of divines. To promote this design, the London ministers, in their petitions, in the year 1641, entreated the houses to use means with the king for a free synod. The commons, accordingly, mentioned it in their grand remonstrance, Dec. 1st, 1641. In the Oxford-treaty, a bill was presented to the same purpose, but rejected. Afterward, Dr Burgess, at the head of the puritan clergy, applied again to parliament, but they were unwilling to take this step without the king, till they were obliged to call the Scots to their aid, who insisted, that there should be an uniformity of doctrine and discipline between the two nations. To make for this, the houses turned their bill into an ordinance, and convened an assembly of learned and pious divines, by their own authority.[a]

Though these divines were illustrious for their learning, and venerable for their piety; yet they come in for their large dividend in the share of misrepresentation, and of gross calumnies. The divine maxim was particularly verified in them: "Yea, and all who will live godly in Christ Jesus shall suffer persecution," 2 Tim. iii. 12. They suffered very much both from the tongue and from the pen of their enemies. They, indeed, were in the regions of the torrid zone of persecution *for righteousness' sake*, when they sat in the assembly at Westminster. We have a remarkable proof of this in Clarendon's history. He says, speaking of this venerable assembly, "There were not above twenty, of the one hundred and twenty members, who were not declared, and avowed enemies to the doctrine, or discipline of the church of England; some of them infamous in their lives, and conversations; and most of them of very mean parts in learning, if not of scandalous ignorance; and of no other reputation, than of malice, to the church of England." [b] This is censure, but little

a Neal's Hist. Purit. vol. iii. chap. ii.
b Clarendon's Hist. Rebellion, vol. i. B. v. p. 415. fol. Ox. 1702.

short of universal. A bold assertion indeed; but without any proof. An assertion which truth keenly stares in the face, and plainly contradicts. Before this remarkable stigma of infamy had been cast on the names of those eminent divines, in the page of history, their principles, their conduct, and their motives, should have been very accurately weighed in a just balance, which certainly was not done by this historian. It is well observed, "Both the actions and the characters of men who render themselves conspicuous in very interesting periods, and during the shock and ebullition of great and singular revolutions, are weighed by cotemporary writers in balances with arms of unequal length; so that they sink down or *kick the beam*, not in exact proportion to their true merit or demerit, but as the prejudice or partiality of the historian has placed them in this or that scale." [a] And such illiberality does not become the historian. It is a very bad assistant to argument; for it disgraces a good, and cannot serve a bad, cause. And, certainly, some evidence may be justly required in support of the charges which the historian brings against this respectable body of ministers, whom he treats with the utmost severity. But, when we carefully examine what he adduces respecting this, we find nothing: and the evidence here rests solely on assertion, and on the construction which the author himself is pleased to put on the characters and conduct of these eminent servants of Jesus Christ. "It has been a good old custom with authors, who were modest enough not to be offended if their readers were not disposed to take assertion for proof, particularly when it was made in opposition to generally received opinions, to elucidate their propositions by examples, and to support them by arguments drawn from reason and authority." [b] I sincerely wish that the earl of Clarendon had strictly adhered to this very laudable custom; and had condescended clearly to state the grounds on which he rested his strong assertions, especially with reference to public and respectable characters,

a Monthly Review Enlarged, vol. xiv. p. 177.
b Monthly Review Enlarged, vol. xiv. p. 274.

to which he has often been very partial. Mr Hume says, "He is less partial in his relation of facts, than in his account of characters: He was too honest to falsify the former, his affections were easily capable, unknown to him self, of disguising the latter." [a] In his account of the characters of the members of the Westminster Assembly, he is undoubtedly very partial, and has greatly disguised them. And the author of the critical history of England, in his treatise entitled, "Clarendon and Whitlocke compared," says, The editors of the lord Clarendon s history have hardly left one fact, or one character on the parliament side, fairly represented. "I was long hesitating on the hard *words* in the title of this treatise, scarce one *fact*, or one *character* fairly represented: and I turned the history of the Rebellion over and over again, to find out *one* that might be called *fair*, which I have not yet found on the side of the parliament." [b] If we deal honestly, we cannot give much credit to the earl of Clarendon's account of the characters of the members of that venerable assembly, according to the above representation of him, which many will account very equitable. A large and respectable body of mankind did and will acknowledge, that the members of that famous assembly, in general, eminently possessed solid learning, true candour, zeal according to knowledge, and a conversation becoming the gospel of Christ: and the opinion of such cannot reasonably be surrendered to the authority of his lordship's *ipse dixit*, whose narrative is very strongly tinctured with prejudice and partiality, and highly impregnated with party spirit. And, certainly, "to load with abrupt obloquy names which the wisest and best of men have for ages agreed to revere, is an offence, not indeed to be punished by the judges, but to be reprobated with indignation by all good men." [c] And it ought to be carefully observed, that the persecutions, which these eminent divines had the honour to suffer, were occasioned by a very close attachment to the best of all causes, that of

a Hume's Hist. Eng. vol. vii. chap. lxii. end.
b Clarendon and Whitlocke compared, title and preface.
c Monthly Review Enlarged, vol. xiv. p. 461.

truth, which makes mankind indeed free. And, as the wisdom and excellencies of Socrates, while they procured him many followers, also created him many enemies;[a] so did the piety, zeal, and faithfulness. of our reforming ancestors, when they signally distinguished themselves by their magnanimous appearance in the cause of God and of truth.

They were much extolled by some, and greatly decried by others, when most diligently employed in the most important services of the church of Christ. What Mr Sulivan observes concerning chymistry, may be fitly applied unto those eminent divines who met in the assembly at Westminster. He says, "Chymistry is an art which, perhaps of all others, has been the most extolled by its admirers, and the most condemned by its opponents."[b] And these divines, perhaps of all others, have been the most extolled by their admirers, and the most decried and condemned by their opponents.

And, there is some probability, that the earl of Clarendon may have been engaged, in writing his history, to expose our reformers, as Aristophanes was to expose Socrates. The Sophists, and other opponents of Socrates, upon finding their own reputation and emoluments daily declining, they became inveterate in their enmity against this bold reformer, and eagerly seized every opportunity of exposing him to public ridicule or censure. And they engaged Aristophanes, the first buffoon of the age, to write a comedy, entitled, "The Clouds," wherein Socrates is introduced hanging in a basket in the air, and thence pouring forth absurdity and profaneness.[c]

But be that as it may, the earl of Clarendon is certainly very partial in his account of characters; and he so holds the candle, that with it's shadow, he industriously endeavours to darken every thing that was excellent and amiable in such as appeared for the glorious work of Reformation. The author of Clarendon and

a Enfield's Hist. of Philosophy, vol. i. B. ii. chap. iv.
b Sulivan's View of Nature, vol. i. let. xiv. p. 137.
c Enfield's Hist. as above.

Whitlocke compared, says, with reference to Clarendon's account of the divines who assembled at Westminster: "If I had met with no other passage but this, to prove that the author of the history wrote unfairly, and partially, this alone would have convinced me, that there was little conscience, or care, taken in the forming of characters. One might have defied the most malicious observer, at that time, to have named only one man of public infamy, of life and conversation." And Dr Calamy says "A very heavy charge upon such a body of men as they were. Though my lord Clarendon was undoubtedly a great man, yet this censure wont recommend his history to posterity, who will be hard put to it, to find men of more exemplary piety, and more eminent ministerial abilities, than those whom he endeavours at such a rate to expose. Who can give credit to him as an historian, who shall represent such men as Dr Twisse, Mr Gataker, Bishop Reynolds, Dr Arrowsmith, Dr Tuckney, and Dr Lightfoot, as men of mean parts? Or who runs down such as Dr Gouge, Mr Oliver Bowles, Mr Vines, Mr Herle, Mr Newcomen, and Mr Coleman, as persons of no reputation, but for malice to the church?" [a]

Neither the characters of our venerable reformers, nor the precious truths of God, which they faithfully maintained, and earnestly contended for, have any thing to fear from the gross calumnies, and malicious efforts, of such enemies, who have dipped their pen in the common sewer. "Parthians might aim their arrows at the sun; wolves may exhaust their strength, by howling at the moon; yet neither the weapons of those could wound the one, nor can the clamour of these so much as alarm the other. The sun persists to shine, and the moon to roll, unextinguished and unimpeded by the impotence of rage, and the emptiness of menace from below." [b]

True and *undiguised candour* is much more amiable and commendable than accusation or censure. And,

a Clarendon and Whitlocke compared, chap. ii.
b Toplady's Historic Proof, vol. i. introduction.

what a celebrated writer justly observes, may be applied here: "If you find that he is either an unfit judge because of his ignorance, or because of his prejudices, his judgment should go for nothing." [a] And, "He whose own house is made of glass, ought not to throw stones at that of his neighbour." [b] "Calumny, though a great, is a temporary evil, but truth and justice will prove triumphant and eternal!"

The compiler of these memoirs pretends not to rank among such as are conspicuous, and have a respectable place, in the roll of the writers of biographical history: but submits himself and the work to the opinion of the public; requesting only equity in their censure, and impartiality in their judging. "The talents of a Plutarch are not implanted in every capacity. To pen the genuine anecdote, the interesting memoir, the correct annal, falls to the lot of very few." [c] The work itself is arduous, it hath been performed under consciousness of the want of abilities for it, and in the intervals of a very labourious life, of much travel and toil in a very extensive congregation, and, therefore, it must be very defective. Accordingly, blame only where ye must, be candid and shew lenity where ye can. And, considering the difficulties that attend such a work, errors, undoubtedly, may be detected in it. Such as discover them, are earnestly solicited to point them out, for future correction, as none have been allowed to pass, in the execution of the work, that could be observed. A strict regard has been paid to truth, the propriety and importance of which all must readily assent unto. And using the words of another, I earnestly wish to be set right: "and I shall be grateful to the friendly hand, which shall point out to me where I am wrong, and shall hold forth farther light, to illuminate the path in which I delight to tread." [d]

In the execution of this *voluntary and pleasing*, though arduous, task, some account is given of the birth, descent,

a Watts' Improvement of the Mind, part i. chap. v. xi.
b Voltaire's Memoirs, English, Dublin, edit. 1786. p. 62.
c Monthly Review Enlarged, vol. iv. p. 361.
d Sulivan's View of nature, vol. i. let. xxviii. end.

education, religion, manners, character, choice sayings, remarkable actions, the afflictions, and the death, of these eminent divines, who met in the famous Assembly at Westminster, as far as authentic information could be obtained. There is, indeed, a lamentable scarcity of biographical materials, relative to some of them; though no pains have been spared to procure these from every quarter where they might be supposed to be found. This deficiency, therefore, can only be regretted, without being remedied, at this distance of time, as far as my knowledge yet extends. And, though from the richness of materials, and other peculiar advantages, voluminous journals, very copious accounts of the lives and opinions of some distinguished characters, have been offered to the public; as in Doctor Parr's life of Archbishop Usher, and in Mr Boswell's life of Doctor Johnson; yet there has been a general complaint, that of many great men, of former times, we know just enough, to make us lament that we know no more.[a] Under the lamentable want of information, I have always been silent. The value of any thing is best known by the want of it. Agreeably to this, having experienced great inconveniences from the want of this information, I have learned thereby to entertain the highest sense of it's worth and importance. And when information could be obtained, nothing that is worthy of notice, or for edification, hath been withheld. A writer of the lives of famous men says, in entering upon the life of Epaminondas, the son of Polymnus, the Theban, "We seem obliged to pass by nothing that may be proper to the setting it clearly forth."[b] We also seem obliged to pass over nothing, which may be serviceable to set forth clearly the genuine character of these illustrious divines, and to preserve the honour of their memory. Very particular attention has been paid to the account of their death. A pleasant and celebrated writer says; "There is nothing in history which is so improving to the reader, as those accounts which we meet with of the deaths of emi-

a See Monthly Review Enlarged, vol. vii. for Jan. 1792.
b Cornelius Nepos, Epam. chap. i.

nent persons, and of their behaviour in that dreadful season."[a] The authorities are carefully annexed to the narrative for confirmation; and sometimes, the reader is informed where he may seek for farther intelligence, with reference to some things. Several pertinent texts of the holy scriptures are interspersed, occasional observations made, and some historical account of the times is given. Perhaps, some may think, that I have been too diffuse, with regard to the last of these. If this is the case, a supposition that some of my readers may have very little knowledge of the history of these times, is my apology. I have written for information and edification. Some lines of poetry are also inserted, in some places, where they appeared to be pertinent, and probably might be beneficial for the relaxation and animation of the reader. And, a particular account also is given of the writings of these divines, as far as they could be traced. This includes a catalogue of these, their several editions, and some partial account where they have been dispersed by divine providence, for the edification of the church and people of God. This hath been a very laborious, difficult, and expensive, part of the work. And, neither labour, nor expences, as far as circumstances would admit, have been withheld.[b] God's Abels, his departed saints, continue to speak both by the holy lives which they maintained, while *they were strangers and pilgrims on the earth.* and by the pious writings which they have left behind them, when their remains are laid in the dust. The hand of death could only reach their mortal part, both their reputation and their writings survive; and will continue to be regarded as their most splendid and lasting monuments. The superlative worth of the writings of these divines appears not to be sufficiently appreciated by us. We ought carefully to collect, to preserve, and to peruse, these writings. It is said concerning Lucretia Gontaga, a lady of uncommon learning, wit, and accomplishments, according to our information, That all that came from her pen was

a Spectator, vol. iv. No. 289.

b Hæc eadem ut sciret, quid non faciebat Amyntas? Virg. Ecl. ii. 35.

so much esteemed, that a collection was made even of the notes which she wrote to her servants, several of which are to be found in the edition of her letters, published at Venice in 1552.[a] And, what came from the pen of several of these eminently learned, very pious, and well accomplished, divines, ought to be highly esteemed by us, carefully preserved, and read with the most attentive consideration. The mind of the authors appears to have been richly impregnated with the celestial dew of the knowledge of the doctrines of the gospel of the Son of God, and with the special influences of the Spirit of all grace. The reader, accordingly, will find, in their writings, the lively vestiges of that knowledge which comes from above, and the genuine signatures of a gracious heart. They contain such rich treasures of heavenly instructions, that one who reads without prejudice, and for real edification, cannot rise from reading them without much advantage. I have correct information, that they have been truly serviceable to some, in acquiring the true knowledge of the truths of the gospel of Jesus Christ, and of reformation principles. The reputation, indeed, of many of these writings, rests more on the value of the materials, than on the elegance of the composition. But the language and the subject are clearly distinguishable; and ought always to be very carefully distinguished; for they are really distinct things in themselves. There is evidently both the beauty of language expressing thought, and likewise the beauty of the thought itself. And these distinct beauties, if we wish either to think, speak or write, correctly, must be particularly distinguished from each other. Language may be considered as the dress of the subject, or of the thought; and, undoubtedly, we can distinguish between the person and the dress. Beside, we are often conscious of the highest pleasure which language can afford, when the subject is very disagreeable: and so on the contrary. And, we frequently find subjects of great dignity, utility, and importance, dressed in very mean language.

a Universal Magazine, vol. xcii.

Theopompus's subject is said to have great force, but his style very little.[a] And style ought not to have the preference over subject. A writer of considerable respectability well observes; "Style is truly valuable and important, but in a frivolous age like the present, we are sorry to see any inclination, among serious men, to give it the preference over subject."[b] The great truths of the gospel of Christ, are usefully illustrated, and judiciously explained, in these writings: and such as prefer substantial food, served up in an homely manner, to the mere garnishings of a dish, may read them with great satisfaction. And some of them want not elegance of composition for the times.

The collecting the writings of these divines has engaged some share of my attention for several years. The place of my residence, hitherto, hath not been very favourable to pursuits of this nature; but correspondence with persons residing in public places, extensive travels, time and assiduity, have, in a considerable degree, remedied this inconvenience. A correspondent in London has been engaged in pursuit of these writings, in my behalf, for several years, in his leisure hours; by whom many of the scarcest and most valuable of them have been procured, and much information of great utility and importance received. Different journeys have been performed to that great metropolis, at the distance of between three and four hundred miles, and close search made for these writings while there, for several weeks, with great success. When in London and in other public places, book-catalogues, book-shops, and stalls in the streets, were diligently searched. Access hath been readily granted to several libraries of great respectability; and the sight and loan of some of the scarcest of these writings have been obtained with an affability and politeness that greatly augmented the favour. I am deeply indebted to several gentlemen, and to others, for the loan of books in composing this work, but as they are

a Elements of Criticism, vol. ii. chap. xviii. sect. i. 7th edit. Edin.
b Universal Magazine.

numerous, and I have not their allowance, I shall not name any of them. I have procured, used, and profited by, a great number of volumes, in composing these memoirs. Such means have been used, that the account both of the lives and of the writings, might be as full and correct as possible.

Usefulness hath been chiefly studied. This is the grand object, both in religious matters, and in philosophical researches. "The *professed* object of philosophical researches, is to discover principles which shall be subservient to the uses of man. Without this object, every inquiry is but the amusement of children." [a] The *professed* object of these memoirs, and of the researches to obtain materials for them, is, to exhibit religious principles and correspondent practices which shall be subservient to the uses of man. There is little expectation, that the accounts of these lives and writings will either be generally circulated, or universally read; but if they are means in the hand of the Lord, of exciting and of exercising the sympathetic emotion of piety, in the minds of a few well disposed readers, the labour, in composing them, will not be wholly lost. Intercourse with pious persons, histories of their religious exercises and experiences, with well authenticated accounts of their generous and disinterested actions, and frequent meditation upon them, keep the sympathetic emotion alive in the mind, and in constant exercise, which by degrees introduces a habit.[b] And this sympathetic emotion, when excited and exercised in the mind of religious persons, is highly advantageous; for it greatly encourages them to imitate the good example which they admire. And good example, having a powerful and commanding influence over the mind of the godly, will strongly operate there, piety and holiness will accordingly gain strength, and thus the church of Christ will be edified, and God's name glorified.

Religious edification being intended, it is expected that such as may be disposed to procure, or to read,

a Monthly Review Enlarged, vol. iv. appendix, p. 517.
b Elements of Criticism, vol. i. chap. ii. part i. sect. iv.

these memoirs, will read them with attentive consideration, and likewise frequently meditate upon what they read. The plan of this work hath required much labour and considerable expence, to execute it; and I should be sorry that the memories, and even the names, of these eminent divines, which are of considerable celebrity among our reformers, should sink back into oblivion as soon as the reader had turned the page. Framing one sentence, and fixing a single date, have been attended oftentimes with much labour and difficulty, by pursuing my researches in several volumes, examining the degree of credit due to the several authorities, and waiting for opportunities of receiving correct information: and, therefore, my progress was not much in the revolution of a year. As the progress of the work hath been very slow, I have endeavoured to make some little improvement, while it was going forward. Plutarch hath observed of Menander, that his later excelled his earlier productions. And, I sincerely wish, and have studied, that for the benefit of the reader, for the credit of religion, for the edification of the church, and for the glory of God, this observation may be in some measure verified in these memoirs.

The memoirs of Dr Twisse, who was the Prolocutor of the Famous Assembly of Divines at Westminster, and of his two Assessors, Dr Burgess, and Mr White, are placed first: after them, the names of the English Divines, who were members of this Assembly, are alphabetically arranged, as they stand in Mr Neal's History of the Puritans; the Scottish Commissioners are next brought forward; and the Scribes, who had no votes, are last in the list.

Having endeavoured, in compliance with the calls of Divine providence, to preach the glorious gospel of the grace of God, in several parts of Scotland, of England, of Ireland, and of America; and considering that I must have been very far deficient in discharging the duties of my office, both at home and abroad, I sincerely wish that this labour of love may partly supply my lack of service. Deficiences, in endeavouring to serve the church one way, may, probably, be partly supplied, by being, in some degree, otherwise serviceable to her interests. That the Divine blessing may accompany this work, as far as it is conformable to the revealed will of God; and that it may be instrumental in carrying the sweet sound of the Saviour's name, which is like ointment poured forth unto those who love him, and in promoting genuine piety, and the knowledge of reformation principles, in all places of the earth where Divine providence may direct its course, is the ardent desire of the author.

JAMES REID.

MEMOIRS, &c.

THE REV. WILLIAM TWISSE, D. D.

PASTOR OF NEWBURY, A VERY LEARNED AND LABORIOUS DIVINE, AN EMINENT LIGHT OF GOD'S CHURCH, AND PROLOCUTOR OF THE ASSEMBLY OF DIVINES AT WESTMINSTER.

WILLIAM TWISSE was born at Speenham-land, near Newbury in Berkshire, England. His grand-father was a German, who, on some occasions had come over into England, and made way, under the providence of God, for his grand-son being left a very choice blessing to that kingdom. His father was a substantial clothier, and educated him at Winchester school, from whence, at eighteen years of age, he was translated to New-College in Oxford, of which he was a fellow. Here he made the closest application to his studies, for sixteen years together; and acquired an extensive and very deep and accurate knowledge of logic, philosophy, and divinity. He adorned the learning of the schools by his literary knowledge. He proceeded Master of Arts in the year 1604; and about the same time he entered into holy orders, and became a diligent and frequent preacher of the everlasting gospel of our Lord and Saviour, Jesus Christ. He was esteemed a popular preacher in the University; and though some judged that his discourses were a little too scholastic, yet they were accompanied with power, and followed with success. He was admired and distinguished among his co-temporaries in the University, on account of his closeness of application to his studies, the vivacity and subtility of his wit, his exact judgment, his holy exemplary life and conversation, and all other valuable qualities which became a man of his profession. And having such advantages, his mind was soon enriched with whatever is valuable, entertaining, or exquisite, in literature.

He proceeded Doctor of Divinity, with general applause, in the year 1614, after having given abundant proof both of his learning and industry, in his catechetical lectures in the college chapel, and in his disputations, as well as in transcribing and judiciously correcting the writings of the famous Dr Thomas Bradwardine, archbishop of Canterbury, which were to be published by Sir Henry Saville.

He was called upon at this time to preach a sermon on a day appointed for baptizing a Jew, one Joseph Barnet, who taught many of the students Hebrew in Oxford then, and deceived many of the University Doctors, especially Dr Lake, provost of New-College, by pretending that he was converted to christianity; but the day before he was to have been baptized, having filled his purse, he ran away. However, being pursued, he was brought back; and Dr Twisse, the next day, laid aside the sermon he had studied, upon a supposition that the Jew was to be baptized, and preached a most excellent and remarkable sermon upon his revolt, wherein he shewed God's just judgment upon that rebellious backsliding nation and people, whom he had given up to a reprobate mind, even to this very day. He acquitted himself on this remarkable occasion in such a learned and masterly manner, that he was applauded and admired by the whole University. As Datames, a very brave and great man, following the business of a soldier, first discovered what he was, in the war with king Artaxerxes carried on against the Cadusians:[a] so Dr Twisse first discovered what he was eminently as a divine and scholar, on this occasion. The short time which he had to study his discourse, and the manner in which he handled it, caused him to be much admired. His celebrated lectures every Thursday, in the parish church of St

a Cornelius Nepos, Dat. i.

Olaves, were so much frequented by the gownsmen, and the inhabitants of the town, that his fame reached the court: and when he lay hid in his academic cell, king James I. made choice of him to be chaplain to his daughter Elizabeth, the princess Palatine, and to accompany her into Germany. Previous to his entering upon his travels into Germany, he very prudently disposed of his patrimony, which was about thirty pounds yearly, and commended it to his brother, requiring him, that out of the rents of it, he should raise portions for his sisters. "A good man sheweth favour, and lendeth: he will guide his affairs with discretion," Psal. cxii. 5.

And when he set out with the princess, to render the journey both profitable and pleasant, he expounded parts of the holy scriptures daily. Every one is delighted with some peculiar pleasure.[a] And they who are born again of water and of the Spirit, John iii. 5. are delighted with the word of God, as their peculiar pleasure. "As new-born babes, desire the sincere milk of the word, that ye may grow thereby," 1 Pet. ii. 2. And as his judicious expositions and observations served to render the way less tedious:[b] so they were also means, along with his many wise and seasonable admonitions, to moderate the grief of the princess, on leaving her dear country. He taught her from the word of God, "that here we have no abiding city;" but ought to "seek a better in the world to come." She was also hereby prepared, under the blessing of God, to encounter all those afflictive dispensations of Divine providence, with which she was afterward visited and tried: for soon after she was crowned queen of Bohemia, she was forced to fly from that country, when pregnant, and excluded from the Palatinate, the paternal inheritance of her husband, and driven to live in exile the remaining part of her days. Then she firmly believed, and sweetly experienced, what the Doctor had very often inculcated, That God's gracious providence doth order all the estates and conditions of all mankind, whether

a Trahit sua quemque voluptas. Virg. Ecl. ii. 65.
b Vide Virg. Ecl. ix. 64.

prosperous or adverse, according to his own good pleasure, and for the everlasting good of those who belong to him, agreeable to that promise, Rom. viii. 28. "And we know that all things work together for good to them who love God, to them who are the called according to his purpose." Thus the princess was both forewarned and forearmed by him. It was probably on account of his eminent service this way, to the queen, that prince Rupert, one of her sons, in the time of the civil war in England, coming to Newbury, where the Doctor was minister, behaved with the greatest courtesy and familiarity to him; making him the largest promises, if he would be of the court party, write in their defence, and live among them. But the Doctor had not so learned Christ, and therefore could not comply with these measures. He had not been quite two months at the court of the elector Palatine, before he was recalled to England, to the great grief of the queen, and also of her husband. They both lamented the loss of such a jewel. The prince shewed his great concern at the Doctor's departure, in a Latin speech which he made to him. The most sanguine projects of life are often wonderfully diverted from their purposed course, by the invisible hand of over-ruling Providence.

Upon his return to England, his native country, he closely and wholly applied himself for the glory of God, and for the good of his church. And, in a country village, and mean house, by very close study, he laid the foundation of those rare and elaborate works, which have been the admiration of all the reformed churches both at home and abroad. Afterward, he was made vicar of Newbury, a mayor and market-town in Berkshire, fifty-six miles distant from London, acccording to Entick.[a] Here he gained

a Newbury is somewhat remarkable for eminent persons. Here flourished John Winscomb, or Jack of Newbury, one of the greatest clothiers in England, who, in the reign of king Henry VIII. maintained 100 of his own men in the expedition to Flodden-field. It is also the birth-place of Mr Kenrick, a merchant of London, who left very considerable sums for encouraging the cloathing trade in this town and in Reading. And Mr Benjamin Woodbridge, who suc-

vast reputation both by his useful preaching, and his exemplary life. And Divine providence so ordered, that where he had first seen the natural light, and drawn his, first breath, he should be *a burning and shining light*, in a spiritual sense, to guide and direct, as a bright star in Christ's right hand, the inhabitants of that place in the way to heavenly glory. Here he passed the remaining part of his time in this world, with much satisfaction, learning in whatever state he was to be content, to the great comfort, profit, and edification of the people.

The disposition of his mind was such, that he neither sought the riches of this world, nor yet ecclesiastical dignities and preferments; but modestly rejected them, when they were offered him. He often congratulated himself on his low retired condition, and accounted himself much indebted to the Lord his God, because he had graciously placed him in a mean condition, as being liable to fewer temptations snd dangers than in the episcopal dignity he might have been exposed to. Like Luther, who is said to have had this passage in his last will and testament:—"Lord God, I thank thee, because that thou hast been pleased to make me a poor and indigent man upon earth. I have neither house, nor land, nor money, to leave behind me."[a] When God raiseth us high by his providence, we are in danger of lifting up ourselves by pride, even against him:—saying to the gold or preferment, "Thou art my hope;" and to the fine gold, or high preferment, "Thou art my confidence." And there is a secret malignity in this world's riches, and in preferments, when they meet with the corruptions of our hearts, to lift us up in pride, and withdraw our hearts from the "living God, who giveth us richly all things to enjoy," 1 Tim. vi. 17. And we may suppose that Doctor Twisse felt this in his own experience: for he was particularly acquainted with the gross corruption of the human heart. He declined being Warden of the College at Winchester, after he was chos-

ceeded Dr Twisse at Newbury, was a very great and eminent man every way.

a Melch. Adam. Vit. German. Theol.

en, and earnestly requested to accept it, though it was a very lucrative place. It is said to have been equal to the greatest ecclesiastic preferment for profit. He requested the offerers to bestow it upon some more worthy person. And hereby he shewed, says Clark, "that he rather desired to attend his studies in private, than to wax old and live idle in a more honourable place." A place of solitude better suited his studious disposition, than a place of honour and preferment. He afterward refused a Prebend at Winchester, when offered him; returning thanks to Dr Moore, his father-in-law, who was prebendary of Winchester, and other friends, but intreating them to give him leave to abide at Newbury to attend the flock over which God had placed him; saying, "he thought himself unfit for a cathedral employment: it was hard for him, among such eminent men as the prebendaries of Winchester, either to sing musically enough, or to preach rhetorically enough." Robert, earl of Warwick, also offered him a Rectory; which, because it was a smaller parish than Newbury, and old age was creeping in upon him, and his bodily strength failing, he thankfully accepted, provided that the earl would take special care to send a pious faithful pastor to Newbury. The Doctor waited upon the archbishop of Canterbury, with whom he had been well acquainted while they were students together at Oxford, concerning this business. The archbishop entertained him courteously, and promised to grant his request; adding, that he would represent him to the king for a pious and learned man, and no puritan. But the Doctor was quick enough to perceive, from such treatment and language, that snares were laid for him. Accordingly, he returned to Newbury, and thought no more of leaving it. Thus we see, that this very eminent man did shrink from the dignities and preferments in the church of England. Like Quintus Sextius, a Pythagorean philosopher, who flourished in the time of Augustus, he seemed formed to rise in the republic; but he shrunk from civil honours, and declined accepting of the rank of Senator when it was offered him by Julius Cæsar, that he might have time to make application unto philosophy.[a] And as Agesilaus, the valiant Lacedemonian prince, preferred a good name to the most wealthy kingdom, and esteemed it far more glorious to obey the laws of his conntry, than to conquer Asia by war:[b] so Twisse preferred the glory and honour of his royal Master to all episcopal preferments; and accounted obedience to the laws of Christ's house far more glorious, than to move in the highest sphere under the noisy applause of men. He came to be so well known in the learned world, and in the church of Christ abroad, by his elaborate and celebrated Latin work, in answer to the much famed book of Arminius against Perkins, that the States of Friesland sent him a pressing invitation to accept the place of Divinity professor, in the University of Francker. This is the highest preferment that a minister of the gospel was capable of in that country. And the States took order to clear the expences of his transportation; but he refused this invitation also. "And how often," says an eminent divine, "do goats clamber up the mountains of preferments, while the poor sheep of Christ feed below?"[c]

Dr Twisse refused to read the king's proclamation, commonly called the book of sports, wherein the people were allowed to use certain sports on the Lord's day; and which was commanded to be read in all churches, on pain of suspension both from office and benefice: yea, he declared against it. Other faithful godly ministers did the same, for which that severe penalty was inflicted upon them. But when king James was informed of Dr Twisse's refusal, he secretly commanded the bishops not to meddle with him. The king knew well, that though Dr Twisse had only a small estate, and lived meanly at home, yet his fame was great in all the reformed churches; and that nothing could be done hardly against him, but it would redound greatly to the disgrace of those who did it.

a Encyclop. Britan. under Sextius, vol. xvii. part i. Edin.
b C. Nep. Agesil. iv.
c Arrowsmith.

This eminent champion for the cause of Christ, now appeared to plead the cause, as it was in the hands of the puritans, wherein he and they laboured as for life, to use his own expression. He faithfully admonished the people under his pastoral care, to beware of the profanation of the sabbath, by sports, pastimes, May-games, dancings, and following carnal worldly pleasures: and he farther enjoined them to remember the sabbath day to keep it holy. And there was a loud call for the continuation of his faithful testimony, with that of others, against the awful profanation of the Lord's day, by that most irreligious and detestable of all proclamations that ever stained the historic page—the blasphemous book of sports. For king Charles I. renewed his father's edict for allowing sports and recreations on the sabbath day, to such as attended public worship; and he ordered his proclamation, for that purpose, to be publicly read by the clergy after divine service. And, the puritans refusing obedience to this disgraceful command, were therefore punished with suspension or deprivation.[a] Dr Twisse still continued to set the trumpet to his mouth, to shew the *people their transgression, and the house of Jacob their sins*, Isa. lviii. 1. And he spared neither king nor parliament, but engaged them with their own weapons set against them: like David, when he cut off the head of Goliah the giant, with his own sword, 1 Sam. xvii. 50, 51. He, with great ingenuity, turned the act of their own parliament, concerning the sabbath, against themselves. He managed this with great propriety and energy, displaying his usual forcible and animated reasoning on the subject.[b] He also appeared against the publications of these times, in support of sabbath profanation, as the translator of Dr Prideaux's lectures, and others, who came on the field in course, concerning the doctrine of the sabbath. And such faithful testimony-bearing, against this very glaring evil, was *not in vain in the Lord*: it had its good fruit; its salutary effect in

a Hume's Hist. of England, chap. liii. 1633.
b See his Morality of the Sabbath, p. 5. &c.

due time. For when the parliament went on vigorously with their intended reformation, in the year 1643, they applied themselves to that of the sabbath also. And on May 5th, this year, the book tolerating sports on the Lord's day was ordered to be burned by the hands of the common hangman in Cheapside, London, and other usual places, which was done the 11th of May 1643; and all persons having copies thereof, were requested to deliver them up to one of the sheriffs of London to be burned.[a] By this instance, we may see, that in due time, the faithful followers of the Lamb shall overcome all opposition by his blood, and by the word of their testimony, Rev. xii. 11. And so long as the evil continues, our testimony against it ought to be displayed. As one of the ancients, when asked how long he would continue to preach against profane swearing, replied, "Until the people cease from swearing profanely."[b] So Dr Twisse continued to testify against the book of sports, until it was abolished. He ever sacrificed his own ease to considerations of public utility in the cause of Christ. And it was probably on account of his spirited appearances against the corruptions and evils of these times, that Dr Prideaux once said, "that the bishops did little consult their own credit because they had not preferred Dr Twisse, though against his will, to some splendid ecclesiastical dignity." He thought, no doubt, that this would have been an effectual mean to stop his mouth from speaking against them, and the sins of the times. Hence it appears, that Dr Twisse was an eminent champion for the grace of God, the morality and sanctification of the sabbath, and that puritan divinity, which the honours of the good old way belong unto.

He was esteemed an able disputant. Dr Baillie, who had considerable opportunity of knowing what his talents were this way, says, in one of his letters addressed to the presbytery of Irvine, dated London, February 28th, 1641, "Dr Twisse, to our great comfort, is here turn-

a Neal's Hist. of the Puritans, vol. iii. chap. i.
b Vicar's Parliamentary Chronicle, p. 382.

ed a remonstrant. Dr Twisse, if there be any dispute, offers to be one. He is doubtless the most able disputer in England." [a]

He generally wished to decline a verbal conference with regard to matters of disputation And, for this, he gives the following reasons:—Because, these things may be done more quietly by writing; the managers of the controversy will then be kept free from foreign discourse; the arguments on each side may be more properly and deliberately weighed; answers returned with due consideration; and the holy things of God may be more decently handled.[b]

At the commencement of the civil war, in the arbitrary reign of Charles I. he was forced to leave Newbury by the cavaliers, or king's soldiers and their party. The king's party spared none who were upon the side of the parliament. And then the Doctor suffered persecution for righteousness' sake.

And upon calling together the Assembly of Divines at Westminster, in the year 1643, he was chosen and appointed by both Houses of Parliament, to be their Prolocutor, in which place he continued until his death. This place he often refused, with his usual modesty and humility. But "he who humbleth himself shall be exalted." Accordingly, he was unanimously chosen to the chair, and filled it, though much against his will. This Assembly of Divines first met at King Henry VII's Chapel, in Westminster-abbey, on Saturday the 1st July 1643. At their first assembling, Dr Twisse, their Prolocutor, preached a sermon unto them, at which the members of both Houses of Parliament were also present. This Assembly was prohibited by the king's proclamation of June 22; and he declared, that no acts done by them ought to be received by his subjects: he also threatened to proceed against them with the utmost severity of the law; which Dr Twisse lamented, in his sermon at the

a Baillie's Letters, let. xxvi. vol. i. when speaking concerning the petition of the English and Scotch against episcopacy.

b See his Riches of God's Love, B. ii. p. 21.

opening of the Assembly, but hoped that in due time his majesty's consent might be obtained. Notwithstanding sixty-nine ministers assembled the first day, who were called to meet there; and after sermon the ordinance of parliament was read, declaring the cause and intention of their convention, viz. the settlement of religion and church government. And then the roll, containing the names of the ministers appointed, was called over, and the names of those who were absent marked. About one hundred and twenty were nominated and appointed. They did not appear there in canonical habits, but chiefly in black coats and bands, in imitation of the foreign protestants.[a] Several of the ablest divines of that age will be found in the list of those who were members of that Assembly. They were both pious and learned; though, perhaps, none have suffered more in their characters and reputations, since the commencement of the christian æra. This Assembly was not a convention according to the Diocesan government; nor was it called by the votes of ministers, in the Presbyterian form; but by the Parliament in extraordinary circumstances, for advice in church affairs. Many of the most learned Episcopal divines were nominated, along with the Presbyterians and Independents; and Archbishop Usher, Bishops Westford, Prideaux, and Brownrigg, Doctors Holdsworth, Hammond, Sanderson, and others;—but they refused, because the king had declared against it. None could enter to hear or see this Assembly without a written order from both Houses of Parliament. They met every work-day, except Saturday, which was allowed the divines to prepare for preaching on the sabbath. Their session was generally from nine o'clock in the morning until two or three afternoon; which the Prolocutor began and ended with prayer. About sixty of the English divines were generally present. These were divided into three committees; and no man was excluded who pleased to come into any of the three. Every committee took a portion of the work prescribed,

a Vicar's Parliamentary Chronicle, p. 352. Neal's History of the Puritans, vol. iii. chap. ii.

and in their afternoon meeting prepared matters for the Assembly, writing their sentiments in distinct propositions, supported by sacred texts. After prayer, the Scribe read the proposition and text, whereupon the Assembly debated in a very grave, learned, ready and accurate manner. "I do marvel," says Mr Baillie, one of the Scotch Commissioners to that Assembly, "at the very accurate and extemporary replies that many of them usually make. They harangue long and very learnedly. They study the question well beforehand, and prepare their speeches; but withal the men are exceeding prompt, and well spoken." [a] None were called up to speak, but all rose of their own accord, and spoke as long as they pleased without interruption. All speeches were addressed to the Prolocutor. And when they had spoken whatever they pleased upon every proposition and text, and the replies and duplies were heard, the most part called to the question. Upon this the Scribe rose from the table, and went to the Prolocutor's chair, who read the proposition from the Scribe's book, and said, "So many as are of opinion that the question is well stated in the proposition, let them say *aye*." When the ayes were heard, the Prolocutor desired those who thought otherwise, to say *no*. When the ayes and noes could be readily known, then the question was ordered by the Scribes, and they went on to debate. If the ayes and noes were nearly equal, the Prolocutor called upon them separately to stand up, and they were numbered by the Scribes and others. When the weather became cold, the Assembly went to the Jerusalem Chamber, a fair room in Westminster-abbey. At the upper end of it there was a chair set on a frame, about one foot above the floor, for Dr Twisse, the Prolocutor. Before it, on the ground, stood two chairs for the Assessors, Dr Burgess and Mr White. Before these two chairs stood a table, where the two Scribes did sit, Mr Byfield and Mr Roborough. The Scotch Commissioners sat on the Prolocutor's right hand. All warrants from the Parliament to sit in this Assembly were presented to

a Baillie's Letters, let. xxxix. vol. i.

the Prolocutor. He welcomed the Scotch Commissioners into the Assembly at their arrival, by a long speech. Mr Baillie, speaking concerning him, as Prolocutor of this Assembly, says, " The man, as the world knows, is very learned in the questions he has studied, and very good, and beloved of all, and highly esteemed."[a] And Dr Calamy says, " That he was very famous on account of his wit, learning, and writings." It hath been said that he spake little in this Assembly. And some have interpreted this as an argument either of his weakness, or at least of the decline of his intellectual powers at that time. But as Sophocles, when his sons charged him with dotage, is said to have recited a tragedy of Oedipus Coloneus, which he had last written, and had in his hands; and to have asked, whether that seemed to be the verse of a dotard.[b] So Dr Twisse could easily have silenced such bold censurers, by the exhibition of those vigorous masculine pieces, which he penned in the different periods of his life. But his disposition to decline verbal conference in matters of disputation, (for reasons already mentioned,) his modesty and humility, with the place which he occupied in this Assembly, may sufficiently account for his speaking little there. Beside, Dr Baillie informs us, that four parts of five did not speak at all; and that among these were many of the ablest divines, and known by their writings and sermons to be much abler than several of the speakers. That silence was no reproach in that Assembly, and did not hinder the work.[c] And some very eminent men, who could speak well, have, notwithstanding, been great lovers of silence, and seldom spoke, except when they reckoned that this was absolutely necessary. It is said, concerning Dr Bradley, one of the greatest English Astronomers of the age wherein he lived, " That he spoke well, and expressed his ideas with great precision and perspicuity; notwithstanding which he was a great lover of silence:— and it has been observed of him, that he seldom spoke,

a Baillie's Letters, let. xxxix. vol. i.
b Cicero, De Senectute.
c Baillie's Letters, let. clxxi. vol. ii.

except when he conceived it absolutely necessary.[a] May we not suppose, that this was the case with Dr Twisse? And that he was like the celebrated Epaminondas, concerning whom Cornelius Nepos says, "He was desirous of hearing others discourse; for by this he thought one might learn in the easiest manner." [b] And, like the Spectator, he hath sufficiently atoned for his speaking little in this Assembly, by writing himself out before he died, in vindication of the cause of God and truth.[c] Beside what he had printed, he left about thirty pieces completed behind him, according to Mr Clark. And therefore, as Sophocles, who composed tragedies in his very old age, was honourably acquitted from the base charge brought against him by his sons, when they appeared before upright and reasonable judges: so will Dr Twisse, in like manner, be acquitted from the charge of speaking little in this Assembly. But supposing that Dr Twisse did not shine equally in extemporary speech or conversation, as in writing, he might very well say with the celebrated Addison, in the famous anecdote. distinguishing between his powers in conversation and in writing, "I have only nine-pence in my pocket; but I can draw for a thousand pounds."

He was eminently distinguished as a writer; as will appear by the testimonies of many learned men, brought forward at the end of this narrative. And as these are sufficient to ascertain his true character, as a writer, and discover the nature of his writings in a general way, we shall say little more concerning this. I shall here favour the reader with an anonymous remark, in manuscript, on this subject, which I received from London, in a book of Dr Twisse's. "The whole scope, and intent of Dr Twisse's writings, is, to set forth the absolute sovereignty and Lordship of God, over all created beings, both angels and men: and to shew, that no man in *nature's state*, with all his acquired abilities, can possibly put forth one act pleasing to God." He often affords consi-

a Universal Magazine for March 1791, vol. lxxxviii. London.
b Nep. Epam. 3.
c Spectator, No. i.

derable entertainment to his reader, by the vivacity of his genius, and the sharpness and elegance of his wit. He sometimes uses jocose or historical diversions, to animate the spirits of his readers, and to preserve them from weariness. Many of his excellent writings are in Latin. One reason of this is, that the Latin language was then more generally a medium of communication and intercourse in divinity, literature, and science, than it is now. Dr Fuller says, "His Latin works give great evidence of his abilities in controversial matters."[a] God seems to have raised him up in his holy and wise providence, at this time, and placed him eminently, with the pen in his hand, against all the adversaries of his grace and truth, like another Bradwardine.[b]

His epistolary correspondence seems to have been considerable: and also the sphere of his literary acquaintance. —He had an epistolary correspondence with Mr Joseph Mede, sometime Fellow of Christ's College, Cambridge, whom he calls his "worthy friend," in his *Morality of the Fourth Commandment*, page 58.

The contentions in church and state broke his heart. He often wished heartily, that the fire of contention might be quenched, though it were with his own blood. "My soul hath long dwelt with him who hateth peace, I am for peace; but when I speak, they are for war." Psal. cxx. 6, 7. He was much grieved and displeased to see liberty given to heresies and blasphemies.—He lived under an abiding sense of the gross corruption and total depravity of his nature, which often filled him with astonishment:—a scripture-mark of a regenerate soul. See Psal. xxxviii. 4. and li. 5. Rom. vii. 23, 24. And he was much employed in the confession of his sins: "I acknowledged my sin unto thee, and mine iniquity have I not hid. I said, I will confess my transgressions unto the Lord," Psal. xxxii. 5. See Psal. li. 3, 4. and Dan. ix. 4. He frequently offered up unfeigned thanks

a Fuller's Worthies of England.

b See Rivet's Latin Preface, to Dr Twisse's Animadversions on Arminius and Corvinus.

to God, who, of his mere grace and love, had kept him from such honours as might have exposed him to temptations and snares. Abounding in the grace of humility, he was still admiring the gifts and graces of God in others, and highly esteeming and commending them, though they were far inferior to his own. He greatly respected and reverenced all good men, and thought only meanly of himself: remembering what is said, Rom. xii. 10. "Be kindly affectioned one to another with brotherly love, in honour preferring one another." He constantly kept a monthly fast in his own family, whereby he endeavoured to quicken his prayers, by which, with great importunity, he sought God in the behalf of his afflicted church, pleading that he would be gracious unto it, and restore it to peace in his own due time. He was particularly mindful of the church of Christ, in his family fasts and prayers. "If I forget thee, O Jerusalem, let my right hand forget its cunning. If I do not remember thee, let my tongue cleave to the roof of my mouth: If I prefer not Jerusalem above my chief joy." Psal. cxxxvii. 5. 6. He applied himself daily to the throne of grace by prayer, with great zeal and fervour of spirit, "That he might obtain mercy, and find grace to help in time of need." Heb. iv. 16. And, always before dinner and supper, he read a portion of the holy scriptures, expounding the more obscure and difficult passages, for the edification of his family. And out of them he gathered arguments, by which he might the more abase himself and his, and with the greater importunity wrestle with God, for the obtaining such blessings and favours as he craved from him. It was a custom, in these times, to read a portion of the holy scriptures at meals, that their souls might be refreshed along with their bodies; that they might see themselves in the glass of the divine law; become better acquainted with the word of God, as their comfort in affliction; and learn to understand the way of his precepts, so as to keep them diligently, and talk of all his wondrous works, Psal. cxix. 4—27—49, 50. As is said concerning Pomponius Atticus, the famous Roman Knight, who lived long at Athens, "He had so learned the precepts of the greatest philosophers, that he made use of them for the conduct of his life, and not for ostentation.[a] And Cornelius Nepos also informs us, concerning Atticus, "That none ever heard any other entertainment for the ears at his meals, than a reader; which we think indeed very pleasant: nor was there ever a supper at his house without some reading, that his guests might be entertained not less in their minds than in their stomachs; for he invited those whose manners were not different from his own." [b] It appears from this passage, that men of learning and taste have had some to read history, or other books, for diverting or instructing their guests at table; and that occasion might hereby be given to some useful or learned discourse. And if so, it certainly becomes christians to read the word of God at their meals, for such noble purposes as Dr Twisse did.

In this eminent character, piety and learning are united: a beautiful constellation, when they meet in the same person. "Learning in religious hearts, like the gold in the ear-rings of the Israelites, is a most precious ornament," says an eminent divine.[c] Piety crowns learning. Dr Twisse's singular ministerial abilities, and his very elaborate useful writings, with his truly amiable and excellent character, rendered him universally respected during his life, and hold him up now when he is dead, as a noble example to christians in general, and to the ministers of Christ in particular. One principal part of the office of a christian minister is, to appear in the defence of evangelical truth. There is a particular necessity for the diligent discharge of this duty in the present time, when both heresy and infidelity abound, and make rapid progress. And it is much to be wished that we were disposed to follow such a laudable example. For, like Constantius, the Roman emperor, he was both amiable and venerable to his flock and acquaintances.[d] But

a Nep. Attic. chap. xvii.
b Nep. Attic. chap. xiv.
c Arrowsmith's Principles, Applic. i. Exer. i.
d Eutrop. chap. x. 1.

as it hath always been the case since the beginning, that *he who was born after the flesh persecuted him who was born after the Spirit, even so it was now:* for this very eminent champion in the cause of God and truth, was designed to ruin by the Canterburian faction—as Mr Henry Jeanes says he found in a manuscript under his own hand.[a]—The chief occasion of this probably was, because his pen was found to be a very heavy hammer in breaking to pieces the modern Pelagian heresy, while he made truth eminently his buckler. For "all who will live godly in Christ Jesus shall suffer persecution," 2 Tim. iii. 12. And persecutors have often attempted to destroy by violence, the man whom they could not vanquish by argument.

He was of an easy disposition, and too prone to be deceived by those whom he judged to be godly. He was a Supralapsarian: considering man not fallen, nor yet created, as the object of predestination. Accordingly, in his writings, he goes into the Supralapsarian way of explaining the doctrine of election and of reprobation. And yet he says, "That he reckons that controversy, relative to the order of God's decrees, to be merely *apex logicus* —a logical nicety," as he calls it, in his riches of God's love, part ii. page 50.

Dr Twisse maintained, as several eminently orthodox divines have done, "That God, by his absolute power, setting aside his decree or free constitution, can forgive sin without any satisfaction." He hath a whole digression against Piscator and Lubbertus, on this subject.[b] And Calvin expressly says, on John xv. 13. That God might, by a word only, or by his command, have redeemed us; but he took this way through his Son, that his love might be made more manifest. And Norton, in his Orthodox Evangelist, chap. iii. says, "God, by his absolute power, could have saved man without a Mediator: he is omnipotent, and could have done what he

a Address to Michael Oldisworth, Esq. prefixed to Dr Twisse's Riches of God's Love.

b Vindic. Grat. l. 1. de elect. digres. 8.

pleased." And Mr Rutherford, Christ dying and drawing sinners to himself, pages 7, 8, says, "If we speak of God's absolute power, without respect to his free decree, he could have pardoned sin without a ransom, and gifted all mankind and fallen angels with heaven, without any satisfaction of either the sinner or his Surety; for he neither punisheth sin, nor tenders heaven to men or angels by necessity of nature—as the fire casteth out heat, and the sun light—but freely." But it appears to me both vain and dangerous to dispute what God can do by his absolute power, especially in the case before us, when he has most solemnly and plainly declared, in the strongest terms, that he *will by no means clear the guilty*, Exod. xxxiv. 6, 7. That is, He will not suffer guilty persons to go unpunished, without a satisfaction. See Numb. xiv. 18. Jer. xxx. 11. Nah. i. 3. Sin is directly contrary to the perfection of God; and, therefore, it cannot go unpunished. It's impunity is incompatible both with the divine nature and government. *And without shedding of blood is no remission.*

Dr Owen opposes Dr Twisse, concerning this point, in his Dissertation on Divine Justice; where he speaks very honourably and respectfully of him as his most learned antagonist. He says, chap. xii. sect 4. "But here, first, of all the antagonists, and who indeed is almost equal to them all, *the very learned Twisse* opposes himself to us." And while Dr Owen, in this controversy with Dr Twisse, follows "this veteran leader, so well trained to the scholastic field;"—as he styles him, he constantly calls him, "This great man; our learned antagonist; the learned Twisse; our justly celebrated antagonist; this renowned man; the very illustrious, and the accurate Twisse." The most grave and judicious divines, as Rivet, Burgess, Rutherford, and others, have also honoured his name with similar distinguishing epithets.

He was allowed to be an excellent casuist. But notwithstanding all his accomplishments, Mr Neal says, that he died in very necessitous circumstances, having lost all that he had by the king's soldiers, insomuch, that when some of the Assembly of Divines at Westminster were deputed to visit him in his sickness, they reported, "that he was very sick, and in great straits." And, Mr Jeanes, in his preface to his Riches of God's Love, complains of his having been shamefully neglected; where he declares against the unnatural vanity of England, in preferring strangers above such of their own countrymen, as far surpassed them. And, he adds, of this unjust partiality, no profession hath tasted more than that of divinity; for of our ministers, such whom God hath best fitted with parts and learning for discussing controversies, have been so undervalued in comparison of some foreign divines, whose learning was little better than systematic, as that they have languished in their private studies, and had died in obscurity, unless the fame of their great abilities had been echoed over to us by the general applause of all christendom.[a] But like Cornelius Nepos, we must measure great men by their eminent qualities, and not by their condition and circumstances in this world.[b]

The great contentions and warm debates in the Assembly of Divines, much disturbed his thoughts; and his disturbed thoughts greatly impaired his bodily health; and his health being impaired, while his private studies and public employments were not abated, he was much reduced. Accordingly, when he spake unto God in the name of the people, and to the people in the name of God, and raised up the hearts of his hearers unto heaven, he fell down in the pulpit. Though his constitution was naturally good, and his disposition cheerful; yet, through age, his body was now become heavy and somewhat burthensome: and therefore, when very warmly employed in spiritual things, his outward strength failed him.—He was carried home, and laid upon his bed, and continued about a year under a lingering indisposition. During this time, he was visited by persons of all ranks, who loved either religion or learning. And, to

a Address to Oldisworth, as above.
b Nep. Eum. chap. i.

his friends who visited him, on the day of his distress, he gave remarkable and very comfortable evidences of his faith, Heb. xi. 13. And, under his affliction, he was a rare example of patience and christian resignation. "Knowing this, that the trying of your faith worketh patience," James i. 3. See Heb. x. 36. And the patience of the saints, which is the peculiar gift of God, and an eminent fruit of the Spirit, is very profitable to them at all times, and especially in trouble and at death, when it *hath its perfect work*, and faith is changed into the beatific vision of God.

"Unaw'd by threats, unmov'd by force,
My steady soul pursues her course,
Collected, calm, resign'd;
Say ye, who search with curious eyes,
The source whence human actions rise,
Say whence this turn of mind?

'Tis *Patience*, heav'n-descended maid!
Implor'd, flew swiftly to my aid,
And lent her fost'ring breast;
Watch'd my sad hours with parent care,
Repell'd th' approaches of despair,
And sooth'd my soul to rest.[a]

When the time of his departure was at hand, he seriously uttered these following words, which were almost his last:—"Now, at length, I shall have leisure to follow my studies to all eternity." He died about the 20th July, 1646, in the seventy-first year of his age. His body was buried with great honour and solemnity, according to his dignity, and former friendship with his brethren, at the request of the Assembly, in the collegiate church of St. Peter, Westminster, near the upper end of the poor folk's table, next the vestry, on the 24th of July, and was attended by the whole Assembly of Divines in a body. There his body rested till the restora-

a Scots Chronicle, Dec. 13, 1799.

tion of king Charles II. when his bones were dug up by an order of council, on the 14th September, 1661, and thrown, with the bones of several others, into a hole in the church yard of Margaret's, before the back door of the lodgings of one of the Prebendaries. Such is the rage of the church's enemies, that when they have no more that they can do, they will even disturb the bones of Christ's members in their graves.

The day after his burial, the parliament voted a thousand pounds to be given to his children, out of the public treasury; but they were cheated out of that, and whatever their father left. Notwithstanding, God was so pleased to appear for them, in his kind providence, that they obtained a decent support.—" Thou art the helper of the fatherless," Psal. x. 14. And in the Lord, the fatherless findeth mercy, Hosea. xiv. 3. " Leave thy fatherless children, I will preserve them alive; and let thy widows trust in me," Jer. xlix. 11.

He was eminently distinguished by his bold, determined. successful opposition to the enemies of God's sovereignty and grace both Arminians and Jesuits. He was an active, unwearied, mighty, and victorious champion in these controversies. And the keen opposition of his antagonists was so far from staggering his faith, that it confirmed his mind the more in the belief of the truth; as the forest oaks are said to be better established in their roots, by stormy winds and beating tempests. He made uncommon exertions in combating the errors of these times, and embraced all opportunities for that purpose; and his abilities always encreased with his work. He was ever glad to meet with the greatest difficulties from his adversaries: the harder the task which they prescribed to him, the better it pleased him. " A great spirited man will overcome not only great difficulties, but seeming impossibilities; yea, he is glad to meet with the greatest difficulties, because they match the greatness of his mind;" says an eminent divine.[a] He observed the movements of Arminian errors with peculiar care; and used the most vigorous

a Caryl on Job, chap. xxxiii. 12.

efforts to stop their progress. His attention was every where in this cause, as is said with regard to bishop Secker. He was the Bradwardine of the age; and he may well be ranked among those eminent characters, who have most successfully contributed their unwearied exertions for the vindication of the truth as it is in Jesus. He was particularly celebrated for his very able defence of the writings of the excellent Mr Perkins, against the Arminians. He hath given abundant proof, in this very accurate and most elaborate defence, that Arminius's much spoken of book was not unanswerable. And he hath displayed, in this remarkable work, such industry, perseverance, and erudition, as are only equalled by the exquisite judgment, and forcible animated reasoning, which he hath therein discovered. This great undertaking appears sufficient to have occupied half the life of an ordinary writer. Here he carefully examines the contents of Arminius's book, with the eagle-eye of a philosopher and sacred critic; and he leaves not the minutest article undiscussed.[a]

But to substantiate more particularly this part of the narrative, we shall here subjoin the joint suffrages of several eminent divines, of different denominations, both at home and abroad, to this purpose.

The learned and judicious Rivet, in his Latin preface to Dr Twisse's Animadversions, above referred to, says, when speaking concerning him:—" Respecting the author, his method, scholastic form of disputation, sharpness, and accuracy, I leave to the judgment of the readers. The most learned men in the whole christian world, even those who are of the opposite party, confess, that there was nothing hitherto published more accurate, nothing more finished and full, touching this controversy, than what was written by Dr Twisse. And this ought to please all the godly at least, that always every where he hath been earnest in a good cause; and hath so vindicated it, if any one ever did, from absurd objections, and the calumnies of the adversaries, that out of his labours, not

a See Rivet's Latin Preface, formerly referred to.

only the learned, but also those who are less exercised in controversies, may find enough to enable them to extricate themselves from the snares of their opponents." And that eminent English divine, Dr Owen, says, in his epistle prefixed to Dr Twisse's "Riches of God's Love," "It is well known what sphere this learned author moved in; how far elevated above any possibility of my reaching the least esteem to him or his labours: this I shall take the boldness to say, that this treatise of our author, comes not any whit behind the choicest of those other eminent works of his; wherein, in this cause of God, he faithfully served his generation.—I doubt not but it will appear to the reader, that he hath dealt with the adversaries of the truth, in their chiefest holds, advantages, and strengths, putting them to shame in the calumnies and lies which they make their refuge."—And the learned Mr Henry Jeanes, the publisher of Dr Twisse's Riches of God's Love, says, in a preface to it, "Were this book, that I now present unto thy view, unto which there is not any peer for solidity, and accurateness in scholastic divinity in the English tongue, translated into Latin, I am persuaded that outlandish divines would have such an estimate of it, as Jerome had of certain books of the martyr Lucian, written with his own hand, which he valued as a precious jewel: or as Beza had of a commentary of Mr Rollock, on the Epistle to the Romans and Ephesians; concerning which he wrote to a friend, that he had gotten a treasure of incomparable worth." And Dr Ridgley, in his Body of Divinity, quest. 12, 13, speaking of Dr Twisse, says, "I am not ashamed to own my very great esteem of this excellently learned and pious writer, who was as considerable for that part of learning, which his works discover him to have been conversant in, as most in his day." And Dr Hall, bishop of Norwich, in a letter to a friend, relative to a small book of Dr Twisse's, entitled, "The Doubting Conscience Resolved," says, "I return you many thanks for the favours you have done me, in affording me the view of this solid and seasonable piece of Dr Twisse, in full answer to this pretended questionist. This sculking and disguised challenger could not have met with a meeter combatant; a man so eminent in school-divinity, that the Jesuits have felt, and for ought I see, shrunk under his strength, in their *Scientia Media.*—The man shall find himself here over-answered; and receive too much honour from such an antagonist, in that it may be said of him, " Thou fallest by the right hand of the great Eneas." The elder Spanhiem styles him, *Subtilissimus Theologus simul & Philosophus,* a most acute philosopher as well as divine. And Mr Neal says, in his History of the Puritans, vol. iii. chap. vii. " He was allowed to be a person of prodigious knowledge in school divinity—a subtle disputant—and withal, a modest, humble, and religious person." The concurring testimony of so many eminent divines must be of considerable importance to establish the truth of the above narrative, and also to ascertain Dr Twisse's true character. And, here we see, that his literary reputation was not confined to England; but also widely extended beyond the seas. And his most learned adversaries have confessed, that there was nothing then extant, more exact, accurate and full, touching the Arminian controversy, than what he published; nor have any written upon this argument since the publication of Dr Twisse's works, without making honourable mention of him. And what Cornelius Nepos, the famous biographer of antiquity, says, with regard to Themistocles, the celebrated Athenian commander, who bravely defended Athens, may well be applied to Dr Twisse with relation to the Arminian controversy. " Themistocles was great in this war, and no less in peace." [a] And a real attachment to the truth, along with an ardent desire to ascertain it unto the satisfaction of his own mind, was his apology for distinguishing himself so much in a controversial way, as appears from his preface to a book against Mr Cotton.

Mr Clark says, That he needed neither trophies, marbles, nor epitaphs. He provided monuments for himself by every volume which he wrote, which will be more durable than either statues of brass or marble.

a Nep. Them. c. vi.

And biographers have done great justice to his memory: —Wood's Athen. Oxon. Leigh's Treatise of Learned Men; and in Fuller's Worthies of England.—He hath a place in Clark's Lives of Eminent Persons, London, 1683, folio;—in Middleton's Biographia Evangelica, vol. iii. London, 1784;—and in the Biographical and Martyrological Dictionary, by a clergyman and others: Newcastle-upon-Tyne, printed by Angus, 1790. And his name well deserves a place in every literary history of England, and in the archives of the reformed churches, both at home and abroad. And, we may well say concerning Dr Twisse, what Eutropius the Roman historian says with regard to Mithridates, king of Pontus, a very valiant man, who maintained a long war against the Romans, when he gives an account of his death, —"He was a man of great activity, understanding, and conduct." [a]

I shall here subjoin a part of a poem, which I lately procured in London, as it especially respects Dr Twisse's death, as Prolocutor of the Westminster Assembly of Divines.

"The great Assembly once renown'd,
Whose fame in foreign parts did sound,
Displac'd on earth, in haste remove
Their session to their house above.
Seraphic TWISSE went first 'tis true,
As Prolocutor, it was his due:
Then Borroughs, Marshall, Whitaker, Hill,
Gouge, Gataker, Ash, Vines, White,—still
Sharp swords soon'st cut their sheaths—Pern, Strong,
Spurstowe, Tuckney, Calamy, they throng
The gate of bliss, as if they fear
That heaven would fill e'er they got there.
He's with the rest, the praise to sing,
Of our most loving Lord and King;
There no dissenting brethren be,
But all as one, in one agree.

a Eutrop. l. 6. 12.

One mouth, one mind, one heart, one way;
No strife, which side shall bear the sway.
All doubts resolv'd, all knots unty'd,
All truth in the God of truth espy'd:
With warmest love they there embrace
Each other, full of perfect grace:
Their glory's great, their wealth is vast;
But O the pleasure that they taste
I' the tree of life, and in the sight
Of that blest face, that's all delight.
What tongue can tell, what mind can think,
What joy 'tis of this spring to drink!
Go fawning world, tempt me no more,
With thy skin-deep fading store,—
Thy best, thy whole is but a toy
To that these happy souls enjoy.
My God invites to angels fare,
To which thy trash cannot compare:
On swinish husks why should I feed,
When I may eat what's meat indeed?
O let my heaven-born soul expire
Itself in sallies, and desire
Only to rest, and make its stay,
Where Thou ART ALL IN ALL *for aye.*"

THE writings of those eminent Divines, who convened in the famous Assembly at Westminster, in the seventeenth century, in general, afford us clear and full views of the nature and perfection of God—of man's fatal apostasy from God—of the evil nature and just demerit of sin—of the total depravity of human nature—the utter impossibility of sinners ever doing any thing which can recommend them to God—the absolute sovereignty and entire freedom of divine grace, as displayed in the eternal choice of the vessels of mercy, their free justification through the finished righteousness of the Lord Jesus Christ, the necessity of divine influence in their regeneration, conversion, sanctification, and perseverance to the end—with the necessity of personal religion, and practical godliness, as expressions of gratitude for redeeming love, and evidences both to themselves and others of their union with Christ as their vital Head, their progress in faith and holiness, and the sincerity of their christian profession.

Dr Twisse's writings, in particular, are chiefly directed against these strong and crafty enemies of God's sovereignty and grace, Arminians and Jesuits, as may be seen at the conclusion of the account of his life, and in the following catalogue of his learned works. The reformers in Britain, as in other European countries, embraced the scriptural and Calvinistic doctrine of predestination and absolute decrees. And, upon this system, they composed all the articles of their religious creed. But these principles having met with strong opposition from Arminius and his party, the important controversy was soon introduced into the British island. Here, it was extensively diffussed, in a short time. The Arminians found much encouragement from the superstitious spirit of the episcopal church of England, and gradually incorporated themselves therewith. And some of that party, by the peculiar indulgence of king James the First, and his son and successor, Charles, attained the highest preferments in the hierarchy.[a]

Doctor Twisse most vigorously and successfully opposed the false tenets both of Arminians and Jesuits, at this critical time. His writings have deservedly obtained a considerable share of reputation, both at home and abroad. They are generally full of very acute, forcible, and animated, reasoning. By them his memory is still preserved; and he continues to *contend earnestly for the faith once delivered to the saints.* They are:

1. *A discovery of Dr Jackson's Vanity:* or, *A Perspective-glass, whereby the admirers of Dr Jackson's profound discourses, may see the vanity and weakness of them, in sundry passages, and especially so far as they*

a Hume's Hist. Engl. vol. vi. chap. li. 1629. and Appendix to the Reign of James I. p. 166. edit. Edin. 1792.

tend to the undermining of the doctrine hitherto received. 4to. pp. 710. Printed in the year 1631. It is not said where it was printed, in the title page; but Wood says that it was printed beyond the sea, which is very probable; for a learned piece of Dr Twisse's against Arminius, was stopped in the press at home about this time. This book was written against Dr Jackson's Treatise of the Divine Essence and Attributes, but the Doctor made no reply.[a] I have one copy of this book; and I have seen another at Lochgoin, in Ayrshire.

2. *Vindiciæ Gratiæ, Potestatis, Ac Providentiæ, Dei.* Folio, Amstelodami, 1632. In Latin.

This very large and most elaborate vindication of the sovereignty and Grace of God, which was written against the Arminians and the Jesuites, was well received, and highly useful at this time. It was much esteemed at home, and an honour to English literature abroad. The learned Rivet informs us, that this excellent work was so acceptable to the public, that, although it was of a great size, when two editions were sold off, a third came forth by the same printer who had printed the first edition. This third edition seems to have been printed at Amsterdam, in the year 1648, according to Wood and Rivet; but I have not yet seen a copy of this edition.[b] I have seen several copies of the folio edition, 1632.—One in Wigtonshire,—one in Renfrewshire,—one in the library of the University of Glasgow,—one in the library of the late Mr Thomson, Quarrelwood,—another in the library belonging to the presbytery of Dumfries; and it is in the catalogue of books in the Theological library, belonging to the students of divinity in the University of Edinburgh, 1757. I have also seen one copy of the second edition, 4to. Amstel. 1632. in the library of the University of Glasgow.

3. *Dissertatio de Scientia Media Tribus Libris Absoluta.* Folio, pp. 498. Arnhemii, 1639. In Latin. I have

a Wood's Athenæ Oxon. vol. ii. p. 81.

b See Wood's Athenæ, vol. ii. p. 81. and Rivet's Pref. to Twisse, de Pred. Amstel. 1649.

seen one copy of this in Renfrewshire, in the year 1807. and another at Quarrelwood. And it is in the catalogue of the books, in the library belonging to the presbytery of Dumfries, 1784. p. 45. foot; and in that of books in the Theological library, belonging to the students of divinity in the University of Edinburgh, above-mentioned.

4. *Of the Morality of the Fourth Commandment, as still in force to bind Christians: delivered by way of Answer to the Translator of Doctor Prideaux's Lecture, concerning the doctrine of the Sabbath.* 4to. pp. 248. London, 1641. In English. It is divided into two parts, 1. An answer to the Prefacer. 2. A Consideration of Dr Prideaux's Lecture. The book will amply repay the trouble of a perusal. It still occurs in the catalogues of books; especially in Edinburgh and London: price 2s. I have seen several copies of it in Scotland; one in the library of the University of Glasgow; and I have seen it in England.

5. *An Examination of Mr Cotton's Treatise concerning Predestination.* 4to. London, 1646. In English. I have seen two copies of it in Scotland.

6. *Animadversiones de Prædestinatione. Amstel.* 1649. Folio, in Latin. This was published by Andrew Rivet. It is a large and learned work, containing animadversions respecting Predestination, Grace, and Free-will, against Arminius, Corvinus, and others. And when this ingenious and indefatigable writer saw that the cause was deserted and betrayed by Tilemus, which he had undertaken to defend, he left nothing untouched on the subject. He took upon himself the burden of answering all the adversaries of truth.[a] I have seen this elaborate work, in the library belonging to the presbytery of Dumfries, two copies of it in Wigtonshire, one in Renfrewshire, and two in the library of the University of Glasgow.

7. *The Scriptures sufficiency to determine all matters of Faith, made good against the Papist: or, That a Christian may be infallibly certain of his Faith and Reli-*

a See Rivet's Preface to this book.

gion by the Holy Scriptures. This is a small book; and it seems to have been first printed, in the year 1652; at least its imprimatur bears that date; but I have not seen a copy of that edition. It was printed at London, 1656. I have a copy of this edition.—Dumfries, 1795. I have some copies of this last edition unsold, which the encouragers of this work may have, if they please. Price 6*d.* A good type, and paper.

8. *The Riches of God's Love unto the Vessels of Mercy, consistent with his absolute Hatred or Reprobation of the Vessels of Wrath.* Small folio. Oxford, 1653. In English Controversial. I have seen several copies of this book, in Scotland.

9. Fifteen Letters to Mr Joseph Mede. In these, there are several things very curious and entertaining, respecting the two witnesses, Rev. xi.—the conversion of the Jews—some obscure passages in the book of Daniel—America—the frequent celebration of the sacrament of the Lord's Supper—and the holiness of times and places. See Mede's Works, folio, 3d edit. London, 1672.

10. Prefaces to the learned works of others; as to Mr Joseph Mede's Apostacy of the Latter Times. London, 1642—1644. And to Mr Mede's Key of the Revelation. London, 1643. Both these Prefaces I have seen.

The learned Thomas Godwin, a very celebrated writer on Roman and Jewish antiquities, in the seventeenth century, was the author of "Three Arguments to prove Election upon Foresight of Faith." This treatise involved the author, in a temporary controversy with the learned Twisse. Godwin seems not to have acquired much fame by this controversy, in the character of a theological disputant.[a] These are all the writings of the learned Twisse that I have seen.

a See Wood's Athenæ, vol. ii. p. 27. Gen. Biogr. vol. iv. under Godwin.

CORNELIUS BURGESS, D. D.

PASTOR OF WATFORD.

CORNELIUS BURGESS was descended from the Burgesses of Batcomb, in Somersetshire, in England. He was educated in the ancient and famous University of Oxford. His first entrance into this University was, in the year 1611; but in what college or hall is uncertain. However, he translated himself unto Wadham college, about the time of its first foundation, and as a member thereof took the degree of bachelor of Arts. Afterward retiring to Lincoln college, he proceeded in the same faculty, received holy orders, and had some care bestowed upon him, which Wood takes to be the rectory of Magnus' church in London, or the vicarage of Watford, in Hartfordshire, or both. In the beginning of the reign of king Charles the first, he became one of his chaplains in ordinary; and in 1627, he took both the degrees in divinity.[a]

He was greatly harassed by that very arbitrary and inquisitorial tribunal, the high-commission court, for opposing the Laudensian faction. The court of high-commission had been erected by Elizabeth, in consequence of an act of parliament, passed in the beginning of her reign. By this act, it was intended, during the great revolution of religious affairs, to arm the sovereign with full powers, in order to discourage and suppress opposition. All appeals from the inferior ecclesiastical courts were carried before the high-commission; and consequently, the whole life and doctrine of the ecclesiastics lay directly under it's inspection. Every breach of the

a Wood's Athenæ Oxon. vol. ii. p 347. 2d edit.

act of uniformity, every refusal of the ceremonies, was cognizable in this court; and during the reign of Elizabeth, had been punished by deprivation, by fine, confiscation, and imprisonment.[a] And this tyrannical court, with all its iniquities and terrors, was continued in the following reigns, whereby many were greatly harassed.

The subject of this memoir was brought into that court, by a powerful adversary, who had formed a strong party against him, for being disaffected to episcopal government, and for permitting some to sit, when they received the sacrament of the Lord's supper, in the year 1622. He was again questioned there, for refusing to read the common prayer in his surplice and hood, before the sermon, in the year 1629. This was upon a Thursday, when he was called to preach for another, who was a Lecturer; and when every Lecturer was enjoined to read divine service before the lecture in his surplice and hood, in order to deter godly ministers from the practice.[b] In the year 1635, he preached a sermon in Latin to the London-ministers, in Alphage church, near Sion-College, by an appointment of the governors thereof. In this sermon, he warmly urged all possible diligence in preaching the *gospel of the kingdom.* Among other arguments, he produced what had been anciently required respecting this, even of the bishops themselves. He reminded them of the third part of the public homily against the peril of idolatry, wherein it is said, of the primitive bishops, "That they were preaching bishops, more often seen in pulpits, than in princes' palaces; more often occupied in his legacy, who said, *Go ye into all the world, and preach the gospel,* than in the embassages and affairs of princes."[c] After this, he recited an old canon of the sixth general council in Trullo, with Zonaras's note upon it; which canon enjoined bishops "to preach often; at least, every Lord's-day, or to be canoni-

a Hume's Hist. of England, vol. vi. Appendix to the Reign of James I. edit. 1792.

b See Neal's Hist. Purit. vol. ii. chap. iv. 1629.

c See the author's Chain of Graces, chap. iv. p. 76.

cally admonished for their neglect: whereupon, if they reformed not, it was farther ordained, that they should be excommunicated, or deposed." Some of his prelatical hearers, though they gave him thanks for his sermon, informed the archbishop of Canterbury against him, who gave in a complaint against him to the king. Upon this, he was summoned by letters missive into the high-commission court, which was then little better than the Spanish inquisition, and peculiarly destructive to all religious liberty, especially after Laud had obtained a grant from the king, that all fines imposed there should go to repair Paul's Cathedral, in London. Upon his appearance there, articles were exhibited against him, charging him with being disaffected to the book of common prayer, the ceremonies, and government of the church by bishops; as also for charging the bishops with conniving at the then too palpable growth of *Arminianism* and *popery*, and their too much conforming thereunto; but chiefly, because he seemed to accuse several prelates and bishops of neglecting to preach often, representing the ancient bishops, as deeply penetrated with the importance of the charge committed to them, and frequently and diligently preaching the gospel of Christ. The bishops now furiously spurned against him, and there party every where said, That he should be both *deprived* and *degraded*. And no doubt, this would have been effected, if he had not given them enough in his answers to the articles exhibited against him, and in his protestation annexed to his sermon delivered to archbishop Laud, professed to stand to what he said in that sermon, against all opposers even to the death. After this, he was not farther troubled.[a] He possessed that spirited and manly character, which eminently distinguished our reforming ancestors; and obtained a signal victory over his powerful opponents. His active zeal in the service of the church was eminently conspicuous, on this, and on several other occasions.

a A Case concerning the Lawfulness of Buying Bishops' Lands, Lond. 1659, p. 28. No Sacrilege nor Sin to Purchase Bishops' Lands, chap. vi. 2d edit. p. 165, 166, & 167.

And, in his sermon, he faithfully and seasonably directed the attention of his hearers to objects both of great utility and importance. It was both seasonable and necessary, to urge diligence in preaching the gospel of the Son of God, when many were very remiss in this great work: and when such faithful ministers as preached twice on the same day, were, by a bishop, in a most scornful manner, compared to Virgil's cow, that came twice a-day to the milking-pail. An ardent desire for the glory of God, in the salvation of souls, raised the faithful preacher above the fear of danger, in performing the duties of his office. And deeply impressed with the great importance of the charge which was committed unto him, he honestly employed the talents which God had given him, in opposing Arminianism, and popery, which now produced it's full growth of superstition. Not like those who sacrifice every thing to the enjoyment of the moment, he supported the honourable cause of truth, with all the energy that he was capable of, even in dangerous times. This zealous champion for the interests of religion, entered the field of contest under the banners of truth and of purity. And our reformers in general, having a superiority of understanding conferred upon them, and of magnanimity and christian courage; and possessing, in an eminent degree, that good quality of a true subject of Christ's kingdom, a sincere and devoted attachment to truth, they boldly resisted the dangerous contagion of prevailing error, and of abounding superstition. And with a determined fortitude, persevered in their resistance, and were seconded, and warmly supported by the state, even the greatest of the nobility. And, unless they had acted in this mannner, instead of enlightening the world, as the stars in Christ's right-hand, and being beneficial to mankind, by the faithful discharge of the duties of their office, they would have added to the darkness and superstitious devices which prevailed, and would have proved a curse and a snare to their fellow-creatures. And they would have been guilty of the prostitution of their ingenuity, learning, and gifts, in the basest manner. But acting as they did, under the gracious influences and sweet smiles of approving Heaven, they were *the salt of the earth*, and *the light of the world.*

When the Long Parliament was opened, Nov. 3d, 1640, the Houses petitioned the king to appoint a fast, and *call a solemn assembly*, that they might *turn to the Lord with fasting, and with weeping, and with mourning*, and pray for a divine blessing upon their counsels. This fast was observed Nov. 17th, 1640. Dr Burgess, and Mr Marshall, were chosen and called to preach to the House of Commons, on this solemn occasion. Dr Burgess pseached from Jer. l. 5. "They shall ask the way to Zion with their faces thitherward, *saying*, Come, and let us join ourselves to to the Lord in a perpetual covenant, *that* shall not be forgotten." [a] Mr Hume says, that the preachers entertained them with discourses seven hours in length. [b] The sermons, undoubtedly, were long: they were both printed, and hitherto they have been preserved, and are very valuable. The principal doctrine exhibited and handled in Dr Burgess's sermon is, "When God vouchsafes any deliverance to his church, especially from Babylon, then it is most seasonable and most necessary to close with God by a more solemn, strict, and inviolable, covenant, to be his, and only his for ever." In prosecuting this doctrine, he first shews, That it hath always been the practice of God's people, upon obtaining any great deliverance, especially from Babylon, to enter into solemn covenant with the Lord. 2. How this ought to be done. 3. The reasons of entering into solemn covenant with the Lord, upon obtaining any deliverance by his hand, especially from Babylon. And the author pays very particular attention to the application of this sermon, dealing plainly and faithfully with his auditory, in reproof, information, and exhortation. The importance of the subject, the author's reputation, and the solemn occasion, seemed to require this particular account of the sermon.

Wood says, that upon the approach of the troublesome times, he, with Stephen Marshall, Edmund Calamy, and

a Neal's Hist. Purit. vol. ii. chap. vii.
b Hume's Hist. vol. vi. chap. liv. 1640.

others, first whispered in their conventicles, and then openly preached, That *for the cause of religion it was lawful for the subjects to take up arms against their lawful sovereign.* Which doctrine being also followed by the rest of the elders, the people of London did violently rush into rebellion, and were found pliable by the faction in parliament to raise tumults, make out-cries for justice, call for innocent blood, subscribe and prefer petitions against the holy liturgy and the hierarchy, and to strike at root and branch, especially if our author Burgess did but hold up his finger to his myrmidons.[a] And the earl of Clarendon says, "Without doubt, the archbishop of Canterbury had never so great an influence upon the counsels at court, as Dr Burgess, and Mr Marshall had then upon the Houses."[b] An author and his reader are not always of the same opinion. And, the above-mentioned authors are much accustomed to enforce opinions, especially against the puritans, only by the weight of assertion. And they are much more intent on upholding a favourite party, by misrepresenting and abusing it's opponents, than by fairly stating the cause, and proving what is right, and what is wrong. They plead for superstition and prejudice, severely censuring the advocates for rational and religious liberty, seriously engaged in sober and free inquiry, and confounding them with those who were unprincipled and licentious. Dr Burgess, and Mr Marshall, were undoubtedly very active men, on the side of the parliament, in the civil war; but they only encouraged taking up arms for the *defence* and *security* of the constitution, and of the religious liberty of the subject, when these were violently attacked by the opposite party, and in the utmost danger. We cannot find by the closest researches, that they concurred in any degree, in those measures, which afterward overturned the constitution, and had a manifest tendency to confusion. Mr Marshall wrote a defence of the side he took in the civil war. Dr Burgess also has published an account of his

a Wood's Athenæ Oxon. vol. ii. p. 347.
b Clarendon's Hist. B. iv. vol. ii. p. 302.

principles and practices, which Dr Calamy thinks deserves to be preserved to posterity.[a] And, in this, and in his writings, the beneficent spirit and pacific principles of the christian religion clearly appear; though he has been treated by the royal party with no small degree of severity. Dr Burgess delivered an animated speech against deans and chapters, in the House of Commons, in the year 1641. The abolition of deans and chapters was now warmly debated in the House; and the application of their revenues to better purposes. This greatly alarmed the cathedral men, and excited them to consult their own safety. Accordingly, one divine was deputed from every English cathedral, to solicit their friends in the parliament in behalf of their several foundations. And addresses were readily presented from both the Universities in their favour. The deputies from the several cathedrals drew up a petition to the Lords and Commons for counsel; but upon being informed, that if they had any thing to offer they should appear and plead their own cause, they selected Dr John Hackett, prebendary of Paul's, and archdeacon of Bedford, for their counsel, who, being admitted to the bar of the House, after the petitions from the Universities had been read, made an elaborate speech in their behalf, chiefly insisting upon the topics of the address from Oxford. He warmly recommended cathedrals, as accommodated to supply the defects of private prayer; the public performance whereof should be in some place of distinction. He affirmed, that at the time of the Reformation, preaching began in cathedrals.—He warmly urged, that cathedrals were serviceable for the advancement of learning, and training up persons for the defence of the church; and that, the removal of them would be very hurtful to the cause of religion, and highly pleasing to their adversaries. That the ancient and genuine use of deans and chapters was to assist the bishop in his jurisdiction; and as some had complained, that bishops for many years had usurped the sole government to themselves and their consistories, the continua-

a Calamy's Contin. vol. ii. p. 737.

tion of chapters rightly used would bring it to a plurality of assistants. He then reminded them of the antiquity of the structures, and the number of persons maintained by them, amounting to many thousands.—He farther enlarged upon the endowments of cathedrals, as greatly encouraging industry and virtue; that several famous protestants of foreign countries had been maintained by being installed prebendaries, as Casaubon, Saravia, Peter du Moulin, Vossius, and others; and that these foundations were highly beneficial to the crown, paying greater sums into the exchequer for first fruits and tenths, in proportion, than other corporations. And finally, he reminded them, That these structures and estates were consecrated to divine service, and barred all alienation with the most dreadful imprecations. Afterward, Dr Cornelius Burgess appeared on the opposite side, against deans and chapters; and made a long and appropriate speech, respecting the unprofitableness of those corporations. He complained that the lives of singing men were debauched, and that their conversation was vicious. He pointedly and extensively replied to the particulars of Dr Hackett's elaborate speech; and, in the concluding passage, said, "Though he apprehended that it was necessary to apply these foundations to better purposes, yet it was by no means lawful to alienate them from public and pious uses, or to convert them to the profit of any private person." [a] He was a strenuous advocate for reformation, at this critical time. And his laudable zeal for the interests of religion, on this remarkable occasion, undoubtedly was attended with beneficial effects. By the prudent and effectual measures, which our reformers adopted, the pressure of the prevailing evils was greatly alleviated. The returning spirit of christian zeal had now taught them to inquire into, and to attempt, under God, a redress of several grievances, and to consult on the most efficacious way to compose the distracted state of the church. In

a Fuller's Eccles. Hist. B. xi. p. 176—179. Neal's Hist. Purit. vol. ii. chap. ix. Or vol. i. 706. 4to. More speeches against Deans and Chapters may be seen in Mr Neal's Hist.

these measures, they were most strenuously opposed by many. But amid all opposition, our reformers, as respectable instruments in the hand of the Lord, completely disentangled truth from error, and purity from corruption. And the immediate consequence was, that many seasonably obtained the sweets of liberty, who had for a long time been held closely in the chains of captivity. These interesting proceedings are detailed more extensively, in the history of the times.

Dr Burgess, taking part with the parliament, was chosen to be one of those pacific divines, who met in the Jerusalem chamber at Westminster, in 1641, for accommodating ecclesiastical differences. They consulted together six several days; and the dean entertained them during that time at his table; but they were not successful in accommodating the differences.[a] He frequently preached before the parliament, especially the House of Commons. Wood says, That he was thought fit by the parliament to be one of those *godly divines*, who were to hold forth before them. And, in this opinion, undoubtedly, the parliament were not mistaken, as the author's sermons, which have been hitherto carefully preserved, in the goodness of Divine providence, abundantly evince. In this, also, Wood said truly, though he sat in the scorner's chair when he wrote it, as clearly appears by his narrative.[b] Wood, generally, is very little scrupulous respecting the characters against whom he levels the shafts of his indignation, especially the puritans: but I shall not trouble either myself, or the reader, here, with retailing his illiberal invective against Dr Burgess.

The Doctor, being highly approved for his zeal, valour and fidelity, and admirably adapted to the nature of the military service, was wisely selected by the earl of Essex, the general of the parliament's army, to be chaplain to his regiment of horsemen. The most eminent and suitable divines were appointed chaplains to the several regiments; and while these continued with them, none

a Neal's Hist. Purit. vol. ii. chap. ix.
b Ath. Oxon. vol. ii. p. 348.

of the enthusiastic follies, which afterward appeared, and were truly reproachable, discovered themselves.[a] Such chaplains were highly beneficial to the parliamentary army, to direct their views aright, to afford them aid in their devotion, and to excite them in the performance of their duty, in defence of their liberty and religion, when the situation of public affairs was truly alarming. They were now called *to add to their faith, virtue*, or military valour, as the word generally denotes in Homer.

Dr Burgess was one of the famous Assembly of Divines at Westminster, and, with Mr John White, was chosen to be Assessor. Two Assessors were joined with the Prolocutor, to supply his place in case of absence or sickness. Mr Robert Baillie, from the church of Scotland, who was present in that assembly, says, " The one Assessor, our good friend Dr Burgess, a very active and sharp man, supplies, so far as is decent, the Prolocutor's place; the other, our good friend Mr White, has kept in of the gout since our coming." [b] When the solemn league and covenant was transmitted to the assembly of divines at Westminster, on the first of Sept. 1643, and generally approved, Dr Burgess argued against imposing it. Mr Baillie says, that he doubted for one night. Dr Calamy says, " He argued against imposing the covenant, and refused the taking it, till he was suspended: but having once taken it, he thought himself obliged to keep it, and was grieved, that he could not prevail with others to be of the same mind, or to act agreeably." [c] Undaunted courage seems to have been the distinguishing characteristic of Dr Burgess. Seemingly, he was never afraid to speak his mind on any occasion, nor in any assembly; and accordingly, he spake freely respecting the covenant, at this critical time. And he seems to have taken it after mature deliberation, which was certainly very proper in so great and interesting a matter. We are told, that even the cautious suspense of Tacitus,

a Wood's Ath. Oxon. as above. Neal's Hist. Purit. vol. ii. chap. xii.

b Baillie's Letters, vol. i. lett. xxxix. p. 399.

c Baillie's Lett. vol. i. p. 390. Calamy's Contin. vol. ii. p. 745.

a most accurate observer, in a doubtful matter, was a proof of his diligent inquiries:[a] and this seems to have been the case here.

When the bishops refused to ordain any who were not in the interest of the crown, and application was made to the assembly at Westminster for their advice in this matter, they advised, That an association of some godly ministers in and about London, and in other places, be appointed by public authority, to ordain ministers for the city and other parts. Agreeably to this advice, the Houses of parliament passed an ordinance, 2 Oct. 1644, for the ordination of ministers for the time, appointing ten, being presbyters, and members of the Assembly, to examine and ordain, by imposition of hands, those whom they should judge admissible into the sacred office of the ministry. Dr Burgess was one of that number, and his name is first in the list. Others were appointed to this work, who were not members of the Assembly.[b]

When Paul's Cathedral was again opened, Dr Burgess was appointed by the parliament at the request of the people, as Lecturer there on the sabbath-evening, and on a work-day, with a settled allowance of £400 yearly out of the revenues of the Cathedral.

When the parliament published the necessity of an advance of money, horses, and plate, by a voluntary *loan*, upon the *public faith, for defence of the king and parliament*, when the king, seduced by evil counsel, had deserted the parliament, and raised an army against them, Dr Burgess did lend several sums of money, in the integrity of his heart, for the defence of both king and parliament. He resolved to have suffered any death, rather than to lend one penny, or to have spoken one word in that cause, upon any other account; as he afterward declared to a committee of the parliament. The parliament, by an ordinance, Nov. 16, 1646, appointed and ordained all the lands and revenues of the bishops to be sold, to raise money for the use of the state. In this

a Gibbon's Hist. Rom. Emp. vol. i. chap. x. edit. 1791.
b Neal's Hist. vol. iii. chap. iv. 1644.

ordinance, they invited all who had before lent money, horses, and plate, for the service of the king and parliament, upon the public faith, to *double* this: and to take the whole out of the lands of bishops, either in money or lands; intimating, that they who did not double, must expect no other security for what they did lend formerly, but the then-despised public faith; nor to be paid, till all *doublers* were satisfied. Dr Burgess seeing this necessity of doubling, to prevent hazarding all, doubled all his bills, which then amounted to £3400, beside his loan for Ireland. He endeavoured to receive all again in money, but could not. Having a wife, and ten children to provide for, who must all be ruined, if that money miscarried; and finding the divisions of the parties, who now managed the public affairs, and pursued several interests, daily increasing; and himself badly requited for all his faithful services, he was obliged to take out his money in *bishops' lands*. And he declares, that this was the only reason of his purchasing these lands.[a] For this he hath suffered severely by the scourge of tongues. The reader who wishes to see this subject minutely handled, may consult the case as here referred to, and the author's book, entitled, "No Sacrilege, nor Sin, to Purchase the Lands of Bishops." Upon the king's restoration he lost all, though about a year before he had been offered above twelve thousand pounds for his house and lands at or near Wells, according to Wood.

Dr Burgess preached a sermon at Mercers chapel, Jan. 14, 1648, in which he inveighed, with great freedom, against the design of taking off the king, and feared not the consequence. And about the same time, he appeared at the head of a number of ministers, who, in exposing themselves, subscribed a paper, entitled, *A vindication of the ministers of the gospel, in and about London, from the unjust aspersions cast upon their former actings for the parliament, as if they had promoted the bringing of the king to capital punishment.* This paper was drawn

a A Case concerning the Buying of Bishops Lands, p. 1, 2, 3. London, 1659. See the following pages of the case.

up by Dr Burgess, and Dr Calamy has given it at length, with fifty-seven names subscribed.[a] It runs thus:

"It cannot be unknown how much we, and other ministers of this city and kingdom, that faithfully adhered to the parliament, have injuriously smarted under the scourge of evil tongues and pens, ever since the first eruption of the unhappy differences and unnatural war between the king and parliament, for our obedience to the commands and orders of the honourable Houses, in their contests with his majesty, and conflicts with his armies. We are not ignorant of the overbusy intermeddlings of prelates and their party heretofore, in overruling civil affairs to the great endangering of kingdoms and of this in particular, when private interests, ambitious designs, revenge, or other sinister ends, engaged them beyond their sphere. Howbeit it cannot reasonably (as we conceive) be denied, that ministers as subjects, being bound to obey the laws and to preserve the liberties of the kingdom, and having an interest in them and the happiness of them, as well as others, may and ought (without incurring the just censure due to busy-bodies and incendiaries) to appear, for preserving the laws and liberties of that commonwealth whereof they are members; especially in our case, when it was declared by the parliament, that all was at stake and in danger to be lost. No, nor as ministers ought they to hold their peace, in a time wherein the sins of rulers and magistrates as well as others have so far provoked God as to kindle the fire of his wrath against his people. And yet, for this alone, the faithful servants of God, have in all ages, through the malice of Satan and his intruments been traduced as Archincendiaries, when only their accusers, are indeed both guilty of laying the train, and of putting fire to it, to blow up a kingdom."

But we cannot insert all the paper here. In it, the subscribers strongly declare their dissatisfaction with the proceedings at Westminster against the king; and accord-

a Calamy's Contin. vol. ii. p. 737—744. See also Neal's Hist. Purit. vol. iii. chap. x.

ing to their covenant, in the name of the Great God, they warn and exhort the people of their respective charges, and any who attended their ministry, or to whom they have administered the covenant; to abide by their vows, and the ways of God, constantly maintaining the true reformed religion, the fundamental constitution, and the government of the kingdom; and not to suffer themselves to be seduced to subscribe the *agreement of the people*, which was the subversion of the present constitution, and opened the way for the universal toleration of all heresies and blasphemies, directly contrary to the covenant, and would effectually divide the kingdoms of England and Scotland. They farther exhort the people to mourn bitterly for their own sins, the sins of the city, army, parliament, and kingdom, and for the woful miscarriages of the king himself in his government, which cast him down from his excellency into an horrid pit of misery, almost beyond example; and to pray, that God would give him effectual repentance, and sanctify the bitter cup of Divine displeasure, which Divine providence had put into his hand; and that God would restrain the violence of men, that they may not dare to draw upon themselves and the kingdom the blood of their sovereign.

They who would judge impartially, in this affair, ought carefully to peruse this paper. It was openly and boldly published, in a very critical time.—Some bitter invectives have been published against Dr Burgess; but many good men have suffered in their reputation, from those who were unfriendly to the cause in which they were engaged.[a]

His name is found among many other respectable names, in Dr Calamy's Account and Index of those who were ejected or silenced by the act for uniformity. He was ejected, from St Andrew's, in the city of Wells, in Somersetshire, after the restoration of king Charles II.

Immediately after the restoration, the royalists and zealous churchmen were the popular party in the nation, and

a See Toulmin's edition of Neal's Hist. vol. i. p. 419. Calamy's Contin. vol. ii. p. 745.

seconded by the efforts of the court, had prevailed in most of the elections. Mr Hume says, that not more than fifty-six members of the presbyterian party had obtained seats in the Lower House; and these were not able either to oppose or retard the measures of the majority. Monarchy, therefore, and episcopacy, were now exalted to as great power and splendour as they had lately suffered misery and depression.

The covenant itself, together with the act for erecting the high court of justice, that for subscribing the engagement, and for declaring England a commonwealth, were ordered to be burnt by the hands of the hangman. The people assisted with great alacriy on this occasion.[a]

Bishops were restored to their seats in parliament, from which they had been excluded by the law which the late king had passed, immediately before the commencement of the civil war. And after an adjournment of some months, the parliament was again assembled, and proceeded in the same spirit as before, Nov. 20. 1661. The church was not less attended to now, than the monarchy. And the bill of uniformity was an evidence of their strong attachment to the episcopal hierarchy, and of their antipathy to presbyterianism. It contained very severe clauses, requiring, that every clergyman, to render him capable of holding any ecclesiastical benefice, should have episcopal ordination, and be re-ordained, if he had not before received episcopal ordination; should declare his assent and consent to every thing contained in the book of common-prayer, adminstration of sacraments, and other rites and ceremonies of the church of England, with the psalter, and the form of making, ordaining, and consecrating bishops, priests and deacons; should take the oath of canonical obedience; should abjure the Solemn League and Covenant; and renounce the principle of taking arms against the king, upon any pretence whatever.[b]

a Hume's Hist. Engl. vol. vii. chap. lxiii. edit. Edin. 1792. Rapin's Hist. Engl. vol. ii. fol. B. xxiii. 1661.

b Hume's Hist. Engl. as above, Macpherson's Hist. of Great Britain, vol. i. chap. i. Neal's Hist. Purit. vol. iv. chap. vi. and Rapin's Hist. Engl. vol. ii. B. xxiii.

Mr Neal says, "It appears from hence, that the terms of conformity were higher than before the civil wars, and the common-prayer book more exceptionable; for instead of striking out the apocryphal lessons, more were inserted, as the story of Bel and the Dragon; and some new holy days were added, as St Barnabas, and the conversion of St Paul; a few new collects and alterations were made by the bishops themselves, but care was taken, says Burnet, that nothing should be altered, as was moved by the presbyterians."—And Mr Hume well observes, that "This bill reinstated the church in the same condition in which it stood before the commencement of the civil wars; and as the old persecuting laws of Elizabeth still subsisted in their full rigor, and new clauses of a like nature were now enacted, all the king's promises of toleration and of indulgence to tender consciences were thereby eluded and broken." And Mr Rapin has some judicious remarks on this act. which the reader, who hath an opportunity, may see in his History of England, or in Neal's History, as referred to here.

This bill, of extreme severity, took it's rise in the House of Lords, and received various alterations when it was sent down to the Commons. Bishop Burnet says, that it passed by no great majority. The 24th of Aug. 1662, the day of St Bartholomew's feast, was the time when the execution of this act commenced. This day seems to have been pitched on, that, if they were then deprived, they should lose the external supports of the whole year, since the tythes are commonly due at Michaelmas. And, in this circumstance, the severity was much greater.[a] When queen Elizabeth enacted the liturgy, and during the dominion of the parliamentary party, a fifth part of each living was left to the ejected minister, for his subsistence; but this indulgence, though at first insisted on by the House of Peers, was now refused to the presbyterians. And to add unto the distress of those who were cast out by the act of uniformity, another was passed, called the five-mile-act, banishing them five miles

a Burnet's Hist. of his own Times, vol. i. p. 268, & 269.

from any city, borough, or church in which they had before served. Hereby they were placed at such a distance from their acquaintance and friends, that they had not opportunity to help them, though they might be disposed to minister unto their relief. The penalty was a fine of fifty pounds, and six months imprisonment. Mr Hume observes, that this act "has given occasion to grievous and not unjust complaints. The church, under pretence of guarding monarchy against its inveterate enemies, persevered in the project of wreaking her own enmity against the nonconformists." And this was an expedient to deprive them of all means of subsistence. And there was another act prohibiting their meeting to worship God any where except in the episcopal churches, or according to the liturgy and practice of the church of England, under the penalties of heavy fines, imprisonments, and banishment to foreign lands. It was now enacted, that wherever five persons above those of the same household should assemble in a religious congregation, every one of them was liable for the first offence, to be imprisoned three months, or pay five pounds; for the second, to be imprisoned six months, or pay ten pounds; and for the third, to be transported seven years, or pay an hundred pounds.[a]

By ejecting the non-conforming ministers from their churches, separating them from their acquaintance and friends, and prohibiting all separate congregations, they reduced them to extraordinary calamities. And these violences were preludes to the most furious and hellish persecution.

Dr Burgess, and many more, absolutely refused compliance with the act of uniformity, though these complicated calamities attended the refusal. And, with great suffering, and much worldly loss, they boldly entered their protest against this presumptuous invasion of Christ's throne and crown-rights: this most schismatical intrusion of strange

a Hume's Hist. Engl. vol. vii. chap. lxiv. Towgood's Dissent, Lett. ii. p. 83. 5th edit. Burnet's Hist. of his Own Times, vol. i. p. 329, & 429. &c.

terms of communion into his church, the house of the living God. With great supernatural courage, and in dependence on the Father of mercies, they sacrificed their temporal interest to their religion, to the astonishment of their avowed enemies: *choosing rather to suffer affliction with the people of God, than to enjoy the pleasures of sin for a season,* in compliance with such measures. And indeed our reforming ancestors, who had taken the covenant, and were really presbyterians, could not comply with the uniformity-act, without being chargeable with the most glaring inconsistency, unfaithfulness, and perjury. And " to their immortal praise be it recorded, they better understood their *rights as men*, and their *duty as Christ's subjects*, the alone King and Head of the church, than basely to comply with these things." By complying, they must have renounced the validity of presbyterian ordination; and consequently have disowned the ministrations of all such as were so ordained: and engaged to maintain episcopacy, which they had sworn to extirpate. And, as the uniformity-act particularly required the abjuration of the Solemn League and Covenant, with a declaration of it's unlawfulness, they could not in conscience comply, while they viewed themselves under the obligations of that covenant. The king, and his episcopal party, were always violently set against this covenant. One observes and says, " There is nothing has whetted the wit of the cavaliers, so much as the Solemn League and Covenant. I imagined by what they said of it, before I read it, that it was some such infernal engagement as witches, or rather as Oliver Cromwell entered into with the devil, in a wood in Worcestershire, according to some." [a] Our venerable ancestors were, therefore, more particularly called to adhere solemnly and stedfastly to this covenant, as they did, by their non-compliance with the act of uniformity. And, who could subscribe and declare, " That it is not lawful upon *any pretence whatever*, to take arms against the king, or any commissioned by him?" " A notoriously false, base and

b Clarendon and Whitlocke compared, chap. v.

scandalous declaration:—a dangerous and important untruth!"[a] By this compliance our respectable reformers would have entirely given up all their rights as men, and their immunities as christians. And this would have been passive obedience, and non-resistence indeed. But their animated refusal added much to their respectability. Mr Towgood, speaking concerning those who were cast out by the act of uniformity, says: To this, "as christians and as protestants they bravely scorned to submit. Noble was the stand which they made in defence of christian liberty and truth. Glorious will their names ever shine in the British annals, while virtue and integrity are sacred among us. Peace and everlasting honour be upon the memory of these christian heroes: future generations will rise and call them blessed!"[b] Mr Locke calls them worthy, learned, pious, orthodox divines, who did not throw themselves out of service, but were forcibly ejected.[c]

And, Dr Burgess was not ejected alone by this act of uniformity. A great and very respectable *cloud of witnesses*, were his brethren and companions in *this tribulation*, and *in the kingdom and patience of Jesus Christ.* Mr Hume says, "The terms of subscription had been made strict and rigid, on purpose to disgust all the zealous and scrupulous among the presbyterians, and deprive them of their livings. About two thousand of the clergy in one day relinquished their cures; and to the astonishment of the court, sacrificed their interest to their religious tenets."[d] Rapin says, "St Bartholomew's-day being come, on which the act of uniformity was to take place, two thousand presbyterian ministers chose rather to quit their livings, than submit to the conditions of this act. It was expected, that a division would have happened among them, and that a great number would have chose rather to conform to the church of England,

a Towgood's Dissent, lett. iii. sect. vi. See Burnet's Hist. of his Own Times, vol. i. p. 329.

b Towgood's Dissent, lett. iii. sect. vi.

c Neal's Hist. Purit. vol. iv. chap. vi.

d Hume's Hist. Engl. vol. vii. chap. lxiii. 1662.

than see themselves reduced to beggary. It was not therefore without extreme surprize, that they were all seen to stand out, not so much as one suffering himself to be tempted." [a] Another says, "By this act, two thousand ministers, who could not chime in with the English hierarchy and service, which was then obtruded upon them, were expelled from their livings and charges." [b]

A celebrated writer and philosopher says, "The desire of truth has made me deviate from established and very favourite principles." [c] And a desire of the truth, and close adherence to it, made the nonconformists deviate from the established and favourite principles of the king and his party. Truth is always truth; it has "an intrinsic and unalterable value, and constitutes that intellectual gold, which defies destruction;" and, therefore, such as perceive its excellence will cleave to it under every hardship.

The subject of this memoir, and his companions in tribulation, being delivered from *the fear of man which bringeth a snare*, and *putting their trust in the Lord*, were determined to take up their cross, and follow Christ. *These are they who follow the Lamb whithersoever he goeth*, Rev. xiv. 4. Fortified by divine grace, clothed with *the whole armour of God*, and helped by society in their sufferings, they were resolved to undergo any hardships, rather than openly renounce their principles; *holding fast the profession of their faith without wavering; for he is faithful who promised*, Heb. x. 23.

And many afterward suffered all the horrors of the most violent and diabolical persecution, for their nonconformity: even females are not excepted, nor Scotland more than England. But here I must imitate Mr Hume, who says: "It were endless, as well as shocking, to enumerate all the instances of persecution. or, in other words, of absurd tyranny, which at that time prevailed in Scot-

a Rapin's Hist. Engl. 1662.
b Christian Mag. vol. x. p. 250.
c Sullivan's View of Nat. vol. ii. lett. 32.

land. One of them, however, is so singular, that I cannot forbear relating it."[a] It is that of three females, who were seized and condemned to a capital punishment by drowning, at Wigtown, for nonconformity, or a stedfast adherence to Christ's crown-rights, and the covenanted-work of reformation.[b] One of them was an elderly woman; about sixty-three years of age: the other two were young, and sisters; the one eighteen years of age, and the other about thirteen. The youngest was not put to death, but was set free at her father's request, upon the footing of a bond of one hundred pounds sterling: but the other two, Margaret M Lauchlan, and Margaret Wilson, were conducted to the place of execution, amid a numerous crowd of spectators, and were tied to stakes within the sea-mark at low water, where they were drowned, and finished their course with joy. The barbarous contrivance of these merciless persecutors rendered the death of these illustrious sufferers both very lingering and most dreadful. They suffered the lingering horrors of a protracted death.

——————" Sex nor age,
Beauty nor innocence, escap'd their rage!"

But the most violent proceedings of the enemies of the nonconformists, never damped the ardour of their zeal for the religion of Jesus. They closely followed the sacred injunctions of their God, amid all the menaces, and cruel measures, of their persecutors. The Lord Jesus Christ, and the peculiar doctrines of his gospel, were the firm foundation of the faith of the nonconformists, and the never-failing source of their comfort: and these raised them above the fear of every calamity. They, accordingly, like Paul, the great apostle of the Gentiles,

a Hume's Hist. Engl. vol. viii. chap. 69. 1682. p. 173, 174.

b For a full, circumstantial, and well-attested, account of these renowned female martyrs, who *loved not their lives unto the death*, See Wodrow's Hist. Sufferings Ch. of Scotland, vol. ii. pages 505, 506, & 507. and Crookshank's Hist. vol. ii. chap. xii. and Hume's Hist. as above: and Laing's Hist. of Scotland, vol. ii. B. ix. p. 145.

cheerfully and patiently suffered the loss of all things, for the sake of truth. The knowledge of the truth as it is in Jesus has been faithfully transmitted to the present generation, at a vast expence of worldly loss, labour and suffering. It is justly and beautifully observed; "Surely if we are to form an estimate of the value from the cost, every iota of divine truth is infinitely more valuable than all the wealth of eastern monarchs, more precious than the gold of Ophir, more desirable than all the "treasures hid in the sand." Let us carefully preserve it pure and entire, and transmit it, with lustre undiminished, to the generation following, that so race unto race may declare the works of the Lord, and the children who are yet unborn may arise and praise him."[a] Our zealous and respectable ancestors, who were inspired with the firm resolution of *quitting all* in this world, for truth, will, no doubt, be censured by many, as rash *enthusiasts*, or *lunatics*, rather than considered as sober christians; but we may charitably hope that they are now reaping the *abundant reward;* that their loss is gain, and their contempt glory, Matt. v. 10, 11, 12.[b] The very reproaches of Christ had such a value stamped upon them, in their estimation, that they far surpassed all the treasures of this present world.

Dr Burgess retired, upon his ejection and loss, to his house at Watford, where he lived privately, and was reduced to distress and straits. In all ages, and in different countries, in the present course of human affairs, good and excellent persons have been often exposed to many hardships and sufferings, and bad and vicious men have been in very prosperous circumstances, and have had great affluence of all worldly enjoyments, even to the end of their lives: hence we may fairly argue, the certainty of a future state of existence, in which all such matters shall be candidly and fully adjusted, by the righteous Judge of the universe. There is nothing, in this mode of reasoning, which is not strictly conformable to the sound-

a Christian Magazine, vol. vi. p. 21.
b See Doddridge's Fam. Exposit. vol. i. sect xlv. Improvement.

est principles of reason and of religion.[a] *Son, remember that thou in thy life time receivedst thy good things, and likewise Lazarus evil things: but now he is comforted, and thou art tormented,* Luke xvi. 25. This sacred text fully corresponds with the remark, and is signally advantageous in corroborating it. Dr Burgess' latter days were embittered with affliction; but we are lame judges of the reasons of God's dispensations. We cannot err in judging, that all events in life are under the wise direction of Divine providence; but when we undertake to assign particular reasons of God's providential dispensations, we may very readily be mistaken. Plato's sentence, which is nearly parallel to the sacred text, Rom. viii. 28. is, "Whether a righteous man be in poverty, sickness, or any other calamity, we must conclude that it will turn to his advantage, either in life, or death."[b] Our author had a very curious collection of the different editions of the book of Common-prayer, which he presented to the public library at Oxford, a few weeks before his death. He died at Watford, in the year 1665; and his mortal remains were buried in the middle of the church of Watford, on the 9th of June that year.[c]

Dr Calamy says, "He was excellently well skilled in the liturgical controversies, and those of church government."[d] Mr Neal says, that he was esteemed a very learned and judicious divine.[e] These eminent writers have certainly given us the true character of Dr Burgess, in few words, here; and more largely in their accounts of him. Though he was reduced to poverty and want, he was not without hope of relief. The gospel of Christ affords hope of relief, under all the calamities of our present state. God in Christ is the well-known refuge of christians; and the gates of this glorious city of refuge

a See Leland's View of Deistical Writers, vol. i. lett. xvii. 5th edit.

b See Plato de Rep. lib. ix. and Doddridge's note on Rom. viii. 28.

c Wood's Athenæ Oxon. vol. ii. p. 350.

d Calamy's Contin. vol. ii. p. 745.

e Neal's Hist. Purit. vol. iv.

are always open to the afflicted, Psal. xlvi. 1. And, when the people of God are loaded with reproaches and persecutions, in this world; or even reduced to poverty and meanness, as many of them have been, they are led, under supernatural influence, to consider Him who voluntarily endured reproach and persecution, who lived a life of poverty and want, and who suffered an ignominious death, for them. By a view of this great object, they are supported under all distress, their hearts are comforted, and they forget their sorrows. *Looking unto Jesus the author and finisher of their faith; who, for the joy that was set before him, endured the cross, despising the shame, and is set down at the right-hand of the throne of God, they run with patience the race that is set before them.* And, though they should be greatly depressed by poverty, or any adversity, at the end of their days in this world, as the subject of this memoir is said to have been, they are not inconsolable, like unbelievers. Believers in the Lord Jesus Christ have no cause to fear, in such circumstances, but rather to *lift up their heads*, with joy and triumph, because then it is, that their *redemption draweth nigh. Then shall the righteous shine forth as the sun in the kingdom of their Father.* Such as are made righteous in the sight of God, by the consummate righteousness of Christ imputed to them, shall *shine forth* in the best robe of Christ's righteousness, in the perfect beauties of holiness, and in the shining garments of glory, incorruption, and immortality, *in the kingdom of their Father.* And notwithstanding all their poverty, affliction, and persecution, in this world, they shall in due time break forth out of obscurity, like the sun from behind a dark cloud, into the most glorious light: and they shall be brought also into the full possession of true honour, of durable riches, and of everlasting felicities. *They shall hunger no more, neither thirst any more; neither shall the sun light on them, nor any heat. For the Lamb who is in the midst of the throne shall feed them, and shall lead them unto living fountains of waters: and God shall wipe away all tears from their eyes.* Rev. vii. 16, 17.

It is the great consolation of Christ's faithful followers, who suffer with him; for his sake, and in his cause, that they shall also be glorified together with Christ. And, *the sufferings of this present time, are not worthy to be compared with the glory which shall be revealed in the children of God.* Rom viii. 17, 18. And these will at last much resemble Christ himself, the glorious sun of righteousness, with whom, and in whose glory, they shall eternally appear.

"Should persecution rage and flame,
Still trust in thy Redeemer's name;
In fiery trials thou shalt see,
That as thy days thy strength shall be.
When call'd to bear the weighty cross,
Of sore affliction, pain, or loss,
Or deep distress, or poverty.
Still as thy days thy strength shall be.
When ghastly death appears in view,
Christ's presence shall thy fears subdue,
He comes to set thy spirit free,
And as thy days thy strength shall be."

IGNOT.[a]

God may visit a people with *cleanness of teeth in all their cities, and want of bread in all their places*, and yet in such extreme distress, the believer in Christ may be fully assured, that *he shall dwell on high:* that *his place of defence shall be the munitions of rocks: that bread shall be given him;* and that *his water shall be sure.* And, we have decisive evidence, in Dr Burgess' writings, that he had previously been taught to comfort himself, in all his afflictions, with the beautiful and important language of an eminent believer and ancient prophet: *Although the fig-tree shall not blossom, neither shall fruit be in the vines; the labour of the olive shall fail, and the fields shall yield no meat; the flock shall be cut off from the fold, and there shall be no herd in the stalls: yet I*

a Christian Magazine, vol. x. p. 260.

will rejoice in the Lord, I will joy in the God of my salvation. Hab. iii. 17, 18.

THE writings of Cornelius Burgess which have been printed:

1. *A Chain of Graces drawn out at length for a Reformation of Manners. Or, A brief Treatise of Virtue, Knowledge, Temperance, Patience, Godliness, Brotherly kindness, and Charity, so far as they are urged by the Apostle, in* 2 Pet. i. 5, 6, 7. London, 1622.

This is a little book; but it contains much. I have perused it, both with great profit, and with much pleasure. Readers who are desirous of acquiring a summary knowledge of this important subject, may reap ample benefit from this small volume, with very little trouble. It is a good pocket-companion for Christians. Several very beautiful Latin citations from the fathers of the church, and from other respectable writers, which increase the value of this interesting treatise, are fairly translated into the English language, or interpreted, by the author. He gratefully dedicated it to the earl of Bedford, and to his religious consort, the lady Lucy, countess of Bedford, in whose family he was sometime a demestic chaplain. It was chiefly intended for the benefit of the people of his own pastoral charge.[a] The author evidently appears to have possessed a mind strongly impressed with a real sense of the truth and importance of religious principles, and to have been earnestly desirous that the knowledge of these should be extensively diffused among mankind, and take fast hold on their minds. He critically examines the original language, gives an accurate and perspicuous description of virtue, knowledge, temperance, patience, godliness, brotherly-kindness, and charity, and subjoins an application, judiciously adapted, to correct and improve the manners of the people. "If the maxim be true, as we firmly believe, that private virtue is the basis

a Epistle Dedicatory.

of public prosperity, no writings can be more useful than those which are honestly designed, and judiciously adapted, to correct and improve the manners of the people."[a]

This little volume is divided into nine chapters, each of which will contribute to the entertainment of a judicious reader. In his third chapter, on virtue, he represents good works as the way to heaven, not the cause of obtaining it, nor of reigning there; as fruits of faith, proving that it is lively; as effects and evidences of our justification by the righteousness of Christ, not contributing to it in the least degree; as testimonies of real gratitude unto God, and of conformity to the image of Christ, *Who gave himself for us, that he might redeem us from all iniquity, and purify unto himself a peculiar people, zealous of good works.* In his chapter on knowledge, he sincerely laments the dismal condition of all those persons, who are closely shut up in the Pope's dark dungeon of brutal ignorance, without the benefit of the holy scriptures; remaining all their days like heathenish Ninevites, not *knowing the right-hand from the left.* And, he justly observes, that it is highly impious to deny the people of God any means of knowledge, especially the *scriptures*, the *key of knowledge.* In the chapter on temperance, he exposes the beastly sin of intemperance, in a very striking manner; considering those who are guilty of it, as debauched monsters, whose lives are disgraceful to human nature, as the companions of beasts, the objects of God's hatred, and the scum of the world; *raging waves of the sea, foaming out their own shame, to whom is reserved the blackness of darkness for ever.* I have seen two copies of this little book in Scotland; one in Wigtonshire, and another in the shire of Renfrew, which wanted the title-page, in the year 1807. In Mr Ogle's Theological catalogue, p. 137. London, 1809, the price of it is marked, 1s. 6d.

2. *New Discovery of Personal Tithes: Or, The Tenth Part of Men's clear gains proved due both in Conscience, and by the laws of this Kingdom.* London,

a Monthly Review Enlarged, vol xix. p. 214.

1625. I have sought for this book some years with fruitless inquiry. It is in the catalogue of his writings, in Wood's Athenæ Oxon. vol. 2. p. 348. and in Palmer's Account. The author handles this subject, in "A Case concerning the Lawfulness of Buying Bishops' Lands, p. 8. &c.

3. *The Fire of the Sanctuary newly uncovered; or, A Complete Tract of Zeal.* A little book, 492 pages, London, 1625. It is divided into eight chapters, in which the nature, the objects, the grounds, the ends, and the qualifications of zeal, are particularly unfolded. This work clearly appears to be composed with care and diligence. It well deserves a serious perusal; and will be found highly useful by those who are earnestly engaged in the pursuit of profitable knowledge. It displays a laudable zeal in the author to promote the interests of religion, and the work of reformation: and it justly claims a particular attention from the public. The following remark of the Monthly Reviewers is applicable to this excellent treatise. "Many a valuable tract is elbowed out of notice, and even out of remembrance, by an unceasing succession of new productions; numbers of which, after all, are only old ideas in a new dress. We therefore are disposed to look favourably on any well formed plan for rescuing the good sense and sententious advice of our forefathers, from that unmerited oblivion to which their brevity exposes them."[a] In Mr Marsom's catalogue, p. 147, High-Holborn, London, 1792, the price of this book is marked, *neat*, 1s. 6d. In Mr Ogle's catalogue, p. 68. London, 1802, the price is marked. 1s. 6d. In Mr Ogle's Theological catalogue, p. 136, London, 1809. the price of it is marked, *frontispiece*, 2s. 6d. All the same edition. Beside mine own, I have seen another copy of this book, in the parish of Fenwick, and county of Ayr, in the year 1802.—A good work generally meets with opposition; accordingly, an anonymous pamphlet, entitled *The Whip*, appeared against this excellent tract, *The Fire of the Sanctuary*, 1643, which was answered

a Monthly Review Enlarged, vol. viii. p. 572.

by a Francis Quarles, who highly commends Dr Burgess, in another pamphlet, entitled, *The Whipper Whipt*, 4to. pp. 44. 1644.[a]

4. *Baptismal Regeneration of Elect Infants, professed by the Church of England, according to Scriptures, the primitive Church, the present Reformed Churches, and many particular divines apart.* Small 4to. pp. 347. Oxford, 1629. This treatise is polemical; and replete with close reasoning from the Sacred Writings. The principal point handled is, *That all elect infants who are baptised, do ordinarily receive from Christ in baptisim the Spirit of regeneration, as the soul and first principle of spiritual life, for their first solemn initiation into Christ, and for their future actual renovation, in God's good time, if they live to years of discretion, and enjoy the other ordinary means of Grace appointed by God to this end.* Objections are answered. In aid of his own opinion, he calls in that of many others. —In Mr Ogle's Theological catalogue, p. 23. London, 1809. the price is marked, 2s. 6d.—I have seen two copies of this book in Glasgow; the one in a private library, and the other in the library of the University.

5. *A sermon Preached from Jer.* l. 5. *to The Honourable House of Commons assembled in Parliament, at their Public Fast*, Nov. 17th, 1640. 4to. pp. 80. 3d edit. 56. London, 1641. See some account of this sermon, in the account of the author's life. I have seen it in the shires of Ayr, Renfrew, and Lanark, in Scotland; and one copy of it belonging to my correspondent at London. Among those, I have seen several copies of the third edition of this sermon, all printed at London, 1641.

6. Another Sermon preached to the Honourable House of Commons, from Psal. lxxvi. 10. 5th Nov. 1641. 4to. pp. 65. London, 1641. In this learned and elaborate sermon the author maintains, that Papists have never been quiet, but continually contriving treasons, ever since the Reformation of Religion. That this practice arises not

a Wood's Athenæ Oxon. vol. ii. p. 348, 349. and The Whipper Whipt.

from the laws made against them, but their very religion itself leads them unto it. That their *priests* are bound to infuse these principles of their religion into them, and to press the use of them upon all occasions. And that to induce their disciples to swallow those principles, and to act from them when occasion offers, they propound great rewards and glory, and defend and magnify those who have formerly miscarried in them, p. 28.—He says to his respectable auditory, "If you would have *peace with Rome*, *Rome* will have *no peace* with you: and that, to pluck up the hedge of your laws, is to lay all waste, p. 23, 24. The sermon is very suitable for the present time, and contains much useful information on the subject of the Roman Catholic emancipation. He concludes, with warmly exhorting the members of parliament, to use all their influence in promoting the interests of the Redeemer's kingdom; and to call a *free synod of grave ministers* to their assistance.

7. *An Humble Examination of a printed Abstract of the Answers to Nine Reasons of the House of Commons, Against the Votes of Bishops in Parliament.* 4to. pp. 77. London, 1641.

8. *The Broken Title of Episcopal Inheritance. Or, a Discovery of the weak Reply, to the Humble Examination of the Answers to the Nine Reasons of the House of Commons, Against the Votes of Bishops in Parliament, their Lordly Dignity, and Civil Authority.* Dedicated to both Houses of Parliament. 4to. pp. 21. London, 1642. I have seen only one copy of each of these pieces, belonging to my correspondent at London.

9. *Two Sermons Preached from* Jer. iv. 14. *to the Honourable House of Commons, at two Public Fasts;* the one, March 30th, 1642. the other, April 30th, 1645. The former, *opening the necessity and benefit of washing the heart;* the latter, *discovering the vanity and mischief of an heart unwashed.* 4to. 1. pp. 50. 2. pp. 53. London, 1645. I have seen a copy of both these sermons belonging to my correspondent at London.

10. *The Necessity of Agreement with God.* A ser-

mon from Amos iii. 3. preached to the House of Peers, Fast, 29th Oct. 1645. 4to. pp. 51. London, 1645.

11. *Prudent Silence.* A sermon from Amos v. 13. preached in Mercer's-chapel to the Lord-Mayor and Citizens, on Jan. 14th, 1648. London, 1660.

Wood says here, He has other sermons extant, which he had not seen, as one from 2 Chron. xv. 2. another from Ezra x. 23. &c. Nor have I seen these; and therefore I cannot give any account of them. The same author also mentions here, "Sion-College, what it is and doth. A vindication of that society against two pamphlets, &c. Lond. 1648. qu. His case as Lecturer in Paul's—A little pamphlet." But I have not hitherto seen any of these.

12. *No Sacrilege nor Sin to Alien or Purchase the Lands of Bishops, or others, whose offices are abolished.* The second edition, revised and enlarged, London, 1659. A small book. I have seen one copy of this edition, in the library of the presbytery of Dumfries: and another in the Stewartry of Kirkcudbright. Mr Wood says, that there was a third edition of this book, Lond. 1660. 4to, revised and abbreviated for the service of the parliament: with a word by way of Postscript to Dr Pearson and his *No Necessity.*[a]

13. *A Case concerning the Buying of Bishops' Lands, with the Lawfulness thereof.* Small and thin 4to. pp. 80. London, 1659. I have one copy of this book, which is all that I could ever see.

a Wood's Athenæ Oxon. vol. ii. p. 349.

JOHN WHITE, M. A.

PASTOR OF TRINITY PARISH IN DORCHESTER, IN THE COUNTY OF DORSET, AND A MEMBER OF THE ASSEMBLY OF DIVINES AT WESTMINSTER.

JOHN WHITE was born at Stanton, St John, in Oxfordshire, toward the end of December, and was baptized there 6th Jan. 1575, where his father, who was John White also, held a lease from New-College. He was descended from the Whites in Hantshire, in England. He was instructed in grammar-learning, at William of Wickham's school, near the city of Winchester. Many eminent men have been educated in this school, where after a certain time, the scholars have exhibitions to study in the New-College at Oxford, founded by the same benefactory. The ancient and famous University of Oxford has for a long time been an eminent seat of learning, and has been emphatically stiled one of the eyes of England.[a] Here the subject of this memoir studied, in New-College, whereof he was Fellow. After he had served two years of probation, in the year 1595, he took the degrees in Arts, holy orders, and became a frequent preacher in these parts. He left his college, in the year 1606, and probably, about that time, became rector of Trinity parish in Dorchester, in the county of Dorset, in England. His mind being deeply impressed with the great importance of the charge which was committed unto him, he now entered upon the arduous duties of his office, which he most faithfully discharged. He appears to have had very strict and just views of the magnitude and importance of the pastoral care. He was a very diligent minister, and faithful pastor, and left himself but few vacant

a. Monthly Review Enlarged, vol. xix. p. 442.

hours for recreation, continually feeding his flock *with knowledge and understanding*. In the course of his ministry he expounded the holy scriptures all over, and half over again; having an excellent faculty in the clear and solid interpretation of them. Dr Manton considers him as excelling in a solid exposition of the text, and deducing pertinent observations, with proper reasons; and for proof hereof, refers the reader to Mr White's commentary upon the three first chapters of Genesis.[a] The knowledge of the holy scriptures is the proper entertainment of immortal souls, as material objects are of the external senses. And by his judicious exposition of the scriptures, and preaching from them, he carefully instructed the people committed to his care, and faithfully administered to them the genuine food of their souls: *the sincere milk of the word, that they might grow thereby.*

Mr White's settlement in Dorchester afforded him an opportunity of doing much good, under God. What is said respecting the celebrated Bernard Gilpin, when his situation afforded him an opportunity of doing much good, may be very justly applied to Mr White. "This object engrossed all his attention, and stimulated every exertion. It concentrated all his views, desires and aims; and it terminated all his prospects. From this point, a circle of benevolent actions diffused themselves, wherever want was an inhabitant, wherever ability could relieve, or influence avail."[b] His exertions were many, and his activity great, for the good of mankind, especially the inhabitants of Dorchester; and by the blessing of God on his labours, they were crowned with success. When he laboured with unwearied diligence, the Lord wonderfully opened a door to him for great usefulness in this place. And in him, the most amiable and exemplary picture of real christianity was clearly seen. Dr Fuller says, that he was "A good governor, by whose wisdom the town of Dorchester was much enriched, knowledge causing piety, piety breeding industry, and industry procuring

a Manton's Pref. Comment. Gen.
b Christian Magazine, vol. vi. p. 22.

plenty unto it. A beggar was not then to be seen in the town, all able poor being set on work, and the impotent maintained by the profit of a public brew-house, and other collections." [a] Religion and industry greatly flourished under his influence, and derived a commanding authority from his laudable and pious example. Like Pertinax, the virtuous Roman emperor, he considered œconomy and industry as the pure and genuine sources of wealth; and from them, under the blessing of God, a copious supply for the public necessities was soon derived.[b] They who wander about in idleness, are a burthen to themselves, and a nuisance to society.

"Health and wealth from honest labour spring;
Th' industrious peasant's happier than a king!"

Mr White seems to have suggested plans for the improvement of the condition of the poor, and heartily concurred with others in the execution of them. And suggesting plans for the benefit of the poor, certainly manifests a very humane and feeling heart. "There is perhaps no problem in the important and intricate science of political œconomy, more difficult than that which regards the employment and support of the poor; and there is certainly none more interesting, whether we consider it in the view of humanity as connected with the advantage of our suffering fellow-creatures,—or in that of policy as it materially affects our hopes of lightening the burdens, increasing the industry and wealth, and even preserving the quiet, of the country." [c] To provide for the helpless poor, and to compel the idle to work, have been the general objects of all systems of poor laws:—but to have supported helplessness without encouraging idleness seems to have too generally surpassed the skill of human policy.[d]

Dr Fuller farther observes, respecting the illustrious

a Fuller's Worthies of England.
b Gibbon's Hist. Rom. Emp. vol. i. chap. iv.
c Monthly Review Enlarged, vol. xix. p. 459.
d See The Monthly Review, as above.

subject of this memoir, that "he absolutely commanded his own passions, and the purses of his parishioners, whom he could wind up to whatever height he pleased on important occasions. He was free from covetousness, if not trespassing on the contrary."[a] In this amiable character, the disposition of doing good to others shewed itself superior to interest, and a public spirit clearly appeared. He diligently instructed his own parishioners in the doctrines and duties of the christian religion, and was eminently useful in reforming their manners, and in preserving good order among the inhabitants of Dorchester.[b] He was commonly called, *Patriarch of Dorchester*, or Patriarch White. And Dr Fuller says, that he had a Patriarchal influence both in Old and New England.

At the beginning of the Long Parliament, when many good subjects and true patriots appeared for the rights of their country, and for the interests of the Redeemer's kingdom, he associated with them. And, his wise counsels, shining example, great influence, and distinguished abilities, greatly contributed to promote the cause of truth, and the interests of the christian religion. But when prince Rupert was in those parts, and the proceedings were known, a party of his horse went to Dorchester, plundered Mr White's house, and took away his library. The great apostle of the Gentiles, for the sake of truth and of the christian religion, suffered the loss of all things. This eminent servant of the church, like Paul, suffered the loss of ease and of property, and endured many hardships, *as a good soldier of Jesus Christ. He took joyfully the spoiling of his goods, knowing that he had in heaven a better and an enduring substance:* and retiring to London, he was appointed to be minister of Savoy parish, for sometime. In the year 1643, he was chosen to be one of the venerable Assembly of Divines at Westminster, and one of the Assessors.[c] He was very highly esteemed in that Assembly. Wood says, he

a Fuller's Worthies of England.
b Wood's Athenæ Oxon. vol. ii. p. 115.
c See Life of Dr Burgess.

"took the *covenant*, and sitting often with them at *Westminster*, shewed himself one of the most learned and moderate among them, and soon after did by order not only succeed Dr Featley in the rectory of Lambeth in Surrey, ejected thence, but had his library conferred on him to keep and enjoy it till such time as Dr Featley could get back our author's from the soldiers under prince Rupert."[a] When both Houses of Parliament, with the Scottish Commissioners, and Assembly of Divines, convened in Margaret's church, Westminster, on the 25th of Sept. 1643 to subscribe the Solemn League and Covenant, for 'reformation, and defence of religion, the honour and happiness of the king, and the peace and safety of the three kingdoms of England, Scotland, and Ireland, Mr White opened the great solemnity with prayer. After him, Messrs Henderson and Nye spake in justification of taking the covenant from scripture-precedents, and shewed the advantage which the church had received from such sacred associations. Mr Henderson spake again, and declared, that the States of Scotland had resolved to assist the English parliament in carrying on the designs of this covenant. Upon this Mr Nye read it from the pulpit with an audible voice, article by article, each person standing uncovered, with his right-hand bare and lifted up to Heaven, worshipping the great and glorious Name of Almighty God, and solemnly swearing to pay his vows. Dr Gouge concluded this solemnity with prayer; after which the House of Commons went up into the chancel and subscribed their names in one roll of parchment, and the Assembly in another, in both which the covenant was fairly transcribed.[b] Mr White subscribed the proposition in the Assembly, when the learned Lightfoot entered his dissent, that "Jesus Christ, as King of the church, hath himself appointed a church-government distinct from the civil magistrate."[c] He uni-

a Wood's Athenæ Oxon. vol. ii. p. 115. See also, p. 679.

b Neal's Hist. Purit. vol. iii. 8vo. chap. ii. Vicar's Parliamentary Chronicle, p. 424.

c Neal's Hist. vol. iii. chap. vii.

formly acted a benevolent and useful part to mankind, especially to the church of Christ; and persevered unweariedly in doing good. He truly lived for the benefit of his country, and hath afforded a shining example, which well deserves to be transmitted unto posterity: and his memory ought to be highly esteemed by us. We are informed, that the ancients held in equal estimation the memory of those worthies who had lived and those who had died for their country. They universally confessed, that they deserved at least the respect of all mankind.[a]

He married the sister of Dr Burgess, by whom he had four sons, who were left behind him.

Dr Fuller says, that he was "a grave man, yet without moroseness, who would willingly contribute his shot of facetiousness on any just occasion." Mr Wood says, "He was a person of great gravity and presence, and had always influence on the puritanical party near to, and remote from, him, who bore him more respect than they did to their diocesan."

When the commotions of the nation ceased, and his work was terminated at London, he returned to Dorchester; and in Nov. 1647, was designed warden of New-College, upon the death of Dr Pink, by Lord Say, and his son; but Mr Wood supposes, that he refused that office, which is very probable. Being old and full of days, *After he had served his own generation, by the will of God, he fell asleep*, on the 21st of July, 1648. And his remains were interred in the church-porch of St Peter in Dorchester, which is a chapel belonging to Trinity-church.[b] And *those who sleep in Jesus will God bring with him*. Death is most beautifully expressed in the holy scriptures by *falling asleep*, and is thus elegantly applied to mankind, in distinction from the beasts that perish, especially to those who die in the Lord, relative to the blessed hope of a glorious resurrection: for *sleeping* evidently

a Monthly Review Enlarged, vol. xix. p. 355. Gibbon's Hist. Rom. Emp. vol. i. chap. ii.

b Wood's Athenæ Oxon. vol. ii. p. 114, 115, 116. Fuller's Worthies of England, fol. 1662.

implies *awaking out of sleep.* See Dan. xii. 2. Acts xiii. 36. 1 Thess. iv. 14. Agreeably to this, the burying-places, especially those wherein the bodies of the saints are laid, may properly be called *sleeping places*, or places designed for *rest* and *sleep*, until the glorious morning of the *resurrection of the dead body.* "The souls of believers are at their death made perfect in holiness, and do immediately pass into glory; and their bodies being still united to Christ, do rest in their graves, till the resurrection."

I am sorry that I have not been able to obtain more materials, respecting the life and death of this eminent servant of Jesus Christ.

I now proceed to give an account of his printed writings which I have seen and read.

1. *The Troubles of Jerusalem's Restoration: Or, The Church's Reformation.* A sermon from Dan. ix. 25. before the House of Lords, in the Abbey church, Westminster, 26th Nov. 1645. 4to. pp. 62. London, 1646.

2. *Way to the Tree of Life: Or, Directions for the Profitable Reading of the Scriptures; wherein is Described occasionally the Nature of a Spiritual Man: and, in a Digression, the Morality and Perpetuity of the Fourth Commandment, in every circumstance thereof, is Discovered and Cleared.*

3. *A sermon* preached from Psal. lxxxii. 6. at Dorchester, in the county of Dorset, at the General Assizes, 7th of March, 1632. 4to. pp. 31. London, 1648.

4. *A Commentary upon the Three first chapters of the Book of Genesis.* Small folio, London, 1656.

JOHN ARROWSMITH, D. D.

A MEMBER OF THE VENERABLE ASSEMBLY OF DIVINES AT WESTMINSTER, MASTER BOTH OF ST JOHN'S, AND OF TRINITY-COLLEGE, SUCCESSIVELY, AND ROYAL OR PUBLIC PROFESSOR OF DIVINITY, IN THE UNIVERSITY OF CAMBRIDGE.

JOHN ARROWSMITH was born near Newcastle upon Tyne, in the county of Northumberland, in England, on the 29th day of March, in the year 1602. It is remarkable, that this eminent divine was born in the same year, on the same day, and almost even at the same hour, with that much celebrated English divine, Dr John Lightfoot.[a] Divine providence raised up most seasonably many very eminent men, about this time, who were great ornaments to the Reformed Church; and who have acquired immortal fame by their valuable writings, and have carefully transmitted their great usefulness to succeeding generations, in their learned and pious productions.

Respecting the early life and education of the illustrious subject of this memoir, I have not been able to procure any particular account: but it is evident by his writings and employments, that he had been highly favoured with a well directed and liberal education. He was sometime preacher of the gospel at Lynn, or King's-Lynn, an ancient sea-port town, in the county of Norfolk. From that place, he was called to sit in the Assembly of Divines at Westminster.[b] Here he was eminently distinguished by his abilities, learning, and piety. Mr Robert

a Lightfoot's Life, prefixed to the folio edit. of his Works, 1684, and 1686.

b See Neal's List of the Assembly of Divines at Westminster, Hist. Purit. vol. iii. chap. ii.

Baillie, one of the commissioners from the Church of Scotland, to the Assembly of Divines at Westminster, says, when writing for Scotland respecting the business of that Assembly: "Our letter to foreign churches, formed by Mr Marshall, except some clauses belonging to us put in by Mr Henderson, is now turned into Latin by Mr Arrowsmith, a man with a glass eye, in place of that which was put out by an arrow, a learned divine, on whom the Assembly put the writing against the Antinomians." [a]

While the Reformation was advancing, several improvements were requisite, highly deserving the attention of our reformers, to render the English Universities more capable of answering the noble ends of their institution. Disgraceful charges were brought against these useful seminaries of learning: and our zealous ancestors consulted both the honour and interest of these venerable foundations, by endeavouring to amend what was amiss in them. Laudable attempts were made to restore the credit of their *Alma Mater.* Learning and piety were now the chief recommendations for offices. Accordingly, the utmost exertions were made, that all departments might be supplied with learned and pious men. The famous Earl of Manchester was appointed to visit the University of Cambridge, in order that he might correct what was wrong in it. Among other things, he ejected some heads of Colleges, and made choice of some divines who were then sitting in the Assembly at Westminster, to be masters in their places; among whom was the illustrious subject of this memoir. Mr Baillie, abovementioned, who was then at Westminster, says, "When we were going to the rest of the propositions concerning the Presbytery, my Lord Manchester wrote to us from Cambridge, what he had done in the University, how he had ejected for gross scandals, the heads of five Colleges;—and that he had made choice of five of our number, to be Masters in their places, Mr Palmer, Vines, Seaman, Arrowsmith, and our countryman, Young, requiring the Assembly's approbation of his choice; which

a Baillie's Letters, vol. i. p. 414.

was unaminously given; for they are all very good and able divines."[a] Agreeably to this account, Mr Arrowsmith having been first examined, and approved, by the Assembly of Divines at Westminster, was constituted master of St John's College, in the University of Cambridge, in the year 1644.[b] By what our reformers did in this affair, they certainly made both the public in general, and the University in particular, their debtors; however little they might both be disposed to acknowledge the obligation. This reformation attracted much notice; and was warmly praised by some persons, and as violently censured by others.[c] Mr Neal says, "The Lord's-day was observed with uncommon rigour; there were sermons and prayers in all the churches and chapels both morning and afternoon. Vice and profaneness were banished, insomuch, that an oath was not to be heard within the walls of the University; and if it may be said without offence, the Colleges never appeared more like nurseries of religion and virtue than at this time." The same author adds, "I have before me the names of fifty-five persons, who, after they had been examined by the Assembly, were put into vacant fellowships in the compass of the year 1644, and within six months more all the vacancies were in a manner supplied, with men of approved learning and piety. From this time, the University of Cambridge enjoyed a happy tranquillity, learning revived, religion and good manners were improved, at a time when the rest of the nation was in blood and confusion. And though this alteration was effected by a mixture of the civil and military power, yet in a little time things reverted to their former channel, and the statutes of the University were as regularly observed as ever."[d]

When our author was promoted to be Master of St John's College one of the *schools of the prophets*, and a principal *seminary* of divines, he conscientiously dis-

a Baillie's Letters, vol. i. p. 439.
b Neal's Hist. Purit. vol. iii. chap. iii.
c See Walker's Attempt, Part i. respecting the Regulation of the University of Cambridge.
d Neal's Hist. as above, where more may be found on the subject.

charged the duties of his office; and pursued his studies and researches, with the most unceasing assiduity. While he had no other public employment, he delivered catechetical lectures in that chapel on the evenings of the Lord's-day, laying a good foundation of the doctrine of Christ, like a wise master-builder. As *Elisha*, when he came to *Jericho*, casting salt into the spring of water, for the preservation, and health of all those persons who were in the place, he used his best endeavours to supply what was wanting, and to correct what was amiss. He explained the genuine sources of religious knowledge, in a most judicious and prudent manner, in order to promote a spirit of practical piety, and vital religion, in the hearts of his hearers, and especially of the candidates for the holy ministry. And he was peculiarly attentive to the advancement of solid and useful learning in his College. Solid learning and true piety were most intimately connected in himself; and they were so connected in all his instructions unto others. They ought always to go hand in hand, in the public teachers of Christianity.—When master of this College, he began to apply himself, with eminent success, to that most elaborate and truly excellent work, *A Chain of Principles.* This most beautiful and very important chain of theological principles was designed to form a complete *Body of Divinity* in *thirty* distinct *Aphorisms*, with their respective *Exercitations.* And the laborious author intended to have prepared these learned and pious productions for the press, if the Lord had spared and afforded him health: but sickness and death put an end to his labours, when he had finished only these six Aphorisms, with their respective Exercitations, which have been published to the world, and are entitled, "A Chain of Principles." [a]

Our illustrious author was removed to be Master of Trinity-College, in the University of Cambridge, which Wood says, is the best preferment in that University.[b] He was also constituted Professor of divinity, in this fa-

a Preface to the *Chain*, by Messrs Horton, and Dillingham.
b Wood's Athenæ Oxon. vol. ii. Col. 505.

mous University. In a situation so peculiarly agreeable to the views and habits of a scholar and of a divine, he eminently displayed his ardent zeal and great fidelity in the honourable service of his great Master. And the infinitely wise and sovereign Disposer of all things certainly regarded the University of Cambridge with peculiar favour, when he placed this learned and pious divine, in such eminent stations there, where he was made the instrument of great usefulness. It was an observation of Tacitus, that advancement rarely mended the disposition of the human mind; only Vespasian was changed into the better. And Evagrius gives it as the high praise of the Emperor Mauritius, that in the height of all his majesty, he retained his ancient piety. It may be considered, by good information, as the high praise of the subject of this memoir, as he was seemingly the subject of the unsearchable riches of divine grace, that in the height of all his preferments, he retained his former piety; and even improved greatly in literature, and in the disposition of his mind. There is growth both in knowledge and in grace.

He was a very eminent and useful preacher of the glorious gospel of the grace of God. There is one remarkable instance of this transmitted to posterity, respecting Mr John Machin, of Jesus' College, Cambridge. Mr Machin was born at Seabridge in Staffordshire, Oct. 2d. 1624. He spent his youth in vanity and sin. When about twenty-one years of age, he went to the University, without any view to the holy ministry, or to a continuance there. But God was pleased, on his first going thither, to effect a gracious change in him, chiefly by the preaching of *Dr Hill;* and that of *Dr Arrowsmith* was much to his comfort and edification. No sooner did he find this blessed change in his heart, than his friends found it by his letters; by which, together with his exemplary conversation afterward, he is said to have been the instrument of converting his three sisters, and there was room to hope, both his parents.[a]

Dr Arrowsmith was also reckoned an eminently

a Palmer's Nonconformist's Memorial, under Whitley, in Cheshire.

learned and highly useful professor of divinity. He was truly *a burning and a shining light*, able to distinguish truth from error, and pure worship from superstitious devices. He was an enlightened leader, and careful instructor of others. He was well qualified to write and discourse upon theological subjects with precision, elegance, ease, and perspicuity. By his great ingenuity and erudition, he was enabled to throw light on many difficult passages of the sacred writings that had been ill understood, and not well applied. Great dexterity, good judgment, profound and admirable learning, and true piety, were very conspicuous, both in his ministry, and in the divinity-chair. He acquired a distinguished reputation in the University, by his excellent wit, amiable manners, singular prudence and plainness. His wit and erudition, being sanctified by the grace of God, were successfully employed by him, as weapons against the adversaries of truth and of religion.

He continued to labour with indefatigable zeal in his Master's service, until he was seized with a lingering sickness, terminating in death, which prevented the completion of his noble designs.[a] I have not been able to obtain any information respecting the manner of the death of this eminent divine; and I must stop short where my information fails me. Respecting the time of his death, Mr Neal says, that he died before the restoration; which exactly agrees with what Wood says, That the headship of Trinity-College in Cambridge was conferred upon Dr John Wilkins, upon the death of Dr John Arrowsmith, in the beginning of 1659.[b]

I shall here avail myself of four lines of a little poem of Mr Smart, on the death of a Mr Newbury, after a lingering illness, which are appropriate.

"Henceforth be every tender tear suppress,
Or let us weep for joy that he is blest;

a See Prefaces to his Chain, and God-man.

b Wood's Athenæ Oxon. vol. ii. Col. 505. and title-page of Arrowsmith's Chain.

From grief to bliss, from earth to heav'n remov'd,
His memory honour'd, as his life belov'd." [a]

Mr Neal says, " Dr John Arrowsmith was of an unexceptionable character for learning and piety. He was an acute disputant, and a judicious divine, as appears by his *Tactica Sacra*, a book of great reputation in those times." [b] He was undoubtedly a real friend to true religion, and has transmitted to posterity a shining example of piety and diligence in his Master's service. And his name ought to be in the list of the eminent divines and men of learning, who were real ornaments to the Reformed Church in the seventeenth century.

Dr Arrowsmith is a writer of distinguished excellence. He may be justly numbered among the benefactors of English literature. In his writings, we clearly see the beautiful image of a mind which was truly judicious and serious; richly furnished and adorned with the comely ornaments both of learning and of piety. His writings are;

1. *The Covenant-Avenging Sword Brandished.* A sermon preached from Lev. xxvi. 25. before the House of Commons, at their solemn fast, Jan. 25th, 1642. 4to. pp. 28. London, 1643. This sermon was also printed at Dumfries, 1797. I have now a few copies unsold, price 3*d*.

2. *England's Ebenezer:* or, *Stone of Help.* A sermon preached from 1 Sam. vii. 12. to both Houses of Parliament, the Lord Mayor and Aldermen of the city of London, being present, on a day of solemn thanksgiving, March 12th, 1644. 4to. pp. 34. London, 1645.

3. *A Great Wonder in Heaven:* or, *A Lively Picture of the Militant Church, drawn by a Divine Pencil.* A sermon preached from Rev. xii. 1, 2. before the Com-

a Monthly Review Enlarged, Jan. 1792. vol. vii.
b Hist. Purit. vol. iii. 1644.

mons, at Westminster, fast, Jan. 27th, 1647. 4to. London, 1647.

4. Tactica Sacra, sive de milite Spirituali Pugnante, Vincente, & Triumphante, Dissertatio, Tribus Libris comprehensa. 4to. pp. 363. Cantabrigiæ, 1657.

This learned dissertation, which is divided into three books, respecting the spiritual soldier fighting, conquering, and triumphing, well deserves the perusal of the scholar, who can read Latin.

5. *A Chain of Principles:* or, *An orderly Concatenation of Theological Aphorisms and Exercitations; wherein the Chief Heads of Christian Religion are asserted and improved.* 4to. pp. 490. Cambridge, 1659.

This is a book of real worth; and it is strange that it has not been oftener printed. It will amply repay the trouble of a perusal. It occurs still in the catalogues of books, especially in London. It was formerly cheap, 3 or 4*s.* but now 7*s.* 6*d.* I have seen it in several parts of Scotland, where it is an ornament to many good libraries.

6. *God-Man.* An exposition of the first eighteen verses of the first chapter of the gospel according to John. 4to. pp. 311. London, 1660. Sells now in London at 7*s.* 6*d.*

Dr Cotton Mather, in his Student and Preacher, says, "Every thing of an Arrowsmith is admirable." "The names of Lightfoot, Selden, Gataker, Greenhill, Arrowsmith, Twisse, Bishop Reynolds, Wallis, &c. will always be famous in the learned world." [a]

a Neal's Hist. Purit. vol. iii. chap. x.

SIMEON ASHE,

MINISTER OF THE GOSPEL IN LONDON, AND A MEMBER OF THE VENERABLE ASSEMBLY OF DIVINES AT WESTMINSTER.

SIMEON ASH, or ASHE, was educated in Emmanuel College, in the University of Cambridge. As several eminent Puritans received their education in this College, the following remark respecting it is, perhaps, worthy of our notice. When Sir Walter Mildmay came to court after he had founded this College, Queen Elizabeth said to him; "Sir Walter, I hear that you have erected a Puritan foundation. No, Madam, said he, far be it from me to countenance any thing contrary to your established laws; but I have set an *acorn*, which, when it becomes an *oak*, God alone knows what will be the fruit thereof." [a]

Biography is most pleasingly instructive and profitable, when it's lessons are given from the examples of those persons who are truly and eminently good; or who have been so, in faithfully serving their own generation. We pass from one event of the lives of those amiable characters to another, with much delight and advantage. Such is the example here before us.

Mr Ashe began his ministry, in preaching the glorious gospel of the grace of God, in Staffordshire, in England, in the neighbourhood of those eminent persons, Mr John Ball, Mr Robert Nicolls, and Mr Langley, with whom he cultivated a particular acquaintance. "*Like loves like.*" And religion greatly improves and refines the social principle of our nature. *Then they who feared the Lord spake often one to another*. The love of God shed

a Fuller's Hist. University of Cambridge, Sect. vii. p. 147.

abroad in the heart, by the Holy Ghost, plainly shews itself, by loving the brethren, and seeking communion with them. And when two or more pious persons meet and converse, they communicate light, experience, and warmth of affection, to each other; and greatly animate each other in the christian race. And our Saviour has graciously promised that *where two or three are gathered together in his name, he will be in the midst of them.* And when he sent forth his apostles, he sent them by *two and two*, in company, that they might mutually encourage and assist each other in their arduous work. The pious subject of this memoir enjoyed much sweet intercourse with his religious brethren, at this time: but he was soon displaced from his living, for not conforming to the ceremonies of the church, and for refusing to read the Book of Sports. The most profitable preferments in the church of England were given to such as were most forward in promoting the new ceremonies and superstitions. New holy-days were introduced, and required to be observed with all possible solemnity, at the same time that the people were encouraged to profane the Lord's-day by a declaration commonly called "The Book of Sports," printed and published by the king's special command. [a] This was first published by King James, dated, Greenwich, May 24th, 1618, as follows: "That for his good people's lawful recreations, his Majesty's pleasure was, that after the end of divine service, they should not be disturbed, letted, nor discouraged from any lawful recreations; such as dancing, either of men or women, archery for men, leaping, vaulting, or any such harmless recreations; nor from having of May-games, Whitson-ales, or Morrice-dances, and setting up of May-poles, or other sports therewith used, so as the same may be had in due and convenient time, without impediment of divine service: and that women should have leave to carry rushes to the church for the decoration of it, according to their old custom; withal prohibiting all unlawful games to be used

a Ludlow's Memoirs, p. 5. Hume's Hist. England, vol. vi. chap. xlvii. and Rapine's Hist. England, fol. vol. ii. B. xviii.

on Sundays only, as bear-baiting, bull-baiting, interludes, and at all times (in the meaner sort of people by law prohibited) bowling."

This declaration was ordered to be read in all the parish churches of Lancashire, a maritime county, in the north-west part of England. Dr Fuller well observes, that when this declaration was brought abroad, "It is not so hard to believe, as sad to recount what grief and distraction thereby was occasioned, in many honest men's hearts, who looked on it, not as local for Lancashire, but what in process of time would enlarge itself all over England, as it did in the reign of Charles I. in the year 1633." Charles, having fully imbibed his father's principles, now revived, enlarged, and keenly urged, his father's declaration. It was to be published in all parish churches, but whether by the minister, or any other person, was left to the direction of the bishop; and therefore putting this hardship on the clergy was the deed of the bishops. And Laud, who was now at the helm, knew well, that the reading of this most impious declaration would greatly distress the Puritans, and free the church from a set of men, to whom he was extremely averse. Many poor clergymen strained their consciences to read it. Some, when they had read it, immediately read the fourth commandment to the people;—adding, "This is the law of God; the other, the injunction of man." Some put it upon their curates; but a great number refused to read it upon any terms; and among these last was Mr Ashe. He had many companions in this tribulation. Many of the most eminently godly ministers were also driven from their places, excommunicated, persecuted in the high-commission court, and some of them forced to leave the kingdom, for not publishing this declaration. They suffered much "for not daring to tell their people, that they might *lawfully* profane the Sabbath by gambols and sports; and to publish from their pulpits the *permission* of the King to break the command of God." [a] And Dr Fuller says, that it is questionable, whether their

a Towgood's Dissent, Let. ii.

sufferings procured more pity to them, or more hatred to the causers thereof.[a]

The reasons of those who refused to read the Book of Sports were enforced in the following manner. 1. That the publication of this declaration would be interpretatively an approbation thereof, whereas on the contrary they are commanded, *to have no fellowship with the unfruitful works of darkness, but rather to reprove them*, Eph. v. 11. 2. That hereby they would draw a just woe upon themselves, pronounced by the prophet of the Lord, *Woe unto them who decree unrighteous decrees, and that write grievousness which they have prescribed*, Isai. x. 1. 3. That the promulgation of a law is a necessary part of it, as persons would neither take notice of this declaration, nor liberty by it, until it were published; and so the publisher should himself become a promoter of sin. 4. That obedience to authority obligeth only in *things lawful and honest.* And the apostle acknowledges, That he himself had power only to edification, and not to destruction, 2 Cor. xiii. 10. whereunto the publication of this declaration did manifestly tend.[b]

The Lord, who hath prepared his throne in the heavens, and whose kingdom ruleth over all, afforded necessary support and help to Mr Ashe, under all his sufferings and temptations. In the goodness of Divine providence, after sometime he obtained a little liberty to preach in an exempt church at Wroxhall, under the protection of Sir John Burgoyne, and elsewhere, under the Lord Brook, in Warwickshire. He was chaplain to the Lord Brook; and upon the breaking out of the civil war, he became chaplain to the Earl of Manchester, and had a considerable part in the Cambridge-visitation.[c] He was at the battle of Edge-hill, which first effectually brake the peace between the King and the Parliament, and was fought on the Lord's-day, 23d of October, 1642. The army belonging to the Parliament, in which Mr Ashe was, under

a Fuller's Church-Hist. of Britain, Cent. xvii. B. x. & xi. Neal's Hist. Purit. vol. ii. chap. ii. & v.

b Fuller's Hist. B. x. 1618.

c Wood's Athenæ Oxon. vol. i. p. 638. Neal's Hist. vol. iv.

the Earl of Essex, designed to rest and observe the Sabbath in Kineton, a small market-town, about three miles from Edge-hill. But in the morning, when the soldiers were going to the church, the news came that the King's army was approaching; and they were, therefore, obliged to go to Edge-hill and fight them. And though Mr Ashe, and other eminent divines, who were chaplains to the army, were much exposed to danger; yet none of them were slain, hurt, or taken prisoners.[a]

Mr Ashe was chosen to be a member of the venerable Assembly of divines at Westminster; and in the list of the Assembly of divines, in Mr Neal's History, he is marked as giving constant attendance there.

He was minister of Michael Basing-shaw, London, and afterward of St Austin's, in London, where he died.[b] He was one of the Cornhill Lecturers. And one of those who subscribed a paper, entitled, *A Vindication of the Ministers of the gospel in, and about London, from the unjust aspersions cast upon their former actings for the parliament, as if they had promoted the King's death.*[c] After the King's death, he vigorously opposed the new commonwealth, under Oliver Cromwell, as established without King and House of Lords, and publicly declaimed against the engagement. He had a considerable hand in bringing in King Charles II.

Dr Walker, among other charges which he brings against him, severely censures him for a sermon, from Psal. ix. 9. before the House of Commons in 1642, as containing large invectives against the government and governors of the church.[d] This author seldom fails to dip his pen in the *very* gall of bitterness, when he meets with the Puritans. But Dr Calamy, upon perusing the sermon, says, that he found it to be a very grave and serious discourse, no way unbecoming either the preacher, or the auditory.[e] Among many sad grievances, Mr

a Vicar's Parliamentary Chronicle, p. 191, 200.
b Wood's Athenæ Oxon. vol. i. p. 638.
c See Dr Burgess's Life, and Calamy's Cont. p. 743.
d Walker's Attempt, part i. p. 48.
e Calamy's Cont. vol. i. p. 2.

Ashe mentions, in this sermon, *subscription* urged upon all *graduates* in both Universities, and upon all men entering into the ministry, as an heavy oppression, driving some promising persons from theological studies, and thoughts of the ministry, and ensnaring the consciences of others;—pressing ceremonies in divine administrations, upon pain of suspension, silencing, deprivation, and excommunication, whereby ministers and their families were exposed to great hardships, congregations deprived of their pastors, and many forced to leave the kingdom;—conniving at a scandalous ministry;—the great abuse of oaths, particularly that of matriculation;—the abuse of church-censures;—and making opposition to the *power of godliness*, by deriding and persecuting those who were forward in it.[a] The charges were heavy, but evidently true; and, therefore, Mr Ashe was blameless. If they are accounted too severe, let this severity be imputed to the authors of these evils, and not to Mr Ashe, who faithfully testified against them, as an honest servant of Jesus Christ. As Luther said, when writing against King Henry VIII. "Should King Henry think that he is treated with more sharpness and severity than is becoming, let him impute it, not to me, but to himself." Massillon well observes, "The righteous man can with boldness condemn in others, that which he disallows in himself; his instructions do not put his conduct to the blush." Mr Ashe eminently distinguished himself, by the ardour of his zeal, and by the faithfulness of his ministry, on this remarkable occasion. Many of the princes and people of Judah, doubtless, would readily think, that the sentiments of Hananiah, the false prophet, who *taught rebellion against the Lord*, prophesying smooth things respecting them, were much more agreeable to their mind, and much more liberal in their nature, than the heavy tidings of Jeremiah; and yet true zeal and faithfulness were only found in Jeremiah.[b]—"They are only minds indifferent about religion, who, colouring their

a See Calamy's Cont. vol. i. p. 2, 3.
b See Jer. xxviii.

secret impiety with a false moderation, dare to censure the indignation of a servant of God in such a conjuncture."[a]

Other charges, seemingly without foundation, are brought against Mr Ashe, by Dr Walker.[b] These are largely and judiciously refuted by Dr Calamy.[c] "Every man ought to endeavour at eminence, not by pulling others down, but by raising himself, and enjoy the pleasure of his own superiority, whether imaginary or real, without interrupting others in the same felicity."[d] "Only to insist on men's faults, to render them odious, is no ingenious employment."[e] The general conduct of our pious reformers, notwithstanding the foul calumnies with which they have been loaded, may court inquiry, and bid defiance to censure.

> "When defamation blasts our name,
> And envy withers at our fame,
> Our Jesus is a friend:
> When he approves, and conscience smiles,
> Both Satan's rage, and world's turmoils,
> We to the tempest lend."

Mr Ashe had a good estate, and a liberal heart. He was very hospitable; and his house was much frequented, and he himself was highly esteemed. He was a christian of the primitive simplicity; and a non-conformist of the old stamp. He was eminently distinguished, by a holy life, and a cheerful mind. Holiness is the bright ornament of the Christian, the glory of angels, the beauty of heaven, and the express image of God himself, who is *glorious in holiness*. And persons who are most strict and holy in their lives ought to be most esteemed and

a Beausobre's Hist. of the Reformation, vol. i. B. i. 1518. respecting Luther.
b Walker's Attempt, p. 113, 114.
c Calamy's Contin. vol. i. p. 4, and 5. See also Dr Fuller's Hist. Univ. Cambridge, p. 168.
d Rambler, Numb. ix.
e Fuller's Church-Hist. Cent. xvii. p. 26.

honoured. But such persons are too often hated, reproached, and persecuted, by the world lying in wickedness, who scoff at holiness, and thereby deride God himself. Holiness is peculiarly becoming, in the ministers of religion, who *minister about holy things*, and ought to be exemplary to the people, in their lives.—And Mr Henry Grove considered cheerfulness of temper, as a kind of habitual gratitude to God, and a proper acknowledgement of his infinite goodness. And while Mr Grove readily paid this just tribute himself, he greatly encouraged all around to concur with him therein.[a] Cheerfulness is, undoubtedly, a distinguishing feature of the Christian religion.[b] One joyful countenance spreads cheerfulness among many. And a friend, at once cheerful and religious, is a great acquisition. He greatly contributes to enliven the exercises of social piety. Mr Calamy, who preached a sermon on the occasion of Mr Ashe's death, represents him as a man of great sincerity, humility, benevolence, prudence, and patience: as eminently diligent in preaching the glorious gospel of the grace of God in season and out of season, so as not to please the ear, but to wound the heart; seeking not the applause of men, but the salvation of souls: as singularly careful in visiting the sick: as excelling in prayer, and in maintaining great acquaintance and communion with God. His death was conformable to his life. He was rich in faith, and in other fruits of the Holy Spirit, and an eminent follower of those who through *faith* and *patience* inherit the promises. He died very comfortably, in the cheerful exercise of faith, and abounding in the consolations of the gospel of Christ, molested neither with doubts nor fears. His conversation was deeply interesting, and very edifying. Like the torch, he illuminated all around him. He did eminently bear witness to the truth and the power of the Christian religion, at this trying season. And he was peculiarly attentive to the spiritual improvement of those who were about him. He warmly recommended Jesus Christ to

a General Biogr. vol. iv. London 1808. under Grove.
b See Matth. v. 12. Phil. iii. 1, 3. iv. 4.

them. This is the last time that we can do any thing for our generation, and it ought to be diligently improved. Dying words are impressive; and those of Mr Ashe deserve our most attentive consideration.

Mr Calamy says, "When I was with him he took occasion to complain much, and not without just cause, that ministers, when they met together, discoursed not more of Christ, of heaven, and of the concernments of the other world; professing that if God should restore him, he would be more careful in his discourses, and more fruitful than ever he had been. He exhorted me and other ministers to preach much of Jesus Christ, and to speak of Christ to him; saying, *When I consider my best duties, I sink, I die, I despair; but when I think of Christ, I have enough; he is all and in all. I desire to know nothing but Jesus Christ and him crucified. I account all things dung and dross, that I may be found in Christ.*"[a] Remarkable to this purpose, and in similar circumstances, are the words of Ernest, duke of Saxony, a prince whose memory should not be buried in oblivion; and who died, in the year 1513. In his sickness, the cordeliers came to visit him, and to offer him the merits of their order to secure and hasten his recovery. The wise prince replied, "I have nothing to do either with your works or your merits: they are of no value in the sight of God. There is nothing but the righteousness of my Lord and of my Saviour, that can be of any service to me."[b] *Surely, shall one say, In the Lord have I righteousness and strength: even to Him shall men come; and all who are incensed against him shall be ashamed. In the Lord shall all the seed of Israel be justified, and shall glory*, Isai. xlv. 24, 25. *For he hath made Him to be sin for us, who knew no sin; that we might be made the Righteousness of God in him*, 2 Cor. v. 21. When the celebrated reformer, Luther, had obtained clear views of justification through the imputed righteousness of the Lord Jesus Christ, apprehended, received, and relied

a Calamy's Fun. Ser. See Phil. iii. 7—10.
b Beausobre's Hist. Reformation, B. i. 1517.

upon, by faith without works, he wrote to a friend of his, in the year 1516, as follows: "I should be glad to know what you think, and whether your soul, at last disgusted with its own righteousness, has learned to place its confidence in Jesus Christ alone, and in his righteousness." [a] This subject is deeply interesting both to an immortal soul, and to the cause of Christianity. I cannot refrain here from transcribing a few sentences of a truly valuable letter of the Rev. John Hill of London, known by a volume of Evangelical discourses. "My dear friend, London, Dec. 1744, from my bed. I have been under a very dangerous fit of sickness; yet one lesson I have learned by this affliction, which I never knew before so perfectly, I am sure not so feelingly, that is, the need and efficacy, and infinite merit and conscience-pacifying virtue, of the blood of Christ. When death and judgment appear in view, and the soul has not one good work he can call *his own*, were he sure he might plead it at God's bar, what must that soul do upon the edge of an eternal world, when he has not one good work he can call his own? whom the law charges with guilt, whom conscience condemns for it; who sees justice armed with vengeance to execute the law's curse, and himself about to fall into the Lord's hand, and be arraigned before the bar of the living God; who has no worthiness to recommend him to the blood of Christ; nothing but guilt and terror, sin and uncleanness all about him? What an hell must there be in such a one's conscience, were there not a Christ ready at hand to help him, and had not his soul liberty, without any merit on his part to venture upon him? Had I been sent to works to recommend me to Christ, to make me welcome to the blessed Jesus, I had been undone. I must have called the man who had preached that doctrine, no messenger, no interpreter, one among a thousand, but have judged of him, as one sent to torment me before the time. Ministers know not what they do, when they send poor souls to the law for life. The law is become weak through the flesh. No

a Beausobre's Hist. Reformation, B. i. 1517.

man can keep the law, therefore none can be saved by it."[a] Jesus Christ crucified, who is our *advocate with the Father, and the propitiation for our sins*, is the very essence of our consolation, under all our external pressures, and our internal conflicts. He is the soul of our religion, and of our happiness: our theme, our crown, our strength in weakness, our light in darkness, and our life in death!

> "Religion! thou the soul of happiness;
> And groaning *Calvary* of thee! *there* shine
> The noblest truths; *there* strongest motives sting!
> *There* sacred violence assaults the soul.—
> My theme! my inspiration! and my crown!
> My strength in age! my rise in low estate!
> My soul's ambition, pleasure, wealth!—my world!
> My light in darkness! and my life in death!
> My boast through time! bliss through eternity!
> Eternity too short to speak thy praise!
> Or fathom thy profound of love to man!
> To man, of men the meanest, even to me;
> My sacrifice! my God! what things are these!"[b]

Such truly sublime and rich sentiments as these, respecting Christ crucified, who is now our advocate with the Father, natively tend to raise believers above themselves, and to transport their hearts to heaven, *where Christ sitteth on the right-hand of God.*

Mr Ashe, *desiring to know nothing but Jesus Christ and him crucified*, in this awful season, said farther: "It is one thing to speak of Christ and of heaven, and another thing to feel the consolation of Christ and of heaven, *as I do*:" when he clapped his hand upon his breast, *rejoicing with joy unspeakable and full of glory*. The Lord Jesus Christ, *the Sun of Righteousness*, is the glorious centre of the Christian system, richly diffusing light, life, health, and unspeakable comfort, throughout the whole

a Christian Magazine, vol. vi. p. 154.
b Night Thoughts, No. iv.

body. And when he *arises with healing in his wings*, and shines gloriously upon the souls of his people, as he does sometimes at their death, he removes the bitterness of their affliction; disarms death of it's sting; divests the grave of it's gloomy effect; and fills them with abundant consolation; *For as the sufferings of Christ abound in us, so our consolation also aboundeth by Christ.* How highly beneficial is the Lord Jesus Christ to us; and how extremely miserable would we be without Him, especially in trouble and at death! Like the world without the sun; all darkness: and like Magor-missabib, *Terror round about!* The pious subject of this memoir received from Christ's *fulness grace for grace.* He enjoyed rich supplies of suffering grace for a suffering hour, and of dying grace for a dying hour.—At another time, he said, "The comforts of a holy life are real, and soul-supporting. I feel the reality of them, and you may know by me, that it is not in vain to serve God."[a] His religious exercises, and his lively edifying conversation, were highly acceptable to those who visited him in his sickness; and they may be highly useful to posterity. He closed an active and holy life, by a pious and edifying death, on the 20th of Aug. 1662, a short time before the fatal Bartholomew-day. His mortal remains were buried on the 23d of Aug. in the church of St Austin.[b]

Accordingly, he was not actually ejected, by the act of Uniformity, but it is allowed that it was his death only that prevented it; for it is well known that he and some others had resolved to quit their livings, rather than to comply with the measures of the times.

The celebrated Mr Calamy, who had the happiness of being intimately acquainted with Mr Ashe, while he was in London, about the space of twenty-two or twenty-three years, said at his funeral, "I can freely and clearly profess, and that with a sad heart, that I and many others, have lost a real, wise, and godly friend, brother, and fellow-labourer in the Lord: the church hath lost an eminent mem-

a Calamy's Fun. Serm.
b Wood's Athenæ Oxon. vol. i. p. 638. Calamy's Fun. Serm.

ber, and choice pillar: and this city hath lost an ancient, faithful, and painful, minister.—And the less sensible the city is of this loss, the greater is the loss.—The ministerial excellencies of many ministers were collected and concentered in one Simeon Ashe. He was a Bezaleel in God's tabernacle, a master-builder, an old disciple,—a burning and a shining light; one whom many ministers, and other good christians, called Father.—And I believe, many experimentally lament over him, as the King did over the prophet Elisha, 2 Kings ii. 12. for he lived desired, and died lamented." [a]

Mr Rutherford, one of the commissioners from the church of Scotland to the Assembly of divines at Westminster, calls him, *Gracious and zealous Mr Ashe.*[b]

A few choice sayings of Mr Ashe, which I have collected from his writings, follow. "*Without me*, saith Christ, *you can do nothing;* neither without him can we endure any thing. And he only can support the sinking soul under the most smarting troubles and heavy oppressions.—We may safely sail through Christ's blood into the bosom of the Father.—Truth, not words, feeds the soul: and I much rather desire, in my ministry, to profit, than to please, my auditory.—Former failings bewailed, shall not interrupt the course of future kindness.—And, execution is the life of law."

Mr Ashe's writings are;

1. *The Best Refuge for the Most Oppressed.* A sermon preached from Psal. ix. 9. to the Honourable House of Commons, at their solemn fast, March 30th, 1642. 4to. pp. 62. London, 1642.

In this elaborate sermon, the author, after representing the *Lord* as a most suitable refuge unto his oppressed people, mentions the English Prelates as great oppressors both in church and commonwealth. He says, " What

a Calamy's Fun. Serm.
b Disput. Lib. Cons. chap. xxi.

county, what city, what town, what village, yea, what family, I had almost said, what person in the kingdom, hath not in one kind or other, in some degree or other, at one time or other, been oppressed by them? They and their officers, by citations, censures, exactions, have been Catholick oppressors. How many wealthy men have been crushed by their cruelty? How many poor families have been ruined by their tyranny? And I beseech you to consider, whether the most pious both among preachers and people, have not met with the hardest measures, from their heavy hands. Alas, alas! How many faithful ministers have they silenced? How many gracious christians have they excommunicated! How many congregations have they starved or dissolved in this kingdom! For the proof of all this, and of more than all this, I appeal unto the many petitions presented to this honourable Parliament."[a]

2. *Good Courage Discovered, and Encouraged.* A sermon preached from Psal. xxxi. 24. before the Commanders of the Military forces, of the city of London, 17th of May, 1642. London, 1642.

3. *The Church Sinking, Saved by Christ.* A sermon preached from Isai. lxiii. 5. before the House of Lords, in the Abbey-church at Westminster, Public Fast, Feb. 26th 1644. 4to. pp. 32. London, 1645.

4. *Religious Covenanting Directed, and Covenant Keeping Persuaded.* A sermon preached from Psal. lxxvi. 11. before the Lord Mayor, the Sheriffs, and Aldermen, his brethren, and the rest of the common council of London, Jan. 14th 1645. Upon which day the *Solemn League and Covenant* was renewed by them and their officers, with prayer and fasting, at Michael Basing-shaw, London. 4to. London, 1646. I have seen this both in Scotland and England. This sermon was printed also at Air, in a small size, good type and decent paper, in the year 1793. I have, at this time, some copies of the Air edition, which the reader may have for 2*d.* each copy. Mr Ashe, in his writings, discovers much zeal for the

a P. 31, 32. See more remarks on this sermon in the author's life.

church of Christ, and for the *Solemn League and Covenant.*

5. *God's Incomparable Goodness unto Israel, unfolded and applied.* A sermon from Psal. lxxiii. 1. before the House of Commons, Fast, April 28th 1647. 4to. pp. 34. London, 1647.

6. *Christ the Riches of the Gospel, and the Hope of Christians.* A sermon from Col. i. 27. at the funeral of Dr Spurstone's only child. London, 1654.

7. *Living Loves betwixt Christ and Dying Christians.* A sermon preached from John xi. 11.—*Our friend Lazarus sleepeth*—At M. Magdalene Bermondsey in Southwark, London, June 6th 1654, at the funeral of that faithful servant of Christ, Mr Jeremiah Whitaker, Pastor of the church there. With a narrative of his exemplary and holy life and death. 4to. pp. 69. London, 1654. I have seen a copy of the second edition of this sermon, same date. Mr Ashe is also said to have preached and published funeral sermons for Mr Ralph Robinson;—Mr Rob. Strange;—Mr Tho. Gataker;—Mr Rich. Vines;—and the Countess of Manchester; but these I have not yet seen. He wrote also several prefaces to the works of others. He published, *The Power of Godliness*, and *A Treatise on the Covenant of Grace*, by the famous *John Ball*, who committed to him all his MSS.

THEODORE BACKHURST.

MR THEODORE BACKHURST, of Overton Waterville, follows in the next place after Mr Ashe, in Mr Neal's List of the Assembly of divines at Westminster. But I have sought in vain for any information respecting this divine, for several years. My researches have been particular and extensive; but always without any success. In looking over the ordinance of Parliament for calling this Assembly, we see the name of *Theophilus Bathurst*, *of Overton Watervile*—and in the list annexed to the promise or vow, is *Theodore Backhurst*. In my researches I have attended to both names. Horace tells us with great energy, that there were brave men before the wars of Troy, but they were lost in oblivion for want of a poet.[a] This is either the case respecting Mr Backhurst, or the information concerning him is very rare. I have not hitherto found one person who could give the least account of him, or of any of his writings. Nor, in all my reading, have I found the smallest hint, respecting either his life or writings, as far as I can recollect. I cannot, therefore, at this time, give any account of Mr Theodore Backhurst. If any person, or persons, into whose hands this publication may come, can give me any intelligence concerning him, I shall account myself much obliged to them.

Mr Thomas Baylie is next in place, in the order of the list.

a "In endless night they sleep, unwept, unknown:
No bard had they to make all time their own."
Horace, Od. iv. ix. xxvi.

THOMAS BAYLIE, B. D.

RECTOR OF MANINGFORD, AND A MEMBER OF THE ASSEMBLY OF DIVINES AT WESTMINSTER.

THOMAS BAYLIE was born in Wiltshire, in England. He was entered of *St Alban's Hall*, in the University of Oxford, in Mich. term, 1600, aged eighteen years, elected Demy of *Magdalen-College*, in 1602, and perpetual Fellow of that house, 1611, he being then Master of Arts. Afterward, he became rector of Maningford Crucis, near Marlborough, in his own country. In the year 1621, he was admitted to the reading of the *sentences*, at which time and after, he was zealously inclined to the puritanical party. There were never, perhaps, men of holier lives than the generality of the *Puritans and Nonconformists* of this period, Their piety and devotedness to God were very remarkable. Their ministers made considerable *sacrifices* for God and religion. They spent their lives, in sufferings, in fastings, in prayers, in walking closely with God in their families, and among their people who were under their pastoral care, in a firm adherence to their principles, and in a series of unremitted labours for the good of mankind. They were indefatigably zealous in their Master's service. Mr Baylie, like our reformers in general, seems to have been strongly attached to his religious principles, and ready to sacrifice every thing in support of them. Accordingly, being zealously attached to the puritanical party, he made an open declaration of his sentiments, took the *covenant*, and was nominated to be one of the Assembly of divines at Westminster. He was a zealous covenanter, and an indefatigable preacher. He had the rich rectory of Mildenhall, in Wiltshire, his own country, conferred on him.

In this he succeeded Dr George Morley, a royalist. After the restoration of King Charles the II, he was turned out from Mildenhall, by the Act for Uniformity.[a] Upon his ejection, he retired to Marlborough, and had a private congregation. He died at Marlborough, in the year 1663, aged 81. His mortal remains were buried in the church of St Peter there, on the 27th day of March that year. Wood says, that upon his death, his conventicle at that place was carried on by another brother as zealous as himself.[b] Thus the Scripture was fulfilled, *A seed shall serve him; it shall be counted to the Lord for a generation.*

Both Wood and Walker say, That he was a Fifth-monarchy man; but Dr Calamy observes very smartly, "That it was not for that he was ejected, but for his *nonconformity.*"

Mr Baylie's writings are;

De Merito Mortis Christi, et Modo Conversionis, Diatribæ duo. Oxon. 1626. 4to.

Concio ad Clerum habita in Templo B. Mariæ Oxon. Wood says he has also, as he has been informed, one or more English sermons extant, but such he has not yet seen, nor have I seen them.

a See Memoir of C. Burgess, and of W. Bridge. Dr Calamy's Acc. p. 754. Cont. vol. ii. p. 864.

b Wood's Athenæ Oxon. vol. ii.

JOHN BOND,

DOCTOR OF THE LAW, MINISTER AT THE SAVOY, LONDON, AND A MEMBER OF THE ASSEMBLY OF DIVINES AT WESTMINSTER.

JOHN BOND was son of Dennis Bond of Dorchester in the county of Dorset. Dennis Bond, his father, who was son of John Bond of Lutton in Dorsetshire, and he the son of Dennis of the same place, was bred up to the trade of a woollen-draper in Dorchester. He was then a constant hearer and great admirer of John White, often called *the Patriarch of Dorchester.*[a] He was elected burgess, with Denzil Hollis, for the Borough of Dorchester, of which he was then alderman, to serve in the Long Parliament. He was accounted a very active man.

John Bond, the subject of this memoir, was educated under the Rev. John White, above mentioned. Mr White's ministry seems to have been highly beneficial to him, in his youthful years. Early impressions are strong; the force of truth is great, and it shall prevail. When young men are, by the blessing of the Lord accompanying his word, the preaching of the glorious gospel of his grace, brought to the knowledge of the truth as it is in Jesus, in connexion with their other learning, they become highly useful to their country; especially when they labour in preaching the gospel of our Lord Jesus Christ. And, by the faithful administration of gospel ordinances, accompanied with Almighty power and free grace, have often been formed those characters, on whom, under God, depend, in a great measure, the important concerns both of churches, and of nations.

Our young scholar, having received a suitable and

a See Memoir of John White.

well directed education at home, was sent to Cambridge, and placed, Wood says, he thinks, in St John's College, where he took the degree of bachelor of civil law. Afterward he became Lecturer in the city of Exeter, the capital of Devonshire. He was very zealously attached to the Puritans, made an open declaration of his sentiments, and was a sufferer for righteousness' sake with that religious body. But it was a common saying among the Puritans, in those times, *That brown bread with the gospel was good fare.* Accordingly, he cheerfully *endured all things* for the gospel's sake. He triumphed over adversity in every frightful shape with true magnanimity, as our reformers in that period generally did. The general language among the ministers of Christ, at the time of the reformation, was,—*None of these things move me, neither count I my life dear unto myself, so that I might finish my course with joy, and the ministry which I have received of the Lord Jesus, to testify the gospel of the grace of God*, Acts xx. 24.

Mr Bond was a zealous covenanter. He shews a very warm attachment, in his writings, to the work of reformation, and to the solemn league and covenant. He says, " The Lord doth absolutely require the *reformation* of religion at this time, in *doctrine*, *worship*, *discipline*, *and government*, in the church.—Also the Lord doth expect that you should promote the late *solemn league and covenant*, that *triple cable* of the three kingdoms, by which the *anchor* of our hope is fastened; that three-fold cord that binds all these kingdoms together and unto God."[a]—He was afterward minister at the Savoy, London, and one of the Assembly of divines at Westminster. About this time, he commenced Doctor of the Laws. Mr Neal says, that he was a superadded divine. Beside those who were originally appointed to sit in the Assembly, in order to supply vacancies which happened by death, desertion, or otherwise, the Parliament named others from time to time, who were called superadded divines. He was sometimes called to preach unto the Long Parliament; and

a Sermon from Isai. xlv. 15. p. 48.

and some of his sermons were published, and are still extant. On the 11th of Dec. 1645, he was made Master of the Hospital called the Savoy under the great seal. He was appointed Master of Trinity-hall, in Cambridge, which Mr John Selden refused. In 1654, he was appointed an assistant to the commissioners of Middlesex and Westminster, for the ejection of ignorant and scandalous ministers and schoolmasters. Wood says, he lived, as he conceives, to the restoration of King Charles II, 1660, being then about 49 years of age; when he retired to Lutton in Dorsetshire, and died there about 1680.[a]

Mr Bond's Writings are; *A Door of Hope: Also Holy and Loyal Activity.* Two Treatises delivered in several sermons in Exeter. 4to. London, 1641.—A sermon before the Deputy-Lieutenants, 4to. 1643.—*Salvation in a Mystery:* or, *A Prospective Glass for England's Case.* A sermon preached from Isai. xlv. 15. before the House of Commons, fast, March 27th, 1644. 4to. pp. 60. London, 1644. I have seen this sermon both in England and Scotland.—*A Dawning in the West.* A thanksgiving sermon from Isai. xxv. 9. before the House of Commons, 22d Aug. 1645. 4to. London, 1645.—*Job in the West.* Two sermons, at two public fasts, for the five associated western counties of England, from Job xix. 21. 4to. pp. 80. London, 1645.—A thanksgiving sermon, from Psal. l. 23. before the House of Commons, 19th of July 1648. 4to. London, 1648.—A sermon, entitled, *Grapes among Thorns,* before the House of Commons: but these two sermons last mentioned, I have not seen.

a Wood's Ath. Oxon. vol. i. Col. 379, 380.

OLIVER BOWLES, B. D.

PASTOR OF SUTTON, IN BEDFORDSHIRE, AND A MEMBER OF THE ASSEMBLY OF DIVINES AT WESTMINSTER.

OLIVER BOWLES was Pastor of Sutton, in Bedfordshire, in England. A Mr Meen at Biggleswade, a town in Bedfordshire, who lately examined the register of Sutton parish very minutely from 1538 to 1700, for some account of Mr Oliver Bowles, says, "It appears to me, that Mr Bowles came to Sutton early in the year 1607. That circumstance is not particularly specified in the register; but there is a new series of entries commencing with that year, in a hand-writing very different from any of the former; and in Dec. 1607 is the following entry among the register of baptisms: "Samuel Bowles filius Mr Bowles baptised Dec. 13th." There are after this, registered the baptisms of ten other sons, who are said to be sons of *Oliver Bowles;* viz. Nathaniel, Benjamin, Joseph, Edward, John, Oliver, Clement, Jonathan, Elisha, and Job. In the register of burials is mentioned another son, *Francis*, buried June 7th 1608, which he most probably had before he came to Sutton; so that it appears certain, this good old patriarch had at least twelve sons." [a] He was chosen to sit in the Assembly of divines at Westminster; and is marked in Mr Neal's list, as giving constant attendance.—He was a very zealous reformer, as appears by his sermon preached from John ii. 17. to the Lords, Commons, and Divines. In his dedicatory epistle to this sermon, he says, "There are many creatures, said the wise man, that are comely in their going; but none so comely as a *zealous reformer*." He was esteemed a very eminent puritanical minister. But through the indolence

a See Theological and Biblical Magaz. for June 1804.

or inattention of contemporaries, and the distance of time, few facts can be fairly stated with certainty respecting him, as far as I know. And I am fully determined to be silent, when I have not authentic information. Conjectures are uncertain, and in many instances false. I have, therefore, resolved to avoid them, in this work.

Mr Bowles' writings which I have seen are;

Zeal for God's House Quickened: or, A Sermon preached from John ii. 17. before the Assembly of Lords, Commons, and Divines, at their solemn fast, July 7th, 1643, in the Abbey church at Westminster; expressing the eminence of zeal requisite in Church-Reformers. 4to. pp. 48. with an epistle dedicatory, of above five pages. London, 1643. Dr Wilkins, in his Preacher, mentions this sermon, in the enumeration of authors who have written on zeal.

De Pastore Evangelico Tractatus. 4to. London, 1649. This is in the catalogue of books, in the Theological Library, belonging to the students of divinity in the University of Edinburgh. Ed. 1757. This excellent treatise, respecting the evangelical pastor, was printed at London, in a small size, in the year 1655. I have seen one copy of it. It is in Latin. Dr Wilkins, in his Preacher, mentions this treatise, in his enumeration of the treatises of learned men, who have written particularly and largely upon the *art of preaching*. It is eminently judicious and useful.

WILLIAM BRIDGE, A. M.

MINISTER OF THE GOSPEL AT YARMOUTH, AND A MEMBER OF THE FAMOUS ASSEMBLY OF DIVINES AT WESTMINSTER.

WILLIAM BRIDGE was a student in Cambridge thirteen years; and sometime Fellow of Emmanuel-College, in that University. He was first minister in Essex, where he continued about five years. He was afterward called and settled in the city of Norwich, the capital of Norfolk, in the parish of St George Tomland. He continued here until he was silenced for non-conformity, by Bishop Wren, in the year 1637. He was afterward excommunicated; and when the writ for taking those who were excommunicated came out against him, he retired to Holland, and became Pastor to the English Church in Rotterdam, where the celebrated Mr Jeremiah Burroughs was preacher. When he was *persecuted in one city*, he *fled into another*. This is allowed, and exemplified both by Christ and his apostles. Wisdom and integrity are indeed necessary, that we may be properly directed in the application of this rule to particular cases. Christ gives liberty to his servants, in imminent danger, when they are violently persecuted, and pursued to their destruction, to retire, both for their own safety, and for the propagation of the glorious gospel of his grace in other places.[a] If their flock be all dispersed by persecution, they may also flee for their own safety. "He who flies may fight again. It is no inglorious thing for Christ's soldiers to quit their ground, provided they do not quit their colours. They may go out of the way of danger, though they must not go out of the way of duty. Observe Christ's care of his disciples, in providing places

a See Acts xiii. 50, 51. & xiv. 5, 6, 7. & viii. 4.

of retreat and shelter for them, ordering it so, that persecution rageth not in all places at the same time; but when one city is made too hot for them, another is reserved for a cooler shade, and a little sanctuary; a favour to be used, and not to be slighted, yet always with this proviso, that no sinful, unlawful means be used to make the escape, for then it is not a door of God's opening." [a] The zealous and pious subject of this memoir, being silenced and excommunicated, and a writ come out against him, could not be useful in this place at that time.

The Puritans were then most severely handled in England, especially by Dr Wren, Bishop of Norwich, for not complying with his Visitation-Articles. The Book contained one hundred and thirty-nine Articles, in which were eight hundred and ninety-seven questions, some very insignificant, others highly superstitious, and several impossible to be answered. The following are a specimen: Is your Communion Table so placed within the Chancel as the Canon directs?—Doth your Minister pray for the King with his whole Title?—Doth he pray for the Archbishops and Bishops?—Doth he observe all the Orders, Rites, and Ceremonies, prescribed in the Book of Common Prayer, and administering the Sacrament?—Doth he receive the Sacrament kneeling himself, and administer to none but such as kneel?—Doth your Minister baptize with the sign of the cross?—Doth he wear the surplice while he is reading prayers and administering the Sacraments?—Doth he in Rogation-days use the Perambulation round the Parish?—Hath your minister read the Book of Sports in his Church or Chapel?—Doth he use conceived prayers before or after sermon?—Are the church-yards consecrated?—Are the graves dug east and west, and the bodies buried with their heads to the west?—Do your parishioners, at going in and out of the church, do reverence toward the Chancel?—Do they kneel at confession, stand up at the creed, and bow at the glorious name of Jesus? with several other articles of the same nature. The weight of these inquiries fell

a Henry on Matth. x. 23. vol. v.

chiefly upon the Puritans, for within two years and four months, fifty able and pious ministers were suspended, silenced, and otherwise censured, to the ruin of their poor families, for not obeying one or other of these articles; among whom were, Mr Ashe, Mr William Bridge, Mr Jeremiah Burroughs, Mr Greenhill, and Mr Edmund Calamy, and others, in the Diocese of Norwich.[a] A complaint was brought to the Commons against Wren, for having, while bishop of Norwich, by oppressions innovations, and requiring certain oaths, compelled above fifty families of that city to withdraw out of England.[b] —And that by his rigorous severities, many of his Majesty's subjects, to the number of three thousand, had removed themselves, their families, and estates, to Holland, and set up their manufactories there, to the great prejudice of the trade of this kingdom.[c] Mr Bridge returned to England, in the year 1642. *Archbishop Laud*, in his annual *accounts* of his province to the King for 1636, thus mentions him; "Mr *Bridge* of *Norwich* rather than he will conform, hath left his Lecture and two Cures, and is gone into *Holland*.—King *Charles's* note upon this is, *Let him go, we are well rid of him.*"[d] But he received encouragement from the Long Parliament to return unto his own country, as many of those who were under banishment and oppression, at this time, also did. He was frequently called to preach unto the Parliament. He was after some time chosen minister of Great Yarmouth, in the county of Norfolk, where he continued his useful labours until the Bartholomew Act, when he was ejected with his brethren in that tribulation, in the year 1662.

He was chosen as a fit person to sit in the Assembly of divines at Westminster; and was one of the dissenting brethren, or Independents, in that Assembly.

The *Independents* were undoubtedly so called from their maintaining that all Christian congregations were so

a Neal's Hist. Purit. vol. ii. chap. v. 1636.
b Rapin's Hist. Engl. vol. ii. fol. B. xx. 1640—1.
c Neal's Hist. vol. ii. chap. vii. 1640.
d Wood's Athenæ Oxon. vol. ii. Col. 364.

many *Independent* religious societies, having a right to be governed by their own laws, without being subject to any other jurisdiction. *Robinson*, their founder, expressly uses this term in explaining his doctrine respecting ecclesiastical government, in his *Apology for the English Exiles.*[a]

The title of *Independents*, probably, was originally derived from that very passage. From the year 1642, this religious denomination is very frequently found in the English *Annals*. The English *Independents* were not displeased with it, but assumed it publicly in a piece which they published in their own defence at *London*, in the year 1644, entitled; *Apologetical Narration of the Independents.* But when in process of time, many sects sheltered themselves under the cover of this extensive denomination, and even seditious persons, aiming at the destruction of the king and the government, employed it as a mask to hide their deformity, then the genuine and religious *Independents* renounced this title, and substituted another in it's place, calling themselves *Congregational Brethren*, and their religious assemblies *Congregational Churches*. The *Independents* chiefly differed from the *Presbyterians* or Calvinists, in ecclesiastical government, as clealry appears by their *Confessions of Faith*, and their other writings, which are extant. Their religious doctrines were nearly the same with those adopted by the church of *Geneva*, and other reformed churches. They were, indeed, averse to episcopacy; but they had fixed and regular ministers, approved by their people; nor did they allow every person to teach publicly, who considered himself qualified for that important office[b] This is the true character of those *Independents*, who come under our view in these memoirs. We are very highly favoured, by the eminently learned Mosheim, with a most candid and judicious account and vindication of the religious Independents in England, as here referred to; which

a Apologia, cap. v. p. 22. as with Mosheim.

b Mosheim's Eccl. Hist. vol. v. Cent. xvii. Sect. ii. part. ii. 21. edit. London, 1790.

the reader who wishes to have a fair view of that community will do well to consult.[a]

Mr Bridge and his brethren were eminently distinguished in the Assembly at Westminster, by their abilities, learning, and piety; especially in pleading the cause of the *Independents*, in the Grand Debate, with the *Presbyterians*. The *Independents*, who took up the cause in opposition to the *Presbyterians*, in the Grand Debate, in this Assembly, and subscribed the reasons that were given in, were called the dissenting brethren. They were Messrs Thomas Goodwin, Philip Nye. Jeremiah Burroughs. Sidrach Simpson, William Bridge, William Greenhill, and William Carter. They entered their dissent respecting the three following propositions, which were made by the *Presbyterians*.

1. "That many particular congregations may be under the government of one Presbytery." The *Presbyterians* endeavoured to prove this, by the instances of the church of *Jerusalem*, and of *Ephesus*, which consisted, they say, of more congregations than one, and were under one Presbyterian government, as appears by the multitude of believers mentioned in several texts of the Acts of the Apostles, the many apostles and preachers in the church, and the diversity of languages among the professors. See Acts ii. 41—46, 47. and iv. 4. and v. 14. and vi. 1—7. and ix. 31. and xii. 24. and xxi. 20. and chap. vi. 2. And these congregations were under one Presbyterial government, because they are one church, Acts viii. 1. and ii. 47. and v. 11. And the apostles did the ordinary acts of presbyters as presbyters in that church, Acts vi. And they meet with the elders for acts of government, Acts xv. 4. and xxi. 17, 18. Rev. ii. 1—7. Acts xx. 17—20. The *Independents* held in the negative, That many particular congregations might not be under the government of one presbytery; but that every particular congregation ought to be under it's own government alone. That the ordinary ruling power of ministers or pastors, did not extend farther than their pastoral charge,

a See Memoir of Mr Burroughs.

or their ordinary teaching. In support of their opinion, they brought in, Acts xx. 28. 1 Pet. v. 2. Heb. xiii. 7. &c. which they considered as holding, that the ruling and teaching power are of equal extent. Mr Baillie, who was in the Assembly, speaking of this proposition, says, "The Independents pressed they might first be heard in the negative. Here they spent to us many of twenty long sessions. Goodwin took most of the speech upon him; yet they divided their arguments among them, and gave the managing of them by turns, to Bridge, Burroughs, Nye, Simpson, and Caryl. Truly, if the cause were good, the men have plenty of learning, wit, eloquence, and, above all, boldness, and stiffness, to make it out; but when they had wearied themselves, and overwearied us all, we found the most they had to say against the presbytery, was but curious idle niceties; yea, that all they could bring was no ways concluding."[a]

2. "That there is a subordination of assemblies or courts." Mat. xviii. proving the subordination of an offending brother to a particular church, by a parity of reason proves the subordination of a congregation to superior assemblies. And he who is wronged by one power, should have recourse to another superior power, to restore his right, and rescind the sentence which injured him; otherwise there would be no powerful remedy against injury and oppression. So appeals may be made from the inferior to the superior respectively, say the *Presbyterians*. But the *Independents* denied all superiority of jurisdiction, or subordination of courts and assemblies.

3. "That one congregation ought not to assume to itself, all and sole power of ordination, if it can associate." Against this the *Independents* gave in their dissent also, reckoning that one single congregation had all and sole power of ordination.[b] The *Independents* entered their dissent only respecting these three propositions in the Assembly.[c]

a Baillie's Letters, vol. i. lett. xlv. p. 436. where the reader may find more on the subject.

b See the Grand Debate.

c Baillie, vol. ii. lett. lxxxviii. p. 78.

Mr Bridge continued to preach the glorious gospel of the grace of God, and to labour among his people in Yarmouth, with uninterrupted zeal and assiduity, until he was cast out by the Act of Uniformity, with his brethren, in the year 1662. His name is found in the respectable list, in Dr Calamy's Index of those persons who were ejected or silenced by the Act for Uniformity.[a]

As this was an event of very great importance in the history of the church of Christ, I have endeavoured to give a particular account of this grievous Act of Uniformity, and of some of it's dreadful consequences, in the memoir of Dr Cornelius Burgess, who was also a sufferer by it.

Mr Bridge and his brethren gave, at this time, plain marks of their candour, and of their sincere love *of the truth, as it is in Jesus.* They have transmitted to posterity edifying and shining examples of faith, piety, patience, and zeal. In them, the glorious gospel of the grace of God has triumphed over the combined malice and wisdom of this world.

The subject of this memoir says, in a sermon which he preached at Westminster, in 1641, "Of all the reformed churches in the world, *England* hath borne the name and worn the crown for the life and power of godliness; yet give me leave with grief of heart, and sadness of spirit, to make a challenge. What reformed church is there in the world, that ever knew so many suspended ministers as England? Speak, O Sun, whether in all thy travels from one end of the heaven to the other, thou didst ever see so many silenced ministers as thou hast done here."[b]

Mr Bridge seems to have had an opportunity of preaching sometimes at *Clapham* in Surrey, after he was ejected. Wood says, "Silenced upon his Majesty's return, he carried on his cause in conventicles at *Clapham* in *Surrey* till about the time of his death."[c] He died at Yarmouth, 12th of March, 1670, aged seventy.

a See Calamy's Cont. vol. ii. Index, and Acc. vol. ii. p. 478.
b Babylon's Downfall, p. 12.
c Ath. Oxon. vol. ii. Col. 364.

Mr Neal says, "He was a good scholar, and had a well furnished library, was a hard student, and rose every morning winter and summer at four of the clock. He was also a good preacher, a candid and charitable man, and did much good by his ministry." [a] This seems to be a very just character of Mr William Bridge.

Some sayings of his follow: *Let your company be always such as you may get good from, and do good unto. When you are alone, think of good things; and when you are in company, speak of good things. Keep the truth, and the truth will keep you. And whatever mercy or blessing you receive, trace it to Heaven's gates, and to Christ's blood; for it flowed from Christ's blood, and leads you to heaven.*

Mr Bridge's writings are numerous. He has several sermons before the Parliament: particularly, *Babylon's Downfall:* A sermon preached at Westminster, from Rev. xiv. 8. before sundry of the House of Commons. 4to. pp. 34. London, 1641.—A sermon from Zech. i. 18, &c. before the House of Commons, Fast, 29th Nov. 1643. 4to. pp. 32. London, 1643.—*The Hiding Place of the Saints in the time of God's anger:* A sermon from Zeph. ii. 3. before the Lords, at Westminster, Fast, 28th Oct. 1646. London, 1647.—Twenty-one Treatises of his were collected into 2 vols. 4to. London, 1657. The 1 vol. contains, - 1. *The Great Gospel-Mystery of the Saint's comfort and holiness, opened and applied from Christ's Priestly office.* - 2. *Satan's power to tempt; and Christ's love to, and care of, his people under temptation.* 3. *Thankfulness required in every condition.* 4. *Grace for Grace; or, the overflowing of Christ's fulness received by all saints.* 5. *The Spiritual actings of Faith, through natural Impossibilities.* 6. *Evangelical Repentance.* 7. *The spiritual life, and in-being of Christ in all believers.* 8. *The woman of Canaan.* 9. *The Saints'*

a Neal's Hist. Purit. vol. iv. 1670.

Hiding-place in time of God's anger. 10. *Christ's coming is at our midnight.* 11. *A Vindication of Gospel Ordinances.* 12. *Grace and Love beyond Gifts.* The 2 vol. contains, *Scripture-light, the most sure Light.* 14. *Christ in Travail, and his Assurance of Issue.* 15. *A Lifting up for the Down-cast.* 16. *Sin against the Holy Ghost.* 17. *Sins of Infirmity.* 18. *The False Apostle Tried and Discovered.* 19. *The Good and Means of Establishment.* 20. *The Great Things Faith can do.* 21. *The Great Things Faith can suffer.* Beside, he has ten sermons of God's return to the soul—Ten sermons respecting Christ and the covenant. London, 1667.—Eight sermons of good and bad company.—Seasonable truths in evil times. Several sermons preached, in and about London. London, 1668.—*The Freeness of the Grace and Love of God to Believers.* London, 1671.—*The sinfulness of sin, and fulness of Christ.*—A word to the Aged.—His *Remains,* containing eight sermons. London, 1673.

Seven of Mr Bridge's sermons were selected, particularly recommend by the Countess Dowager of Huntingdon, to the congregations in connexion with her ladyship, and reprinted in the year 1789. The first three are entitled, The Spiritual Actings of Faith through all natural impossibilities. 4th. No ground of Discouragement for Believers, whatever their condition be. 5th. The Cure of all Discouragements by Faith in Christ Jesus. 6th. The Great Things Faith can do. 7th. The Great Things Faith can suffer. Price 2s. stitched.

Mr Bridge is a very pious and practical writer.

ANTHONY BURGESS, A. M.

SOMETIME FELLOW OF EMMANUEL-COLLEGE IN CAMBRIDGE, PASTOR OF THE CHURCH OF SUTTON-COLDFIELD, IN WARWICKSHIRE, AND A MEMBER OF THE ASSEMBLY OF DIVINES AT WESTMINSTER.

ANTHONY BURGESS was the son of a learned schoolmaster at Watford in Hartfordshire, in England, where Dr Cornelius Burgess was minister, and in this succeeded Dr John Burgess; but he was not a-kin to either of them. He was educated at St John's College, in the University of Cambridge. And from thence he was chosen to a Fellowship in Emmanuel-College merely for his scholarship and worth. He was eminently distinguished in the University, by his piety, his learning, and being a good disputant, and a good tutor. The learned Dr John Wallis, who was his pupil, says, "About Christmas 1632, I was sent to the University of Cambridge, and there admitted in Emmanuel-College, under the tuition of Mr Anthony Burgess, a pious, learned, and able scholar, a good disputant, and a good tutor."[a] A good tutor, in an English University, is highly beneficial to his scholar. It is well known that the tutors, public and private, and not the professors, are the dispensers of that knowledge which is commonly sought in an English University. The case is very different here from what it is abroad, or even in Scotland. There, the professors are the fountains of knowledge. All that is learned must be drawn from that source; but this is not so at Oxford and Cambridge.[b] Where the tutors are the dispensers of useful knowledge, they must be of very great importance. This was the character of

a Memoirs of Dr Wallis prefixed to his sermons, London, 1791. p. 15.

b The Monthly Review Enlarged, vol. iii. p. 285. and 286.

Mr Burgess. He afterwards became pastor of the church of Sutton-Coldfield, in Warwickshire, where he soon gained much reputation. He was esteemed an eminent preacher, a sound and solid divine. When the celebrated Mr Matthew Henry removed from Chester to Hackney, near London, he visited Sutton-Coldfield, or Colefield, as some write it, and preached there from Psal. xxii. 30. *A seed shall serve him; it shall be accounted to the Lord for a generation.* Mr Henry's biographer says, That he was the more willing to see this place, on his way, for the sake of the eminent Mr Anthony Burgess, who had laboured so much among the people there.[a]

Mr Burgess continued to labour among his people with great diligence, until by plundering and other terrors of the soldiers, in the time of the civil war, he was obliged to retire to Coventry for safety. The common people who filled up the king's army were of the looser sort; the chief officers were men of profligate lives, and made a jest of religion; the private sentinels were soldiers of fortune, and not having their regular pay, lived for the most part upon free plunder. When they took possession of a town they rifled the houses of all who were called Puritans, and turned their families out of doors. Mr Baxter says, that when he lived at Coventry after the battle of Edge-hill, there were above thirty worthy ministers in that city who had fled thither for refuge from the soldiers and popular fury, as he himself also had done, though they had never meddled in the wars: among these were the Rev. Messrs Vines, Anthony Burgess, and others.[b] Famous preachers, and pious persons, chiefly suffered. They who prayed in their families, who were heard repeating sermons or singing psalms, were accounted rebels, and most severely handled.[c] The disciples of Jesus were now subjected to great hardships, on account of their religion. When Mr Burgess retired to Coventry for safety, the same garrison was full of such men, and they had a lecture every morning, in

a Henry's Life by Tong, chap. vi.
b Neals Hist. Purit. vol. ii. chap. xii. 1642.
c Neal, as above.

which Mr Burgess had a frequent course. From thence he was called to sit in the Assembly of divines at Westminster, where he was generally and highly respected. He was eminently distinguished here, by his solid learning, and genuine piety.

During the time that he was at London, he was repeatedly called to preach unto the Parliament, at their solemn fasts, and on other public occasions. And he was sometime preacher at Lawrence-Jury, there. He was earnestly solicited, by the ministers of London, to give a course of Lectures against the Antinomian errors of these times, which were delivered at Lawrence-Jury, and afterward published. The learned society, at whose solicitation these excellent lectures were given, earnestly desired their publication, as follows: "We the President and Fellows of Sion-College, London, earnestly desire Master *Anthony Burgess* to publish in print his elaborate and judicious lectures upon the law and the covenants against the Antinomin errors of these times, which at our entreaty he hath preached, and for which we give him most hearty thanks, that so as well the kingdom, as this city, may have the benefit of those his learned labours. Dated at Sion-College, the 11th of June, 1646, at a general meeting of the ministers of London there. *Arthur Jackson*, President, in the name and by the appointment of the rest."[a] In the year 1538, John Agricola, a native of Eisleben, made a declaration against *the law*, maintaining that it was neither fit to be proposed to the people as a rule of manners, nor to be used in the church as a mean of instruction; and that *the gospel* alone was to be inculcated and explained both in the churches and in the schools of learning. The followers of Agricola were called *Antinomians*, that is, enemies of the law.[b] They held that the law is of no use or obligation under the gospel-dispensation; and taught

a This is prefixed to the Lectures.—Sion-College was founded in 1627, by Dr Thomas White, Vicar of Dunstan's in the West, for the benefit and improvement of the London clergy. Here is a public library, containing about fifteen thousand books, printed and in manuscript. Description of England and Wales, vol. vi. under Middlesex.

b Mosheim's Eccl. Hist. vol. ii. p. 168.

doctrines that evidently supersede the necessity of good works and a holy life. The *Antinomians*, greatly prevailed in England in the seventeenth century. Dr *Crisp*, who was born in London, in the year 1600, was a flaming preacher among them.[a] Great disputes were occasioned by the publication of the Posthumous Works of *Crisp*, who died 27th of Feb. 1643.

The errors and sophistry of the *Antinomians* are unmasked and refuted, by Mr Burgess in his lectures at Lawrence-Jury, in the most satisfactory manner. Their opinions are brought to the test of a judicious examination, by the lively oracles of God: and they are completely deprived of the fallacious arguments by which they maintained their errors. These lectures were very necessary when they were delivered; and they may undoubtedly be highly beneficial to the christian church in every age, especially when Antinomian errors prevail. "For the christian world in general, it is most requisite to urge and persuade them to yield a careful and diligent attention to that moral law, the law of God, of rectitude and truth, the authority and obligation of which they do not hesitate to acknowledge. If there be others who disclaim such *obligation*, and hold themselves exempted from religious obedience, it is of great moment to convince them of their error, and to endeavour to stem its progress."[b]

Mr Burgess, having finished his labours at London, returned to discharge the duties of his pastoral office at Sutton-Coldfield. He conformed before the wars, but he was so far from the new conformity, as it was settled at the restoration, that upon his death-bed he professed great satisfaction in his having refused it. He was ejected from Sutton-Coldfield, by the act for Uniformity in 1662.[c] After his ejectment, he lived at Tamworth, a town in Staffordshire, in a very cheerful and pious manner. Before he left his place, the new Bishop of Coventry and

a See Mosheim's Eccl. Hist. vol. v. Cent. xvii. Sect. ii. Part ii. xxiii. Wood's Ath. Oxon. vol. ii. Col. 26.

b The Monthly Review Enlarged, vol. xix. p. 464.

c See Memoirs of Dr Cornelius Burgess, and of Mr William Bridge.

Litchfield sent for him, as he did also for several other worthy dissatisfied ministers in his diocese, hoping to gain upon them. This design failed, but he gave encomiums of several of them. He said respecting Mr Burgess, "That he was fit for a Professor's place in the University." He was eminently learned and pious; every way possessing the highest claims to public esteem and deference. A judicious writer well observes, "The primitive dissenters from our ecclesiastical establishment, were not less eminent for learning than for piety; of the two thousand ministers, who, in the reign of Charles the Second, so nobly resigned emoluments and dignities, for conscience-sake, few were destitute of literary accomplishments, while some possessed and exhibited them in a degree which will immortalize both their names and their usefulness."[a]

Mr Flavel, Fountain of Life, serm. 25, says, that Mr Anthony Burgess was *a grave divine.* Dr *John Wallis*, who was a member of the Assembly of divines at Westminster, was his pupil, and gives him the following character: he says, "I was sent to the University of Cambridge, and there admitted in Emmanuel-College, under the tuition of Mr Anthony Burgess, a pious, learned, and able scholar, a good disputant, a good tutor, an eminent preacher, a sound and orthodox divine, and afterward minister of Sutton-Coldfield, in Warwickshire."[b]

Mr Burgess is an eminent writer. Dr Fuller, in his History of the University of Cambridge, in the account of Emmanuel-College, page 148, says, "Among the *learned writers* of this College, I have omitted many still alive, as Mr *Anthony Burgess*, the profitable expounder of the much mistaken nature of the *two covenants*." Dr Wilkins, in his Preacher, enrols Mr Anthony Burgess among some of the most eminent of the English divines, for sermons and practical divinity. Dr Cotton Mather, in his Student and Preacher, speaks thus: "Of an A. Burgess, I may say, he has written for thee excellent things."

a The Instructer, No. 33. p. 257. See Dr Calamy's Account of the Ejected Minrs. and Palmer's Nonconformist's Memorial.

b Memoirs of Dr Wallis, as above. See also Dr Calamy's Cont. vol. ii. p. 853.

His style is neat and plain. His writings are;

1. *The Difficulty of, and Encouragements to Reformation:* A sermon preached from Mark i. 2, 3, before the House of Commons, at the public fast, 27th Sept. 1643. 4to. pp. 28. London, 1643.

2. *Judgments Removed, where Judgment is Executed:* A sermon preached from Psalm cvi. 30, 31. to the Court-Martial in Lawrence-Jury, London, 5th of Sept. 1644. Being the day of their solemn seeking the Lord for his blessing upon their proceedings. 4to. pp. 13. London, 1644.

3. *The Magistrate's Commission from Heaven:* A sermon preached from Rom. xiii. 4. in Lawrence-Jury, London, the 28th of Sept. 1644. at the election of the Lord Mayor. 4to. pp. 20. London, 1644.

In this sermon, there are some very judicious remarks respecting the extent of the magistrate's power in the church. He says, "It extends unto the reforming and redressing of all the corruptions that creep into the church and the worship of God. This the magistrate's power reaches unto, in Deut. And so we read of *Josias*, *Moses*, *Hezekiah*, all these worthy governors, their power did reach to the redressing of the abuses that were in the church of God, when idolatry and superstition came in: so that it is made their sin, that the high places were left. Why the magistrates had power then, and should not have power now, there can no solid reason be given. Indeed the manner of the punishment, belonging to God's judicial law, may be altered, but their duty to preserve the worship of God, which floweth from the moral law, cannot cease."—He adds, "Their power extendeth yet farther, and that is to restrain heresies and errors, or any thing that may spread itself to the destruction of the church."—

4. *Rome's Cruelty and Apostacy:* A sermon preached from Rev. xix. 2. on the 5th of Nov. 1644, before the House of Commons. 4to. pp. 21. London, 1645.

In this sermon, the author, after giving a particular account of the great *Cruelty* and *Apostacy* of the idolatrous church of Rome, says to his learned auditory, "The way to keep out popery is to encourage learning. The heathens in their sacrifice to *Apollo* offered Ivy to him, to shew, that learning could not grow unless the magistrates would bear it up. God forbid, therefore, that ever you should discourage it; for at the same time when God brought truth into the world, human literature flourished, and was a great help thereunto."

5. *The Reformation of the Church to be endeavoured more than that of the Commonwealth:* A sermon preached from Judges vi. 27, 28, 29. before the House of Lords, at the public fast, 27th Aug. 1645. 4to pp. 27. London, 1645.

In this excellent sermon the reformation of the church of Christ is a chief object of attention, and warmly recommended to the illustrious auditory. In it, the author discovers much zeal for the purity of divine institutions, and for the glory of God.

6. *Public Affections Pressed.* A sermon preached from Numb. xi. 12. before the House of Commons, 25th Feb. 1645. 4to. London, 1646. I have seen these sermons both in Scotland and England.

7. *Vindiciæ Legis:* or, *A Vindication of the Moral Law, and the Covenants, from the Errors of Papists, Arminians, Socinians, and more especially, Antinomians:* In twenty-nine lectures, preached at Lawrence-Jury, London. Small 4to. pp. 271. London, 1646. The second edition, 4to. pp. 281. London, 1647. I have seen copies of both editions, both in England and Scotland.

8. *The True Doctrine of Justification Asserted and Vindicated, from the Errors of Papists, Arminians, Socinians, and more especially Antinomians*: In thirty lectures preached at Lawrence-Jury, London. Part 1. 4to. London, 1648. 2d edit. 1651. The third edition, with the addition of the contents of each sermon, by a friend of the author. 4to. pp. 300. London, 1655.

9. *A Treatise of Justification.* Part 2. *Of the Natural Righteousness of God, and Imputed Righteousness of Christ.* 4to. London, 1654. In forty-five sermons.

10. *Spiritual Refining:* or, *A Treatise of Grace and Assurance.* Folio pp. 696. London, 1652.

In this excellent treatise, are handled, the doctrine of

assurance; the use of signs in self-examination; how true graces may be distinguished from counterfeit; several true signs of grace, and many false ones; the nature of grace under several scripture-notions or titles, as regeneration, the new creature, the heart of flesh, vocation, sanctification, &c. Many chief questions occasionally controverted between the Orthodox and the Arminians. Also many cases of conscience; the whole tending to comfort and confirm saints, undeceive and convert sinners.

11. *Spiritual Refining:* Part 2. or, *A Treatise of Sin, with it's Causes, Differences, Mitigations, and Aggravations.* 4to. pp. 368. London, 1654. Second edition, both parts, folio, London, 1658.

The main scope of this work is to bring not only the ungodly, but the believer also into more acquaintance with his own heart. I have seen this useful work; both parts, in the valuable library belonging to the presbytery of Dumfries, in several counties in Scotland, and in England.

12. *One Hundred and forty-five Expository Sermons upon the whole seventeenth chapter of the Gospel according to John:* or, *Christ's Prayer before his Passion explained, and both practically and polemically improved.* Folio. pp. 702. London, 1656.

Dr Edward Williams, in his Preacher's Library, says, "Burgess's expository sermons on John xvii. are full of sound doctrine, methodically arranged, and closely applied, in very plain language."

In Mr Ogle's Theological catalogue, p. 5. London, 1809, the price is marked, 10*s.* I have seen this volume of sermons, in several parts of Scotland.

13. *The Doctrine of Original Sin, Asserted and Vindicated against the old and new Adversaries thereof, Socinians, Papists, Arminians, and Anabaptists. And practically improved for the benefit of the meanest capacities.* Folio. pp. 555. London, 1659.

This excellent work is divided into four parts; the first proving, *That Original Sin is,* by pregnant texts of scripture vindicated from false glosses; the second shewing what it is, and how communicated; the third handling it's subject, in what part it resides, and what powers of the soul are corrupted by it; and the fourth setting forth it's immediate effects. To which is added a digressive epistle concerning *Justification* by faith alone, excluding the conditionality of works in that act.

I have seen this elaborate work, in the library belonging to the presbytery of Dumfries, and two copies of it, in the library of the University of Glasgow, and several copies of it, in different parts of Scotland; and I have seen it in England.

14. *The Scripture Directory, for Church Officers and People:* or, *A Practical Commentary* upon the whole third chapter of 1 Cor. To which is annexed the Godly and the Natural Man's Choice, upon Psal. iv. 6, 7, 8. Folio, London, 1659.

15. *An Expository Commentary on the whole first Chapter of* 2 *Cor.* Fol. pp. 697. London, 1661.

Dr Edward Williams, in his Preacher's Library, says, "Burgess's Expository Comment. on 2 Cor. i. fol. Lon. 1661, deserves the same character as his work on John xvii."—I have seen it in different parts of Scotland.

It is said, that Mr Burgess has a Treatise of Self-judging, in order to the Sacrament, with a Sermon on the Day of Judgment; but these I never saw.

JEREMIAH BURROUGHS, A. M.

A FAMOUS PREACHER TO TWO OF THE LARGEST CONGREGATIONS ABOUT LONDON, STEPNEY AND CRIPPLEGATE; AND ONE OF THE DISSENTING BRETHREN IN THE ASSEMBLY OF DIVINES AT WESTMINSTER.

JEREMIAH BURROUGHS was educated in the University of Cambridge; but he was obliged to remove both from the University and the kingdom for nonconformity, in these evil times. He had now his season of adversity; but he was sufficiently supported under it. He was *persecuted, but not forsaken.*—He was among those pious and faithful ministers and followers of Christ, who suffered severely by Bishop Wren's Visitation-Articles.[a] *Laud*, archbishop of *Canterbury*, was now high in place, and carried things to excessive and intolerable lengths, through his warm and violent attachment to the ancient rites and ceremonies of the church. The king was entirely directed by his counsels.[b] And Rapin says, "If it was endeavoured in Scotland to ruin Presbyterianism (Calvinism) by indirect ways, it was thought proper to proceed in England with less caution. Accordingly, all possible efforts were used to destroy it utterly, by persecuting the Puritans, for whom there was not the least condescension."—Samuel Ward, a minister in Ipswich, boldly preached against the king's Book of Sports, and also said, *That the church of England was ready to ring changes in Religion:* for which he was suspended by the high commission-court, and afterward committed to prison for refusing to make a public recantation.[c]

Mr Burroughs cheerfully renounced every temporal in-

a See Memoir of Mr William Bridge.

b Mosheim's Eccl. Hist. vol. v. cent. xvii. sect. ii. part i. chap. i. x.

c Rapin's Hist. England, fol. vol. ii. B. xix. 1633. p. 289.—1636. p. 294.

terest for the sake of truth, and with determined courage, trusting in the Lord, he retired to Holland.[a] There he became minister of an English congregation at Rotterdam, He continued here sometime; but returned to England, when he received encouragement by the Long Parliament, and became preacher to two of the largest and most numerous congregations about London, Stepney and Cripplegate He was called to sit in the Assembly of Divines at Westminster, and was one of the dissenting brethren in that Assembly; but shewed himself to be a divine of great candour, modesty, and charity. Mr Baxter was accustomed to say, If all the Presbyterians had been like Mr Marshall, and all the Independents like Mr Burroughs, their differences might have been easily compromised. Mr Burroughs made a declaration in the name of the Independents, in their difference with the Presbyterians, "That if the Independent congregations might not be exempted from that coercive power of the classes; if they might not have liberty to govern themselves in their own way, as long as they behaved peaceably toward the civil magistrate, they were resolved to suffer, or go to some other place of the world, where they might enjoy their liberty."[b]. It was said, That the divisions which prevailed in these times broke his heart, because one of the last subjects which he preached upon, and printed, was his *Irenicum*, to the lovers of truth and peace, or an attempt to heal divisions among Christians. He never gathered a separate congregation, nor accepted of a parochial living, but wore out his strength in continual preaching, and other services of the church. *He endured all things for the elect's* sakes, that they may also obtain the *salvation which is in Christ Jesus with eternal glory*. He denied himself, that he might promote the eternal happiness of his fellow-creatures. Like Paul, he *travailed as in birth*, in order that *Christ might be formed in the souls of his hearers*. In his preaching, he did not use "those gaudy ornaments which too often put the preacher in the

a See Memoir of W. Bridge.

b Neal's Hist. Purit. vol. iii. chap. vi. 1645. where the reader may find more on the subject.

place of his text; or, as one has well expressed it, serve only to evaporate weighty truths, and to make them appear as light as the style."—His great aim was to guide his hearers in the way to heaven; and accordingly, plainness and persuasion were the chief objects of his attention.[a] The plain Calvinistic doctrine of the Reformation was honoured with wonderful success, in promoting the interests of the Redeemer's kingdom, at that time. Mr Burroughs's sermons were pregnant with important instructions. He, in a peculiar manner, warmly charged home the evil of sin, and proclaimed solemnly the benefits of redemption through Christ's atoning blood. An ingenious writer says, "Presumption and despair are the two dangerous extremes to which mankind are prone in religious concerns. Charging home sin precludes the first, proclaiming redemption prevents the last." In both these, Mr Burroughs excelled; as may be clearly seen, by his two remarkable treatises, *The Exceeding Sinfulness of Sin*, and *Gospel-Remission.* He neither flattered the pride of his hearers, nor cherished their presumption; but unfolded clearly to them the way of saving sinners through an atonement, in which mercy and truth meet together, righteousness and peace embrace each other; in which God *is just, and the justifier of him who believes in Jesus.* Such doctrine natively tends to humble us, and to endear God's name to us. And it claims, in a particular manner, the attention of ministers of the gospel.

Mr Burroughs was esteemed a great ornament of the pulpit. He used to preach at Stepney-church in the morning, at seven o'clock, and Mr Greenhill in the afternoon at three; which occasioned Hugh Peters, in a sermon which he preached there, to call the one the morning star of Stepney, and the other, the evening star.

Mr Burroughs died of a consumptive illness on the 14th of Nov. 1646, about the forty-seventh year of his age. Mr Neal says, "He was an excellent scholar, and a good expositor, and most popular preacher."[b] He is

a See Mr Walker's Sermons, of Edin. vol. i. ser. i.
b Hist. Purit. vol. iii.

eminently distinguished, and best known to us at this time, by his pious and useful writings. He wrote, and published several treatises while he lived, and his friends published more after his death, which have met with general acceptance. He is a writer of great penetration, pays much attention to his subject, handles it very extensively, and often brings to view very uncommon things. He is both evangelical and practical He sacrifices not the truth of his subject to the splendor of composition. His style is homely; but his subject is excellent. Dr Wilkins, in his Preacher, reckons him among some of the most eminent of the English divines for sermons and practical divinity. And he gives him a place also, as a commentator on Hosea. Dr Cotton Mather, in his Student and Preacher, says, "And some things of a Burroughs, especially his Moses's Choice, will not make you complain that you have lost your time in conversing with them." His name is enrolled among the learned writers of Emanuel-College, in the University of Cambridge, by Dr Fuller.[b] He discovers a strong attachment to the solemn league and covenant, and the work of reformation, in his writings. They are numerous; and I cannot say that I am able to give a proper account of them all; but I shall give a correct account, as far as my knowledge extends.

---

1. *The Excellency of a Gracious Spirit:* A treatise on Numb. xiv. 24. A small book. London, 1638.—1640.—1649.—and 1657.

2. *The Sea-Man's Direction in time of Storm:* A sermon from Psalm cxlviii. 8. delivered upon occasion of a stormy wind. London, 1640.

3. *Moses's Self-Denial:* A treatise upon Heb. xi. 24. Small book. London, 1641.—1649.—1657.

4. *Moses's Choice, with his eye fixed upon Heaven: discovering the happy condition of a self-denying heart:* A treatise upon Heb. xi. 25, 26. 4to. pp. 754. London, 1641.—1650.—and 1659.

a Fuller's Hist. Univ. Cambr. p. 147.

5. *Zion's Joy:* A sermon preached from Isai lxvi. 10 to the House of Commons, at their Public Thanksgiving, for the Peace concluded between England and Scotland, Sept. 7th, 1641. 4to. pp. 64. London, 1641.

6. *The Glorious Name of God, The Lord of Hosts:* Two sermons from Isai. xlvii. 4. At Michael's Cornhill, London: Vindicating the commission from this Lord of Hosts, to subjects, in some case, to take up arms. With a postscript, briefly answering a treatise by Henry Ferne, D. D. 4to. London, 1643.

7. *An Exposition with Practical Observations on the Prophecy of Hosea.* In 4 vols. 4to. Vol. i. London, 1643. vol. ii. and iii. Lond. 1650. and vol. iv. Lond. 1651. I have seen a copy of the 2d edition of vol. i. on the first three chapters, London, 1652.—This exposition of the prophecy of Hosea extends only to chapter xiii. 11. the author dying before he had finished what he intended on it. Respecting this exposition, Dr Edward Williams, in his Preacher's Library, says, "Burroughs on Hosea is a pleasing specimen, to shew how the popular preachers of his time applied the scriptures to the various cases of their hearers, in their expository exercises."

8. A Sermon preached from Phil. iv. 12. before the House of Peers, in the Abbey at Westminster, Fast, 26th Nov. 1645. 4to. pp. 50. London, 1646.

9. A Sermon preached from Mat. v. 6. before the Commons, at their solemn Fast, 26th Aug. 1646. London, 1646.

10. *Irenicum, to the Lovers of Truth and Peace. Heart-divisions opened, in the causes and evils of them: With cautions that we may not be hurt by them, and endeavours to heal them.* 4to. pp. 302. London, 1646.—1653.

11. *Gospel-Worship:* or, *The Right Manner of Sanctifying the Name of God in general. And particularly in these three great ordinances, Hearing the Word, Receiving the Lord's Supper, and Prayer.* Small 4to. pp. 297. London, 1648.

12. *Gospel-Conversation:* Shewing, 1. How the conversation of believers in Christ ought to exceed what could be by the light of nature. 2. Beyond those who

lived under the law. 3. And suitable to those truths which the gospel reveals: In seven sermons, preached from Phil. i. 27. in the years, 1645, and 1646. And three sermons, from John xviii. 36. wherein the nature of Christ's kingdom is explained; and a Gospel-Conversation answerable thereunto is warmly recommended. Unto which is added, *The Misery of those Men who have their Portion in this Life*, from Psal. xvii. 14. Small 4to. pp. 358. London, 1648.—1650.

13. *The Rare Jewel of Christian Contentment.* 4to. Lon. 1649. pp. 239. Lon. 1651.—1666.—1670.—1685.

Perhaps this book was printed before 1649; but the edition in 1649 is the first that I have seen. The book has been often printed, and may be read with interest. Good judges have recommended it as worthy of a perusal.

14. *Two Treatises:* 1. *Of Earthly Mindedness.*—2. *Of Conversing in Heaven, and Walking with God.* Small 4to. London, 1650.—1656

15. *A Treatise of the Evil of Evils:* or, *The Exceeding Sinfulness of Sin.* 4to. London, 1654.

The subject is very important, and calls for more than ordinary attention at this time, when sin greatly abounds. And the author has shewn much zeal and concern in his manner of treating it. The book will amply repay the trouble of a perusal.

16. *The Saints' Treasury; Holding forth, The incomparable excellency and holiness of God.—Christ's All in All—The glorious enjoyment of Heavenly things by Faith.—The Natural Man's bondage to the Law, and the Christian's liberty by the Gospel.—And a preparation for judgment:* Several sermons preached in London. A thin small quarto, 131 pages. London, 1654.

His pieces on *Precious Faith*, *Hope*, and *Walking by Faith*, seem to have been published about this time; but I have not seen them, and therefore cannot give any particular account of them.

17. *Gospel-Reconciliation:* or, *Christ's Trumpet of Peace to the World.* 2 Cor. v. 18, 19, 20. Two sermons are added; one from Hos. ii. 14. and another from Prov. xvi. 31. 4to. London, 1657.

18. *Christ Inviting Sinners to Come to Him for Rest:* Sermons from Mat. xi. 28, 29, 30. In four Books. A thick quarto. London, 1659.

19. *The Saints' Happiness; together with the several steps leading thereunto:* Forty-one sermons, or discourses, on the Beatitudes, Mat. v. These were the last sermons which our author preached: and they were published about thirteen years after his death, by his friends. 4to. pp. 662. London, 1660.

20. *Gospel-Revelation: In three Treatises.* 1. *The Nature of God.* 2. *The Excellencies of Christ.* 3. *The Excellency of Man's Immortal Soul.* 4to. pp. 370. London, 1660.

21. *The Excellency of Holy Courage in Evil Times.* 4to. pp. 215. London, 1661.

22. *Gospel-Remission:* or; *A Treatise shewing, that True Blessedness consists in Pardon of Sin.* 4to. pp. 220. London, 1668. The second edition, London, 1674.

23. *Four Useful Discourses.* 1. *The Art of Improving a full and prosperous Condition, for the Glory of God; an Appendix to the art of Contentment, in three sermons from* Phil. iv. 12. 2. *Christian Submission, from* 1 Sam. iii. 18. 3. *Christ a Christian's Life; and Death his Gain,* Phil. i. 21. 4. *The Gospel of Peace sent to the Sons of Peace:* Six sermons, from Luke x. 5, 6. 4to. London, 1675.

24. *The Difference between the Spots of the Godly, and of the Wicked.* A small book. London, 1687.

I have been informed that this laborious author has a piece, entitled, *Jerusalem's Glory;* but I have not seen it, though I expected it before this time.

I have seen part of Mr Burroughs' writings in the Stewartry of Kirkcudbright, in the shires of Dumfries and Wigton, and especially in the shires of Ayr, Renfrew, and Lanark; and some of them belonging to the library of the University of Glasgow. I have seen part of them in England, especially about London. They often occur in catalogues of books, and chiefly in the British metropolis.

RICHARD BYFIELD, M. A.

PASTOR IN LONG DITTON, IN SURREY, AND A MEMBER OF THE ASSEMBLY OF DIVINES AT WESTMINSTER.

RICHARD BYFIELD was born in Worcestershire, in England. He was brother or half brother to the famous English divine and writer, Mr Nicholas Byfield. Richard Byfield, at sixteen years of age, in the year 1615, was entered at the University of Oxford, in Queen's College, at Mich. term. When he had taken the degrees in arts, he left the University. He had the Curacy or Lectureship of *Isleworth* some time. Afterward he became rector of Long Ditton, in the county of Surrey.[a] He was a pastor who really fed the people with knowledge. He was now eminently distinguished as a zealous reformer, and strenuous opposer of superstitious devices. He was eminently zealous for the sanctification of the Sabbath-day, as clearly appears by his vindication of the doctrine of the Sabbath. And he seems to have suffered suspension and sequestration for not reading the Book of Sports: for he says, in his epistle dedicatory, prefixed to his two sermons from 1 Cor. iii. 17. "I sat down under their unjust illegal sentence, with this saying to some of my acquaintance: *There is no coming in for me again, but with the breaking of the whole state; an alteration that must change the kingdom and the laws thereof.* I sat down willingly to see *the way of God in his work.* The desires of my soul were toward him in that hour and power of darkness.—In the time of that four years and four weeks' suspension and sequestration that I suffered, my thoughts, among other things, were on that text, in Zech. ii. 13." It appears here, that this respects his suspension for not reading the Book of Sports. He also

a Wood's Ath. Oxon. vol. ii. Col. 340.

mentions here, that he was formerly a teacher of the congregation of Kingston on Thames.

He was chosen to be one of the Assembly of divines at Westminster; and he was a respectable member in that brilliant constellation.—He was a very zealous covenanter.—In the year 1654, he was appointed an assistant to the commissioners of Surrey for ejecting scandalous ministers and schoolmasters.

There was once a difference between him and his patron, Sir John Evalyn, respecting the reparation of the church. Mr Byfield complained to Oliver Cromwell, then Protector, who brought them both together, in order to reconcile them. Sir John said, that Mr Byfield reflected upon him in his sermons. Mr Byfield most solemnly declared he never intended any reflection upon him. Oliver, thereupon turning to Sir John, said, Sir, *I doubt there is something indeed amiss; the word is penetrating, and finds you out: Search your ways.* This he spake so pathetically, and with so many tears, that Sir John, Mr Byfield, and others present, weeped also. The Protector made them good friends before he dismissed them. And to bind the friendship the faster, he ordered his secretary to pay Sir John £100 toward the repair of the church.

Mr Byfield was ejected from Long Ditton for non-conformity, by the Act for Uniformity, above-mentioned. He was the oldest minister in the county before he was ejected. He retired after this to Mortlake, a pleasant village in the county of Surrey, seated on the Thames, a few miles from London. Here he spent his time in preparing for his approaching death. He preached usually twice every Lord's-day in his own family; and he did so the very Lord's-day before his death. The next day he intimated to those about him, that his departure was at hand. He gave many serious exhortations and admonitions to his wife and children, and particularly charged the latter to live in love, that the God of love and of peace might be with them. On the Thursday, a friend desired his judgment on Rev. viii. 1. to which he spake with great freedom for a considerable time together; and then rising from his seat, he fell into an apoplectic fit, and only saying that he desired to rest his head, he slept in the Lord, Dec. 1664. aged 67.

He is allowed to have been a man of great piety and zeal.[a]

Mr Byfield's writings are;

1. *The Light of Faith, and Way of Holiness; shewing how and what to believe in all estates and conditions.* London, 1630.

2. *The Doctrine of the Sabbath Vindicated, In confutation of a Treatise of the Sabbath, written by Mr Edward Breerwood against Mr Nicholas Byfield.*

In this Vindication of the Sabbath, Mr Byfield maintains the five following things: 1. That the fourth commandment is given to the servant and not to the master *only*. 2. That the fourth commandment is moral. 3. That our own light works as well as gainful and toilsome works are forbidden on the Sabbath. 4. That the Lord's day is a divine Institution. 5. That the Sabbath was instituted from the beginning. An elaborate and valuable work. 4to. pp. 227. London, 1631.

3. *The Power of the Christ of God:* or, *a Treatise of the Power, as it is originally in God the Father, and by him given to Christ his Son,* &c. 4to. London, 1641.

4. Zion's Answer to the Nation's Ambassadors, according to Instructions given by Isaiah from God's mouth: A sermon from Isai. xiv. 32. before the House of Commons, fast, 25th June, 1645. 4to. London, 1645.

5. *Temple-Defilers Defiled; Wherein a true Visible Church of Christ is described:* Two sermons preached from 1 Cor. iii. 17. at the Lecture in Kingston-upon-Thames, Feb. 20th, and 27th. 1644. London, 1645.

6. *The Gospel's Glory without Prejudice to the Law, shining forth in the Glory of God the Father, Son, and Holy Ghost, for the Salvation of Sinners, who through Grace do believe according to the draught of the Apostle Paul in* Rom. iii. 24. London, 1659.

7. *The Real Way to Good Works.*

8. A Treatise of Charity.

a Wood, Calamy, and Palmer.

EDMUND CALAMY, B. D.

AN EMINENT DIVINE AMONG THE ENGLISH NONCONFORMISTS OF THE SEVENTEENTH CENTURY, PASTOR OF ALDERMANBURY, LONDON, AND A MEMBER OF THE VENERABLE ASSEMBLY OF DIVINES AT WESTMINSTER.

EDMUND CALAMY was born in London, in the month of February, in the year 1600. His father was a citizen of London. The subject of this memoir was educated in Pembroke-hall, in the University of Cambridge, where he was admitted on the 4th of July, 1616. He took the degree of Bachelor of Arts, in the year 1619; and that of Bachelor of Divinity, in the year 1632. He very early discovered his hostility to the prevailing Arminian party, which greatly hindered him from obtaining a Fellowship in that society, even when he was justly entitled to it by his standing, his useful learning, and his unblemished character. In *England*, the face of religion was considerably changed, in a very little time after the famous Synod at *Dort*, in the year 1618. And this remarkable change was entirely in favour of *Arminianism*. And it was principally effected by the counsels and influence of *William Laud*, archbishop of *Canterbury*. This strange revolution gave new courage to the Arminians; whose leaders were eminently distinguished by their eloquence, sagacity, and learning. And the decisions and doctrines of the Synod of *Dort*, respecting the points in debate between the Arminians and the Calvinists, were now treated, in *England*, with something more than mere indifference, beheld by some with aversion, and by others with contempt.[a] And the genius and spirit of the

a Mosheim's Eccl. Hist. vol. v. cent. xvii. sect. ii. part ii. chap. ii. xii.

Church of *England* was very favourable to the Arminian tenets, at this time. In these circumstances, a person warmly attached to the Calvinistic system, and hostile to Arminians, as Mr Calamy certainly was, could not readily expect much preferment, either in the University, or in the Church of England, during this period. At last, however, he was elected *Tanquam Socius*, as it were Fellow, of Pembroke-hall. This was peculiar to that Hall. Beside the society of the Fellows, the *Tanquam Socius* had his dividend in the garden; liberty to take pupils; and the honour of the cup; together with a certain stipend, but he had no share in the government of the house. Yet take it altogether, though there was less profit, there was at least as much honour in being *Tanquam Socius*, as in being Fellow; for it was an evident sign, that, though the College conferred only this, they thought him on whom they conferred it worthy of the other, since they might otherwise have saved themselves this expence.[a] The *Tanquam Socius* held his office but for three years, unless he was re-chosen. Respecting Mr Calamy, he was within that time better accommodated in the goodness of Divine Providence.—Hence we may see. that it is not, therefore, at all likely, that he should be then of the Laudensian Faction, as Dr Walker unworthily insinuates.[b] Our author's grand-son says, that he had good evidence of the contrary.[c] Mr Calamy's studious disposition, and his religious character, greatly recommended him to Doctor Felton, the eminently pious and learned Bishop of Ely, who took particular notice of him, made him his domestic Chaplain, and paid him, during his residence in his family, uncommon marks of respect. The prudent bishop gave particular directions, that Mr Calamy should not be called down to family-prayers, nor upon any other occasion, without half an hour's notice, that his studies might not be abruptly interrupted. The generous bishop gave him also, as another signal mark of his

a Biogr. Britannica, 2 edit. vol. iii. fol. under Calamy.
b Walker's Attempt, part ii. p. 255.
c Calamy's Cont. vol. i. p. 7.

respect, the Vicarage of Mary's in Swaffham-Prior, in his neighbourhood, in Cambridgeshire, where he did much good, and was highly beneficial to many souls. Mr Calamy served the church in this place, while he was in the house of Bishop Felton, and resigned that charge about the time that he removed to Bury. The good bishop also very obligingly directed and assisted Mr Calamy in his studies, which he pursued with unwearied assiduity. He was an illustrious example of the literary diligence of these times. He studied now at the rate of sixteen hours each day. Lord Chief Justice Hale told himself, That for two years after he came to the inn of Court, he studied sixteen hours a-day. His lordship added, however, that by this intense application he almost brought himself to his grave, though he had a very strong constitution [a] But the times, and the all-important work of the Reformation, required much study; and the Divine promise was most seasonably accomplished, *And as thy days, so shall thy strength be.* In this favourable situation, Mr Calamy relinquished all unprofitable amusements, and devoted himself entirely to his studies. He read over the controversies of Bellarmine entirely, one of the most celebrated controversialists of the Church of Rome, and the answers which were written by Chamier, Whitaker, Reynolds, and others, who, by parts undertook the refutation of his voluminous work. Mr Calamy also perused several writings of the Schoolmen; particularly those of that dexterous hair-splitter, and eagle-eyed Doctor, Thomas Aquinas, whose Sums he read with the most attentive consideration, and thoroughly mastered. And we are informed, that he read over Augustine's works five times. Beside, he perused many other eminent writers, both ancient and modern. By this laborious course, he acquired that large fund of solid and useful learning, which enabled him to discharge with great ability, and with much reputation, the duties of the several offices to which he was afterward called.

Though his reading was very extensive, and his intel-

a Boswell's Life of Johnson, vol. iv. p. 326. 3d edit. London.

lectual treasures were great, yet he never affected quotations, but contented himself with a plain and familiar manner of speaking, which did not at all savour of the schools. His mind was greatly enriched with valuable stores of profitable knowledge, which he did not lock up, but freely and generously communicated them for the benefit of others. And in all his reading and studies, he much preferred the Holy Scriptures, *which are able to make us wise unto salvation, through faith which is in Christ Jesus.* He read part of them daily, and the Commentators upon them. And, by frequently reading the Sacred Writings, and meditating upon them, he appears to have early imbibed a great veneration for them, and to have had his mind amply enriched with their most precious truths. And it is worthy of our observation, that the most eminent reformers, in the Christian Church, have always devoted themselves to the reading and study of the Holy Scriptures. When the famous Luther commenced a Doctor of Divinity, in the University of Wittemberg, on the 19th of October, in the year 1512; and his sentiments underwent a great change, he devoted himself entirely to the reading of the Holy Scriptures, and of the Fathers, especially of Augustine.[a] The celebrated Calvin also devoted himself to the reading and study of the Holy Scriptures, when he discovered the abominations of the Romish church, and became acquainted with the Reformed Religion.[b] And the illustrious John Knox, the prime Instrument, under God, of spreading and of establishing the Reformed Religion in Scotland, pursued the same plan. He took his degrees, and was admitted into orders, when very young. He then applied himself unto the reading of the Fathers, particularly the writings of Jerome and of Augustine. At length, he became an earnest and close student of the Holy Scriptures, by which, through the blessing of Heaven, he was well informed respecting *the truth as it is in Jesus.* Upon obtaining this highly useful, and truly important, informa-

a Beausobre's Hist. Reformation, Book i. An. 1517.
b Clark's Marrow of Eccl. Hist. under Calvin.

tion, he very willingly and cheerfully embraced the truth, most freely and boldly confessed it, and with indefatigable zeal and great faithfulness, taught it unto others.[a]

After Bishop Felton's death, in the year 1626, Mr Calamy was chosen one of the Lecturers of Edmund's-Bury, commonly called Bury, in the county of Suffolk, where he had Mr Burroughs as his fellow-labourer. Having resigned the Vicarage of Swaffham, about the time that he removed to Bury, he now applied himself wholly to the discharge of the duties of his function at Bury, where he continued about ten years. Some writers say, that during his residence in this place, he distinguished himself for the most part as a strict Conformist: but himself and others say the contrary. Wood has taken considerable pains to shew, that he altered his opinion respecting Church-government and ceremonies:[b] and Mr Walker hints, that he was once as high in his opinions as Archbishop Laud. Their testimonies, however, will not affect his character much, if the authors themselves, and the authorities which they produce, are fairly answered. The author of a quarto pamphlet, printed at Oxford, in the year 1643, entitled, *Sober Sadness; or, Historical Observations upon the Pretences, Proceedings, and Designs, of a prevailing Party, in both Houses of Parliament*, &c. says, " That Mr Calamy complied with Bishop Wren, his Diocesan, preached in his surplice and hood, read prayers at the rails, bowed at the name of Jesus, and undertook to satisfy and reduce such as scrupled at these ceremonies." Page 5. And Mr Henry Burton, in a pamphlet, printed at London, in 1646, entitled, *Truth still Truth, though shut out of Doors*, asserts nearly the same things. In answer to which, Mr Calamy published *A Just and Necessary Apology against an Unjust Invective, published by Mr Henry Burton*, in a late book of his. In this apology, Mr Calamy affirms, " That during the time he was at Edmund's-Bury, he never bowed to, or toward the Altar, to, or toward the East, never read

a Clark's Marrow of Eccl. Hist. under J. Knox.
b Wood's Fasti. Oxon. vol. i. col. clxxxi.

that wicked Book of Sports upon the Lord's day, never read prayers at the high altar, at the upper end of the church, where the people could not hear. I have often preached against innovations; and once I did it, at a public visitation, and was called in question for my labour: I never justified the oath *ex officio*, nor ever prosecuted any man or woman at the High commission; I never, to my best remembrance, preached at any time for the justification of any innovations. In some few things, I confess, I did conform, according to the light I then had, out of the uprightness of my heart." Page 8. Whoever considers this impartially, and that Mr Calamy was only Lecturer at Edmund's-Bury, will be readily inclined to think, that these writers were mistaken respecting his conformity, or might, perhaps, be misled by misrepresentations, which were very common in those days. The truth seems to be, that he was unwilling to oppose ceremonies, or to create disturbances in the church respecting them, so long as this might be avoided, with *a conscience void of offence, toward God, and toward men.* But when Bishop Wren's Articles, and the reading of the detestable Book of Sports, were enforced, he found himself obliged to alter his conduct. He now resolved not only to avoid conforming for time to come, but he also avowed his dissent, and made a public apology for his former behaviour from the pulpit, with equal modesty, freedom, and candour.[a] He, with about thirty other worthy Ministers, were driven out of the Diocese, by Bishop Wren's Visitation-articles, and the unhallowed *Book of Sports.*[b] With these abominations, he could not comply. Pure and ardent zeal for the honour of his royal Master, and the most generous love to the souls of his fellow-creatures, were happily united in him, and very feelingly expressed in the native language of a warm and upright heart.

Mr Calamy was now considered, and eminently distinguished, as an undisguised and active Nonconformist, of

a See his Apol. 1646. 4to.

b Neal's Hist. Purit. vol. iv. under Calamy, Dr Calamy's Account, 2d edit. vol. ii. p. 5.

great respectability. And, with a determined courage, he appeared as a good and faithful soldier of Jesus Christ, *contending earnestly for the faith which was once delivered unto the saints.* Like his brethren in the same cause, he was *persecuted, but not forsaken; cast down, but not destroyed.* Being in great favour with the famous Earl of Essex, he presented him to the living of Rochford, a Market-town in the marshes of Essex, a Rectory of considerable value, but it proved a fatal present to Mr Calamy; for removing from one of the best and most wholesome airs in England, that of Edmund's-Bury, into the Hundreds and marshes of Essex, he contracted such an illness, as broke his constitution, and left behind it a dizziness in his head, which he complained of as long as he lived.

Upon the death of Dr Stoughton, he was chosen Minister of Mary Aldermanbury, London, in the year 1639. He is mentioned among the ministers of Aldermanbury, by Newcourt.[a] Here he soon acquired a very shining reputation. He now made a conspicuous appearance, and was eminently distinguished, by taking an active part, and a very large share, in the great controversy respecting Church-government, which was then greatly agitated. In July 1639, he was incorporated of the University of Oxford, which, however, did not take him off from those with whom he was engaged.[b] In the year 1640, he was employed with some other writers in the composition of that very famous book, entitled, "Smectymnuus," which both Mr Calamy himself and others say gave the first deadly blow to Episcopacy in England. The mysterious word *Smectymnuus* is made up of the first letters of the names of the authors, who were, Stephen Marshall, Edmund Calamy, Thomas Young, Mathew Newcomen, and William Spurstow. This treatise is allowed to have been very well written, and therefore we find frequent references thereto in the defences and apologies for Non-

a Newcourt's Repertorium Eccl. vol. i. page 918. as with Dr Calamy, Cont. vol. i. p. 7.
b Wood's Fasti. vol. i.

conformity which were afterward published. The title is: *An Answer to a Book entitled, An Humble Remonstrance; in which, the Original of Liturgy and Episcopacy is discussed: and Queries propounded concerning both. The Parity of Bishops and Presbyters in Scripture demonstrated. The occasion of their Imparity in Antiquity discovered. The Disparity of the Ancient and our Modern Bishops manifested. The Antiquity of Ruling Elders in the Church vindicated. The Prelatical Church bounded.* Written by Smectymnuus. Printed in the year 1641. 4to. containing with the Appendix or Postscript 94 pages. It is divided into eighteen sections; and then follow sixteen queries respecting Episcopacy, with a postscript. Doctor Joseph Hall, Bishop of Exeter, who wrote the Humble Remonstrance, published a vindication of it in answer to this book; and to this answer the Smectymnuus replied. An appeal was now made to the legislature, or high court of Parliament, on both sides, which may be viewed as containing the substance and merits of the controversy.[a] Beside, of this answer of Smectymnuus a Confutation was attempted by the learned Usher: and to the Confutation, the celebrated English poet, Mr John Milton, who was engaged in the controversies of those times, and now on the side of the Puritans and Presbyterians, published a Reply, entitled, "Of Prelatical Episcopacy, and whether it may be deduced from the Apostolical Times, by virtue of those testimonies which are alledged to that purpose in some late treatises, one whereof goes under the name of James Lord Bishop of Armagh." [b]—Smectymnuus was of such reputation, that it has been considered, not only by the Nonconformists, but also by Dr Wilkins, afterward the famous Bishop of Chester, in his Ecclesiastes, as a capital work against Episcopacy. As such it is mentioned by Dr Calamy, in his Postscript to the Preface of his Abridgement to Mr Baxter's Life, in which Postscript, he professes to instruct the inquisitive reader respecting the

a See Neal's Hist. Purit. vol. ii. chap. viii.
b Johnson's Lives of English Poets, vol. i. Milton.

books most proper to be read, in order to have a true notion of the merits of Nonconformity. And Mr Neal considers this work in the same light.[a] Mr Calamy had now acquired a shining reputation, in the metropolis. He was eminently distinguished by his intrepid integrity, ministerial faithfulness, solid learning, and genuine piety. He made vigorous efforts, for the progress of useful knowledge among mankind, in overthrowing error, and in defending and propagating truth. He was made an instrument of great usefulness in London, at this time; and highly esteemed, especially by the Presbyterians. In the year 1641, he was appointed by the House of Lords a member of the Sub-committee for accommodating Ecclesiastical matters, which consisted of very eminent Divines.[b]

When the Protestants in Ireland were overwhelmed with dreadful calamities, by the unrelenting barbarity of the Roman Catholics, and could hardly subsist without some immediate help from their neighbours, a very liberal collection was advanced for them, at the church of Aldermanbury, upon Mr Calamy's representation of their distressed condition, and his very pathetic motion in their behalf. As his name was now regarded with much veneration in London, and he made an eminent appearance for the relief of misery, the collection which was gathered, at this time, at the doors of his church, and in the houses of the parishioners, amounted to between six and seven hundred pounds at least.[c] A large sum for one parish at that time. This instance of Mr Calamy's pure and active benevolence deserves to be transmitted to posterity, as every kind of distinguished excellence should be. His heart was richly stored with that liberality which marks the Christian and the Gentleman. Mr Calamy having now given some signal proofs of his superior abilities as a divine; and his talents having become so conspicuous as to attract the notice of many, he was appointed a

a Hist. Purit. vol. ii.
b Fuller's Ch. Hist. Cent. xvii. p. 174.
c Vicars's Parliamentary Chronicle, p. 74.

Member of the Assembly of Divines at Westminster. He was a very active man in all their proceedings; and eminently distinguished both by his learning and moderation.

> "Honour unchang'd, a principle profest,
> Fix'd to one side, but moderate to the rest."

In the important contest, in that famous Assembly, respecting Ruling Elders in the church, when several eminent Divines of that brilliant constellation were positively against the institution of any such officer by divine right, as Dr Smith, Dr Temple, Messrs Gataker, Vines, Price, Hall, and others, Mr Calamy, with many more, appeared for the divine institution of the ruling elder, and reasoned bravely for it. In this serious debate, all were willing to admit ruling elders in a prudential way; but this was peremptorily rejected by others, as very dangerous.[a]

Mr Calamy was one of the most popular preachers in London; and a frequent preacher before the Members of the Long Parliament, for which his memory has been very severely treated.[b] He was also one of the Cornhill Lecturers. He was a very zealous and steadfast Covenanter. He was the first who did openly defend, before a Committee of Parliament, that in the Holy Scriptures a Bishop and a Presbyter were one, as Wood affirms. He was generally accounted a firm Presbyterian. He had very great interest in the city of London; and preached to a numerous and respectable audience, twenty years, composed of the most eminent citizens, and even persons of quality. And seldom so few as sixty coaches came to the church where he preached. He was one of those ministers of the city, who declared against the proceedings of the army in 1648, testifying his disapprobation of the violent measures which brought on the King's death, an

a Baillie's Letters, vol. i. p. 401.

b Wood's Fasti. Oxon. vol. 1. Col. 281. Echard's Hist. Eng. vol. iii. p. 178.

event which he ardently deprecated. The representation of the London-ministers to the General of the army, and his Council of war, presented 18th Jan. 1648, was drawn up to enforce what Mr Calamy, and some other ministers of the same persuasion, had delivered in two conferences; the first with the General and his Council, the second with the chief Officers of the army. Collier, in his Church-History, styles this, an instance of handsome plain-dealing, and a bold reprimand of a victorious army.

In Cromwell's time, Mr Calamy lived as privately and quietly as he could: but he sometimes opposed the Protector's measures. It is said, in the Life of Oliver Cromwell, as with Dr Calamy, that Harry Nevill, who was one of the Council of State, used to tell the following anecdote upon his own knowledge. Cromwell, having a design to set up himself, and bring the crown upon his own head, sent for some of the chief of the Divines in the city, as if he accounted it a matter of conscience to be determined by their advice. Among these was the leading Mr Calamy, who very boldly opposed the project of Cromwell's single government, and offered to prove that it was both *unlawful and impracticable*, that one man should assume the government of the country. Cromwell answered readily upon the first head of *unlawful*, and appealed to the safety of the nation being the supreme law. But says he, pray, Mr Calamy, why is it *impracticable?* He replied; telling him, Oh, it is against the voice of the nation; there will be nine in ten against you. Very well, replied Cromwell; but what if I should disarm the nine, and put the sword in the tenth man's hand, would not that do the business?[a] Mr Calamy readily concurred with the Presbyterian party, in opposing the Sectaries, in Cromwell's time. He was much against them; and his influence was at that time highly beneficial.

In the year 1659, he concurred with the Earl of Manchester, and other eminent men, in encouraging and persuading General Monk to bring in the King, in order

a Calamy's Cont. vol. i. p. 8. Anecdotes, vol. i.

to put an end to the public confusions. He had a considerable hand in bringing home the King, but he soon repented having done it without a previous treaty. He preached before the Parliament the day before they voted the King home, and was one of those Divines who were sent over to the King in Holland. He was reckoned to have the greatest interest in court, city, and country, of any of the ministers, and therefore he was very much caressed at first; but he soon saw the design and tendency of things. As an evidence of this, having General Monk for his auditor in his own church soon after the King's restoration, on a sacrament-day, he had occasion to speak of *filthy lucre;* "And why, said he, is it called *filthy*, but because it makes men do base and *filthy* things? Some men, said he, will betray three kingdoms for *filthy lucre's* sake." Saying this, he threw his handkerchief, which he generally waved up and down while he was preaching, toward the General's pew. He commonly spoke his sentiments with great freedom, and did not fear man.

In the year 1660, after the King was restored, he was encouraged by the Earl of Manchester, who was made Lord Chamberlain, and other great men at court, to hope for considerable favour, both for himself and for his brethren. In June that year, he was sworn Chaplain in ordinary to his Majesty, as some other ministers also, who were counted Presbyterians. But none of them preached more than once before the King in that capacity. About this time, Mr Calamy was often with his Majesty at the Chamberlain's lodgings, or elsewhere; and was always smiled on, and kindly received. He had a chief hand in drawing up the Proposals made at that time to the King, respecting Church-government, which laid the foundation of the Savoy-conference: and was also concerned in the concessions which were made by the Declaration dated Oct. 25th, the same year. And being one of the Commissioners appointed, he was employed with others, in drawing up *Exceptions against the Liturgy* which were then delivered; and also the *Reply to the Reasons of the Episcopal Divines,* against the

Exceptions which were given in by the Presbyterians, and the *Petition for Peace*, which was drawn up in a very moving strain, and not duly considered. In 1661, he was one of those chosen by the Ministers of London to represent them in *Convocation*, but was not allowed to sit there. He attended the several meetings at the Savoy, and thought it his duty to do what he could in order to an accommodation, though without any effect.

Mr Calamy preached his Farewell Sermon, 17th of August 1662, a week before the Act of Uniformity took place, from 2 Sam. xxiv. 14. *And David said unto Gad, I am in a great strait: let us fall now into the hand of the Lord, for his mercies are great, and let me not fall into the hand of man.* It may not be amiss, to give a brief abstract of this discourse, as a specimen of the author's spirit and manner. The chief design of it is to illustrate and improve this point, "That sin brings persons and nations into great perplexities." He observes, That beside many outward troubles, this brings a spiritual famine upon a land: a famine of the word.—Use 1. This reproves those who commit sin to avoid perplexity—who to escape suffering will do any thing, who will be sure to be of the religion that is uppermost, be what it will. Consider—It is sin only that makes trouble to deserve the name. There is more evil in the least sin, than in the greatest calamity. Whosoever goes out of God's way to avoid danger, shall meet with greater danger. 2. This should teach us above all things, to abhor sin. Cautions against twelve sins, among which, slighting the gospel. 3. What cause to fear that God should bring this nation into great distress? And what reason, you of this congregation and parish have to expect to be brought into great straits, because of your unfruitfulness under the means of grace? You have long enjoyed the gospel.—Are there not some of you who begin to loathe the manna, and to look back to Egypt? Have not some of you *itching ears* who would fain have a preacher who would feed you with dainty phrases; and who begin not to care for a Minister that unrips your consciences, and speaks to your hearts: some who by often hearing sermons are become sermon proof? There is hardly any way to raise the price of the gospel-ministry, but the want of it. —I may not flatter you who have not profited by it. You may justly expect God may bring you into straits, and take away the gospel from you: may take away your Ministers by death or otherwise. What God will do with you I know not: a few weeks will determine. He can make a great change in a little time. We leave all to him. But let me commend one text of Scripture to you. Jer. xiii. 16, 17. *Give glory to the Lord your God, before he cause darkness, and before your feet stumble,* &c. *But if ye will not hear, my soul shall weep in secret places for you—because the Lord's flock is carried captive.* Give glory to God by confessing and repenting of your sins, before darkness come; and who knoweth but that may prevent that darkness.—Having consulted with his great friends at court, a Petition was drawn up to the King, and signed by a considerable number of the Ministers in and about the city, who were affected with the Act of Uniformity. It was in the following words.

To the King's Most Excellent Majesty, the Humble Petition of several Ministers in your City of London.

MAY IT PLEASE YOUR MOST EXCELLENT MAJESTY,

" Upon former experience of your Majesty's tenderness and indulgence to your obedient and loyal subjects, in which number we can with all clearness reckon ourselves, we some of the Ministers within your City of London, who are likely by the late Act of Uniformity to be cast out of all public service in the ministry, because we cannot in conscience conform to all things required in the said Act, have taken the boldness humbly to cast ourselves and concernments at your Majesty's feet, desiring that of your Princely Wisdom and Compassion, you would take some effectual course whereby we may be continued in the exercise of our ministry, to teach your people obedience to God and your Majesty. And we doubt not but by our dutiful and peaceable carriage therein, we shall render ourselves not altogether unworthy of so great a favour."

This Petition was presented to his Majesty, Aug. 27th, three days after the Act took place, by Mr Calamy, Dr Manton, Dr Bates, and others. And Mr Calamy made a speech upon the occasion, intimating that those of his persuasion were ready to enter the list with any, for their fidelity to his Majesty, and did little expect to be dealt with as they had been: and they were now come to his Majesty's feet, as the last application they should make, &c. His Majesty promised that he would consider their business. And the very next day the matter was fully debated in Council, his Majesty himself being present, who was pleased to declare, that he intended an *indulgence*, if it were at all feasible. The great friends of the silenced Ministers, whose hopes were much encouraged by a variety of specious promises, were now allowed to suggest freely their reasons, against putting the Act in execution; and they argued most strenuously. But Dr Sheldon, Bishop of London, in a warm speech, declared, that it was now too late to think of suspending that law; that he had already, in obedience to it, ejected such of his Clergy as would not comply with it; and should they now be restored after they were thus exasperated, he must expect to feel the effects of their resentment, and should never be able to maintain his Episcopal authority among such a Clergy, who would not fail to insult him as their enemy, being countenanced by the court.—Should the Sacred Authority of this law be now suspended, it would render the Legislature ridiculous and contemptible. And if the importunity of such disaffected people were a sufficient reason to humour them, neither the church nor state would ever be free from distractions and convulsions. And upon the whole it was carried, that no *indulgence* at all should be granted.[a]

The justly celebrated Mr Calamy was cast out from Aldermanbury by the Act of Uniformity. He refused a

a Calamy's Cont. vol. i. p. 9, 10, 11.

Bishoprick, because he could not have it upon the terms of the King's Declaration; and he considered several things in the Conformity to be intolerable sins, and therefore he could not comply. Like Moses who *refused to be called the son of Pharaoh's daughter: Choosing rather to suffer affliction with the people of God, than to enjoy the pleasures of sin for a season.*—Bishop Wilkins had such an opinion of his knowledge in the controversy respecting Church-government, that he heartily wished he could have conformed, that he might have confronted the bold and confident assertors of the *Divine right* of Episcopacy in the Convocation, in which he was not allowed to sit, though he was chosen one of the Clerks for the city.[a] He preserved his temper and moderation after he was ejected, and lived pretty much retired. Upon the 28th of Dec. after the Act passed, Mr Calamy went to the church of Aldermanbury, where he formerly preached, with an intention to be a hearer; but he who was expected to preach at that time failed; and to prevent a disappointment, and answer the importunity of the people who were assembled, Mr Calamy preached on that occasion from 1 Sam. iv. 13. respecting old Eli's concern for the Ark of God. This sermon was printed, though unpremeditated, and may be seen in the Collection of Farewell Sermons. It discovers much concern for true religion, which was then in no small danger. Upon this, the worthy Author was put into Newgate-prison, by the warrant of the Lord Mayor, as a breaker of the Act of Uniformity, the great Dagon in these times of tyranny, and much like the *golden image* which was set up in the Plains of Dura, in the province of Babylon. As Paul when at Rome, Mr Calamy was now, *A prisoner of Jesus Christ.—Behold, the devil shall cast some of you into prison, that ye may be tried; and ye shall have tribulation ten days: be thou faithful unto death, and I will give thee a crown of life.* Innocence has often the hard lot to be thrust into a prison.—A Popish lady passing through the city during Mr Calamy's confinement, found

a Calamy's Account, vol. ii. p. 6.

it difficult to get along Newgate-street, on account of the many coaches attending there. Being surprised at this incident, curiosity led her to enquire into the occasion of this stoppage, and the number of coaches, where she did not expect them. The people who were standing by, who seemed greatly concerned and disturbed, informed her, that one Mr Calamy, a person much beloved and respected, was imprisoned there for a single sermon. This so struck the Lady, that she took the first opportunity of waiting upon the King at Whitehall, and frankly told him the whole affair; expressing, at the same time, her apprehensions that, if such steps were taken, his Majesty would lose the affections of the city, which might be attended with very bad effects. It was partly in consequence of this representation that Mr Calamy was soon discharged from prison, by the King's express order.[a] And the general resentment of this severity, with the many respectable persons who visited Mr Calamy in Newgate, may also be considered as partly contributing to his release. This being afterward complained of in the House of Commons, it was signified in the House that his release from imprisonment was not owing to the sole command of the King, but to a deficiency in the Act of Parliament, that had not fully provided for his longer confinement. Whereupon the following entry was made in their Journal: Die Jovis, Feb. 19th, 1662, or —63. "Upon complaint made to this House, that Mr Calamy being committed to Prison, upon Breach of the Act of Uniformity, was discharged upon pretence of some defect in the Act: Resolved, That it be referred to a Committee to look into the Act of Uniformity, as to the matter in question, and to see whether the same be defective, and wherein." And soon after this, a Committee was appointed, *to bring in the Reasons of the House, for their advice to the King against a Toleration, with an Address to his Majesty.* And thus an effectual door was opened for all that most dreadful severity which followed.[b] Dr Robert Wilde, a

a Biogr. Britan. vol. iii. fol. 2 edit. Calamy.
b Calamy's Cont. vol. i. p. 12.

Poet among the Nonconformists of that period, published a copy of verses on the occasion of Mr Calamy's imprisonment in Newgate, which was spread through the kingdom. It follows.

"This page I send you, Sir, your *Newgate* fate,
Not to condole, but to congratulate.
I envy not our mitred men, their places,
Their rich preferments, nor their richer *faces:*
To see them steeple upon steeple set,
As if they meant that way to Heaven to get.
I can behold them take into their gills,
A dose of churches, as men swallow pills,
And never grieve at it: Let them swim in wine
While others drown in tears, I'll not repine.
But my heart truly grudges, (I confess)
That you thus loaded are with happiness;
For so it is: And you more blessed are
In *Peter's* chain, than if you sat in's chair.
One sermon hath preferr'd you so much honour,
A man could scarce have had from Bishop *Bonner*.
Whilst we, your brethren, poor erraticks be,
You are a glorious fixed star we see:
Hundreds of us turn'd out of house and home;
To a safe habitation you are come.
What though it be a gaol? shame and disgrace
Rise only from the crime, not from the place.
Who thinks reproach or injury is done
By an eclipse, to the unspotted *sun?*
He only by that black upon his brow,
Allures spectators more; and so do you.
Let me find honey, though upon a rod,
And prize the prison, where my keeper's God.
Newgate or *Hell* were *Heaven*, if Christ were there:
He made the stable so, and sepulchre.
Indeed the place did for your presence call:
Prisons do want perfuming most of all.
Thanks to the *Bishop*, and his good Lord *Mayor*,
Who turn'd the den of thieves to a House of Prayer.

And may some thief by you converted be,
Like him who suffered in Christ's company.
Now, would I had a sight of your *mittimus;*
Fain would I know how you are dealt with thus.
Jaylor, set forth your prisoner at the bar.
Sir, you shall hear what your offences are.
First, It's proved, that you being dead in law,
(As if you car'd not for that death a straw.)
Did walk and haunt your church, as if you'ld scare
Away the reader and his *Common Prayer:*
Nay, 'twill be proved you did not only walk,
But like a *Puritan*, your *Ghost* did talk.
Dead, and yet preach! these *Presbyterian* slaves
Will not give over preaching in their graves.
Item, You play'd the thief; and if't be so,
Good reason, Sir, to *Newgate* you should go:
And now you're there, some dare to swear you are,
The greatest pick-pocket that e're came there.
Your wife, no better than yourself you make,
She's the receiver of each purse you take.
But your great theft, you acted in your church,
I do not mean you did your sermon lurch,
That's crime *canonical*, but you did pray
And preach, so that you stole men's hearts away.
So that good man to whom your place doth fall,
Will find they have no heart for him at all.
This felony deserved imprisonment;
What can't you Nonconformists be content
Sermons to make, except you preach them too?
They that your places have, this work can't do.
Thirdly, 'Tis proved, when you pray most devout
For all good men, you leave the *bishops* out.
This makes Seer *Sheldon* by his powerful spell,
Conjure and lay you safe in *Newgate*-Hell:
Would I were there too, I should like it well.
I would you durst swapt punishment with me;
Pain makes me fitter for the company
Of roaring boys: and you may lie in bed,
Now your name's up; pray do it in my stead.

And if it be deny'd us to change places,
Let us for sympathy compare our cases;
For if in suffering we both agree,
Sir, I may challange you to pity me:
I am the older gaol bird; my hard fate
Hath kept me twenty years in *Cripplegate;*
Old *Bishop Gout*, that Lordly proud disease,
Took my fat body for his Diocese;
Where he keeps court, there visits every limb,
And makes them (*Levite*-like) conform to him;
Severely he doth article each joint,
And makes enquiry into every point.
A bitter enemy to preaching, he
Hath half a year sometimes suspended me;
And if he find me painful in my station,
Down I am sure to go, next visitation.
He binds up, looseth; sets up, and pulls down;
Pretends he draws ill humours from the crown:
But I am sure he maketh such a do,
His humours trouble head and members too.
He hath me now in hand, and ere he goes,
I fear for hereticks, he'll burn my toes.
Oh! I would give all I am worth, a fee,
That from his jurisdiction I were free.
Now, Sir, you find our sufferings do agree,
One *Bishop* clapt up you, another me:
But oh! the difference too is very great,
You are allow'd to walk, to drink, to eat;
I want them all, and never a penny get.
And though you be debarr'd your liberty,
Yet all your visitors I hope are free:
Good men, good women, and good angels come,
And make your prison better than your home.
Now may it be so, till your foes repent,
They gave you such a rich imprisonment.
May for the greater comfort of your lives,
Your lying-in be better than your wives.
May you a thousand friendly papers see,
And none prove empty except this from me.

And if you stay, may I come keep your door,
Then farewell *Parsonage*, I shall neer be poor."

Mr Calamy lived to see the dreadful fire of London, which broke out in the year 1666, and destroyed a great part of the city. This fire is said to have over-run 373 acres of ground within the walls, and to have burned 13,200 houses, 89 parish churches, beside chapels, and that only eleven parishes within the walls were left standing.[a] This awful sight is said to have broken his heart. "The conflagration of a city, with all its tumults of concomitant distress, is one of the most dreadful spectacles which this world can offer to human eyes."[b] This most dreadful spectacle very much affected our author. He was driven through the ruins of the city in a coach, and upon seeing its very desolate condition, his affectionate mind received very deep impressions; and he went home, and never came out of his chamber again, but died within a month, in Oct. 1666, in the 67th year of his age.

Mr Calamy was well acquainted with the subjects appropriate to his profession: as a preacher, he was plain and practical; and he boldly avowed his sentiments on all necessary occasions. He generally had the chair among the ministers of the city in their meetings, and was highly esteemed for his prudence and good conduct.

Mr Calamy's writings, though not numerous, are sufficient to maintain his reputation, and to transmit his name, and make his abilities known to posterity. He was one of the authors of the famous book, which was entitled, *Smectymnuus*, above-mentioned. He had also a hand in drawing up the *Vindication of the Presbyterial Government and Ministry*. Printed in the year 1650, and the *Jus Divinum Ministerii Evangelici, et Anglicani*, Printed in the year 1654. He has several sermons extant, as

a Granger's Wonderful Museum, vol. ii.
b Johnson.

1. *England's Looking-glass:* a sermon from Jer. xviii. 7—10. before the House of Commons, at their solemn Fast, 22d Dec. 1641. 4to. pp. 62. London, 1642. The design is to shew, that national repentance will divert, and national sins draw down, national judgments.

2. *God's Free Mercy to England:* a sermon from Ezek. xxxvi. 32. before the Commons, at their solemn Fast, 23d Feb. 1641. 4to. London, 1642. The intention of this sermon is, to represent England's mercies, as precious and powerful motives and means of England's humiliation and reformation.

3. *The Nobleman's Pattern of true and real thankfulness:* a thanksgiving sermon from Josh. xxiv. 15. before the House of Lords, 15th June, 1643. 4to. pp. 59. London, 1643.

4. *England's Antidote against the Plague of Civil War:* a sermon from Acts xvii. 30. before the House of Commons, on their solemn Fast, 22d Oct. 1644. 4to. pp. 45. London, 1645.

5. *An Indictment against England because of her self-murdering Divisions; with an Exhortation to Concord:* a sermon preached from Mat. xii. 25. to the House of Lords, on the monthly Fast, 25th Dec. 1644. 4to. pp. 41. London, 1645. The monthly Fast, when the sermon was preached, was on Christmas-day. Respecting that day, Mr Calamy, in his sermon, has the following expressions. "This day is commonly called *The Feast of Christ's Nativity*, or, *Christmas-day;* a day that has formerly been much abused to *superstition, and profaneness.* It is not easy to say, whether the superstition has been greater, or the profaneness. I have known some who have preferred *Christmas-day* to the *Lord's-day.* I have known those who would be sure to receive the sacrament upon Christmas-day, though they did not receive it all the year after.—Some persons, though they did not play at cards all the year long, yet they must play at Christmas; thereby, it seems, to keep in memory the birth of Christ. This, and much more hath been the profanation of this Feast. And truly I think that the superstition and profanation of this day is so rooted into it, as that there is

no way to reform it, but by dealing with it as Hezekiah did with the brazen serpent. This year God, by his Providence, has buried this *Feast* in a *Fast*, and I hope it will never rise again. You have set out, Right Honourable, a strict order for keeping the Fast, and you are here this day to observe your own order, and I hope you will do it strictly. The necessities of the times are great; never more need of prayer and fasting. The Lord give us grace to be humbled on this day of humiliation for all our own and England's sins, and especially for the old superstition, and profanation of this Feast."

6. *The Great Danger of Covenant-refusing*, and *Covenant-breaking:* a sermon preached from 2 Tim. iii. 3. —*Truce-breakers;* or, *Covenant-breakers*, on the 14th of Jan. 1645—46, before the Lord Mayor of the city of London, with the Sheriffs, Aldermen, and Common Council of that city, at their taking the Solemn League and Covenant, at Michael Bassingshaw, London. 4to. pp. 40. London, 1646. This sermon was also printed at Edinburgh, in the year of Covenant-breaking, in a small collection, entitled, *A Phenix.*[a] I saw one copy of the Phenix, including Mr Calamy's sermon, at London, in the year 1797. The substance of this sermon was printed in the year 1706. We are not told where; but I suppose that it might be at Edinburgh, because I have generally seen this edition in Scotland, and it is often bound with sermons of the same size, printed that year at Edinburgh. It was also printed at Glasgow, in 1741; and again in 1799, in a collection of sermons at taking the Covenant. This famous sermon has been printed at London, Edinburgh, and Glasgow. And it's illustrious author was a very respectable and steadfast covenanter, always abounding in the work of the Lord.

a This contains, beside a very short epistle to the reader, The Solemn League and Covenant, subscribed by many of the House of Commons.—The ordinance of the Commons, for the public reading of this Covenant, in every church and congregation within the kingdom.—The form of the coronation of King Charles II. at Scoon, 1 Jan. 1651, with Mr Douglas's sermon on that occasion.—The King's Declaration to all his loving subjects in Scotland, 1650; and Mr Calamy's sermon.

7. *The Door of Truth Opened: A Just and Necessary Apology against an Unjust Invective* of Mr Henry Burton. 4to. London, 1646. Containing a Vindication of himself from Mr Burton's Calumnies.

8. *The Saints' Rest*; or, *Their Happy Sleep in Death:* a sermon from Acts vii. 60. at Aldermanbury, London, 24th Aug. 1651, being the next Lord's-day after Mr Love's death. London, 1653.

9. *The Doctrine of the Body's Fragility; with a Divine Project, discovering how to make these vile bodies of ours glorious by getting gracious souls:* a sermon preached from Phil. iii. 21. at the funeral of Dr Samuel Bolton. London, 1655.

10. *The Monster of sinful self-seeking anatomized; together with a description of the heavenly and blessed self-seeking:* a sermon from Phil. ii. 21. at Paul's, Dec. 10th 1654. 4to. pp. 34. London, 1655.

11. A sermon at the funeral of the Earl of Warwick, 1658.

12. A sermon from Isai. lvii. 1. at the funeral of Mr Simeon Ashe, preached at St Austin's, London, Aug. 23d 1662. London, 1662. I have seen in the county of Surrey, England, a second edition of this sermon, which was annexed to the collection of Farewell Sermons, by the London Ministers, printed in the year 1662. His Farewell Sermon, and that on the 28th of Dec. above mentioned. London, 1662—1663.

The Godly Man's Ark, or City of Refuge, in the day of his Distress. This is a small book, containing five sermons from Psal. cxix. 92. with an epistle dedicatory to the inhabitants of Aldermanbury parish, with all others who attend constantly upon the Word of God there preached, and more especially to such of them who are admitted to partake of the Lord's supper there administered. The first of these sermons was preached at the funeral of Mrs Elizabeth Moore; and the other four were afterward preached, and they were all published, for the support and consolation of the saints of God in the hour of tribulation. Mrs Moore's Evidences for Heaven, which were composed and collected by her in the time of her health, for her comfort in the time of sickness, are annexed. All the parts of this work are really excellent, and justly entitled to a serious perusal. They will amply repay the well-disposed reader. The book has been very popular. I have not been able to procure a copy of the first edition, after a close search for several years; and therefore I cannot inform the reader when it was first printed. But I have seen a copy of each of the following editions. The 3d edition, London, 1661 —The 4th edition, London, 1664.—The 7th edition, London, 1672.—The 8th edition, London, 1682. —The 17th edition, London, 1693.—The 18th edition, 1709.

He has a sermon in the Morning-Exercise at St Giles's upon the Resurrection of the Dead, from Acts xxvi. 8. but I cannot at this time give any particular account of it. And after his death, there was a *Treatise of Meditation*, printed in a hidden way; not by his son, nor from his manuscript, but from imperfect notes which were taken by a hearer. He also wrote and subscribed several prefaces to the works of others; as to pieces of Mr Christopher Love, and to Mr John Ball's Treatise of the Covenant of Grace, and Mr Hutcheson's Exposition of John's Gospel, and of the small Prophets. Edmund Calamy is a name of great celebrity; and it has been transmitted to posterity through several channels.

Mr Calamy's eldest son was ejected from Moreton, in the county of Essex, by the Act of Uniformity. His grand-son, Dr Edmund Calamy, a Dissenting Divine of great eminence, is well known by his learned works.

* See Wood's Ath. Oxon. Calamy's Account & Cont. Palmer's Nonconf. Mem. Biographical Dict. Biogr. Brit. & Gen. Biogr. vol. ii. London, 1801.

WILLIAM CARTER,

MINISTER OF THE GOSPEL IN LONDON, AND A MEMBER OF THE ASSEMBLY OF DIVINES AT WESTMINSTER.

WILLIAM CARTER was educated in Cambridge, and afterward he became a very popular preacher in London. He was a good scholar, a person of great seriousness; and though but a young man, he was appointed a member of the Assembly of Divines at Westminster. After some time, he joined the Independents, and became one of the Dissenting Brethren, in that Assembly.[a] He was one of those members in the Assembly who appeared for the divine institution of a doctor in every congregation, as well as a pastor. Mr Robert Baillie, one of the Commissioners from the Church of Scotland to that Assembly, speaking of his arrival there with his brethren, says: "At our first coming, we found them in a very sharp debate anent the office of doctors. The Independent men, whereof there are some ten or eleven in the Synod, many of them very able men, as Thomas Goodwin, Nye, Burroughs, Bridge, Carter, Caryl, Phillips, Sterry, were for the divine institution of a doctor in every congregation as well as a pastor. To these the others were extremely opposite, and somewhat bitterly, pressing much the simple identity of pastors and doctors. Mr Henderson travelled between them, and drew on a committee for accommodation; in the whilk we agreed unanimously upon some six propositions, wherein the absolute necessity of a doctor in every congregation, and his divine institution, in formal terms, was eschewed; yet where two ministers can be had in one congregation, the one is allowed, according to his gift, to apply himself most to teaching, and the other to exhortation, according to the Scriptures.[b]

a See Life of William Bridge, pp. 140, 141.
b Baillie's Letters, vol. i. p. 401.

Mr Carter had offers of many places, but he refused them, not being satisfied with the parochial discipline of those times. Nevertheless, he laboured constantly in the Lord's vineyard, with indefatigable ardour. He was most attentive to the work of the ministry, *not seeking his own profit, but the profit of many, that they might be saved.* Having tasted that the Lord is gracious, he was unwilling to eat his spiritual morsels alone; but earnestly wished that others should be partakers of these sweet and satisfactory refreshments with himself. He ardently desired to advance the interests of the Redeemer's kingdom, and to promote the spiritual and eternal welfare of precious and immortal souls. He had learned cheerfully to sacrifice both his own humour and ease to the work and glory of his God and Saviour. He preached twice every Lord's-day to two large congregations in the city, beside Lectures on the work-days, and his other labours. Labouring night and day, he faithfully preached the glorious gospel of the grace of God to the inhabitants of London. *Being affectionately desirous of them, he willingly imparted to them, not the gospel of God only, but also his own soul, because they were exceedingly dear unto him. Having known the terrors of the Lord,* he had a very tender compassion for those thoughtless persons who had no pity for themselves. His pious soul mourned for them in secret places, and he was greatly grieved with the hardness of their hearts. He earnestly longed to impart unto them *some spiritual gift,* by which they might be *edified and established.* Having spent his time and strength, in endeavouring to save souls from death, he fell asleep in the Lord, about mid-summer, in the year 1658, and in the fifty-third year of his age.[a]

I have seen only one sermon of his, which is entitled, *Light in Darkness,* from Psal. lxv. 5. before the House of Commons, 24th Nov. 1647, at their solemn Fast. London, 1648.

a Neal's Hist. Purit. vol. iv.

THOMAS CARTER,

MINISTER OF DYNTON, IN BUCKINGHAMSHIRE, IN ENGLAND, AND A MEMBER OF THE FAMOUS ASSEMBLY OF DIVINES AT WESTMINSTER.

THOMAS CARTER was Minister of Dynton, in Buckinghamshire, in England; but I cannot give much account of him. He preached a sermon to the House of Commons, from Exod. xxxii. 9, 10. June 28th, 1643. This sermon is entitled, *Prayer's Prevalence for Israel's Safety.* 4to. pp. 38. London, 1643. In the epistle dedicatory to the House of Commons, he says: "In the fathomless depths of infinite goodness and wisdom, a design is laid through the clear discoveries of God's perfections and glory, to complete and accomplish the happiness of his servants. There is not any thing that befals them in this valley of tears, but by his contrivances, it brings with it a secret influence, and activity, to raise them to the mount of joy. I need not tell you how near the dust God's people of this kingdom were, they yet retain the dints of contempt and scorn: but hath not a strong reflection of God's power been cast upon us, from that very cloud under which we were? Are there not deliverances created for us, even beyond our hopes? Hath not the Lord raised you up, most Noble Senators, as once he did that pillar to the Israelites, to be a light to us, and darkness to our enemies?" This will give the reader a small specimen of the author. I am sorry, that I cannot give any farther account of Mr Thomas Carter.

JOSEPH CARYL, A. M.

MINISTER OF THE GOSPEL IN LONDON, AND A MEMBER OF THE ASSEMBLY OE DIVINES AT WESTMINSTER.

JOSEPH CARYL was born of genteel parents in London, in the year 1602. He was educated in Exeter-College, Oxford, where he became a commoner or sojourner, in the beginning of 1621, aged seventeen years. Here, by the benefit of a good tutor, and the use of proper means, he soon became a noted disputant. In the year 1627, he proceeded in arts, and entering into holy orders, he exercised his function in, and near, Oxford for some time. Afterward, he became preacher to the honourable society of Lincoln's-Inn, when he came to London, where he continued several years, and acquired a good reputation. The respectable and intelligent society of Lincoln's-Inn, have long been favoured with preachers of very great celebrity.—In the year 1642 and afterward, Mr Caryl was frequently called to preach to the Long Parliament at their solemn Fasts and Thanksgivings, and upon other occasions. Several very valuable sermons which he preached to the Parliament, and upon other occasions, were printed at that time, and are still extant.

Being now become very conspicuous, justly entitled to respectable notice, and eminently distinguished by his zeal for the interests of the Redeemer's kingdom, and for the Reformation, he was chosen to be a member of the venerable Assembly of Divines at Westminster, in the year 1643. In this and in every other station, he gave proofs of his great abilities, learning, piety, and modesty. He was a moderate Independent; and one of those Divines in this Assembly, who were for the divine institution of a doctor in every congregation as well as a pastor.[a]—He was appointed a Licenser of Books of

a See Memoirs of Mr Will. Bridge and Mr Will. Carter.

divinity, about this time. The first volume of Burroughs on Hosea has Mr Caryl's *imprimatur*, or, *it may be printed*, Aug. 10th, 1643.—He was an eminently zealous and judicious Covenanter, as very clearly appears from that excellent sermon, which he preached at Westminster; at that public Convention, which was ordered by the honourable House of Commons, for taking the Covenant, by all such persons, of all degrees, as willingly presented themselves, upon Friday, October 6th, 1643. This sermon claims the particular attention of all Covenanters, and subjects of God's moral government.

Mr Caryl became pastor of the church of Magnus, near London-bridge, in the year 1645. In this important station, he laboured several years with very singular diligence and success. He was much respected for his piety, integrity, amiable temper, and great fidelity in discharging the duties of the pastoral office. His faithful and eminent services were highly acceptable and useful, both to his own people and to the public. His discourses were well adapted to general edification; and in the delivery of them, he appeared like one who was really standing in the presence of Almighty God, animated with a true zeal for the Redeemer's glory, and for the everlasting salvation of immortal souls. He was esteemed one of the most judicious, learned, and respectable, ministers of the gospel of the age in which he lived; and one of the best expositors of the Holy Scriptures.—He and Mr Stephen Marshall were appointed chaplains to the commissioners, who were sent by the Parliament to the King, who was then at Newcastle, for an accommodation of peace. By easy journies, they accompanied the King and the commissioners to Holmby-house in Northamptonshire. Here his Majesty continued sometime without any of his chaplains in ordinary to wait upon him. Wood says, that the said ministers, Caryl and Marshall, upon the desire of the commissioners, did offer their service to preach before the King, and say grace at meals, but they were both by him denied, the King always saying grace himself, with an audible voice, standing under the state.[a]

a Wood's Ath. Oxon. vol. ii. Col. 512.

Mr Neal says, "While the King was at Holmby-house he was attended with great respect.—The Parliament appointed two of their clergy, Mr Caryl and Mr Marshall, to preach in the chapel mornings and afternoons on the Lord's-day, and perform the devotions of the chapel on week-days, but his Majesty never gave his attendance. He spent his Sundays in private; and though they waited at table he would not so much as admit them to ask a blessing."[a] In September 1648, Mr Caryl was one of those divines who went with other commissioners appointed by Parliament to the treaty of peace at Newport in the isle of Wight. The Parliament appointed five noblemen, ten commoners, and four divines to assist them in their religious debates; Messrs Caryl, Marshall, Vines, and Dr Seaman. Mr Caryl preached here on this occasion. Wood says, that in September 1650, he and John Owen, an Independent minister, were by order of Parliament sent to Scotland to attend Oliver Cromwell, who desired their company in order that he might receive comfort by their prayers and preachings.[b] In the year 1653, Mr Caryl was appointed one of the *Triers* for the approbation of ministers. And in 1654, he was constituted an assistant to the commissioners of London, who were appointed by Parliament for ejecting scandalous, ignorant, and insufficient, ministers and school-masters. In 1659, he was sent into Scotland to give General Monk an account of the state of affairs in England, with a letter from Dr Owen, expressing their fears of the danger of their religious liberties upon a revolution of the government.—And Wood says, That on the 14th of March following, he was, with Edward Reynolds and others, appointed by act of Parliament to approve of and admit ministers according to the Presbyterian way. But that being nulled at the King's Restoration, he receded to his charge at Magnus, where he continued till the Act of Uniformity ejected him.

The worthy Mr Caryl was cast out from the church of

a Hist. Purit. vol. iii. chap. vii.
b Ath. Oxon. vol. ii. Col. 513.

Magnus, near London-bridge, by the Act of Uniformity, in the year 1662. On this very mournful occasion, he preached his farewell sermon at Magnus from Rev. iii. 4. —*And they shall walk with me in white; for, they are worthy.* The author says, the design of this discourse, badly taken, is, to represent the honour and happiness of those, whom he had described in a former one, who like those *few names in Sardis, have not defiled their garments*, by a sinful conformity to a degenerate world. —They shall walk *with Christ.* They shall enjoy peace, and intimacy with him, as his friends, and be indulged with peculiar favour from him.—They shall walk *in white* garments: denoting their *state* of justification; but particularly their *character*, which is truly honourable in the sight both of God and of men: and also their inward *peace* and *joy*;—arising from the testimony of their own consciences—the witness of the Spirit—and a well grounded hope of future glory; in consequence of which they may now glory in tribulation. Thus it was with *Job*, chap. xvi. 19. and with *Paul*, 2 Cor. i. 12. What Christ says of the lily, may be said of those who keep themselves pure, in matters of faith, practice and worship; *Solomon in all his glory was not arrayed like one of these.* To such persons may the words of the preacher be addressed, Eccl. ix. 7. *Go thy way, eat thy bread with joy,—for God now accepteth thy works: let thy garments be always white.* Though the world give thee nothing but the bread of adversity, and the water of affliction; and clothes thee in mourning, and causes thee to prophesy in sackcloth, yet be of good comfort; thou hast the fruit of thy labour: whether present or absent thou art accepted of God, therefore rejoice in it. Here is the happiness of those who keep themselves from a defiled and a defiling world. Hence he takes occasion to caution Christians against every thing that would wound their consciences and defile their garments. They who neglect this shall *walk in black*, in garments of mourning. He earnestly exhorts them to adopt the laudable resolution of that eminent believer, Job, chap. xxvii. 6. To maintain purity of heart and life, that angelic robe which the world can neither strip off, nor sully with its reproaches. He adds, The blessed martyrs, though cast into black dungeons, have preserved their white garments, and though dressed so as to make them look like devils, have been filled with peace and joy.—Finally, this walking with Christ in white has respect to the heavenly glory, of which his transfiguration was a type, when it is said, *his raiment was white, so as no fuller on earth could whiten it.* Having told his hearers, that it had been the great object of his labours among them, to bring them into this holy and happy state, he concludes thus:—It shall be the desire and prayer of my heart that, if I should have no more opportunities among you, as you have been stirred up to obtain this *white robe of grace,* you and I may meet in *glory,* where we shall never part. That is the best of all. That is the answer of all our prayers; and that is the issue of all our working. Then shall we have as much *joy* as we can hold for ever.

He continued to live in London, after he was cast out from Magnus, and soon gathered a congregation in the neighbourhood, by London-bridge, to which he preached as the times would permit. His congregation so much increased, that at his death, he left one hundred and thirty-six communicants. He died universally lamented by all his acquaintance, at his house in Bury-street, in London, Feb. 1673, and in the seventy-first year of his age.

The following account of Mr Caryl's death, given in a letter of Mr Henry Dorney to his brother, well deserves to be inserted here. "That famous and laborious minister, Mr Joseph Caryl, your ancient friend and companion, is departed this life, aged 71 years. His death is greatly lamented by the people of God throughout this city. About the beginning of his sickness I was with him, and he inquired concerning you, as he was wont to do; and perceiving him to be somewhat weak, though he did not then keep his chamber, I desired him, while he was yet alive, to pray for you, which motion he cheerfully and readily embraced. And coming to him again, about three days before his death, found him very weak and past hope of life. He told me, as well as I could understand him, for his speech was low, that he remembered his promise to me concerning you. I think good to mention this particular (circumstance) to provoke you to all seriousness in regard to your own soul, whose eternal welfare lay so much upon the heart of this servant of Christ. His labours were great; his studies incessant; his conversation unspotted: his charity, faith, zeal and wisdom gave a fragrant smell among the churches and servants of Christ. His sickness, though painful, was borne with patience and joy in believing; and so he parted from time to eternity under the full sail of desire and joy in the Holy Spirit. He lived his sermons. He did at last desire his friends to forbear speaking to him, that so he might retire in himself; which time they perceived he spent in prayer; oftentimes lifting up his hands a little; and at last his friends, finding his hands not to move, drew near and perceived he was silently departed from them, leaving many mourning hearts behind."[a]

Mr Wood says, that Mr Caryl was a learned and zealous Nonconformist. A considerable character from an avowed adversary. Dr Calamy says, that he had universally the character of a *learned man*. Messrs Neal and Palmer say, that he was a man of great piety, learning and modesty: a character which is sufficiently supported by his writings.—The Oxford-historian informs us, that several elegies were made on him after his death, of which two or more he had seen extant. I have seen an elegy on his death, entitled, *London's Lass*. Part of it follows:

"Room for our tears; for here are thousands come
To vent our founts at his commanding tomb.
But oh! what mortal's genius can devise
A decent flood for such a sacrifice?—
His pious sermons did declare his worth,
His expositions set his learning forth;

a Dorney's Divine Contemplations, Lett. 113. p. 343. As with Palmer, Nonconf. Mem. second edit. vol. i.

And whilst we here lament his being gone,
Angels with Anthems welcome him at home.
Caryl, whose conversation, free from ill,
Can be expressed but by an angel's quill:
As in some mirror you might clearly see
In him, a perfect map of Piety;
The beauty of whose virtues may incite
The world to imitation and delight."—

The summer after Mr Caryl died, his congregation chose Dr John Owen for their pastor, and all united with that which was before under his care, which consisted of several persons of rank in the army. This united respectable society had afterward the eminently learned Mr David Clarkson for their pastor, who was succeeded by Dr Chauncey, as he was by the late very eminent Dr Isaac Watts, for whom they built a new meeting-house in Berry-street, near St Mary-Axe.[a]

I have collected a few choice sentences from Mr Caryl's writings, which follow; and will give the reader some idea of this eminent author. Speaking of what constitutes *a good work*, he mentions three things. 1. That the work may be good, we must be sure that the matter of it be good. It must be good in itself, as being according to Rule.—2. The aim, or the end of the work, must be good; and chiefly the glory of God, Mat. v. 16.—The *end* doth denominate the action.—3. The principle or spring of the work must be good—Unless the *principles* be good, the work is not good. As the fountain is, such are the streams that come from it. As the tree is, such is the fruit that grows upon it. *Do men gather grapes of thorns, or figs of thistles?* Mat. vii. 16. The thorn hath not a principle in nature to put forth a grape: The thistle hath not a principle in nature to put forth a fig: and therefore saith Christ, *A corrupt tree cannot bring forth good fruit.*——Gospel-charity is of a nobler extract, than to be found in the whole compass of nature; and godliness moves in a higher sphere, than the best dress

a Palmer's Nonconf. Mem.

that the gayest moralist ever reacht unto, Mat. v. 20.—Hence see the necessity of regeneration—We are not born with this *pure heart—good conscience and faith unfeigned*, which are the requisites to a *good work* in the text, 1 Tim. i. 5. These are the issues of the new birth.—You must be God's workmanship, before you can do God's work. You must be new creatures, created in Christ Jesus unto good works, before you can do them, Eph. ii. 10.—God makes us good, before we can do good.—We by union to Jesus Christ, come to have a spiritual principle to carry us out in the doing of all good works. As we are grafted into Christ, he changes the branch. Being planted into Christ, by the power of the Spirit, we are then made like him; and then we bring forth fruits of righteousness, which are to the glory of God *by him*. Mark the expression, *Being filled with the fruits of righteousness, which are by Jesus Christ*, Phil. i. 11. That is, by virtue of union with Christ, of implantation and ingrafture into Christ. Then all our fruits are sweet, pleasant, and well tasted.—They are from a principle of life in Christ; and from a principle of love unto Christ.

Mr Caryl is eminently distinguished by his learned and judicious writings, of which an account here follows:

1. *The Works of Ephesus;* explained in a sermon from Rev. ii. 2, 3. before the House of Commons, at their solemn Fast, 27th April, 1642. 4to. pp. 60. London, 1642. An excellent sermon.

2. *David's Prayer for Solomon;* containing the proper endowments and duty royal of a king, with the consequent blessings upon a kingdom. A sermon from Psal. lxxii 1—3. at Christ-church, London, before the Lord Mayor, and Aldermen, 27th of March, 1643. The commemoration of his Majesty's inauguration. 4to. pp. 38. London, 1643.

3. *The Nature, Solemnity, Grounds, Property, and Benefits of a Sacred Covenant: Together with the Duties of those who enter into such a Covenant:* A sermon from Neh. ix. 38. preached at Westminster, at that

public Convention, ordered by the House of Commons, for taking the Covenant, by all such, of all degrees, as willingly presented themselves, upon Friday, Oct. 6th, 1643. 4to. London, 1643. This excellent sermon was printed again at Glasgow, in a Collection of Sermons and Speeches at taking the Covenant, in the year 1741. And again, in the same Collection, Glasgow, 1799. I have seen copies of all these editions, in different parts of Scotland.

4. *The Saints' Thankful Acclamation at Christ's Resumption of his Great Power and the Initials of his Kingdom:* A sermon at Westminster, from Rev. xi. 16, 17. before the House of Commons, at their solemn Thanksgiving, 23d April, 1644. 4to. pp. 50. London. 1644.

5. *The Arraignment of Unbelief, as the Grand Cause of our National Non-establishment:* A sermon to the House of Commons, Fast, 28th of May, 1645. from Isai. vii. 9. the latter part of the verse. 4to. pp. 48. London, 1645.

6. *The Present Duty and Endeavour of the Saints:* A sermon at Paul's from Eph. v. 10. upon the Lord's-day, Dec. 14th, 1645. London, 1646.

7. *Heaven and Earth Embracing:* or, *God and Man Approaching:* A sermon preached from Jam. iv. 6. the former part of the verse, before the House of Commons, upon the day of their public Fast, at Margaret's Westminster. 4to. pp. 44. London, 1646.

8. *Joy Out-joyed:* or, *Joy in overcoming evil spirits and evil men, overcome by better joy:* A sermon preached from Luke x. 20. to the House of Peers, at Martin's in the Fields, on a day of Thanksgiving. 4to. pp. 30. London, 1646.

9. *England's Plus Ultra, both of Hoped Mercies, and of Required Duties:* A sermon preached from Psal. cxviii. 17. to both Houses of Parliament, the Lord Mayor, the Court of Aldermen, and Common-council of London, together with the Assembly of Divines, at Christ-church, on a day of public Thanksgiving, April 2, 1646. 4to. pp. 42. and 4 pages of an epistle dedicatory. London, 1646.

Wood observes here, that he has other sermons which

he had not seen, as, A Fast sermon before the House of Commons, 29th July, 1646. Thanksgiving sermon before the Parliament, at Margaret's Westminster, Oct. 8th, from Psal. cxi. 1—5. Fast sermon before the Parliament, 24th Sept. 1656. And Fast and Thanksgiving sermon before the Parliament, Aug. and Oct. 1659. Nor have I seen these sermons. But I have seen his sermon, entitled, *The Oppressor destroyed*, from Psal. cxix. 134. before the Lord Mayor, 21st Sept. 1651. And his Farewell sermon at Magnus, from Rev. iii. 4. 4to. London, 1662—1663. with other Farewell sermons.

Mr Caryl has also written and published, *An Exposition with Practical Observations upon the Book of Job.* This most elaborate, learned, judicious, and pious, work, was first printed in London, in twelve volumes in quarto, and afterward in two large volumes in folio. The 1st vol. 4to. 1644, 2d vol. 1645, the other vols. in the following years, and the 12th in the year 1666. 1036 pages. I have also seen vol. 1. 4to. pp. 479, London, 1651, and 1669. vol. 2d 4to. pp. 725. London, 1656.—All the 12th vols. I have seen were printed in the year 1666.—The 1st vol. folio edit. pp. 2281. London, 1676: 2d vol. pp. 2410. London, 1677. Wood says that these volumes are epitomised in the second volume of *Poole's Synopsis Criticorum.* Dr Calamy informs us, that some have very unworthily represented this work as a Commentary on Pineda, or a translation of it; but he who will but be at the pains to compare them a little, by reading a dozen leaves in each, will find that this is a gross mistake.[a]—The whole work is strongly marked with the characters of sound judgment, extensive erudition, and genuine piety. Dr Edward Williams, in his Preacher's Library, gives this work the following character: "Caryl's Exposition, with practical observations upon the book of Job, is a most elaborate, learned, judicious, and pious work; containing a rich fund of critical and practical divinity." Dr Cotton Mather, in his Student and Preacher, says, when speaking respecting Commentators on the Holy Scriptures;

a Calamy's Acc. 2 edit. vol. 2. p. 8.

" How happy should we have been, if an Hutcheson, who has done so well on Job, and on the smaller prophets, and on John, had left us the like operations on the rest of the Bible? Or, if a Caryl on Job, a Greenhill on Ezekiel, a Burroughs on Hosea, an Owen on the Hebrews, a Manton on James, and a Jenkins on Jude, were accompanied with others like them on the rest of the sacred pandects." Dr Wilkins, in his Ecclesiastes, reckons Mr Caryl a most eminent Commentator on Job. He certainly explains with perspicuity, and maintains with dignity, the peculiar characteristic doctrines of the gospel. He gives the most judicious and clear expositions of many other parts of the Holy Scriptures, in this work, and in all his writings. Mr Brown very properly places Mr Caryl among the best Commentators on the Holy Scriptures, in his Dictionary of the Bible, under the word Bible.

The quarto edition of this large and celebrated work is in the catalogue of books in the Theological library, belonging to the students of divinity in the University of Edinburgh, 1757. I have seen both editions in the libraries of Gospel-Ministers, in several counties of Scotland; and this luminous work well deserves a place in the library of every Christian divine. I have seen it plentifully in many families, in different parts of Scotland. It continues to be often advertised for sale, in the London-catalogues. It was in Mr Hamilton's catalogue, Pater-noster Row, 1809, p. 4. 2 vols. folio, £2. 18*s*. In Mr Ogle's, under the same date, 2 vols. imperial folio, strongly bound in calf, £3. 10*s*. And in 1811, 2 vols. folio, £3. 13*s*. 6*d*. and 12 vols. 4to. neat, £3. 3*s*.

Mr Caryl had also a hand in a book, entitled, *An English Greek Lexicon, containing the derivations and various significations of all the Words in the New Testament.* Oct. 1661.

And after his death, was published, *The Nature and Principles of Love, as the end of the Commandment:* being some of his last sermons, with an epistle to the reader by Dr Owen, and a fine Portrait of the author. A small book, London, 1673.

THOMAS CASE, M. A.

MINISTER OF THE GOSPEL IN LONDON, AND A MEMBER OF THE ASSEMBLY OF DIVINES AT WESTMINSTER.

THOMAS CASE was born in the county of Kent, in England. He was the son of Mr George Case, Minister of Boxley in that county. His father, who was eminently distinguished both by his parts and his piety, was peculiarly attentive to him, and gave him a well-directed and religious education in early life, which is commonly the best time for instruction. *Train up a child in the way he should go; and when he is old he will not depart from it.* "The importance of early instruction is written upon the whole system of nature, and repeated in every page of the history of Providence. You may bend a young twig and make it receive almost any form; but that which has attained to maturity, and taken its ply, you will never bring into another shape than that which it naturally bears."—Children may undoubtedly receive much benefit by the use of means, in a very early period of life And when parents use the means, they ought carefully to remember the beautiful connexion between the duty and the promise—*Train up a child in the way he should go; and when he is old he will not depart from it.* We ought to believe the certainty of the promise, as well as the obligation of the duty; and take a full view of the connexion. The beautiful connexion here was very clearly seen, in the pious subject of these pages. Under the seasonable and wholesome instructions of the religious and careful father, accompanied with the divine blessing; the amiable and tractable son, drinking in spiritual and good instructions with much earnestness and delight, gave very signal proofs of his eminently pious disposition, and of his great ingenuity, even in his child-hood, upon the first dawn of reason, which continued with him until old age.

We are informed, that he was a very young convert; and that his conversion began with prayer in very early life, *God working in him both to will and to do of his good pleasure*, when he was only six years of age. The solemn transaction with the Lord God of his salvation appears to have been very deeply engraved upon his young mind; for he himself related it to Dr Jacomb, who preached his funeral sermon.[a] And at that age, through the influence of divine grace, he was inclined to pray by himself, every morning and evening, shewing forth with a grateful heart the loving-kindness of God in promising salvaion in the morning, and his faithfulness in accomplishing it every night, which are inexhaustible subjects for morning and evening prayers and praises. And he prayed, not by the help of any *book* or *form*, either read or remembered; but by the gracious assistance of the Holy Spirit. He readily performed the duty, not upon any *precept* or *direction*, either from his father, or from any other person; but solely upon God's drawing and inclining his heart to it. That saying of Tertullian is very applicable to his prayer—*Without a monitor*, *because from the heart.*[b] His management of prayer with others, when advanced to eight years of age, is said to have been very remarkable, but I cannot give any particular account of that.—In the account of the remarkable conversion of the apostle Paul, it is said, *Behold*, *he prayeth*, Acts ix. 11. He no longer breathed out threatenings and slaughter against the disciples of Jesus; but earnestly prayed for mercy. Prayer is the breath of regenerate persons, and shews that they are spiritually alive; especially prayer with the spirit and with the understanding; frequent and fervent prayer, from a feeling sense of our want of spiritual blessings, such as we had no knowledge of before, nor desire after. The subjects of God's regenerating grace, always cry unto him; whether they are called after a course of opposition to God, as Paul, who therefore styles himself—*One born out of due time*, or in

a Jacomb's Fun. Serm. p. 48.
b Jacomb.

early life, as the subject of these pages. Our blessed Lord and Saviour has said—*Suffer the little children to come unto me, and forbid them not: for of such is the kingdom of God*, Mark x. 14. Our Saviour's words here undoubtedly imply, that even little children may be the subjects of divine regenerating grace, and thereby become really holy, and enjoy communion with God. If they can bear the dark impression of Adam's corrupt nature in their infancy or childhood, they may certainly be then *renewed in the spirit of their mind, after the image of Him who created them.* Almighty power, and the unsearchable riches of divine grace, can very easily accomplish this desirable change in children, as in the remarkable instance which is now before us. Our young and pious convert gave afterward sufficient proof of the sincerity of his conversion, by actively promoting the cause of religion, and by acquitting himself, under supernatural influence, in his proper station, with the spirit and temper of a real Christian. *In his calling, he did abide with God.*

At the proper season, he was sent to school at Canterbury, and afterward to Merchant-Taylor's school in London. He continued there, until his father, meeting with troubles, was obliged to remove him from these seminaries, and to take him home to himself; where he gave him all instruction in the arts and languages, that his circumstances would admit. In due time, he was sent to the famous University of Oxford, and became student of Christ-church there, in the year 1616, aged seventeen years, or thereabout, as Wood informs us. His industry and improvement were such, that he was unanimously elected *Student* of that House, by the Dean and Canons. He resided there until he commenced Master of Arts, and a year or two after. He took the degree of Master of Arts, June 26th, in the year 1623.[a]

Being now in some measure fitted for the work of the holy ministry, he commenced a preacher of the gospel. Wood says, that he preached sometime in these parts,

a Wood's Fasti. Oxon. vol. i. Col. 225.

and afterward in Kent, at, or near the place of his nativity. By the great importunity of a most intimate and affectionate friend in Norfolk, he was prevailed with to go and reside sometime with him. But he was soon called to the exercise of his ministry at Erpingham, a town in the county of Norfolk, where he continued eight or ten years. He was remarkably laborious in the work of his pastoral charge here, preaching twice every Lord's-day, expounding the Holy Scriptures, catechising the young people, and repeating in private what he had delivered in public, as several eminent ministers did in those times, in England His mind was enlightened, and his heart animated, by the Spirit of truth and of love; and he sincerely endeavoured *to divide rightly the word of truth;* instructing the ignorant, and arousing the careless, reproving the sinner, and comforting the saint. He attracted the esteem of many persons, who readily attended him, in order to enjoy the benefit of his profitable labours. And he was an eminently successful labourer in the Lord's vineyard, in the conversion of many souls. But meeting with much trouble there, he was forced to remove from that place by Bishop Wren's extreme severity, which we frequently meet with in this work. He was summoned to the high commission-court, and bailed; but before answer could be given to the articles preferred against him, the court was taken away by act of Parliament. His very intimate and affectionate friend above-mentioned, being made Warden of Manchester, took Mr Case with him into Lancashire. Our faithful and persecuted servant of Jesus Christ was, in a short time, presented to a place in the neighbouring county. But great revolutions and confusions prevailing soon after in the nation, he was, by the importunity of some persons of quality, persuaded to accompany them to *London.* Divine Providence conducted him safely to this famous metropolis, and afterward settled him comfortably there. He was first chosen lecturer, and afterward pastor of Mary Magdalen church in Milk-street, in London. Here he was eminently laborious and faithful in his ministerial work. Beside his labours in the congregation, and on the Lord's-day, he carried on a weekly lecture every Saturday, in order that the people might be the better prepared for the Sabbath. And here he first set up the *Morning Exercise*, which was highly beneficial to many persons, and has been long continued.[a] Many citizens of London having some near relation or friend in the army of the Earl of Essex, so many bills were sent up to the pulpit every Lord's-day for their preservation, that the minister had neither time to read them, nor to recommend their cases to God in prayer. Some divines in London therefore agreed to separate an hour for this purpose every morning, one half to be spent in prayer, and the other half in a suitable exhortation to the people. Mr Case began it in his church at seven o'clock in the morning, and when it had continued there a month, it was removed by turns to other churches at a distance, for the accommodation of the several parts of the city, and was called the *Morning Exercise*. The service was performed by different ministers, with fervent prayer both for the public welfare and for particular cases, in the presence of a large auditory. When the heat of the war was over, it became a casuistical lecture, and was carried on by the most learned and eminent divines of those times till the restoration of King Charles the Second. Their sermons were afterward published in several volumes in quarto, under the title of the *Morning Exercises*, each sermon being the resolution of some practical case of conscience. This lecture, though in a different form, was afterward continued among the Prostenant Dissenters.[b]

Mr Case's labours were not confined to his parish in Milk-street, he also carried on a lecture at Martin's in the Fields every Thursday; which he kept up above twenty years. Being eminently zealous for the Reformation, he was chosen a member of the Assembly of Divines at Westminster, and displayed his abilities there with success, in the service of the church. He was called frequently to preach to the members of the Parliament, and on public occasions.—Mr Walker reflects severely upon

a Jacomb's Fun. Ser. pp. 39, 40, 41.
b Neal's Hist. Purit. vol. ii. chap. xii. 1642.

him from a sermon which he preached before the Commons, in the year 1644, and for his *invitation* of those persons to the Sacrament, *who had contributed freely and liberally to the Parliament, for the defence of God's cause and the gospel.*[a] And the following passage in the sermon before the commissioners for the Court-martial, in 1644, is mentioned by Mr Granger, assanguinary and reprehensible. "Noble Sirs, imitate God, and be merciful to none that have sinned of malicious wickedness;" meaning the royalists. And the following observation has been made here: "It is painful to reflect that so venerable and amiable a man should have been so transported by the fury of the times, as to have uttered, and especially to have printed, so unchristian a sentence."[b] In order that the reader may have just conceptions of the author's meaning in this sentence, which is reckoned *unchristian*, I shall exhibit it as it stands in the sermon, and he may judge for himself. The sermon is preached from 2 Chron. xix. 6, 7. before the commissioners for the Court-martial, and is entitled, *Jehoshaphat's Caveat to his Judges.* In the eighteenth page of this sermon, the author says, "Noble Sirs, in your execution of judgment upon *delinquents*, imitate God: *And be merciful to none that have sinned of malicious wickedness,* Psal. lix. 5." He adds: "Let not your eye pity any who in this bloody quarrel have laid the foundation of their Rebellion and Massacres in *irreconcileable hatred* to Religion and the Government of Jesus Christ: Those his enemies that would not have him reign over them, slay them before his face.—Let not them find mercy in your eyes, in whose eyes a whole nation, and our posterity, could find no pity: spare not, but where you think in your consciences God himself would spare, if he himself were upon the bench in person. Imitate God in your justice." After this exhortation, the author insists warmly and largely upon imitating God in their mercy. *Be merciful as your heavenly Father is*

a Walker's Attempt, Part i. p. 17. Wood's Ath. vol. ii. Col. 707.

b See Toulmin's edit. of Neal's Hist. vol. iv. p. 599. Note.

merciful.—The other expressions, in Mr Case's writings, which have been severely censured by his enemies, are similar to those above-mentioned. Respecting the sentence which is reckoned *unchristian*, and similar expressions in the author's writings, we ought to observe, that he is not addressing private Christians, but such as are God's deputies, and should act always conformably to his law in their station, *taking heed what they do; for they judge not for man, but for the Lord, who is with them in the judgment.* Beside, it is unfair, in giving the sentence, to leave out the expression, "Execution of judgment upon *delinquents*," or those persons who have committed crimes; to make no reference to the sacred text, Psal. lix. 5. which the author does; and to say without qualification, that he means the royalists. He undoubtedly means the royalists when they were found to be *delinquents;* but not otherwise. And he only means that the royalists, or any persons, should be punished as the divine law directs, according to their crimes, which the sermon sufficiently proves. He insists chiefly upon the imitation of God, and acting in strict conformity to his law, in judgment. It is readily allowed that he was quick and passionate; this seems indeed to have been his infirmity; but his memory should not on that account be treated with partiality. And the severe persecution which he and his brethren endured from Bishop Wren and his court, ought to plead something in his excuse, admitting that he expressed himself sometimes with too much warmth.[a] The cruel treatment of the most zealous and useful preachers, while the most loose and careless were warmly encouraged, would probably have excited the indignation of persons of a very calm temper, who had God's glory at heart, and who had suffered as much as Mr Case had done. I do not intend, however, to plead for what is wrong in any degree, in any person. The real followers of Jesus have their peculiarities, and their infirmities, in their state of imperfection; and too fre-

a See Walker's Attempt, Part i. pp. 48, 49. Calamy's Cont. vol. i. p. 23.

quently give proof to those who are around them that they are renewed but in part. "It is obvious from the history of the first disciples of our Lord and Saviour—that while the grace of God has a holy influence, it seldom if ever changes the constitutional complexion—and that while it sanctifies the powers of human nature, it does not give us new ones. It renders the possessor open to conviction, and makes him willing to retract when he has done amiss, but it does not lay him under an impossibility of doing wrong. Hence a diversity of character in the church of God. Hence a variety of degrees in the spiritual life. Hence blemishes mixed with excellencies and defects rendered the more observable by the neighbourhood of some very praise-worthy qualities in the same individual. And hence, while religion appears to be divine in its origin and its tendency, we can easily discern that it is human in its residence and its exercise."[a] Let us therefore be tender, and consider ourselves, lest we also be tempted; and not censure indiscriminately, but praise as far as we can with truth and justice. Let the strong bear the infirmities of the weak, and not please themselves.

Mr Case was an eminently zealous Covenanter, as very clearly appears by his judicious and valuable sermons, which he preached at taking the Covenant. His first sermon on this occasion was preached at Laurence Church, on the Fast-day, Sept. 27th, 1643. His second sermon was preached at Milk-street, upon Saturday evening, Sept. 30th. for the Preparation to the Covenant. And his third sermon was preached on the Sabbath-day in the morning, the first of October; immediately before taking the Covenant, in Milk-street-church.—In the preface to these three sermons, he says:—"To every soul that shall enter into this holy league and covenant; my request is, that they would look around them: life and death is before them; if we break with God now, we have just cause to fear, God will stand to covenant no more with us, but will avenge the quarrel, with our utter destruc-

a Jay's Discourses for Families, vol. i. Disc. viii.

tion; if we be sincere and faithful, this covenant will be a foundation of much peace, joy, glory, and security, to us, and our seed, to the coming of Christ, which that it may be, shall be the earnest prayer of him, who is thy servant for Jesus' sake,

THOMAS CASE."

He was one of those ministers who subscribed the two Papers, declaring against the proceedings of the Parliament, in the year 1648, and the bringing King Charles to a trial.[a]

He was turned out of his place of Mary Magdalen, Milk-street, for refusing the *Engagement*, when it was vehemently urged, in the time of Oliver Cromwell, or of the Commonwealth, after the death of King Charles the First. The oaths of allegiance and supremacy were now abolished, and a new oath was appointed, called the *Engagement*, which was, "To be true and faithful to the Government established without King or House of Peers." Such persons as refused this oath were declared incapable of holding any place or office of trust in the Commonwealth; but as many of the excluded members of the House of Commons as would take it resumed their places. —And in order to bring the Presbyterian ministers to the test, the Engagement was strongly urged, and required to be sworn and subscribed by all Ministers, heads of Colleges and Halls, Fellows of Houses, Graduates, and all Officers in the Universities.—No minister was to be admitted to any ecclesiastical living; nor to be capable of enjoying any preferment in the church, unless he qualified himself by taking the Engagement within six months, publicly in the face of the congregation.[b] Mr Baxter says, that most of the Sectarian party swallowed the Engagement; and so did the King's old Cavaliers, very few of them being sick of the disease of a scrupulous conscience: but the moderate Episcopal men, and Presbyterians, generally refused it, as Mr Case did. Though

a Calamy's Cont. vol. i. p. 14.
b Neal's Hist. Purit. vol. iv. chap. i.

he was put out of his place on this account, Divine Providence soon opened another door for him. Christians should never despair. Our heavenly Father can always provide for his children. His resources are innumerable and inexhaustible. *O fear the Lord, ye his saints: for there is no want to them who fear him.* Mr Case was now called to preach as Lecturer, at Aldermanbury, and at Giles' Cripplegate. He continued preaching the glorious gospel of the grace of God in these congregations, until he was sent prisoner to the Tower, where he was confined about six months for his concern with the celebrated Mr Love. Upon the death of King Charles First, the Scots proclaimed the Prince of Wales King of Scotland, and sent commissioners to the Hague, to invite him into that kingdom, *if he would renounce Popery and Prelacy, and take the Solemn League and Covenant.* The body of the English Presbyterians acted in concert with the Scots, for restoring the King upon the footing of the Covenant. Several English Ministers carried on a private correspondence with the chiefs of the Scottish nation; and instead of taking the *engagement* to the present powers, called them *usurpers*, and declined praying for them in their churches: they also declared against a general Toleration, which the army and Parliament contended for.[a] In this cause, Mr Love lost his life, and Mr Case was imprisoned about six months, under the new government, or commonwealth. He made the best use he could of his imprisonment, falling then into the meditation which he afterward preached and printed, under the title of *Correction, Instruction.* The prison-house, where persons are confined for a good cause, is not a bad school for the ministers of Christ. Some of Paul's epistles were dated there, and greatly savour of prison-supports. And we are told, that Cervantes wrote his adventures of Don Quixote in a prison; and, from so vigorous an exercise of all his faculties in that situation, we may conclude that a person may be in jail without being miserable.

Mr Case, after his release, was invited to be Lecturer

a Neal's Hist. Purit. vol. iv. chap. i.

at Giles' in the Fields, near London. He continued here, till the King's restoration, when the former incumbent was re-admitted.

Mr Wood says, that "when the Presbyterians began to lift up their heads in the latter end of 1659, upon the generous proceedings of General Monk, he was constituted by Act of Parliament, dated 14th of March that year, one of the Ministers for the approbation and admission of Ministers according to the Presbyterian way." [a]

In the year 1660, he was one of the ministers deputed by his brethren in London, to wait upon the King at Breda, to congratulate him on his Restoration.—Mr Baxter says, that the King gave them very encouraging promises of peace, and raised some of them to high expectations. He never refused them a private audience when they desired it; and to amuse them farther, while they were once waiting in an anti-chamber, his Majesty said his prayers with such an audible voice in the room adjoining, that the ministers might hear him: "He thanked God that he was a covenanted King; that he hoped the Lord would give him an humble, meek, forgiving, spirit; that he might have forbearance toward his offending subjects, as he expected forbearance from offended Heaven." Upon hearing which old Mr Case lifted up his hands to Heaven, and blessed God, who had given them a praying King.[b]

In the year 1661, Mr Case was one of the commissioners at the Savoy-conference. In the year 1662, he was ejected or silenced with his brethren, by the Act for Uniformity. Wood says; "Yet ever after so long as he lived, he was not wanting to carry on the *beloved Cause* in Conventicles, for which he sometimes suffered."—In this *trying* season, he was chiefly concerned, that *divine grace might be sufficient for him*, to preserve him from *sin;*—that he might derive advantage from his crosses, and be able to say it is *good for me that I have been afflicted;*—that he might enjoy the light of God's countenance, as

a Wood's Ath. Oxon. vol. ii. Col. 707.

b Neal's Hist. Purit. vol. iv. chap. iv. 1660.

his support and comfort;—that he might in due time *come forth as gold;*—and that he might *glorify the Lord in the fires.* And when his public ministry was at an end, he ceased not in private with the utmost diligence to do all the good he could. He preached his Farewell-sermon, at the conclusion of his public ministry, from Rev. ii. 5. He says, Christ here prescribes precious Physic for the healing of this languishing church of Ephesus, compounded of three ingredients,—self-reflection—holy contrition—and thorough reformation. He warmly urges these upon his hearers, in order to prevent the threatened removal of their religious privileges.—In the close of the last head, respecting the necessary Reformation,—"We should do something by way of extraordinary bounty and charity to the relief of God's indigent servants"—He enlarges upon the pertinent passage, Dan. iv. 27. and concludes thus: "That which I would exhort you to is, for every one to set apart some considerable part of your estate, and account it as a hallowed thing, dedicated to God; as a thing which to touch were sacrilege; that you may be ready on all occasions, in all due and regular ways, to bring out for the relief of the poor. You know objects abounding in every place, and you may expect warrantable means for dispensing of what God shall put into your hands, in this manner." This wholesome advice furnishes us with one eminently distinguishing and pleasing trait in the character of this venerable servant of Jesus Christ. God has made rich men stewards, but not proprietors. And they who have, as the gift of *the living God, all things richly to enjoy,* should *be rich in good works, ready to distribute, willing to communicate,* to the poor and distressed. *It is required in stewards, that a man be found faithful.* And the tender care of Divine Providence extends to the poor as well as to the rich.

Mr Case was eminently distinguished in his relative capacity, and praise-worthy. He had a prudent wife from the Lord; *a help meet for him.* They lived together nearly forty-five years; and he often said, that *in all that time there had been no contention between them, except in this, who should love one another most.* They were *equally yoked together*, being both very pious and affectionate. They were worthy of imitation in their whole deportment. —Mr Case had no children of his own body; but his wife had children, to whom he was peculiarly attentive, and highly useful.—As soon as God had crowned his wishes, by placing him over a family, he endeavoured to glorify God as the master of a family. He now worshipped God, not only in the closet, but also in the parlour, with his wife, the children and servants in the train. He zealously used all proper means to render the family truly religious. He was eminently attentive to the welfare of all persons who came under his roof. He instructed them carefully in the principles of religion, by helping them to understand the Holy Scriptures; which were read in his family morning and evening. And his custom was, to cause every child and servant remember something that had been read; which he opened to them, in a plain and familiar manner, and afterward proceeded to prayer. He mingled instruction with devotion. Many servants, who lived with him, blessed God that ever they came into his house.[a]

He died in a good old age, on the 30th of May, in the year 1682, aged eighty-four years. His life was holy, and his death was easy. He was allowed to escape, in a great degree, from the alarming approaches of the last enemy. He endured no sickness, no pain, no agonies, at the last. " The garment of mortality easily dropt off; and the servant of God fell asleep in the Lord." Rising from dinner he desired some repose upon his bed; where as soon as he was laid, he *gathered up his feet, and so yielded up the ghost, and was gathered unto his people.* This easy death he had much desired, and often prayed for, and he was mercifully favoured with it, in answer to his prayers. His mortal remains were decently interred in Christ-church within Newgate in London, on the 14th of June, 1682. Soon after his body was buried, a large white stone was laid over his grave; just below the steps

a Jacomb's Fun. Serm. pp. 51, 52.

going to the altar, with the following inscription upon it in Latin, which I shall translate into English: *Here sweetly sleeps Thomas Case, a most faithful Minister of Jesus Christ, an excellent preacher in this city and elsewhere for many years. Educated in Christ-church, Oxford, in this church of Christ at last buried. He died 30th of May, in the year of his age* 84, *and in the year of our Lord,* 1682.[a] Mr Case lived the longest of any of those who composed the Assembly of Divines, who continued among the Dissenters. He was a man of good abilities, of sound judgment, of quick invention, of a warm spirit, and of steady principles; an open plain-hearted man; an ardent and hearty lover of God, and of all good men; of *a broken and a contrite heart,* heavenly minded and charitable.—He was an excellent scripture-preacher; an eminent man in prayer, and a very diligent and successful labourer in the Lord's vineyard.—In doctrine, he was a very strict Calvinist.—*Mark the perfect man, and behold the upright: for the end of that man is peace. And let us be followers of them who through faith and patience are now inheriting the promises.*

Mr Case has left several written works:

Two sermons preached from Ezek. xx. 25. and Ezra x. 23. at Westminster before sundry of the House of Commons. 4to. London, 1641, Second edit. 1642.—Sermons respecting God's Waiting to be gracious, at Milk-street, from Isai. xxx. 18. 4to. pp. 168. London, 1642.—*God's Rising, his Enemies' Scattering:* A sermon from Psal. lxviii. 1, 2. before the Commons, Fast, 26th Oct. 1642. 4to. pp. 51. London, 1644.—*The Root of Apostacy, and Fountain of true Fortitude:* A sermon from Dan. xi. 32. before the House of Commons, 9th April, 1644. 4to. pp. 34. London, 1644.—*Jehoshaphat's Caveat to his Judges:* A sermon from 2 Chron. xix. 6, 7. before the Commissioners for the Court-Martial, 17th Aug. 1644. London, 1644.—*The Quarrel of the Covenant, with the Pacification of the Quarrel:* Three

a Wood and Jacomb.

sermons from Lev. xxvi. 25. and Jer. l. 5. 4to. London, 1644; Glasgow, 1741, and 1799.—A Thanksgiving sermon from Isai. xliii. 14. before the Commons, 22d Aug. 1645. 4to. London, 1645.—*Deliverance, Obstruction;* or, *The Set-backs of Reformation:* A sermon from Exod. v. 22, 23. before the House of Lords, Fast, 26th March, 1646. 4to. London, 1646.—*A Model of True Spiritual Thankfulness:* Sermon from Psal. cvii. 30, 31. before the Commons. 4to. London, 1646.—*Spiritual Whoredom:* Fast sermon, before the Commons, from Hos. ix. 1. London, 1647.—*The Vanity of Vainglory:* Funeral sermon for Kinsmet Lucy, Esq. from 1 Cor. i. 29—31. London, 1655.—*Sensuality Dissected:* Sermon to divers citizens of London, born in Kent. London, 1657.—*Elijah's Abatement, or Corruption in the Saints:* A sermon preached at Chatham in Kent, from James v. 17. at the funeral of Mr Rosewell, Minister of the Gospel there. London, 1658.

He has other funeral sermons; but I have not seen them; One for Mrs Elizabeth Scott, in 1659.—Another for Darcy Wivil, Esq. in 1659.—The first and last sermon in the Morning Exercise at St Giles', 1659, are his.—And a sermon on the Sanctification of the Sabbath, from Isai. lviii. 13, 14. in the Supplement to the Morning Exercise at Cripplegate.—And his Farewell sermon.

Mr Case has also written, *Correction, Instruction:* or, *A Treatise of Afflictions.* Small book, the second edit. corrected and enlarged, London, 1653; and again, 1671.

Imitation of the Saints opened in Practical Meditations. 4to. London, 1666.

Mount Pisgah: or, *A Prospect of Heaven.* This volume contains An Exposition of the 4th chap. of 1 Thess. from ver. 13. to the end of the chap. divided into three parts. 4to. London, 1670.

DANIEL CAWDREY, A. M.

MINISTER OF THE GOSPEL AT GREAT BILLING IN NORTHAMPTONSHIRE, AND A NOTABLE MEMBER OF THE ASSEMBLY OF DIVINES AT WESTMINSTER.

DANIEL CAWDREY was the son of an old Nonconformist, Mr Robert Cawdrey, who struggled hard with the Bishops upon his deprivation for Nonconformity. His case was published, and the injustice which he suffered was preserved upon record. This son was the youngest of many sons. He was educated in Peter-House, in the University of Cambridge. We must regret the want of information respecting the particulars of the life of the subject of this Memoir. It is certain, however, that he was eminently distinguished in his day, in the character of a Christian minister. It appears, by the title-page of his sermons, which are entitled, *Humility the Saints' Livery*, that he was sometime, in 1624, Minister of the Word of God, at Little Ilford, in Essex. He was afterward settled at Great Billing, in the county of Northampton, in England. Dr Calamy says, He was a considerable man, eminently learned, and a noted member of the Assembly of Divines. He preached sometimes to the members of Parliament. In a sermon preached to the House of Commons, from Prov. xxix. 8. at their solemn Fast, he testifies against these seminaries of sin, stage-plays, which are often well attended, when many churches are almost empty. Speaking of open scorners, who are professed mockers of Religion, he says; "Among these you may reckon your *Stage-players*, who had scoffed Religion out of countenance with many. *You have done well to put them down, and shall do better, if you keep them down.*"

This eminently good man, and faithful servant of Jesus Christ was cast out from Great Billing, by the Act for Uniformity, after he had been a very laborious minister of the gospel there, about thirty-six or thirty-seven years. He removed afterward into Welling-borough, where he had a daughter married. There he lived in great pain, receiving, however, all who came to him, and encouraging them in the ways of holiness and piety, till Oct. 1664, when he fell asleep in the Lord; aged forty days short of seventy-six years.

Mr Cawdrey's written works are;

1. *Humility the Saints' Livery:* Substance of two sermons, from 1 Pet. v. 5. London, 1624.
2. An Assize sermon at Northampton, in 1627, from Psal. lxix. 9.
3. *Superstitio Superstes.* 4to. 1641.
4. *The Good Man a Public Good:* A sermon preached from Prov. xxix. 8. to the House of Commons. 4to. pp. 43. London, 1643.
5. *Vindiciae Clavium:* or, A Vindication of the Keys of the Kingdom of Heaven, into the hands of the right Owners. 4to. pp. 90. London, 1645. in English.
6. *The Inconsistency of Independency with Scripture & itself:* A threefold Discourse. 4to. pp. 219. Lon. 1651.
7. *Sabbatum Redivivum:* or, *The Christian Sabbath Vindicated:* A large and elaborate work, in two quarto volumes. The first Part by him and Mr Herbert Palmer; the second Part by Mr Cawdrey alone. London, 1645.
8. *Independency a great Schism.*
9. A Diatribe against Dr Hammond, on Superstition and Festivals.
10. A Vindication of this Diatribe.
11. *A Sober Answer to a Serious Question:* Against Mr Giles Firmin.
12. A sermon at Paul's, July 1st 1655. from 1 Tim. i. 19. London, 1655.
13. *Self-examination for Preparation to the Lord's-table.*
14. *Family Reformation Promoted.* Small book, London, 1656.
15. *Church-Reformation Promoted.* Small book, London, 1657.
16. Bowing to or toward the Table Superstitious.
17. *An Essay against Usury.*
18. *The Grand Case, with Reference to the New Conformity.*[a]

a Dr Calamy's Account, vol. ii.

HUMPHREY CHAMBERS, D. D.

PASTOR OF CLAVERTON AND OF PEWSEY, SUCCESSIVELY, AND A MEMBER OF THE ASSEMBLY OE DIVINES AT WESTMINSTER.

HUMPHREY CHAMBERS was born in Somersetshire, in England. He was a gentleman's son, and he was educated in University-College, Oxford, where he became a Commoner, in the year 1614, aged fifteen years. After he had taken the degree of Master of Arts, he entered into holy Orders, and in June 1623, he was made Rector of Claverton in his own country, on the death of John Bewshen. Afterward, he took the degree of Bachelor of Divinity, and was much esteemed by the neighbouring ministers as an orthodox divine. But he was silenced by Bishop Pierce, his diocesan, for maintaining and preaching up *the morality of the Sabbath.* He boldly discovered, on this occasion, a true Christian spirit. His faithfulness, in contending earnestly for the truth, exposed him to heavy sufferings. Dr Calamy says, that this created him two years trouble, imprisonment, and sequestration, by Archbishop Laud's taking the cause into his own hands, who was seldom backward in severity, in cases of that nature.[a] Mr Chambers was, at this time, eminently distinguished by his self-denial and holy courage, qualities which are highly ornamental to the Christian character. He was entirely devoted to the honourable service of his blessed Lord and Saviour; and made an illustrious appearance, at this period, for the morality of the Lord's-day, or Christian Sabbath. He was willing to sacrifice every personal consideration for the good of the church, and for the glory of his Redeemer, whom he cheerfully followed to the gloomy prison. *Jesus said unto his disciples, If any man will come after me, let him deny himself, and take up his cross, and*

a Calamy's Account, vol. ii. 2d edit. p. 754.

follow me. He was firmly resolved, that, through the strength of divine grace, nothing should stop him in the course of his duty. And *he took joyfully the spoiling of his goods, knowing in himself, that he had in heaven, a better and an enduring substance.* By such remarkable dispensations, God, *whose foolishness is wiser than men,* exercises the faith and patience of his servants, and gloriously displays the power of his own arm, and the unsearchable riches of his grace, in carrying on his own eternal designs, in spite of the utmost efforts of his most formidable adversaries. And the behaviour of Christ's zealous and faithful servants, under their grievous sufferings, exhibiting noble examples of undaunted courage, admirable patience, unshaken firmness, cheerful resignation, and disinterested love, affords a very strong testimony to the truth of the Christian religion. Thus, *the wrath of man,* and of Satan also, against the church, is made *to praise the Lord;* and *the remainder of it, he* most mercifully *restrains.* And Christ always furnishes his servants completely, for whatever service he requires from them; rendering *his yoke easy, and his burden light,* to them. And persons may sometimes be converted and encouraged by the sufferings of Christ's faithful servants, as well as by their ministry. And, when we reflect upon the numerous and grievous sufferings of the primitive Christians, and of the faithful followers of the Lamb in succeeding ages, we should cheerfully submit, without murmuring, yea, with grateful hearts, to our very small inconveniences in Christ's service. *Verily, there is a reward for the righteous; verily he is a God who judgeth in the earth.*

When the times changed, and the civil war broke out between the King and Parliament, Mr Chambers took part with the Parliament. He maintained a man and a horse at his own expence, in actual service, in the defence of civil and religious liberty. He took the *Covenant,* and was constituted a member of the Assembly of Divines at Westminster. He preached a sermon before the House of Commons, in Margaret's, Westminster, at their public Fast, on the 27th of Sept. 1643. In his address to the

House of Commons, which is prefixed to this sermon, he says, "Suffer a word of exhortation, and be intreated, in the fear of God, to continue ever faithful to the God of heaven, and to our dread Sovereign, the King's Majesty, then, although you be esteemed enemies, for speaking the truth, and seeking righteousness, yet may you wait with comfort, for a time, wherein the Lord will cause your righteousness to shine forth as the morning, and your just dealing as the noon day." In the sermon, he greatly laments the divisions among the worshippers of the one living and true God; and warmly recommends Christian unity in all matters of religion, to all those who love the Lord Jesus Christ in sincerity, not only in England, but also in Scotland, and in Ireland, as now notified and ratified by a solemn Covenant. Addressing the House of Commons, he says, "Honourable and beloved, It is greatly to be hoped and desired, that that solemn Covenant, into which yourselves with some others, have already exemplarily entered, shall in God's due time, notwithstanding all oppositions, bring forth a blessed Church, unity in the united kingdoms of England, Scotland, and Ireland, which if ever attained, will be a blessed and heavenly pledge and assurance to us and our posterities after us, that the Lord will make good to us and them that blessed promise which he made of old unto his people; *I will set my tabernacle among you: and my soul shall not abhor you. And I will walk among you, and will be your God, and ye shall be my people*, Lev. xxvi. 11, 12. Oh! that we might live to see that happy day, wherein the three kingdoms, united under one Sovereign Commander on earth, may be sweetly united in the service and worship of the one God of Heaven, *that the Lord may be one, and his Name one in them all.* Then doubtless would the Lord, the God of peace, set his tabernacle among us, and rejoice over us to do us good."—Toward the end of the sermon, he says, "Worthy patriots—be exhorted, in the name of God, seriously and undauntedly to set forward a holy Reformation of our kingdom, regulated by the word of God. That solemn peaceful Covenant, into which you have lately entered, engageth you thereunto. That Covenant obligeth you to labour to *bring the Churches of God in the three kingdoms to the nearest conjunction, and uniformity in religion, according to the word of God, to endeavour the extirpation of whatsoever shall be found contrary to sound doctrine and the power of godliness.* In the accomplishment of this Covenant, the work of public Reformation, which I now press upon you, will be accomplished, prosecute it, and in the prosecution thereof you cannot but promote that Reformation, which the Lord calls and looks for, as the fruit and ornament of all your days of solemn humiliation. Take this for your comfort; they who are for God in sincerity, shall have the Lord God for them, and with them, in abundant mercy, to guide them by his counsel till at length he receive them to eternal glory. Let the Apostle's Christian exhortation, therefore, sound ever in your ears, and prevail upon your hearts, *Let us not be weary in well doing; for in due season we shall reap, if we faint not.*" In the whole sermon, the author discovers much genuine piety, solid learning, and true zeal for the Reformation. He was also one of the three ministers who preached before the House of Lords, on the 22d of Oct. 1644, on the uniting of the army. Wood says, that he was Minister of Stretchley, in Shropshire, in the year 1648. Soon after he had the rich Rectory of Pewsey, near Marlborough, in the county of Wilts, conferred on him by the Earl of Pembroke. He commenced Doctor of Divinity, on the 12th of April, in the year 1648. He was married to a daughter of the eminently learned and pious Dr Richard Brett, who was appointed one of the translators of the Bible into English, by King James, in 1604.[a] Dr Chambers was appointed an assistant to the commissioners for ejecting scandalous, ignorant, and insufficient, ministers and schoolmasters. Oliver Cromwell, with the advice of his Council, published an ordinance, under the date of Aug. 28th, 1654, entitled, "An ordinance for ejecting scandalous, ignorant, and insufficient, ministers and school-

a Wood's Ath. Oxon. vol. i. Col. 608.

masters." This ordinance appoints, and nominates certain lay-commissioners for every county, and joins with them ten or more, of the gravest, and most notable, ministers, as their assistants, and empowers any five, or more of them, to call before them any public preacher, lecturer, parson, vicar, curate, or schoolmaster, who is, or shall be reputed ignorant, scandalous, insufficient or negligent; and to receive all articles or charges which should be exhibited against them; and to proceed in the examination and determination of such offences, according to certain rules which were agreed to.

The Wiltshire commissioners summoned Mr Walter Bushnel, Vicar of Box, near Malmsbury, before them, to answer to a charge of drunkenness, profanation of the Sabbath, gaming, and disaffection to the government; and after a full hearing, and proof upon oath, they ejected him. The Vicar prepared for the press a narrative of the proceedings of the commissioners appointed by Oliver Cromwell for ejecting scandalous and ignorant ministers, in the Case of Walter Bushnel, &c. but it was not printed till the King's restoration; and even then the commissioners did themselves justice in a reply, which they called, "A Vindication of the Marlborough Commissioners, by the Commissioners themselves." And Dr Chambers, who was reproached by Bushnel, justified himself, in a distinct vindication.[a]

After the King's Restoration, he kept his place until the very day when the Act of Uniformity commenced. Then, having preached his Farewell sermon from Psal. cxxvi. 6. that this life is a seed time for eternity, he went home, was seized with sickness presently and died. His mortal remains were buried in the church of Pewsey, on the 8th day of Sept. 1662, without the service of the church, which had just at that time taken place. And his wife was buried there also, about the same time. And by the favour of the noble Earl, who was his constant friend, the family obtained permission to remove the household-goods.[b]

a Neal's Hist. Purit. vol. iv. chap. iii.
b Wood's Ath. vol. ii. and Calamy's Acc.

Dr Chambers' writings are;

Some sermons before the Parliament, and on other occasions; as, *A Divine Balance to weigh Religious Fasts in:* A sermon preached from Zech. vii. 5—7. before the House of Commons, Fast, Sept. 27th, 1643. 4to. pp. 44. London, 1643.—*Paul's Sad Farewell to his Ephesians:* A sermon preached from Acts xx. 37, 38. at the Funeral of Mr John Grayle, Minister of Tidworth, in the county of Wilts. 4to. London, 1655.—*Motives to Peace and Love.* 4to. 1649.—*Animadversions on Mr W. Dell's Book*, entitled, *The Crucified and Quickened Christian.* 4to. London, 1653.—*An Apology for the Ministers of the county of Wilts.* 4to. London, 1654. It is said, That in writing this *Apology*, Dr Chambers was assisted by Messrs J. Strickland, Adoniram Byfield and Peter Ince. And *an Answer to Mr Walter Bushnel, about the Proceedings of the Commissioners for ejecting Scandalous Ministers.* 4to. 1660.

FRANCIS CHEYNELL, D. D.

SOMETIME FELLOW OF MERTON-COLLEGE, OXFORD, PASTOR OF PETWORTH, AND A MEMBER OF THE ASSEMBLY OF DIVINES AT WESTMINSTER.

FRANCIS CHEYNELL was born in Catstreet, in St Mary's parish, within the city of Oxford, in the year 1608; and he received baptism there, on the sixth of July, the same year. He was the son of John Cheynell, an eminently learned Doctor of Physic, and sometime fellow of C. C. College. His father is said to have been the most celebrated physician in Oxford, at that time. He bred his son, the illustrious subject of this Memoir, a scholar, and lived to see him Fellow of Merton-College. After he had been educated in grammar-learning, either in the school of that very notable Grecian, Edward Sylvester, who taught, at that time, in Allsaints parish, or, in the free-school of Magdalen-College, or, in both, he became a member of the famous University of Oxford, in the beginning of the year 1623. And when Bachelor of Arts, of two years standing, or more, he was elected probationer Fellow of Merton-College, in 1629, where he resided several years. After he had proceeded in Arts, he entered into the sacred function, and was a curate in or near Oxford for some time. He took the degree of Bachelor of Divinity, and was invited by Mr Holman, to accept a living from him, near Banbury, of several hundreds yearly. Here he lived sometime, and had a ruffle with Archbishop Laud, while in his height.

In every situation, he diligently cultivated those talents, which qualified him for his future and important services. Having spent much of his time in the College, he had acquired a very correct and extensive knowledge of books and of what belonged to his profession. And he constantly used his endeavours to promote his growth in the divine life, in the knowledge of the Lord Jesus Christ, and in fitness for his office, by reading, meditation, and prayer. He possessed a proper mixture of a studious disposition, and of an active spirit, which rendered him highly useful to the church. His real personal character was very plainly and fully unfolded, in those trying and troublesome times, in which he lived. Whatever he believed, he thought himself obliged to profess, and what he professed he was ready to defend. He was peculiarly bold in the cause of truth, and in the way of duty. He says, in a sermon before the House of Commons, from Zech. ii. 7.—" What upon prayer and study, God hath revealed by the clear texts of the *Revelation*, I will this day deliver unto you, though I were sure to die St John's death, or to be banished into St John's island.

When the civil war broke out between the King and Parliament, he took part with the Parliament. In the beginning of the war, he was mostly with the Earl of Essex. When he was with the Earl in Cornwall, he was a very goodly person, of great strength and undaunted courage. He now, indeed, added the praise of true valour to that of solid and useful learning. An eminent writer says, " He seems indeed to have been born a soldier, for he had an intrepidity which was never to be shaken by any danger, and a spirit of enterprize not to be discouraged by difficulty, which were supported by an unusual degree of bodily strength."[a] Dr Calamy says, That his commands were as readily obeyed by any Colonels in that army as the General's own. He was,

> "In vice untaught, but skill'd where glory led
> To arduous enterprize."

Brave in action, and full of intelligence. He possessed true fortitude derived from the best sources. And fortitude, in the estimation of the Romans, was the principal quality of human nature, and the defeat of an enemy the chief of it's fruits. When he appeared in the field, and displayed his eminent zeal and undaunted resolution, he did not fight against either his king or his country; but for the right of both. He appeared in defence of the rights of both king and country; and chiefly of civil and religious liberty. During the time in which the illustrious Mr Hampden was engaged in the Civil Wars, he wore round his neck an ornament, consisting of a small silver chain, inclosing a plain Cornelian stone. Round the silver rim of the stone was inscribed,

> "Against my King I never fight,
> But for my King and Country's right."

Our reformers, in general, both in church and state, at that time, appeared for the right of both their King and their country, as their writings and testimonies fully evince. And, it was Mr Cheynell's daily prayer, That God would unite the King and Parliament, in the cause of Christ. He says, "Lord, be pleased to decide the controversy, let that side prevail which doth most sincerely desire thy glory, the King's good, the kingdom's welfare by an happy Reformation, and a Christian peace."[b] He had a very public spirit, and was a real lover of his country, and rendered signal services to it, but did not accumulate wealth. Among the Romans, riches were of no account in constituting rank. Men became eminent by rendering signal services to their country, not by accumulating wealth. In this manner, Cheynell became eminent. Ardent love to the Redeemer, excited him to proclaim his

a Johnson. b Epistle to his Serm. from Zech. ii. 7.

ineffable glories, appear openly and boldly in his cause, and to offer his invaluable benefits to the sons of men. In his ministry, he used not flattering words, nor a cloak of covetousness. He *renounced the hidden things of dishonesty, not walking in craftiness, nor handling the word of God deceitfully; but by manifestation of the truth commending himself to every man's conscience in the sight of God.*

Being now eminently distinguished by his useful learning, genuine piety, great abilities, and signal services to his country, he was appointed a member of the famous Assembly of Divines at Westminster, in the year 1643. He preached frequently before the members of Parliament. He embraced the Covenant, and was a very zealous covenanter, as appears by his writings. He was voted Parson of Petworth, a town in the county of Sussex, a rich parsonage then let for £700 yearly, by an Ordinance of Parliament. He was one of the select Committee, which was appointed by the Assembly of Divines, for the examination and approbation of such clergymen already in orders, as petitioned for sequestered livings.[a]

Mr Cheynell has been greatly blamed respecting his behaviour at Mr Chillingworth's funeral. Mr Chillingworth was born and educated at Oxford. He afterward turned Roman Catholic, and went to the Jesuits' College at St Omer's; but not being thoroughly satisfied in some of their principles, he returned to England, in 1631, and having embraced the Religion of the Church of England, he published a Treatise, entitled, "The Religion of Protestants a safe way to Salvation." It was the general opinion that he was a Socinian; but in his last Letter at the end of his Works, he appears an Arian, according to Neal.—He served as engineer in Arundel Castle in Sussex, in the King's army, where he was taken prisoner, and when indisposed had the favour of being lodged in the bishop's house at Chichester, where he died, Jan. 20th, 1644. By the interest of Mr Cheynell, who attended Mr Chillingworth in his sickness, he was kindly used. Mr Cheynell wished that he would renounce some of his dangerous principles, and reasoned with him for

a Neal's Hist. Purit. vol. iii. ch. ii.

that end, but could not prevail. He prayed fervently for him while he was alive, and excited others to join with him in his behalf: but he was greatly grieved and provoked by his obstinacy, and by the errors in his book, above-mentioned. At Mr Chillingworth's interment, he cast his book into the grave, saying, "Get thee gone, thou cursed Book, which hast seduced so many precious souls; get thee gone, thou corrupt rotten Book, earth to earth, and dust to dust; get thee gone into the place of rottenness, that thou mayest rot with thy author, and see corruption."

Mr Cheynell's behaviour on this occasion was certainly very unbecoming and offensive. But the spirit of that man of God, the singularly meek Moses, was sometimes so stirred within him, that he both acted and spake in an improper manner. On a particular occasion, when highly provoked by the gross corruption of the children of Israel, and his anger waxed hot, he dashed the two tables of God's holy law to the ground, and brake them beneath the mount. And, he also spake unadvisedly with his lips, and incurred the displeasure of his heavenly Father. Beside, it should be observed, that Mr Cheynell's temper was hot, his zeal for God was ardent, the temptation was strong, and he was sometimes disordered in his brain. In such circumstances, it is not very strange, though a man's actions and words are sometimes unaccountable. He was not one of those cold-complexioned persons, nor probably wished to be regarded as such, who could endure to see men foaming out their own shame, in promoting error and corruption, without rising into indignation at the thought, and yielding to such animated expressions of his feeling, as that indignation must supply.

He was one of those Divines who were sent down by the Parliament to the Treaty of Uxbridge. He was also sent with other eminent Divines, for the reformation of the University of Oxford, about the beginning of Sept. 1646.[a] The University of Oxford was in the most deplorable condition, when it fell into the hands of the Parliament. The two Houses appointed seven of their most popular Divines to go to Oxford, with authority to preach in any pulpit in the University for six months, in order to soften

a See Life of Arrowsmith.

the spirits of the people, and to give them a better opinion of their cause. Mr Cheynell was in that number. The Ministers were very diligent in discharging their trust, preaching twice every Lord's-day. And they had a weekly conference every Thursday, in which they proposed to solve such objections as should be raised against their new Confession of Faith and Discipline; and to answer any other important cases in Divinity. The question, or case, was to be propounded the week before, that it might be well considered; a moderator was also appointed to keep order, who began and concluded with a short prayer; and the whole business was conducted with great decency and gravity. And, like Paul at Athens, *some mocked them, others slighted them; but certain men clave unto them, and believed.*

There being no prospect of reforming the University by these means, the Parliament proceeded to a visitation, and past an Ordinance for that purpose, May 1st, 1647. Mr Cheynell was also appointed one of the visitors of the University; and he was made President of St John's-College, and also Margaret Professor of the University, in the room of Dr Lawrence. He gave up both these places after some time for refusing the Engagement. He had now proceeded Doctor of Divinity, and retired to Petworth, where, Wood says, he remained an useful member for the Covenanting cause till the King's Restoration. He was unremittingly attentive to his charge there, and God crowned his labours with great success. He was very hospitable and charitable; and he never increased his estate by any of his preferments. He was sometimes disordered in his head, as above-mentioned, but he was perfectly recovered to a sound mind, some years before his death. He was cast out from the rich Living of Petworth by the Act for Uniformity. He afterward lived privately in a little village near Preston and Brighthelmstone in the county of Sussex, where he had an estate. He died at his house there, in Sept. 1665.

Dr Cheynell was exactly orthodox, and generally allowed to be a very pious and learned divine, and a man of great abilities, a good disputant and preacher.

Dr Cheynell has left several valuable written works *to praise him in the gate:*

1. *Zion's Memento, and God's Alarum:* A sermon from Zech. ii. 7. Fast, before the House of Commons, May 31st, 1643. 4to. pp. 45; with 7 pages of an Epistle prefixed; London, 1643. An excellent sermon.—2. *The Rise, Growth, and Danger, of Socinianism.* 4to. pp. 79. London, 1643. This learned work was ordered to be printed by a Committee of the House of Commons for printing, 18th April, 1643. It contains a plain discovery of the desperate design of corrupting the Protestant Religion, shewing, that what was so violently contended for by the Abp. of Canterbury and his adherents, is not the true and pure Protestant Religion, but a hotch-potch of Arminianism, Socinianism, and Popery. The author also maintains, That the Atheists, Anabaptists, and Sectaries, so much complained of, have been raised or encouraged by the doctrines and practices of the Arminian, Socinian, and Popish, party.—3 *Chillingworthi Novissima:* Or, *The Sickness, Heresy, Death, and Burial, of William Chillingworth.* 4to. pp. 61. London, 1643, and 1644.—4. *The Man of Honour Described:* A sermon from Psal. xlix. 20. Fast, before the House of Lords, March 26th, 1645. 4to. London, 1645.—5. *A Plot for the Good of Posterity:* A sermon from Gen. xviii. 19. to the House of Commons, March 25th, 1646. 4to. London, 1646.—6. *Divers Letters to Dr Jasp. Mayne, concerning false Prophets.* 4to. 1647.—7. A copy of some Letters which passed at Oxford, between him and Dr Hammond. 4to. London, 1647. —8. A Relation of a Disputation at Oxford, between Mr Cheynell, and Mr Erbury, a Socinian. 4to. London, 1646 -1647.—9. *The Divine Trinunity of the Father, Son, and Holy Spirit.* 12mo pp. 480. London, 1650. This elaborate work is in the catalogue of books in the Theological library, belonging to the students of divinity in the University of Edinburgh, 1757. And I have seen this and the author's other writings both in England and Scotland, in different places.—10. *A Discussion of Mr Fry's Tenets lately condemned in Parliament: and Socinianism proved to be an Unchristian Doctrine.*

PETER CLARK, M. A.

A MEMBER OF THE ASSEMBLY OF DIVINES AT WESTMINSTER, MINISTER AT CARNABY, AND KIRKBY-UNDERHILL, IN YORKSHIRE.

PETER CLARK was born at Beverly, a town in Yorkshire, in England, of pious parents. A Mr Peter Vinke, an eminently learned and pious divine, was often heard saying, "That he reckoned it a greater honour to have descended from pious ancestors, than if he could have derived his pedigree from the greatest princes." The subject of this memoir had the honour to have descended from pious parents. He received his first education at the place of his birth. He was eminently distinguished for his great proficiency at the school, in the early period of life. In due time, he was sent to Cambridge, and admitted student of St John's College, of which he was afterward Fellow. When he left the University, he settled at Carnaby, where his ministerial labours were acceptable and crowned with success. When the civil war commenced, he was forced to seek shelter at London, and was chosen a Member of the Assembly of Divines at Westminster. When the troubles came to an end, he returned into Yorkshire, where he was settled at Kirkby-Underhill, and he continued there until he was cast out by the Act of Uniformity. His name stands among the ejected or silenced Ministers, in the county of York, in Dr Calamy's Account. After his ejection, he retired with his wife and four children to Walkington near Hull, where he had a pretty estate which descended to him from his father. There he employed himself in teaching a private school, boarding gentlemen's sons in his house, some of whom were afterward both great ornaments and great blessings to their country. He continued there until the time of his death.[a] As the earth

a. Dr Calamy's Account, vol. ii. 2d edit. p. 822.

is the Lord's, and the fulness thereof, and he has the hearts of all flesh in his hand, and all events at his disposal, he can very easily make comfortable provision for his servants, and their families, and find useful employment for them, as seems good in his sight. *The Lord knoweth the days of the upright, and their inheritance shall be for ever. They shall not be ashamed in the evil time.* Psal. xxxvii. 18, 19.

I have not seen any of Mr Clark's writings; nor have I ever heard that he had any.

RICHARD CLEYTON, M. A. OF SHOWELL,

A MEMBER OF THE ASSEMBLY OF DIVINES AT WESTMINSTER.

RICHARD CLEYTON was one of the Assembly of Divines at Westminster, and his name occurs in the list of the members of that Assembly in this manner, in my copy of Neal's list: "Mr Richard Clayton, of Showel." Dr Calamy mentions this; but he says, "It should be Mr *Richard Cleyton*, for that was his name." And I find in the ordinance of the Lords and Commons assembled in Parliament, for calling an assembly of learned and godly divines, to be consulted with by the Parliament, for settling the government and liturgy of the church of England, he is called, *Richard Cleyton of Showell.* And in a list of those divines, which was printed with their Confession of Faith, Edinburgh, 1708, his name is, Richard Cleyton. Dr Calamy says, that he was told, Richard Cleyton was M. A. if not B. D. That he found his name to the Testimony of the Ministers in the province of Essex, to the truth of Jesus Christ, sent to the Ministers of London, and printed in 1648: But he subscribed there as Minister of Easton Magna in Essex. He removed from Essex to Showell; which is a place near Lutterworth in Leicestershire. After some time, he removed to Seighford, in the county of Stafford, from which he was cast out, in the year 1662, by the Act of Uniformity. His name stands, among many worthy names, in the venerable list of the ejected or silenced Ministers, in the county of Stafford, in England, in Dr Calamy's Account and Continuation. Afterward, he removed to Nuneaton, in Warwickshire, where he lived several years. Dr Wild was there at the same time, and these two were like David and Jonathan, most harmoniously and affectionately united, in peculiar intimacy and friendship. Their sweet social intercourse afforded them much pleasure, and was highly beneficial to themselves, in their tribulations through which they must enter into the kingdom. *Then they who feared the Lord spake often one to another; and the Lord hearkened and heard: and a book of remembrance was written before him for them who feared the Lord, and who thought upon his name.*—Dr Calamy says, that "Mr Cleyton was a good scholar, a sound divine, and one of strict piety. He was very courteous and obliging in his temper and carriage, and at the same time very sedate and grave, but not morose. His whole life adorned religion and his sacred character. He was that perfect and upright man whom the Psalmist speaks of, whose *end* is said to be *peace.*"[a]

I have not received information whether Mr Cleyton has left behind him any writings *to praise him in the gate.*

a Calamy's Continuation, vol. ii. p. 784.

THOMAS COLEMAN, M. A.

MINISTER OF GOD'S WORD AT BLYTON, IN LINCOLNSHIRE, AND A MEMBER OF THE ASSEMBLY OF DIVINES AT WESTMINSTER.

THOMAS COLEMAN was born in Oxfordshire. Wood says, that seemingly he was born within the city of Oxford, where several persons of his name and time have lived. And Neal says, that he was born at Oxford. He received his education in the ancient and famous University of Oxford. He made his first entry into Magdalen-Hall, in the beginning of the year 1615, in the seventeenth year of his age. He took the degrees in Arts, and in due time he received holy orders, and entered upon the ministerial work.

The Father of lights, the great author of every good and perfect gift, had conferred upon him distinguished genius and talents for learning the Hebrew language. For "No advantages of education, no favourable combination of circumstances, produce talents, where the Father of spirits dropped not the seeds of them in the souls which he made." [a] The Father of spirits having dropped the precious seeds of singular talents for Oriental learning in Mr Coleman, these talents were roused into exertion, unfolded, and greatly improved, by his education, and a favourable combination of circumstances, under Divine Providence. This plantation of the Lord was early and carefully watered and cultivated. And, by the close application of his vigorous mind to study, he became so complete a master of the Hebrew language, that he was commonly called *Rabbi Coleman*. His learning shed a peculiar lustre round his name. The powers of his mind were well cultivated by a liberal education.—Afterward, he was made Rector of Blyton, in Lincolnshire. At the beginning of the civil war, in

a Dr Erskine, Disc. viii. 1 Chron. xxix. 12.

1642, being persecuted by the cavaliers, or King's party, he was obliged to leave his Rectory of Blyton, and retire to London. Upon his arrival there, he was preferred to the Rectory of St. Peter's Church in Cornhill. And in 1643, he became a member of the Assembly of Divines at Westminster. Mr Wood says, " that he was chiefly called to sit in the Assembly for his knowledge in the Hebrew tongue; and that he behaved modestly and learnedly, maintaining among them the tenets of Erastus." It is certain, that Mr Coleman maintained very strenuously the tenets of Erastus in the Assembly, and was one of the chief patrons of this scheme.[a]

In order that every reader may have just conceptions of this subject, it may be necessary here to state what the sentiments of Erastus were respecting church government. He maintained, That the Lord Jesus Christ and his apostles had prescribed no particular form of discipline for the Christian church in after ages, but had left the keys in the hands of the civil magistrate, who had the sole power of punishing transgressors, and of appointing such particular forms of church-government from time to time, as were most subservient to the peace and welfare of the commonwealth. The pastoral office, in his view, was only persuasive, as a professor of the sciences over his students, without any power of the keys annexed to it. He maintained, that the Lord's Supper and other ordinances of the gospel, were to be free and open to all. That the minister might dissuade the vicious and unqualified from the communion, but might not refuse it, nor inflict any kind of censure; the punishment of all offences, either of a civil or religious nature, being reserved to the civil magistrate.—The learned Dr Lightfoot was also a great patron of this scheme, in concurrence with Mr Coleman, in the Assembly of Divines. And some of the greatest names in the House of Commons appeared keenly for it. The several parties, in this famous Assembly, of Presbyterians, Independents, and Erastians,

a Baillie's Letters, vol. ii. p. 195. Neal's Hist. Purit. vol. iii. under Erastians.

earnestly demanded that they should all make a very strict inquiry into the constitution of the primitive Christian Church, in the days of the apostles of our Lord Jesus Christ. That church being considered as founded upon the model of the Jewish synagogues, this investigation gave to Dr Lightfoot, Mr Coleman, Mr Selden, and other eminent masters of Jewish antiquities, an opportunity of displaying their superior learning, by strange interpretations of some parts of the Holy Scriptures.

When committees were chosen to prepare materials for a new form of discipline and church-government, the Independents agreed with the Presbyterians, that there was a certain form of church-government laid down in the New Testament, which was of divine institution. But when they came to the questions, What was that government? and, Was it binding in all ages of the church? both the Erastians and the Independents divided against the Presbyterians. The proposition was, "That the Scripture holds forth, that many particular congregations may, and by divine institution ought to be under one Presbyterial government." Mr Neal says, that the debate lasted thirty days; and that the Erastians did not except against the Presbyterial government as a political institution, proper to be established by the civil magistrate, but they were against the claim of a *divine right.*[a] And Mr Coleman was so very zealous upon this head, that he keenly declaimed against the Divine Right, not only in the Assembly, but also in the pulpit, apprehending that Presbytery would prove as arbitrary and tyrannical as Prelacy, if it came in with a divine claim. He therefore proposed, that the civil magistrate should have the sole power of the keys, in the mean time, until the nation should be at peace, or in a more settled state. The Independents opposed the proposition of the Divine Right of Presbytery, by advancing a contrary divine right of their own scheme. Fifteen days they stated themselves as opponents; and fifteen days they appeared in a defensive manner. The chief inquiries, in this grand debate, were,

a Neal's Hist. Purit. vol. iii. under Erastians.

respecting the constitution and form of the first church at Jerusalem; the subordination of synods, and of lay-elders. Much learning was displayed on both sides; but the main pillars of the Presbyterian government were voted to be of divine appointment by a very great majority. The Independents entered their dissent in writing, and complained of unkindly usage in the Assembly. The Assembly replied, that they were not conscious of having done them any injustice. When the Erastians saw how affairs were managed in the Assembly, they reserved themselves for the House of Commons, where they were certain, that they would be readily joined both by their own party, and by all the patrons of the Independents. Accordingly, the clause of divine right was lost in the House of Commons, to the grief and disappointment both of the Scottish Commissioners, and of their English friends in the Assembly. And the Assembly's proposition was made to stand thus, "That it is lawful and agreeable to the Word of God, that the church be governed by Congregational, Classical, and Synodical Assemblies."[a] It is not strange, that the clause of divine right was lost in the House of Commons, if Mr Baillie writes correctly; for he says that "The most of the House of Commons are downright Erastians; they are like to create us much more woe than all the sectaries of England."[b]

The Erastians endeavoured to maintain their principles, by contending strenuously, that the Jewish church and state were all one. That they knew no distinction of ecclesiastical and civil laws, nor causes; for the church of the Jews was their commonwealth, and their commonwealth was their church, and the government of church and state among them was the very same. And consequently, that in the Jewish church, there was no church-government distinct from the civil government. Mr Coleman says, "I am sure the best reformed church that ever was went this way, I mean the church of Israel, which had no distinction of church-

a Neal's Hist. Purit. vol. iii. under Erastians.
b Baillie's Letters, vol. ii. p. 96.

government and civil government."[a] In opposition to this opinion of Mr Coleman, and of other Erastians, the learned, laborious, and pious, Mr Gillespie, with many other able divines, maintained, 1. That the Jewish church was formally distinct from the Jewish state. 2. That there was an ecclesiastical Sanhedrim and government distinct from the civil. 3. That there was an ecclesiastical excommunication, distinct from civil punishments. 4. That there was also in the Jewish church a public confession or declaration of repentance, and thereupon an admission again of the offender to fellowship with the church in the holy things. 5. That there was a suspension of the profane person from the temple and passover.[b]

Mr Gillespie, in tracing the rise, growth, decay, and reviving, of Erastianism, says, That it has not the honour of being descended from honest parents. The *father* of it is the *old serpent;* it's mother is the enmity of our nature against the kingdom of our Lord Jesus Christ; and the midwife, who brought this unhappy brood into the light of the world, was Thomas Erastus, Doctor of Medicine, at Heidelberg. The Erastian error being born, the breasts which gave it suck were *profaneness* and *self-interest;* it's strong food, when advanced in growth, was arbitrary government; and it's careful tutor was Arminianism. But, nevertheless, it afterward fell into a deadly decay, the Reformed churches refusing to receive and entertain it, and so leaving it exposed to hunger and cold, to shame and nakedness; Erastus himself making some concessions, respecting the ecclesiastical censure of profane persons; and several very eminent divines making their appearance with great courage and force of solid argument against it.[c]

a Mr Coleman's Brotherly Examination Re-examined, p. 16.

b Aaron's Rod Blossoming, book i. chap. 2. Readers who wish to have a clear view of the Erastian controversy, in that period, and to see an able confutation of Erastian principles, respecting church-government, may consult, with interest, this learned, elaborate, and masterly performance, by Mr Gillespie.

c As Beza, de Excomm. & Presb. contra Erast. Ursinus, Judicium de disciplina Eccl. et Excommunicatione. Casp. Broch-

When Erastianism is said to have been at the gates of death, Mr Coleman endeavoured, with all his abilities and learning, to raise it up again. Mr Gillespie says, that though Mr Coleman was the first man, he was not the only man, who appeared in the Erastian controversy in England. He appeared publicly in this controversy, in a sermon which he preached to the House of Commons, from Job xi. 20. in Margaret's Westminster, July 30th, 1645, at the monthly Fast. It is observable, that Mr Coleman was not thanked for this sermon, according to custom, but only ordered to print it. The order runs thus: "Ordered by the Commons assembled in Parliament, That Mr Coleman be injoined to print his sermon he preached before the House of Commons the last Fast, as near as he can as he preached it. And Sir John Wray is appointed to give him notice of this Order." Mr Coleman, in his epistle dedicatory to the House of Commons, says, "There was never a sermon preached on these public Fasts, that was received with such contrary affections, and censures, as this; some approving above commendation, others disliking below detestation." He brought forth in this sermon some things which produced much speculation, and engaged him in a warm debate respecting the Erastian controversy, with the celebrated Mr Gillespie, who was one of the Commissioners from the Church of Scotland to the Assembly of Divines at Westminster.

Mr Coleman in this sermon says, "All eyes are upon government, they look upon it, as the only help. If any where, here let wisdom be used. To prescribe is above me, only let me offer two or three rules, which may either be helpful to the work, or useful to the workmen.

1. *Establish as few things by Divine Right, as can well be.* Hold out the practice, but not the ground: it will gather more, nay all, that hold it not unlawful, men differently principled may meet in one practice. It may

mand, a Lutheran, System. Theol. Tom. 2. Artic de disciplina Eccl. and many others.

be will be of larger extent than it must be. This (the Divine Right) was the only thing, that hindered union in the Assembly. Two parties came biased, the one with a National determination, the other with a Congregational engagement. The reverend Commissioners from Scotland were for the *Divine Right* of the Presbyterial. The Independents for the Congregational government. How should either move, where should they both meet? Here was the great bar, which if you can avoid, you may do much.

2. *Let all precepts, held out as divine institutions, have clear Scriptures.*—I could never yet see, how two co-ordinate governments exempt from superiority and inferiority can be in one state, and in Scripture no such thing is found, that I know of. That place, 1 Cor. v. takes not hold on my conscience for excommunication, and I admire, that Mat. xviii. should upon any; yet these two are the common places on which are erected the chiefest acts of ruling. And when I see not an institution, nor any one act of government in the whole Bible performed, how can it be evinced, that a Ruling Elder is an instituted officer? Let the Scripture speak expressly, and institutions appear institutions, and all must bow.

3. *Lay no more burden of government upon the shoulders of Ministers, than Christ hath plainly laid upon them.*—The Ministers have other work to do, and such as will take up the whole man, might I measure others by myself.—It was the king of Sodom's speech to Abraham, Give me the persons, take thou the goods: so say I, Give us doctrine, take you the government. As is said, Right Honourable, give me leave to make this request, in the behalf of the ministry, give us two things, and we shall do well;—learning and a competency.

4. *A Christian Magistrate, as a Christian Magistrate, is a governor in the Church.*—Christ has placed governments in his church, 1 Cor. xii. 28. Of other governments, beside magistracy, I find no institution; of them I do, Rom. xiii. 1, 2. I find all government given to Christ, and to Christ as Mediator, Eph. i. 22, 23. I desire all to consider it.—To rob the kingdom of Christ of the

magistrate, and his governing power, I cannot excuse, no not from a kind of sacrilege, if the magistrate be his."

These are Mr Coleman's four rules for promoting unity, and settling controversies respecting church government. The celebrated Mr Gillespie, in his Brotherly Examination of these rules, says, That Mr Coleman's cure is worse than the disease, and that instead of making any agreement, he was likely to have his hand against every man, and every man's hand against him. Mr Gillespie proceeds, after this remark, to examine the above-mentioned rules, in their order, in the following manner.

1. *Establish as few things by Divine Right, as can well be.* Which is by interpretation, as little fine gold, and as much dross, as can well be. *The words of the Lord are pure words; as silver tried in a furnace of earth, purified seven times*, Psal. xii. 6. What you take from the Word of God is *fine gold tried in the fire.* But a holy thing of man's devising is the dross of silver. Can he not be content to have the dross purged from the silver, except the silver itself be cast away? The very contrary rule is more sure and safe, which I prove thus. If it be a sin to diminish, or take any thing from the Word of God, so that it is forbidden under pain of taking away a man's part out of the book of life, out of the holy city: then as many things are to be established by Divine Right, as can well be. But it is a sin to diminish, or take any thing from the Word of God, so that it is forbidden under pain of taking away a man's part out of the book of life, and out of the holy city. Therefore, as many things are to be established by Divine Right, as can well be. The question is not now, whether this or that form of church-government be by Divine Right; but whether a church-government be by Divine Right? Has Jesus Christ so revealed his will in his word, that there should be church-censures, and that those should be dispensed by church-officers? Mr Coleman is for the negative.—*The Divine Right* is said to be *the only thing which hindered union in the Assembly.* Mr Gillespie says, If it was so, how shall Mr Coleman make himself blameless, who made union in the Assembly yet more difficult, because he

came biased a third way, with the Erastian tenets? He asks, Where the Independents and we should meet? I answer, in holding a church-government by Divine Right, that is, that the pastors and elders ought to suspend or excommunicate, according to the degree of the offence, scandalous sinners. Who can tell, but the purging of the church from scandals, and keeping the ordinances pure, when it shall be actually seen to be the great thing which is carefully attended to on both sides, may make union between us and the Independents more easily than many persons imagine. Respecting his exception against us, who are Commissioners from the Church of Scotland, I thank God, it is but such, yea not so much as the Arminians objected against the foreign divines who came to the Synod of Dort. They complained, that those divines were pre-engaged, and biased, respecting the judgment of those churches from which they came: and therefore they did not help but hinder union in that Assembly. And might not the Arians have thus objected to Alexander, who was engaged against them before he came to the Council of Nice? Might not the Nestorians have made the same objection to Cyril, because he was under an engagement against them, before he came to the Council of Ephesus? —It is no fault to be engaged for the truth, but against the truth. It is not blame-worthy, but praise-worthy, to hold fast our attainments. Notwithstanding, we have also from the beginning professed, *That we are most willing to hear and learn from the word of God, what needs farther to be reformed in the Church of Scotland.*

2. *Let all precepts, held out as divine institutions, have clear Scriptures—let the Scripture speak expressly.* Mr Gillespie says, The Scripture speaks in that manner, which seemed fittest to the wisdom of God, that is, so as it must cost us much searching of the Scripture, as men search for hidden treasure, before we find out what is the good and acceptable and perfect will of God respecting the government of his church. Will any divine deny, that it is a divine truth, which by necessary consequence is drawn from Scripture, as well as what in express words and syllables is written in it? Are not several

articles of our profession, as baptism of infants, certainly proved from Scripture, though it make no express mention thereof in words?—He says, *I could never yet see how two co-ordinate governments exempt from superiority and inferiority, can be in one state.* I suppose he has seen the co-ordinate governments of a general, and of an admiral; or if we should come lower, the governments of parents over their children, and masters over their servants, though it often fall out, that he who is subject to one man as his master, is subject to another man as his father. In one ship, there may be two co-ordinate governments, the captain governing the soldiers, and the master governing the mariners. In these, and in such like cases, you have two co-ordinate governments, when the one governor is not subordinate to the other. After other remarks here, Mr Gillespie adds, "But the reverend brother might well have spared this. It is not the independency of the church-government upon the civil government, which he intended to speak against. It is the very thing itself, a church-government, as is manifest by his other two rules."

Then he comes to his third rule, *Lay no more burden of government upon the shoulders of Ministers, than Christ has plainly laid upon them.* He means none at all, as is manifest not only by his fourth rule, under which he says, That he finds no institution of other governments beside magistracy, but also by the next words here, *The Ministers have other work to do, and such as will take up the whole man.*—You see his words tend to the taking away of all church-government out of the hands of church-officers.—Respecting Mr Coleman's observation on the king of Sodom's speech to Abraham, Gen. xiv. 21.—*learning and a competency*, Mr Gillespie very ingeniously remarks: This calls to mind a story which Clemens Alexandrinus tells us. When one had painted Helena with much gold, Apelles, looking upon the picture, said, *Friend, when you could not make her fair, you have made her rich.* Learning and competency enrich. The Jesuites have enough of both. But *government and discipline;* the removal of scandals, and the preservation of the ordinances from pollution, make the church externally fair: *beautiful as Tirzah, and comely as Jerusalem.* He had spoken more for the honour of God, and for the power of godliness, if he had said in behalf of the ministry, It were better for us to want competency and helps to learning, than to partake with other men's sins, by admitting the scandalous and profane to the Lord's table.—

Mr Coleman, under his fourth rule, says, *Of other governments, beside magistracy, I find no institution; of them I do.* Mr Gillespie says, I am sorry that he sought no better, else he had found more. Subjection and obedience are commanded, as due, not only to civil, but also to spiritual governors, to those *who are over us in the Lord,* 1 Thes. v. 12. so 1 Tim. v. 17. Heb. xiii. 7—17. And what understands he by him who rules, Rom. xii. 8? If the judgment of Gualther and of Bullinger has any weight with him, as I suppose it has, they do not there exclude, but take in, under that word, the ruling officers of the church.[a]

This debate, between Mr Coleman and Mr Gillespie, was carried on in writing, by several pamphlets, to a great extent. Beside what Mr Gillespie advanced on the subject, in his sermon from Mal. iii. 2. before the House of Lords, 27th Aug. 1645, he added to that sermon, " A Brotherly Examination of some passages of Mr Coleman's Sermon from Job xi. 20." Both were printed. Upon the publication of these, Mr Coleman published, " A Brotherly Examination Re-examined." This was followed by " *Nihil Respondes,* Thou answerest nothing," by Mr Gillespie. Mr Coleman published A Brief Reply to Mr Gillespie's Nihil Respondes, which is entitled, " *Maledicis Maledicis,* Thou Indeed Speakest Amiss." Mr Gillespie published An Answer to Mr Coleman's Maledicis, which is entitled, " *Male Audis,* Thou Hearest Amiss."—I have seen some other pamphlets on the Eras-

a Mr. Gillespie's Brotherly Examination of some passages of Mr Coleman's Sermon, from Job xi. 20. where the reader may find more on the subject.

tian controversy, on both sides, which were written at that time, and have a particular reference to this controversy, as it was carried on by Mr Coleman and Mr Gillispie. As Mr Hussey's Plea for Christian Magistracy, on Mr Coleman's side; and A Brief View of Mr Coleman's New Model of Church-government, by an anonymous author, on Mr Gillespie's side.

Mr Coleman engaged also in a public debate, respecting the Erastian controversy, in the Assembly of Divines at Westminster, against the following proposition: *Jesus Christ, as King and Head of his church, hath appointed a government in the church, in the hands of church-officers, distinct from the civil government.* He argued some days against this proposition, having full liberty both to argue and to reply as much as he pleased. But he was visited with sickness, at that time, and could not proceed in the debate. Under his sickness, he caused intimation to be made to the Assembly, that he wished them to lay aside that proposition for some time, that if God should be pleased to give him health again, he might resume his debate. The Assembly complied with his request; but the Lord, who has the hearts of all flesh in his hand, and all events at his disposal, was pleased to remove him by death, before he could accomplish his designs in this, and in some other particulars. It is said, that he intended to translate and to publish in English the book of Erastus against excommunication.[a] Mr Neal says, that Mr Lightfoot entered his dissent respecting the above proposition, with whom Mr Coleman would have joined if he had not fallen sick at this juncture and died.[b]

Mr Coleman was also much against Prelacy. He sufficiently raises his testimony, in all his writings, against the ambitious tyrannical prelacy of those times, and the gross corruption which abounded. He preached several times to the Parliament, and closely applied his doctrine to the sins of the times; the then prevailing evils. In one of his sermons to the House of Commons, he says:—

a Aaron's Rod Blossoming, Book ii. chap. i. p. 168.
b Neal's Hist. vol. iii. chap. vii. 1646.

"Our formalities and government, in the whole hierarchy, are become a fretting gangrene, a spreading leprosy, an insupportable tyranny. Up with it, up with it to the bottom, root and branch, hip and thigh: destroy these Amalekites, and let their place be no more found. I mean not the persons, but the pride, and power, and offices, of the whole rabble."[a]—"What kind of men were ordinarily seated in our Cathedrals? In a great part of late they are become the nests of idle drones, and the roosting places of superstitious formalities."[b] And, "Let popery find no favour, because it is treasonable; prelacy as little, because it is tyrannical: but establish God's truth and ways."[c]

A zealous historian, speaking in a scornful manner, says, "This was rare stuff for the blades at Westminster, and pleased them admirably well." And speaking of those divines who preached before the Parliament, the same author says, "Another of these brawlers, who seldom thought of a bishop, or the king's party, but with indignation, was Mr Thomas Coleman."—*Blessed are ye, when men shall revile you, and persecute you, and shall say all manner of evil against you falsely, for my sake.* I suppose that those persons who had felt the iron rod of the prelates, at that time in England, would readily allow, that there was certainly too much truth in Mr Coleman's remarks.

Wood says, that he was *a grand covenanter.* It is certain, that he was eminently zealous for the covenant, and preached a sermon, which has been published, at the public entering into it. In this sermon, he says, "You of our brethren of Scotland, come you and enter into this sure covenant. Lay the foundation of such an eternal league and peace, that the sun shall never see broken: all your countrymen, your kingdom are not here. Let your forwardness to this work tell us, what they would do, if they were."

During the grand debate in the Assembly at Westminster respecting church-government, he was attacked

a Serm. from Jer. viii. 20. p. 24. b Ibid. p. 39. c Ibid. p. 64.

with sickness, and his complaint rapidly increasing, he died in a few days, and the whole Assembly paid the last tribute of respect to his memory by attending his funeral in a body, on the 30th of March, 1647.

Mr Coleman was of Erastian principles respecting church-government; but he is generally allowed to have been a very learned and pious divine. Fuller says, that he was "a modest and learned divine, equally averse to Presbytery and Prelacy."

Mr Coleman has written and published;

1. *The Christian's Course and Complaint, both in the pursuit of Happiness desired, and for Advantages slipped in that pursuit:* a Sermon preached to the Honourable House of Commons, from Jer. viii. 20. on the day of the Monthly Fast, Aug. 30th, 1643, at Margaret's Church, Westminster. 4to. pp. 71, with an Epistle Dedicatory to the Honourable House of Commons, consisting of four pages, closely printed, under the date of Sept. 11th, 1643. London, 1643. At the end of this sermon is added, "A Thanksgiving unto God taken out of the Form of Prayer and Administration of the Sacraments used in the Church of Scotland, after their deliverance from the tyranny of the Frenchmen, by the English: with prayers made for the continuation of peace between the realms of England and Scotland. Printed at Edinburgh, by Thomas Bassandine, in the year of our Lord, 1575." A truly valuable and pious piece of curiosity.

2. *The Heart's Engagement:* a Sermon preached from Jer. xxx. 21, last clause of the verse, at Margaret's Church, Westminster, at the public entering into the Covenant, Sept. 29th, 1643. 4to. London, 1643. Glasgow, 1741, and 1799, in a Collection of Sermons and Speeches at taking the Covenant.

3. *God's Unusual Answer to a Solemn Fast:* a Sermon preached from Psal. lxv. 5. before both Houses of Parliament, at an extraordinary Fast, Sept. 12th, 1644. 4to. pp. 30. London, 1644.

4. *Hopes Deferred and Dashed:* a Sermon preached from Job xi. 20, to the Honourable House of Commons,

in Margaret's Church, Westminster, July 30th, 1645, the day of the Monthly Fast. 4to. pp. 35. London, 1645.

5. *A Brotherly Examination Re-examined:* or, a clear Justification of those Passages in a Sermon, against which Mr Gillespie did both preach and write. 4to. London, 1646. To this piece is added, A short Discovery of some Tenets which intrench upon the Honour and Power of Parliaments.

6. *Maledicis Maledicis:* or, A Brief Reply to Mr Gillespie's Nihil Respondes. Also,

7. *The Brief View Briefly Viewed.* Being Animadversions upon a nameless author, in a book, called, A Brief View of Mr Coleman's New Model. 4to. pp. 39. London, 1646.

JOHN CONANT, D. D.

AN EMINENT ENGLISH DIVINE.

JOHN CONANT was born at Yeatenton, a small village in Devonshire, England, upon the 18th of October, in the year 1608. He was descended from a very good family, of a competent estate. The family had flourished many years in that county, but was originally *French.* The illustrious subject of these memoirs was educated in classical learning at private schools, under the inspection of his uncle. the Rev. John Conant; who entered him a student of Exeter-College in Oxford, in the year 1626. In that famous Seminary, he studied with unremitting diligence, and exhibited those distinguishing abilities which he displayed in the succeeding part of his life. To men of such indefatigable industry, we are much indebted. The vigour and activity of his mind were great. And by close application, he was soon eminently distinguished, as a linguist, for the purity and perspicuity of his Latin style, and his particular acquaintance with the Greek language. He was so complete a Master of the

Greek, that he often disputed publicly in that language in the schools. He gained the esteem and respect of his superiors; and was accounted one of the most able disputants in the public schools. He maintained at the same time the most regular and irreproachable manners. His extraordinary accomplishments recommended him very highly to Dr John Prideaux, then Rector of Exeter-College, who applauded him by the following witticism upon his name: *Conanti nihil difficile.* To him who *endeavours* nothing is difficult. The force of the expression is lost in a translation. In one sense, it implies, to him who endeavours, every thing is easy; and in another, there is nothing difficult to Conant. Dr Prideaux was also at that time the King's Professor of Divinity; and he was accustomed to say, respecting this excellent scholar, "*Jack Conant* will have my place." And it is remarkable, that both those eminent places then enjoyed by Dr Prideaux, were afterward conferred on Dr Conant. He took his degrees regularly; and, upon the third of July 1633, he was chosen Fellow of Exeter-College, in which he became a very eminent tutor. It is said, that his fame, as a tutor, procured him pupils from the best families in England.

Upon the commencement of the civil war, between the King and the Parliament, the greater part of his pupils left the University; and he thought it most expedient to retire himself, which he did in the year 1642, after having first obtained Deacon's orders, and been qualified by the more appropriate studies for the useful discharge of the ministerial function. He went first to Lymington, in Somersetshire, where his uncle and namesake was minister. His uncle being fled, in these troublesome times, and he then in orders, he officiated there as long as he could continue with safety. It is said, That while he was at Lymington, he was constituted by the Parliament a member of the Assembly of Divines at Westminster; but that he never sat among them, or at least very seldom, since it is certain, that he never took the covenant.[a] Be that as

a Middleton's Biogr. Evan. vol. iv. Gen. Biogr. vol. iii.

it may, he followed his uncle to London, and assisted him sometime in the discharge of the pastoral duties, in a parish of that city. He became a domestic chaplain to Lord Chandos, in whose family he lived at Harefield, near Uxbridge, in Middlesex. While he continued with his Lordship, he had a gratuitous lecture at Uxbridge, upon a work-day, to numerous audiences, with very great applause. He resigned his Fellowship of Exeter-College, on the 27th of Sept. in the year 1647; but, upon the 7th of June 1649, he was unanimously chosen Rector of that College, on the death of Dr Hakewell: a strong proof of the high esteem in which he was held, by that learned Society where he had been educated. He obtained that place without any application of his own; and keeping up a severe discipline, Exeter-College flourished, during his time, more than any College in Oxford, according to Wood. In a very short time, however, after he was comfortably settled, in that honourable office, he was in great danger of being driven again out of all public employment, by the Parliament's enjoining what was called the Engagement, which he did not take within the time which was prescribed. His principles, and the regulations of the then ruling powers, did not agree. He was allowed a fort-night for deliberation on the subject, and permitted to subscribe with a very peculiar explanatory declaration, his character being held in very high estimation. The terms of the engagement were: "You shall promise to be true and faithful to the Commonwealth of England, as it is now established without King or House of Lords." Mr Conant's declaration before the commissioners, when he took the engagement, was in this form: "Being required to subscribe, I humbly promise, First, That I be not hereby understood to approve of what hath been done in order unto, or under this present government, or the government itself: Nor will I be thought to condemn it, they being things above my reach, and I not knowing the grounds of the proceedings. Secondly, That I do not bind myself to do any thing contrary to the Word of God. Thirdly, That I do not so hereby bind myself, but that, if God shall remarkably call me to submit to any other power, I may be at liberty to obey that call, notwithstanding the present engagement. Fourthly, In this sense, and in this sense only, I do promise to be true and faithful to the present government, as it is now established without King or House of Lords."

Having surmounted this difficulty, he went on to discharge the duties of his office of Rector of Exeter-College with peculiar zeal and diligence. In this dignified situation, he soon acquired the esteem and approbation of all whose support could afford him any encouragement. He applied himself, with great success, to restore the reputation of the revenues of his College, which, by sums of money advanced for the king's assistance, and by different calamities, had become very much embarrassed. What was of far greater utility and importance, he was peculiarly attentive to the restoration and maintenance of proper discipline. To this great object he cheerfully devoted himself with indefatigable ardour, intense application, great watchfulness, and prudence, until he had secured to his College so high a reputation in that fundamental point, that it overflowed with students from every part of the nation, and even from foreign countries. Many of these students were eminently distinguished for their literary attainments, or afterward filled respectable situations, both in the state, and in the church. In the year 1654, he was admitted to the degree of Doctor in Divinity, and in Dec. the same year, he was appointed Professor of Divinity in the University of Oxford, in the place of Dr Hoyle, who was deceased. This appointment afforded great satisfaction to numerous and learned auditors who attended his lectures. In the year 1657, he accepted the impropriate Rectory of Abergeley near St. Asaph in Denbighshire, as some satisfaction for the benefices, formerly annexed to the Divinity-chair, which he never enjoyed, but knowing that it had belonged to the Bishopric of St Asaph, he immediately quitted it, upon the establishment of episcopacy. On the 19th of Oct. 1657, he was raised to the high dignity of Vice-chancellor of that famous University, which he held until the first of

August 1660. He preached often both on Sabbath and work-days in different churches in Oxford, without accepting any compensation for his services. In the honourable office which he now filled, he eminently distinguished himself by the correction of abuses; the regulation of the public exercises, in such a manner as proved highly beneficial to the interests of religion and of solid learning; by being instrumental in procuring Mr Selden's large and valuable collection of books for the public library; and by great vigilance and firmness in his attention to the rights and privileges of the University. He is also said to have had a considerable share in defeating a design for erecting an University at Durham, to which the Protector, Oliver Cromwell, had given his consent. His prejudices in favour of the body over which he presided, and of the other University, might lead him to hinder this measure, which might have proved highly beneficial to the northern counties of England. Their distance from the grand seats of learning occasions much inconvenience and expence, and may deprive some persons of the advantages of a liberal education, who might enjoy it, if there was an University at Durham, or some more central place.

Upon the restoration of King Charles Second, Dr Conant, as Vice-chancellor of the University of Oxford, came up to London, attended by the Proctors of the University, and many of the most illustrious and learned members thereof, to present a congratulatory address to his majesty. The Doctor was introduced to the king, to whom he made a Latin speech, and presented a book of verses, which were written by the members of the University. On the 25th of March 1661, the king issued a commission for reviewing the Book of Common Prayer. Dr Conant was appointed one of the Commissioners, and assisted in conducting the conferences at the Savoy. He is placed among those divines who were for alterations in the hierarchy of the Church. And afterward, when the act of uniformity had passed, he could not submit to its terms. He refused to conform to the ceremonies and discipline of the Church of England. He was then deprived of his preferments, and disabled from the public exercise of his ministerial duties, and accordingly his Rectory of Exeter-College was pronounced vacant, upon the first of Sept. 1662.

He continued in this state about eight years. A Mr Edmund Trench, who had been determined for the ministry, and was very willing to have conformed, but had some scruples which he could not remove, sent his scruples to Dr Conant for his resolution. After half a year's expectation, the Doctor sent him the following message; That *upon the most serious thoughts he could hardly satisfy himself; and therefore would never persuade any to conform while he lived.*[a] But, after eight year's deliberation upon the interesting subject of conformity, Dr Conant himself complied, and was re-ordained upon the 28th of Sept. in 1670, by Dr Reynold's, bishop of Norwich; whose daughter he had married in Aug. 1651, and by whom he had six sons and as many daughters. Preferments were offered him immediately, and on the 18th of Dec. 1670, he was elected Minister of Mary Aldermanbury, in London; but having spent some years in the town of Northampton, where he was much respected and beloved, he fixed his choice rather on that place, and accepted the invitation of his acquaintance and neighbours to remain among them. And Dr Simon Ford, who was then Minister of All-Saints, in the ancient burough of Northampton, going to Mary's Aldermanburry, Dr Conant was nominated to succeed him at Northampton, where he continued until his death.

On the 20th of Sept 1675, he had the mortification to see the greatest part of his parish, together with his church, burned to the ground, though in the goodness of Divine Providence his own house was mercifully preserved. He makes some very pertinent remarks, enforcing religious duties, respecting this alarming dispensation of Divine Providence, in his Sermon from Ezra ix. 13, 14. vol. 1. He says, " Though God hath severely handled us, yet he *hath in wrath remembered mercy*, *and*

a Calamy's Account, vol. ii. pp. 389, 390.

punished us less than our iniquities deserve. If we take a true estimate of his dealings with us, we cannot chuse but discern much lenity and moderation, much tenderness and compassion to have been mingled with his severity, in many respects. 1. He who turned your houses into ashes and rubbish, and took away a great part of your substance, might have taken all, and left you nothing. 2. He might by the same terrible fire that deprived you of your estate, have also deprived you of your children and dearest relations. The loss of one child in such a way of terrible Providence would have troubled you more, and have gone nearer your heart than the loss of all your estate. 3. It might have been your own lot to have perished in the flames. God who mercifully spared you, and rescued you from the violence of the fire, might by it have hurried you out of this world into hell, and sent you from one fire to another. This fire was terrible, but the unquenchable fire of hell had been much more terrible.—How mercifully and favourably hath God treated you amid his greatest severities, seeing none of these things have befallen you, or any of your's! O then go one step further with Ezra in the text, and say, *After all that is come upon us for our evil deeds, and for our great trespass, and seeing thou hast punished us less than our iniquities deserve, should we again break thy commandments?"*

A word fitly spoken is like apples of gold in pictures of silver. This able spiritual instructor very wisely adapted his public discourses to the particular circumstances and necessities of his hearers, as the prudent householder *gives to every one his portion of meat in due season.* On the 8th of June in 1676, he was installed Archdeacon of Norwich, in the place of Mr John Reynolds, his brother-in-law, deceased. The Bishop offered him that preferment, with this singular compliment, "I do not expect thanks from you, but I shall be very thankful to you if you will accept of it." He accepted it after some deliberation, and discharged the office in a very becoming manner, as long as health permitted him.

It should be observed here, that he constantly resided

in his parish, except when his other offices absolutely required his attendance, and always officiated in person, preaching twice every Lord's day, and carefully inculcating practical religion in the plainest and most pathetic language. He composed his sermons in such a manner, that the meanest person might understand them, and the most judicious had no cause to despise them. He neither offended the weak brother, nor gave advantage to the malicious critic. In the evenings he catechised the children; and among them his own were always present. He was peculiarly attentive to the visitation of the sick. His clerk had strict orders to inform him when any persons were sick; and then, without staying to be sent for, he readily waited upon the meanest of his flock. He entered the cottages of the poor, as willingly as the houses of the rich. He was no respecter of persons. He was not afraid to speak freely when it was necessary. Where he saw the appearance of indigence, he relieved in a bountiful manner. He was very charitable in general. At Northampton, for twenty years together, he paid for the schooling of poor children, never fewer than twenty-four, and sometimes nearer forty; and these he placed out with several needy widows, that what he gave might contribute to their assistance. He was, upon all occasions, ready to promote the relief sought by strangers; of which various instances are given in his son's memoirs. He was one of the most remarkable casuists in his time, and was not only resorted to by some persons who lived at a great distance, but his advice was also asked, by letters, even from foreigners. As his duties occupied a great part of his time, his necessary relaxations were short, and such as few persons would have accounted recreation. Reading a few pages in the classics, hearing some remarkable piece of history, and discoursing upon it to his children, or explaining to them some point in Natural Philosophy, that they might have just conceptions of the wisdom of Divine Providence, and an early impression of the reverence due to it's glorious Author, are said to have been his only diversions. "He knew the worth of time too well, to trifle it away in vain amusements, in idle visits, in unprofitable studies, or needlessly to immerse himself in secular business, in political schemes, or any thing else foreign to his office. Impatient of whatever would divert him from his work, or retard him in it, he counted those hours lost, in which he was not either getting good to his own soul, doing good to the souls of others, or acquiring greater fitness for his important trust." But with all his strictness of manners, he had nothing either of moroseness or pride. He possessed great evenness of temper, which never rose higher than being cheerful. He was not depressed by temporal losses or bodily pain. He was clothed with humility, which appeared with peculiar lustre upon all occasions. He despised form and ceremonies; yet, from natural sweetness of temper, he was affable, kind and condescending to all, even to the meanest person in his parish.

Upon the 3d of Dec. 1681, he was installed a Prebendary in the church of Worcester. The Earl of Radnor, an old friend and contemporary of his at Exeter-College, asked it for him from King Charles Second, in the following terms: "Sir, I come to beg a preferment of you for a very deserving person, who never sought any thing for himself;" and upon naming him, the king very kindly consented.

In the year 1686, after his eyes had been sometime weak, he lost his sight entirely; but he did not die until the 12th of March, 1693, when he was in the eighty-sixth year of his age. He bore his affliction with very much Christian resignation. His mortal remains were buried in his own parish church of All-Saints in Northampton, where a monument was erected over him by his widow with a suitable inscription. He left behind him a son of both his names, Doctor of the Civil Law, sometime Fellow of Merton-College, and an eminent Advocate.

Doctor Conant was a man of very solid and extensive learning; yet so modest, it is said, that though he understood most of the Oriental languages, and was particularly versed in the Syriac, few people knew it. Dr Calamy, in his Account of the ejected Ministers, vol. ii. p. 76, says: "Neither must I forget that excellent person, John

Conant, D. D. Rector of Exeter-College, who having been one of the Commissioners at the Savoy, left his place in 1662, and continued a Non-conformist seven years or thereabouts, and at last conformed, and became a Minister in Northampton. But his temper was so like that of his ejected brethren, and he preached with that plainness, and that care to approve himself to the consciences of all, that both by such as were in the Church, and such as were out of it, he was generally ranked with the Presbyterians all his days.

Six volumes of Dr Conant's Sermons have been published: The first, London, in 1693, and dedicated by himself to the inhabitants of Northampton, and more especially to those of the parish of All-Saints there; the second after his death, in 1697, by John Bishop of Chichester; the third in 1690; the fourth in 1703; the fifth in 1708, by the same Editor; the sixth in 1722, by Digby Cotes, M. A. Principal of Magdalen-Hall in Oxford; all in 8vo. Dr Conant's Sermons were advertised for sale in Mr Ogle's Theological Catalogue, London, 1811, p. 119, 6 vols. 18s.

There were two men of the name of John Conant, in England, at that time, who were both very eminent and learned divines; the uncle and the nephew. They were both Fellows of Exeter-College in Oxford; and they seem to have been confounded by several writers. It has been said by different writers, that while Dr Conant, who was born at Yeatenton in 1608, was at Lymington officiating in his uncle's place, he was constituted by the Parliament one of the Assembly of Divines at Westminster. This is seemingly a mistake; for in the ordinance of Parliament, for calling an Assembly of Divines, John Conant of Lymington, Bachelor in Divinity, is mentioned. This John Conant was Rector, or Pastor, of Lymington, several years; at least from 1620 to 1643, when he was called to sit in the Assembly of Divines at Westminster; but how long before or after these dates, I cannot tell.

In writing the above account of the learned and pious Dr Conant, who went to the College in the year 1626, and removed from the University in the year 1642, I very much doubted if he was the John Conant, who was the member of the Assembly of Divines. Having always endeavoured to render this work as correct and full as possible, the account of Dr Conant was written with the utmost care and caution respecting this matter; and all sources of information which I had have now been carefully consulted. Wood, who is generally very correct in such matters, in his Account of Dr Conant, makes no mention of his being a member of the Assembly of Divines at Westminster, nor of his being called to sit there, which he would very readily have done, if he had been a member of that conspicuous body. But Wood says, that John Conant, who was Rector of Lymington Somersetshire, was one of the Assembly of Divines. Giving an account of his commencing Bachelor of Divinity, in the year 1620, he says: "John Conant, lately Fellow of Exeter-College, now Rector of Lymington in Somersetshire.—He was afterward one of the Assembly of Divines, and the writer and publisher of *The Woe and Weal of God's People:* Fast. Sermon before the House of Commons, 26th July 1643, on Jer. xxx. 7. London, 1643. 4to.; and another on Lam. iii. 31, 32, printed the same year in 4to. But this last I have not yet seen, or any thing else of his extant." [a]

It is now my opinion that not Dr Conant, but John Conant, B. D. and Pastor of Lymington in Somersetshire, was the member of the Assembly of Divines at Westminster. If I am wrong, I wish to be set right; but this now seems to be the truth. I shall, therefore, give what account I am able of the Rev. John Conant of Lymington.—He was sometime Fellow of Exeter-College in Oxford. It is said, that he was nine years a Fellow of that College. When he became Rector or Pastor of Lymington, I cannot tell; but he proceeded Bachelor of Divinity on the

a Wood's Ath. Oxon. vols. i. & ii. under John Conant. Second edition.

28th of June, in the year 1620, and he was at that time Pastor of Lymington. In this situation, he seems to have met with much opposition and trouble, for want of strict conformity, and on account of some zealous and laudable exertions in his ministerial work. Something of his real spirit and temper, and also of his history, and of the troubles which he met with on account of his zeal and faithfulness in the honourable service of his Master, may be readily collected from the following papers.

No. I. *The Testimony of John Conant, Rector of Lymington, within the Diocese of Bath and Wells,* Jan. 1640.

Having continued in my own parish church a Lecture for the space of ten or eleven years, viz. from 1622, until 1633, first once every fortnight, and afterward weekly, without any considerable intermission, without any prohibition or the least discouragement from Bishop Lake and his successors, until Bishop Pierce his coming into this Diocese, and after his, the said Bishop Pierce, coming to Wells, I being told that he was an adversary to Lectures, that a storm was coming, and having heard that some more public Lectures were already suppressed, I thought it a meet and inoffensive way to repair unto the said Bishop and crave his leave and liking for the continuance of my Lecture, which I did, taking with me a grave and orthodox minister of mine ancient acquaintance, viz. Mr John Vivian, that he might, if need required, give testimony unto such passages as should intercede between the Bishop and myself. But the Bishop taking me into an inner room beckoned unto Mr Vivian, as he himself told me, signifying that he should stay behind, notwithstanding which I yet earnestly and humbly intreated the said Bishop Pierce to afford me his approbation and encouragement in my said Lecture, alledging to this purpose, that I was Bachelor in Divinity, and a preacher licensed by the University, also that the Lecture was within mine own parish, and upon a day appointed for Common Prayer by our Church, and that I was willing to employ the time and talent which God had vouchsafed me for the benefit and instruction of my people, who much needed the same. Yet the said Bishop utterly denied me any such leave or approbation, telling me that such as come to my church on Wednesdays should hear the Litany and be gone, withal requiring me once and again not to proceed any once more in my said Lecture or Exposition, (which he called preaching) on Wednesdays, as I would answer the contrary. And when I humbly desired to know the reason why he should so strictly prohibit me beyond some others, who then continued their wonted weekly preaching in their own churches, and within the same Diocese without any such restraint; alledging no reason for his so doing, he answered, that it was in his power to inhibit or licence whom he would, though within their own cures, to preach any such weekly Lecture within his Diocese, and therewith promised me as a pretended favour, that if any else within his said Diocese did continue any such Lecture, I should enjoy the like liberty; but added, that his purpose was not to permit any. That this was the sum of my suit unto Bishop Pierce, and of his Lordship's answer returned unto me, or in words to this effect, I can and by these presents do truly testify, and shall be ready by oath, if called upon, to confirm the same. *John Conant.*

No. II. *Another Testimony of the said John Conant,* May 4th 1640. (Written after his Lecture was discontinued.)

Being demanded whence it came that I discontinued my Wednesday's Exposition,—my answer is this—(repeating the substance of his former interview with the Bishop, and adds) he told me that it was not in my power to make holy days: that by preaching on Wednesdays, I drew men from their callings, &c.—When a Mr Ford said to the Bishop, What if I should go on with my Lecture? The Bishop replied, that he would suspend him. Mr Ford said, What if Mr Conant appeal? He answered, that he knew the Archbishop's mind well enough already. The Bishop gave charge publicly, that in catechising children and servants, no other question should be asked, nor any other answers given than such as in express words are mentioned in the Catechism contained in the Book of Common Prayer. For transgressing this unreasonable charge, the Bishop enjoined an ancient and laborious minister of his Diocese open penance in the public congregation. Mr Conant entreated the Bishop that he might enjoy his former liberty, for asking some other questions, and receiving some other answers, tending to unfold more plainly those which are expressed in the Catechism in the Book of Common Prayer. But this liberty was denied.[a]

I have given an account of John Conant, D. D. because some eminent writers have represented him as a member of the Assembly of Divines at Westminster, at least, as called to sit in that Assembly. I have also given what information I could respecting John Conant, B. D. Rector, or Pastor, of Lymington, in Somersetshire, because it appears to me that John Conant of Lymington was really the member of the Assembly of Divines at Westminster.

It may be added, that Mr Conant was appointed one of the Select Committee for the examination and approbation of ministers who petitioned for sequestered livings. In the year 1644, he was also upon the Committee for the examination and ordination of ministers.[b]

I have not seen any of Mr Conant's writings, except the above-mentioned sermon from Jer. xxx. 7, in Wood's Account of him. This sermon is found in the volumes of sermons, which were preached to the Long Parliament. In it, the author discovers much faithfulness in his station, and true zeal for the Reformation. 4to. pp. 46, with an Epistle Dedicatory to the House of Commons, of 4 pages. London, 1643.

a Palmer's Nonconf. Mem. 2d edit. vol. i. p. 229, &c.

b Neal's Puritans, vol. iii. chap. ii. & iv.

EDWARD CORBET, D. D.

OF MERTON-COLLEGE, OXFORD,

A MEMBER OF THE ASSEMBLY OF DIVINES AT WESTMINSTER, AND PASTOR OF GREAT HASELY, IN OXFORDSHIRE.

EDWARD CORBET was born at Pontesbury, in Shropshire, in the year 1602. He was descended from the ancient family of Corbets in that County, and educated in Merton-College, Oxford, where he was chosen Fellow, having taken the degrees in Arts. He was made Proctor of the University, but, upon refusing conformity in certain points, he was called before the Vice-chancellor. It is said, that he was no enemy to the Church of England, but he could not with a good conscience observe all her superstitious ceremonies. And while the Vice-chancellor laid his case before Archbishop Laud, Chancellor of the University, he petitioned his Lordship for relief; but it was not likely that he could obtain the least redress. Upon the commencement of the civil war, Oxford being garrisoned by the King's forces, he was deprived of his Fellowship, and expelled from the College, because he refused to espouse the Royal cause. Archbishop Laud, being afterward prisoner in the Tower, refused him the Rectory of Chatham, in Kent, because he was a Puritan; and when he was appointed Rector of that place, by an ordinance of Parliament, May 17th, 1643, his Lordship still continued to refuse his allowance, but his refusal was unavailing. Mr Corbet was a witness against Archbishop Laud at his trial, and deposed "that, in the year 1638, his Grace visiting Merton-College, by his Deputy, Sir John Lamb, one article propounded to the Wardens and Fellows was, Whether they made due reverence, by bowing toward the altar, when they came into the Chapel—That he and Mr Cheynell were enjoined by the Visitors and Commissioners to use this ceremony; but they refused;

for which, though he assigned his reasons for refusing, he was particularly threatened.—That, after this, Dr Frewin, the Vice-chancellor, told him that he was sent to him by the Archbishop, requiring him to use this ceremony.—That the Archbishop afterward sent injunctions to Merton-College, requiring them to bow toward the altar, and the Visitors questioned those who refused.—And that in Magdalen-College there was a crucifix placed over the communion table, and pictures in the windows; and a new crucifix was set up in Christ's Church, none of which innovations were ever heard of before the time of the Archbishop."

Mr Corbet was chosen one of the Assembly of Divines at Westminster, became a member, and in Neal's list is marked as giving constant attendance. He is also said to have been one of the Committee for the examination and ordination of Ministers, and one of the Preachers before the Parliament. He was likewise appointed one of the Preachers with a view to reconcile the scholars in Oxford to the Parliament, in the year 1646; but, according to Wood, he soon quitted that employment, whereby that duty lay on the shoulders of only six persons. Walker says, "The Parliament made a farther advance toward the more immediate appearance of their authority in a *visitation*, by sending their harbingers to prepare the way for it. These were seven Divines whom they dispatched to Oxford to reduce the University to a better temper; and to dispose them to a reconciliation with the Parliament and their proceedings. The persons pitched on for this purpose, were Mr Robert Harris of Hanwell, in Oxfordshire; Mr Edward Reynolds, formerly of Merton-College; Mr Henry Wilkinson, Senior of Magdalen-Hall; Mr Francis Cheynell, Mr Edward Corbet, both of Merton-College; Mr Henry Cornish, formerly of New-Inn-Hall, and Mr Langley, formerly of Pembroke-College.[a] Mr Corbet was also appointed one of the Visitors of that University, and Orator and Canon of Christ's Church, in the room of

a Walker's Sufferings of the Clergy, Part i. p. 125. See Cheynell's Life, pp. 230, 231.

Dr Henry Hammond. It has been observed, "that, though he was one of the Visitors, he seldom or never sat among them. And when he usually preached at Mary's Church, the year before the King was beheaded, he would, in his long prayer before sermon, desire *that God would open the King's eyes to lay to heart all the blood that he had spilt. And that he would prosper the Parliament and their blessed proceedings.*" However, he did not continue long in this situation; but, being made Rector of Great Hasely, in Oxfordshire, he removed to the charge of his flock, *over which the Holy Ghost had made him overseer, to feed the church of God, which he has purchased with his own blood.* He continued there until his death. He took his degree of Doctor of Divinity on April 12th, in the year 1648. He died in London, in January, in 1657, aged fifty-five years, or thereabout. His remains were conveyed to Great Hasely, and interred in the chancel of the church.

Dr Corbet is allowed to have been a good divine, a valuable preacher, and very remarkable for his integrity. His wife was daughter of Sir Nathaniel Brent, and granddaughter of Dr Robert Abbot, bishop of Salisbury. She is said to have been a lady of most exemplary piety. Her funeral sermon was preached by Dr Wilkinson, and afterward published, with some account of her excellent character. Some of Bishop Abbot's manuscripts fell into Dr Corbet's hands, particularly his Latin Commentary upon the whole Epistle to the Romans. This learned and laborious work, in four volumes folio, Dr Corbet deposited in the Bodleian library, Oxford, where, we are told, it still remains.[a]

Dr Corbet seems to have been the author of *The Worldling's Looking-glass; or, The Danger of Losing his Soul for Gain*, 1630. And he has published, *God's Providence;* A sermon preached from 1 Cor. i. 27, before the House of Commons, at their Solemn Fast, Dec.

a Wood's Ath. vols. i. and ii. Brook's Lives of the Puritans, vol. iii.

28th, 1642. 4to. London, 1647. Probably he has some other writings which I have not seen.

PHILIP DELME

WAS A MEMBER OF THE ASSEMBLY OF DIVINES AT WESTMINSTER.

HE is, in Mr Neal's list, marked as giving constant attendance. He is also said to have been a superadded divine. And he was one of those who subscribed that proposition, That "Jesus Christ, as King and Head of his Church, hath appointed a government in the Church, in the hands of Church-officers, distinct from the civil government." But I cannot give the reader any farther account of Mr Philip Delme.

CALIBUTE DOWNING, D. D.

WAS CHOSEN ONE OF THE ASSEMBLY OF DIVINES AT WESTMINSTER; BUT, IN NEAL'S LIST, HE IS MARKED AS WITHDRAWING, OR SELDOM APPEARING, THOUGH HE SEEMS TO HAVE BEEN SOMETIME IN THE ASSEMBLY, AND TO HAVE TAKEN THE PROTESTATION.

CALIBUTE DOWNING was born at Shenington, in Gloucestershire, in the year 1604. He was descended from an ancient and respectable family, and educated in Oriel-College, Oxford. After he had finished his studies at the University, and entered upon the Ministerial work, he became successively Rector of Ickford, in Buckinghamshire, of West Ilsley, in Berkshire, and Vicar of Hackney, near London.

In the year 1640, Dr Downing, in a sermon before the artillery company, maintained, "that for the defence of religion, and the reformation of the Church, it was lawful to take up arms against the King, if it could be obtained no other way." For this, he was forced to abscond, and he retired to the house of the Earl of Warwick, in Essex, until the meeting of the Long Parliament. In the year 1643, he resigned his Vicarage, and was succeeded by Dr Spurstowe, who was afterward one of the ejected Non-conformists. Upon the commencement of the civil war, he became Chaplain to Lord Roberts, in the army of the Earl of Essex. In that office, he has incurred the very heavy censure of the High-church historians.—He was appointed one of the licensers of the press. Wood says, That "in 1643, he shewed himself a grand Covenanter, and thereupon was made one of the Assembly of Divines." Dr Downing died, in the year 1644, aged forty years; and he has left behind him the character of a pious man, a warm preacher, and a very zealous promoter of the interests of the Redeemer's kingdom, and of the welfare of his country. Sir George Downing, of East Hatley, in Cambridgeshire, was a son of his.

Dr Downing's writings are;

1. *A Discourse of the State Ecclesiastical of this Kingdom, in relation to the Civil*, 1633.

2. *A Digression* discussing some ordinary Exceptions against Ecclesiastical officers, 1633.

3. A Discovery of the False grounds which the Bavarian Party have laid to settle their own Faction, and shake the peace of the Empire. 4to. London, 1641.

4. A Discourse upon the Interest of England, 1641.

5. A Discoursive Conjecture upon the Reasons which produce the present Troubles of Great Britain, different from those of Lower Germany. 4to. London, 1641. And several Sermons.[a]

a Wood's Athenæ Oxon. vol. ii. Brook's Lives of the Puritans, vol. ii.

THE REV. JOHN DURY,

A SCOTCHMAN, AND LEARNED DIVINE, WHO WAS EMINENTLY DISTINGUISHED BY HIS INDEFATIGABLE INDUSTRY TO PROMOTE UNION AMONG CHRISTIANS, AND A MEMBER OF THE ASSEMBLY OF DIVINES AT WESTMINSTER.

JOHN DURY was born in Scotland; but in what part of it, or at what time, I cannot inform the reader. Wood says that he was a Scotchman, and became a sojourner in the University of Oxford, in the month of July, in the year 1624, for the sake of the public library, but how long he continued there, he could not tell. Afterward, he travelled into various foreign countries, particularly through most parts of Germany, where he visited the recesses of the Muses. Having continued a considerable time in those parts, he spoke the German language so well and fluently, that, upon his return to England, he was taken for a native of Germany. Wood adds, that he was by profession a Divine and a Preacher, but whether he took orders according to the Church of England, which he always scrupled, doth not appear. He is said, however, to have overcome these scruples, by some means. For, though he had been ordained in one of the foreign Reformed Churches, he was required to be re-ordained before he could be admitted to a benefice in England. He, accordingly, submitted to the renewal of his ordination under the hands of Bishop Hall of Exeter.[a]

Mr Dury was for several years employed in a design of promoting a reconciliation between the Calvinists and Lutherans abroad; or as he himself usually expressed it, "for making and settling a Protestant union and peace in the Churches beyond the seas." He was eminently distinguished by his extraordinary zeal and activity in endeavouring to promote this desirable union. Strongly possessed with hopes of success, he applied for a dispensation of non-residence upon his Living, in order that he might

a Prynne's Cant. Doome, p. 390. as with Brook.

travel through the Christian world, with a view to accomplish this object. And he not only procured a license for that purpose, but seems also to have at first obtained the approbation and recommendation of Archbishop Laud, though he appears afterwards to have thrown some difficulties in Mr Dury's way. Mr Dury, however, was assisted, in this great undertaking, by Bishop Hall, and Bishop Bedell of Kilmore in Ireland. Bishop Bedell loved to bring men into the communion of the Church of England, in a voluntary way, and was of opinion, that Protestants would agree well enough if they could be brought to understand each other. He was therefore induced to promote Mr Dury's design, and, toward defraying the expenses of which, he subscribed twenty pounds a-year. Mr Dury began by publishing his plan of an union, in the year 1634; and, the same year, he appeared at a famous Assembly of Lutherans at Frankfort in Germany. The Churches also of Transylvania sent him their advice and counsel the same year; and he afterward transacted with the Divines of Sweden and Denmark. He quickly turned his attention to every quarter. He consulted the Universities, communicated their answers, and he was not discouraged by the ill success which he met with. He had conference with the learned Divines on this subject, in most places on the Continent, and obtained their approbation of his design. It is said, that he afterward endeavoured to unite, not only the Lutherans and Calvinists, but even the whole Christian world.

Both Mr Dury and his enterprise have been very warmly censured, by some writers; but it is evident, that he was honest in his intention, and his undertaking has received the warmest patronage and encouragement of many very celebrated divines. In the year 1635, he exchanged several letters upon the interesting subject, with the eminently learned Mr Joseph Mede, Fellow of Christ's College, Cambridge, in England. He first solicited this celebrated scholar to give his thoughts upon the best method of pursuing the design; and then stated the method in which he had addressed the Batavian churches, earnestly desiring his remarks respecting it. Mr Mede most cordially approved of his endeavouring to promote a pacification among the Reformed Churches, but he very much doubted his success. He commended Mr Dury's method of addressing the foreign Churches; readily owned his good intentions; and spoke of his rare abilities in terms of the highest approbation. In his answer to Mr Hartlib, excusing his passing judgment on Mr Dury's Address, he says, "Mr Hartlib, I received yours on Saturday, with the copy inclosed, and Mr Dury's courteous letter; to which yet I doubt I shall make no answer; but use the liberty he there vouchsafes me; *that each of us either speak freely or be silent, as seems most proper.* For he desires me to give my judgment of his manner of address and treaties with those of the Batavian churches: what may be expected from them, and what course were best to be taken in case they grant or deny. But what were this, but for Phormio to teach Hannibal stratagems of war?—And for my part, *in the present state of things*, I cannot conceive any way better than what Mr Dury there relates he took; whose wisdom and ability therein, I am fitter to receive knowledge and information by, than to censure or give direction unto." In another letter to Mr Hartlib, Mr Mede says,—"It grieves me not a little, yea, perplexes me, to hear that Mr Dury is come off with no better success." [a]—Mr Dury communicated his design to the most celebrated Divines in New England, who expressed their most hearty concurrence in his generous undertaking. And the famous Mr Baxter observes, that "Mr Dury having spent thirty years in his endeavours to reconcile the Lutherans and Calvinists, was again going abroad upon that work, and desired the judgment of our association how it might be most successfully accomplished; upon which, at their desire, I drew up a letter more largely in Latin, and more briefly in English." [b]

Upon the commencement of the civil wars in England,

a Mede's Works, Letters.

b Sylvester's Life of Baxter, Part i. p. 117.

Mr Dury espoused the cause of the Parliament, was one of the preachers before them, and was also chosen one of the superadded members to the Assembly of Divines at Westminster. He is marked in Neal's list, as giving constant attendance. He took the Covenant with the rest of his brethren, and was appointed one of the Committee of accommodation. He was undoubtedly a man of a very amiable character, and was much respected and beloved by many persons who were eminently distinguished for both learning and piety; among whom, it would certainly be a very great omission not to mention the justly celebrated Sir Robert Boyle, who was eminently his kind friend. In the great and deeply interesting design of promoting concord among Christians, Mr Dury plainly discovered a most excellent spirit, and was indefatigably laborious. His laudable endeavours were, without doubt, highly useful, though they were not crowned with such eminent success, as the best Christians sincerely desired. He seemingly acted, in the whole undertaking, upon the most generous and honourable principles. This will very clearly appear from his letter, under the date of July, 1660, which was addressed to the Lord Chancellor Hide, and which was as follows:

My Lord,

In the application which I made to your honour when you were at the Hague, I offered the fruit of my thirty years labours towards healing the breaches of Protestants; and this I did as one who never had served the turn of any party, or have been biassed by particular interests for any advantage to myself; but walking in the light by rules and principles, have stood free from all in matters of strife, to be able to serve through love. My way hath been, and is, to solicit the means of peace and truth among the dissenting parties, to do good offices, and to quiet their discontents, and I must still continue in this way if I should be useful. But not being rightly understood in my aims and principles, I have been constrained to give this brief account thereof, as well to rectify the misconstructions of former actings, as to prevent farther mistakes concerning my way: that such as love not to foment prejudices may be clear in their thoughts concerning me; and may know where to find me, if they would discern me or any of my talents which God hath bestowed upon me for the public welfare of his churches, which is my whole aim; and wherein I hope to persevere unto the end, as the Lord shall enable me, to be without offence unto all, with a sincere purpose to approve myself to his Majesty in all faithfulness.

Your Lordship's most humble servant in Christ,

John Dury.

During the same month he sent another letter, giving an account of certain proceedings respecting the universal pacification among Christians. It was addressed to the Earl of Manchester, Lord Chamberlain of his Majesty's Household. In Dec. 1660, Mr Dury was presented, by favour of the Earl of Manchester, with so much of the Lithuanian Bible as was then printed, which was down to the Chronicles. Mr Dury has been called *the Lithuanian scholar*. He lived till after the King's restoration in 1660; but he does not appear to have conformed, nor yet to have been ejected. Most probably, he discontinued his ordinary ministerial exercises sometime before that period, making every thing give way to his peculiar favourite object.

Wood says, that he has written and published about twenty books and pamphlets; among which are;

1. *Consultatio Theologica super negotio pacis Eccelsiast.* 4to. London, 1641.

2. *A Summary Discourse concerning the work of Peace Ecclesiastical, &c.* 4to 1641. Cambridge.

3. *Petition to the House of Commons for Preservation of true Religion, &c.* 4to. London, 1642.

4. *Certain considerations shewing the necessity of Correspondence in spiritual matters between all professed Churches, &c.* 4to. London, 1642.

5. *Epistolary Discourse to Tho. Goodwin, Phil. Nye, and Sam. Hartlib.* 4to. London, 1642-1644. This,

being written against Toleration, was answered by H. Robinson.

6. *Israel's Call to March out of Babylon unto Jerusalem;* A Sermon from Isai. lii. 11. before the House of Commons, Fast, Nov. 26, 1645. 4to. pp. 49. London, 1646.

7. *Of Presbytery and Independency.* 4to. 1646.

8. *Model of Church Government.* 1647.

9. *Peace-maker the Gospel way.* 1648.

10. *Seasonable Discourse for Reformation.* London, 1649.

11. *An Epistolical Discourse* to Mr Thorowgood, *concerning his Conjecture that the Americans are descended from the Israelites.* 4to. pp. 16. London, 1650. To this piece he added the History of a Portugal Jew, Antonie Monterinos, attested by Manasseh Ben Israel, to the same effect.

12. *Considerations concerning the Engagement.* 1650.

13. *The Reformed School.* 1650.

14. *Supplement to the Reformed School.* London, 1651.

15. *The Reformed Library-keeper.* London, 1650.

16. *Bibliotheca Augusta Sereniss Princ.* D. Augusti Ducis Brunovicensis, &c. 1650.

17. *The unchanged, constant, and single-hearted Peacemaker drawn forth into the world:* or, *A Vindication of John Dury from the aspersions cast upon him in a nameless Pamphlet, called, The Time-serving Proteus, and ambidexter Divine, uncased to the World.* 4to. London, 1650.

18. *Conscience eased,* or *the main scruple which hath hitherto stuck most with conscionable Men against taking the Engagement, removed.* 4to. London, 1651.

19. *Earnest Plea for Gospel Communion.* 4to. London, 1654.

20. *A Summary Platform of Divinity.* 1654.

21. *A Declaration of John Dury,* to make known the Truth of his Way and Deportment in all these Times of Trouble. 1660.

22. *Irenicorum Tractatuum Prodromus,* 1662.

Beside these, I have in my possession three letters in

Latin, which were written by Mr Dury to Mr Mede. And Mr Dury translated from French, *A Copy of a Petition as it was tendered by him to* Gustavus Adolphus, King of Sweden, when he was at Elbing in Prussia, in 1628. 4to. London, 1641.[a]

It appears that there were some eminent divines of this name, who were natives of Scotland, about that time. Dr Calamy mentions a Mr David Dury, who was ejected from Henly, in the county of York, in England, by the act of uniformity. He says, "After his being silenced, he went into Scotland, which was his native country. There he was eminent for his piety, and particularly for his gift in prayer. He fared better there than many of his brethren in the reign of King Charles II, though he was continually changing his place. He lived till after the Revolution, in 1688, and died in Edinburgh about the time of the first General Assembly, in the reign of King William."[b]

THOMAS FORD, M. A.

A MEMBER OF THE ASSEMBLY OF DIVINES AT WESTMINSTER, AND MINISTER OF THE GOSPEL AT EXETER.

THOMAS FORD was born at Brixton, in Devonshire, in England, in the year 1598. The family from which he descended was respectable; and his parents left his eldest brother above two hundred pounds yearly. His father died when he was young, and his education devolved upon his mother. In his childhood, he had a strong inclination to learning, and to serious impressions. He was trained up in school education under Mr Durant, a pious schoolmaster at Plympton. His master reckoned that he was fit for the University when fifteen years of age; but for some reasons he was not sent to it, till the year

a Wood's Athen. vol. i. 2 edit. Brook's Lives of the Purit. vol. iii.
b Calamy's Cont. vol. ii. p. 949.

1619, or 1620, when he was entered as student in Magdalen-Hall, in Oxford. He applied diligently to his studies at the University, and made great improvement in the knowledge of the learned languages, and in the different branches of literature, which are more immediately connected with theological science. He proceeded Bachelor of Arts, in the year 1624; and Master of Arts, in the year 1627. Wood says, that he entered into Orders, and became a very faithful tutor in his House for several years. Dr Calamy says, "Here he was as celebrated a tutor as any in the University." He was warmly attached to the principles of the Puritans. And the lively interest which he felt in these principles, led him to use some expressions publicly in the University, which, with similar expressions used by other persons, made a considerable noise at that time. The case was this: Dr Frewen, President of Magdalen-College, had changed the communion table in the chapel into an altar, which was the first set up in the University since the Reformation. Several preachers at St Mary's exclaimed against this innovation; particularly Mr Thorn of Baliol-College, in a sermon from 1 Kings xiii. 2. respecting the altar at Bethel: and Mr Hodges of Exeter-College, from Numb. xiv. 4. *Let us make a captain, and let us return into Egypt.* Mr Ford preached also in his course from 2 Thess. ii. 10, 11. *And with all deceivableness of unrighteousness in them who perish; &c.* His sermon was preached on the 12th of June, in the year 1631. He made some smart observations respecting the innovations which were then creeping into the church, the magnifying tradition, making the eucharist, or Lord's supper, a sacrifice, altars instead of tables, bowings to the altar, and the like.

Laud and his party were greatly exasperated at these sermons, made bitter complaints against them, and pretended that they were reflections on some eminent churchmen, and a violation of the King's declaration for silencing the Arminian controversies. Next Saturday, the Vice-chancellor convented Mr Ford before him, and demanded a copy of his sermon. Mr Ford offered to give him one, if he demanded it according to the statutes. The Vice-chancellor ordered him to surrender himself prisoner at the castle. Mr Ford offered to go, if he would send a beadle or servant with him. That not being complied with, he did not surrender himself. Next Saturday the Vice-chancellor, highly enraged, seals up Mr Ford's study, and afterward searches his books and papers, but found nothing which could be urged against him, he having with precaution removed whatever his enemies could take hold of. In the mean time, Archbishop Laud, who was then their Chancellor, received information respecting this affair. He returned orders to punish the preachers. Upon this, a citation in Laud's name was fixed on St Mary's, July 2, commanding Mr Ford's appearance before the Vice-chancellor, on the 5th. Mr Ford appearing on the day appointed, he was urged to an oath *ex-officio*, to answer any questions respecting his sermons; but he refused, because there were no questions in writing. He offered again a copy of his sermon, if demanded according to the statute; and next day he delivered a copy, which was accepted. But on pretence of former contumacy, the Vice-chanceller commanded him again to surrender himself prisoner. Mr Ford appealed from the Vice-chancellor to the convocation, and delivered his appeal in writing to the two Proctors, who were men of eminent integrity and ability, according to Dr Fuller, Messrs Atherton Bruch, and John Doughty.[a] They carried the appeal to the convocation, who referred the cause to sixteen delegates; the greater part of whom, viz. ten in fifteen, upon a full hearing acquitted Mr Ford from all breach of peace. From them the Vice-chancellor appealed to the convocation, who appointed delegates also; but the time limited by statute expired before they came to sentence. Upon this, Laud brought the whole matter before the King and Council at Woodstock. Mr Ford appearing there, the King examined him upon three questions. 1. *Why he refused a copy of his sermon?* He answered that he had not denied it, but offered it ac-

a Fuller's Church-Hist. Book xi. p. 141.

cording to the statutes. 2. *Whether Dr Prideaux dissuaded him from giving it?* He assured the King, that he had never consulted the Doctor respecting it. 3. *Why he did not go to prison, when the Vice-chancellor commanded him thither upon his Faith?* He gave the same answer to the King as before to the Vice-chancellor; adding, *That he hoped his Majesty's poor scholars in the University should not be in a worse condition than the worst of felons, who were imprisoned by a Mittimus, and with legal officers to conduct them to it.* The King spake no more to Mr Ford. And Laud, though present, did not interpose one word. But the following sentence was passed: That Messrs Ford, Thorn, and Hodges, be expelled the University; that both the Proctors be deprived of their places for receiving their appeals, though they could not legally refuse them; and that Dr Prideaux, Rector of Exeter-College, and Dr Wilkinson, Principal of Magdalen-Hall, receive a sharp admonition for meddling in this affair in their behalf.

Messrs Thorn and Hodges, upon a recantation and a year's suspension. were fully restored, and afterwards promoted to be Archdeacons. But Mr Ford, by the final sentence, was obliged to remove from the University within four days, and was conducted out of the town with much honour, by a great multitude of scholars in their habits. He was soon invited by the magistrates of Plymouth to be their Minister: but Laud obtained a letter to them from the King, signed with his own hand, and accompanied with another from himself, forbidding them to admit him, upon pain of his Majesty's highest displeasure; and in case that he was chosen, the bishop of Exeter was commanded not to admit him. The inhabitants of Playmouth were obliged to give up the object of their choice. Mr Ford now finding that the bishop was determined to exclude him from all preferment in England, embraced an opportunity of going beyond sea, as Chaplain to an English regiment under the command of Colonel George Fleetwood, in the service of Gustavus Adolphus. He travelled with the Colonel into Germany, and lay sometime in garrison at Stode and Elbing. His eminent abilities and erudition recommended him to learned men of all professions in his travels. While abroad, he was invited by the English merchants at Hamburgh, to be their minister, with the promise of a salary of two hundred pounds yearly.

Mr Ford was well qualified for improvement and useful observation when he travelled into Germany; but not finding satisfaction in a foreign country, he returned home. At his return, he met with no opposition in a presentation to the Rectory of Aldwinckle or Orendle, in Northamptonshire. There he laboured in his ministerial work with great diligence some years, and married the daughter of —— Fleetwood of Graye's-Inn, Esq. by whom he had several children. He was chosen Proctor for the clergy of the diocess of Peterborough to the famous convocation 1640, who framed the &c. oath. When the civil war broke out between the King and Parliament, he retired to London, and was made minister of St. Faith's, London, and a member of the Assembly of Divines at Westminster. When the wars were over, he settled at Exeter, the capital city of Devonshire, in England. At this time, he found the city and country around over-run with many errors; and the inhabitants greatly under the influence of those persons of an enthusiastical turn, who pretended to be above ordinances. He was now eminently distinguished by his preaching with great zeal and fervour, and with surprising success, against the mad errors of this visionary tribe. His extensive labours in this place were highly acceptable and useful. The whole city was greatly reformed, and a good relish of the best things generally appeared.—He preached in the Cathedral, though for sometime he was once put out of it, in the year 1649, by Major General Desborough, who quartered there, for refusing the Engagement. He was much esteemed not only by the body of the people, but also by the magistrates and neighbouring gentlemen. And he generously maintained a very friendly corresponedence with the other ministers of the city. He induced them to set up a Tuesday's Lecture, in which they all took their turns, and were well attended. This lecture was undertaken with holy zeal, and performed with remarkable success. Mr Ford also prevailed with his brethren to have communions once a-fortnight in each church alternately, at which the members of any of the other congregations might communicate. These measures had a strong tendency to prevent all jealousies among the ministers, and to unite the people firmly among themselves.

The ministers of Exeter enjoyed the best harmony and the most endearing friendship about thirteen years, in the diligent and comfortable discharge of the duties of the pastoral office, until the dismal Bartholomew-day, in the memorable year 1662. Then the respectable subject of this Memoir was cast out with his brethren, but still resided among his people. Upon the coming out of the Oxford-Act, he and twelve other Ministers who resided in that city, not being satisfied with all the particulars of the oath which was prescribed, and knowing that their refussal would be misconstrued, thought that it was prudent to present a petition to the magistrates of Exeter, "Begging leave to declare, that they could swear, That they were so free from all thoughts of raising a new war, or resisting the Powers which by Divine Providence were over them, that they were fully resolved never to take up arms against the King's person, crown, dignity or authority, or to aid, abet, countenance, or encourage any other in any tumultuous or unpeaceable endeavours toward the disturbance of his Majesty's kingdoms; but to behave themselves peaceably in all things and at all times, under His Majesty's government in church and state. Adding, that this they humbly offered, not as expecting to escape the penalties of the Act by it, but that they might not be represented as disloyal or disaffected to His Majesty's person and government." But the magistrates, being such as had no favour for men of their principles, rejected the petition, and the petitioners were obliged to leave the city for sometime.

Mr Ford now retired to Exmouth, about nine miles from Exeter. He lived privately there in those evil days, depending upon the care and faithfulness of his heavenly Father. And under the direction and kindness of Divine

Providence, he obtained a competent support. They who are enabled to trust in the Lord's promise, shall never be forsaken by him. *There is no want to them who fear him. The young lions do lack and suffer hunger: but they who seek the Lord shall not want any good thing.* When the indulgence came out, though he did not esteem the persons who obtained it, nor approve their design in it, yet it was his judgment, that they should embrace the opportunity of preaching the Gospel. Though his health was now greatly impaired, he returned to Exeter, but he was not able to preach more than two sermons in public. But he was highly useful to many persons by private advice and conversation, and his fervent prayers for them. While many persons were flattering themselves with the approach of flourishing times, he plainly told them, that there was a more dreadful storm behind which would unavoidably fall upon the churches. This prediction was completely verified, in the most terrible persecutions, during some following years, in different parts of the earth. Mr Ford declined daily in his bodily health after his last sermon, and was soon confined to his bed, and could speak little to those persons who visited him. But when two Ministers of that city came to see him, he spake much to them respecting his own unworthiness, and the all-sufficiency of Christ. He said, *That he would repose himself upon that Rock in the storms of approaching death.* When his ancient colleague, Mr Burtlet, recited those divinely inspired words, *The sting of death is sin, and the strength of sin is the law;* he stopped him short, and added, *But thanks be to God for Jesus Christ, through whom we have the victory.* These were his last words. Dr Calamy says, He died in his 76th year, in Dec. 1674. Mr Wood says, He died in the latter end of Dec. 1676. They both agree, that his mortal remains were buried in St Lawrence Church in Exeter.

Mr Wood says, " A certain Doctor of Divinity of his time and persuasion, who knew him well, hath several times told me, that this our author was *a man of very good parts and of unbiassed principles, one and the same in all times and changes.*"[a]

Mr Ford published two sermons, one before the Lords, and the other before the Commons.—*Singing of Psalms The Duty of Christians under the New Testament.* Or, A Vindication of that Gospel-Ordinance, in five sermons from Eph. v. 19. Wherein are asserted and cleared; 1. That, 2. What, 3. How, 4. Why, we must sing. London, 1653-1657.—*The Sinner condemned of himself; being a Plea for God against all the ungodly, proving them alone guilty of their own destruction.* London, 1668. And *Scripture's self-evidence, proving it to be the only Rule of Faith; against the Papists,* 1677.

JOHN FOXCROFT, A. M.

MINISTER OF THE GOSPEL AT GOTHAM, AND A MEMBER OF THE ASSEMBLY OF DIVINES AT WESTMINSTER.

JOHN FOXCROFT received his education in Magdalen-Hall, Oxford. He took his degree of Master of Arts on the 29th of October, in the year 1617. And, having finished his studies at the University, he entered upon the ministerial work. He was afterward minister of Gotham, in Nottinghamshire; where, according to Wood, he continued several years a Puritanical preacher. Upon the commencement of the civil war, he joined the Parliament, and was much molested by the royal party, when he was employed in the work of his pastoral office at Gotham. In the year 1643, he was chosen one of the Assembly of Divines at Westminster, and he constantly attended. Removing to London, he became a frequent preacher in that city; and he preached sometimes to the Parliament.[b]

a Wood's Ath. Oxon. vol. ii. Col. 577. And Calamy's Account, vol. ii. 2 edit. pp. 207—214.

b Wood's Athenæ Oxon. vol. i. Brook's Lives of the Puritans, vol. iii.

Mr Foxcroft still retained a strong affection for Nottinghamshire, where he had been a diligent labourer in the Lord's vineyard, as appears by his epistle dedicatory to the House of Commons, before his sermon from Isa. xxxii. 1, 2. in which he says, "Give me leave only to shed a few tears upon the neck of the bleeding County of Nottingham, my dear *Ithaca*, now as beloved as that which gave me breath; having been the place of my ministry the longer half of my life."

I have seen one sermon of Mr Foxcroft's, which is entitled, "The Good of a Good Government, and Well-grounded Peace," from Isa. xxxii. 1, 2. preached before the House of Commons, in Margaret's Church at Westminster, Dec. 31, 1645, the day of their monthly Fast. 4to. pp. 24. London, 1645-46.

HANNIBAL GAMMON, A. M.

MINISTER OF MAUGAN IN CORNWALL, WAS CHOSEN ONE OF THE ASSEMBLY OF DIVINES AT WESTMINSTER;

But he is marked in Neal's list as not appearing there at all; and his name is not enrolled among those Divines who were members of that Assembly. Many persons who were called to attend that Assembly never appeared in it. My plan is, to give some account of those Divines only who were members, and constantly attended the Assembly, including the Scribes and Commissioners from Scotland. But as Mr Gammon is classed among the Puritans, and was chosen one of that Assembly, I shall here give a short account of him.

HANNIBAL GAMMON was born in the city of London, in the year 1585. He was a Gentleman's son, and educated in Broadgates-Hall, Oxford. He took the degrees in Arts, and in due time became minister of Maugan in Cornwall, where he was soon esteemed a very popular preacher. Wood says, that he was much followed by the Puritanical party for his edifying and practical preaching. On the commencement of the civil war, he espoused the cause of the Parliament, and in 1643, he was chosen one of the Assembly of Divines.

Mr Gammon was the author of "An Assize sermon," 1621.—"A sermon at Lady Robert's Funeral," 1627.—"Praise of a Godly Woman; a Wedding sermon," 1627.—"God's Smiting to Amendment; an Assize sermon," 1629.[a]

THOMAS GATAKER, B. D.

A VERY LEARNED ENGLISH DIVINE, CRITIC, AND COMMENTATOR, WHO FLOURISHED IN THE SEVENTEENTH CENTURY, PASTOR OF ROTHERHITHE, AND A MEMBER OF THE ASSEMBLY OF DIVINES AT WESTMINSTER.

THOMAS GATAKER was born in the Parsonage-house of St Edmund the King, in Lombard-street in London, on the 4th of Sept. in the year 1574. He was descended from a very ancient family, in Shropshire, in England, and from those of his name of Gatacre-Hall, where that name is said to have been found from the time of Edward the Confessor. His father was also Thomas Gataker, or Gatacre, as the name has been often written; sometime a student in Oxford, and afterward Pastor in St Edmund's church in Lombard-street in London. He was eminently distinguished by his self-denial, and forsaking all to follow Christ.

The subject of this Memoir received the first principles of his education, in his father's house. He gave very early indications of an uncommon genius, a most retentive memory, and surprising application. He entirely devoted himself to literature in very early life. He had pe-

a Wood's Athenæ, vol. ii. Brook's Lives, vol. iii.

culiar delight in his book; and a very quick apprehension. His manners were amiable, and his conversation grave. He exhibited learning above his age, and manners above his learning. Enjoying the advantages of a good education, and very seasonable early instructions, his youthful and vigorous mind soon imbibed those principles, which afterward ripened to a very happy maturity. His progress in learning, in the grammar-school, was very rapid, and he exceeded many of his fellow-scholars. Having passed through the classes in the grammar-school by the time that he was sixteen years of age, he was sent by his father in the year 1590 to St John's College in Cambridge. As he very early began to seek and taste the peculiar sweetness of all useful learning, and had an uncommon thirst for knowledge, he now pursued his academical studies with unremitting attention, and indefatigable industry. He was also eminently distinguished here by his examplary and agreeable manners. He was one of those diligent students who constantly attended the Greek lectures of the famous and eminently learned Mr John Bois, which he read in his bed. This learned Grecian and divine, who was one of the translators of the Bible, in 1604, read a Greek lecture in his bed to such scholars as preferred their nightly studies to their rest. Under his instructions, Mr Gataker acquired an accurate acquaintance with the Greek language. And he carefully preserved the notes of those lectures as a precious treasure; and when he was visited by Mr Bois, several years afterward, he produced them to him, to the great joy of the good old man, who professed that he was some years younger by that very grateful entertainment. Mr Gataker continued to pursue his studies with the closest application, and made very great proficiency in the knowledge of the Hebrew language, with the good assistance which he derived from the very celebrated Mr Edward Lively, who was the Professor of Hebrew in Cambridge, and eminently skilful in that language.

Not long after he was settled at the College, his father was called to *go the way of all the earth.* He sustained a considerable loss by his father's death, in several respects.

His father was not in circumstances to leave him a sufficient provision of maintenance during the course of his academical education. The early hopes, however, which he had afforded, under divine Providence, of future proficiency, and of being highly useful to the Church of Christ, induced some friends to contribute to his assistance. Being thus encouraged, he prosecuted his studies with uncommon diligence and success. *The hand of the diligent makes rich.* He, accordingly, soon acquired, by his great diligence, under the divine blessing, a very great stock of intellectual riches. His high attainments in learning, and his amiable deportment, so recommended him, that he was chosen a scholar on the foundation of his College. At the statutable periods, he took his degrees in Arts with uncommon applause. His good disposition and sentiments were greatly cherished by associating with eminently learned and pious Christians and Divines; and particularly with that eminent servant of our Lord Jesus Christ, Mr Richard Stock. Mr Stock and Mr Gataker were united by the closest ties of mutual affection and friendship, which continued until Mr Stock's death, as appears by Mr Gataker's testimony given unto him at his funeral.

Mr Gataker was now held in so very high esteem for his learning and piety, that the trustees of Sidney-College, of which the foundation was laid in 1596, appointed him one of the Fellows of that Institution, even before the building was erected. He is enrolled among the learned writers of this College by Dr Fuller, in his History of the University of Cambridge. The uncommon circumstance which has been mentioned occasioned an offer to be made to him, to reside, until the College should be completed, at the house of William Ayloffe, Esq. afterward a Baronet, of Barksted, in the County of Essex, as tutor to that gentleman's eldest son, and as assistant to himself in the study of the Hebrew language. While he continued in this family, he was accustomed every morning to read a portion of the Holy Scriptures, giving the sense from the original languages with great perspicuity, and afterward deducing pertinent and practical observations. He went over, in this manner, the apostolic epistles, the prophecy of Isaiah, and a good part of the book of Job. This learned and pious exercise was highly beneficial both to himself and to the whole household. It was highly beneficial to himself for promoting those biblical or theological studies, which are of the greatest utility and importance to ministers of the gospel, for enabling them to understand and to explain the Sacred Writings. It was also highly beneficial to the family, for enabling them to understand the *Holy Scriptures which were able to make them wise unto salvation, through faith which is in Christ Jesus.* At one of these exercises on the first chapter of Paul's epistle to the Ephesians, Dr Sterne, Suffragan bishop of Colchester, who was nearly related to the Mistress of the family, was present, under Divine Providence. The Doctor was so very highly pleased with Mr Gataker's performance, that he most earnestly pressed him to enter into orders, or to be ordained to the work of the ministry, that his gifts might be authoritatively exercised for the public good, and generously offered him his assistance. For some time, Mr Gataker's modesty and diffidence led him to decline undertaking the ministerial character. His views of the holy ministry were of a very serious and exalted nature. He considered the office of an ambassador of the Lord Jesus Christ, as of the highest importance, and was disposed to say, *Who is sufficient for these things?* But being repeatedly solicited by Dr Sterne and other friends, not to with-hold from the Public the benefit of his services, and considering that his *sufficiency was of God*, he at length acceded to their wishes, and was ordained by the Suffragan above mentioned.

When in the year 1599 Sidney College was finished, and prepared for the reception of its society, Mr Gataker repaired to his proper station, and commenced the office of tutor with great reputation and success. He warmly recommened to his young students piety and learning. While he was engaged in this very useful employment, he also united with Mr Abdias Ashton, and with Mr William Bedell, afterward bishop of Kilmore, in Ireland, in the truly pious and laudable plan of preaching the glorious gospel of the grace of God in places lying near to Cambridge, where, from different circumstances, the people were in great want of able ministers. In conformity to this plan, Mr Gataker constantly preached for six months every Lord's-day at Everton, a village on the borders of the Counties of Cambridge, Bedford, and Huntingdon. The Vicar of this place was rendered incapable of performing the duties of his office by the infirmities of an advanced age.—The universal establishment of the spiritual kingdom of the Lord Jesus Christ, our glorious Redeemer, is the work of ages. And the ambassadors of Christ, of every age, and in every country, should use their utmost endeavours for promoting the interests of his kingdom. " The prophecies stand recorded in the sacred volume, as pledges to assure us of the final event; and they then produce in our minds their intended influence, when they excite our most active endeavours to bring that event to pass. The Almighty can, doubtless, effect his purposes, without the intervention of human assistance; but, since he has been pleased to take us in, as fellow-workers with him in the execution of his gracious plan, it is our indispensable duty to perform with diligence those various parts of it, which he has committed to our charge.—In this supreme work, then, of Christian charity, which is no less honourable to ourselves, than beneficial to those, on whom it is employed, let us not grow *weary or faint in our minds.* The cause of religion is the cause of God, which he will never suffer finally to sink or fail. He ruleth over all the kingdoms of the earth; and has the hearts of their inhabitants, all, in his hands. And, as he opens the hearts of some to make liberal contributions for promoting his gospel; so will he open the hearts of others to receive the truths of that gospel, which we are thus enabled to impart." [a]

Some reasons, which are not explained, having determined Mr Gataker to remove from the University, and to settle in London, he was prevailed upon by his friend

a The Edinburgh Christian Instructor, vol. iv. No. iii. p. 165.

Mr Ashton to reside with Sir William Cooke, near Charing-cross, in the capacity of his Chaplain. In this distinguished situation, he was readily introduced to many persons of eminence and learning, particularly in the profession of the law: and as several of the latter, who were members of Lincoln's-Inn, had frequent opportunities of knowing and admiring his peculiar ministerial gifts, and excellent talents for the pulpit, when he preached for different ministers of his acquaintance, they earnestly wished that he would take the necessary and legitimate steps to be chosen Preacher to their Society. But his native modesty and diffidence of his own abilities would not allow him to become a candidate for that honourable office. He resisted even the importunity of his good friend Mr Stock. However, upon his being chosen to that office about the year 1601, without any solicitation on his part, he was prevailed upon to accept it; and he fulfilled the duties of the office for ten years, in such a manner as reflected the highest credit on himself, and greatly contributed to advance the interests of religion, in that honourable Society. He was much admired and caressed by his very respectable and learned auditory. He prosecuted his studies with judicious and successful application. And he carefully adapted his labours to the sphere in which he moved, and to the circumstances under which he was placed, by Divine Providence. Among other objects which engaged his attention, he was particularly active in promoting the reformation of some abuses of the Lord's-day, and was successful. He studied zealously to promote the religious observance of that day, among all ranks of the community.

Dr Montague, Master of Sidney-College, designed to invite Mr Gataker to return to the College, that he might read a Hebrew Lecture; which had a salary annexed to it by Lord Harrington; but the Doctor had laid that design aside, upon hearing that Mr Gataker was chosen to be Preacher to the honourable Society of Lincoln's-Inn, and warmly urged his acceptance of the call of this respectable body. By accepting the office of Preacher at Lincoln's-Inn, Mr Gataker did not dissolve his connexion with Sir William Cooke's family, notwithstanding that in term time he thought that it was his duty to reside in Lincoln's-Inn; but in the vacations he went down to Sir William's seat in Northamptonshire, and during his stay there he preached constantly, either in the domestic chapel, or in the parish church. *He went about doing good*, with an apostolic mind. He preached the gospel, not for filthy lucre, but freely. Next to the glory of God, he seems to have had the good of his fellow-creatures in view, as the great object which regulated his life. He engaged with much diligence and earnestness in whatever could promote in any degree their temporal and eternal welfare. This laborious and generous preacher of the gospel, aimed more at the good of others, than at his own temporary advantage.—In the year 1603, he took his degree of Bachelor of Divinity at Cambridge, and was afterward often solicited to proceed to take his degree of Doctor in Divinity; but he declined it, for economical reasons. The great reputation which he acquired by his learned discourses at Lincoln's-Inn, occasioned several offers of valuable preferments to be made to him, which, it was supposed, he might have held without relinquishing his situation of Preacher to that Society. But he entertained very proper and conscientious scruples against pluralities; and no arguments could persuade, nor examples induce, him to believe that one man, at the same time, could discharge his duty, in a proper manner, having two cures of souls. He wished also to continue in that situation, though his income was much smaller than that of Livings to which he might have been inducted, because of the advantage which it afforded him of time for pursuing his learned studies. He devoted much of his time to his studies, and especially to his improvement in an acquaintance with the Holy Scriptures in their original languages, with the Fathers of the first ages in the Christian Church, and with the best Greek and Roman writers. A celebrated Divine says, " The best natural powers will need to be well cultivated by a liberal education. Without an ability to read the Scripture in the languages in which it was originally written, and some aquaintance with natural and moral philosophy, history, antiquity, the best Greek and Roman authors, and the arts of logic, rhetoric, and criticism, in an age of so much learning as the present, a minister can scarcely fail to be despised; and a despised ministry is seldom successful. Besides, on many occasions, the teacher will need all his learning to unfold to him the meaning of difficult passages in sacred writ; especially if, as sometimes happens, his commentaries fail him, where he most wants their help. Nor will one, wholly ignorant of philosophy, history, and criticism, be able to give satisfying answers to the reasonings of infidels founded upon those, to detect their sophistry, beat them out of their strong holds, and so, if he convince not their conscience, at least to stop their mouths. There are some Scriptures, from which, if they stood in the original as they do in our translations, almost unanswerable objections might be drawn against our holy faith. And what advantages must this give the infidel to triumph over the illiterate teacher! And, indeed, if the hedge of a learned ministry were once removed from these lands, as I am afraid some wish it to be; what could we expect, but that ignorance and infidelity, error and heresy, superstition and enthusiasm, should quickly overspread them! Those who, by the blessing of God on their studies, have acquired considerable measures of learning, have been the best explainers and defenders of Christianity, and recommended practical religion in the most distinct and persuasive manner. And, without a miracle, which we have no ground to expect, illiterate ministers can never equal them."[a]

In the year 1611, Mr Gataker, having entered into the matrimonial state, accepted the Rectory of Rotherhithe in the County of Surrey, near London-bridge. He was much importuned to retain his former office, of Preacher at Lincoln's-Inn, with his Rectory of Rotherhithe; but in consistency with his principles, which have al-

a Dr Erskine's Discourses, Dis. 1. from James iii. 1. The Qualifications necessary for Teachers of Christianity, where the reader may find many excellent things on the subject.

ready been mentioned, he now resigned his former office, to the great regret of the learned body who had profited much under his ministry. Respecting the grounds and motives of this settlement, Mr Gataker has given a large account to the public, in his defence of himself against Lilly. Devoting his whole attention to the particular flock over which the Holy Ghost had made him the overseer, he now applied himself in discharging the duties of the pastoral office with great diligence and fidelity, notwithstanding that for a long time he was afflicted with an almost perpetual head-ach, to which, very probably, his late and early studies did not a little contribute. To the work of his public ministry upon the Sabbath-day, he added a catechetical weekly lecture on Friday, in the evening, which was chiefly designed for the instruction and benefit of children and young persons. This benevolent and useful Institution was for some time well attended; and had a strong tendency to fix on the young mind lasting impressions of the all-important truths of religion. The religious education of youth is certainly a most interesting and important object. Society at large is deeply concerned in it. "There is no man, however obscure his condition, however low his attainments, or however limited his means of usefulness, whose character is a matter of indifference to the public. The more generally, then, religious knowledge is disseminated, the greater is the good done to the community, the surer is the foundation on which its happiness and prosperity depend. How widely may those blessings be diffused, which arise from the religious education of a few children!" [a] At Mr Gataker's lecture, a certain number, every evening, were called to give an account of their knowledge, by answering questions which were before delivered out to them for their instruction. He considered the religious instruction of young persons highly beneficial to the public; and under the blessing of the Almighty, which makes rich, his labours were crowned with success, in their instruction. In this profitable ex-

a Edinburgh Christian Instructor, vol. iv. No. iii. p. 206.

ercise, he explained the whole body of divinity, in a most accurate and methodical manner; and Christians who had made considerable progress in religious knowledge carefully attended his discourses. And let pastors, and parents, and instructors of the rising generation of every class, seriously remember and feel,

"That they are bound to cast the minds of youth,
Betimes, into the mould of heavenly truth,
That taught of God, they may indeed be wise,
Nor ignorantly wandering miss the skies." [a]

Mr Gataker performed this work with much zeal and accuracy, until he had completed an excellent summary of divinity. He continued his highly useful and disinterested labours as long as those persons attended who were chiefly designed in the Institution. And he was honoured to be the instrument of dispensing the inestimable blessings of religious and saving knowledge to a number of that rising generation.

In the year 1616, and in some following years, Mr Gataker maintained a literary correspondence with Dr Usher who was afterward Archbishop of Armagh, on the subject of some curious manuscripts which he had in his possession of some ancient divines, and among others of the famous Robert Grosthead, bishop of Lincoln. I have seen and read three letters from Mr Gataker to Dr James Usher, afterward Archbishop of Armagh, under the dates of 1616, 1617, and 1621, which are preserved in a collection of letters subjoined to the Life of Archbishop Usher, by Dr Richard Parr, his Lordship's domestic chaplain, at the time of his death, London, 1636, 1686. These letters afford sufficient evidence of Mr Gataker's profound erudition, and critical skill, and also of his great modesty and humility, and of the very high esteem in which he was held by that learned Prelate.

While Mr Gataker had been Preacher at Lincoln's-Inn, among other curious subjects more particularly adapted to his learned auditory, he had devoted several discours-

a Cowper.

es to the consideration of the nature, use, and abuse, of lots, or lotteries. These discourses were intended by our learned preacher to shew the lawfulness of lusorious, or entertaining games of chance, and the unlawfulness of the divinatory lots. What he had delivered on this subject is said to have been much misrepresented; and he was accused of having pleaded the cause of gamblers, and of having given encouragement to the abuse and misemployment of precious time. Finding that these charges were propagated not only in conversation but also by the press, he was obliged to overcome his reluctance to sending any of his learned labours into the world, and by way of self-defence he published the substance of his discourses on this subject, under the title "Of the Nature and Use of Lots; A Treatise Historical and Theological," in the year 1619. This very elaborate work is allowed to be eminently distinguished by great accuracy of method, acutness of reasoning, profound learning, perspicuity and elegance of style, considering the time in which it was written. It was readily received with much applause by a great part of the learned world; but at the same time it excited the strictures of several persons, with whom the learned author afterward engaged in controversy. He protests, in the most solemn manner, in his epistle to the reader, which is prefixed to this book, that he undertook the task for no sinister end; and that he neither had averred nor defended any thing, but what he was verily persuaded to be agreeable to the word of God. That if any man could better inform him in any thing therein, he should very readily hearken unto him.—That the clearing of Truth has been in this work his main aim. And he further says, "That whosoever shall take no more liberty than by me is here given, shall be sure to keep within the bounds of piety, of sobriety, of equity, and of charity."

In the year 1620, Mr Gataker set out on a tour through the Spanish and United Netherlands, in company with two eminent friends, and with a nephew of his, who was then a student. He had a laudable curiosity to see some of the churches in those parts of the earth; and he wished also to form an acquaintance with men who were eminently distinguished for their learning and piety. With these objects before him, he entered upon his travels, and gained considerable information in a short time, worthy the attention of the scholar and the divine. When he was at Middleburgh, in Zealand, in the United Netherlands, he preached in the English church there, to the very great satisfaction of his Protestant countrymen. His friends in that town were both very glad to see him, and very desirous to hear him preach, and he yielded to their importunity. He very eminently distinguished himself by the spirit and ability with which he disputed against the English Catholic priests who resided in those parts, together with the fugitives of their persuasion who had been obliged to remove from England, for being concerned in the base plots against the government in the reigns of Elizabeth and her successor. While he was in Holland, he had formed a very high opinion of the peculiar zeal of the Dutch for the Protestant religion. And he was fully convinced, that the English could never differ from the Dutch, even upon points of national policy, without very great injury to the Protestant interest. This opinion was very warmly maintained for some time by those men who opposed the measures of the English court; but when they had succeeded in overturning the royal authority, they proceeded upon a very different system, as the reader may very readily learn from the history of those times.

Upon Mr Gataker's return to his native country, from which he was absent only about a month, he soon found that his Treaties on Lots had been attacked by a Mr John Balmford, whose work, on account of the angry spirit in which it was written, and the illiberal insinuations which it is said to have contained, was, by the licenser of the press, refused permission to be published. Very much to Mr Gataker's honour, he immediately most generously interested himself to obtain the removal of the prohibition against the work of his adversary; and after that it had been permitted to appear, he employed himself in preparing a learned and very elaborate answer to it. This answer was published in the year 1623, under the title of

"A Just Defence of Certain Passages in a former Treatise concerning the Nature and Use of Lots, Against such Exceptions and Oppositions as have been made thereunto by Mr J. B. Wherein the Insufficiency of his Answers given to the Arguments brought in Defence of a Lusorious Lot is Manifested; the Imbecility of his Arguments produced against the same further Discovered; and the Point itself in Controversy more fully Cleared." This Defence consists of three parts, An Answer to Mr Balmford's Preface and Postscript; A Reply upon Mr Balmford's Answer to Mr Gataker's Arguments; and a Rejoinder to Mr B's Reply in Defence of his own Arguments. Mr Balmford's entire context is inserted; and Mr Gataker's own arguments and answers are transcribed from his former book, that neither of them may be wronged, nor the reader obliged to turn from book to book, to search for what is either confirmed or confuted, or otherwise handled, having all represented together unto his view. Several years after this, he found himself under the necessity of publishing a Latin defence of his opinions respecting the nature and use of lots against two very learned men who had written upon the same subject; the celebrated Amesius and Voetius. The reader will find the title of this Latin defence in the list of Mr Gataker's writings. In the year 1624, our author's peculiar zeal for the Protestant religion led him to publish a learned work, which was very highly valued at the time when it first appeared, and still deserves a respectable rank among the controversial treatises against the Roman Catholics. It was entitled, "A Discussion of the Popish Doctrine of Transubstantiation: Wherein the same is declared, by the confession of their own writers, to have no necessary ground in God's word: As also it is further demonstrated to be against Scripture, Nature, Sense, Reason, Religion, the judgment of the Ancients, and the Faith of our Ancestors." Afterward he also published "A Just Defence of the same Discourse, and Arguments against the Answer of a nameless Popish Priest thereunto." This indefatigable and respectable writer, very much to his honour, as a zealous friend to the Reformation, heartily engaged in the discussion and confutation of the doctrine of transubstantiation, at this time. This most absurd doctrine, that a person who had received holy orders in the Romish church could convert, by a word, the bread and wine, the signs and memorials of the death of Christ, into his real body and blood, equally mocks our senses and our reason. It should be utterly condemned, without any hesitation, by every friend to Christianity. Mr Gataker most steadily directed the efforts of his enlightened and vigorous mind against this most absurd doctrine, and the other corrupt doctrines of the Roman church. He first examined these doctrines, with the utmost care and candour, bringing them all, with peculiar zeal and diligence, to the test of a severe examination by the word of God; and having clearly discerned their inconsistency with the word of God, he confuted and rejected them. Having great abilities and a liberal education, he examined with the most scrupulous care, the foundation of all those received opinions, which prevailed at that time, and had any connexion with the salvation, or with the interest and happiness of mankind. And it was a maxim with him, that Truth, so far from being injured by discussion, which some persons greatly fear, will uniformly derive much advantage from it; and that the sharper the scrutiny is, the more glorious will be her triumph.—"In tracing the general or local progress of the Reformation, let not the evils which it struggled to remove be cast out of sight; let us contemplate the system of Popery, not modified by the expanded reason of mankind, but as it exerted its energy in the ages of intellectual darkness. Thus shall we justly appreciate the labours of those who sapped its strength; thus shall we ascribe to the proper cause, that amazing improvement in the social and moral condition of man, which has succeeded its weakness or its destruction."[a]

In the year 1624, Mr Gataker also published "A Short Catechism." About this time, and in the following years, he published several other learned and very

a Cook's Hist. Reformation in Scotland, vol. i. p. 33.

elaborate pieces, which are mentioned in the account of his writings. On the 19th of April, in the year 1640, he began in the course of his ministry to unfold that remarkable portion of the Holy Scriptures, *We conclude, therefore, that a man is justified by faith without the deeds of the law*, Rom. iii. 28. In due time, he, by divine assistance, accomplished what he had intended in his explanation of the entire doctrine of justification. He handled and illustrated this highly useful and important doctrine, with his usual accuracy of method, solidity of reasoning, profound learning, and clearness of expression, to the great satisfaction of his judicious hearers. He preserved by him, the rude draughts of his meditations respecting this deeply interesting doctrine, and they were extant after his death. He was frequently urged to publish those meditations; but his great modesty and averseness to appear in public hindered him some time from printing, what he had preached with much cheerfulness and freedom. At last, however, not so much by the importunity of friends, as through the love of the truth, as it is in Jesus, he was prevailed upon to engage in preparing the work for the press, as an antidote to the prevailing errors respecting justification. He recollected his loose papers, revised his notes, new-modelled his treatise, and was diligently employed in making it ready for a public appearance in the world, and for the benefit of the Church and of posterity, when he was summoned by the inexorable messenger of eternity, and diverted from communicating his conceptions to the Church on the earth, to resign his spirit to God who gave it, before he had fully finished this work, which, though unfinished was published after the author's death by his son.[a] Mr Gataker had very carefully collected much information, and a great number and variety of writers, respecting justification. He read most extensively, and seems to have had access to many sources of information, by which his views were greatly enlarged and matured. And by his intense application, and the

a Preface unto this Antidote to Error concerning Justification, by the Author's son.

vivacity of his genius, he made great progress in the pursuits to which he directed his attention. He applied with peculiar zeal and diligence to the study of all subjects which he handled, and discussed them in a very able manner.

In the year 1642, he was attacked by a violent colic, which brought him to the very gates of death; but the Lord, who is rich in mercy, to relieve all who call upon him, raised him from the gates of death, for his further service. The people of God meet with their afflictions in this world, like the waters of Marah, in their way to the heavenly Canaan; and they are sometimes, by those afflictions, brought very low. But He, whose high prerogative it is literally to *raise from the gates of death*, can always find the means of recovering and of preserving his servants, when he has more work for them.

When the famous Assembly of Divines was appointed to sit at Westminster, in the year 1643, Mr Gataker, before his strength was well recovered, was nominated one of that respectable body, and constantly attended in his place, from a pure desire of promoting truth and peace, and of rendering what service he could to the religious interests of his country at that very critical time. And he undoubtedly was a very great ornament and credit to that brilliant constellation. When the discussion took place in the Assembly on the important subject of justification, and he found that the majority were determined to adopt a definition of it different from the sense in which he understood that doctrine, his great love of unity led him to impose silence upon himself, as far as respected the public, and to with-hold from the press some discourses from Rom. iii. 28, which he had composed in defence of his sentiments. In the dispute respecting ruling elders, he was entirely against the institution of any such officer by divine right. Mr Baillie from Scotland, who was present, speaking of this dispute, says, "Sundry of the ablest were flat against the institution of any such officer by divine right, as Dr Smith, Dr Temple, Mr Gataker, Mr Vines, Mr Price, Mr Hall, and many more."[a]

a Baillie's Letters, vol. i. p. 401.

It is said, that upon the introduction of the *covenant* into the Assembly, Mr Gataker declared his judgment to be in favour of what was called moderate Episcopacy, denying the distinction of that order from that of Presbyters, divesting the Prelates of their baronies and seats in the House of Lords, and abolishing the rest of the hierarchy. And, that though he and other members who united with him in opinion, could not carry their point, yet they obtained a considerable qualification before they were brought to subscribe.[a] Some men, at that time, were exceedingly zealous for the whole hierarchy, and for all the exorbitant power of the bishops. When Mr Gataker came to sit in the Assembly of Divines at Westminster, he drew upon himself the dislike at least, if not the hatred of such men. Others were for destroying or extirpating Episcopacy root and branch, reckoning that it was a great impediment to the Reformation and to the life and power of godliness. Some were only for a reformation of the hierarchy, or for what was called moderate Episcopacy, as Mr Gataker seems to have been.—During his attendance upon the work of that famous Assembly, the Earl of Manchester, who was well acquainted with his eminent abilities, profound learning, and peculiar accomplishments for academical services, offered him the Mastership of Trinity College in Cambridge, which was the greatest preferment in that University; but he declined to accept of that preferment, notwithstanding the earnest solicitations of his friends, partly on account of his bodily weakness through age, and his ill state of health, and partly because of his ardent desire of devoting what time he could spare from his pastoral duties to such pursuits as might be beneficial to the learned world. He was deeply interested in enlightening mankind; and having vast intellectual abilities, which were brightened and diligently cultivated by much study, his learned labours were crowned with surprising success. This important object he kept constantly in view even when under the visitation of a very distressing disease. He was again attack-

a Gen. Biogr. vol. iv. See Middleton's Biogr. Evang. vol. iii. under Gat.

ed by an alarming illness; but it pleased the Lord, though he sorely chastised him, not to give him over to death. When confined to his chamber by illness, he composed two works, in which his eminent learning and critical talents were very advantageously displayed. The first was a profound and ingenious treatise respecting the name by which God made himself known to Moses and to the people of Israel, the most glorious name of God, JEHOVAH. In this elaborate piece, the author strenuously defends the common way of pronouncing the word Jehovah in England. The second work was respecting diphthongs, wherein he endeavours to prove that in reality there are no diphthongs, and that two vowels cannot be united in such a manner as to form one syllable.

Mr Gataker also engaged with other eminent divines in writing the learned Annotations upon the Bible, which were published under the name of the "English Annotations," and not the "Assembly's Annotations," as they have been frequently called. I have long used a copy, which is entitled on the back "English Annotations." And Messrs Baillie and Gillespie, who were Commissioners from the Church of Scotland to the Assembly of Divines at Westminster, call these the English Annotations.[a] And Dr Cornelius Burgess, who was an eminent man in that Assembly, and had the best opportunity of correct information respecting these Annotations, gives the following account of them: "It is indeed true, that some members of that Assembly, joining with some others, did compile some Annotations upon the Bible, which many take to be the work of the Assembly. But take this for an undoubted truth, those Annotations were never made by the Assembly, nor by any order from it; nor after they were made ever had the approbation of the Assembly; or were so much as offered to the Assembly at all, for that purpose or any other."[b] The same Parliament which called that Assembly, employed the authors of

a Baillie's Letters, vol. ii. pp. 22, and 167. Gillespie's Aaron's Rod, pp. 20—68—97.

b Dr Burgess's No Sacrilege nor Sin to purchase Bishops' Lands, chap. iv. 2d edit. pp. 87, 88.

those Annotations. And some Divines who were members of that Assembly were concerned in writing these Annotations. Such mistakes are not here pointed out with any envious intention, but solely from a love of truth. Mr Gataker was, in particular, the author of those Annotations upon Isaiah, Jeremiah, and the Lamentations of Jeremiah, which have been generally very much esteemed; and they are, without doubt, justly entitled to very high esteem. In these, his extraordinary reading, talents, learning, diligence, and piety, are clearly seen. And it has been said, that Mr Gataker's part of these learned Annotations is exceeded by no Commentator, ancient or modern, on those books.[a] The other parts of these Annotations, according to my best information, were done by the following authors: The Pentateuch, or five books of Moses, by Mr Ley, Sub-dean of Chester: The two books of Kings, of Chronicles, Ezra, Nehemiah, and Esther, by Dr William Gouge of Black-Friars, London: The Psalms, by Mr Meric Casaubon: The Proverbs, by Mr Francis Taylor: Dr Reynolds wrote upon Ecclesiastes; and Mr Smallwood, on Solomon's Song.—Ezekiel, Daniel, and the lesser prophets, were done, in the first edition, by Mr Pemberton, and in the second edition, by Bishop Richardson. The Notes on the four Evangelists are Mr Ley's; and those on Paul's Epistles are Dr Featly's. Messrs Downham and Reading were also concerned in this great work, and might perhaps do the other parts which are not here mentioned.[b]

Our illustrious author also wrote some very able treatises against the Antinomians.—When his health was in some degree re-established, he returned to the duties of his profession, and laboured in these, until by the bursting of one of the vessels of his lungs, which was followed by frequent alarming discharges of blood, he was obliged to decline the service of the pulpit; though he still continued to administer the sacraments, and to deliver short discourses at funerals suitable to the occasions. These ex-

a Johnson's Lives.

b Dr Calamy's Account, vol. i. chap. vi. Neal's Hist.

ercises, though short, were painful to him; but he always delighted in doing good to his fellow-creatures. The chief part of his time was now spent in study. And he enjoyed favourable opportunities of study and retirement, in which he greatly delighted, and improved with much activity and diligence. In the year 1648, he presented to the world an excellent work on the style of the New Testament, which very justly gained him the character of being one of the ablest philologists of his age. This eminently learned work was but the forerunner to a larger one of the same nature, which is highly useful in illustrating the sense of difficult passages in both the Old and New Testaments; the primitive Fathers, modern critics, and also in profane authors both Greek and Latin. At first, only two books of the six into which it is divided, were published, in the year 1651. The remaining books of this collection were published after the author's death by his son Charles, under the title of Adversaria Miscellanea-Posthuma, &c. in 1659. In the year 1651, Mr Gataker also published a learned Latin discourse on infant baptism. Three years after he published another treatise on the same subject. In 1652, he favoured the public with his excellent edition of the Emperor Antoninus' Meditations, with a very valuable preliminary discourse respecting the philosophy of the Stoics, an exact translation and commentary.

When Mr Gataker was obliged to desist from preaching, he was deeply interested in the welfare of his flock, and did not desert it; but retained his title until they had an opportunity of being provided with a faithful and orthodox minister, to whom he might comfortably devolve both the charge and the benefit. At the same time, he was equally attentive to his duty in instructing his family in private. On Friday night, weekly, he was accustomed, after supper, to expound that short Catechism which he had published for the use of his parishioners. In this course, he most beautifully unfolded the nature and attributes of God; the state of man, both as he was created and fallen; the means of his fall and recovery; the nature of faith and repentance, and the doctrine of the sacraments. His parlour was an excellent school for profitable instruction. And, for some time, he maintained a private seminary in his house for the instruction of several young English gentlemen; and many foreigners also went and lodged with him, in order that they might enjoy the benefit of his advice in their studies. Under his tutorage and direction, those students were equally built up in piety and learning. And several persons who were afterward great ornaments to the churches, both at home and abroad, were brought up, at least, under his eye, as Paul was at the feet of Gamaliel.—His polite literature was much admired by eminently learned men both at home and abroad; and he maintained a literary correspondence with Salmasius, Hornbeck, and other learned foreigners.

When some desperate officers of the army, and their dependants, assuming and maintaining the military sword in a most arbitrary manner, had determined to bring the King to a trial, and were proceeding to take their measures for that purpose, Mr Gataker was one of those ministers of the gospel, within the Province of London, who subscribed a very bold and judicious remonstrance to the General and army against that design; and he made no scruple to condemn it, both in public and in private, as he also did the putting of the King to death. He, in like manner, condemned and testified against the subsequent changes which were introduced into the constitution of both the civil and ecclesiastical government. The sentiments which he readily avowed respecting these subjects rendered him an object of suspicion to the rulers of that period. Some of his ungrateful parishioners speedily took advantage of this circumstance, and refused to pay him any longer their share of the composition for the tythes of their houses, which upon a law-suit amicably conducted, had been decreed him in the court of Exchequer. He bore this unkind treatment with great patience, and clearly shewed that he *had not received the spirit of the world, but the spirit which is of God.* Kindness reigned in his heart, and appeared in his life. In the evening of his days, when he earnestly desired that repose to which he was very justly entitled, by his unwearied labours, he was most warmly attacked by an active and angry adversary, Mr William Lilly, the famous astrologer. But Mr Gataker, who possessed all the sacred and profane literature respecting astrology, not only defended himself with great strength of argument, but also very clearly detected all the plausible sophisms which could be urged in support of that pretended science. The ground of this controversy was Mr Gataker's Annotations on Jer. x 2, in which he had, with solid sense and sound learning, completely destroyed the credit of that delusive art, by which, in all ages and countries, weak and unstable minds have been much misled. These Annotations roused the whole tribe of astrologers against him, from the highest to the lowest. They were greatly offended, and wrote against him without mercy. Mr Gataker was thus induced to publish in vindication both of his Annotations and of himself; which he did in a very satisfactory manner. Respecting himself, he speaks of the most considerable transactions of his life, relates at large how he came to his several preferments, and completely refutes all the idle and malicious reflections of Lilly and his associates. Declares that he never was an advocate for the power and splendour of the Prelacy; but on the contrary, had always inclined to a moderate Episcopacy.

Mr Gataker undoubtedly was one of the most able, learned and pious, divines and writers of his age. He had an extraordinary strength of memory. He retained what he had read, without the help of a common-place book. And his reading was very extensive, as clearly appears by his manifold quotations, in all his writings. By his unwearied application to reading and to study, he had acquired a vast stock both of divine and of human learning. In his course of reading and study, he had made a very judicious selection, which, like the rich treasures of the hive, unites in one precious mass, all the sweets of numerous flowers. He was very charitable; but he gave his alms generally in secret, unless he found it necessary to give them openly, for exciting other persons to their duty. In his last will, he left to the poor of the parish of Rotherhithe fifty pounds. To ten of his brethren in the ministry, who were oppressed by the iniquity of the times, fifty pounds; that is, to each five pounds. And to eight ministers' widows, five pounds each. He pursued a peaceable and useful course, until his constitution was worn out with years, infirmities, and continual labours. He brought forth fruit in great abundance, even in old age. *They shall still bring forth fruit in old age; they shall be fat and flourishing; to shew that the Lord is upright.* His mental abilities were not abated; but his understanding and memory continued strong, even unto his end.

He was seized with a fever which terminated in his death. He gave order that his dear friend Mr Ashe should be certified of his weakness, that he might be remembered before the Lord in his prayers, and that he might prepare for preaching his funeral sermon. Mr Ashe, upon receiving such intelligence, went to see his dying friend, and found him very weak, and not able to speak much, but what he said was both weighty and savoury, and has been faithfully related by Mr Ashe. His words were; *I am now conflicting with my last adversary, though I believe the sting is taken out. Nature will struggle, but I humbly submit unto the good pleasure of God. I heartily beg the pardon of my many sins, especially of my want of sedulity and fidelity in my public and private charge, hoping to be washed with Christ's blood, and desiring to be translated out of this restless condition. I expect daily, yea hourly to be translated into that everlasting rest, which God hath prepared for them who are interested in his Christ. And I pray God to bless you, and his whole ministery every where.* These were his last words to Mr Ashe.[a] During all the time of his last sickness, his faith, patience, and resignation unto the will of the Lord, were very conspicuous. His mind was deeply impressed with a sense of his sin, and the necessity of the Saviour, whose name is called *Jesus*, because he saves his people from their sins. To an ancient servant who waited upon him. and who said to him that his head did not lie right, he said, *It will lie right in my coffin.* The day before his departure, be-

a Mr Ashe's Fun. Ser. pp. 38, 39.

ing exercised with extreme pain, he cried, *How long, Lord, how long? Come speedily!* In the afternoon of that day, feeling a great change in himself, he called his son, his sister, and his daughter, to each of whom he delivered his dying charge, saying, *My heart fails, and my strength fails; but God is my fortress, and the strong rock of my salvation. Into thy hands, therefore, I commend my soul; for thou hast redeemed me, O God of truth.* Then he turned his discourse to them respectively, in the following manner—*Son, you have a great charge, look to it. Instruct your wife and family in the fear of God, and discharge your ministry conscientiously.—Sister, I thought you might have gone before me, but God calls me first. I hope we shall meet in heaven. I pray God bless you.—Daughter, mind the world less, and God more; for all things, without religion and the fear of God, are nothing worth:* Or,—*all things without piety and the true fear of God are worth nothing*, as one copy has it. He also gave his advice, that his son Draper, being a man of worldly substance, should entertain some godly minister in his house to teach his children and instruct his family. He warmly exhorted them all to concord, and after some enlargement in the parts of his discourse, or dying charge, he earnestly wished them all to lay to heart the words of a dying man. He then desired them all to withdraw and leave him to his rest, which he hoped was at hand. He expired on the 27th of July 1654, aged seventy-nine years, having been forty-three years pastor at Rotherhithe. His funeral sermon was preached from Prov. xvi. 31, by his much esteemed friend, Mr Simeon Ashe, and afterward published under the following title: "Gray Hayres crowned with Grace; A sermon preached at Redrith, near London, Aug. 1. 1654, at the funeral of that reverend, eminently learned and faithful Minister of Jesus Christ, Mr Thomas Gataker." *He came to his grave in a full age, as a shoke of corn cometh in in his season*, being nearly fourscore years old.

This venerable divine would never suffer his picture to be taken; but the following is said to be a just description of his person. He was of a middle stature, of a thin body, of a lively countenance, and of a fresh complexion. He was temperate in diet, free and cheerful in conversation, and much addicted to study, but he did not seclude himself from useful company. He enjoyed a quick apprehension, and solid judgment, and a very extraordinary memory. He was a loving husband, a discreet parent, a faithful friend, and a kind benefactor. He was an ornament to the University, a light to the church, salt to society, a stout champion for the truth, and an eminent lover of peace. The frame of his soul may be collected from a pious epigram which is supposed to have been his. It follows;

"I thirst for thirstiness; I weep for tears;
Well pleased I am to be displeased thus:
The only thing I fear is want of fears;
Suspecting I am not suspicious.
I cannot chuse but live, because I die;
And, when I am not dead, how glad am I!
Yet, when I am thus glad for sense of pain,
And careful am, lest I should careless be;
Then do I greive for being glad again,
And fear lest carelessness take care from me.
Amid these restless thoughts this rest I find,
For those who rest not here, there's rest behind."

Echard says, "He was remarkable for his skill in Greek and Hebrew, and the most celebrated among the Assembly of Divines; and adds, It is hard to say which was most remarkable, his exemplary piety and charity, his polite literature, or his humility and modesty in refusing preferments." Among foreigners, Morehoff gives him a very high character. It is said, "Of all the critics of this age, who have employed their pens in illustrating polite learning, there are few, if indeed any, who deserve to be preferred to Thomas Gataker for diligence and accuracy, in explaining those authors whose writings he has examined." He is styled "a writer of infinite learning and accurate judgment." And his name as a scholar is paralleled with those of Selden and Usher.

Mr Gataker's writings are numerous.

1. *Of the Nature and Use of Lots.* Small 4to. pp. 360. 1st edit. London, 1619. 2d edit. reviewed, corrected, and enlarged, 1627.

2. *A Just Defence of the same against Mr J. B.* 4to. pp. 275. London, 1623.

3. Thomae Gatakeri Londinatis Antithesis, Partim Gulielmi Amesii, Partim Gisberti Voetii, De Sorte Thesibus reposita. 4to. pp. 61. London, 1638.

4. A Discourse of Transubstantiation, with a Defence thereof. 4to. pp. 233. London, 1624.

5. David's Instructor.

6. The Christian Man's Care.

7. *The Spiritual Watch;* or *Christ's General Watch-Word.* A Meditation on Mark xiii. 37. 4to. pp. 130. The 2d edit. amended and enlarged, London, 1622. An excellent piece of practical divinity.

8. The Gain of Godliness, with its self-sufficiency. A Meditation on 1 Tim. vi. 6.

9. The Just Man's Joy, with signs of Sincerity.

10. Jacob's Thankfulness.

11. David's Rememberancer.

12. Noah's Obedience.

13. Memorial of England's Deliverance from the Spanish Invasion, in 1588.

14. Sorrow for Zion.

15. God's Parley with Princes, with an appeal from them to Him.

16. Eleazer's Prayer; A Marriage Sermon.

17. A Good wife God's Gift.

18. A Wife Indeed.

19. Marriage Duties.

20. Death's Advantage.

21. The Benefit of a Good Name, and a Good End.

22. Abraham's Decease, delivered at the Funeral of Mr Richard Stock, late Pastor of All-hallows, Bread-street.

23. Jeroboam's Son's Decease.

24. Christian Constancy Crowned by Christ.

The above sermons, of which the pious Bishop Wilkins, gives a very high character, were published separately, in 4to. but, in 1637, they were collected and published in one volume folio.

25. The Decease of Lazarus.

26. St Stephen's last Will and Testament, 4to. and also folio. London, 1638.

27. Fran. Gomari Disputationis Elencticae, de Justificationis materia & forma, 1640.

28. Animadversiones in J. Piscut. &c.

29. Mr Anthony Wotton's Defence, 1641.

30. A true Relation of Passages between Mr Wotton and Mr Walker, 1642.

31. An Answer to Mr Walker's Vindication, 1642.

32. Stricturae in Barth. Wigelini Sang. de obedientia Christi, &c. 1653.

33. A Defence of Mr Bradshaw against Mr J. Canne.

34. *God's Eye on his Israel*, 4to. pp. 99; to which is prefixed a large epistle to the Religious, Judicious, and Ingenuous, Reader. London, 1645. This valuable work contains an explication and application of Balaam's words which are recorded Numb. xxiii. 21, clearing them from Antinomian abuse.

35. De Nomine Tetragrammato Dissertatio. A small book in Latin, Londini, 1645. The learned work was reprinted in 1652; it is also inserted among our author's Critical Works, which were printed at Utrecht, in 1698. And it has deservedly found a place among the ten Discourses upon this subject, which were collected and published by Hadrian Reland. The first five of these discourses were written by John Drusius, Sextinus Amama, Lewis Capel, John Buxtorff, and James Alting, who opposed the received usage of that glorious name of God, JEHOVAH, which is strenuously defended in the other five dissertations, the first of which was written by Nicolas Fuller, the second by Gataker, and the three others by the celebrated John Leusden. Mr Gataker, in his judicious and laborious discourse on the glorious name by which God made himself known to Moses and the people of Israel, has shewed that he was a very great master of Hebrew: and this curious and instructive treatise has been well received by competent judges, and found its way

under Divine Providence, into some very respectable libraries.

36. The English Annotations upon Isaiah, Jeremiah, and the Lamentations of Jeremiah, folio, 1st edit London, 1645. the 2d edit. 1651, so enlarged as to make an entire Commentary on the Sacred Scriptures. The 3d edit. London, 1657. These Annotations upon all the books of the Old and New Testaments were published in the 1st edit. in one vol. folio, and in the 2d and 3d edit. in 2 vols. The celebrated Mr Boston of Etterick informs us, in his Memoirs, Period 9th, 1711, that he had the English Annotations, 1st edit. in his library.

37. De Diphthongis sive Bivocalibus Dissertatio Philologica, 1646. In this learned and critical work, he endeavours to establish the point, that there are in reality no diphthongs, and that it is impossible two vowels should be so blended together as to enter into one syllable. This was certainly one of Mr Gataker's singularities. We pretend not to enter into this controversy, nor to decide whether our learned author was right or wrong in his views of orthography. This may seem to some persons beneath the attention of so great a man; but it appears that he was firmly resolved to vindicate such inquiries, and to shew that a thorough knowledge of grammatical learning greatly contributed to the improvement of true science. He had uncommon skill in Greek literature, his work was well received, and highly commended, by some able and candid judges, and it was also printed among his Critical Works.

38. A Mistake or Misconstruction removed, (whereby little difference is pretended to have been acknowledged between the Antinomians and us,) and Free Grace, as it is held forth in God's Word, as well by the Prophets in the Old Testament, as by the Apostles and Christ himself in the New, shewed to be other than is by the Antinomian party in these times maintained. In way of Answer to some Passages in a Treatise of Mr John Saltmarsh, concerning that Subject, 4to. 1646. This is written in answer to Mr Saltmarsh's Free Grace, or the Flowings of Christ's blood freely to sinners; being an Experiment

of Jesus Christ upon one who hath been in *bondage* of a troubled spirit at times for twelve years. Mr Gataker, in his work observes, " That it seems a thing much to be feared, that this course which I see some effect, and many people are much taken with, of extracting divinity in a kind of chymical way, even chimerical conceits, will, if it hold on, as much corrupt the simplicity of the Gospel, and the doctrine of faith, as ever the quirks and quillets of the old School-men did "

39. Shadows without Substance; or, Pretended New Lights, in Answer to Saltmarsh's Shadows flying away. 4to. pp. 124. London, 1646. Published by authority.

40. Mysterious Clouds and Mists, in Answer to Mr John Simpson. 4to. pp. 13; small and closely printed. London, 1648.

This celebrated scholar and divine employed both his learning and his zeal in the Antinomian controversy. He soon after published his learned work on the Style of the New Testament, in which he opposed the sentiments of Pfochenius, who maintained that there were no Hebraisms in those sacred writings, which he endeavoured to prove both by authorities and arguments. These sentiments Mr Gataker undertook to overthrow, which, in the opinion of able critics, he has most completely accomplished. Beside, he has most clearly and concisely explained the true sense of many texts both in the Old and New Testaments; corrected numerous passages in ancient authors; and discovered such consummate skill in the languages, such accurate judgment, and uncommon penetration, as very justly gained him the character of one of the best critics of the age. This work is entitled, " Thomae Gatakeri Londinatis de Novi Testamenti stylo Dissertatio." 4to. 1648. He informs us, in the first chapter, that, meeting with the treatise of Pfochenius, a German divine, published in 1639, he read it with much attention, and found it both weighty in matter, and replete with good learning. But he found many of the author's sentiments contrary to his own, and in his judgment not agreeable to truth. He saw also, that many eminent men were censured without cause, and sometimes represented as speaking very differently from what he considered to be their real sentiments. These observations induced him to examine many questions started in that treatise, or what naturally flowed from them. He begins by refuting a principle which Pfochenius has assumed, viz. that the Greek, Latin, German, &c. are original tongues. Mr Gataker thinks, it is very difficult to know what are original tongues, but respecting the Latin, he maintains that it is not. Thus he saps the very foundation of Pfochenius' system, by shewing, that there can be no assurance of the purity of any language, in the sense in which he understands it.—In the forty-fourth chapter, Mr Gataker gives a recapitulation of the whole dispute, and observes, that the true state of the question is, whether the style of the New Testament in Greek is every where the same with that which was used by the ancient writers, at the time when the language was in its greatest purity? Or, whether it is not such as frequently admits of Hebraisms and Syriasms? Pfochenius affirms the former, and denies the latter; but Gataker maintains the opposite sentiments. He concludes by observing, that, notwithstanding all that Pfochenius has urged, he does not doubt that nearly *six hundred* phrases might be produced from the New Testament, and a far greater number from the Greek version of the Old Testament, the purity of which Pfochenius seems tacitly to maintain, in which there are plain characters of the Hebrew or the Syriac tongues, and not the least resemblance of the real ancient Greek, so far as the most laborious and learned men have hitherto discovered. Archbishop Usher, the venerable Primate of Ireland, a competent judge, shewed his great respect both to our learned author, and to this performance of his, by sending a copy of it with his own Annals, as a present to the learned Dr Arnold Boate, who was then residing at Paris.[a]—Though this literary production was a very considerable work, and much increased the author's reputation, it was only a specimen of a larger work, in which he had been many years em-

a Parr's Life of Usher, p. 559, folio, 1686.

ployed; but of this an account has already been given; and also of his Latin discourses on infant baptism, a controversy in which he was deeply versed. He wrote several discourses on infant baptism, in which he treated the main questions with great seriousness and solid argument. The two Latin discourses, which he published on this subject, are said to be, for modesty, learning, and argumentation, not at all inferior to any of the other productions of his pen. The first of these is entitled, "De Baptismatis Infantilis vi & Efficacia Disceptatio privatim habita inter V. C. Dom Sam. Wardum, & Th. Gatakerum," 1651. The other is entitled, "Stricturae ad Epistolam J. Daven, de Baptismo Infantum," 1654.—His admirable edition of the Emperor Marcus Antoninus' Meditations has also been already mentioned. The work was reprinted in 1697, with the addition of the Emperor's Life, by Mr Dacier, together with some select notes of the same author, by Dr George Stanhope, who, in his dedication to the Lord Chancellor Somers, gives a very high character of our learned author. The most valued editions of these Meditations are said to be those with Gataker's notes, particularly that of Cambridge, 4to. 1652; of London, 4to. 1697; and of Utrecht, folio, 1698. Mr Gataker now appeared as an editor and annotator of ancient writings. In this walk, he was eminently distinguished, as he had formerly been in others; and his labours of this kind have been very much esteemed by the learned world. —These Meditations are collections of maxims and thoughts, in the spirit of the Stoic philosophy, without much connexion, or skill of composition, but breathing peculiar sentiments of piety and benevolence. They were written in Greek, Gataker has given a good Latin version, with a commentary, and the English reader is particularly indebted to Mr Graves for giving to them a modern English dress. This translator has added a few notes: others might very properly and advantageously have been selected from Gataker.—He published a vindication of his treatise on the name by which God made himself known to Moses and the people of Israel, in Latin, which is entitled, "Thomae Gatakeri Londinatis, Dissertationis De Tetragrammato suæ, adversus Capellum Vindicatio." Londini, 1652. Small piece.—He published a Vindication of the Annotations on Jer. x. 2. 4to. 1653. And A Discourse Apologetical, 4to. pp. 104. London, 1654, which has been formerly mentioned.—And "An Antidote against Error Concerning Justification," which has also been already brought to view, was published by his son, Charles, 4to. pp. 58. London, 1670. The celebrated Hermannus Witsius, in the year 1698, collected and published in one volume all Mr Gataker's critical works, entitled, "Opera Critica;" which probably will stand a monument to his memory as durable as time. His works *praise him in the gate*, and reflect much honour on the literary character of his country. In these, his zeal and courage in the Protestant cause are manifest. His learned performances in the Popish controversy about transubstantiation proved a very great and seasonable service to the cause of Protestants, and most deservedly rendered him conspicuous in the eyes of the most enlightened and respectable persons of those times, who admired his erudition and his fortitude as much as his humility and his readiness to serve the Church of Christ. His writings have a strong tendency to enlarge the sphere of critical knowledge, and of genuine piety; and in these he shews himself well read in biblical learning. They are full of large and learned marginal references or notes. They are works of laborious meditation, and of accurate and extensive inquiry. They *come home*, like Bacon's Essays, *to men's business and bosoms, and will, therefore, live as long as books last.*

Mr JOHN GIBBON, OF WALTHAM,

A MEMBER OF THE ASSEMBLY OF DIVINES AT WESTMINSTER.

I HAVE sought much in vain for some particular information respecting Mr John Gibbon, of Waltham. In my researches, I have only found that he had a son of both his names, who was ejected by the Act of Uniformity from Blackfriars, London; that he was minister at Waltham, was chosen one of the Assembly of Divines at Westminster, and is in Neal's list marked as giving constant attendance.

SAMUEL GIBSON,

PASTOR OF BURLEIGH, AND ONE OF THE ASSEMBLY OF DIVINES AT WESTMINSTER.

MR SAMUEL GIBSON had the character of a learned, pious, and judicious divine. He was also very modest and humble, as pious and judicious men generally are. He was Pastor of Burleigh, or Burley, as it is also written, in Rutlandshire, in England. He was chosen one of the Assembly of Divines at Westminster, and constantly attended that learned body. While he was at London attending the Assembly, he was some time minister at Margaret's, Westminster. He was one of those who agreed to and subscribed the proposition, "That Jesus Christ, as King of the Church, has himself appointed a church-government, distinct from the civil magistrate." He preached to the House of Commons. In his sermon to them, he says, "Honourable Senators, ye do well that every morning before ye go to the work of the day, ye begin with prayer to God, for his direction, and assistance, and blessing. I hope every member doth it with an humble heart, apprehensive of his own impotency, and nothingness; for certainly neither the ablest church-men in spiritual affairs, nor the wisest statesmen in temporal, can do any thing well without God, and therefore it is good to follow the old rule, and that is, to begin with God, lest errors be committed for want of his direction."[a]

Mr Gibson has written and published;

The Ruin of the Authors and Fomentors of Civil Wars;

a. Ab Jove principium.

as it was delivered in a sermon before the Honourable House of Commons, in Margaret's Church, Westminster, Sept. 24th, being the day of the monthly Fast, 1645. 4to. pp. 35. London, 1645. The text is 2 Sam. xvii. 14. The author says in it, "Many will say they stand for the *Common Prayer Book*, and they will fight for that as long as they can stand on their legs. A resolution fitter for the vulgar *Welch*, than for understanding *Englishmen;* for that Book was never of God's making, and no wise man will venture his life, and shed his blood, for any book made by man, were it never so good, for he can look for no reward of God for it.—But it hath been often said, *Take away the Common Prayer Book, take away our Religion.* Nay, our Religion is in the Bible, there is our God, and our Christ, and our Faith, and our Creed in all points. The whole Bible was Paul's belief; there are the Psalms of David, and his Prayers, and the Lord's Prayer, and other prayers, by which we may learn to pray. We have still the Lord's Songs, the Songs of Zion, sung by many with grace in their hearts, *making melody to the Lord*, though without organs. There we have all the commandments." He gives his testimony also against the Book of Sports, adding: "Our Court-prelates made the King Lord of the Sabbath, and themselves Lords of misrule: compelling parents, and masters, and ministers, and magistrates, to suffer their sons and daughters, and servants of both sexes, to play, and sport, and dance, if they had a mind to it, and to profane a great part of the day. Here was trenching upon God's prerogative.—They who were for the Book of Sports, would not endure the name *Sabbath.*" Mr Gibson was a stout champion for the Parliament, for the Reformation, and for *the Truth as it is in Jesus.* He gives, in his sermon above mentioned, the highest commendation to the Brethren and Church of Scotland for reformation. He says, "They shewed zeal and courage, and quickened us when we in a manner had lost ourselves, and there was little life in us. They have been instruments to promote the Reformation which we have."

GEORGE GIPPS,

RECTOR OF AYLESTON, AND A MEMBER OF THE ASSEMBLY OF DIVINES AT WESTMINSTER.

GEORGE GIPPS was Rector of Ayleston, in Leicestershire, a County almost in the centre of England. He was chosen one of the Assembly of Divines at Westminster, and is marked by Mr Neal as constantly attending. He preached to the House of Commons. He published at their desire a sermon which he preached from Psal xlvi. 1. This is entitled, "A Sermon preached (before God, and from Him) to the Honourable House of Commons, at a publike Fast, Novemb. 27, in the yeare *God is our refuge, our strength; a helpe in troubles verie abundant we finde.*" This was in the year 1644. 4to. pp. 32. London, 1645.

Mr Gipps seems to have been a self-denied and pious man, and not a bad casuist. Dr Calamy informs us, that a son of his, John, was cast out for non-conformity. But I cannot give any farther account of him.

Mr William Good, or Goodie, as he seems to have written his name, is another of those Divines respecting whom I have not found much information. At this distance of time, we cannot expect much information respecting all those divines who met at Westminster in the seventeenth century. I have, however, received large accounts of some of those eminent men, in the goodness of Divine Providence, and shall endeavour to give the reader, from a considerable collection of materials, whatever authentic information has appeared to me interesting, curious, and useful. Great defects are now unavoidable; especially respecting those persons who lived in some degree of obscurity, and were less employed in the great transactions of the times.

WILLIAM GOODE, B. D.

PASTOR OF DENTON, AND A MEMBER OF THE ASSEMBLY OF DIVINES AT WESTMINSTER.

WILLIAM GOODE was Pastor of Denton, in the County of Norfolk, in England. He was chosen one of the Assembly of Divines, and superadded. He constantly attended; and was one of those divines who subscribed the proposition, respecting church-government, which has been repeatedly mentioned.

I have seen two good sermons which he published; the one is entitled, "The Discovery of a public spirit, presented in a sermon before the Honourable House of Commons, at Margaret's, Westminster, at their public Fast, 26th March 1645." 4to. pp. 32. London, 1645. The other is entitled, "Jacob Raised; Or, The means of making a Nation happy both in spiritual and temporal Privileges:" A Sermon from Amos vii. 5, before the Lords at Westminster, Fast, Dec. 30th, 1646. 4to. London, 1647.

THOMAS GOODWIN, D D.

MINISTER OF THE GOSPEL IN LONDON, A MEMBER OF THE ASSEMBLY OF DIVINES AT WESTMINSTER, AND PRESIDENT OF MAGDALEN-COLLEGE, IN OXFORD.

THOMAS GOODWIN was born at Rolesby, a small village in the County of Norfolk, in England, on the 5th of October, in the year 1600. He was the eldest son of Richard and Catharine Goodwin, the name of whose family was Collinwood. His parents watched over his infant-mind with peculiar care, and they endeavoured to bring him up *in the nurture and admonition of the Lord.* Being religiously educated and early intended by his parents for the holy ministry, he received a suitable education in grammar-learning, and on the 25th of August, in the year 1613, he was sent to Christ-Church-College, in the University of Cambridge. He continued about six years in that college, which was then in a very flourishing condition, having about two hundred students. He applied there with great diligence to his studies, and soon secured the esteem of his tutors, and attracted much notice in the University. In the year 1619, he removed to Catherine-hall, in the same University, of which he became afterward a Fellow, and was also chosen Lecturer for the year 1620. For some time he was an admirer of Doctor, afterward Bishop, Senhouse, whose sermons were adorned with flowers of wit and human learning, collected from the Fathers, Poets and Historians. This mode of preaching was at that time much applauded by many scholars in the University. Mr Goodwin was then ignorant in a great degree both of the corruption of his nature, and of the necessity and worth of Jesus Christ. He pursued vain wisdom, and leaned unto his own understanding. He walked in the vanity of his mind, seeking applause and preferment. But Almighty God, in the unsearchable riches of his grace, was pleased to change his heart, and to turn the course of his life to his own service and glory. Mr Goodwin kept a diary, of which his son says he had above a hundred sheets written with his father's own hand, and in which are recorded, the account of the work of the Holy Spirit on his soul, in converting him to God, and many of his religious exercises and experiences. As nothing so clearly and fully unfolds the work of the Holy Spirit, and the exercise of the soul, in conversion, as a person's diary, I shall partly give the account of these in Mr Goodwin's own words, which may be both acceptable and useful to readers who have a taste for such things. He says,

"Though by the course of nature in my first birth, I was not like to live, being born before my time, and therefore of a weak constitution; yet God so kept and strengthened me, that he preserved me, as David says, *When I hung upon my mother's breasts;* as one in whom he meant to manifest his grace, in the miraculous conversion of my soul to himself. He did often stir up in me in my childish years, the sparks of conscience, to keep me from gross sins, and to set me upon performing common duties. I began to have slighter workings of the Spirit of God, from the time I was six years old; I could weep for my sins, whenever I did set myself to think of them, and had flashes of joy upon thoughts of the things of God. I was affected with good motions and affections of love to God and Christ, for their love revealed to man, and with grief for sin, as displeasing them. This shewed how far goodness of nature might go, as well in myself as others, to whom yet true sanctifying grace never comes. But this I thought was grace, for I reasoned with myself, it was not by nature. I received the sacrament at Easter, when I was fourteen years old, and for that prepared myself as I was able. I set myself to examine whether I had grace or not; and by all the signs in Ursin's Catechism, which was in use among the Puritans in the College, I found them all, as I thought in me. The love of God to such a sinner, and Christ's dying for me, did greatly affect me: and at that first sacrament I received, with what inward joy and comfort, did I sing with the rest the ciii. Psalm, which was usually sung during the administration! After having received, I felt my heart cheared in a wonderful manner, thinking myself sure of heaven, and judging all these workings to be infallible tokens of God's love to me, and of grace in me: All this while not considering that these were but mere strong fits of nature's working. God hereby made way to advance the power of his grace the more in me, by shewing me how far I might go, and yet deceive myself, and making me to know that grace is a thing surpassing the power of nature; and therefore he suffered me to fall away, not from these good motions, for I could raise them when I would, but from the practice of them; insomuch as then my heart began to suspect them as counterfeit.—I made a great preparation for the next ensuing sacrament, and in the mean time, I went to hear Mr Sibbs, then Lecturer at Trinity Church to the town of Cambridge, whose lecture the Puritans frequented. I also read Calvin's Institutions, and O how sweet was the reading of some parts of that book to me! How pleasing was the delivery of truths in a solid manner then to me? Before the sacrament was administred, I looked upon the holy men in Christ's College, where I was bred, and how affected was I, that I should go to heaven with them!—When I was in my place in the chapel, ready to receive the sacrament, being little of stature, the least in the whole University then, my tutor seeing me, sent to me that I should not receive it, but go out before all the College, which I did. This so much dampt me, as I greatly pitied myself, but chiefly for this, that my soul, which was full of expectation from this sacrament, was so unexpectedly disappointed of the opportunity. For I had long before verily thought, that if I received that sacrament, I should be so confirmed, that I should never fall away.

But after this disappointment I left off praying; for being discouraged I knew not how to go to God. I desisted from going to hear Dr Sibbs any more. I no more studied sound divinity, but gave myself to such studies as should en:ble me to preach after the mode, then of high applause in the University, which Dr Senhouse brought up, and was applauded above all by the scholars.—Arminianism was now set a foot in Holland, and the rest of these provinces, and it continued hottest at that very time when I was thus wrought upon. I perceived by their doctrine, which I understood, being inquisitive, that they acknowledged a work of the Spirit of God to begin with men, by moving the soul; but free-will then from its freedom carried it, though assisted by these helps. And this work of the Spirit they called grace, sufficient in the first beginnings of it, exciting, moving and helping the will of man, to turn to God, and giving him power to turn, when being thus helped he would set himself to do it: But withal they affirmed, that though men are thus converted, yet by the freedom of the same will, they may, and do often in time, fall away totally; and then upon another fit, through the liberty of the will, again assisted by the like former helps, they return again to repentance.

Farthermore, I am yet to tell you, how I was acquainted, during this season, with several youths in Christ's College, who had made known to me the workings of God upon them, in humiliation, faith, and change of heart. And I observed that they continued their profession stedfast, and fell not off again. Though the Arminian doctrines suited my own experience, in these natural workings of conscience off and on in religion; yet the example of those godly youths, in their constant perseverance therein, made so strong an impression on me, that in my very heart and judgment, I thought the doctrine of Arminianism was not true. And I was fixed under a conviction, that my state was not right; but yet I could not imagine wherein it was defective. But notwithstanding my falling thus away, yet I still upon every sacrament set myself of new to examine myself, to repent, and turn to God: but when the sacrament was over, I returned to a neglect of praying, and to my former ways of unregenerate principles and practices, and to live in hardness of heart and profaneness. When I was thus given over to the strength of my lusts, and farther from all goodness than ever I had been, and utterly out of hope, that God would ever be so good to me, as to convert me, and being resolved to follow the world, the glory, applause, preferment, and honour of it, and to use all means possible for these attainments.

When I was one day going to be merry with my companions at Christ's College, hearing a bell toll at St Edmund's for a funeral, one of my company said, There was a sermon, and pressed me to hear it. I was loth to go in, for I loved not preaching, especially that kind of it that good men used, and which I thought to be dull stuff: but yet seeing many scholars going in, I thought it was some eminent man, or if it were not so, that I would come out again. I went in before the hearse came, and took a seat, and fain would I have been gone, but shame made me stay. I was never so loth to hear a sermon in my life. Enquiring who preached, they told me it was Dr Bambridge, which made me the more willing to stay, because he was a witty man. He preached from Luke xix. 41, 42. I remember the first words of the sermon pleased me so well, as to make me very attentive all the while. He spake of deferring repentance, and of the danger of doing so. Then he said, that every man had his day, it was, *This thy Day*, not to-morrow, but to-day. He shewed also that every man had a time, in which grace was offered him; and if he neglected it, it was just with God, that it should be hidden from his eyes. And that as in things temporal, it was an old saying, That every man had an opportunity, which, if he took hold of, he was made for ever: so in spiritual things, every man has a time, in which if he would know the things which belong to his peace, he was made for ever; but otherwise, they would be hid from his eyes. This a little moved me, as I had wont to be at other sermons. Then he came to shew that the neglect of this had final impenitence, blindness of mind, and hardness of heart; concluding with this saying, Every day thou prayest, pray to God to keep thee from blindness of mind, and hardness of heart. The matter of the sermon was vehemently urged on the hearer, whoever he was who deferred his repentance, not to let slip the opportunity of that day, but immediately to turn to God, and defer no longer, being edged with that direful threatening, lest if he did not turn to God in *that day*, the day of grace and salvation, it might be eternally hidden from his eyes. I was so far affected, that I said to a companion of mine who came to church with me, and indeed had brought me to that sermon, *That I hope to be the better for this sermon as long as I live.* That companion and I had come out of our own chambers at Catherine-hall, with a fixed design to have gone to some of my like acquaintance at Christ's College, on purpose to be merry and spend that afternoon; but as I went along, was accidentally persuaded, to hear some of the sermon. This was on Monday in the afternoon, 2d October 1620. As soon as we came out of the church, I left my fellows to go to Christ's College; but my thoughts being retired then, I went to Catherine-hall, and left all my acquaintance, though they sent after me to come.—I thought myself to be as one struck down by a mighty power.[a] The grosser sins of my conversation came in upon me, which I wondered at, as being unseasonable at first; and so the working began, but was prosecuted still more and more, higher and higher; and I, endeavouring not to entertain the least thought of my sins, was passively held under the remembrance of them, and affected, so as I was rather passive all the while in it than active, and my thoughts held under, while that work went on.[b]

I remember some two years after, of preaching at Ely in the Minster, for Dr Hill, Master of our College, I told the auditory, meaning myself, that for a man to be converted, who is ordinarily ignorant of what the work of conversion should be, and what particular passages it consists of, and that yet he should be guided through all the dark corners and windings of it, would be a wonder to think of, and would be as if a man were to go to the top of that lanthorn, to bring him to all the passages of the Minster, within and without doors, and knew not a jot of the way, and were in every step in danger to tread awry and fall down. So it was with me, I knew no more of that work of conversion than these two general heads, that a man was troubled in conscience for his sins, and afterward was comforted by God's favour manifested to him. And it was one evidence of the truth of the work of grace upon me, when I reviewed it, that I had been so strangely guided in the dark. In all this intercourse, and those that follow to the end, I was acted all along by the Spirit of God upon me, and my thoughts passively held fixed, until each head and sort of thoughts were finished, and then a new thought began and continued, which made me view them as so many conferences God had with me, by way of reproof and conviction.—An abundant discovery was made unto me of my inward lusts and concupiscence, and how all sorts of concupiscences had wrought in

a See Acts ix. 3—9. b See Rom. vii. 9.

me; and I was amazed, to see with what greediness I had sought the satisfaction of every lust."[a]

Mr Goodwin proceeds, informing us, that by the Divine illumination which he now enjoyed, he had obtained a very full and affecting discovery of the most secret sins of his heart; it being searched, as it were with candles, agreeably to the prophet's phrase. That he now clearly saw his inward corruption, as the root, or fountain, of all his sinful courses; and ceased from *going about to establish his own righteousness;* which he never before had done. He now saw, that the sinfulness of his sin was exceedingly enlarged, *Wherefore he abhorred himself, and repented in dust and ashes.* He *was humbled under God's mighty hand,* with whom only and immediately he had to do.—Under a full conviction of the original corruption of his nature, and vitiated state of all his faculties, he was much affected with a sight and sense, that his heart was entirely empty of all spiritual goodness. *For I know that in me, that is, in my flesh, dwelleth no good thing.* Finding himself altogether destitute of any spiritual good thing toward the Lord God of Israel; and having a strong propensity unto all evil, he was very much inclined to trace his sinfulness, both in heart and life, unto it's proper source. Here he says, " And after I had well debated with myself, that one place, Rom. v. 12, *By one man sin entered into the world, and death by him, and passed upon all men, in whom, or in that all had sinned:* That it was in him they all sinned, for they had not in and of themselves sinned actually, as those who die infants, *after the similitude of Adam's transgression,* which limitation is there cautiously added by the apostle, to shew that they had not actually sinned of themselves, but are simply involved in his *act* of sinning; and that sin wherein we were all involved, as guilty of it, is expressly said to be the *disobedience of that one man;* for by one man's disobedience, many of his children of the sons of men, were all made sinners; for disobedience notes an act of sinning, not a sinful nature or habit. This caused me necessarily to conceive

a See Rom. vii. 8.

thus of it, that it was the guilt or demerit of that one man's disobedience, that corrupted my nature. Under such apprehensions as these, did my spirit lie convicted so strongly of this great truth, that being gone to bed some hours before, and filled with these meditations, I rose out of bed, being alone, and solemnly fell down on my knees before God, the Father of all the family in heaven, and did of my own accord, assume and take on me the guilt of that sin, as truly as any of my own actual sins."—

Having had a most affecting discovery made unto him of the vanity of his mind, the deceitfulness of his heart, and of the wretchedness and sinfulness of his condition, he was entirely shut up, and, for sometime, he saw no way of relief; but together with the deplorable sight of his own sinfulness and vileness, he saw also hell opening it's mouth ready to receive and devour him. And, the very alarming consideration of the eternity of misery, *Where their worm dies not, and the fire is never quenched*, greatly disquieted his soul, and pierced it through with many sorrows. He lay bound very closely under the pressure of divine wrath, as being subject to the righteous judgment of the Lord, as the word, he says, should be translated. How long his soul continued filled with these thoughts, he did not remember, but says, that the time was short. He was now, indeed, under a solid and strong conviction of God's wrath abiding on him, as being in a state of unbelief; but God, *who is rich in mercy to relieve all who call upon him*, soon set his soul free from trouble. He, whose faithfulness never fails, sent his word and healed his patient.

"At the noise of thy water-spouts
  deep unto deep doth call;
Thy breaking waves pass over me,
  yea, and thy billows all.
His loving-kindness yet the Lord
  command will in the day,
His song's with me by night; to God,
  by whom I live, I'll pray."

God was mindful of his word of promise to Mr Goodwin, *and did not suffer him to be tempted above that he was able; but did with the temptation also make a way to escape, that he might be able to bear it.* When his soul was dead in trespasses and sins, the Father of mercies, the Lord of life, and the God of all comfort, said unto him, *Live; yea, He said unto him, Live.* The Lord God of salvation was graciously pleased, in a very unexpected manner, to change the whole of his former dispensation respecting the subject of this memoir, to his inexpressible comfort and advantage: and having imparted a new life and spirit unto his soul, He also said to him, for his farther encouragement under his distress, *Thy sins, which are many, are forgiven. Come now, and let us reason together, saith the Lord: Though your sins be as scarlet, they shall be as white as snow; though they be red like crimson, they shall be as wool.* Mr. Goodwin, through patience and comfort of the Holy Scriptures, now enjoyed the real pleasures of hope. Like Saul, who was afterward called Paul, he *obtained mercy;* and really found that *the grace of our Lord was exceedingly abundant with faith and love which is in Christ Jesus.* And that *This is a faithful saying, and worthy of all acceptation, that Christ Jesus came into the world to save sinners; of whom he was chief.* And having formerly a strong guard set upon him, as the prisoner of hell, he now, in his sweet experience, through the grace of the divine Spirit, found the Lord Jesus Christ speaking a word in season unto his weary and distressed soul. And he reckoned, that the example of Paul, and similar examples of conversion, are exhibited by God, "as flags of mercy before a company of rebels to win them in." *For whatsoever things were written aforetime were written for our learning, that we, through patience and comfort of the Scriptures, might have hope*, Rom. xv. 4. Examples are used both for the illustration and confirmation of rules. And, "that God pardoned such a man in such a condition, is often brought home to another man in the same condition, and contains implied in it; a secret promise, that he may do so to me, in the like condition."

Mr Goodwin now, in a particular manner, found that he was endowed with a new nature, new dispositions of soul, natively inclining him to good, whereas before he was only inclined to evil. He now found not only good temporary motions from the Spirit of God, when he applied himself to holy duties; but a new indweller, or habitual principle of opposition to indwelling sin, and a real hatred of it, to which he was formerly an entire stranger. He now found, that the beautiful image of God was happily restored unto his precious and immortal soul. Being really renewed in the spirit of his mind, he was effectually taught *to put on the new man, which after God is created in righteousness and true holiness. He was renewed in knowledge after the image of him who created him.* He found, in his sad experience and also to his comfort, that there were two very contrary principles in him, spirit against flesh, and flesh against spirit. The internal principle of grace against the corruption of nature, and the corruption of nature against the internal principle of grace. These two very contrary principles are found in all regenerate persons, while they are strangers and pilgrims on the earth. *For*, in them *the flesh lusteth against the spirit, and the spirit against the flesh*, Gal. v. 17. And, Mr Goodwin found also the wide difference of that opposition, which the natural conscience only makes against a lust, and that which the spirit, or internal principle of grace, makes against the flesh, or corruption of our nature. He found that the *spirit* not only contradicted and checked the *flesh*, but also made a real natural opposition to it, such as fire does to water; so that the spirit did as truly lust against the work of the flesh, as the flesh against that of the spirit. He here farther remarks, that he did not discover this difference, either by reading, or hearing any person speak of it, but solely from his own experience. He now concluded, that this contest between grace and corruption was peculiar to a regenerate person. He argued in the following manner: It is not in God; for he is only and infinitely holy. It is not in devils; for they are wholly sin. It is not in good angels; for they are entirely holy. It is not in wicked men; for they have no internal principle of grace in them, to fight with the corruption of their nature, in such a manner.—He could now bless God, and say, " I am what I was not." He was quite contrary to what he was in the past years of his life, in judgment, in heart, and in conversation. Upon this, he heartily resolved to turn from all known sins unto God, under the influence of his grace snd Spirit; and became an eminent example of strict and serious godliness, entertaining the truth of it, as far as he had received it from the word of God. And under divine direction and assistance, he looked back on his former ways and sinful state, and took a summary survey of his chief sins and lusts; and readily found that he had been *a lover of pleasures more than a lover of God.*—That he had formerly sought, with his whole soul, vain glory, and academical praise. *I thought on my ways, and turned my feet unto thy testimonies.* He now chiefly aimed at the glory of God, in all his thoughts, words, and actions. And with the fear of God before his eyes, he turned his attention in a particular manner to his aim in his studies, upon which he had spent all his time. Having been early devoted by his parents to the work of the holy ministry, he was now made duly sensible of the importance of that service in the church of God, to which he had been devoted. As he improved in learning, he did grow also in grace, which enabled him to lay out all his other attainments to the glory of God, and especially in the deeply interesting work of the ministry. Having now a peculiar zeal for the glory of God, a great regard for the interests of the Redeemer's kingdom, and a most tender concern for the everlasting salvation of precious and immortal souls, he readily found, that affectation of wit, vain glorious eloquence, which he formerly pursued with great eagerness, *and every high thing which exalts itself against the knowledge of God, were all brought into captivity and obedience to Christ.* He had formerly sought his own glory, the honour and applause of men; but now he sought the glory of Him who sent him. And he concluded, That *he who seeks his glory who sent him, the same is true, and no unrighteousness is in him.* He says, " I came to this resolved principle, that I would preach wholly and altogether sound wholesome words, without affectation of wit and vanity of eloquence. And in the end, this project of wit and vain glory was wholly sunk in my heart, and I left all, and have continued in that purpose and practice these threescore years; and I never was so much as tempted to put in any of my own withered flowers which I had gathered and valued more than diamonds, nor have they offered themselves to my memory, to the bringing them into a sermon to this day; but I have preached what I thought was truly edifying, either for conversion of souls, or bringing them up to eternal life." He earnestly *longed to impart to them some spiritual gift, by which they might be edified.* His inquiry now was not, how he might raise his own reputation; but how he might glorify God and be the instrument of saving sinners.

He was a great admirer at this time of Dr Preston, and became a frequent hearer of him, and of Dr Hill, who were thorough Calvinists, and whose sentiments and views of things he now adopted. He considered those eminent divines as his models, while he was preparing for the important office of the Christian ministry. It was a considerable time before he came to have a clear knowledge of the gospel, and a full view of Christ by faith, and to have joy and peace in believing. He says, "I was diverted from Christ several years, to search only into the signs of grace in me. It was almost seven years ere I was taken off to live by faith on Christ, and on God's free love, which are alike the object of faith." His thoughts for such a length of time were chiefly and intensely set on the conviction which he was under of the heinousness of sin, and of his own sinful nature and miserable state, as a child of wrath; and on the difference between the workings of the natural conscience, though enlightened, and the motions of the heaven-born soul, when changed and under the influences of the Holy Spirit, in an effectual work of peculiar and saving grace.—

He entered into a very great intimacy with that eminently pious minister of Jesus Christ, Mr Price of Lynn, who was the instrument employed by God to lead him into the innermost temple of divine love and a gracious and experimental acquaintance with his Divine Saviour. From Mr Price's conversation, letters, example, and prayers, through the grace of the Eternal Spirit, Mr Goodwin was much enlightened into the sublime mysteries of the Redeemer's kingdom, and led into the real spirit of the gospel, to live by faith in Christ, and to derive from him life and strength for sanctification, and all comfort and joy through believing. By his means, he was led into the comfortable, heart-felt enjoyment, and gracious experience of true Christianity. Mr Price, in one of his letters to Mr Goodwin, writes as follows: "As for trials of your own heart, they are good for you, only remember this, that Christ, in whom you believe, has overcome for you, and he will overcome in you; the reason is in 1 John iv. 4. And I say trials are good for you, because else you would not know your own heart, nor that need of continual seeking to God; but without these trials your spirit would soon grow secure, which of all conditions of those who fear God, is most dangerous, and most uncomfortable. Therefore, count it exceeding cause of joy not of sorrow, when you are exercised with any temptations, because they are tokens of your being in Christ; which being in him, Satan would disquiet, and carnal reason would call in question: Yet stand fast in the liberty of Christ, maintain the work of God's free love, which his good Spirit has wrought in you. Say unto the Lord, Lord, thou knowest I hate my former sinful course, it grieves me that I have been so long such a stranger to thee, my Father. Thou knowest now I desire to believe in Jesus Christ, I desire to repent of my sins, and it is the desire of my heart to do thy will in all things. Finding these things in your heart, cast yourself upon the righteousness of Christ, and fear nothing; for God will be a most merciful God in Christ unto you. Strive but a little while and you shall be crowned." Mr Price, in another letter to him, says—"All your complaints are good, and will bring abundance of thankfulness in the end; for mark it in the Scripture, where the saints of God have complained for want of Christ or any good thing from God in Christ, they have had ere long their hearts and tongues filled with thanksgiving and praise, Rom. vii. 24, 25." By similar letters and conferences, Mr Price poured the balm of the grace of the gospel of Christ into Mr Goodwin's wounded soul, which, through the blessing of God, healed and comforted it. These truly evangelical instructions turned his thoughts to Christ, who is *the way, and the truth, and the life*, to find that relief in Him which he had in vain sought for in other objects. As the result of that highly useful correspondence, Mr Goodwin wrote in the following manner to Mr Price,—" I am come to this pass now, that signs will do me no good alone: I have trusted too much to habitual grace, for assurance of justification—I tell you, *Christ is worth all.*" Mr Goodwin, coming thus to the Lord Jesus Christ, his weary soul most readily found true and everlasting rest in Him. *Come unto me, all ye who labour and are heavy laden, and I will give you rest.* Mat. xi. 28.

Disclaiming now all vain wisdom and self-dependence, he was most happily brought, under divine influences, to sit down at the feet of the Lord Jesus Christ, his blessed Master, to learn the mysteries of the kingdom of heaven from Him, who teaches as never man taught. At his school, he learned how widely different that knowledge of divine things is, which is accquired by mere human learning, from that sublime wisdom which comes from above.—He was admitted, upon preparatory examination, to preach the glorious gospel of the grace of God, and soon became a very celebrated preacher in Cambridge. He was now acquainted with *personal religion*, which has been considered as a necessary qualification in the Christian teacher. An eminent writer says, " God has not, indeed, limited the efficacy of ordinances by the character of the dispenser. But yet the Scriptures warrant us to say, that wicked ministers run unsent, and that God generally frowns upon, and blasts their labours.[a] When souls are entrusted to the slaves of Satan, we cannot but dread a

a Psal. l. 16. Jer. xxiii. 21—23.

bad account of them. For what concern will those feel, or what care will they take, about the salvation of others, who feel no concern for their own salvation? Ministers are men of God; an expression which surely implies that they are men devoted to his service, conformed to his blessed image, zealous for his honour, animated by his Spirit, and breathing after communion and fellowship with him. But a man of God, living without God in the world! a master of Israel, ignorant of the new birth! a guide to Zion, walking in the paths that lead to destruction! a soldier of Christ, in league with Satan! is a shocking and monstrous absurdity. The light of the world, and the salt of the earth, are too honourable titles for any under the power of darkness and corruption.—An infinitely wise God would scarcely appoint those to help others to Christ, who themselves are strangers to him; or commission those as his ambassadors, to negotiate a treaty of peace with an apostate rebel world, who themselves are obstinately persisting in treachery and rebellion."[a]

Mr Goodwin was chosen Lecturer of Trinity-Church in Cambridge, in the year 1628, though not without opposition from Dr Buckridge, bishop of Ely. The bishop, at first, made some difficulty in admitting him to that place, unless he would solemnly promise, in pursuance of the King's proclamation, not to preach respecting any controverted points in divinity. Mr Goodwin ingeniously remarked, that the most essential articles of the Christian faith, being controverted by some persons, such a promise would scarcely leave him any subject to preach upon. That it was not his Majesty's intention to inhibit him or any other person, from preaching against the gross errors of Popery. After some opposition he was admitted. And he was presented by the King to the vicarage of the same church, in the year 1632. In this situation he was much followed and admired by the Puritans, who were now rapidly increasing in numbers in the University, as well as in the kingdom at large. In the

a Dr Erskine's Disc. from James iii. 1.

Memoirs of his Life, he is said to have been a happy instrument in turning many persons to the love and practice of serious religion. He says himself, "After I had been seven years from Cambridge, coming out of Holland, I had for some years after, well nigh every month, serious and hearty acknowledgements from several young men, who had received the light of their conversion by my ministry, while I was in the University of Cambridge. And this was the great encouragement I had to return again to an University, having enjoyed so frequently a testimony of the fruit of my labours while I was preacher of Cambridge; and what the success has been at Oxford, I leave to Christ till the latter day." His preaching at first was for the most part, if not wholly, much calculated to produce conviction and terror; to alarm the conscience and wound the heart. But upon his obtaining the sweet experience of the heavenly refreshing comforts, which flow plentifully into the soul from the knowledge of Christ, and free justification by his finished righteousness alone, he became a zealous preacher of the glorious gospel of the grace of God, for the consolation of such distressed consciences, as his own had been. He seems to have made a good improvement of a hint which the celebrated Dr Sibbs gave him, in a familiar manner, as follows: "Young man, if you ever would do good, you must preach the gospel, and the free grace of God in Christ Jesus." He readily complied with his friend's advice; and he called his sermons of the glory of the gospel, which were printed in the fifth volume of his works, his *Evangelical First-Fruits*. The only copy of these sermons was very remarkably preserved and recovered, by the special and unremitting care of Divine Providence. The portmanteau in which they were, was, by a thief, cut off from Mr Goodwin's horse, in the dark of the evening, just against St Andrew's church-yard in Holborn. The clerk or sexton, coming on the morning of the Lord's-day to ring the bell, found a bundle of papers, lying at the foot of a large tree. In it there were some acquittances, which a bookseller of Cambridge, who had accompanied Mr Goodwin to London, had from some of his customers. By these only, the clerk could know to whom the bundle belonged, who brought it to the bookseller, who was his particular friend.

Mr Goodwin, becoming dissatisfied with the terms of conformity, relinquished his preferments, and quitted the University, in the year 1634. In giving up his preferments, and removing from the University, he sincerely followed the light which God had given him from his word; and though he was thereby subjected to great outward trouble, he had much inward comfort, and especially from these appropriate words of his blessed Saviour, which are recorded in Luke xviii. 29, 30. *And he said unto them, Verily I say unto you, there is no man that hath left house, or parents, or brethren, or wife, or children, for the kingdom of God's sake, Who shall not receive manifold more in this present time, and in the world to come life everlasting.* That exceedingly great and precious promise, and the performance of it, afforded him strong, lasting, divine, and inexpressible inward comfort, in all his outward trouble. The people of God have generally enjoyed most inward comfort, when they were under the greatest outward trouble. *For as the sufferings of Christ abound in us, so our consolation also aboundeth by Christ.* Mr Goodwin left all for the sake of Christ, and of his gospel. He was made willing on the memorable day of divine power, to live in the meanest and most afflicted condition, if so he might serve his Royal Master in all godly sincerity. He says, "I cheerfully parted with all for Christ, and he has made me abundant compensation, not only in the comforts and joys of his love, which are beyond comparison above all other things, but even in this world. What love and esteem I have had among good men, He gave me. He alone made my ministry in the gospel acceptable, and blessed it with success, to the conversion, and spiritual good and comfort of many souls."

In the year 1638, he married Elizabeth Prescott, the daughter of Alderman Prescott. She was really a help meet for him, being a woman of a very sweet temper, of lively wit, and of sincere piety, which rendered her peculiarly agreeable to her husband, and to all her acquaintance. By her, God gave him an only daughter, Elizabeth, who was married to Mr John Mason, a citizen of London.

When the terms of conformity were closely urged, and the Puritans were severely persecuted by the Episcopal consistories, he was one of those ministers, who, in the year 1639, went over into Holland, to enjoy that Christian liberty which he could not enjoy in his own native land. In that country, he became pastor of an independent congregation at Arnheim. During the time of his abode in that place, some differences arising in the English Church at Rotterdam, he and the elders of the church at Arnheim, went to Rotterdam, and God was pleased to bless their friendly advice, to compose the differences, and to re-establish the disturbed peace of that Church. About the beginning of the long Parliament, he returned to London, and was chosen a pastor of a church in that famous city, and also a member of the venerable Assembly of Divines at Westminster. He took a brief account of the transactions of that memorable Assembly, in fourteen or fifteen volumes octavo, which his son says he had in his possession, written with his father's own hand. He was one of the dissenting Brethren in that assembly.[a] Wood says, that he was one of "the atlasses and patriarchs of Independency." In the year 1647, he had invitations from the reverend, pious and learned John Cotton, and other worthy ministers in New England, to go over to them. He was much inclined to comply with their invitation, and had put a part of his library on board a ship; but through the advice of his friends, to which he paid a great respect, he changed his resolution.

In the year 1649, he married Mrs Mary Hammond, who was descended from the ancient family of the Hammonds in Shropshire, whose ancestor was an officer in the army of William, Duke of Normandy, when he invaded England, in the year 1066. She was an help meet

a See Life of W. Bridge, pp. 141, 142.

for him, as his former wife had been; and by her, God gave him two sons, and two daughters.

He was a great favourite with Oliver Cromwell, who highly commended him as an eminent instrument in propagating the gospel, and a great luminary in the church. Through Cromwell's influence, Mr Goodwin was appointed President of Magdalen College in Oxford, in the year 1649. Here he formed a church upon the Independent plan, and was very diligent in promoting the interests of piety and learning. He was also made one of the triers of ministers, or commissioners for the approbation of preachers. In the common register of the University, he is said to be *well known to the world by many theological writings.* It has been supposed that he was the Independent minister, and head of a College, described in the 494th No. of the Spectator.—Having been bachelor of divinity of several years standing, he proceeded Doctor in divinity, Dec. 23, 1653. He attended Cromwell upon his death-bed. Soon after the Restoration, in 1660, he was dismissed from his Presidentship, when he retired to London, where he continued the exercise of his ministry until his death.

He now spent much of his time in religious retirement, in prayer, reading, and meditation. He read much, and the authors he esteemed and studied were, Augustine, Calvin, Muscuhus, Zanchius, Pareus, Walaeus, Gomarus, and Amesius; and among the schoolmen, Suares, and Esthius. But he chiefly read and studied the Holy Scriptures. And having furnished his library with a very good collection of commentators, he made good use of them. The everlasting love and free grace of God, and the glorious excellencies of the Lord Jesus Christ, were the truths in which he peculiarly delighted, in his meditations. These most precious truths were the life and food of his soul. And as his heart was deeply affected with them, he wrote and delivered these with a spiritual warmth which is better felt than can be expressed. Though he read much, he spent more time in thinking, and it was by intense thought that he made himself master of the subject of his discourse.

In the dreadful fire at London, in 1666, he lost above the half of his library, to the value of five hundred pounds. But his books of divinity, which were chiefly useful to him, were remarkably preserved. On this occasion, he wrote a discourse on patience, and it's perfect work, which soon after was published.

We come now to the account of Dr Goodwin's death. He was seized with a fever, which in a few days put an end to his life in this world. As his life was exemplary, his death was edifying. In all the violence of his fever, he discoursed with such strong faith, and assurance of Christ's love, with such holy admiration of free grace and joy in believing, and with such heavenly expressions of gratitude and praise, as deeply affected all persons who heard him. When one prayed earnestly for him, "That God would return into his bosom all those comforts, which he had by his ministry of *free grace*, poured into many distressed souls," he found that the prayer was speedily answered, in the abundant consolation which he enjoyed. Divine comforts now filled his soul. He had great joy and peace in believing. He rejoiced in the thoughts that he was dying, and going to enjoy full and uninterrupted communion with God. He said, "I am going to the Three Persons, with whom I have had communion: they have taken me, I did not take them. I shall be changed in the twinkling of an eye; all my lusts and corruptions I shall be rid of, which I could not be here. These croaking toads will fall off in a moment." And mentioning these illustrious examples of faith, Heb. xi. he said, "All these died in faith. I could not have imagined, that I should ever have had such a measure of faith in this hour. No, I could never have imagined it. My bow abides in strength. Is Christ divided? No, I have the whole of his righteousness. I am found in Him, not in my own righteousness which is of the law, but in the righteousness which is of God, which is by faith of Jesus Christ, *who loved me, and gave himself for me.* Christ cannot love me better than he doth; I think I cannot love Christ better than I do. I am swallowed up in God." The Lord Jesus Christ was "as honey to his mouth, music to his ears, and joy to his heart," as He is to all true believers. *Christ* was all to him; and he found inexpressible delight in the love of Christ, *which passes knowledge.* He saw the vast importance of a Mediator between God and sinners.—That *Jesus* was a necessary and an all sufficient Saviour; and the only support for a departing soul. And he did not build the hopes of his salvation upon the quicksand of his good works, but alone on the firm and eternal rock, *Christ Jesus.* Directing his speech to his two sons, he exhorted them to value the privilege of the Covenant. He said, "It has taken hold on me. My mother was a holy woman, she spake nothing diminishing of it. It is a privilege, which cannot be valued enough, nor purchased with a great sum of money," alluding to the words of the chief captain to Paul, Acts xxii. 28. Then he exhorted them to be careful that they did nothing to provoke God to reject them. And upon that he said; *Now, I shall be ever with the Lord.* With this assurance of faith, and fulness of joy, his soul left this world, and went to enjoy the reality of that blissful state of glory, which, in a discourse on that subject, he beautifully unfolded.—He died, Feb. 23d, 1680, in the 80th year of his age. His mortal remains were buried in a little vault toward the east end of the new burial place for dissenters, joining on the north side of the new Artillery-yard by Bunhill-Fields.[a]

Dr Goodwin, in doctrinal sentiment, was a Calvinist of the Supralapsarian cast. And zealously recommending what he considered to be the genuine doctrines of Christianity, he neglected not to remind his hearers or his readers of the strong incitements which these sublime doctrines presented to purity both in heart and life. Dr Calamy says that "he was a very considerable scholar, and an eminent divine; and had a very happy faculty in descanting upon Scripture so as to bring forth surprising remarks, which yet generaly tended to illustration." He was a writer of very considerable eminence. Dr Wilkins,

a His Life by his Son, Calamy's Account, Neal's Hist. Purit. and Wood's Athenæ.

in his Gift of Preaching, places him among some of the most eminent English divines for sermons and practical divinity. And Dr Cotton Mather, in his Student and Preacher, says, "If you would see sound doctrine, the works of an Owen have it for you.—You have a Goodwin who will place you among the children of light, and will give you the marrow of the doctrine which is according to godliness. He often soars like an eagle; perhaps, you would have been content, if sometimes a little more concisely." His style is plain and familiar; but diffuse, homely, obscure and tedious, though not disagreeable to a sober mind. He handles his subject with much gravity and decency, and at great length. Fiery declamations, or appeals to the passions, discover more enthusiasm than judgment. But Dr Goodwin's discourses are very judicious, pious, grave, and well digested. They are temperate, and attended with conclusive reasoning, having a tendency to make an impression on the mind of the sensible reader and of the practical Christian, which reflection confirms, the understanding approves, and the memory retains. He had a remarkable talent for exposition. He delighted much in searching into difficult texts, and was successful in his attempts. The least particles of speech came under his notice, and in many instances he has made it appear, how much depends upon *little words*, in the Sacred Writings, which are too generally overlooked. It is said, that his writings continue to be much read and esteemed by the Calvinistic Independents. They are numerous, and some were printed in his lifetime, and others after his death. The sentiment is valuable.

---

1. *A Child of Light walking in Darkness:* Or, A Treatise shewing the causes by which the cases wherein, and the ends for which, God leaves his children to distress of conscience. Together with directions how to walk so as to come out of such a condition. With other observations upon Isai. l. 10, 11. Quarto, of 255 pages. London, 1636—1644—1647, and London, 1651, 4to. pp. 165. in a collection of the author's other pieces,

which follow, entitled, *Certain Select Cases Resolved;* especially tending to the comfort of believers, in their chief and usual Temptations. Very useful for afflicted souls.

2. *Return of Prayers:* A Treatise, in which this case, How to discern God's answers to our prayers, is briefly resolved; with other observations upon Psal. lxxxv. 8. respecting God's speaking *Peace unto his people, and to his saints.* I cannot tell when the first edition of this treatise was printed; but I have seen an edition of it, 4to. pp. 100. London, 1651, and another in a small size. Glasgow, 1748.

3. *The Trial of a Christian's Growth, in Mortification, and Vivification;* or, *in Purging out Corruption, and bringing forth more Fruit,* on John xv. 1, 2. This treatise was printed when the author was absent from his native country, under considerable disadvantage both in style and matter, which, upon his return, he amended, as he informs us in a preface to it, under the date of April 26th, 1643. It was also printed, London, 1650. 4to. pp. 110.

4. *The Vanity of Thoughts Discovered: with their Danger and Cure.* London, 1638-43, 1650. 4to. pp. 33.

5. *Aggravation of sin; and sinning against Knowledge and Mercy;* in several sermons delivered on different occasions. London, 1643—& 1650. 4to. pp. 92.

6. *Christ set forth in his Death, Resurrection, Ascension, Sitting at God's right-hand, and Intercession, as the Cause of Justification, and the Object of Justifying Faith,* upon Rom. viii. 34. Together with a Treatise discovering the affectionate tenderness of Christ's heart now in heaven, unto sinners, on earth. These treatises are said to have been first printed in 1642. I have seen a second edition of them both, London, 1642. And another edition, London, 1651.

7. *Christ the Universal Peace-Maker:* Or, The Reconciliation of all the People of God, notwithstanding all their differences and enmities. London, 1651. I have seen all these treatises collected into one volume, in quarto.

8. *Zerubbabel's Encouragement to Finish the Temple:* A sermon preached from Zech. iv. 6—9, before the House of Commons, at their solemn Fast, April 27th, 1642. 4to. pp. 59. London, 1642.

9. *The Great Interest of States and Kingdoms:* A sermon from Psal. cv. 14, 15, before the House of Commons, Fast, Feb. 25th, 1645. 4to. pp. 59. London, 1646.

10. *The World to Come:* Or, The Kingdom of Christ asserted; in two Expository Lectures on Eph. i. 21, 22. London, 1655.

11. *Patience and its perfect work under sudden and sore Trials;* which was written upon his loss by the great fire of London.

12. After his death; A Treatise of the Punishment of Sin in Hell, was published by Mr Thankful Owen and Mr Barron; which was followed by five volumes in folio. His Works in folio, 1681, have been advertised for sale lately in London, 5 vols. £5. Fine copy, £5 15s. 6d. And a very fine copy, £7 17s. 6d.—His pieces which were published in his life-time, are accounted by some the most valuable. Wood says, that Mr Jemmat translated into Latin some part of Dr Thomas Goodwin's works, which were printed at Heidelberg in 1658. I have seen his writings both in England and Scotland.

WILLIAM GOUGE, D. D.

AN EMINENT ENGLISH DIVINE, WHO FLOURISHED IN THE FORMER PART OF THE SEVENTEENTH CENTURY, PASTOR OF BLACK-FRIARS, LONDON, AND A MEMBER OF THE VENERABLE ASSEMBLY OF DIVINES AT WESTMINSTER.

WILLIAM GOUGE was born at Stratford-Bow, in the County of Middlesex, in England, on the 1st of Nov. in the year 1575. His parents were very respectable. His father, Mr Thomas Gouge, was a devout gentleman;

careful in the worship of God, and in the duties of religion. His mother was a virtuous and pious woman; the daughter of Mr Nicholas Culverwell, a merchant in London: and she was the sister of those two famous preachers, Messrs Samuel and Ezekiel Culverwell. And she had two sisters who were married to those two famous and learned divines, Dr Chaderton, the Master of Emanuel College in Cambridge, and Dr Whitaker, the Royal Professor of Divinity in the same University.[a]

The subject of this memoir received his classical education, partly in Paul's school, London, partly at Felsted in Essex, and partly at Eton-school. He was three years at Felsted, and during that time, he was trained up under the gospel ministry of his uncle, Ezekiel Culverwell. This ministry was highly beneficial to his soul. He often said, That if he was not thereby first begotten again to a lively hope, he was much built up in his holy faith. He was six years at Eton; and during that time, the pleasant blossoms of his early piety were amply unfolded. He possessed a large share of the fear of God. He was remarkably attentive to secret prayer, and to the sanctification of the Lord's day. With grief he observed the profanation of that day, by sports and amusements, which the Great Lawgiver has required to be kept holy. "Perhaps at no period of our history were the fashionable world ever so much devoted to pleasure and amusement as at the present, nor indeed was there ever a less regard paid to that law of God, *Remember the Sabbath day to keep it holy.*"[b] Many persons seem to indulge themselves in letting the world see, that they neither fear God, nor regard man. And an unblushing profanation of the Lord's-day is a sure prognostic of destruction. "The most solemn observance of this day is a duty of so commanding a nature, that we hazard in the breach of it our individual and national safety: for there cannot be a more unerring prognostic, which I hope neither we nor our latest posterity shall ever behold, of the approaching

a Clarke's Lives.

b The Instructor, No. xlv. 1808. p. 365.

downfal of this country, than an open and unblushing disregard of the Sabbath "[a] We ought to observe the open and unblushing disregard of this holy day with much grief; and to be particularly attentive to the sanctification of it, as our religious scholar was.—He was also remarkably attentive to every branch of his education at the schools; and persevered in his learning with indefatigable diligence. Having at length attained, by his indefatigable diligence, a considerable degree of classical knowledge at the grammar-schools, he was elected to King's College in Cambridge, in the year 1595. He pursued his academical studies with uncommon assiduity, and with proportionate success. He was a notable example of the great literary diligence of those times. He began his studies early in the morning, and continued them until a late hour at night. During the first three years, he did not sleep one night without the walls of the College. At the expiration of that time he was chosen Fellow, and then he paid a visit to his friends, but he soon returned to resume his studious labours. He was an acute disputant; and he took his Degrees in Arts at the regular periods, when he performed all those exercises with great applause in the public schools, which were required by the statutes of the University.

He continued nine years in the College. And during all that time, he was never absent from morning prayers in the chapel, which were usually performed about half an hour after five o'clock in the morning, except when he went out of town to visit his friends. He rose so long before, that he might have time for his secret devotions, and for reading his morning task of the Holy Scriptures. He resolved to read fifteen chapters of these every day; five in the morning, five after dinner, before he entered upon his other studies, and five before he went to bed.[b] And when he could not sleep during the watches of the night, he meditated upon these, and enjoyed then a spiritual and an intellectual feast upon the Word of God. " In whatever point of view we contemplate the Word

a The Instructor, No. xii. p. 91. b Clarke's Lives.

of God, under the sweet, the irradiating influence of the Divine Spirit, it shews a lovely and interesting countenance; every feature charms, astonishes and delights. How sublime its theory! How lovely its practice! How sweet its experiment! How glorious its perfection! If the planetary system afford pleasure to the Astronomer, far more wonderful discoveries attract the Christian in this system of grace:

The heavens declare thy glory, Lord,
In every star thy wisdom shines;
But when our eyes behold thy Word,
We read thy name in fairer lines.

Truth, wisdom, power, goodness, mercy, grace, and love, are the bright constellations of this system of everlasting beauty, while Christ, the sweet sun of righteousness, with majestic lustre, sheds the beams of glory over every page:

O may these heav'nly pages be
My ever dear delight,
And still new beauties may I see,
And still increasing light." [a]

He who is renewed in the spirit of his mind, and enjoys the supernatural influences of heaven, will make the Holy Scriptures his companions both by day and by night. "He will have recourse to them for direction, in the bright and chearful hours of prosperity; to them he will apply for comfort, in the dark and dreary seasons of adversity." [b] The knowledge of the Holy Scriptures is highly beneficial for our spiritual improvement, especially in holiness. "By continual meditation in the sacred writings, a man as naturally improves and advances in holiness, as a *tree* thrives and flourishes in a kindly and well watered soil." [c] Our pious student also wrote in a little book, which he always carried with him, the distinct heads of every particular passage in every chapter of the

a The Instructor, No. xviii. p. 140.

b Horne's Comment. on Psal. i. 2. c Horne on Psal. i. 3.

Bible, which was highly useful to him afterward. And he had stated times for making a more particular search into the meaning of difficult places of the Holy Scriptures. By such means, accompanied with the Divine blessing, he was one mighty in the Scriptures, as our reformers generally were. "Blessed are they, who seek in the Scriptures the true riches; who traffic for the spiritual gains of celestial wisdom; for surely *the merchandise of it is better than the merchandise of silver, and the gain thereof than fine gold*, Prov. iii. 14."[a]

While he was at the College, a Jewish Rabbi came to Cambridge, and was admitted into several Colleges to teach the scholars the Hebrew language. Mr Gouge, with others, readily embraced the opportunity of learning that useful language from him. Many of the scholars soon tired, and left their Jewish teacher; but Mr Gouge continued with him as long as he remained there. The value of any thing is best known by the want of it. They who did not avail themselves of the advantage of their instructor while he was among them, were obliged to lament their folly and loss when he was gone. They immediately turned their eyes toward Mr Gouge, and applied to him for instruction in the Hebrew language. He generously attended unto their request, and afforded them his assistance. By teaching them he at length attained an extensive and accurate knowledge of the Hebrew himself, and became an excellent Hebrew scholar.

He was chosen a Lecturer both in logic and in philosophy in the College, and acquired great reputation by the able manner in which he discharged the duties of that useful and important appointment.

In the first year of his Fellowship he began his Common-place-book for divinity, in which he referred to what he read. He had also white or clean paper bound between the leaves of his Bible, on which he wrote such short and energetic interpretations, and observations, on the text, as could not well be referred to any head in his Common-place-book.

a Horne's Comment. on Psal. cxix. 72.

Having continued in the College the space of nine years; and being intimately acquainted with the various branches of literature, and particularly with divinity and with the Hebrew language, he was called home by his father, and soon afterward entered into the matrimonial connexion. He was greatly delighted with an University-life, and resolved to spend more time in it than he did, if not his whole life: but Divine Providence over-ruled matters otherwise, which greatly contributed to the benefit of the church of Christ. Upon his entering into a matrimonial connexion, that he might wholly devote himself unto his studies, he committed the whole care of the secular affairs of his family to the management of his wife. Having completed his regular courses, he was admitted into Orders, or into the holy office of the ministry, in the year 1607; and in June, in the year 1608, he was called to the particular exercise of his ministry in the parish of Black Friars, in the city of London. In this settlement he continued until his death, though he had the offer of several eminent places. He often said, That the height of his ambition was to go from Black-Friars to heaven. A good man only desires power and opportunities of doing good to his fellow-creatures, and of shewing forth his praises who hath called him out of darkness into his marvellous light. Mr Gouge discharged the duties of the pastoral office with exemplary diligence and fidelity. The able and impressive manner in which he conducted the public services of the Sabbath-day, and the amiable and condescending spirit which he shewed in the useful and important duties of visiting and catechising, were highly commendable. He commonly prayed eight times in public, on the Sabbath; both before and after reading and expounding the Holy Scriptures; and before and after each sermon; which he performed both forenoon and afternoon. Mr Leigh informs us, That he began his prayer very audibly and distinctly, which was the more commendable, because of his great congregation at Black-Friars.[a] He was eminently labori-

[a] Leigh's Treatise of Religious and Learned Men, Book iv. Chap. ii.

ous and faithful in dispensing the *will* of God to his hearers, and not his own fancies, nor the inventions of men; sincerely instructing them in the way of salvation, and constantly breaking to them the bread of life; always endeavouring to comfort and encourage the weak. He is said to have excelled in the logical analysis of his text, and in expounding difficult places of the Holy Scriptures when they occurred. His expressions were plain, and his style familiar. "Remember, we do not mount the pulpit to say fine things, or eloquent things, we have there to proclaim the good tidings of salvation to fallen men; to point out the way of eternal life; to exhort, to cheer and support the suffering sinner; these are the glorious topics upon which we have to enlarge—and will these permit the tricks of oratory, or the studied beauties of eloquence? Shall truths and counsels like these be couched in terms which the poor and ignorant cannot comprehend? Let all eloquent preachers beware lest they fill any man's ear with sounding words, when they should be feeding his soul with the bread of everlasting life!—Let them fear lest instead of honouring God, they honour themselves! If any man ascend the pulpit with the intention of uttering *A Fine Thing*, he is committing a deadly sin."[a]

Mr Gouge's ministry was highly beneficial to many souls. After he had finished his public labours, on the Sabbath-day, some neighbours, who were without helps in their own families, came to his house, where he repeated his sermons to them in a familiar manner, which they found to be highly useful. Afterward, he visited the sick in his parish, or such as could not attend the public ordinances. And he knew well how to avail himself of the advantages of their circumstances. He also carefully examined his parishioners, especially before they were admitted to the sacrament of the Lord's supper. He considered himself as the devoted servant of the Lord Jesus Christ, and of his church; and he highly esteemed, and greatly delighted in, the service of his Royal Master.[b]

a The Instructor, No. xlix. p. 394.
b See his Epistle to the Reader, before his Whole Armour of God.

He lived in all humility, and in singleness of heart, unto the Lord Jesus Christ. Beside preaching twice every Sabbath, he also set up a weekly lecture, which was much frequented for thirty-five years, not only by his own parishioners, but likewise by several ministers in London, by members of the Inns of Court, and by the more respectable and religious citizens, and even by those who came occasionally to London, respecting their secular affairs. He so highly esteemed the work of the holy ministry, that he ardently wished that all his sons might be preachers of the glorious gospel of the grace of God. He said to Lord Coventry, keeper of the great seal of England, "That he envied not his great place and employment." When we consider him as ministring to his people, and associating with his family, it is difficult to imagine a more respectable and truly amiable character. His family resembled a church in the house, for prayer, morning and evening, and reading the Holy Scriptures; and for catechising, and government. He was the delight both of his friends and of his family. His truly respectable character adorned his sacred profession. His example, both in public and in private life, may be imitated with great advantage; and ought to be considered as having a tendency to inflame our piety and zeal, and to excite our love of God and of divine things. "The great and shining examples, which display their lustre, more or less, in every period of the Christian history, must have an admirable tendency to inflame our piety, and to excite, even in the coldest and most insensible hearts, the love of God and virtue."[a] And, "It must be useful to perpetuate the memory of some of these excellent men, who are now gathered to their fathers, and to exhibit them as models to an age in which domestic religion is grown unfashionable, and families are consequently deprived of those sweet charities of life which are the fruits of true and undefiled religion."[b]

The subject of this memoir was now particularly atten-

a Mosheim's Eccles. Hist. vol. i. Introduction, xx.

b The Christian Magazine, vol. vi. p. 50.

tive to the sanctification of the Lord's-day, both publicly and privately. His servants were not required to provide any supper the evening before the Sabbath, that they might go to bed in good time, and prepare for the approaching day. And he would not allow any servant to remain at home to prepare meat upon the Lord's-day for the entertainment of any friend. The Sabbath is a very ancient institution, Gen. ii. 3. And that it might never be forgotten, God himself was pleased to engrave it on tables of stone, and to insert it in the middle of the decalogue, with a particular note, *Remember the Sabbath-day to keep it holy*. See Exod. xxxi. 12—18. and xx. 8—11. " Men, by the manner in which they " regard this day to the Lord," discover the real complexion of their minds relative to him. This day will declare whether they have any knowledge and fear of God, any faith, hope, and delight in him, any love to, or desire after him." [a] I observed with much pleasure, that at Watlington, in the County of Oxford, a Society has been formed for the purpose of promoting the orderly and religious observance of the Lord's-day. The clergy, gentlemen, and tradesmen, of that town, and eleven or twelve neighbouring parishes, impressed with the idea that it was their duty to prevent, as far as their influence extends, the violation of that sacred day, agreed to the following Resolutions: 1. To pay their servants and labours their wages on the Saturday, or on some other day, in sufficient time to enable them to procure their provisions or other articles before the Sabbath. 2. To abstain from buying or selling, or suffering to be bought or sold, on their account, any goods or commodities whatsoever on the Lord's-day. And while these resolutions were framing, the clergymen observed a very laudable and exemplary conduct. They waited personally on the farmers belonging to their respective parishes, and with very general success, submitted to them the propriety of paying their labourers their wages in good time, as expressed in the first Resolution; thereby removing,

a The Instructor, No. lvi. p. 455.

so far as they are concerned, the complaint of late payment, too often made by servants of that class, and uniformly urged as an apology for violating the Sabbath.[a] A religious observance of the Lord's day is enjoined upon us by the high authority of heaven: and we ought to prevent, as far as our influence extends, the violation of that sacred day; and, as friends of vital godliness, to excite and encourage others in the sanctification of it by our laudable example and just authority. It should be observed agreeably to the tenor of Isaiah's heavenly language, who speaks to us in the name of the Lord of the Sabbath, Isai. lviii. 13, 14.

"What says the Prophet? Let that day be blest
With holiness and consecrated rest.
Pastime and business both it should exclude,
And bar the door the moment they intrude;
Nobly distinguish'd above all the six,
By deeds in which the world must never mix.
Hear him again. He calls it a delight,
A day of luxury, observ'd aright;
When the glad soul is made Heaven's welcome guest,
Sits banquetting, and God provides the feast.
But triflers are engag'd, and cannot come:
Their answer to the call is—*Not at Home*."[b]

Mr Gouge was so eminently exemplary and religious in the whole course of his life, that he was called an Arch Puritan by some scoffers. He highly esteemed the religion of Jesus, which too many treat with contempt. "A set of miserable and unthinking creatures treat with negligence, nay sometimes with contempt, the religion of Jesus, not considering that they are indebted to it for all the good things which they so ungratefully enjoy.[c]

He was admitted to the degree of Bachelor of divinity, in the year 1611; and to that of Doctor in the same faculty, in the year 1628. About this time, he became one

a The Instructor, No. lvi. p. 451. Sept. 28, 1808. b Cowper.
c Mosheim's Eccles. Hist. vol. i. Cent. i. p. 1. chap. i. end.

of the trustees of the society which had united for the purpose of buying impropriations, to bestow them on such clergymen as should be distinguished by their piety and ministerial qualifications; which occasioned his being prosecuted in the Star-Chamber. This society intended to plant a learned and powerful ministry, especially in cities and market-towns, in several parts of the kingdom, which were most destitute, for promoting the glorious gospel of the grace of God in those parts: but the court adjudged their proceedings as illegal, and dissolved the society.[a]

In the year 1643, Dr Gouge was nominated one of the Assembly of Divines at Westminster, and was held in such reputation by that learned body, that he was often called to the moderator's chair in his absence. He was a very respectable and useful member; and preferred that public employment to any private business. He constantly attended the Assembly: and that he might not lose any time, he carried his Bible, and some other books in his pocket, in order to use them during any intermission in the affairs of the Assembly. When Episcopacy was voted down, and the bishops refused to ordain any who were not in the interest of the crown, and application was made to the Assembly at Westminster for their advice respecting this affair, they advised, That an association of some godly ministers in and about London, and in other places, be appointed by public authority, to ordain ministers for the city and other parts. Agreeably to this advice, the two Houses of Parliament passed an ordinance, 2d Oct. 1644, for the ordination of ministers for the time, which appointed ten persons, being Presbyters, and members of the Assembly, to examine, and ordain, by imposition of hands, all those whom they should judge admissible into the sacred office of the ministry. Dr Gouge was one of that number.[b] And as these ordinations were accompanied with fasting and prayer, he was observed to be peculiarly attentive to these solemn exercises on such occasions.

a Clarke's Life of Gouge. b Neal's Hist. Purit. vol. iii. chap. iv. Calamy's Cont. vol. i. pp. 66, 67,—550.

He was also chosen by a committee of Parliament, with others, to write Annotations on the Bible, being well known to be very judicious, and eminently skilful in expounding the Holy Scriptures. His share was from the beginning of the first book of the Kings to Job. "In which the intelligent reader may observe such skill in the original, such acquaintance with the sacred story, such judgment in giving the genuine sense of the text, and such acuteness in raising pertinent observations, that without the help of any other Commentators, a man may accommodate himself with the sense, doctrines, and uses of most of those Scriptures that came under his hand, in those brief annotations." [a]

Being chosen President of Sion-College, according to custom, when he resigned his office, he preached a learned and polite sermon in Latin to the clergy, which he delivered by the strength of his memory, without the help of his notes; which shewed that though his body was weak, his mental powers were strong.

He was an excellent casuist: a sweet comforter of dejected souls, and distressed consciences. Many applied to him, both in town and country; both private Christians, and public teachers. He was esteemed the father of he London Ministers for several years. He was highly useful in composing differences. *Blessed are the peace-makers: for they shall be called the children of God.* He was eminently charitable; *doing good unto all, especially unto them who are of the house-hold of faith.* To do good was the great object of his pursuits. He disdained to accumulate useless wealth. He studied the decent advancement of his family, the generous assistance of his friends, and the benevolent relief of the indigent. He often exerted his abilities, *in the cause of the widow, the fatherless, and of him who had none to help him.* He maintained some poor scholars in the University wholly at his own expence, and contributed liberally toward the maintenance of others. He set apart a sacred stock, as he called it; a portion fcr the poor, proportionate to his income,

a Clarke's Lives.

which he faithfully distributed. "He got riches to use them, and used them so as to be honoured on their account."[a] He was a bright example of benevolence.—His temperance was very great, in his eating, drinking, clothes, and recreations. Like Luther, "He was a stranger to the elegancies of life, being superior to all selfish considerations." A great economist of time, from his youth until his death. He generally rose about four o'clock in the morning, during the summer; and in winter, he rose before it was light, that he might have the better opportunity for his own devotion, in imitation of his blessed Lord and Master, Mark i. 35. The blessed Jesus rose before it was light, that he might enjoy God and himself, in religious retirement. "It surely becomes us sometimes willingly to deny ourselves the gratifications of sleep, that we may have the better opportunity for devotion. And it should be the peculiar care of those who are employed in God's public service, to cultivate communion with him in private; lest while they keep the vineyard of others, their own be *neglected* and impoverished."[b]—Dr Gouge was singularly modest and affable; and very richly adorned with humility. He was very friendly; and his friendship, founded on religion, was highly beneficial to many; like the gentle dew upon herbs, and as the clear shining after rain. He delighted much in communion with God, and in the emanations of his love, which a stranger intermeddleth not with; and which this world can neither give nor take. Such persons possess a joy which is unspeakable and full of glory.

"While others vain delights pursue,
They taste God's love for ever new."

He was accustomed to look up constantly to God, as the author of every good and of every perfect gift; the generous dispenser of every blessing, and the wise orderer of every event. His mind was deeply impressed with a sense of God's kindness displayed in favours which had been

a Plutarch's Lives, vol. iii. Cimon. b Doddridge's Family Expositor, 4to. vol. i. Sect. 36. Improvement.

received. He was singularly warm, vigorous, and extensive, in expressing his gratitude to God for all his benefits. His gratitude increased with his years, and kept pace with the countless, and signal instances of divine goodness, and mercy which followed him all the days of his life. "The more kindness we receive, and the longer we live, we should abound the more in thanksgiving to God.—It is a service very pleasant in itself, and highly creditable to Christianity.—It approaches nearer than any other service in this world, to the employments of the blessed in heaven, who praise Jehovah without weariness, without interruption, and without end! The angels are continually employed in this delightful exercise."[a] *They shall abundantly utter the memory of thy great goodness, and shall sing of thy righteousness.* The laudable examples of the saints, whom we find frequently employed in thanking God for his goodness, are recorded for our imitation. The sweet Psalmist of Israel is eminently exemplary in this heavenly exercise; and the subject of this memoir should not be overlooked. Mr Clarke says, That there was none like him in thanksgiving He also often engaged in the solemn and extraordinary exercises of fasting and prayer, when he discovered a truly contrite heart, a very deep sense of sin, and much sorrow for it. When public *fasting* had not the countenance of the bishops, he was very helpful to Christians in their private *fasts*. In dangerous times, he united with others in humble acknowledgment of their transgressions against Almighty God, sometimes in monthly and even weekly fasts, of which many were observed in his own house, and others in his vestry. On these solemn occasions, like a genuine son of Jacob, he earnestly wrestled with God, with supplications and tears of godly sorrow, humbly imploring a removal of those evils which they professedly lamented, and that the Lord their God *would return and repent, and leave a blessing behind him.*

He was singularly inquisitive respecting the state of the

a Christian Magazine, vol. vi. pp. 27,—29.

Church of Christ, both at home and abroad; and eagerly wished to obtain the interesting intelligence of her condition, that he might know how to supplicate God in her behalf. *If I forget thee, O Jerusalem, let my right-hand forget her cunning If I do not remember thee, let my tongue cleave to the roof of my mouth; if I prefer not Jerusalem above my chief joy.*

He studied much to magnify Christ, and to debase himself. He was accustomed to say,—" When I look upon myself, I see nothing but emptiness and weakness; but when I look upon Christ, I see nothing but fulness and sufficiency." Every thing that we need is found in Christ, and may be derived from him as the vital head of the Church. *And of his fulness have all we received and grace for grace.* " Of what worth Christ is to us, is a question, says an old writer, which would non-plus all the saints on earth, and angels in heaven, to answer. One thing we are certain of—that no being in the universe can fill his place, and do for us what he is able to do."[a] Of this Dr Gouge was fully convinced; and to this truth he here bears ample testimony. When the hand of his body was weak and tremulous, the hand of his soul, his faith, was strong and steady. When he could scarcely hold the cup at the sacrament of the Lord's Supper, with his paralytic hand, while he carried it to his mouth; with a firm and fixed confidence he took hold of Christ, and with an holy and spiritual thirst applied his blood to his soul. When he returned to his house from the Lord's Supper, he very joyfully offered to God thanksgivings and praises for the abundant refreshment which he had received from the flesh and blood of his Redeemer. We always ought to serve our God with joyfulness and gladness of heart, for the abundance of his goodness.

Particular circumstances in the lives of illustrious characters may be perused with advantage, and especially those respecting their afflictions and death. Affliction and death are *trying* seasons, when Christians are concerned

a Jay's Discourses for Families, vol i. Disc. 28.

to *come forth as gold.* They then require much divine support and comfort, that they may not *faint*, and strong faith and great patience and resignation that they may not *sin.* When the subject of this memoir was afflicted with sharp and bitter pains, which were occasioned by the stone, asthma, or disease of the lungs, and other distempers, he never complained of God for his sufferings, but often of himself for sinning. He was now particularly attentive to the sovereignty and holiness of God,—the evil nature of sin, which is the cause of all trouble, and of his own sin in particular. He often said, "A great sinner, but I comfort myself in a great Saviour." Jesus is *a name above every name.* It *is as ointment poured forth* to sinners. It hath a high relish with the people of God, who are sinners saved by grace. Jesus affords comfort to his people, whom he saves from their sins, in all their afflictions, as he did to this servant of his.—In the most violent paroxysms, he said,—"Well, yet in all these there is nothing of hell, or of God's wrath." His sufferings were never so deep, but he could see the bottom of them, and say, "Soul, be silent: soul, be patient. It is thy God and Father who thus ordereth thy condition. Thou art his clay, and he may tread and trample on thee as he pleaseth. Thou hast deserved much more. It is enough that thou art kept out of hell. Though thy pain be grievous, yet it is tolerable. Thy God affords some intermissions. He will turn it to thy good, and at length put an end to all: None of which things can be expected in hell." His afflictions greatly contributed to the exercise of his grace. *Tribulation worketh patience; and patience, experience; and experience, hope: And hope maketh not ashamed; because the love of God is shed abroad in our hearts by the Holy Ghost which is given unto us.*

In his extreme pains, he often repeated the words of holy Job,—*Shall we receive good from the hand of God, and shall we not receive evil?* He often warmly commended his soul unto Christ, saying,—*I am persuaded that he is able to keep that which I have committed to him against that day.* When any of his friends proposed to to comfort him, by mentioning the gifts which God had conferred on him, and the works which he had peformed by him as an instrument, he readily answered,—"I dare not think of any such things for comfort. Jesus Christ, and what he hath done and endured, is the only ground of my sure comfort." Similar to this, is the pathetic language of the Rev. John Willison of Dundee, in a letter to the Rev. Ralph Erskine, in like circumstances.—"Though I sometimes aimed to be concerned for the truth and interest of our Lord Jesus, and to appear as I could for the same; yet I renounce all these appearances, and all my other doings, as filthy rags, and desire only to take up my rest in Christ as the Lord my righteousness; and to lay down my head in his bosom, when my heart, flesh, and strength, fail me, as they are presently doing. O that I may die like Simeon, with Jesus in my arms, saying, *Now lettest thou thy servant depart in peace, according to thy word; for mine eyes have seen thy salvation.* I acknowledge my attainments small, and manifestations few; yet sometimes I would be saying, *I'll remember the Lord from the land of Jordan and the hill Mizar,*—though, in the mean time, I would flee from all past experiences to a present offered Christ, and a present offered perfect righteousness, and depend entirely thereon. I rest, I hope, I *live* on this righteousness: I die leaning and resting wholly on this bottom: all other bottoms are false and deceiving."[a] This subject deserves our best attention, and ought to be seriously considered. Dr Gouge was highly useful to mankind both living and dying. He was particularly attentive to the spiritual improvement of those around him on his death-bed; recommending the Saviour and his ways. His friends and acquaintances visited him now with interest, and retired highly satisfied; for he was truly exemplary in his death, as well as in his life. In this most eventful and trying season, he clearly shewed the absolute necessity of *repentance toward God, and faith in our Lord Jesus Christ,* and that it was extremely dan-

a Christian Magazine, vol. vi. pp. 152, 153.

gerous to die trusting to the general mercy of God, or to some fanciful righteousness of our own. The Great Mediator between God and men was his only comfort in death.

When death approached near, his pains increased; but in the lucid interval, he diligently improved his time, and made some farther progress in his much desired commentary upon the epistle to the Hebrews, which he eagerly wished to finish, and did finish within half a chapter, under the goodness of Divine Providence. When he was so weak that he could not arise out of his bed, he said,—"Now, I have not long to live in this world. The time of my departure is at hand. I am going to my desired haven." He often said to his friends who came to visit him in his sickness,—"I am willing to die, having, I bless God, nothing to do but to die." He called death his best friend, next to Jesus Christ. He had much familiarity with death, which was highly advantageous to him, at this time. When his sister said to him, Brother, I am afraid to leave you alone: He said to her,—"Why, sister, I shall, I am sure, be with Jesus Christ when I die." *Mark the perfect, and behold the upright: for the end of that man is peace.*

When the time of his departure was at hand, his spirit became more lively and cheerful, than it had been for several days before, probably from the pleasing prospect, that his death was near. His speeches were now very heavenly, as if he were already in heaven. He spake much in the admiration of God's free grace, and the riches of his mercy in Jesus Christ. He greatly rejoiced in Christ Jesus. "Jesus Christ is the very object-matter of a believer's joy; *Our rejoicing is in Christ Jesus.* Take away the knowledge of Christ, and the Christian is the most sad and melancholy creature in the world: again, let Christ but manifest himself, and dart the beams of his light into their souls, it will make them kiss the stakes, sing in flames, and shout in the pangs of death, as men that divide the spoil."[a] This remark was particularly

a Flavel's Works, vol. i. Sermon i.

verified in the illustrious subject of these pages, who was an eminent follower of them who through *faith* and *patience* inherit the promises. The power of religion, and the energy of divine grace in the soul, were clearly seen in him, in the last eventful and trying hour. He died very comfortably and piously, falling asleep in Jesus, December 12th, in the year 1653, in the 79th year of his age, having been Minister of Black-Friars almost forty-six years.[a]

Mr Neal says, "He was a modest, humble and affable person, of strict and exemplary piety, an universal scholar, and a most constant preacher, as long as he was able to get up into the pulpit." Dr Calamy gives him a similar character.[b] His name is enrolled in the catalogue of King's-College Worthies, among the learned writers of that College, in Dr Fuller's History of the University of Cambridge. His memory has been carefully preserved, and his real character transmitted to posterity, by his writings, by the biographical writers here referred to, and also in Burnham's Pious Memorials. Wood styles him a *pious and learned preacher*, and says, "He is often honourably mentioned by Voetius, Streso, and other foreign divines; and was always accounted by the Puritans eminent for his humility, patience, and faith." Granger says, he was offered the Provostship of King's-College, Cambridge, but declined to accept it; and that he was laborious, exemplary, and so much beloved that none ever thought or spoke ill of him, excepting those who were inclined to think or speak ill of religion itself.[c] Mr William Jenkin was assistant to Dr Gouge about twelve years, preached his funeral sermon, and succeeded him in the pastoral office. Mr Thomas Gouge, on whose death Dr Watts wrote an excellent elegiac poem, was the Doctor's son, and Mr Richard Roberts married his eldest daughter. These three excellent divines were ejected by the Act of Uniformity, in 1662.[d]

a Clarke's Lives of eminent Divines; Neal's Hist. Purit. vol. iv. General Biogr. vol. iv. London, 1803. b Calamy's Cont. vol. i. p. 12. c Granger's Biog. Hist. vol. ii. p. 179.

d Palmer's Noncon. Mem.

Dr Gouge's Writings are;

1. *The Whole Armour of God:* Or, The Spiritual Furniture which God hath provided to keep safe every Christian Soldier from all the assaults of Satan. A Treatise on Eph. vi. 10—20. 4to pp. 523. London, 1616—1619—1627. Folio, the 4th edit. corrected and enlarged.

2. *Eight Treatises on Domestic Duties:* viz. Particular Duties of Wives—Husbands—Children—Parents—Servants—and Masters. 4to. 1622. The 2d edition, London, 1626, folio.

3. *A Guide to go to God.*

4. *God's Three Arrows, the Plague, Famine, and Sword, in three Treatises:* 1. *A Plaister for the Plague.* 2. *Dearth's Death.* 3. *The Church's Conquest over the Sword.* 4to. London, 1631.

5. *A Treatise on the Sin against the Holy Ghost.* Folio, London, 1626.

6. *The Extent of God's Providence;* A Sermon from Mat. x. 29—31.

7. *The Dignity of Chivalry;* A Sermon preached from 2 Chron. viii. 9. before the Artillery Company of London, 13th of June, 1626. The 2d edition, 4to. 1631.

8. *The Saint's Sacrifice;* or a Comment on Psal. cxvi. 4to. 1632.

9. Two Treatises; 1. On the Sabbath. 2. On Apostacy.

10. *The Saint's Support;* a Sermon from Neh. v. 19, before the House of Commons, Fast, 29th June, 1642. 4to. pp. 40. London, 1642.

11. Mercie's Memorial.

12. *The Progress of Divine Providence;* a Sermon before the House of Peers, Fast, 24th Sept. 1645, from Ezek. xxxvi. 11. 4to. pp. 40. London, 1645.

13. A Funeral Sermon for Mrs Duck.

14. *The Right Way;* a Sermon from Ezra viii. 21, before the House of Lords.

15. Two Catechisms.

16. *A Commentary on the Epistle to the Hebrews,* 2 vols. folio, London, 1655. This is accounted a learned and highly useful work. And the pious Bishop Wilkins classes Dr Gouge's sermons among those which he calls

the most excellent of his time. Dr Gouge's part in the English Annotations has been already mentioned; and a particular account has been given of these Annotations in Gataker's Life.—Dr Gouge was, through the instigation of Bishop Neile, cast into prison for publishing again Finch's book on *The Calling of the Jews.* Having remained in prison nine weeks, he was released.

STANLEY GOWER,

MINISTER AT BRAMPTON-BRYAN, AND A MEMBER OF THE ASSEMBLY OF DIVINES AT WESTMINSTER.

STANLEY GOWER was a Puritan divine of considerable eminence in the church of Christ. He was sometime Minister of Brampton-Bryan, in the County of Hereford, in England. He was chosen one of the Assembly of Divines at Westminster, and he constantly attended during the session. Upon his removal to London, he preached at Martin's in Ludgate-street, and was also one of the preachers to the Parliament. In a sermon which he preached to the House of Commons, he entreats them to receive it for a divine *maxim,* "That piety is the best policy, and godly men are in the Holy Ghost's judgment the wisest men." He was appointed by the Assembly one of the committee for the examination and approbation of ministers who petitioned for sequestered livings. In the year 1644, he was also upon the committee appointed for the examination and ordination, by imposition of hands, of those candidates who were found qualified to be admitted into the sacred ministry.[a] He united with his brethren, the ministers in London, in their declaration against the death of the King.[a] According to Kennet's Chronicle, he was living in 1660, was then minister at Dorchester, and is denominated a zealous and eminent Presbyterian.

a Neal's History, vol. iii. chap. ii. & iv. b Neal, chap. x. vol. iii.

Mr Gower wrote the Life of Mr Richard Rothwell, published in Clarke's Lives annexed to his Martyrology. I have often seen one of his sermons which has the following singular title, "Things Now-a-doing: or, the Church's Travail of the Child of Reformation Now-a-bearing" This sermon was preached from Dan. xii. 10, before the House of Commons, at their solemn Fast, July 31st, 1644. 4to. pp. 30, including an Appendix. Lond. 1644. In the application of this sermon, he warmly exhorted his auditory to display their zeal in reforming the House of God, by denying themselves and giving up thereto that which may make it glorious. And, he says, in the conclusion, for their comfort, "If any of you die before you see this great salvation of the Lord, your posterity shall inherit the blessing; and for you, it is honour enough that you expire in so great a cause."

JOHN GREENE, M. A.

PASTOR OF PENCOMBE, AND A MEMBER OF THE ASSEMBLY OF DIVINES AT WESTMINSTER.

JOHN GREENE received a liberal education, and was eminently learned and pious. He was sometime pastor of Pencombe, in the County of Hereford; and he carefully fed his people with knowledge, and warned them of danger. He was much against the unhallowed Book of Sports. The appearance of that declaration was a great grievance to him, and he freely expressed his sentiments upon the subject. In his sermon from Neh. i. 3, 4. p. 19, which he preached to the House of Commons, he says: "They were my meditations upon the coming forth of that book for that sinful *liberty* on the Lord's-day, (and I did not forbear to express them) when I too often heard, in neighbouring parishes, drums beating up for a Marrice or a May-pole on that day, we had just cause to fear lest the Lord should punish that sin, with beating up drums for a *march* on that day; and the Lord hath brought our fears upon us. How many *marches* have been on that day, since the beginning of these wars? I have long thought it one of the highest provoking sins of this land." Mr Greene seems, with others, to have considered the Lord of Hosts, as punishing that general and leading sin, the heaven-daring profanation of the Lord's-day, by the mournful battle at Kineton, or Edge-hill, on that day.[a] He adds, "But I hope those many ordinances for suppressing this profaneness will be a good means, through God's mercy, to quench our unnatural flames, if to good laws, which are the life of a state, be added careful execution, which is the life of laws."

In 1643, Mr Greene was chosen one of the Assembly of Divines at Westminster; and he is in Mr Neal's list marked as giving constant attendance. He preached to the Parliament.

Mr Greene wrote and published a sermon which is entitled, "Nehemiah's Tears and Prayers for Judah's Affliction, and the ruins and repair of Jerusalem." This sermon was preached from Neh. i. 3, 4, in the church of Margaret, Westminster, before the House of Commons, upon the day of their Monthly Humiliation, April 24th, 1644. 4to. pp. 40. London, 1644.

WILLIAM GREENHILL, A. M.

MINISTER OF THE GOSPEL AT STEPNEY, AND A MEMBER OF THE ASSEMBLY OF DIVINES AT WESTMINSTER.

WILLIAM GREENHILL was born in Oxfordshire. He was entered a student of Magdalen-College, Oxford, in the year 1604, aged thirteen years. He took the Degrees in Arts, that of Master being completed, in the year 1612. When and where he entered upon the holy ministry, I cannot inform the reader; but in the year

a See Mr Ashe's Life.

1643, when he was chosen one of the Assembly of Divines at Westminster, he was at Stepney. Wood says that "expressing himself then a rank Covenanter he was made one of the Assembly of Divines by the Long Parliament, in the year 1643, and much about the same time an Afternoon-Lecturer at Stepney, near London." Mr Greenhill constantly attended the Assembly, and was one of the Dissenting Brethren.[a] He was a zealous Puritan, greatly against the Prelates, the superstitious ceremonies, and corruptions, of the Church of England. He suffered much for his Nonconformity, while the bishops were high in place.—He was one of those divines who agreed to and subscribed the proposition, "That Jesus Christ, as King of the Church, has himself appointed a church-government distinct from the civil magistrate."—He was the person pitched upon to be chaplain to the King's children, the Dukes of York, and Gloucester, and the Lady Henrietta Maria, according to Dr Calamy. He is said to have been in favour with Oliver Cromwell, in his time. He was appointed one of the thirty-eight commissioners for the examination and approbation of preachers or ministers of the gospel, in the year 1654, who were commonly called *triers*. Bishop Kennet pours a torrent of calumny upon those eminently learned and pious divines who received this appointment. He says, "By the questions they were wont to ask, a man could not tell what they aimed at, except it was to advance Quakerism, or make way for Mahometism."[b] Mr Greenhill was cast out from Stepney, in the County of Middlesex, by the Act of Uniformity. When he died, I cannot tell; but his library was sold in 1677, and probably he might die about that time. Dr Calamy says, in his Account of the ejected ministers, vol. ii. p. 471, that he was "a worthy man, and much valued, for his great learning, and unwearied labours" Mr Howe, in his funeral sermon for Mr Mead, speaking of his connexion

a See Mr Bridge's Life.

b Neal's Puritans, vol. iv. chap. iii. Kennet's Chronicle, p. 714.

with Mr Greenhill, styles him, "That eminent servant of God Mr Greenhill, whose praise is still in the churches."

Mr Greenhill's writings are;

1. *The Axe at the Root;* A Sermon preached from Mat. iii. 10, before the House of Commons, at their public Fast, April 26th, 1643. 4to. pp. 50. London, 1643.

2. An Exposition of the Book of the Prophet Ezekiel, with useful observations thereupon; in 5 vols. 4to. Vol. 1st, pp. 468. London, 1645. Vol. 2d, pp. 565.—1649. Vol 3d, pp. 621. London, 1651. Vol. 4th, pp. 592. London, 1658. Vol. 5th is considerably larger than any of the other volumes. It was finished in the latter end of the year 1654; but not published until the year 1662. This valuable Exposition of Ezekiel was delivered in several lectures in London. It is still advertised for sale, both in London and in other places; but is now become very scarce, and the price is greatly advanced. In Mr R. Ogle's Divinity Catalogue for 1802, 5 vols. *neat* and *scarce*, £1 8s. In his Catalogue for 1809; 5 vols. *very scarce*, £1 11s. 6d. In Mr Steven and Co.'s Sale Catalogue, Glasgow, for 1811, *very scarce*, *neat*, £2 10s.

3. *Sermons of Christ's last Discovery of himself;* viz. 1. *Christ the Root of all.* 2. *His Royal Descent*, &c. from Rev. xxii. 16, 17. London, 1656.

4. Sermon before the Parliament, Ezek. xliii. 2.

5. Sermon on Ezek. xviii. 32; in the Morning Exercise at Cripplegate. 4to. London, 1661.

6. *The Sound-hearted Christian*, with several other Sermons; small piece, pp. 319. London, 1670. I have seen Mr Greenhill's writings both in Scotland and England.

END OF VOL. I.

CONTENTS

OF VOLUME I.

MEMOIRS

OF THE

LIVES AND WRITINGS

OF THOSE

Eminent Divines,

WHO CONVENED IN

THE FAMOUS

ASSEMBLY AT WESTMINSTER,

IN THE

SEVENTEENTH CENTURY.

BY JAMES REID,

MINISTER OF THE GOSPEL.

"The righteous shall be in everlasting remembrance," PSALM cxii. 6.

VOL. II.

PAISLEY:

PRINTED BY STEPHEN AND ANDREW YOUNG,

High Street.

1815.

PREFACE

TO THE SECOND VOLUME.

MEMOIRS of men of distinguished eminence are both instructive and interesting. In those books, we may see the goodness of Divine Providence, in raising and furnishing proper instruments for every work. In the Memoirs of the brilliant constellation at Westminster, we may see, in particular, sound principles, Christian dispositions, and a conversation becoming the gospel of Christ. In these, we may clearly see the power of divine grace shining forth in all its glory, in real life, subduing the inbred corruptions of our fallen nature, and animating to every good word and work. In these, we may see pious and learned men eminently zealous in the advancement of true religion, and *earnestly contending for the faith which was once delivered unto the saints.* In these volumes, we may see the reproaches and persecutions which the faithful servants of Jesus Christ have endured *for righteousness' sake;* those gracious and heavenly principles which supported them in all their tribulations, and the course which they uniformly followed in their way to the better world.

We are very much indebted to the Assembly of Divines at Westminster, as we are to our illustrious Reformers in general, both in early and later times, for our civil and religious liberty. They were zealous advocates for all that liberty wherewith Christ has made his people free. And their labours were not in vain. We enjoy the fruits of these labours. And to rescue from oblivion genuine and impartial accounts of those eminent divines, is a tribute which we owe to their memory.

The very interesting history of their diligent researches both in literature and in divinity, and of their unwearied labours in the cause of their God and their country, well deserves to be faithfully transmitted to the latest posterity. And, true accounts of their avowed and warm attachment to the cause of Christ, of their painful sufferings in that cause, and of their triumphant deaths, are justly entitled to all our attention and esteem.

The author of these Memoirs has spared neither labour nor expense in the collection of materials, and has carefully preserved whatever appeared interesting, entertaining, and useful. When the excellencies of those divines have been exhibited, neither their infirmities, nor the accusations of their adversaries, have been suppressed. Impartiality has been studied.—There is always reference to the authorities; but sometimes only at the end of the life.—Attention has been given to the true orthography of the names both of persons and of places.

After all efforts to obtain information, the account of several lives is very defective, to the great loss of the inquisitive reader. This defect was unavoidable at the distance of time, and in my circumstances. After the utmost research, for some years, no more information could be procured. The work will be found very defective in its execution, as well as through want of information; and it requires much indulgence from the reader. The author has done what he could, and availed himself of every advantage within his reach, to make the whole work as full and useful as possible. And, having given a larger account of it, in the preface to the first volume, he now concludes with wishing, that both the reader and himself may be taught to imbibe the principles and spirit of those divines, to follow them as far as they followed Christ, in adhering firmly to the cause of true religion, and in propagating it with the same holy zeal.

MEMOIRS, &c.

HENRY HALL, B. D. OF NORWICH,

AND A MEMBER OF THE ASSEMBLY OF DIVINES AT WESTMINSTER.

HENRY HALL is marked in Mr Neal's list of the Assembly of Divines at Westminster, as giving constant attendance. He was appointed one of the select Committee for the examination and approbation of those ministers who petitioned for sequestered livings. He appears to have been a divine of considerable eminence; for he was employed by the Assembly in work of very great utility and importance. Mr Robert Baillie, one of the learned Commissioners from the Church of Scotland, to the Assembly at Westminster, reckons Mr Hall among the ablest divines in that venerable Assembly, where he is speaking of him being against the institution of ruling elders by divine right.[a]

One Henry Hall, B. D. some time Fellow of Trinity-college, in Cambridge, has published a Sermon, which is entitled, *Heaven Ravished; or, A Glorious Prize, achieved by an Heroical Enterprise.* Probably, he was the same person, who sat in the Assembly at Westminster; but I am not able to say, certainly. That Sermon was preached from Mat. xi. 12. to the Honourable House of Commons, at their solemn Fast, May 29, 1644. 4to. pp. 71.—In it he says, "A Christian is never so glorious, as when he suffers most reproach and ignominy for Christ's sake." Speaking of zeal in religion and reformation, according to knowledge, he says, "Let us all labour to blow up, and to keep alive this sacred fire, upon the altar of our hearts, that it may inflame our devo-

a Baillie's Letters, vol. i. p. 401.

tion toward God, kindle our love toward men, and burn out all our own corruptions. Let it never cool with age, nor abate with opposition, nor be quenched with any floods of persecution." It is a good Sermon.

HUMPHREY HARDWICK,

MINISTER OF THE WORD AT HADAM MAGNA, IN THE COUNTY OF HARTFORD, AND ONE OF THE ASSEMBLY OF DIVINES AT WESTMINSTER.

HUMPHREY HARDWICK was one of the superadded divines, in the Assembly. He is represented by Neal as attending constantly during the Session. He seems to have been a considerable sufferer under the oppressions of the persecuting prelates, and by the civil war. In his Sermon before the House of Commons, from Psalm cxxvi. 5, 6. he speaks of himself as among the silenced ministers. And in his epistle dedicatory to the House of Commons, which is prefixed to that sermon, he says,—" No man, I suppose, hath more cause to be large in apology than I, having long since had my poor library totally plundered, and myself not able, until this day, to buy one book of considerable value. Besides from the beginning of this war, until the last month, being conversant among arms, where studies are interrupted. But those things I account part of my chief happiness on earth, to have suffered much, and done a little good in the cause of Christ, and service of the state." He was very zealous in the noble cause of the Reformation. He says, in the Sermon above-mentioned, " Search through the holy Book, and tell me whether any men are so precious in the eyes of Heaven, and the account of God himself, as those who have been zealous for the reformation of his Church, the carrying on of his cause, the help of his people against their wicked and profane opposers. How highly were Caleb and Joshua esteemed of God for being courageous, when others flagged in the business, and shrunk at evil tidings?" Mr Hardwick was a great advocate for the National Covenant.—I have seen only one sermon of his, which is entitled, "The Difficulty of Zion's Deliverance and Reformation; together with the Activity which her friends should manifest, during the time that her cause is in agitation." It was delivered at Margaret's, Westminster, before the Honourable House of Commons, on Wednesday morning, the 26th day of June, 1644. 4to. pp. 36. London, 1644. A valuable Sermon.

ROBERT HARRIS, D. D.

PASTOR OF HANWELL, A MEMBER OF THE ASSEMBLY OF DIVINES AT WESTMINSTER, AND PRESIDENT OF TRINITY-COLLEGE IN OXFORD.

ROBERT HARRIS was born at Broad Campden in Gloucestershire, in England, in the year 1578. His father had the character of a very prudent and intelligent man; and his mother was allowed to be a very religious and charitable woman. Under the tuition of these parents he passed his childhood. He discovered, in this early period of his life, a strong propensity to his play. He acknowledged with compunction, that he greatly preferred his sport to reading the Holy Scriptures at the call of his affectionate parents. This natural averseness to read the Sacred Writings was matter of much grief to him, during his whole life. *I acknowledge my transgressions: and my sin is ever before me. The carnal mind is emnity against God; for it is not subject to the law of God, neither indeed can be.* This all mankind must feel whether they acknowledge it or not. The subject of this memoir was *made to possess the iniquities of his youth. Surely after that I was turned I repented; and after that I was instructed I smote upon my thigh: I was ashamed, yea, even confounded, because I did bear the reproach of my youth.* He found always, while he was a stranger and a pilgrim on the earth, sufficient reason for that appropriate prayer, *Remember not the sins of my youth, nor my transgressions: according to thy mercy remember thou me, for thy goodness sake, O Lord*, Psalm xxv. 7. His youthful folly, and disobedience to parental authority and the law of the Lord, made a deep and permanent impression upon his tender mind, and occasioned much serious exercise of soul. But, according to the proverb, "An untoward boy may make a good man." This was indeed fully verified, in the notable example which is now before us.—His parents, having designed him either for the Law-business, or for the holy ministry, according as his parts and inclination might lead, sent him in due time, to receive his early education at the free-school of Chipping-Campden, in his native county. Here he was very far from being comfortable in his school-masters. They were often changed upon him, through want of salary; and some of them beat their scholars in a brutal and savage manner, without mercy. Such a mode of correction is certainly a disgrace to civilized life. It made very fearful and lasting impressions upon the mind of our young scholar. Though for his own part, he never felt as far as he remembered, the smart of the rod in any school, yet the daily executions upon others, brought such a trembling and sadness on his spirit, that he could not be entirely delivered from so long as he lived. He often said, that such treatment was the bane (ruin) of many school-boys. The inhabitants of Gloucestershire were in a very rude state, at that time; which should be here observed. He was removed from Chipping-Campden to the school at Worcester, where he was placed under the tuition of Mr Bright, and on the Sabbath day he was a hearer of that learned pastor, Dr Robert Abbots. When accomplished in school-education, he removed to Magdalen-college, Oxford, in the latter end of the year 1595. There he shewed an uncommon thirst for knowledge; and very soon began to seek and taste the sweetness of all useful learning. He became an excellent scholar, and a famous logician and disputant. And he was called by his tutor, Mr Goffe, or Gough, to concur with his other pupils in reading the Bible, in prayer, and in the repetition of sermons.[a] Not being accustomed to this yoke of our Lord Jesus Christ, he found it at first somewhat galling. He observed, that he knew few, if any, of the serious, who followed that practice, and yet he was not able to confute it. In this case, he very properly applied unto the Father of Lights for direction. Prayer is the natural language of the soul, imploring, in its distress, Divine direction and help. It was, accordingly, an excercise most exactly suited to the condition of our young pupil, who now required light to direct him in the way in which he should go. He humbled himself before the Lord in prayer. He fell down in his study, and entreated that the infinitely wise God would either discover the falsehood, if his tutor had any design upon him to seduce him; or, if this way were pleasing to God, that then He would confirm him in it. He was very soon fully resolved to comply with the wholesome measures of his pious tutor. He bought a Bible, read and studied it, with indefatigable diligence and care, along with some good authors in divinity. *In all thy ways acknowledge him, and he shall direct thy paths.* He also made great advances in philosophy, and in the Greek and Hebrew languages. He was singularly happy in his tutor. And when Mr Goffe ceased to be his tutor, they agreed to continue their studies and reading together, for their mutual benefit. In the Hebrew, they had also the concurrence of some other of the fellows, who joined them, one of whom was afterward president. And though Mr Harris was not then complete bachelor in the hall, yet he was readily accepted by the company, being found to be a very diligent student, and equally expert in his grammar, as his companions were. Beside these useful studies, his tutor and he mutually agreed to read the celebrated Calvin's Institutions by turns. These Institutions appear to have been much read at that time by students, in England. Dr Saunderson, bishop of Lincoln, says; "When I began to set myself to the study of divinity as my pro-

[a] See Wood's Ath. Oxon. vol. ii. p. 261. 2d edition.

per business, Calvin's Institutions were recommended to me, as they were generally to all young scholars in those times, as the best and perfectest system of divinity, and the fittest to be laid as a ground-work in the study of that profession. And indeed my expectation was not at all deceived, in the reading of those Institutions." [a]—

Mr Harris, having taken one degree in arts, and continued some time bachelor of arts, turned his attention more particularly to the work of the holy ministry. By the Divine blessing upon his studies, and the pious instructions of his excellent tutor, he was brought to a saving knowledge of the glorious Gospel of the grace of God, and soon after became a very eminent Puritan. He generously offered his service in preaching the Gospel, at Chipping-Campden, in his native county. But such is said to have been the ignorance of the times, and the state of religious affairs in that place, that when he came to the church there was no Bible to be found, from which he might read his text. Even in the greater town, he did not know where one could be procured. At length, he was directed to the house of the vicar of the parish, who had a Bible in his possession; but, as it had not been seen for some months, it could scarcely be found. Having, however, at last obtained the sacred volume, he went to the church, and preached an admirable sermon from Rom. x. 1. *Brethren, my heart's desire and prayer to God for Israel is, that they might be saved:* This sermon met with much applause; but the preacher often said, that he lost by the bargain. He found himself in danger of *being exalted above measure, through the abundance* of his success and popular applause, which was against the prosperity of his soul. Beside, his friends solicited him to cease now from pursuing any longer his studies in the University, and come among them, declaring that he already had a sufficiency of human literature. His father also, having yet many other children to provide for, wished to have him settled in some place in the church. But he then declined public employment in the church,

a See Toplady's Hist. Proof, vol. ii. sect. 20.

and importuned his father to allow him what more patrimony he was pleased to give him, for the farther prosecution of his studies at Oxford. With much difficulty, he obtained his request, and, with great joy, he returned to the University. But very soon after his return, a dreadful plague invaded that famous seat of learning. The students were dispersed, and he was in great perplexity. He was averse to return home, and where to go he knew not. But according to the Jewish proverb, "When the bricks are doubled, then comes Moses." He was, in the extremity of his distress, mercifully relieved, by Divine Providence. One Mr Doyly, who lived not far from Oxford, a gentleman of a very ancient family, and very friendly to the Gospel of Christ, invited Mr Harris to his house. Mrs Doyly was eminently pious and intelligent, and he was peculiarly comfortable in that family. He there met with one Mr Prier, a pious minister, who was then in a very weakly state, and over-burdened with preaching, both on the Lord's-day, and at extraordinary Fasts, which were appointed on account of the prevalence of the plague. Mr Harris preached some times, through compassion, for Mr Prier, with much approbation. His labours being highly acceptable and useful, he was solicited to continue there for some time, which he did, until the Lord appeared in another call to him.

The venerable and justly celebrated divine, Mr John Dod, being silenced for non-conformity, and ejected from Hanwell in Oxfordshire, by Dr Bridges, bishop of Oxford, Sir Anthony Cope invited Mr Harris to become his successor. He complied with the invitation, and, accordingly, he removed to Hanwell, though with very much grief and fear. Mr Dod, whose labours at Hanwell were very numerous, and most extensively useful, being driven from his truly affectionate and beloved people, they would acknowledge no man as their pastor except him who had been ejected from Hanwell. It was, however, agreed upon that Mr Harris should preach so long as there was any hope of recovering Mr Dod, their former faithful pastor. During this very unsettled state at Hanwell, archbishop Bancroft presented the place to one of his chaplains, upon pretence of a lapse. But Sir Anthony Cope, who was then sitting in parliament, together with some other members of the house, waited upon the archbishop, and presented Mr Harris, whom his grace, after a long contest, with very great reluctance, admitted. Sir Anthony having formerly spoken in that parliament against insufficient ministers, not without some reflection upon the insufferable proceedings of the archbishops and bishops, Bancroft very readily embraced this opportunity of shewing his resentment; and, therefore, he referred Mr Harris to be very strictly examined by his most learned chaplain. The chaplain, after sufficient examination, returned Mr Harris *moderately learned.* This return proving unsatisfactory to the archbishop, Mr Harris was afterward committed to the examination of bishop Burlow, a man who was most exactly suited to Bancroft's wishes. The bishop was a person of great wit and learning, and exceedingly glad of the opportunity. He examined Mr Harris first in divinity, then in other branches of learning, especially in the Greek language, in which his lordship was allowed to be a celebrated critic. As the story is related, " They Greeked it until they were both run a-ground for want of words, upon which they burst into a fit of laughter, and so gave it over." Burlow returned to the archbishop, and, delivering a most favourable testimony, his grace, it is said, was satisfied. But Mr Harris expressed his fear to become the successor of so eminent a divine as Mr Dod, which was not very pleasing to the archbishop, though at that time he courted Mr Dod.

Mr Harris being now settled as pastor at Hanwell, Mr Seudder at Drayton, and Mr Whately at Banbury, they soon became very intimate, and were united in judgmen, in brotherly affection, and also by affinity. Mr Harris married Mr Whately's sister, and Mr Seudder his wife's sister. These divines commonly met together once a-week, to translate and analyse a chapter of the Bible. This laudable practice had a strong tendency to promote brotherly love, their mutual edification, and to excite them to greater diligence in their studies. They continued the practice as long as their employments and circumstances admitted.

Though Mr Harris was comfortably settled, he was called by Divine Providence to endure many trials. *Man is born unto trouble, as the sparks fly upward.* His faith and patience were much exercised by his wife's long and painful illness, upon the birth of her first child. Mr Dod told him, That this affliction was designed to season him, and fit him for his arduous work. And Mr Harris himself often said, "That he should have been quite spoiled, had he not been thus taken down. Young ministers know not on what ground they tread, till God make them humble."—*Now for a season, if need be, ye are in heaviness through manifold temptations: That the trial of your faith, being much more precious than of gold that perisheth, though it be tried with fire, might be found unto praise, and honour, and glory, at the appearing of Jesus Christ.* Mr Dod was accustomed to say, "Sanctified afflictions are spiritual promotions." Mr Harris had the experience of the truth of this judicious saying. After some other troubles, he found much encouragement in his labour in the Lord's vineyard. His people now began to relish his ministry, and the Lord, who alone gives the increase, greatly blessed the works of his hands. He did not feed the flock, over which the Holy Ghost had made him an overseer, with airy notions, and dry speculations, but with genuine knowledge, *the sincere milk of the word, that they might thereby grow.* His discourses, in general, were adapted to persons of the meanest capacity. His people received least benefit from what cost him most labour, his sermons upon the whole epistle to the Colossians. This has often been verified. When he preached these sermons, he thought that he could not speak in too high a style to a people who were so well instructed, but at last he found that he was mistaken. Some of his hearers afterward told him, that his labour upon that epistle was lost to them. A lesson to all ministers of the Gospel. He greatly excelled in handling and illustrating historical passages of the Sacred Writings. He dispensed to his hearers the substantial provision of the Gospel. And he carefully provided milk for babes, and strong meat for men. He had much zeal for God, and great compassion on precious and immortal souls. And *a great and effectual door was opened to* him. He had many seals to his ministry. And God is said to have so remarkably blessed his labours, that for some time there was not one prayerless family in Hanwell, nor any person who refused his examination and instruction previous to receiving the Lord's supper.

The Father of mercies, and the God of all comfort, was pleased to bless both his ministerial labours, and his outward estate. He was blessed in his basket and store. He observed a sensible blessing on the provision of his family. His income was not great, his children numerous, for whom he kept a tutor, and he was a lover of hospitality, yet he was increasing, which made him conclude, that there was a secret blessing on house-keeping. He said, that he was not able to give an account of his expences, and of God's supplies. In this situation he continued about forty years, blessed himself, and made a blessing to his people at Hanwell, and to the people in that neighbourhood, being a constant and laborious preacher, both upon the Lord's day, and upon other occasions, until the commencement of the dreadful civil wars. The bloody battle of Edg-hill, only a few miles distant from Hanwell, was fought on October 23, 1642, being the Lord's day; yet, the wind being contrary, he did not hear the least noise of it until the public exercises of the day were over; nor could he believe the report of a battle till soldiers, besmeared with blood, came to make it known. From that time his troubles greatly increased; but he bore these with great meekness of spirit, and holy resignation to the sovereign will of God. The civil war spread its terrors through that country. Rude soldiers were quartered upon him, some calling him *round-head*, others *malignant;* but he continued to attend upon his numerous duties as at other times. Some of his guests joined with him in family-duties, others scoffed at these, because they were not mingled with book-prayers. He continued the course of his ministry every Lord's-day, and most of those persons who quartered upon him, being commanders and officers, they were civil, both to him and to his family. But one company which was quartered upon him was so outrageous in swearing, that he could not forbear preaching from James v. 12. *But above all things, my brethren, swear not.* This discourse so highly offended the company, that they swore they would shoot him if he preached again from that text, supposing it had been by design chosen against them. Undismayed by their fearful threatenings, he courageously proceeded to preach from the same words on the following Sabbath, trusting in the Lord his God, and boldly confirming what he had formerly advanced on the subject. When he was preaching, he observed a soldier preparing his firelock, as if he designed to shoot; but Mr Harris went on without fear, apprehending that the soldier intended only to disturb him, and he finished his discourse without interruption. He endured the severe storm until he had suffered very material injury; but was at length driven from the place. He continued in his station, however, until he saw his tenements in the neighbourhood fired, wood and nurseries of wood destroyed, himself threatened, and at last forced by a Scottish commander to shift for himself, and found some of his neighbours now ready to betray him.

Mr Harris, being forced from his flock, fled to London, and was chosen one of the Assembly of Divines at Westminster, and preached at St Botalph's church, Bishopsgate, during his attendance upon the Assembly. It is said, that in the Assembly, he heard all, and said little. In the year 1646, he was appointed one of the preachers to the University of Oxford; and, the year following, one of the visitors of that University. Dr Walker, with his common slander, when he meets with the Puritans, observes, that when the visitors proceeded to open their visitation, they began, as they did all the other distinguished wickednesses of these times, according to their usual hypocrisy, with *prayers*, and a *sermon!* The person pitched upon for the office of preaching was, Mr Harris, one of the visitors.[a] Mr Harris, at the same time, took

a Walker's Attempt, Part I. p. 127.

his degree of Doctor of divinity, was made president of Trinity-college, and became rector of Garlington, near Oxford. He governed his college with much prudence, gaining the affections of all the fellows and students, who reverenced him as a father. He was ten years president of that college. He preached on the Lord's day at his parsonage, once a-week in the city of Oxford, and constantly in his turn at the University, both in English and in Latin.

Dr Walker and other royalists have stigmatized him as a notorious pluralist. The Doctor rests the evidence of this slanderous accusation upon the authority of a very scurrilous and abusive letter, which was published in those troublesome times, with a view to expose and pour all manner of contempt upon the Puritans. He also observes, "that he had somewhere read, that in those times, Dr Harris's picture was drawn with one steeple upon his head, and with others coming out of his pockets."[a] Pluralities should not be justified. They are certainly indefensible. Respecting this charge, Dr Harris himself made the following generous and open declaration. He says, "That though he stood clear in his own conscience, and in the consciences of those persons who best knew him, that he was far from allowing non-residence and a plurality of livings; yet, to such persons as were ignorant of all circumstances, there was some appearance of evil. And that it would, and should be to him, matter of humiliation and of caution while he lived, that he had given the least advantage to the adversary. He undoubtedly possessed several benefices; but whether he received the profits of them all, and enjoyed them all at the same time, appears very doubtful. Though Dr Grey denominates him "a fanatical hero, and a professed enemy to the constitution, both in church and state;" yet he partly acquits him of that vile charge, and invalidates, in a great degree, the authority of the above scurrilous letter, upon which it rested.

Wood, the famous Oxford historian, brings accusations

a Walker's Attempt, Part I. p. 127.

against Dr Harris, which, if true, would prove him to have been one of the very basest of men. He charges him with having taken for his own use two bags of gold, containing one hundred pounds each, which he found among some old rubbish in Trinity-college, soon after he became president. He also affirms, that Dr Harris told most glaring falsehoods, with a view to secure the money to himself.[a] One very judiciously observes here; "Though our documents will not afford us materials for a complete refutation of these charges; yet the whole of what is asserted, and especially the worst part of it, is so contrary to the uniform spirit and deportment of this learned and pious divine, that the account appears extremely suspicious, and only designed to reproach the memory of the Puritans."[b] Many attempts, in those times, were made to reproach the memory of the Puritans. They were, like the apostles and followers of the Lord Jesus Christ, in former times, accounted as *the off-scouring of all things*.

Dr Harris was eminently distinguished by his prudent government of himself and of his family, as well as of his college and of his flock. His government of himself was very remarkable. *He who has no rule over his own spirit is like a city that is broken down, and without walls.* But the prudent subject of this memoir had much rule over his own spirit, and was like the standing city, having strong walls. He was most exactly temperate in the use of all things, confining himself strictly to hours for food, sleep, labour, and recreation. He ate sparingly and seasonably, which had a strong tendency to preserve in him much vigour, even to a great age. His principal time for recreation was the afternoon of Saturday, when he would unbend his mind, and allow himself some harmless recreation, in order that he might be more vigorous for the important and deeply interesting work of the Lord's-day.—He was very seldom seen angry; but, if at any time, his mind was discomposed by the improper conduct of other persons, he had such a remarkable

a Wood's Fasti Oxon. vol. ii. p. 67. 2d edition.

b Brook's Lives of the Puritans, vol. iii. p. 308.

command of himself, that he could very quickly turn his passion into wholesome instruction. In his censures of others, he was very sparing, gentle to all, and severe only to himself. He had a very peculiar gift of forgetting injuries, without offering any. He was very mindful of favours. And, in the government of his family, he was not less remarkable. *He ruled well his own house.* He carefully maintained his authority over his children, which was equally tempered with lenity and gravity. He loved them without shewing fondness, and he ruled them without rigour. As soon as they could speak, they were taught to repeat some historical passages of the Holy Scriptures. As soon as they could walk, they were sent to school. When they were able to recollect any part of a chapter, which had been read, or commit to memory, and bring home any passage of a sermon which they had heard, he began to instruct them in the first principles of religion. When they were farther advanced, he enjoined upon them the practice of religion, and he diligently observed their private performance of religious exercises. He was very attentive unto them every way, carefully observing their capacities, inclinations, and constitutional sins. And he used all caution and means, that they might be enabled, through divine grace, to avoid those sins. His laudable endeavours were crowned, by the blessing of God, with success equal to his largest wishes. He was an example of strict and serious godliness in his family. He was an affectionate and good husband. To his servants he was a kind and gentle master, carefully instructing them and exhorting them unto their duty; and some of them had much reason to bless the Lord that ever they came under his roof.

He found very much sweet delight in God, and in divine things. He accounted those his best days, when he enjoyed most intercourse with Heaven. Upon a person in his sickness asking him how he did, he said, "O, this has been a sweet day, I have had sweet communion with God in Jesus Christ." He had an early sense of religion, though he neither knew the preacher, nor the sermon, by which he was converted. In his self-examination, he marked down in writing his evidences for heaven, some times in propositions from the Holy Scriptures, and at other times in syllogisms. These evidences he often subscribed in a book which he had for the purpose: but they were best read in the course of his life, which was an exact walking with God, in piety, charity, humility, patience, and an entire dependance upon Him.

When he had settled his worldly affairs and his children, and left himself nothing to do but to turn his attention more particularly to preparation for death, the Lord was pleased to visit him with a very sore affliction. His wife, who was eminently religious, having lived about fifty years with him, was now delivered up to such strong temptations of Satan and horrors of mind, as terrified all spectators. On this mournful occasion, he often said, "God made it appear to all beholders, that the best man is no more than God makes him. Grace and comfort are all from Him." He bore this heavy affliction with much meekness and patïence, and it served only, under the blessing of God, to throw greater lustre on his graces, and to excite him unto more diligence and fervour in religious exercises. *Now, no chastening for the present seemeth to be joyous, but grievous: nevertheless afterward it yieldeth the peaceable fruit of righteousness unto them who are exercised thereby.*

We come now to the close of this laborious and valuable life, in this world. The following lines were strikingly verified in our celebrated preacher, both in the course of his life, and at his death.

"I preach, as if I ne'er should preach again;
And, as a dying man, to dying men."

Dr Harris, in his last sickness, being desired to admit company, said, "It is all one to me whether I am kept alone, or have my friends with me. My work is now to arm myself for death, which assaults me, and to apply myself unto that great encounter." Accordingly, he spent his time in prayer, meditation, and reading the Holy Scriptures; especially the book of Psalms, the prophecy of Isaiah, and the Gospel by John. He delighted exceedingly in the 10th, 14th, 15th, 16th, and 17th, chapters of that Evangelist And when he became unable to read himself, he desired his friends to read unto him. He collected the principal things which were contained in the chapter, and expounded what seemed to be difficult in it, feeding most sweetly on this spiritual food. *Trouble and anguish have taken hold on me; yet thy commandments are my delights.* He warmly exhorted those persons who visited and attended him, to seek above all things to obtain the precious grace of faith. He said to them, "You must put on all the spiritual armour of God, and then go forth in the Lord's strength. Stand in the fight, and the issue shall be glorious: only forget not to call in the help of your General. Do all from him, and under him." He hindered none, on the Lord's-day, from public worship, to attend him; but greatly encouraged them to go unto the house of God. And upon their return, he said, "Come, what have you for me?" meaning that they should repeat to him some part of the sermons which they had heard, to which he carefully attended. And having given a summary of every sermon, he said, "O what excellent truths are these! Lay them up charily, you will have need of them." When his friends came to visit him, being weakly, he said, "I cannot speak, but I can hear." Notwithstanding, upon being asked where his comfort lay, he answered, *In Christ, and in the free grace of God.* He derived his comfort from the Lord Jesus Christ, and the unsearchable riches of divine grace, *reigning through righteousness unto eternal life.* When it was observed that he might take much comfort from his labours and usefulness, he replied, "All is nothing without a Saviour. Without Him my best works would condemn me. Oh! I am ashamed of them, being mixed with so much sin. Oh! I am an unprofitable servant. I have not done any thing for God as I ought. Loss of time sits heavy upon my spirit. Work, work apace. Be assured nothing will more trouble you, when you come to die, than that you have done no more for God, who has done so much for you." He farther said, "I never in all my life saw the worth of

Christ, nor tasted the sweetness of God's love, in so great a measure as I now do." Here we may observe, That the Lord Jesus Christ is indeed an all-sufficient Saviour, and the only real support of a departing soul. I cannot refrain transcribing in this place the admirable words of the celebrated Mr Davies, president of the college of New Jersey, in America, in a letter to his dear friend and brother, when he was beginning to creep back from the valley of the shadow of death, to which he had made a very near approach, using his own words. Mr Davies, in that letter, says, "In my sickness, I found the unspeakable importance of a Mediator in a religion for sinners. O! I could have given you the word of a dying man for it, that that *Jesus* whom you preach is indeed a necessary, and an all-sufficient Saviour. Indeed he is the only support for a departing soul. None but *Christ*, none but *Christ*. Had I as many good works as Abraham or Paul, I would not have dared to build my hopes upon such a quicksand, but only on this firm eternal rock." [a]

When Dr Harris's friends asked what they should do for him, he replied, "You must not only pray for me, but also praise God for his unspeakable mercy to me; and in particular, that he has kept Satan from me, in my weakness. O, how good is God! Entertain good thoughts of him. However it be with us, we cannot think too well of him, nor too ill of ourselves." The inexpressible goodness of God in Christ seems to have made a very deep and lasting impression upon his religious mind; for in all his *wills* the following legacy was always renewed; "Also, I bequeath to all my children, and their children's children, to each of them a Bible, with this inscription, *None but Christ*." He said to his particular friends, "I am now going home, even quite spent. I am now at the shore, but leave you still tossing on the sea. Oh! it is a good time to die in." Nearer the time of his departure, being asked how he did, he said, "In no great pain, I praise God, only weary of my useless life. If God has no more service for me to

a Middleton's Biogr. Evang. vol. iv. p. 349.

do here, I could be gladly in heaven, where I shall serve him better, delivered from sin and distractions. I pass from one death to another, yet I fear none. I praise God that I can live, and dare die. If God has more work for me to do here, I am willing to do it, though my infirm body be very weary." Afterward, he said, "I do now no good, I hinder other persons who might be better employed, if I were removed. Why should any desire to live, but to do God service? Now I cease from that, I do not live." When both the violence of his trouble and the advice of his physicians prohibited speech, he called upon those persons who attended him, to read the Holy Scriptures unto him, and upon his son to pray frequently with him. In the immediate views of an approaching eternity, he desired that the eighth chapter of the epistle to the Romans should be read unto him. And he professed that he lived and died in that faith which he had preached and printed, and that he now, in the near prospect of death, found the unspeakable comfort of it; desiring that intimation should be made thereof in that country where he had been longest known. Having given strong evidence of the excellence and power of that religion, which can support the precious and immortal soul, and make the, otherwise very gloomy, prospect of death easy and cheerful, he closed his eyes in peace, pleasingly resigning his soul to God, on the 11th of Dec. 1658, aged eighty years.

The following brief account has been given of the excellent endowments of Dr Harris.—He was a very hard student, a man of great abilities, and richly furnished with all learning which is necessary to a divine. He was a pure and elegant Latinist, he had a considerable knowledge of the Greek, and was an exact master of the Hebrew language. He was greatly admired as a subtle, clear, and very ready, disputant. He excelled in chronology, church-history, the councils, case-divinity, and in the knowledge of the fathers. But his parts were best seen in the pulpit. His gifts and graces eminently appeared, in prayer; his affections were warm and elevated; his petitions weighty and substantial; and his language, pertinent, unaffected, and without tautology. He was accounted a judicious divine, and an accomplished preacher. He preached with much learned plainness, beautifully unfolding the grand mysteries of the glorious Gospel of the grace of God unto persons of the meanest capacities. In his younger days, about twenty years together, he wrote his sermons exactly, and committed them to memory, which he could do with much ease. He was very large and particular in the application of his sermons. In prayer and preaching, he had an admirable faculty of engaging the attention, and of warming and raising the affections of his auditory. He was exceedingly charitable to the poor, and eminently distinguished for humility, mortification, and self-denial. In short, he was a person of eminent piety and gravity, and was richly furnished with every necessary qualification to render him a complete scholar, a wise governor, a profitable preacher, and an excellent Christian.

Some of his choice sayings follow. He used to say, "That a preacher has three books to study: the *Bible*, *himself*, and the *people*.—That preaching to the people was but one part of the pastor's duty: he was to live and die in them, as well as for, and with them."— He advised young preachers to pen largely, and to keep their notes for all emergencies. He observed, That the humblest preachers converted the greatest number of souls, not the most choice scholars while unbroken.—That he valued no man for his gifts, but for his humility under them.—Nor did he expect much from any man, were his parts ever so great, until he was broken by afflictions and temptations. —That so much humility as any man had, so much grace and worth, and no more.—That it was just with God to deny us the comforts of our graces, when we deny him the glory of them. He used to say, that some duties which were often in men's mouths, were very difficult to him: as, *to deny himself*, in all the extent of that expression; *to live only by faith, and a bare promise witht out a pawn; to ascribe all to free grace, and to Chris. alone; and to love where we meet with the want of love, and contempt.*—He said, "That it was a hard thing for a saint to forgive himself some faults, even when God has forgiven these. It is hard to continue long in holy thoughts, and to confine our thoughts to the prayers of another person. We know but little of Christ's love, till all be perfected, and spread before us in heaven." [a]

Dr Harris's last will and testament contains much excellent advice to his wife and to his numerous children, but it is too long for insertion in this place. His writings came forth at different times, in their first appearance to the public eye. "The Way to True Happiness, in twenty-four Sermons upon the Beatitudes," Mat. v. and "A Treatise of the New Covenant," from Ezek. xi. 19, 20. were both printed at London, in quarto, in 1632. But these and his other writings were afterward collected and published in one volume, small folio, London, 1654. The eminently pious bishop Wilkins passes an high encomium upon his English Sermons. And his Latin Sermons to the clergy have been very highly commended. These are said to have gained the approbation of all persons who were skilful in that language. Wood says, that one of his Latin Sermons, from John xxi. 17, 18. with another Latin Sermon of Dr Dan. Featly were printed at Utrecht, in 1657, and both entitled *Pedum Pastorale*, &c.

CHARLES HERLE, A. M.

PASTOR OF WINWICK, IN LANCASHIRE, A MEMBER AND SOME TIME PROLOCUTOR OF THE ASSEMBLY OF DIVINES AT WESTMINSTER.

CHARLES HERLE was born at Prideaux-Herle, near Lystwithyel, or Lostwithiel, in the county of Cornwall, in England, in the year 1598. He was descended from a good family, and born of honourable parents.

a Clark's Lives, and Durham's Life of Dr Harris.

He was the third son of Ed. Herle, Esq. Wood says, that though his ancestors had lived several generations in that place above-mentioned in genteel fashion, yet they were originally of West Herle in Northumberland. He received his education in Exeter-college, in Oxford, where he entered a student, in the year 1612. He took his degrees in arts, that of master being completed in the year 1618. Having finished his studies at the University, he entered upon the ministerial work. He was first settled at some place in Devonshire, where, being always accounted a Puritan, he suffered persecution on account of his non-conformity. For, *All who will live godly in Christ Jesus shall suffer persecution.* Afterward, he became rector of Winwick, in Lancashire, which is said to have been one of the richest livings in England. Upon the commencement of the civil war, he took part with the Parliament, was elected one of the Assembly of Divines at Westminster, and, upon the death of Dr Twisse, in the year 1646, he was chosen prolocutor to the Assembly. He took the Covenant, preached frequently before the Parliament, was appointed one of the licensers of the press for books of divinity, in 1643, one of the morning lecturers at the Abbey-church, Westminster, and one of the select committee for the examination and approbation of ministers of the Gospel who petitioned for sequestered livings. And, in the year 1644, he and others, to the number of twenty-one, had full power given them to ordain ministers for a time in the county of Lancaster. Mr Herle was also appointed one of the committee of accommodation, in 1645; and he was one of the committee of learned divines appointed by the Assembly to prepare materials for their Confession of Faith. He subscribed the proposition, "That Jesus Christ, as King of the church has himself appointed a church-government distinct from the civil magistrate." He was accounted a moderate presbyterian. In his imprimatur to the Apology of the Independents, he calls it a Performance full of peaceableness, modesty and candour; and though he wrote against it, yet in the preface to his book, which is entitled, "The Independency on Scriptures of the Independency of Churches," he says, "The difference between us and our brethren who are for Independency, is nothing so great as you seemed to conceive it;—at most it does but ruffle a little the fringe, not any way rend the garment of Christ; it is so far from being a fundamental that it is scarcely a material difference." —When the Scottish commissioners proposed to leave the Assembly of Divines at Westminster, with a view to return home, Mr Herle, who was then prolocutor to the Assembly, spoke in the name of his brethren, and thanked the honourable and reverend commissioners from the church of Scotland for their seasonable assistance. Upon this occasion, he excused, in the best manner that he could, the Directory's not being so well observed as it ought; and lamented that the Assembly had not power to call offenders to an account. He confessed, that their affairs were very much embarassed, and that they were still in great confusion. He observed that the Parliament was in great distress, while the common enemy was high and strong. He added, that their extraordinary successes hitherto were owing to the prayers of their brethren of Scotland, and of other Protestants abroad, as well as to their own. He then mentioned with deep concern some other restraints which the Assembly lay under, but that this was not a proper time for redress.[a] In the year 1647, Mr Herle and Mr Stephen Marshall were appointed to attend the commissioners of Parliament to Scotland, with a view to give the Scots a just account of the affairs of England. After the King's death, Mr Herle retired to his flock and stated ministerial labours in the Lord's vineyard at Winwick, where he continued the remainder of his days, and was very much beloved by his brethren in the ministry in that country.

In the year 1651, the Earl of Derby having raised a regiment of soldiers for Charles Second, who was then on his march from Scotland, he sent Lieutenant Arundal, with about forty horses, to Mr Herle's house at Winwick, which filled the whole family with the utmost consterna-

a Neal's Hist. Puritans, vol. iii. chap. viii.

tion, expecting that they would be immediately plundered and ruined. When Arundal arrived at the house, he said to Mr Herle, " My business is to tell you, that the Earl of Derby wishes you to come to him with all speed; and if you will go, there shall be no farther trouble to you nor your family." Mr Herle replied, " I will go immediately, and wait upon the right honourable the Earl of Derby, my patron;" and ordered his horse to be brought out. After some kind entertainment of the lieutenant and his soldiers, Mr Herle accompanied them to the Earl's quarters, who received and treated him with the utmost civility. After some friendly conversation with him, his lordship sent him back, attended by a guard of soldiers. It has also been observed, that, after the battle of Warrington-bridge, in this year, Arundal's forces being routed, and himself wounded, he retired to Mr Herle's house, where he was treated with the utmost kindness.[a] Mr Herle was appointed, together with Mr Isaac Ambrose, Mr Edward Gee, and some others, assistant to the commissioners for ejecting ignorant and scandalous ministers and school-masters in Lancashire. Dr Grey says, that, in this office, he acted " with great severity; and how well he was qualified for such dirty work, his public sermons sufficiently testify." He then transcribes from those sermons the following expressions, in order to prove the charge which he has brought against him: " Do justice to the greatest. Saul's sons are not spared; no, nor Agag; nor Benhadad, though themselves kings. Zimri and Cosbi, though princes of the people, must be pursued to their tents. What an army of martyrs has God given to the fire for our reformation at first! What a calendar of traitors has he given to the gallows, for our preservation since!" Mr Brook, in his account of Mr Herle, well observes here,—" Whether these expressions afford sufficient evidence of the doctor's charge, or whether he designed it only to reproach the memory of this celebrated divine, every intelligent reader

a Brook's Lives of the Puritans, vol. iii. p. 325.

will easily judge. The character of Mr Herle is too well established to be at all impaired by any such calumny."

The very famous Mr John Howe was ordained at Winwick, by Mr Herle, with the assistance of several other ministers; on which account Mr Howe would sometimes say, "That he thought few in modern times had so truly primitive an ordination; for he considered Mr Herle as a primitive bishop."[a] Dr Fuller says, that he was a good scholar, and esteemed by his party a deep divine; and that he was so much the Christian, the scholar, and the gentleman, that he could agree in affection with those who differed from him in judgment.[b] He died at Winwick, toward the end of September, in the year 1659, aged sixty-one years; and his remains were interred in his own church.[c]

A few choice sayings of Mr Herle, which have been collected from his writings, are here subjoined, in order that the reader may obtain a fuller view of his true character. *By their fruits ye shall know them.*— "Thankfulness is the best tenure; it gives the surest title to new mercies.—Religious families are the surest nurseries of religion." And speaking of the influence which the bad example of parents has on their children, he says, "That a Cain will not want others *to go on in his way*, nor a Jeroboam followers *in making Israel to sin.*—The highest office of government is, to be the nurse, the guardian, of religion.—Peace without *contentment*, is but lethargy; safety without it, is but a prison; but *contentment* without both, is a *continual feast*, a kingdom. The proud man hath no *God*, the unpeaceable man hath no *neighbour*, the distrustful man hath no *friend*, but the discontented man hath not *himself*.—As use gives things perfection, so *usefulness* gives them value.—Let *divine* truths be believed, *others* proved.—Long discourses are over-feathered arrows, that over-shoot the mark, and ordinarily lose both game and labour by wearying the attention. Our *discourse* should be to the matter,

a Middleton's Biogr. Evang. vol iv. Howe.
b Worthies of England, and Church Hist. B. xi. p. 213.
c Wood's Athenæ Oxon. vol. ii.

as trimming to clothes, rather *proper* than *gaudy*, rather *fit* than *fine*. *Affectation* in any thing, especially in words, argues more ambition, than ability; and discovers a narrow soul, that is fain to take up forms and examples instead of reason, and dares not write but by a copy.—*Injuries*, if we are not wanting to ourselves, are the greatest *advantages*, as well as *trials*, in our whole lives. Courtesies, applauses, successes, steal us out of ourselves. Injuries restore us to ourselves again; it is *in our patience we possess our souls*. Would we instead of making a return of injuries on others, make a retirement by them into ourselves, we should find them the best restoratives of our minds to themselves.

Mr Herle was the author of several practical and controversial writings, which praise him in the gate.

1. *Microcosmography, in Essays and Characters*, 1628; small book.—2. *Contemplations and Devotions on the several Passages of our blessed Saviour's Death and Passion;* a small volume, pp. 546. London, 1631.—3. An Answer to misled Dr Hen. Fearne, according to his own method of his book; 4to. London, 1642.—4. Several Sermons, among which are the following:—*A Pair of Compasses for Church and State;* a Sermon from Zech. viii. 19. at Margaret's, Westminster, before the Honourable House of Commons, at their monthly Fast, Nov. last, 1642. 4to. London, 1642.—*David's Song of* three Parts; a Sermon from Psal. xcv. 1. before the Honourable House of Lords, 15th of June, 1643. 4to. pp. 29. London, 1643.—*David's Reserve and Rescue;* a Sermon from 2 Sam. xxi. 16, 17. before the Honourable House of Commons, Nov. 5th, 1644. 4to. pp. 18. London, 1645.—Three Sermons, 1 Kings xxii. 22. Wood mentions other Sermons by Mr Herle, but says that he had not then seen these, nor have I seen them; to wit, *Abraham's Offering*, before the Mayor and Aldermen of London, from Gen. xxii. 2. London, 1644. And a Sermon from 2 Sam. xxii. 22. London, 1644. A Thanksgiving Sermon, before the House of Commons, 12th of May, 1646, and a Fast Sermon before the House

of Lords, the same year.—5. *The Independency on Scriptures of the Independency of Churches.* In this performance the Question of the Independency of Church government is temperately stated, fairly argued, and particularly cleared from objections. 4to. pp 44. London, 1643.—6. *Worldly Policy and Moral Prudence; the vanity and folly of the one, and the solidity and usefulness of the other, in a moral Discourse;* a small book, London, 1654. This book was printed again, in the year 1655, under the title of *Wisdom's Tripos*, in three Treatises. 1. Of Worldly Policy. 2. Of Moral Prudence. 3. Of Christian Wisdom. The vanity of the first, the usefulness of the second, and the excellency of the third. An excellent book. It was also printed, London, 1670.

RICHARD HEYRICK, A.M. OF MANCHESTER,

A MEMBER OF THE ASSEMBLY OF DIVINES AT WESTMINSTER.

RICHARD HEYRICK was born in London, and educated in Merchant Taylor's school. He was a younger son of Sir William Heyrick of Beaumannour in Leicestershire. He became commoner of St John's college in Oxford, in the beginning of the year 1617, aged seventeen years. In due time, he took the degrees in arts, and was elected fellow of All-Soul's-college, in the same University, in the year 1624, and about that time he entered into holy orders. Afterward he was pastor of a church in Norfolk, and made warden of Christ's college in Manchester, in Lancashire in England, by means of Archbishop Laud. Upon the commencement of the civil wars, he espoused the cause of the Parliament, and was chosen a member of the Assembly of Divines at Westminster. He is called in Neal's list, "Mr Richard Heyrick of Manchester," and marked as constantly attending the Assembly. He took the Covenant, and is said to have been very zealous in promoting the interests of the Reformation. In the year 1644, Mr Heyrick, and other ministers, to the number of twenty-one, had full power given them by an ordinance which passed the Houses of Parliament, for the benefit of the county of Lancaster, to ordain ministers for a time in that county.[a] He was concerned in that affair respecting the restoration or expedition of Charles II. into England, after his father's death, which has been called *Love's* plot, as he was a principal sufferer on account of it. It was formed by a number of gentlemen and ministers, and designed to raise money by private contribution, to forward the expedition of Charles II. into England; but the object was soon discovered and defeated by the great vigilance of the commonwealth, which had its active spies in all places. The celebrated Mr Christopher Love and Mr Gibbons were made public examples, as a terror to other persons, when some, by petitioning for mercy, and promising submission to the government in time to come, were released, and escaped the severity of the storm. Several persons absconded; but in what manner Mr Heyrick came off, I cannot tell. Be that as it may, he was afterward appointed an assistant to the commissioners for ejecting ignorant and scandalous ministers and school-masters in Lancashire. Wood says, "Upon the approach of his Majesty's Restoration, he seemed to be zealous for it, and turning about, as many of his party did, he kept his wardenship to his dying day." He died on the sixth day of Aug. 1667, aged 67 years, and his remains were interred in the collegiate church of Manchester. Soon after there was a comely monument put over his grave at the charge of Anna Maria, his widow, with a large inscription thereon, which was composed by his ancient and real friend, Thomas Case, Minister of the Gospel in London, who had been intimately acquainted with Mr Heyrick while he was a student in the University of Oxford. This inscription gives Mr Heyrick a very eminent character, as a person of genteel extraction, a most diligent student, a

a Neal's Hist. Purit. vol. iii. chap. iv.

most faithful pastor, and a most watchful guardian of his college. A man of solid judgment, with acute penetration, of singular zeal mingled with remarkable prudence, of great gravity, accompanied with much sweetness of manners and true humility. He is allowed to have beeu a man of great learning.[a]

He has published several sermons, among which are the following:—Three sermons preached in the collegiate church of Manchester, from Psalm cxxii. 6. 2 Thess. ii. 15. and Gen. xlix. 5, 6, 7. London, 1641.—*Queen Esther's Resolves:* or, *A Princely Pattern of Heaven-born Resolution, for all the Lovers of God and their country;* a Sermon preached from Esther iv. 16. before the House of Commons, at the monthly Fast, 27th of May, 1646. 4to. London, 1646. I have seen this sermon, in Wigtonshire, and in Ayrshire, in Scotland. It is said, that he has a sermon from Gal. iv. 16. And Wood mentions a sermon of his from 2 Kings xi. 12. 4to. London, 1661. But these two I have not seen.

GASPAR HICKES, A. M.

PASTOR OF LAUDRAKE IN CORNWALL, AND A MEMBER OF THE ASSEMBLY OF DIVINES AT WESTMINSTER.

GASPAR HICKES was the son of a Minister, and was born in Berkshire, an inland county in England. He was educated in Trinity-college in Oxford, where he entered in the year 1621, aged sixteen years. He took the degrees in arts, and entered upon the holy ministry, and at length became pastor of Laudrake, or Lawrick, in the county of Cornwall. Here he continued a constant, diligent, and faithful preacher, several years, under the name of a Puritan. Upon the commencement of the

a Wood's Athenæ Oxon. vol. ii. 2d edit.

civil war, he espoused the cause of the Parliament, openly and plainly expressed his sentiments in his sermons, and shewed his zeal in that cause. When the royalists entered that country and were prevalent, he found his situation uneasy, and retired to London. He was chosen a member of the Assembly of Divines at Westminster, took his seat there, and constantly attended. He preached frequently in London, and sometimes before the Parliament. Afterward, upon the declining of the King's interest, he returned to his pastoral charge in Cornwall. In the year 1654, he was appointed an assistant to the commissioners of Cornwall for ejecting ignorant and scandalous ministers and school-masters in that county. And Wood says, that "ever after, till the Act of Conformity came forth, he was esteemed there the chief of the Presbyterian Ministers." Being ejected, by the Act of Uniformity, in 1662, from Laudrake, he continued to live there, and near that place, several years, preaching always as he had opportunity; but in that honourable and good work he met with much trouble and disturbance. Continuing, after May 30, 1670, to preach in his family, to the number which the Act against Conventicles allowed, with some other persons under sixteen years of age, Mr Winnel, the young parson of Laudrake, was greatly enraged, and informed against him, as keeping conventicles, and caused his house to be searched by the officers of the parish, who found but four persons there above the age of sixteen, beside his own family. The furious zealot rode from Justice to Justice to convict Mr Hickes, but the gentlemen in the neighbourhood would not give him any countenance, being sensible that the law was not violated. Upon this he went into Devonshire, where he found some Justices for his purpose, who convicted Mr Hickes; and taking it for granted that he preached, though there was no proof of it, they levied £40 upon him. Mr Hickes appealed to the next general sessions, where, contrary to law, he was denied a Jury, and the Justices passed sentence of judgment upon him by vote, and his appeal hereby being made unjust, they beside the £40 gave treble cost against him, and at the same time loaded him with foul reproaches. Poor dissenters sometimes have not had common justice. But, *Blessed are ye when men shall revile you, and persecute you, and shall say all manner of evil against you falsely, for my sake. Rejoice, and be exceeding glad; for great is your reward in heaven: for so persecuted they the prophets who were before you.*

Mr Hickes died in the year 1677, about the seventy-third year of his age. His remains were buried, according to his own desire, in the porch of the parish church of Laudrake, and many pious persons attended his funeral.

He has published some sermons, as, *The Glory and Beauty of God's Portion*, a sermon from Isai. xxviii 5 6. before the Honourable House of Commons, at the Public Fast, June 26, 1644. 4to. pp. 43. London, 1644. *The Life and Death of David*, a sermon at the Death of Will. Strode, Esq. from Acts xiii. 36. 4to. Lond. 1645. *The Advantage of Afflictions*, a sermon from Hos. v. 15. before the House of Peers, Fast, 4to. pp. 31. London, 1645. Dr Calamy says, that he was a good scholar, and a celebrated preacher.[a]

THOMAS HILL, D. D.

PASTOR OF TICHMARSH, IN THE COUNTY OF NORTHAMPTON, A MEMBER OF THE ASSEMBLY OF DIVINES AT WESTMINSTER, AND MASTER OF EMANUEL AND OF TRINITY COLLEGE, CAMBRIDGE.

THOMAS HILL was born in Worcestershire, in England, of godly parents, who solemnly dedicated him unto God in his childhood. This duty, which is shamefully neglected by us, was, among our forefathers, an object of chief attention. His parents also, with great cheerfulness, resolved to educate him for the important work of

a Calamy's Acc. vol. ii. p. 136. Cont. p. 175. Wood's Ath. vol. ii.

the holy ministry. And, having received a well directed education in the country, he was afterward sent to Emanuel college, in the University of Cambridge Here, he was eminently distinguished by his close application to his studies, and by his sobriety. The grace of God, which sanctifies our natures, and refines our manners, did now shine in him, with peculiar lustre, in his early youth. In this critical season of life, he was taught to despise the allurements, the deceitful, and transitory pleasures of sin: and to devote the first and the best of his days to the service of his Maker and Redeemer. Such deportment is most beautiful and becoming in young persons, and highly worthy of imitation. This justly entitled him to respectful notice among the governors of the College; who, upon examination, elected him *scholar of the house*.

Afterward, he went to spend some time, for his farther improvement in useful knowledge and true piety, with the eminently pious and learned Mr Cotton, at Boston, in Lincolnshire. Mr Cotton's suitable directions, and his striking and exemplary piety, were highly beneficial to this well-disposed scholar, and had a powerful tendency to improve his mind, and his religious principles, which continued with him through the whole journey of life.

He gained a shining and lasting reputation, in a short time, by his piety and learning: and upon his return to the College, he was soon chosen a Fellow, with general approbation, after an uncommonly strict examination. And now, he became a very careful, diligent, and successful, tutor to young scholars, for some time. He afterward commenced a preacher of the glorious Gospel of the grace of God. His fame soon spread, and he was called to the pastoral charge of Tichmarsh, in Northamptonshire, in England, where he discharged the duties of his ministerial office with much steadiness and fidelity, about eight or nine years. He was chosen into the respectable Assembly of Divines at Westminster, for the county of Northampton. He was very useful in this public and important service. He was often employed by the Parliament to preach before them at their Fasts, and upon other solemn occasions. While he was at London, he preached on the Lord's-day at St Martin's in the Fields, a large congregation, where he was highly beneficial to many souls. And he was chosen to be one of the Morning Lecturers at Westminster Abbey. He was afterward elected to be Master of Emanuel-college, in the University of Cambridge; and from thence he was removed to the Mastership of Trinity-college. In these superior stations, this illustrious luminary of the Christian church behaved with great prudence and circumspection. He was principally attentive to promote piety and learning, in these seminaries. He preached very frequently in their chapel, and wrote to their seniors. His views were really noble, and his conduct very suitable to the genius of the religion which he professed. He always seconded his arguments, by the victorious power of an exemplary life. That gentleness of manners, which greatly sweetens the intercourse of human society, was very conspicuous in him. In his general behaviour, he was meek and condescending; but he always retained the dignity of his character, and was readily moved with just indignation, at the least appearance of sin and corruption. He was also eminently distinguished by his ardent zeal for the honours, privileges, and emoluments, of the University. He was two years vice-chancellor. This eminent divine firmly believed, constantly preached, and strenuously defended, the all-important doctrines of God's sovereignty in his decrees;—of his free love and grace in election;—of justification by the imputed righteousness of Christ;—and of the final perseverance of the saints in a state of grace. At his death, he intimated to one of his friends, that he then derived singular comfort from these doctrines, as many other eminent Christians have also done, in this very trying season.

In his preaching, he was plain, powerful, spiritual, and frequent. Both our blessed Saviour and his apostles preached the glorious Gospel of the grace of God, in the plainest manner. They wisely adapted their discourses even to the meanest capacities of their hearers, whose knowledge often was as low as their external condition, *that all men might know the Lord from the least to the greatest.* This mode of preaching, as one well observes, "hath always an air of candour and sincerity, and thereby the labour of tedious inquiry is prevented."—Some preachers, in order to conceal unpopular opinions, and to put on an air of orthodoxy, use expressions which may be interpreted, with equal ease, to divers, and even contrary, purposes.—Remarkable, in this case, is that very striking passage, 1 Cor. xiv. 8, 9. *For if the trumpet give an uncertain sound, who shall prepare himself to the battle? So likewise ye, except ye utter by the tongue, words easy to be understood, how shall it be known what is spoken? for ye shall speak into the air.* "If this be a good argument against preaching in an unknown tongue, it is equally good against every thing else that disguises, instead of unfolding our sentiments of Christianity. The apostles used great plainness of speech; and it is an apostolical injunction, "If any man speak, let him speak as the oracles of God." Let his style be plain and clear, like that of the sacred writings; not dark and ambiguous, like the oracles of the Heathen."[a] And powerful preaching, calculated to command a reverent attention, to strike the conscience, and to warm and affect the heart, well becomes ministers of the glorious Gospel of the Son of God. They ought to speak with dignity and holy boldness, not fearing the face of man. "Favour should not bribe, nor frowns nor dangers affright us, from delivering our Master's message."[b] Insipid sermons, in which a pathetic address is wanting, seldom warm the heart, or arouse the hearer. "Soft and drowsy harangues, instead of rousing a secure generation, will rather increase their spiritual lethargy; and a cold preacher will soon have a cold auditory. Jesus has intrusted us with the concerns of his people, a people dearly bought, and greatly beloved; we have to do with souls, that must be happy or miserable for ever; we address them, in the name of God, upon matters of infinite importance; and is it not

a The Scotch Preacher, vol. i. ser. v. Dr Erskine. 2d edit.
b Dr Erskine, as above.

an indignity to Him whose ambassadors we are, to execute our commission coolly, and as if half asleep? Will it not tempt others to slight our message, if, by the manner of delivering it, we appear to slight it ourselves? When our own hearts are most impressed with the inestimable worth of immortal souls; when out of the abundance of the heart the mouth speaketh, when our sentiments, style, voice, and gesture, discover how much we are in earnest; then we are most likely to touch the hearts of our hearers, and make them feel the force of what we say."[a] And, spiritual preaching, suited to the spiritual state of the flock, and to the dispensations of Divine Providence respecting them, is, undoubtedly, highly useful and important. And, the Lord Jesus Christ, and salvation through his name, ought to be frequently preached. The subject of this memoir was a most diligent, faithful, and laborious, preacher of the Gospel of Christ, during the whole of his public ministry, and especially toward the period of his life in this world. Beside his preaching in the University, he set up a lecture every Sabbath-morning, in one church in the town, which was performed only by himself, and cheerfully frequented both by many scholars and inhabitants of the town; and one lecture in another church, every Lord's-day in the afternoon, in which he did bear at least, the fourth part of the burden; and both *gratis*. He also preached occasionally in several adjacent towns and villages; and was instrumental in setting up lectures in some of them, and often assisted at these lectures. When near the end of his journey to the promised land, he was eminently distinguished by his unwearied zeal, and his unremitting industry, in faithfully discharging the trust which was committed to him. He continued *stedfast and immoveable, always abounding in the work of the Lord;* and his labours were attended with much success.

Though naturally modest, yet when the case required, he appeared with boldness and with spirit, in a good cause. Being endowed with a very public spirit, he was deeply in-

a Dr Erskine's Ser. as above.

terested in the interests of the Redeemer's kingdom. His other eminent qualities were richly adorned with much humility, very low thoughts of himself, an agreeable, familiar, and instructive, conversation, an affable condescending manner in society, and with true benevolence, which shed its kindly beams for the relief and comfort of many really indigent persons. Like the good Samaritan, he often poured balm into the wounded mind, *delivered the poor who cried, and the fatherless, and him who had none to help him.*

He was seized with a long continued quartan-ague, which did bear the marks of mortality. In the lucid intervals of his trouble, he improved his time, in making close inquiry respecting his peace with Heaven, and his readiness for his passage into the world unknown.—In his short sickness, he expressed to one of his friends, his great comfort and joy, in God's free discriminating electing love. To Dr Tuckney, about half an hour before his departure, who made inquiry respecting the settlement of his outward estate, and of his inward peace, he readily, and without any hesitation, answered, *Through the mercy of God in Christ, his peace was made, and that he quietly rested in it.* Then, with tranquillity, he suddenly departed, Dec. 18th 1653, in an advanced age, very much lamented by his acquaintance and brethren.

Having settled his peace with God, through the Lord Jesus Christ, the Prince of Peace, who has made peace by the blood of his cross, the king of terrors appeared now to be transformed into an angel of peace, to waft his immortal soul into the blissful mansions in a better world, where neither sin nor sorrow can enter. The Redeemer's death is the Christian's strongest consolation, and best antidote to the fears of death. And there is always some peculiarity in the death of the real Christian. "There is a majesty in the death of the Christian: He partakes of the spirit of that world to which he is advancing, and he meets his latter end with a face that looks to the heavens." [a]

a Logan's Sermons, vol. i. ser. vii. end.—See Dr Tuckney's Ser. at Dr Hill's Fun. Lon. 1654. and Clark's Lives.

Mr Neal, in his History of the Puritans, says, that Dr Hill "was a good scholar, and very careful of the Antiquities and Privileges of the University: a strict Calvinist, a plain, powerful, and practical, Preacher, and of an holy and unblameable conversation." "A holy life is the most persuasive sermon, expressed too in a language which men of all nations equally understand. It even explains what other sermons mean, instead of needing to be explained by them. Men will see more beauty in a truly virtuous action, than in the most rhetorical description we can give of it; and then they lose no time, for they see it at once: whereas, besides the necessary expence of time, much skill and address must likewise be employed, to unfold it in such a manner as to make it thoroughly understood and relished."[a]

Our reformers were eminently distinguished by a holy life, the importance of which is well expressed by Mr Walker. In this way, the ministers of the glorious Gospel of the grace of God preached without ceasing. They exhibited continually the amiable religion of Jesus, in their practice, and afforded an easy opportunity of reading the wholesome laws of Christ's house every day.—*That* alone can be accounted true religion, which dwells in the heart, and which constantly displays its peculiar influence in the life.—Dr Hill was a divine very eminent for humility and holiness, an excellent and useful preacher, and of great learning and moderation; but no friend to Arminianism. He used to lay his hand upon his breast, and say, "Every true Christian has something here, that will frame an argument against Arminianism."[b] Mr Henry Oatland, one of the ejected ministers, who was one of his pupils, and admitted into Trinity college while he was master, observes, that he derived unspeakable advantage from Dr Hill's plain but truly excellent method of preaching and advancing Christ. He says, "that he learned more of Christ in one year, from Dr Hill's preaching, and almost daily expositions in the chapel,

a Mr Walker's Sermons, of Edin. vol. i. ser. i.
b Firmin's Real Christian, p. 26. Edit. 1670.

than he had all his time before in the country."[a] Mr John Machin, another of the ejected ministers, going to the University, without any view to the ministry, or to continue there, on his first going thither, had a gracious change effected in him, chiefly by the preaching of Dr Hill; and that of Dr Arrowsmith was much to his comfort and edification. No sooner did he find this blessed change in his heart, than his friends found it by his letters; by which together with his exemplary conversation afterward, he was the means of converting his three sisters, and there was room to hope, both his parents, as Mr Palmer informs us, in his Nonconformist's Memorial. Dr Hill was very highly esteemed by the Earl of Warwick in whose family he became acquainted with Mrs Willford, governess to the Earl's daughter, whom he afterward married. When the committee of accommodation was appointed by the House of Lords, to consider the innovations in religion, Dr Hill, with several bishops and other learned divines, was chosen a member of the sub committee, to prepare materials for their debate. And, when the committee of accommodation was revived by order of Parliament, he was appointed one of its learned members.[b]—In the University, he diligently employed all his talents and zeal in the advancement of sound learning and genuine piety, and in the due observance of college exercises.

He was the author of several pieces, chiefly sermons before the Parliament, among which are: 1. *The Trade of Truth Advanced*, in a Sermon from Prov. xxiii. 23. to the Honourable House of Commons, at their solemn Fast, 27th of July, 1642. 4to. pp. 59. London, 1642. —2. *The Militant Church Triumphant over the Dragon and his Angels*; a Sermon preached from Rev. xii. 11. to both Houses of Parliament, at an extraordinary Fast, 21st of July, 1643. 4to. pp. 31. London, 1643.—3. *The Good Old Way, God's Way to Soul-refreshing Rest;*

a Calamy's Contin. vol. ii. p. 885.
b Brook's Puritans, vol. iii.

a Sermon from Jer. vi. 16. to the Lord Mayor, and Court of Aldermen of London, 24th April, 1644, Fast. London, 1644.—4. *The Season for England's Self-Reflection, and Advancing Temple-Work;* a Sermon preached from Hag. i. 7, 8. to the two Houses of Parliament, Aug. 13, 1644. being an extraordinary day of Humiliation. 4to. pp. 37. London, 1644.—5. *The Right Separation Encouraged,* in a Sermon preached from 2 Cor. vi. 17, 18. to the Right Honourable the House of Lords, in the Abbey-church at Westminster, on Wednesday, Nov. 27th, 1644, being the day of the monthly public Fast. 4to. pp. 35. London, 1645. It is said, that Dr Hill has several other Sermons; but I have not seen these.

THOMAS HODGES, B. D.

MINISTER OF THE GOSPEL AT KENSINGTON, AND A MEMBER OF THE ASSEMBLY OF DIVINES AT WESTMINSTER.

THOMAS HODGES was Minister of the Gospel at Kensington, in the county of Middlesex, near London, several years. He was at Kensington when he was chosen to be a member of the Assembly of Divines at Westminster. He took his seat in that Assembly, and gave constant attendance during the session. He was a Covenanter, and preached sometimes before the Parliament. Some sermons which he preached before the Parliament were then printed, and are still extant. In a sermon which he preached before the Honourable House of Commons, from 2 Pet. ii 2. and in his epistle dedicatory, which is prefixed to that sermon, he complains very much of the growth and spreading of heresy, and of the fruitfulness of the press in producing many monstrous misshapen births. He says, in his address to the learned and brave patriots, "Is it not time to cry to you for help? There is nothing more excellent than God's truth, nor of more concernment than man's soul; both lie a-bleeding." Mr Hodges maintained, as our reformers did, in general, that the care and reformation of religion belonged to civil rulers, and constituted one of the principal duties of their office. Accordingly, he farther adds, in the above-mentioned sermon, in addressing the House of Commons, "I beseech you shew mercy to lovely *Truth*, that beam of glory, daughter of heaven, that clue of mercy let down into this dark erring world, to lead us through the many labyrinths of a benighted mind, erring thoughts, misleading examples, and dark temptations, to bliss and happiness. For she suffers, and is here like to perish from us, and be utterly lost, or at least shrewdly eclipsed, if you relieve her not." What have we to leave posterity, so precious as this *Way of Truth?* If that be gone, the glory is departed from Israel, and farewell all. Have we received it from our ancestors in lustre and purity, and is it not grievous to us, that in our time it should be so mangled and defaced, that our children after us, except it be timely prevented, will scarcely be able to distinguish between it and error? Why did the valiant Martyrs shed their precious blood, but to maintain this *way of truth?* And shall we lose and let it go at so cheap a rate, and not mourn for it? The Jews of old, when they heard blasphemy, used to rend their cloaths, to testify the inward rending of their hearts: Can ours be whole when the foolish people so much defame God's truth, and blaspheme his name?" He concludes his sermon, with recommending to the learned auditory, to encourage catechising, whereby poor souls may be taught the principles of religion in the plainest manner, and that there might be milk for babes.—To plant a learned and able Ministry in every eminent place. And here, he says, "Give me leave to suggest unto you, That there are many learned men in this kingdom, whom God hath not gifted with elocution and other the like abilities for pulpit-work, yet would be very fit to maintain the Truth by their pen, against destroying errors, might they but have encouragement." He adds, "Settle with all convenient speed your Confession of Faith, wherein people may take notice what is allowed for Truth, upon mature debate;—and with little pains discern what is right or wrong." And that error might be effectually suppressed, and truth established. he advises the worthy senators, as the guardians and foster-fathers of Truth, to take special care of the Universities, that learning and piety be sufficiently encouraged in these useful fountains. And that reading the Holy Scriptures, and pious exercises, might be more in use among them. Wood says, that after his Majesty's restoration, Mr Hodges became rector of St Peter's church in Cornhill London, and dean of Hereford in the place of Dr H Croft who was made bishop thereof in 1661; and that holding that deanery to the time of his death, he was succeeded therein by Dr George Benson about Mid-summer, in the year 1672.[a]

His writings.—1. *A Glimpse of God's Glory;* a Sermon from Psalm cxiii 5, 6. before the House of Commons, at their solemn Fast, 28th Sept. 1642. 4to. pp. 41. Lond. 1642.—2. *The Growth and Spreading of Heresy;* a Sermon from 2 Pet ii. 2 before the Honourable House of Commons, at their public Fast for the growth of heresy, 10th of March 1646 4to. pp. 60. London, 1647. —3. *Inaccessible Glory: or The Impossibility of seeing God's Face while we are in the body;* a Sermon from Exod. xxxiii. 20. at the funeral of Sir Theod. de Mayerne, in the church of St Martin's in the Fields, on the 30th of March, 1655. 4to. London, 1655. It is said, that he has a Sermon from Gen. i. 31. but I have not seen it.

a Wood's Fasti Oxon, vol. ii. p. 31. 2d edit.

JOSHUA HOYLE, D. D.

PROFESSOR OF DIVINITY IN THE UNIVERSITY OF DUBLIN, A MEMBER OF THE ASSEMBLY OF DIVINES AT WESTMINSTER, MASTER OF UNIVERSITY-COLLEGE, OXFORD, AND KING'S PROFESSOR OF DIVINITY IN THAT UNIVERSITY.

JOSHUA HOYLE was born at Sawerby, near Halifax, in Yorkshire, in England, and educated in Magdalen-college, Oxford. Afterward, being invited into Ireland, he became fellow of Trinity college, Dublin. He took his degrees in divinity, and was chosen professor of divinity in that University. He was exceedingly eager to *redeem the time*, and indefatigable both in his studies and other labours. He seems to have been for some time greatly captivated with scholastic studies, and to have prosecuted these with much success, as many eminent reformers have done. But he greatly preferred the study of the Holy Scriptures to that of scholastic theology. He was led to the Sacred Writings as the alone pure fountain of divine truth. He soon became a profound divine; and being now placed in a sphere of great usefulness, he laboured with unwearied assiduity, in promoting the interests of religion. In his daily lectures, as professor of divinity, he expounded the whole Bible, seldom taking more than one verse at a time, which lasted about fifteen years. Some time before he had ended that great work, he began the second exposition of the whole Bible in the church of Trinity college, and in about ten years he went through the greatest part of the sacred volume. He preached and expounded thrice every Sabbath for the far greater part of the year, and also on many extraordinary occasions. To these unwearied labours may be added his learned weekly lectures, as professor, in the controversies, and his elaborate answers to the great champion Bellarmine, one of the most celebrated controversialists of the Romish church. Bellarmine was very highly esteemed by the court of Rome, and had the reputation of being one of the most strenuous defenders of the Catholic religion against the reformers. And so very formidable were his controversial labours accounted, that for many years almost every eminent protestant divine endeavoured to make the arguments of Bellarmine a particular object of refutation. The great work which has furnished matter for this critical warfare, is a Body of Controversy, which was written in Latin, and has been often re-printed, in 4 vols. folio. Dr Hoyle boldly and successfully attacked the system of error and corruption in the Romish church. He has discovered to the world that *Mystery of Iniquity*, as Hercules did Cacus's den. Or, as Theodosius used those idolatrous temples in Egypt, when all the ridiculous toys of Pagan priests, and their cheating tricks were brought upon the stage. He prepared answers to all Bellarmine, both in word and writing. He began with the cardinal's work respecting the seven sacraments, which he was more than eight years in finishing. Afterward, he proceeded in his answers to the other controversial pieces of the great champion of the Romish church. Dr Hoyle was one of our eminent reformers, " who, having forced the strong-hold of superstition, and penetrated the recesses of its temple, tore aside the veil that concealed the monstrous idol which the whole world ignorantly worshipped, dissolved the magic spell by which the human mind was bound, and restored it to liberty." In the year 1634, he sat in the convocation which was held at Dublin. But, upon the commencement of the rebellion in Ireland, in the year 1641, he fled from the terrible effusion of blood. According to the computation of the popish priests themselves, who were actively employed in this dreadful rebellion, upward of *one hundred and fifty-four thousand* protestants were massacred in Ireland in the space of a few months: but, during the continuance of that horrid rebellion, according to Sir J. Temple, there were above *three hundred thousand* cruelly murdered in cold blood, or ruined in some other way. Cardinal Richelieu was deeply concerned in this barbarous massacre; and, according to Rapin, in his History of England, King Charles I. spread abroad that the Roman Catholics had his authority for what they did. Dr Hoyle's life being exposed to the most imminent hazard, he now returned to England, and became vicar of Stepney, near London; but, according to Wood, he, being too scholastical, did not please the parishioners. Be that as it may, he was always esteemed an eminent Puritan, and a zealous advocate for civil and religious liberty. While he remained at Stepney, the celebrated Mr Burroughs preached there in the morning, and Mr Greenhill in the afternoon. In the year 1643, Dr Hoyle was appointed a member of the Assembly of Divines at Westminster, and constantly attended. Dr Calamy says, "This Dr Hoyle was a member of great esteem and honour in the Assembly of Divines, as a master of all the ancient learning of the Greek and Latin fathers, and one who reigned both in his chair and in the pulpit."[a] He was witness against Archbishop Laud at his trial, when he attested that the Archbishop had corrupted the University of Dublin, by the arbitrary introduction of the errors of popery and Arminianism, while he was chancellor of that University.—He was appointed one of the select committee for the examination and approbation of ministers who petitioned for sequestered livings. In the year 1645, he was elected one of committee of accommodation; and in 1648, he became master or head of University-college, Oxford, and King's professor of divinity in that University, in the room of Dr Saunderson. In the office of professor of divinity he has incurred the severe and unjust animadversion of Dr Walker, who seldom fails to dip his pen in the *very* gall of bitterness, when he meets with the Puritans. This illiberal and abusive writer says, that Dr Hoyle opened his lectures by a speech void of all spirit or learning; and that his lectures had neither method nor argument in them, and shewed him to be ignorant even of the most common rules of logic.[b] Wood, however, says, that "he was a person of great reading and memory, much devoted to

a Calamy's Account, vol. ii. p. 472.
b Attempt, part. i. p. 141.

study, and in a manner a stranger to the world and things thereof, profound in the faculty of divinity, a constant preacher, and a noted Puritan." He was eminently learned, indefatigably industrious, and is allowed to have been as well qualified for an academic as any person of his time. He was eminently distinguished by the unwearied assiduity with which he laboured in the stations which were assigned to him. He died on the 6th of Dec. 1654, and his remains were interred in the old chapel belonging to the University-college. His successors in the offices of master and professor were Mr Francis Johnson and Dr John Conant, who were both silenced nonconformists, in 1662. Dr Hoyle was very highly respected by the famous Archbishop Usher. In vindication of this eminently learned prelate, he wrote " A Rejoynder to Mr Malone's Reply concerning Real Presence." 4to. pp. 662. Dublin, 1641. This is a very learned and elaborate work.

JOHN JACKSON, A. M.

A MEMBER OF THE ASSEMBLY OF DIVINES AT WESTMINSTER.

JOHN JACKSON, in the ordinance of the Parliament, for calling an Assembly of learned and godly divines, is said to be, John Jackson of Marske. In Mr Neal's list of that Assembly, he is styled, John Jackson, A. M. of Queen's college, Cambridge. Wood mentions several persons of the name, as John Jackson, M. A. of Cambridge, it seems, born in Lancashire, beneficed in Essex, and author of several tracts of practical divinity, as of *A Taste of the Truth as it is in Jesus*, &c. A John Jackson, who translated from Latin into English, a book entitled, De Immortalitate Animae. John Jackson, who has an exact Concordance of the Bible. Wood adds: " There

a Wood's Athenæ Oxon. vol. i. Fasti, p. 279. 2d edit.

was also one John Jackson, Parson of Marsh in Richmondshire, who hath written, *The faithful Minister of Jesus Christ, described by polishing the twelve Stones in the High Priest's Pectoral*, &c. London, 1628. This John Jackson was one of the Assembly of Divines, in the year 1643, and Preacher of Gray's-Inn."[a] Mr Jackson is represented as constantly attending the Assembly during the session. I have not received any farther information respecting him.

JOHN LANGLEY,

A MEMBER OF THE ASSEMBLY OF DIVINES AT WESTMINSTER.

JOHN LANGLEY was Minister of West-Tuderly, in the county of Southampton, in England. He was elected one of the Assembly of Divines at Westminster, in the year 1643. He gave constant attendance during the session He preached to the House of Commons. Wood says, that he became a publisher of several matters of divinity. I have seen and read a sermon of his, which is entitled, *The Mournful Note of the Dove.* It was preached from Psalm lxxiv. 19, 20. at Margaret's, Westminster, before the Honourable House of Commons, at their solemn Fast. Dec. 25, 1644. 4to. pp. 32. London, 1644. I am not able to give any further account of Mr Langley.

a Wood's Athenæ Oxon. vol. i. Fasti, p. 279. 2d edit.

JOHN LEY, A. M.

MINISTER OF GREAT BUDWORTH, IN CHESHIRE, AND A MEMBER OF THE ASSEMBLY OF DIVINES AT WESTMINSTER.

JOHN LEY was born in the ancient borough of Warwick, in England, on the 4th day of Feb. in the year 1583. He was descended from those of that name in Cheshire. In due time, he was sent to the free Grammar-school in Warwick. He became a student of Christ's Church-college, Oxford, in the year 1601, where, having continued a considerable time, he proceeded master of arts. Having finished his studies at the University, he was presented to the vicarage of Great Budworth in Cheshire, where he continued a constant preacher for several years. He was minister of Great Budworth in the year 1643, when he was chosen a member of the Assembly of Divines at Westminster. He was made prebendary of the Cathedral church at Chester, and sub-dean thereof, where he had a weekly lecture at St Peter's church, and was once or twice elected member of the convocation. But having always been puritanically inclined, he, upon the commencement of the civil war, espoused the cause of the Parliament, took the covenant, his seat in the Assembly of Divines, and he was appointed examiner in Latin to that famous Assembly.

Mr Ley became rector of Ashfield in Cheshire, and for a short time, rector of Astbury in the same county, chairman of the committee for the examination and approbation of ministers, one of the committee of printing and one of the committee for the ordination of ministers according to the Presbyterian form. About the year 1645, he was chosen president of Sion College, and about the same time, he was inducted into the rich living of Brightwell in Berkshire. In the year 1653, he was appointed one of the tryers of ministers, and, in the following year, an assistant to the commissioners of Berkshire for ejecting ignorant and scandalous ministers and school-masters. After some time he resigned his living of Brightwell, and was presented to that of Solihull in Warwickshire. He continued in that place some time; but by too much exertion and constant preaching, he broke a blood-vessel; and being disabled in such a manner that he could not fulfil the duties of his office, he resigned his charge, and retired to Sutton Colfield in the same county, where he lived privately the rest of his days.

A certain writer has placed Mr Ley at the head of those divines who, he says, "encouraged tumults," and whom, in great derision, he styles "able, holy, faithful, laborious, and truly peaceable preachers of the Gospel." The proof of his accusation is contained in Mr Ley's own words, which are as follows:—"It is not unknown, nor unobserved by the wise, that the ministers have been very serviceable to the civil state, and to the military too; not only by their supplications to God for good success in all their undertakings, and their happy proceedings in all their warlike marches and motions, as at the removal of the ark, Num. x. 35. *Rise up, Lord, and let thine enemies be scattered: Let them who hate thee, flee before thee;* but by their informations and solicitations of the people to engage both their estates and persons in the cause of God and their country" The author, having produced these, and some other citations which are similar, most triumphantly adds: "After these proofs and declarations of the ministers' zeal and industry for promoting, supporting, and carrying on the late bloody, impious, and unnatural war; let any man take upon him any longer to acquit the non-conformist divines of the guilt and consequence of that execrable rebellion."[a] Such heavy charges should certainly be supported, by very substantial and clear evidence. Though some of the most celebrated nonconformist divines were eminently zealous in the cause of the Parliament, which they firmly believed to be the cause of God and of Truth, will any unpre-

a L'Estranges' Dissenters' Sayings, part ii. pp. 51, 55. as with Brook, Lives Puritans, vol. iii. under J. Ley.

judiced person affirm, that they *encouraged tumults*, any more than those divines who were conformable? No person who is properly acquainted with the history of those very distracted times, and is without the unreasonable influence of a bigoted party spirit, will affirm any such thing. Respecting what is called the *execrable rebellion*, it is well known to all parties, that it originated in the most arbitrary and cruel proceedings of the haughty King and his tyrannical courtiers. Their barbarous and oppressive measures, after many woful years, led to all the horrors of a civil war. If, therefore, there was any such thing as an *execrable rebellion*, it may be easily seen who were the guilty persons, in raising, promoting, supporting, and carrying it on.

This eminently learned and laborious divine died on the 16th day of May, 1662, aged seventy-nine years, when he *rested from his labours*, and his remains were interred in the church at Sutton Colfield. Mr Ley was accounted an excellent preacher, an eminently learned and pious divine, deeply read in the fathers and councils, and one of the chief pillars of Presbyterianism.[a]

His writings.—1. *An Apology in Defence of the Geneva Notes on the Bible.* These Notes were in Mary's church in Oxford, publicly and severely reflected on by Dr John Howson. I cannot inform the reader when Mr Ley's Defence was printed; but it is said to have been written about 1612, and examined and highly approved by the celebrated Bishop Usher.—2. *A Pattern of Piety: or, the religious Life and Death of Mrs Jane Ratcliff of Chester.* Lond. 1640.—3. Several occasional Sermons, in 1640 and the following years, one from Ruth iii. 11. Lond. 1640. *A Monitor of Mortality*, in two funeral Sermons, which were occasioned by the death of John Archer, Esq. son and heir of Sir Simon Archer, knight of Warwickshire, and of Mrs Harper of Chester, and her daughter, aged 12 years. 4to. London, 1643. A Sermon which is entitled, *The Fury of War, and Folly of*

a Wood's Athenæ Oxon. vol. ii. 2d edit.

Sin, before the House of Commons, Fast, April 26, 1643, from Jer. iv. 21, 22. 4to. pp. 74. London, 1643 — 4. *Sunday a Sabbath:* or, a Preparative Discourse for discussion of Sabbatarian Doubts, 4to. London, 1641. He was assisted in this work, by the MSS. and advice of Archbishop Usher.—5. *The Christian Sabbath maintained*, in Answer to a Book of Dr Pocklington, styled, 'Sunday no Sabbath.' 1641 —6. Defensive Doubts, Hopes, and Reasons, for refusal of the Oath, imposed by the sixth Canon of the Synod, 4to. London, 1641.—7. A Letter against the Erection of an Altar, written June 29th, 1635, to John, Bishop of Chester, 1641.—8. *Case of Conscience concerning the Sacrament of the Lord's Supper.* 4to. London, 1641.—9. A Comparison of the Parliamentary Protestation with the late Canonical Oath, and the Difference between them; as also the opposition between the Doctrine of the church of England and that of Rome. 4to. London, 1641.—10. A farther Discussion of the Case of Conscience touching the receiving the Sacrament —Printed with the Comparison.—11. A Discourse concerning Puritans. 4to. 1641.—12. Examination of Mr Saltmarsh's New Query, 4to. pp. 106. with an Epistle prefixed to the Right Honourable Thomas Adams, Lord Mayor of London, of ten pages, closely printed, London, 1646. Mr Saltmarsh's New Query was published with a view to delay the establishment of the Presbyterian Government. And Mr Ley's Examination and Resolution of that New Query, very clearly shews, that it is unseasonable, unsound, and opposite to the principles both of true *religion* and of the *state*.—13. *Light for Smoke;* or, a clear and distinct Reply to a dark and confused Answer, in a book, made and entitled, 'The Smoke in the Temple, by John Saltmarsh.' To this book is added, *Novello-Mastix;* or, *A Scourge for a scurrilous News-monger*, in answer to the malevolent aspersions cast upon that Rev. and learned divine, Mr John Ley. 4to. Lon. 1646. —14. An After-reckoning with Mr Saltmarsh; or, an Appeal to the impartial and conscientious Reader, 1646. —15. Annotations on the Pentateuch, and on the four

Evangelists, in the English Annotations.[a]—16. A learned Defence of Tithes, 1651–1653.—17. General Reasons grounded on Equity, Piety, Charity, and Justice, against the payment of a fifth part to sequestered Ministers, their Wives and children. 4to. London, 1654–55.—18. An Acquittance or Discharge from Dr E. H. (Edward Hyde) his demand of the fifth part of the Rectory of Brightwell in Berks, pleaded as in the Court of Equity and Conscience, 4to. London, 1654.—19. A Letter to Dr Edward Hyde, in Answer to one of his, occasioned by the late Insurrection at Salisbury, 1655.—20. A Debate concerning the English liturgy, between E. Hyde, D. D. and J. Ley, 4to. London, 1656.—21. A Discourse, or Disputations, chiefly concerning Matters of Religion, 4to. Lon. 1658.—22. Animadversions on two printed books of J. Onely, a lay-preacher, 1658.—23. A consolatory Letter to Dr Bryan, upon the death of his dear son, 1658.—24 Equitable and necessary considerations for the Association of Arms in England and Wales.—25. A Petition to the Protector, by divers, for establishment, as Ministers of the Gospel, without induction by Bishops.—26. Comparison of the Oath of the 6th Canon of the last Synod of Bishops.—27. Attestation against errors, &c.—28. Exceptions many and just.

a See Gataker's Life and Writings.

JOHN LIGHTFOOT, D.D.

A VERY LEARNED ENGLISH DIVINE, AND ABLE COMMENTATOR, WHO FLOURISHED IN THE SEVENTEENTH CENTURY, AND WAS A MEMBER OF THE ASSEMBLY OF DIVINES AT WESTMINSTER.

JOHN LIGHTFOOT was born in the Rector's house of Stoke-upon-Trent, near Newcastle under Line, in the county of Stafford, in England, upon the 29th day of the month of March, in the year 1602. He was born in the same year, on the same day, and almost at the same hour, with the celebrated Dr Arrowsmith. His father was Mr Thomas Lightfoot, a native of a little village called Shelton, in the parish of Stoke, above-mentioned; a man of great respectability, and was vicar of Uttoxeter, in Staffordshire, thirty-six years. His mother was Elizabeth Bagnall, a gentlewoman of a very respectable family, of which three males were made knights by Queen Elizabeth, for the martial skill and courage which they displayed in the wars in Ireland against the rebels. The subject of this memoir, was the second of five sons in his father's family. When he had arrived to the age, in which he was capable of learning the rudiments of grammar, he was committed to the care of Mr Whitehead, who was school-master at Morton-green, near Congerton, in the county Palatine of Chester. He continued in that place until the month of June, in the year 1617, and then he was sent to Christ's college in Cambridge. He was there admitted under the tuition of the very learned and pious Mr William Chappel, who was then Fellow of that house, and afterward was Doctor of Divinity, and Professor in Trinity-college, Dublin, and at length Bishop of Cork in Ireland. Mr Lightfoot seems to have profited much, by being, in his early years, committed to the care of eminently learned men. It was the opinion of Tasso's father, when he committed his son to the care of Angehezzo, a man of learning, "that a boy could not be put too soon under the tuition of men."

In the college, Lighfoot gave great specimens of a promising genius and lively wit. He made very great proficiency in his studies; especially in the knowledge of the Latin and Greek languages. His tutor said to some of the heads of the University, that he had a young pupil, meaning Lightfoot, whom he accounted the best orator of all the under-graduates in the town. He continued in the college, until he took the degree of bachelor of arts. He afterward was admitted as an assistant to his former master, Mr Whitehead, who was at that time master of a famous school at Repton in Derbyshire, where he continued a year or two, and made great proficiency in the Greek language. In that station, he was equally agreeable both to the master, and to the boys who were committed to his care. Some time after that, he entered into the holy ministry; and his first settlement was at Norton under Hales, in the county of Salop, or Shropshire in England. When he was there, Sir Rowland Cotton took him into his family, as his chaplain, being much pleased with his hopeful parts, upon hearing him preach. There he laid the foundation of that Rabbinical learning, for which he has been very justly and eminently distinguished, both at home and abroad. His eminently learned patron, Sir Rowland Cotton, often questioned him in the Hebrew language, in the knowledge of which he was then only a novice. His great ignorance of that beautiful language made a very deep impression upon his mind. He was greatly ashamed to be baffled by a country gentleman as he confessed he frequently was, especially in a branch of learning which belonged to his profession. The example of his patron was highly useful to him. His singular talents for the Oriental learning began now to be unfolded. Indefatigable in his literary researches, while he enjoyed a sound constitution, a vigorous mind, with a friend's company, conversation, and example, he soon acquired an extraordinary store of very useful Rabbinical knowledge, which has certainly made a great accession to the republic of letters, and contributed much to the understanding of the Holy Scriptures.

Wagenseil says, "John Lightfoot, an Englishman, a

man well versed in Hebrew literature, performed a laudable work, in explaining the four Evangelists; when out of the Talmud chiefly, he studied to bring light on the sacred writers, and to illustrate some of the more obscure sayings in them. That laborious work I highly value; for the whole is filled with deep learning, and furnishes many things, of which no interpreter ever thought, nor could think of, without skill in the Talmud. Would to God he had lived to handle all the Sacred books in the same manner."

Dr Gill, in the preface to his Exposition of the New Testament, edition 1774, says, "Some may think, I have made too much use of Jewish authorities in the following Exposition; my concern is, that I have made no more use of them; and that my reading and observations have not furnished me with more materials of this kind, which I am very well satisfied might be obtained from them.—I have used all diligence, both from my own reading, and from the observations of others, to make it as perfect in this way as I could; and from none have I had so much help and assistance as from the great Dr Lightfoot, who has broke the ice for me, and pointed out the way in which I should proceed, as Wagenseil observes."

Our late commentators on the Holy Scriptures have, in general, made much use of Dr Lightfoot's valuable writings. He was without doubt one of the best Oriental scholars of his age; and also well acquainted with the Greek language—An able commentator, who has thrown much light on the Gospel History. The accurate knowledge of the original languages of the Holy Scriptures, is certainly of the greatest utility and importance, for understanding these writings. And such persons as devote themselves to the work of the holy ministry, should study, not only a competent, but also a very accurate and critical, knowledge of these deeply interesting languages. As they undertake to explain the Sacred Writings to their fellow-creatures, they should spare no pains to understand the languages in which these were originally written. Our author's laudable example may be highly useful to us, in that very delightful and interesting study.

When Sir Rowland Cotton, his good friend, went to reside at London with his family, he followed him in a short time, and having been with him there some space, he returned again to the country, and visited his parents at Stoke. He had formed a design of going into foreign countries for his improvement, but he was persuaded to change his resolution, to the great joy of his parents and friends, upon being chosen and importuned by the inhabitants of Stone in Staffordshire to be their minister. He continued there about two years. During that time, May 21, 1628, he married Joice, the daughter of William Crompton of Stone-Park, Esq. and widow of George Copwood of Dilverne in the county of Stafford. He removed from Stone to Hornsey, near London, with a view to enjoy the benefit of Sion-college library, in prosecuting his studies. To that famous library, he frequently resorted. Afterward, in the spring of the year 1630, he and his family having gone to Stoke, they remained there until the following September, when Sir Rowland Cotton preferred him to the rectory of Ashley, in the county of Stafford, where he continued in great esteem for twelve years, carefully discharging the duties of his office, and pursuing his Rabbinical studies with indefatigable application. By his unremitting diligence, his stock of knowledge very much increased.—*The hand of the diligent maketh rich.*

In the month of June 1642, he went up to London, and was chosen minister of St Bartholomew's behind the Exchange, and next year he was nominated a member of the Assembly of Divines at Westminster. He is marked in Neal's list, as giving constant attendance during the session. He was appointed one of the select committee for the examination and approbation of ministers who petitioned for livings which had been sequestered. He had a fair opportunity, in that famous Assembly, of displaying his eminent abilities, and extraordinary learning; and of both he gave good specimens. He was then not much above forty years of age; and yet he discovered a very extensive knowledge in divinity, in Oriental learning, and in church-government. He very often spake, when enquiries into the primitive constitution of the Christian church were under consideration; and also when places of the Holy Scriptures were produced to stand for proof of such points of doctrine or discipline as were under decision. He often gave very remarkable interpretations of controverted places; I say not whether he was right or wrong, leaving the reader to judge for himself.

When some divines in the Assembly were for gathered churches, consisting *only* of *Saints*, and produced for that purpose, Rev. xv. 3.—*Thou King of Saints;* Dr Seaman objected to it, because the reading was doubtful, some copies reading, *Thou King of Ages*, or *Everlasting*. And Lightfoot backed him, by shewing, that the Syriac and Arabic read to the same import, *King of the World*, or *of Ages*.—When a debate commenced respecting the persons who should read the Holy Scriptures in public, and some were for the pastors doing it themselves, and Gouge and Marshall seemed to be for some expert and sober persons of the laity, Lightfoot shewed at large, that none in the Jewish synagogue read the law and the prophets, but public officers, and of the Levitical order. He produced the following arguments for the support of his assertion: Their multitude of universities for the education of the Levites for such purposes, viz. forty-eight; and their curiosity, that not a tittle of the law should be mistaken by those persons who read it. But Mr Reyner urged, that the Levites were not types of the pastors, but the priests were. To this Lightfoot answered, that the Levites in the Temple were one thing, and in the Synagogues another; for though these at the Temple were servants to the priests, yet in their Synagogues they were their pastors.—When the bishops, who had been employed to ordain, were voted out of the House, and their jurisdiction laid aside, the Assembly brought in this position respecting Ordination, That in extraordinary cases, some things extraordinary may be done, until a settled order may be had. Lightfoot was of this mind, shewing, that even some positive laws of God gave place not only to necessity, but even to convenience; as the steps to Solomon's altar, and many candlesticks and tables in the Temple. But when as a proof of it, that place was produced, 2 Chron. xxix. 34, *The priests were too few, so that they could not flay all the burnt-offerings; wherefore their brethren the Levites did help them till the work was ended, and until the other priests had sanctified themselves.* And Bathurst spake to that place to prove it pregnant; and also out of Numb. xviii. 4, 5, 6. and Levit. i. would prove that the Levites had nothing to do in slaying the sacrifices. Lightfoot answered them, and so did Coleman and Selden, who declared the contrary. When voted, it was carried that it was a pregnant place; but Lightfoot gave his negative.—When some in the Assembly called in question the equality of Matthias with the rest of the apostles, because he was chosen by lot, and not immediately called by Christ, he answered, That the lot did argue his immediate call. Because the apostles could not ordain him for an apostle by imposition of their hands, but sought to the immediate imposition of Christ's hands by a lot.—A question arose in the Assembly, whether *excommunication* should be done in a Presbytery, or in the presence of the whole church. Some were for it done in the presence of the whole church, bringing as proof, 1 Cor. v. 4.—*When ye are gathered together*, &c. Lightfoot said, That *the gathering together* here respected the heart-burnings among them. That they triumphed one against another in the very act of the incestuous person; and, therefore, he commands them to convene, unite in affection, and agree among themselves. And after two or three debates upon the case of the incestuous person, Lightfoot said again, That this case of the Corinthians was such as cannot be among us; for they were hedged in with the heathen, and the apostle plainly tells, that there was an iniquity among them more than heathenish, v. 1. Therefore, if he would have the whole church to come together, and cast out this member, for the vindication of the whole church, it is a singular example, and cannot be paralleled among us.—Several members offered 1 Cor. v. 2. for excommunication, and for excluding from the communion; where direction is given that the incestuous person be *taken away from among them.* But Lightfoot's judgment was, that this place did not at all respect excommunication. The dispute continued the whole day. And when the place was carried for a proof of excommunication, he gave his denial. Nor did he relish Mat. xviii. 17. which was also brought for excommunication. He considered it as speaking of offence given from a member to his pastor.—That it spake of *shaming* an offender, and not of *censuring.* For that the two or three, ver. 16. not the church, had to do with the offender.—That the Heathen and Publicans had access *to sacred things;* but the Jews abhorred their civil society. And this was *to be as an heathen man and a publican,* to have no society with such: but *to be as a publican* included not excommunication. Again, after Herle and Reynolds had spoken for that passage as proving excommunication, he answered them, 1. with the question, Are the *two or three* here named witnesses, as they would have them? For it is plain, that these must be admonishers. 2. He shewed that the text and speech of our Saviour was upon occasion of the disciples quarreling. Now how improper is it, when he is speaking of offence between brother and brother, to conclude what such an one shall be to the church, and not to the party offended?

When the dispute came on between the Independents and the other party respecting *Congregations,* whether there were more than one in a city, especially in Jerusalem? and Dr Temple doubted whether there were many fixed congregations in that city, and it seemed to him there were not; Lightfoot answered in several particulars. 1. That such a multitude of pastors as were there at Jerusalem could not suit with one congregation. 2. That there were divers languages, that understood not one another; therefore there could not be but divers congregations. 3. That one part of the church had deacons, the other not; therefore we must make a distinction of their congregations. 4. In Acts xii. 12, we are informed that *Many were gathered together praying;* and yet James and the brethren were not there.—Burroughs and Lightfoot had a controversy respecting the *five thousand who were added to the church*, Acts iv. whether they were new converts, which Lightfoot positively declared, and Burroughs denied. And when Lightfoot had done, Palmer supported him in that.—Lightfoot contended, in the Assembly, for general admission unto the sacrament of the Lord's Supper, explaining the institution of it from the passover, and using the following arguments in support of his opinion. 1. That though the law forbid the unclean to come to sacred things, yet it gave not power unto any person to repel those who offered themselves to come: nor find we any such example. 2. Circumcision was indifferently administered to all the seed of Abraham; and therefore all ought to be admitted unto the sacrament of the Lord's Supper. 3 Judas received that sacrament; and therefore the admission should be general. When an instance was produced against his opinion, in his first argument, in the repulsion of Uzziah, 2 Chron. xxvi. he replied, that Uzziah's repulsion was from office and place, and not from the use of holy things. And he added, Grant that the priest then did and might repel the unclean, yet the case was now different; for that uncleanness was external, and it might be known whether the persons were purified or not. But a minister cannot now so judge of a man's conscience; for though he were scandalous yesterday, yet his repentance may be unfeigned to-day, for aught he knows. When the Assembly opposed to his opinion, Mat. vii. 6. *Give not that which is holy unto the dogs, neither cast ye your pearls before swine, lest they trample them under their feet, and turn again and rend you*, he replied, That this was spoken respecting the safety of the apostles.—That the Jews themselves, who use this proverb, by dogs and swine understand the bitter enemies and prsecutors of the truth. And so our Saviour hereby warrants his disciples, though they preach not to persecutors and enemies, lest it cost them their lives. Respecting Judas, it was urged against his opinion, That though Christ knew the heart, yet the villany of Judas was not known among the disciples. He replied, That Christ had publicly marked him out for a traitor before.

It was also argued, *After the sop he went out.* He replied, That was no passover nor sacrament, but before it. Upon this the contest became warm, for he seemed in that debate to oppose the whole Assembly. Liberty was publicly given to him and another member to dispute the matter respecting Judas; which they did at large, but in that debate we cannot farther follow them.

Our author being eminently distinguished in that venerable Assembly, by his learning and integrity, he was by them promoted to the church of Much Munden in Hartfordshire, about the end of the year 1643.

He was some times appointed to preach before the House of Commons. In a sermon, which he preached before them, at the public Fast, from Luke i. 17. he speaks very warmly against placing the Apocrypha, in the midst of the Bible, between the two Testaments. He says, "It is not a little to be admired, how this *Apocrypha* could ever get such place in the hearts, and in the Bibles of the primitive times, as to come to sit in the very centre of them both." He reckons that this might be partly accounted for, because both the Apocrypha, and the Old and New Testaments, came to the converted Gentiles from among the Jews. And because that the Jews alone, for a long time, had enjoyed the knowledge of divinity and religion among them, the converted Gentiles could not but highly esteem their writings. Thus the Apocrypha gained esteem among mankind, in primitive times. He also allows that the prevalence of superstition contributed much to retain the Apocrypha in our Bibles: many persons, without consideration, persisting in doing as their forefathers had done, and in retaining what they had retained. And after admitting, that while ignorance and superstition prevailed, and it became a religion to do as their forefathers had done, retaining the Apocrypha in the Bible might be accounted for, he expresses his great wonder, that the Reformed Churches should still continue to allow it a place in their Bibles, upon their having shaken off the yoke of superstition. He adds, "It is true indeed that they have refused these books out of the *canon*, but they have reserved them still in the Bible: as if God should have cast Adam out of the state of happiness, and yet have continued him in the place of happiness. Not to insist upon this, which is some digression, you know the counsel of Sarah concerning Ishmael, and in that she outstripped Abraham in the spirit of prophecy, *Cast out the bond woman and her son; for the son of the bond woman may not be heir with the son of the free woman.*" He here calls the Apocrypha, "The wretched *Apocrypha*, and this patchery of human invention." In the same sermon, he says, That Christ and Antichrist are plainly *the seed of the woman, and the seed of the serpent.* And that "he who will seek to make conjunction of *Rome* and us, will marry light and darkness, God and the Devil, Christ and Antichrist together, and make a friendship between those, between whom God himself hath doomed an enmity while the world endureth." At the conclusion of that sermon, he says, "Let scattered Popery never cloud us again, nor superstition overwhelm us. Let Religion and the Gospel be in all our borders, and peace and truth in all our times."—

In another sermon, which he preached before the House of Commons, from Rev. xx. 1, 2. he says, "It is a groundwork, necessary to be laid by him who will make any thing of the book of Daniel and of the Revelation; That where Daniel ends John begins, and goes no farther back, and where John begins Daniel ends, and goes no farther forward. For Daniel sheweth the state and the persecutors of the Church of the Jews, from the building of Jerusalem by Cyrus, to the destruction of it by Titus, and he goes no farther. And where the beloved prophet concludeth the beloved disciple begins, and shews the state and the persecutors of the Christian church, from the destruction of Jerusalem to the end of the world, and revealeth a new Jerusalem coming down from heaven when the old one on earth is destroyed, and one persecuting monarchy and state of Rome equalling in mischief and cruelty against the church all the four that had gone before it."—In the same sermon, he warmly recommended to the House, a Review and Survey of the Translation of the Bible. He said, "I hope you will find some time among your serious employments to think of a review and survey of the translation of the Bible; certainly that might be a work which would very well become a reformation, and which would very much redound to your honour. It was the course of Nehemiah, when he was reforming, that he caused the law not only to be read, and the sense given, but also caused the people *to understand the reading*, Neh. viii. 8. And certainly it would not be the least advantage that you might do to the three nations, if not the greatest, if they, by your care and means, might come to understand the proper and genuine reading of the Scripture, by an exact, vigorous, and lively, translation. I hope, (I say it again) you will find some time, to set a-foot so needful a work. And now you are about purging the Temple, you will look into the Oracle, if there be any thing amiss in that, and remove it."—He also earnestly recommended to the House, to take care that none intrude upon the ministry, or to preach the Gospel, who have not a call to that work, and some competent ability for it. He observed, "This is a main well-head from whence flow all the errors that are among us, when mechanics, unlettered and ignorant men will take upon them to be preachers, and to instruct others when they need teaching themselves; and this, if it be not stopped, will overflow all with a puddle of errors and heresy. You have made good orders for stopping and preventing this, but execution is all." He likewise recommended to them, a speedy and effectual settlement of the church; and he expressed his joy in seeing what they had done, in *Platforming Classes and Presbyteries*, which, says he, *I verily and cordially believe is according to the Pattern in the Mount.* In the same sermon, he spake very warmly, and with great energy, against the sin and folly of allowing an unrestrained liberty of conscience. He says, That *error is more dangerous than open persecution;* for persecution can only destroy the body, but error destroys both body and soul.—"And for Zion's sake, who can hold his peace? Souls lie a-bleeding by this, as well as bodies by the enemy. The church is undone by this, as the land by them. This spoils our truth, as they do our peace." He adds, "There is great talk of, and pleading for *liberty of conscience;* that men may do in matters of Religion, as Israel is said to have done in the book of Judges, that which seemeth right in their own eyes.—I shall not determine the question, whether the conscience may be bound or not, though for mine own satisfaction I am resolved that it may." And he maintains, that it is a truer point in divinity, that *an erring conscience may be bound*, than to hold the contrary opinion. He adds, "But certainly the devil in the conscience may be, nay, he must be bound, or else you act not according to what Christ requireth at your hands. It is true indeed which is so much talked of, that Christ alone must reign in the conscience, but it is as true also, that he doth so by the power that he hath put into the hands of the magistrate, as well as by his word and Spirit."

The learned Lightfoot became master of Katherine-hall, Cambridge, when Dr Spurstow was ejected from that place, for refusing the Engagement. Lightfoot is enrolled among the masters of Katherine-hall, in Dr Fuller's History of the University of Cambridge, page 83, and among the learned writers, page 84, where the author says, that he was *an excellent linguist.* He enjoyed that mastership, with the sequestered living of Much Munden, which was given him by the Assembly of Divines, till the Restoration, when he would have resigned it back into the hands of Dr Spurstow, but he declining it, Lightfoot conformed, and upon his application to the King was confirmed in both his preferments until his death. In 1652, he took the degree of Doctor in Divinity. His Latin discourse was from these words, *If any man love not the Lord Jesus Christ, let him be Anathema Maranatha.* When he was in the University, he preached frequently; and his discourses were highly useful to the students. He always warmly recommended unto them a blameless life, and diligence in their studies. He faithfully warned them to avoid enthusiasm, which at that time greatly prevailed in England.—In the year 1655, he was chosen Vice-chancellor of the University of Cambridge; and he most carefully discharged the duties of his office.—Beside his labours in the University and in the church, and writing many learned books, he also contributed to promote the elaborate works of other eminently learned men. He afforded considerable assistance to Dr Walton, who was afterward bishop of Chester, in his Biblia Polyglotta, or Polyglott Bible, which was printed at London, in 6 vols. folio, 1657. In that very elaborate work, the sacred text was, with peculiar care, printed, not only in the vulgar Latin, but also in the Hebrew, Syriac, Chaldee, Samaritan, Arabic, Ethiopic, Persic, and Greek, languages, each having its peculiar Latin translation annexed to it; and an *apparatus* fitted for each, that those different tongues might be the better understood. We are informed, that our author was consulted by Dr Walton respecting the whole work, when he proposed to engage in it. Dr Lightfoot seems also to have assisted Dr Custell, Arabic Professor of Cambridge, in his *Lexicon Heptaglotton*, and the learned Poole, in his *Synopsis Criticorum*.

Dr Lightfoot maintained some peculiar sentiments. 1. That the *Jews* shall not be called, but are utterly rejected. And that the time of their rejection happened before the times of Christ; and was on account of their fond and impious traditions; rather than, as is commonly asserted, after Christ, for their wickedness in murdering their Messiah, and persecuting the Gospel. And that their last and only calling was in the times of Christ and his apostles; when some few of them, viz. *A Remnant*, were brought in to the faith of Christ. But that neither then there was, nor ever shall be, any universal calling of them. And that Rom. xi. 5. was very unfit to prove this calling of the *Jews* to be either universal, or after a great many ages. 2. That the Greek Translation of the Bible by the Seventy was hammered out by the Jews, with more caution than conscience, more craft than sincerity; and that it was done out of political ends to themselves. 3. That the Keys were given to Peter alone, as Christ spake only to him, Mat. xvi. 19. That is, to open the Gospel to the Gentiles; which was designed, he said, by *the kingdom of heaven*. And that it was to this purpose Peter spake,

Acts xv. 7. This opinion he openly held in the Assembly of Divines. 4. He did not allow that *Binding* and *Loosing* related to discipline, but to doctrine. And that because the phrases, to *bind* and *loose* were Jewish, and most frequent in their writers; and that it belonged only to their teachers, to bind and to loose. And that when the Jews set any apart to be a preacher, they used these words, *Take thou liberty to teach, what is bound, and what is loose.* And we may here add, his peculiar interpretation of God's words to Cain, *If thou dost not well, sin lieth at the door. Sin*, that is not *punishment*, to take hold of thee, but a *sin-offering*, to make atonement for thee. And that, he said, was the common acceptation of the Hebrew word, which is rendered *sin*, in the books of Moses. And that God did not intend to terrify Cain by those words, but rather to keep him from despair.

Upon the restoration of King Charles the Second, it is said, that he was in danger of being deprived of his preferments, but by the good offices of Archbishop Sheldon, and others, he was not only confirmed in the possession of these, but was also presented, by the lord-keeper Bridgeman, to a prebendary's place in the cathedral of Ely. He died there of a fever, Dec. 6th, 1675. His remains were interred at Munden.

Some of Dr Lightfoot's writings were first published separately, in small pieces. His *Miscellanies Christian and Judaical, and Others:* Penned for Recreation at vacant hours. A small book, 203 pages. London, 1629. It was dedicated to Sir Rowland Cotton. The epistle dedicatory was dated at Hornsey, near London, March 5, 1629. In that epistle, he says, "My creeping and weak studies, neither able to go, nor to speak for themselves, do, like Pyrrhus in Plutarch, in silence crave your tuition.—Your encouragement and incitation did first set me forward to the culture of holy tongues, and here I offer you the first fruits of my barren harvest. Your tried learning and tried love assure me, that you can judge soundly, and yet will not judge too heavily of my weak endeavours; and such a patron my book desireth." He published that book, when he was about twenty-seven years of age; and, by the quotations in it, he appears to have studied and read to a very great extent.—His Harmony of the Old Testament was also first published separately. And his Harmony of the four Evangelists among themselves and with the Old Testament, Part 1st, from the beginning of the Gospel to the baptism of our Saviour. 4to. pp. 214. London, 1644.—Part 2d, 4to. pp. 136, from the baptism of our Saviour, to the first passover after. London, 1647.—Part 3d, from the first passover after our Saviour's baptism, to the second. 4to. pp. 295. London, 1650.—A Commentary on the Acts of the Apostles, chronical and critical, Part 1st, from v. 1, to the end of chap. 12th, with a brief survey of the contemporary story of the Jews and Romans. 4to. pp. 331. London, 1645.—And, The Harmony, Chronicle and Order, of the New Testament—The text of the four Evangelists methodized—The story of the Acts of the Apostles analized—The Order of the Epistles manifested—And the times of the Revelation observed. All illustrated, with variety of observations upon the chiefest difficulties Textual and Talmudical, for clearing of their sense and language. With an additional Discourse concerning the Fall of Jerusalem, and the condition of the Jews in that land afterward. This learned and elaborate work was published, in a small folio-form. pp. 195. London, 1655.—I have seen three sermons of his, before the House of Commons, Fast, which were published separately; one from Luke i. 17. 4to. pp. 50. Lond. 1643. Another from Rev. xx. 1, 2. 4to. pp. 31. Lond. 1645. And a third from Psalm iv. 4. 4to. pp. 35. Lond. 1647. —The Temple-service as it stood in the days of our Saviour. 4to. pp. 200. The Temple: especially as it stood in the days of our Saviour. 4to. pp. 286. Lond. 1650. Horae Hebraicae, &c. Leipsic, 1675.

His Works were published by Mr Strype, in two volumes folio. London, 1684. The first volume contains The Harmony of the Old and New Testaments—Observations on Genesis—An handful of Gleanings out of the book of Exodus—A Commentary on the Acts of the Apostles—The Temple-service—Miscellanies—The Temple described, with a map of it drawn by himself. The second volume contains, Horae Hebraicae, or Hebrew and Talmudical Exercitations, on the four Evangelists, the Acts of the Apostles, some chapters of the Epistle to the Romans, and on 1 Cor. translated into English, and published by Mr John Strype, with above forty Sermons, which were preached on several subjects and occasions, and a short tract on the fourth article of the Creed, never before published: All in English. And his Works were printed in Latin at Rotterdam, in 2 vols. folio, 1686. with a very beautiful frontispiece. And Mr Strype informs us, in his Preface to his Remains, that this learned man's usefulness has been so well known abroad, that there have been two or three impressions of his works there, since his death, the last of which was finished at Franeker, in the year 1698, with the addition of different tracts of his Remains. Remfertus, the Professor, and several learned men in that place, had earnestly desired to obtain every production of Dr Lightfoot's pen for publication, that no notions of so great a man might be lost. Some of his Genuine Remains were published by Mr Strype. London, 1700. Octavo, pp. 295.[a] I have seen Dr Lightfoot's writings in different parts of Scotland, and in England.

JOHN DE LA MARCH.

JOHN DE LA MARCH was minister of the French Church. In the year 1643, he was appointed one of the Assembly of Divines at Westminster, and assisted his brethren in their arduous work in that Assembly. He was one of those divines who subscribed the proposition, " That Jesus Christ, as King of the Church, hath himself appointed a church-government, distinct from the

a Lightfoot's Life prefixed to his Works, both Latin and English, and the Preface to some of his Genuine Remains.

civil magistrate." Lightfoot entered his dissent respecting that proposition, with whom very probably Mr Coleman would have joined, if he had not been seized with sickness at that juncture and died.[a] But many eminent divines readily subscribed it.—From what John de la March has published to the world, he appears to have been a considerable sufferer in the cause of Truth, and a very zealous covenanter and reformer. He has published a Treatise on Rev. xviii. 17. which is entitled, "A Complaint of the False Prophet's Mariners, upon the drying up of their Hierarchical Euphrates, as it was publicly preached, in the island of Guernsey, before a sett order of Ministers, expounding in their turns the Revelation of John." 4to. pp. 112. London, 1641. In this publication, the author speaks very warmly against the innovations, the usurpations, and tyrannical government of the prelates, with their attempts to introduce popery. He speaks against the government of the church by Archbishops, diocesean bishops, and all ecclesiastical officers depending on that hierarchy; and in favour of the Presbyterian form of church-government. In the last page of the book, he says, "But above all be careful to commend the rooting out to the very stumps, yea stumps and all of that hierarchical antichristian-like church-government, with all the officers thereof, to those who are now fighting the battles of the Lord; and, in place thereof, labour to have the holy church-discipline of Christ established, countenanced, and fully authorised among us; seeing that no man usurp, under what colour or title, how favourable and specious soever it be, any dominion over the Lord's inheritance."—A dedicatory epistle to the House of Commons, an Address to the faithful witness of Christ, Mr Henry Burton, and a short Preface, are prefixed to that Performance. In the Address to Mr Burton, the author says; "Worthy Sir, the first draught of this Treatise was conveyed unto you presently after the matter therein contained had been preached in our monthly Propositions, and public meetings duly observed among us, according

a Neal's Puritans, vol. iii. chap. vii.

to the order prescribed in our Discipline, not unknown unto you. The reason was because of the great interest you had therein, not only in regard of the spiritual brother hood, and former acquaintance, but especially in respect of the subject thereof You being one of the eminent witnesses of Christ, who had suffered for the testimony of his truth, according to the prophecy, Rev. xi. 7. &c. yet then lying unburied, in one of the public places *of the great city*, Castle-cornet in Guernsey, where some few years before two other brethren, and the author also, for a whole week of months had been unjustly imprisoned, and unlawfully detained for the same testimony."—Mr Henry Burton, B. D. to whom our author wrote that Address, was eminently courageous in the cause of truth, and a very great sufferer in the cause of non conformity, under the iron rod of the English prelates. He felt the shocking cruelties of the ruling prelates in his time, and especially those of Laud, the arch-enemy of the Puritans. Mr Henry Burton, and Mr John de la March, seem to have been *companions in tribulation, and in the kingdom and patience of Jesus Christ.*

This is all the account that I am able to give of Mr John de la March. The reader, who has an opportunity, may see an interesting account of his brother and companion in tribulation, Mr Henry Burton, in that excellent and seasonable work, Brook's Lives of the Puritans, vol. iii.

STEPHEN MARSHALL, B. D.

MINISTER OF FINCHINGFIFLD IN ESSEX, AND A MEMBER OF THE ASSEMBLY OF DIVINES AT WESTMINSTER.

STEPHEN MARSHALL was born at Godmanchester in Huntingdonshire, in England He received his education in Emmanuel-college, Cambridge. Dr Fuller says, " Thence he went very early a *Reaper in God's Harvest*, yet not before he had well sharpened his sickle for that service." He was some time minister at Wethersfield in Essex, and afterward he became minister of Finchingfield, in the same county. He gained there a very high reputation And Dr Fuller informs us, that after several years discontinuance, he came up to Cambridge, to take the degree of Bachelor of Divinity, where he performed his exercise with general applause.—It is said, that when he was at Finchingfield, he was silenced for non-conformity; and that he continued a considerable time under suspension. He was greatly despised and reproached by the opposite party; but he was a man of great worth, and was often called to preach before the Long Parliament, who consulted him in all affairs of importance respecting religion. Dr Fuller says, "No man was more gracious with the principal members. He was their trumpet, by whom they sounded their solemn Fasts, preaching more public sermons on that occasion, than any four of his function. In their sickness he was their confessor, in their assembly their counsellor, in their treaties their chaplain, in their disputations their champion." Clarendon says, "And without doubt, the Archbishop of Canterbury had never so great an influence upon the councils at court, as Mr Marshall and Dr Burgess had upon the Houses of Parliament." November 17, 1640, was observed as a day of solemn fasting by the House of Commons, at Margaret's church, Westminster, when these two eminent divines were appointed to conduct the public service of the day. On that solemn occasion, it is said, that they prayed and preached at least *seven hours.* Upon the important service being ended, the House voted thanks to both the preachers, desiring them to print their sermons; and for their encouragement in time to come, a piece of plate was, by order of the House, presented to each person.

Clarendon, with some other writers of a similar spirit, brings a very heavy charge against Mr Marshall; a charge which is indeed altogether unworthy of any honest man. It respects the ministers' petition which was presented to the Parliament for a reformation of certain grievances in the hierarchy in 1640, or 41. It follows: "The paper which contained the ministers' petition was filled with very few hands, but many other sheets were annexed for the reception of numbers who gave credit to the undertaking. But when their names were subscribed, the petition itself was cut off, and a new one, of a very different nature, annexed to the long list of names; and when some of the ministers complained to Mr Marshall, with whom the petition was lodged, that they never saw the petition to which their names were annexed, but had signed another petition against the canons, Mr Marshall is said to have replied, that it was thought fit by those who understood the business better than they, that the latter petition should be preferred rather than the former." This is certainly a charge of a very high nature, and should have been well substantiated. Dr Walker, notwithstanding his extreme bigotry and enmity against the Puritans, seems not here to give full credit to the noble historian. After he has affirmed that the petition was only the contrivance of some few of the ministers in and about London, and *probably* of Mr Marshall in particular, he adds only, " that it is *probable* that Mr Marshall was deeply enough concerned in the affair." He clearly appears unwilling to affirm it as a matter of fact. If, however, the above account had been true, why did not the ministers complain to the Committee which was appointed by the house of Commons to inquire into their regular methods of procuring hands to petitions? The royal historian answers, that they were prevailed upon to sit still and pass it by; for the truth of which we have only his lordship's word, where we should have had reference to clear proof. It has also been observed here, that nothing of that kind appears in Rushworth, Whitlocke, or any other impartial writer of those times. The whole affair seems, therefore, to have the appearance of a mere forgery, designed to defame the memory of Mr Marshall and of the rest of the Puritans.

Wood says, that " upon the approach of the troublesome times in 1640, Mr Marshall, Mr Calamy, Dr Burgess, and some others, did first whisper in their conventicles, then openly preach, that *for the cause of religion it was lawful for the subjects to take up arms against their lawful sovereign.*" The celebrated Dr Calamy says, "As to Mr Stephen Marshall, he was an active man, and did encourage the taking up arms for securing the constitution, when it appeared not only to him and his brethren, but to a number of as worthy gentlemen as ever sat in St Stephen's chapel, to be in no small danger; but I am not aware that he can be justly charged with any concurrence in those things, which afterward overthrew the constitution, and tended to confusion. He wrote a defence of the side which he took in our civil broils, and I cannot hear that it was ever answered."[a]

Mr Marshall, at the same time, took a very active part in the controversy respecting church-government. He was one of the authors of *Smectymnuus.*[b] The learned Dr Kippis says, "it was a production of no small importance in its day; and was drawn up in a style of composition superior to that of the Puritans in general, and, indeed, of many other writers at that period."

In the time of the civil war, Mr Marshall was appointed chaplain to the Earl of Essex's regiment in the Parliament's army. Dr Grey, in contempt, calls him and Dr Downing "the two famed casuistical divines, and most eminent camp chaplains;" and charges them on the authority of Clarendon and Echard, with publicly avowing, "that the soldiers lately taken prisoners at Brentford, and released by the king upon their oaths, *that they would never again bear arms against him*, were not obliged by that oath; but by their power they absolved them, and so engaged those miserable wretches in a second rebellion." This has the appearance of forgery, with a view to defame these eminent divines. Priestly absolution was exceedingly remote from their practice, and the object of their utmost abhorrence. Beside, the Parliament's army stood in so little need of these prisoners, who are said to have been only 150 men, that there is great reason to suspect the truth of the whole account.

a Calamy's Contin. vol. ii. p. 737.

b See the account of that famous piece, Life of Mr Calamy, vol. i. pp. 171, 172.

In the year 1643, Mr Marshall was chosen one of the Assembly of Divines at Westminster, and was a most active and valuable member. He was one of those divines in that famous Assembly, who appeared for the institution of the ruling elders by divine right.[a] He seems to have been employed in writing to foreign churches, for Mr Baillie says: "Our letter to foreign churches, formed by Mr Marshall, except some clauses belonging to us put in by Mr Henderson, is now turned into Latin by Mr Arrowsmith."[b] In this very public office he could not expect to escape the bitter censures of the opposite party. One of them, speaking of him as a member of the Assembly, says, "He quickly grows to be master, and is so called by all. They sit, not to consult for the reformation of religion in things that are amiss, but to receive the Parliament's commands to undo and innovate religion. In which work, or rather drudgery of the devil, our active Stephen needs neither whip nor spur; tooth and nail he bends himself to the overthrow of the hierarchy, root and branch."

Mr Marshall and Mr Nye were sent, by order of the English Parliament, to attend the commissioners to Scotland, whose great object was to establish an agreement with the Scots, desiring their aid in the war, and some of their divines to join those at Westminster, for settling an uniformity of religion and church-government in both nations. The commissioners arrived at Edinburgh, Aug. 9th, 1643, and were favourably received by the Assembly, who proposed, as a preliminary, that the two nations should enter into a perpetual covenant for themselves and their posterity, that all things might be done in God's house according to his will. Having appointed some of their number to consult with the English commissioners respecting a proper form, they chose delegates for the Assembly at Westminster, and unanimously advised the Convention of States to assist the English Parliament in the war, chiefly because they apprehended that the war was for religion. The Committee for drawing up the

a Baillie's Letters, vol. i. p. 401. b Letters, vol. i. p. 414.

solemn League and Covenant, delivered it into the Assembly, Aug. 17th. where it was read, and highly applauded, both by ministers and elders, none opposing it except the King's commissioner. It readily passed both the Assembly and Convention in one day, and was dispatched the next morning to Westminster, with a letter to the two Houses, wishing that it might be confirmed, and solemnly sworn, and subscribed in both kingdoms, as the surest and strictest obligation to make them stand and fall together in the noble cause of Religion and Liberty.—Messrs Marshall and Nye, in their letter to the Assembly at Westminster, under the date of Aug. 18th, 1643, assure their brethren, that the Scottish ministers were wholly on the side of the Parliament.[a] They conclude their valuable letter, in the following words: "We scarcely ever saw so much of Christ for us as this day, in the Assembly's carrying of this business, such weeping, such rejoicing, such resolution, such pathetical expressions, as we confess hath much refreshed our hearts, before extremely saddened with ill news from our dear country; and hath put us in good hope that this nation, which sets about this business, as becometh the work of God and saving of the kingdoms, shall be the means of lifting up distressed England and Ireland."

Mr Marshall frequently united with his brethren in the observance of public fasts, when the services were protracted to a great length. On one of these occasions, it is said, that Dr Twisse having commenced the service with a short prayer, "Mr Marshall prayed large two hours, most divinely confessing the sins of the members of the Assembly, in a wonderful, pathetick, and prudent way. After, Mr Arrowsmith preached an hour, then a psalm; after which, Mr Vines prayed nearly two hours, Mr Palmer preached an hour, and Mr Seaman prayed nearly two hours, then a psalm. Mr Henderson then spoke of the evils of the time, and how they were to be

a Neal's Hist. vol. iii. chap. ii. Baillie's Letters, vol. i. Letter xxxvi.

remedied, and Dr Twisse closed the service with a short prayer and blessing."[a]

In the year 1644, Mr Marshall attended the commissioners of Parliament at the treaty of Uxbridge. In 1645, he was chosen one of the Committee of accommodation, to secure the peace of the church, and to promote, as far as possible, the satisfaction of all parties. The following year, he was appointed, together with Mr Joseph Caryl, chaplain to the commissioners who were sent to the king at Newcastle, in order to an accommodation for peace. Removing thence, by easy journies, to Holmby-house, in Northamptonshire, the two chaplains performed divine worship there; but his Majesty never attended. He spent his Lord's day in private; and though they waited at table, he would not so much as allow them to ask a blessing. Wood, who mentions this circumstance, relates the following curious anecdote:—"It is said that Marshall did, on a time, put himself more forward than was meet to say grace; and, while he was long in forming his chaps, as the manner was among the saints, and making ugly faces, his Majesty said grace himself, and was fallen to his meat, and had eaten up some part of his dinner, before Marshall had ended the blessing; but Caryl was not so imprudent."[b]

In the year 1647, Mr Marshall was appointed, together with Mr Vines, Mr Caryl, and Dr Seaman, to attend the commissioners at the treaty of the Isle of Wight, when he conducted himself with great ability and moderation. The house of Commons having now many important affairs under consideration, Mr Marshall and Mr Nye, by order of the House, Dec. 31, 1647, were desired to attend the next morning to pray with them, that they might enjoy the direction and blessing of God in their weighty consultations.

In the year 1654, when the Parliament voted a toleration of all who professed to hold the fundamentals of Christianity, Mr Marshall was appointed one of the

a Ballie's Letters, vol. ii. pp. 18, 19.

b Wood's Athenæ Oxon, vol. ii. under Caryl.

committee of learned divines, to draw up a catalogue of fundamentals to be presented to the House. About the same time, he was chosen one of the triers. He was justly accounted a very useful as well as admired preacher. Lady Brown, wife to an eminent member of the Long Parliament, was once under great trouble of mind, respecting the salvation of her soul. For some time she refused to attend public worship, though it had formerly been her very great delight. She even asked what she should do there, and said it would only increase her damnation! In that dismal state of mind, she was persuaded, and almost forced into the coach to hear Mr Marshall. The sermon was so exactly suited to her case, and so powerfully applied to her disconsolate mind, that she received great satisfaction, was filled with hope of her salvation, and returned home in transports of holy joy.[a] He seems to have given great satisfaction, when he preached in Edinburgh. Mr Baillie says, in his letter above-mentioned: "On the Sabbath, before noon, in the New Church, we heard Mr Marshall preach with great contentment." His sermons which have been printed abound with striking comparisons, and pointed appeals to the hearers; and though they are not adapted to the taste of modern eloquence, it may be very easily seen how they might gain much admiration in those times.

Mr Marshall has suffered greatly in his name and reputation. Dr Heylin, with his usual modesty, calls him "the great bell-wether of the Presbyterians." Mr Echard, with his usual candour, denominates him "a famous incendiary, and assistant to the Parliamentarians." Newcourt calls him "The Geneva-Bull, and a factious and rebellious divine." And Wood styles him "a notorious independent, and the archflamen of the rebellious rout." The truth however is, that he never was an independent, but he both lived and died an avowed Presbyterian. And respecting his rebellion, what has been before observed will afford every impartial reader a sufficient refutation of that charge. Dr Fuller had a better opinion of him, and

a Calamy's Contin. vol. i. pp. 466, 467.

has classed him among the learned writers of Emmanuel-college, Cambridge, and accounted him a minister well qualified for his work.

Although some persons have suspected him of deserting his Presbyterian principles; yet upon his death-bed he gave full satisfaction of the contrary. Echard says, "This great Shimei, being taken with a desperate sickness, departed the world *mad* and *raving;*"[a] than which there never was a more unjust aspersion. He was, indeed, taken ill, and obliged to retire into the country for the benefit of the air, when the Oxford Mercury published to the world that he was distracted, and in his rage continually cried out, that he was damned for adhering to the Parliament in their war against the king. But he lived to refute that unjust calumny, and also published a treatise to prove the lawfulness of defensive war, in certain cases of extremity. Upon his retirement from the city, he spent his last two years at Ipswich. Mr Giles Firmin, minister in Shalford, who knew him in life, and attended him at his death, observes, in a preface to one of Mr Marshall's posthumous sermons, "That he left behind him few labourers like himself; that he was a Christian in practice as well as in profession; that he lived by faith, and died by faith, and was *an example to the believers, in word, in conversation, in charity, in faith, and in purity*. And when he, together with some other persons, conversed with him respecting his death, he said, "I cannot say, as one did, I have not so lived that I should now be afraid to die; but this I can say, I have so *learned Christ*, that I am not afraid to die." He enjoyed the full use of his understanding to the last; but, for some months previous to his death, he lost his appetite and the use of his hands. He died in the month of November, 1655, when his remains were interred with great funeral solemnity in Westminster-abbey, but were dug up, together with several others, at the restoration.[b] The court and bishops were not content with their tri-

a Echard's Hist. of Eng. vol. ii. p. 183.

b Fuller's Worthies of Eng. fol. 1662. Wood's Athenæ Oxon. vol. ii. edit. 2d. Neal's Hist. vol. iv. Brook's Puritans, vol. iii.

umphs over the living Presbyterians, but they descended into the grave, and dug up the bodies of those who had been buried in Westminster-abbey in the late times. When the Emperor Charles the Fifth was at Wurtemberg in 1547, some of his officers desiring him to order the bones of Luther to be dug up and burnt, he most nobly told them, "I have now nothing further to do with Luther. He has henceforth another Judge, whose jurisdiction it is not lawful for me to usurp. Know that I make not war with the dead, but with the living who still continue to attack me." [a]

Mr Baxter, who was well acquainted with Mr Marshall, calls him "a sober and worthy man;" and used to observe, on account of his great moderation, that if all the bishops had been of the same spirit as Archbishop Usher, the independents like Mr Jeremiah Burroughs, and the Presbyterians like Mr Stephen Marshall, the divisions of the church would soon have been healed. Mr Marshall appeared and wrote with considerable ability against the baptists, and published many sermons which were preached before the Parliament, the titles of some of which have been with diligent search collected for this work.

Mr Marshall's writings.—1. A Sermon preached from 2 Chron. xv. 2. before the honourable House of Commons, at their public Fast, Nov. 17, 1640. 4to pp. 50. Lond. 1641–1645.—2. *A Peace-offering to God;* a Sermon preached from Psal. cxxiv. 6, 7, 8. to the honourable House of Commons, at their public Thanksgiving, for the peace concluded between England and Scotland, Sept. 7, 1641. 4to. pp. 51. Lond. 1641.—3. *Meroz Cursed;* or, a Sermon preached from Judges v. 23. to the honourable House of Commons, at their solemn Fast, Feb. 23, 1641. 4to. pp. 54. London, 1641.—4. *Reformation and Desolation;* or, a Sermon tending to the Discovery of the Symptoms of a People to whom God will by no means be reconciled, preached from 2 Kings xxiii. 25, 26.

a Anecdotes, vol. iii.

before the Commons, at their public Fast, Dec. 22, 1641. London, 1642.—5. *The Song of Moses the servant of God, and the Song of the Lamb*, opened in a Sermon preached from Rev. xv. 3, 4. to the honourable House of Commons, at their solemn Thanksgiving, June 15, 1643, for the discovery of a dangerous, desperate, and bloody, design, tending to the utter subversion of the Parliament, and of the famous city of London. 4to. pp. 48. Lond. 1643.—6. A Copy of a Letter written by Mr Stephen Marshall to a Friend of his in the city, for the necessary Vindication of himself and of his Ministry, against that altogether groundless, most unjust, and ungodly Aspersion cast upon him by certain Malignants in the city. 4to. pp. 30. London, 1643.—7. *The Church's Lamentation for the Good Man's Loss;* delivered in a Sermon from Micah vii. 1, 2. to the Right honourable the two Houses of Parliament and the reverend Assembly of Divines, at the Funeral of that excellent Man, John Pym, Esquire, a late Member of the honourable House of Commons, on the 15th of Dec. 1643. 4to. London, 1644.—8. *A Sacred Panegyrick;* or, a Sermon of Thanksgiving, preached from 1 Chron. xii. 38, 39, 40. to the two Houses of Parliament, his Excellency the Earl of Essex, the Lord Mayor, Court of Aldermen, and common Council of London, the reverend Assembly of Divines, and Commissioners from the Church of Scotland. 4to. pp. 32. London, 1644.—9. *A Divine Project to save a Kingdom*, opened in a Sermon from Numb. xxv. 10, 11. to the Right honourable the Lord Mayor, and Court of Aldermen, of the city of London, at their anniversary meeting, April 22, 1644. 4to. pp. 44. Lond. 1644.—10. A Sermon of the Baptizing of Infants, preached from 1 Pet. iii. 21. in Abbey-church, Westminster, at the Morning Lecture appointed by the House of Commons. 4to. London, 1644–1645, pp. 61.—11 *God's Master-Piece;* a Sermon from Psal. cii. 16. tending to manifest God's glorious appearing in the Building up of Zion, preached before the Right honourable the House of Peers. March 26, 1645. 4to. 1645.—12. *The Strong Helper;* or, the Interest and Power of the Prayers of the

Destitute, for the Building up of Zion, opened in a Sermon from Psal. cii. 17. before the Commons, monthly Fast, April 30, 1645. 4to. 1645.—13. *A Sacred Record to be made of God's Mercies to Zion:* a Thanksgiving Sermon preached from Psal. cii. 18. to the two Houses of Parliament, the Lord Mayor, Court of Aldermen, and common Council of the city of London, at Christ's church, June 19, 1645.—1645.—14. *A Defence of Infant-Baptism:* In Answer to two Treatises, and an Appendix, published by Mr John Tombes. In this treatise, the controversy is fully discussed. The ancient and generally received use of infant-baptism, from the days of the apostles of Christ, until the Anabaptists sprung up in Germany, is manifested; and the arguments for it from the Holy Scriptures maintained, and the objections against it answered. This learned and elaborate piece was dedicated, under the date of April 2, 1646, to the reverend Assembly of Divines and Commissioners of the Church of Scotland, then sitting at Westminster. 4to. pp. 256, Lond. 1646. —15. *A Two-edged Sword out of the mouth of Babes, to execute vengeance upon the enemy and avenger;* a Sermon from Psal. viii. 2. before the Lords at Westminster, monthly Fast, 28th Oct. 1646. 4to. London, 1646.—16. *The Right Understanding of the Times;* a Sermon before the Commons, Dec. 30, 1646, Fast, from 1 Chron. xii. 32. 4to. pp. 46. London, 1647.—17. A Thanksgiving Sermon from Joshua xxii. 33. preached to the two Houses of Parliament, in the Abbey church, Westminster, 12th Aug. 1647. 4to. London, 1647.—18. A Sermon preached from Rom. xii. 4, 5. to the Right honourable the Lord Mayor, and Court of Aldermen of the city of London, at their anniversary meeting, April 1652, wherein the Unity of the Saints with Christ the Head, and especially with the Church the Body, with the duties thence arising, are endeavoured to be cleared. 4to. Lon. 1652. The second impression, 1653. It is said that he has sermons from Isai. viii. 9. Zech. vii. 12. & Mat. xi. 12. but I have not seen these. I have seen, "The Power of the Civil Magistrate, in matters of Religion, vindicated; and the extent of his power determined, in a Sermon preached before the Parliament, on a monthly Fast-day," by Mr Marshall, and published by Mr Firmin, London, 1657.

JOHN MAYNARD, A.M.

MINISTER OF THE GOSPEL AT MAYFIELD, AND A MEMBER OF THE ASSEMBLY OF DIVINES AT WESTMINSTER.

JOHN MAYNARD was born of a genteel family in Sussex, at, or near, Riverfield, in England. He became a commoner of Queen's-college, Oxford, in the beginning of the year 1616, compounded for the degree of bachelor of arts as a member of that House, and afterward translated himself to Magdalen-hall, in the same University. In the year 1622, he took the degree of master of arts, entered into the holy ministry, and at length was settled at Mayfield, in his own country. Upon the commencement of the civil war, he espoused the cause of the Parliament, openly avowed his sentiments, was appointed one of the Assembly of Divines at Westminster, took the Covenant, and preached sometimes before the members of Parliament. In 1654, he was appointed one of the assistants to the commissioners of Sussex, for the ejection of ignorant and scandalous ministers and school-masters. A Mr Elias Paul d'Aranda was sometime assistant to Mr Maynard, who was so generous as to allow him all the tithe, reserving to himself the parsonage-house only, and the glebe. Mr Maynard was ejected from Mayfield, by the Act of Uniformity. After his ejection, he lived in that town, and was generally respected. He was a considerable benefactor to Magdalen-hall, where he received part of his education. Mr Peck, who succeeded him, was fixed on by the patron, with his approbation. He died June 7th, 1665. His remains were interred in the church yard of Mayfield, where he has a tomb-stone, with the following inscription: Thus translated. "Sacred to the Memory of the very Reverend John Maynard, of Queen's-college, Oxford, M. A. He was endowed with a penetrating genius; well skilled in History; a divine of irreproachable manners, and of the most venerable gravity. very pious and learned, and a good public speaker. He shone during the space of forty years the light and glory of his flock at Mayfield (by so much the more happy or unhappy.) At length weary of this world, and ripe for heaven, he departed hence that he might enjoy Christ for ever and ever, June 7th, 1665. He fixed on this spot as the depository of his mortal part."

Mr Maynard's writings.—1. A Sermon before the House of Commons at their solemn Fast, from Prov. xxiii. 23. Feb. 26, 1644. 4to. London, 1645.—2. *A Shadow of the Victory of Christ;* a Sermon from Phil. iii. 21. before the House of Commons, at Westminster, at their solemn Fast, 28th Oct. 1646. 4to. London, 1646.—3. The Young Man's Remembrancer, and Old Man's Monitor, 1660.—4. The Law of God ratified by the Gospel of Christ; or, the Harmony of the Doctrine of Faith with the Law of Righteousness, wherein many of the types and rites of the Ceremonial law are unfolded, in several sermons, London, 1674.—5. The Beauty and Order of the Creation Displayed in the six days' work.[a]

WILLIAM MEWE, B. D.

WILLIAM MEWE was Rector of Essington, or, Eastington, in the county of Gloucester, in England, and one of the members of the Assembly of Divines at Westminster. He is marked in Mr Neal's list as giving constant attendance during the Session. He preached a Sermon at Westminster from Isai. xlii. 24, 25. before the honourable

a Wood's Athenæ Oxon. vol. ii. Calamy's Account, vol. ii. Cont. vol. ii.

House of Commons, at their solemn Fast, Nov. 29, 1643. This Sermon is entitled, "The Robbing and Spoiling of Jacob and Israel." 4to. pp. 48. London, 1643. He has an epistle which is addressed to the House of Commons, and is prefixed to that sermon, dated Chancery-lane, 19th Dec. 1643. I am not able to give any farther account of Mr Mewe.

THOMAS MICKLETHWAIT.

THOMAS MICKLETHWAIT was a member of the Assembly of Divines at Westminster, and is marked in Mr Neal's list as constantly attending. He was Minister at Cherryburton in Yorkshire. From that place he was called to sit in the Assembly of Divines at Westminster; and from thence he was cast out by the Act of Uniformity. He was father to Sir John Micklethwait, the celebrated physician. John Micklethwait, the son, had taken the degree of doctor of physic, at Padua in Italy, in 1638, was one of the college of physicians, and president thereof, physician in ordinary to King Charles II. from whom he received the honour of knighthood. And Dr Calamy says "the father was no less famous in the country, for his piety, gravity, prudence, and learning, in his profession of divinity, than his son was at London for his skill in the art of medicine."[a] I have neither seen any writings by Mr Micklethwait, nor found any more information respecting him, in all my researches.

a Wood's Athenæ Oxon. vol. ii. Calamy's Account, vol. ii. Cont. vol. ii.

MATTHEW NEWCOMEN, M. A.

MINISTER OF THE GOSPEL AT DEDHAM IN ESSEX, AND A MEMBER OF THE ASSEMBLY OF DIVINES AT WESTMINSTER.

MATTHEW NEWCOMEN received his education in St John's college, in Cambridge. He was very highly esteemed there, and eminently distinguished by his wit and his curious parts; which, being afterward sanctified by the power of divine grace, rendered him peculiarly serviceable to the church of God. He succeeded the famous Mr John Rogers at Dedham. Their gifts were very different. Mr Rogers was a grave, severe, and solid, divine. His great gift lay in the delivery of the solid matter which he had prepared with a peculiar gesture and elocution, so that few persons heard him without trembling at the word of God. He was indeed one of the most awakening preachers of the age. But Mr Newcomen's gifts lay almost every way. And his greatest enemies must allow, that he shewed as much art as piety in his sermons and prayers, and in all his religious services. Dr Collins, in his preface to Mr Fairfax's sermon which he preached upon the occasion of his death, gives the following account of him. He says, "That he had thirty years acquaintance with him, and in that time had been well acquainted with many learned and pious persons; but that he never knew any who excelled him, considering him as a *minister in the pulpit, a disputant in the schools*, and a *desirable companion*. In the first capacity, his gift in prayer was incomparable. He was a solid, painful, pathetick, and perswasive, preacher." He was a member of the Assembly of Divines at Westminster, and constantly attended during the session. And he then preached with Mr Calamy at Aldermanbury. He was employed together with Dr Arrowsmith and Dr Tuckney in drawing up that admirable piece, the Assembly's Catechism. He was also one of the commissioners at the

Savoy. His management of the argument against the Toleration of the Jews, though never printed, made him to be admired by all persons who heard it. He had both many and great offers of preferment, after he was settled at Dedham; but he refused all these offers, and continued there until he was turned out by the Act of Uniformity, in the year 1662. Soon after he was ejected, he was invited to the pastoral charge of the English Church at Leyden in Holland. He accepted that charge more readily, because he knew that he should there have the full liberty of his public ministry, which he preferred to any thing in this world. He was there exceedingly acceptable to Dr Hoornbeck, and the other professors and learned men of those parts. And there he died of a fever, which prevailed much in that city, in the year 1668, or 1669. He was a most accomplished Scholar and Christian. He was eminently distinguished by his universal learning and piety, and by his extraordinary humility and pleasant conversation.[a] Mr Baxter, in his own life, frequently mentions Mr Newcomen with great respect, as one of the principal ministers concerned in the transactions of those times.

Mr Newcomen's writings.—Irenicum, a work much commended; but I have not seen it.—A Sermon preached from Neh. iv. 11. before the honourable House of Commons, Nov. 5, 1642. 4to. pp. 48. Lond. 1643. —A Sermon preached from Isai. lxii. 6, 7. before both Houses of Parliament, and the Assembly of Divines, at their solemn Fast, July 7th, 1643. 4to. pp. 34. London, 1643.—A Sermon tending to set forth the Right Use of the Disasters that befall our Armies, from Joshua vii 10, 11. preached before both Houses of Parliament, at their extraordinary Fast, Sept. 12th. 1644. 4to. pp 41. London, 1644.—*The All-Seeing Unseen Eye of God;* a Sermon from Heb. iv. 13. before the Commons, Fast, Dec. 30th, 1646. 4to. Lond. 1647.—*The Duty of Such as would Walk worthy of the Gos-*

a Calamy's Account, vol. ii.

pel, to endeavour Union, not Division, nor Toleration; opened in a Sermon from Phil. i. 27. at Paul's, upon the Lord's day, 8th Feb. 1646–47. 4to. Lond. 1646–47.—A Sermon at the Funeral of Mr Samuel Collins, Pastor of Braintree in Essex, 1657.—A Farewell Sermon in the London Collection, from Rev. iii. 3.—Another Sermon in the Country Collection, which is the last in the volume, from Acts xx. 32. entitled, *Ultimum Vale;* or, The last Farewell of a Minister of the Gospel to a beloved people. It consists of 78 pages. Lond. 1663.—*The Best Acquaintance, and Highest Honour of Christians.* A Discourse on Job xxii. 21. A small book; but a great treasure. London, 1668 & 1679.

PHILIP NYE, M. A.

MINISTER OF KIMBOLTON, AND A MEMBER OF THE ASSEMBLY OF DIVINES AT WESTMINSTER.

PHILIP NYE was born of a genteel family in Sussex in England, in the year 1596. He entered a commoner of Brazen-nose college, Oxford, 21st of July, 1615. He did not continue long there, but removed to Magdalen-hall, in the same University, where, being put under the care of a Puritanical tutor, he remained until he had taken the degrees in arts. He was a very diligent student, while he continued at Oxford. In due time, he entered into the holy ministry, and officiated sometime at Michael's church, in Cornhill, London, where he was in the year 1630.

In the year 1633, upon the death of Archbishop Abbot, Laud was made Archbishop of Canterbury; when he and his brethren renewed their blind zeal in the violent persecution of the Puritans. Many lecturers were silenced, and their lectures put down. The most eminent divines were often silenced, driven from place to place, and some of them were driven out of the country. Mr Nye, and others, to escape the fury of the storm, fled to Holland. He crossed the seas, that he might avoid the severe censures of the Episcopal inquisitions, and be free from impositions, with which he was much dissatisfied. Wood says, that there he continued for the most part at Arnheim in Guelderland. He returned to England about the beginning of the Long Parliament, and, by the favour of the Earl of Manchester, he became minister of Kimbolton in Huntingdonshire. In the year 1643, he was appointed one of the Assembly of Divines at Westminster, sitting in which he had the rectory of Acton near London conferred upon him. He was one of the dissenting brethren in that Assembly. Mr Baillie says, speaking of Mr Nye, " When it came to his turn in the Assembly to oppose the presbytery, he had, from Mat. xviii. drawn in a crooked unformal way, which he never could get in a syllogism, the inconsistence of a presbytery with a civil state. In this he was cried down as impertinent. The day following, when he saw the Assembly full of the prime nobles and chief members of both Houses, he entered on that argument again, and very boldly offered to demonstrate, that our way of drawing a whole kingdom under one national assembly, is formidable; yea, thrice pernicious to civil states and kingdoms. All cried him down, and some would have had him expelled the Assembly as seditious. Mr Henderson shewed, that he spake against the government of our's, and all the Reformed churches, as Lucian and the Pagans were wont to stir up princes and states against the Christian religion. We were all highly offended with him. The Assembly voted him to have spoken against the order; which was the highest of their censures. Maitland was absent; but enraged when he heard of it. We had many consultations what to do: at last, we were resolved to pursue it no farther, only we would not meet with him, except he acknowledged his fault. The Independents were resolute not to meet without him, and he was resolute to recal nothing of the substance of what he had said. At last, we were intreated by our friends, to shuffle it over the best way might be, and to go on in our business. God, who brings good out of evil, made that miscarriage of Nye a mean to do him some good; for, ever since, we find him, in all things, the most accommodating man in the company."[a]

When Mr Baillie is speaking respecting the Independents having the communion every Sabbath, without any preparation before, or thanksgiving after; little examination of the people, and the like, he adds: "Mr Nye told us his private judgement was, that in preaching he thinks the minister should be covered, and the people uncovered; but in the sacrament, the minister should be uncovered, as a servant, and the guests all covered."[b] Mr Baillie also says, "As for the Assembly, these three weeks, Mr Nye, and his good friend Mr Herle, has kept us on one point of our directory alone, the recommending of the communicants coming up to the table to communicate. Their way of communicating, of some at the table, and some about it, without any succession of companies to more tables, is that whereon we stick, and are like to stick longer."[c]

In 1643, Mr Nye and Mr Stephen Marshall were sent with the commissioners who went from the English Parliament into Scotland, in order to obtain and establish an agreement with the Scottish nation, and to desire their assistance. The reader may see more respecting that important business, in the Life of Mr Marshall.—Mr Hume says, in his history of England, chap. lvii, 1463, "That Marshall and Nye were two clergymen of signal authority."—Mr Nye was exceedingly zealous and active in promoting, and in recommending, the Solemn League and Covenant. He delivered an excellent speech, before the subscribing of that covenant, to the honourable House of Commons, and to the reverend Divines of the Assembly, at Margaret's, Westminster, 25th of Sept. 1643. This speech was published by special order of the House of Commons, and has been repeatedly printed. He was one of the chaplains who attended the commissioners, who went from the Parliament to King Charles I. into the isle of Wight, in the year 1647.

a Baillie's Letters, vol. i. p. 437.

b Letters, vol. i. p. 440.

c Letters, vol. ii. p. 33.

In the year 1653, he was appointed one of the Triers of ministers. In the year 1654, when the Parliament voted a toleration of all who professed to hold the fundamentals of Christianity, Mr Nye was appointed one of the committee of learned divines, to draw up a catalogue of the fundamentals to be presented to the House; and he acted in that business. He was also constituted an assistant to the commissioners of London for ejecting ignorant and scandalous ministers and school-masters. He was a principal man in managing the meeting of the congregational churches at the Savoy by the Protector's order, where the Declaration of the Faith and Order and Practice in the congregational churches in England was agreed upon, by their elders and commissioners, Oct. 12, 1658. This Declaration was printed, 1659, and in the following year was translated into Latin by Professor Hornbeck, and published at the end of his *Epistola ad Duraem de Independentismo*. There was scarcely a book upon the disciplinarian controversy, which Mr Nye had not looked into; as may be seen by his little book which is entitled, *Beams of former Light*, &c. Soon after the restoration of King Charles II. there was an order of Parliament for lodging his papers with the Archbishop of Canterbury at Lambeth, where these are said to have remained a considerable time. He was a great politician; and it was debated in council after the King's restoration, for several hours, whether he should be excepted for life, because he had acted highly against the King, and had been a particular instrument in bringing all things into confusion. The result was, "That if Philip Nye should after the first of September, in the same year, accept or exercise any office, ecclesiastical, civil, or military, he should to all intents and purposes in law stand as if he had been totally excepted for life." He was ejected from Bartholomew behind the Exchange, London, and lived and preached privately as opportunity offered, to a congregation of dissenters. He died in the parish of Michael, Cornhill, or near it, in London, in the month of September, in the year 1672, when he was about seventy-six years of age. His remains were buried in Michael's church, Cornhill. He left behind him the character of a man of uncommon depth, and one who was seldom if ever out reached. Dr Calamy says, that he had a complete History of the Old Puritan Dissenters in manuscript, which was burned at Alderman Clarkson's, in the fire of London.[a]

Mr Nye's writings.—1. A Letter from Scotland to his Brethren in England concerning the Success of Affairs there. 4to. London, 1643. Stephen Marshall's name is also subscribed to that Letter.—2. An Exhortation to the taking of the Solemn League and Covenant, for Reformation and Defence of Religion. London, 1643, and there again once or twice.—3. The Excellency and Lawfulness of the Solemn League and Covenant, in a speech to the House of Commons, and to the reverend Assembly of ministers, 25th Sept. 1643. 4to. 2d edit. Lond. 1660. In a collection of Sermons and Speeches, at taking the Covenant, Glasgow, 1741 & 1799.—4. An Apologetical Narration submitted to the honourable Houses of Parliament. 4to. London, 1643. He was assisted in this by Goodwin, and others.—5. An Epistolary Discourse about Toleration. 4to. London, 1644. In this Discourse, Thomas Goodwin and Samuel Hartlib are joined with him.—6. The Keys of the Kingdom of Heaven, and Power thereof, according to the Word of God, &c. Lond. 1644. 2d edition. Wood says, Thomas Goodwin had also a hand in this book.—7. Mr Anthony Sadler examined.—8. The Principles of Faith, presented by Thomas Goodwin, Philip Nye, &c. to the committee of Parliament for Religion, by way of explanation to the Proposals for propagating the Gospel. 4to. Lond. 1654.—9. Beams of former Light, discovering how evil it is to impose doubtful and disputed Forms for Practices upon Ministers, especially under the penalty of ejection for non-conformity unto the same. 4to. Lond. 1660.—10. Case of great and present use, &c. 1677.—11. The Lawfulness of the

a Wood's Athenæ Oxon. vol. ii. edit. 2d. Calamy's Account, vol. ii. Cont. vol. i. p. 28. and Neal's Puritans, vol. iv.

Oath of Supremacy, and Power of the King in Ecclesiastical Affairs, with Queen Elizabeth's admonition, &c. 4to. Lond. 1683. It was then reprinted, and in 1687 being printed again, it was dedicated by Henry Nye, the author's son, to King Charles II.—12. A Vindication of Dissenters; Proving that their particular Congregations are not inconsistent with the King's Supremacy in Ecclesiastical Affairs—1683.—13. Some Account of the Nature, Constitution, and Power of Ecclesiastical Courts: Printed with the former.—14. The Lawfulness of hearing the Public Ministers of the Church of England. 4to. Lond. 1683.—He has also a Sermon extant, which was preached from Neh. vi. 11. to the honourable Citizens of London, 29th Sept. 1659, being the day of the election of their Lord Mayor. 4to. pp. 29. London, 1661.

HENRY PAINTER, B. D. OF EXETER,

AND A MEMBER OF THE ASSEMBLY OF DIVINES AT WESTMINSTER.

HENRY PAINTER of Exeter was bachelor in divinity. When an ordinance passed both Houses of the English Parliament for calling an Assembly of pious and learned divines, with a view to settle the doctrine, worship, government, and discipline, of the church, Mr Henry Painter was chosen one of that venerable Assembly, which met at Westminster, in 1643; and he did sit in that Assembly with his brethren, according to the list of those divines which has been transmitted unto us. But in all my researches among the writings of those times, I have not yet found any more particular account of Mr Painter. He might probably have his education in the University of Cambridge, as he is not mentioned in Wood's Athenæ Oxonienses. Nor have I found his name among those divines who preached before the Parliament.

HERBERT PALMER, B. D.

PASTOR OF ASHWELL, IN HARTFORDSHIRE, A MEMBER OF THE ASSEMBLY OF DIVINES AT WESTMINSTER, AND MASTER OF QUEEN'S COLLEGE IN CAMBRIDGE.

HERBERT PALMER was born at Wingham, in the county of Kent, in England, and baptized there on the 29th of March, in the year 1601. He was descended from an ancient and respectable family of that name, which was related to several other notable families, both of the gentry and nobility. His father was Sir Thomas Palmer of Wingham, above-mentioned, and his mother was the eldest daughter of Herbert Pelham of Sussex, Esq.

The subject of this memoir had a polite and religious education in his father's house, when he was very young. His parents carefully trained him up in the nurture and admonition of the Lord; and also exerted themselves to improve his intellectual powers in the rudiments of learning. Their instructions were very successful. He learned the French language almost as soon as he could speak. The progress of his opening mind was very remarkable and pleasant. It was soon adorned, both with the precepts of piety and with the principles of literature. Being early impressed with religious thoughts, he applied unto his mother for information respecting God, when he was about four or five years of age. From his childhood, he was well acquainted with the Holy Scriptures, *which are able to make us wise unto salvation, through faith which is in Christ Jesus.* All other knowledge is but trifling, when compared with the knowledge of the important truths of Divine Revelation. He read these with great delight, and committed portions of them to his memory, which he accounted a very pleasant task. By persevering in these exercises, he soon acquired an accurate knowledge of the Sacred Writings, which was highly beneficial to him afterward. And this most useful knowledge, formed his taste, enlarged and elevated his mind, and afforded him the noblest views of God, and of divine things, at the present time. The pious parents persevered in their duty. Many inconsiderately imagine, that parents are free from that carefulness and authority which are indispensably necessary, when the blooming youth goes out from the nursery. But it is then that the carefulness and authority of the parents ought to be particularly manifested, in *training up their children in the way in which they should go.* The *youthful mind* cannot be too early circumscribed by the judicious limits and restrictions of parental discrimination and appointment, and while the preceptive part of education is laudably dictated, example should *conspicuously shine* to establish and enforce its salutary tendency and effects, to allure the observer to an imitation.[a] The training of youth in a proper manner is, undoubtedly, a very difficult and labourious work. It requires great patience, much firmness of mind, and peculiar prudence, accompanied with pure and devout principles. But the benevolent exertions, and the laudable endeavours, of parents, in training up their children in the way in which they should go, shall not be in vain in the Lord. They shall be crowned with success. The salutary fruits have sometimes immediately appeared; but in other instances, not until a considerable time elapsed. See Prov. xxii. 6. And the supposition is entirely false, that the vigour and activity of youth will be blunted, and the temper soured, and become gloomy and austere, by being too early attentive to religious knowledge.[b] Sin produces such dismal effects; but not the religion of Jesus, which has a very different tendency.

The illustrious subject of these pages appears to have been really sanctified from the womb, like that eminent and faithful servant of the Lord, Jeremiah. When our religious youth was asked what course

a The Instructor, No. 32. p. 250.
b See The Instructor, as above.

of life he should pursue; whether he inclined to be a lawyer, a courtier, a country gentleman, or the like, he constantly replied, *That he would be a Minister of Jesus Christ.* When some of his friends suggested in order to try him effectually, and seemed to dissuade him, by telling him, that this was too mean an employment for a gentleman, and that the ministers of Jesus Christ were hated, despised, and accounted as the off-scouring of the world, and the like, he always replied, "It was no matter for that; for if the world hated him, yet God would love him." Persons, who have just conceptions of the excellency of Jesus Christ, of the goodness of his cause, and of the importance of his service, and who know, that they are the objects of his love, are inspired with a magnanimity and gladness of heart, which will make them undaunted, easy and happy, in the frightful prospect of the hatred of the world, and even under any persecutions from earth or from hell. What the friends of this pious youth suggested unto him, in his early years, afforded him a fair opportunity of counting the cost, before he actually engaged in Christ's public service. Christ warmly recommends this to all his ministers and followers, with the greatest candour. See Mat. x. 16—25. This devout youth deliberately counted the cost, before he publicly appeared in Christ's service; and he also attentively considered what support and comfort Christ had promised to his faithful servants, in their difficulties and sufferings, especially that they should be beloved by his Heavenly Father, who would always countenance and assist them. See John xiv. 23. When he looked seriously around him, he saw no interests, which he thought fit to prefer to the interests of the Redeemer's kingdom. And he was very early dedicated to the honourable service of Jesus Christ: *Choosing rather to suffer affliction with the people of God, than to enjoy the pleasures of sin for a season: Esteeming the reproach of Christ greater riches than the treasures in Egypt.*

His progress in his education was truly admirable. And while others, at vacant hours, pursued their sports and recreations, he constantly attended to his lesson.—

He had very just views of parental authority; and most readily obeyed his parents in the Lord, in his early years; and afterward warmly recommended this unto others.

When he was well instructed in grammar-learning, and in other necessary branches of education, he was admitted Fellow-commoner in St John's-college, in Cambridge, in the year 1615, when he was about fourteen years of age. Here he prosecuted his academical studies with great diligence: and the fervour of his spirit in serving the Lord was nothing abated. He took the degree of master of arts, in the year 1622. He was chosen fellow of Queen's-college in the University of Cambridge, in the year 1623. He was a gentleman, and had an estate of his own, beside his fellowship, which probably were sufficient for his external support; yet he cheerfully undertook the charge of many scholars, as this charge was considered to belong to the office. And having been accustomed to religious exercises, and to learning, from his early years, devotion and literature were now very conspicuous in him. And this eminent tutor combined a religious and learned education in his plan of instruction. He prayed fervently with and for those who were under his tuition in his chamber, and carefully instructed them in the principles of the Christian religion, and of genuine literature. He also warmly recommended to their attentive consideration the public exercises, which were required from them by the college. These divinely appointed means of carrying truth into the heart, and of improving the opening mind, in concurrence with the Divine Blessing, produced their appropriate fruit, and were highly beneficial to many. As this respectable teacher of youth was both very pious, and an accomplished scholar, he was peculiarly attentive to the eternal interests of his pupils, and also to their learning. Religion and learning ought always to be combined in the education of youth. And both the teacher and the scholar ought to pray fervently to God, that his blessing may accompany their instructions. Without the Divine Blessing, no instructions can be truly profitable to any person.

This celebrated tutor, while he was fellow of Queen's-college, was called and solemnly ordained to the sacred work of the Christian Ministry, to which he was entirely devoted from his childhood, in the year 1624. The Anointed Saviour was exceedingly precious to his soul, and, therefore, he solemnly devoted himself to preach to poor perishing sinners *the unsearchable riches of Christ.* Some have thought, that it is dangerous to encourage any one to think of devoting himself to the work of the Christian Ministry, until the Saviour has become precious to his soul, whatever his learning may be. "Those who are acquainted with Gospel Truth and believe it, will be able to conceive of reasons why danger is to be apprehended, in this quarter, without it being necessary that they should disrespect literary attainments. The plain Gospel has nothing in it pleasing to the natural man, and while persons are in this state the pride of learning only leads them to despise it. It is therefore a wise precaution, which congregational Churches have for some time used, not to encourage any one to think of devoting himself to the work of the Ministry, till the Saviour has become precious to his soul; and they have not been without frequent warnings that this precaution is not greater than is necessary."[a] To pay to learning as much respect as is really due to it, and no more, is highly interesting to the Religious World, but the task is very difficult. And any plan that confines the ministerial office to those who have made very considerable advances in learning, seems to be dangerous, as it is founded on a principle which, if it had been always admitted, would have excluded. many valuable characters from public usefulness in the Christian church. These remarks are not designed as unfriendly to learning, but the contrary; and that learning may have as much respect paid to it as is really due, and no more; and chiefly, that the great beauty of the combination of real learning and of saving grace, in the Minister of the Gospel of Jesus Christ, may be clearly seen. God is especially jealous of the honours of his grace, and when learning tends to degrade these, it must become foolish-

a The Instructor, No. 36. p. 286.

ness. " And while *to the poor the Gospel is preached*, so important is its *simplicity*, that when this is endangered by any undue deference paid to learning, every friend to vital Christianity should be alarmed." [a]

The subject of this memoir, beside having an experimental knowledge of the power of Divine grace in his own soul, had also a large measure of gifts conferred on him for the work of the ministry. He had a peculiar delight in that work; chiefly aiming at the good of souls and the glory of God. And the Supreme Lord, who sends labourers into his vineyard at his pleasure, did, in his own time, by his special Providence, open a door for the exercise of his gifts in his public Ministry, at Alphage church, in the city of Canterbury, about the year 1626.

It becomes us here to trace the steps of Divine Providence, which gradually terminated in placing him in the Ministry at Canterbury. He was induced to pay a visit to his brother, Sir Thomas Palmer at Wingham. On this occasion, at the solicitation of some friends, he preached a sermon at the Cathedral church in Canterbury, which was highly acceptable to his auditory; especially to those who were truly religious among them. The report of this soon reached an eminently pious and faithful minister of the French church in Canterbury, who went to Wingham, to obtain an acquaintance with Mr Palmer. " *Like loves like*." This interview was very satisfactory to both persons, and the foundation of a profitable and lasting friendship between them. Mr Delme, the minister of the French church, above-mentioned, solicited Mr Palmer to preach another sermon in Canterbury, which was also highly acceptable to the pious people in that city. They immediately turned their views toward Mr Palmer as a suitable object for them, and expressed their earnest desire to enjoy his ministry among them. And feeling themselves deeply interested in this affair, they applied to the Father of Lights for direction, and succeeded in obtaining the object of their desire, whom they received with the most lively demonstrations of joy and gratitude. At a

a The Instructor, as above.

Lecture here, he preached on the afternoon of the Lord's-day. The oil of divine grace in his heart, and the gracious presence of Christ with him, rendered him a burning and a shining light in that place. This faithful servant of Jesus Christ now laboured with all diligence, and with much godly sincerity, in discharging the duties of his office; and especially, in endeavouring to be instrumental in turning men from darkness to light, and from the power of Satan unto God. His sermons were heavenly and practical. He preached the peculiar doctrines of the glorious Gospel of the grace of God, which are the foundation of our faith and the source of our comfort. And he was jealous for the honour of the truth as it is in Jesus; earnestly contending for purity both in doctrine and in worship, against the false innovations and growing corruptions of the times. He had not such clear views, at this time, respecting the unlawfulness of the government and of some ceremonies in the church, as he afterward obtained; but he strenuously opposed the corrupt innovations which were now coming in like a flood, and successfully fortified his hearers against their pernicious influence, by his wholesome instructions. He was faithful according to his knowledge. His ministry was remarkably useful, in promoting the interests of religion, and the welfare of Zion. He was highly beneficial to many, by his heavenly doctrine, by his holy example, and his religious and private conversation. His speech, like that of a genuine disciple of Christ, was *always with grace*, with sweetness and courteousness, which rendered it highly acceptable to the hearers, and well *seasoned* with salt. It is a just complaint, that religious conversation does not greatly prevail even in religious circles. But ministers of the Gospel of Christ ought to excite others unto this, and set an example themselves. *The lips of the righteous feed many.* " Spiritual discourse is spiritual food." And appropriate discourse is often highly beneficial. Mr Palmer excelled in this. And he always endeavoured to gain the affections of his hearers, by giving them his friendly advice, especially in difficult and important cases; and by affording them opportunities of private conference, that he might the better understand their spiritual condition. This genuine friend of godliness used all means to instruct persons in the righteous ways of the Lord. He visited them, even those of the meanest rank, as often as he could; and allowed them to apply unto him in their distress. He was an excellent casuist; and very helpful to many who came to him with distressed consciences. He was also very serviceable to many by his epistolary correspondence, being instrumental in promoting solid piety both in hearts and in families, in the neighbourhood of Canterbury. Mr Clarke, who wrote a large account of his life, says, That great numbers of his Christian letters were then to be seen.

This pious and benevolent preacher also contributed to the welfare of the French congregation in Canterbury. He could both converse and preach fluently in the French language. And at the request of their eldership, he preached twice to that congregation in the French language, on solemn days. His labours on these days were highly acceptable to his auditory, and very beneficial to many souls. An aged French lady was so struck with his small stature and child-like look, upon seeing him the first time when he was coming into the pulpit, that she said with a loud voice, *Alas! what shall this child say to us?* But upon hearing him pray and preach with great fervency, and with much spiritual vigour, she lifted up her hands toward heaven with admiration and joy, blessing God for what she had heard.[a] We are told, That the Scythians, much impressed with the fame of Alexander, were astonished when they found him a little man.

Mr Palmer's success in his ministry was not without opposition. The Gospel of Christ has been very commonly opposed by wicked and unreasonable men: but when the arm of Jehovah is engaged on the side of those who are employed in preaching it, they may confidently defy the most formidable opposition. Greater is he who is with them, than all who can be against them. Almighty God can make the wrath of man to praise him,

a Clarke's Lives of eminent divines.

and the remainder of this wrath he can easily restrain. He can make his grace sufficient for his servants, and readily supply all their wants, and confer upon them such honour and happiness as this world cannot purchase. Mr Palmer's piety, zeal and faithfulness, raised enemies against him in this place, among carnal, lukewarm, and Gallio-like, men, who *cared for none of those things;* and especially among the cathedralists. His high birth and powerful friends partly intimidated them; yet some of their leaders adventured to exhibit articles against him: but the goodness of his cause, and the solidity of his answers, under Divine Providence, brought him off, at this time. Nevertheless, his lecture in Canterbury was afterward put down with the rest of the Afternoon sermons, which greatly grieved his pious hearers. By the influence of several persons of great respectability, he was restored for sometime; but removed from Canterbury at last.

While he was there, his friends at court employed their influence, to have him made one of the prebendaries of Canterbury; but were not successful, for which he often thanked God. He afterward clearly saw, that by this disappointment, he was mercifully delivered from many temptations; for that company were afterward chiefly employed, by the succeeding archbishop, in promoting superstitious innovations. Religious characters sometimes have suffered considerable injury by a successful change in their circumstances; and disappointment has often proved highly beneficial to them.

The subject of this memoir removed to Ashwell, in Hartfordshire, in the year 1632. He was presented to the vicarage there by Laud, who, in his defence before the House of Peers, insisted upon this as one of his good deeds.[a] Now, as formerly, he was indefatigably laborious, in discharging the duties of his office. He had just views of the importance of the pastoral charge, the great charge of immortal souls: and his care was chiefly exercised respecting *the flock, over which the Holy Ghost had made him an overseer, to feed the church of God, which*

a Clarke's Lives.

he hath purchased with his own blood. He knew that the important work in which he was engaged was the Lord's, and he persevered in it with unshaken confidence, and with unimpaired vigour. He was now eminently distinguished, by his increasing diligence and disinterested zeal, in earnestly endeavouring to awaken the people in that place to attend unto the proper business of life, the salvation of their immortal souls; and to personal religion, and practical godliness, as expressions of gratitude for redeeming love, and evidences of union with Christ, and of progress in the ways of the Lord. He preached twice every Lord's-day, and frequently beside at other times, when he had opportunity. His heart glowed with a strong desire of promoting the spiritual and eternal interests of the people. He particularly studied plainness or simplicity, in his preaching; carefully condescending to the capacities of his hearers. He rather wished to edify them, than to discover his own learning; which he could easily have done. He accommodated his language and expression to the manners and habits of his auditory. The plainness of preaching was most beautifully and advantageously exemplified, in the public discourses of our Lord Jesus Christ. *With many such parables spake he the word unto them, as they were able to hear it.* He compared spiritual things with natural, intentionally alluding to those scenes of life and particular objects with which his hearers were best acquainted, in the respective places where he preached. By such means, these spiritual things are better understood, and make deeper impression on the mind of the serious and attentive hearer. And ministers of the Gospel, in their preaching and official duties, ought to follow the laudable example of our Lord Jesus Christ.

Our exemplary and edifying preacher was also highly useful to the people, in the time of their trouble. He pointedly availed himself of the advantages of sickness, or of any heavy affliction, that he might be instrumental in impressing their minds more effectually respecting their spiritual and eternal interests, when the Lord had softened their hearts, and opened their ears to receive instruction.

As their sympathising friend, he endeavoured *to stir up their pure minds, by way of remembrance*, "to review those precious sources of everlasting consolation and good hope through grace, which our Lord Jesus Christ, and God even our Father himself hath given us, that they might thankfully improve them, for establishment, growth, and comfort." From the same principles, he was favourable to funeral sermons, thinking that the minds of mankind, especially of those who were nearly related, might be advantageously impressed, by exhibiting suitable views of death, and of the eternal world, from appropriate texts of the Holy Scriptures, on such affecting occasions.—He also carefully catechised the people of his charge, both publicly and privately; instructing them in the principles of the Christian religion, especially those who were young and ignorant among them. And for their help and encouragement, he composed and published a Catechism, entitled "An endeavour of making the Principles of the Christian Religion plain and easy;" which was highly approved. His glowing piety, lively zeal, and ministerial faithfulness, also appeared in using all means to reduce disorderly persons into order. The evils which prevailed, as drunkenness, the profanation of the Lord's day, stealing, profane swearing, cursing, slander, whoredom, quarreling, disobedience to parents and superiors, were the subjects of his severest censures. And he repeatedly pressed and enjoined those duties which were either neglected or carelessly performed among the people, industriously promoting reformation in the place. He engaged some of his parishioners to concur with him in this arduous work, which they jointly carried on with great vigour and success, according to some excellent resolutions which they unanimously approved and subscribed. He accounted it his greatest honour and principal work to be instrumental in doing good to the souls of those who attended his ministry. He fully complied with the following admonition of a celebrated author to his younger brethren in the ministry. "I hope my younger brethren in the ministry will pardon me if I intreat their particular attention to this admonition, Not to give the main part of their time to the *curiosities* of learning, and only a few fragments of it to their great work, the *cure of souls;* lest they see cause in their last moments to adopt the words of dying Grotius, perhaps with much more propriety than he could use them: *I have lost a life in busy trifling.*"[a] He did not leave his people uninstructed; but was constant and zealous in this service of God, that they might be intimately acquainted with their Bibles, and with the method of salvation by the Lord Jesus Christ. "The divine who spends all his time in study and contemplations, on objects ever so sublime and glorious, while his people are left uninstructed, acts the same part the eagle would do, that should sit staring all day at the sun, while her young ones were starving in the nest."[b]

Mr Palmer was truly and extensively charitable. God's goodness claims our particular attention. It is very conspicuous, and shines with peculiar lustre, both in his works and in his word. *The Lord is good to all; and his tender mercies are over all his works*, Psal. cxlv. 9. And real Christians, who have the image of God restored to their souls, and the love of God shed abroad in their hearts, by the Holy Spirit given unto them, will natively imbibe, according to their limited capacities, the same benevolent and amiable dispositions which they behold and admire in God. The love of Christ constrains them not to live to themselves, but unto Him who died for them, and in doing good to his followers. Their faith works by love, and excites them to perform works of love. Agreeably to this, our author was peculiarly charitable and exemplary, especially in giving Bibles to the poor who could read, and money to those who could not read, to assist and encourage them in learning. He also contributed readily and largely to the other necessities of indigent persons. The commands of our blessed Lord and Saviour, the exhortations and examples of his apostles, and of the primitive Christians, and the nature of the

a Proh! vitam pendidi, operose nihil agendo.
b Christian Magazine, vol. vi. p. 366.

holy calling of ministers of the glorious Gospel of the grace of God, all harmoniously unite their voice in saying, *Feed the hungry, clothe the naked, do good to all, but especially unto those who are of the household of faith.* The poor of this world, who are *rich in faith, and heirs of the kingdom which God has promised to them who love Him*, are members of that one glorious body, of which our blessed Lord, Jesus Christ, is the head, as well as the rich. When any member of our natural body suffers, we strenuously endeavour to relieve it. We ought to act in the same manner, respecting the members of Christ's mystical body. And, the gratuitous distribution of Bbles, among the poor, for the supply of their spiritual wants, is certainly highly commendable. We should also, undoubtedly, assist those persons who cannot read, in learning to read. Reading the Bible is necessary, in order that we may enjoy benefit by it, and comply with the authoritative command of our blessed Lord, *Search the Scriptures; for in them ye think ye have eternal life.* And we should contribute also to the other necessities of poor persons, that they may comfortably enjoy the use of the Holy Scriptures, in imitation of Mr Palmer, and of other eminently pious persons, and above all of our blessed Lord and Saviour. And the proper maintenance of an able ministry, to enable persons the better to understand and apply the Bible, in which institution the poor should have gratuitously their share, ought not here to be overlooked.—*How shall they hear without a preacher?* And *to the poor the Gospel is preached.*

The order of Mr Palmer's family was very exemplary, like that both of a real Christian and of a faithful minister of the Gospel. His house was, in an eminent sense, a school of religion, where the best instructions for the advantage of souls were always enjoyed. He was peculiarly careful that none should be admitted into his family, but such persons as were either really godly, or at least willing to be instructed in the ways of God. He was constant in family-worship twice every day, not allowing any member of the family to be absent, when he read to them some portion both of the Old and New Testaments, and prayed with them. He also catechised his family twice every week, and likewise required from them some account of the sermons which were preached on the Lord's day, when he repeated these sermons to them, for their edification. He had firmly resolved, that *he and his house would serve the Lord.* Religion, in the power of it, will not be confined within the walls of the church, but will also appear and shine in the family and in the whole conversation. True religion will be family-religion. While he was at Ashwell, the sons of several respectable persons of the nobility and gentry desired to spend some time in his house, that they might have the benefit of his family-instructions and of his learned and pious conversation. He maintained in his house an assistant as a tutor to these young gentlemen. And he required of them the same account in catechising and repetitions as of his own servants. A chapter of the Holy Scriptures was also daily read by one of those gentlemen in course, after dinner and supper, and he whose turn it was to read, was also required to repeat from memory the substance of what he had read. By this practice, much useful knowledge was obtained. Mr Palmer afterward explained what appeared difficult, and made some observations from the most remarkable passages. Beside, he required that after every meal his servants should have some portion of Scripture read among them, or a part of some important religious treatise. He was peculiarly careful that all his family should *remember the Sabbath-day, to keep it holy.* He required them to cease from their work sooner the night before the Sabbath than on other nights, that they might be better disposed for the religious exercises of the following day. On that day, he called his family together, and engaged in prayer, reading the Holy Scriptures, and in singing psalms with them; and in due time, he carefully collected all his family to go with him to the solemn assembly, that they might be present at the whole of the public divine service. In the evening of the day, he required of all his servants, and of the young gentlemen who were in his house, an account of such portions of the Sacred Writings as had been read in public; and warmly exhorted them to meditate in private upon what they had heard in public. Neither family-worship nor secret devotion were neglected. Mr Palmer allowed no food for the body to be prepared on the Lord's-day in his house, except what was necessary for a comfortable refreshment. No feasting on that day. If he had known, that any dish which was brought to the table had hindered any of his servants, in preparing it, from attending divine ordinances, he would not eat any part of that dish. He found very great delight in communion with God, and was much employed in secret prayer, both on the Lord's-day, and on other days. In that divine fellowship, he enjoyed a rich spiritual feast for his soul. He indeed *walked with God.* He scarcely ever entered upon any business, either by himself, or in company, without first *asking counsel at the mouth of the Lord.* He had a very quick and deep sense of his own failings seemingly, in the most minute instances. And though he walked very closely, yet he also walked very humbly, with his God, in a life of evangelical repentance and much self-denial. He often set days apart with a view to humble himself in secret, by solemn fasting and prayer, at the calls of Divine Providence. He also observed times of solemn thanksgiving for mercies received. *Giving thanks always for all things unto God and the Father, in the name of our Lord Jesus Christ.* He entered God's *gates with thanksgiving, and his courts with praise. He served God with fastings and with prayers night and day.* He was a very great admirer of the Holy Scriptures; and his accurate knowledge and readiness in these were very remarkable. Beside what he read and heard read in his family, he very frequently read by himself some part both of the Old and New Testaments, and wrote short meditations and observations on the passages which he thus read. Some hundred sheets of these meditations were left behind him. He could very readily quote chapter and verse of the Sacred Writings, in a great number of instances, with surprizing exactness. He was a most careful observer of Divine Providence, and of its exact agreement with the Word of God.

During the year 1632, he was chosen one of the preachers to the University of Cambridge, by which, having proceeded bachelor of divinity about two years before, he had authority to preach as he should have occasion, in any part of England. In the year 1640, he and the celebrated Dr Tuckney were chosen clerks of the convocation for the diocese of Lincoln. Being now eminently distinguished by his learning and piety, he was, in the year 1643, appointed one of the Assembly of Divines at Westminster, and afterward one of their Assessors, in which place he behaved with great prudence and integrity. In that venerable Assembly, he was an illustrious and highly useful member. He was peculiarly distinguished by his excellent talents, and unwearied industry, and was very seldom absent, and never but upon urgent and unavoidable occasions. That public and honourable service of the church of Christ, which the members of that famous Assembly were employed in, was very delightful to him, and he was richly furnished for it. He had a quick apprehension, a very tenacious and vast memory, a solid and steady judgment, and a very ready elocution. In matters which required deliberation, he discovered much Christian prudence. In debates, whether respecting doctrine or discipline, he shewed very great sagacity in searching out the true sense of the Holy Scriptures, a clear understanding, and much strength of reason, in the accurate statement of questions for debate, in confirming the truth, and dissolving objections against it. In his judgment, he was for the Presbyterian form of church-government, the principles of which he well understood, and had great ability to defend. He was an eminent instrument in promoting that form of church-government. At first, indeed, he was much unsatisfied respecting the divine right of ruling elders, but by the learned debates in the Assembly, he received satisfaction on that subject; especially by the authority of 1 Cor. xii. 28, where government is attributed to a distinct rank of officers who are inferior to teachers, and of 1 Tim. v. 17, which implies, that there are other elders who rule well, beside those who labour in the word and doctrine. Mr Baillie, speaking of the dispute in that Assembly, respecting the divine right of ruling elders, says, "When all were tired, it came to the question. There was no doubt but we would have carried it by far most voices; yet because the opposites were men very considerable, above all gracious and learned little Palmer, we agreed upon a committee to satisfy, if it were possible, the dissenters."[a] It appears that the celebrated Mr Palmer, at last, received satisfaction respecting that matter.

Upon his being called to attend the Assembly of divines at Westminster, he was obliged to give up his ordinary residence at Ashwell, and could only make some occasional visits to that place. He was succeeded at Ashwell by the eminently pious Mr John Crow, who was afterward silenced, in the year 1662, as Dr Calamy informs us in his Account of the ejected ministers. Mr Palmer having tasted that the Lord was gracious, resolved to employ all his time and talents in the honourable work of the ministry, and in promoting the interests of the Redeemer's kingdom. He accordingly preached when desired in different churches in and about London. But he was determined in his own mind, to accept the first invitation for the constant exercise of his ministry. And he readily accepted an invitation to Duke's-place, London, though the external support was small. But afterward, having received a very pressing invitation, he became pastor at New Church, Westminster. He was the first pastor of that church. He was succeeded at Duke's-place by Mr, afterward, Dr Thomas Young, an eminent and worthy divine. In each of these situations, Mr Palmer was highly esteemed, and his preaching, expounding, catechizing, and other ministerial labours, as formerly, were most abundant. He was always abounding in the work of the Lord. He was also one of those divines, who, by appointment of Parliament, carried on the morning lecture at the Abbey-church, Westminster. It is truly wonderful, that a person of such a weakly constitution could perform so much work. But *as his day was, so was his*

a Baillie's Letters, vol. i. p. 401.

strength. He continued frequently to speak in public for the space of six or eight hours on a Sabbath-day, beside spending a considerable time in more private exercises of prayer, repetition of sermons, pious exhortations, and the like, in the family. When his friends advised him to spare himself, suggesting that so much labour was hurtful to him, and beyond what his constitution admitted; he replied, "That his strength would spend of itself, though he did nothing; and it could not be better spent than in God's service." Having now obtained a very high reputation both for learning and piety, he was, on the 11th of April, in the year 1644, constituted master of Queen's-college, in Cambridge, by the Earl of Manchester, who was at that time employed by an ordinance of Parliament, for the reformation of that University. In that place, he succeeded Dr Edward Martin, who was one of Archbishop Laud's chaplains, and a man of very high principles. Under the peculiar care and encouragement of the celebrated new master, the college flourished exceedingly, even to the great admiration of all persons. He laboured with indefatigable industry in promoting both religion and learning, in his college. He was exceedingly careful that no person should be admitted to a scholarship or fellowship, who was not both religious and learned; that the whole society should attend the public worship of God, and strictly observe the Lord's-day. He also closely attended to the instruction both of the young scholars, and of the college-servants, in the principles of religion. The exercises of common places, or sermons in the chapel, which had formerly been in use, only in term-time, he caused to be continued weekly all the year. And when he was present in the college, he frequently either preached himself, or expounded some part of the Holy Scriptures to them. He looked particularly into the several conversations of all persons. He required the constant performance of public exercises, by persons of all ranks. He used his utmost endeavours to have the college library furnished with good authors. He readily gave himself, and excited other persons to give, considerable sums of money for that purpose. And some dues, which were payable to the college, and had been formerly employed in feasting, were, by his means, converted to purchase valuable books for the library. He bestowed also a considerable part of his profits in that place, upon the yearly maintenance of poor scholars.—When any persons solicited him for preferment of their friends, he constantly replied, " That if they were found to deserve it better than others, they should have it; but if otherwise, they must expect to go without it." And his actings were always exactly conformable to his words.—In his converse with the fellows of the college, he was peculiarly careful to preserve unanimity. His laudable exertions for the benefit of that college were, by the blessing of God, crowned with surprizing success. And scarcely, perhaps, was ever any head of a society taken from them with more deep and general sorrow.—In the year 1645, he was appointed, by order of Parliament, one of the committee of accommodation. He was one of those divines who subscribed the proposition, " That Jesus Christ, as King of the church, has himself appointed a church-government distinct from the civil magistrate."

Mr Palmer always firmly adhered to his principles. Though he would very readily deny himself when only his own interest was concerned, he was constantly zealous and unmoved in whatever respected the glory of God and the interests of the Redeemer's kingdom. Accordingly, upon his being called to preach at the Bishop of Lincoln's visitation, at Hitchin, he spoke with much faithfulness and freedom against the existing corruptions of the church, not fearing the consequences, though he was very sensible of his great danger. When the disgraceful Book of Sports, bowing to the altar, reading part of the service in the chancel, and other innovations, were enjoined, he firmly resolved rather to lose all, than offend God by encouraging superstition and profaneness. But the haughty prelates seem to have been more favourable to him than to some others. He constantly and vigorously opposed the superstitious and unrighteous oath of canonical obedience. He was always a most consistent and conscientious nonconformist.

This eminently learned and pious divine was several times called to preach before the Parliament, when he faithfully and plainly declared what God expected from them, and freely reproved what was amiss. He was accustomed to say, "that he did not in that place preach before them, *as before a judge*, but to them authoritatively, as by commission from God. And how much soever they might be superior to him in other respects, yet he was in that place superior to them, as acting in God's name; and therefore would not be afraid to speak, whatever was the will of God that he should tell them, notwithstanding any displeasure or danger which might by this means befal him for so doing." By his sermons before the Parliament, he has incurred the great displeasure and severe censure of some historians. But what such writers have advanced, evidently with a design to blacken the memory of one of the best of men, only requires to be fairly stated in the author's own words, that it may be completely refuted. And what these scurrilous writers have brought forth against that eminently learned and pious divine, will remain a stigma upon their own character, and a reproach to their memory, as long as men are disposed to read and to examine with candour the impartial records of history.

Mr Palmer was eminently distinguished for his temperance and sobriety. He abstained altogether from strong drink, and he drank wine very sparingly, and only when necessity required. He commonly eat only of one dish at a meal, and that was often not the most delicate. He scarcely used any recreation; but instead of that, he refreshed himself with the Christian conversation of his friends. He accounted time very precious.

His last sickness was not long, his constitution being weakly, and his natural strength much spent; but his behaviour was highly pleasing. His conversation was holy and heavenly. He lived piously, and died cheerfully, in the exercise of faith, patience, and submission to the will of God. He was much engaged in prayer, for himself, that God would heal the sinfulness of his nature, pardon all his transgressions, deliver him from an evil heart of unbelief, and from temptation;—teach him to improve all providences, and to live upon Christ and the promises. He also prayed much for the nation, for the church of God, and for all with whom he stood connected. He prayed particularly for Scotland, the churches in France, New England, and foreign plantations.—Afterward, having forgotten to crave a blessing upon something which was given him, he prayed, "Lord, pardon my neglect and forgetfulness of thee.—Lord, glorify thy name in my poor spirit; and let none of thy people ever see me shrink from thee, for Jesus Christ's sake." When his friends recommended him to cast the burden of his pains and sickness upon the Lord his God, he said, "I should act very unworthily, if after I have preached to others, that they should cast their burdens upon God, I should not do so myself."—Having spent his life in the most laborious study, and in promoting the cause of Christ and the interests of true religion, he resigned his spirit to God who gave it, in the firm hope of eternal life, through the Lord Jesus Christ, in the year 1647, aged forty-six years. His remains were interred in the New church, Westminster.[a]

Mr Palmer was a gentleman of a low bodily stature, and had a weakly constitution; but his soul was richly adorned with a splendid variety of talents and graces. He was highly distinguished by constancy and courage, in the most trying situations, and by unshaken fidelity to his engagements. He was indefatigably laborious. He had a competent estate, and chose a single life, and was therefore able to do much for the benefit of his fellow-creatures. He generously maintained several poor scholars at his own expence, in the college, and at his death, he left a considerable sum of money for that purpose. Granger styles him "a man of uncommon learning, generosity, and politeness;" and also observes, "that he possessed a most excellent character; that he wished for peace during the civil war; and that he spoke the French language with as much facility as his mother tongue."[b]

a Clark's Lives, and Neal's Puritans.
b Granger's Biog. Hist. vol. ii. pp. 182, 183.

Mr Palmer's writings.—1. *An endeavour of making the Principles of the Christian Religion plain and easy.* In modern times, this book is entitled, *The Principles of the Christian Religion made plain and easy.* The sixth impression was printed, in 1645.—2. *Of making Religion one's Business.*—This last and several other pieces were afterward published together, entitled, *Memorials of Godliness and Christianity;* the eleventh edition of which was printed, London, 1673, and the thirteenth edition, recommended, in a short preface, by Mr Tong of London, was printed in 1708.—3. Sermons preached before the Parliament, one of which is entitled, "The Necessity and Encouragement of Utmost Venturing for the Churches Help, together with the Sin, Folly and Mischief of Self-idolizing; a Sermon from Esther iv. 13, 14. before the honourable House of Commons, on the day of the monthly solemn Fast, 28th June, 1643." 4to. pp. 71. London, 1643. Another is entitled, "The Glass of God's Providence toward his Faithful Ones; held forth in a Sermon preached from Psal. xcix. 8. to the two honourable Houses of Parliament, at Margaret's Westminster, Aug. 13, 1644, being an extraordinary Day of Humiliation." 4to. pp. 66. full and close. London, 1644. In this most elaborate and excellent sermon, the learned and pious author exhibits the great failings which the best of men are liable unto, and upon which God is sometimes provoked to take vengeance. The whole is faithfully applied, in a special manner, to a more careful observation of the *Solemn National Covenant,* and most particularly against the ungodly Toleration, pleaded for under pretence of *Liberty of Conscience.* In the application of the Sermon, he made a motion, that the Covenant should be read every Fast-day. He adds, "I cannot but again say, I am much afraid, it hath been little pondered by the most of us since we have taken it. And undoubtedly *the great business aimed at in every rightly observed Fast, is the renewing of a Solemn Covenant with God.* It is a duty altogether indispensible. And unto this Covenant we have very great bonds lying upon us to tie us most strictly. *We lifted up our hands to God in it,* in the day of our calamity, in the time of our fear and trouble, when we were *very low*. And since that time God hath raised us *very high*, in comparison of our condition then, and afforded us a great deal of help, from men and from Himself; and it contains both the general of all our duties to God and man, and very many and most necessary particulars, justly and wisely limited." p. 42.—His remarks respecting Toleration, and other things, may be read with interest. I have seen another Sermon of his from Isai. lviii. 12. London, 1646.—4. "The Christian Sabbath Vindicated, in a full Discourse concerning the Sabbath and the Lord's-day," in which he was assisted by Mr Daniel Cawdrey. 2 vols. 4to. London, 1645, and 1652.[a]—5. "Scripture and Reason pleaded for defensive Arms," in which he was assisted by some other persons; but Mr Clark says, he had the chief hand in that work.—It may be observed here, That though Mr Palmer's judgment was clear respecting the lawfulness of defensive arms, he was positively against offensive arms.—I have in my possession an ancient Letter of Mr Palmer's, under the date of Aug. 14, 1632. which was printed in the Baptist Annual Register, Jan. 1. 1801. at London. It is a valuable and religious letter. And it is said, at the end of the printed letter, "This, with other papers, in Mr Herbert Palmer's *own hand writing*, are in the possession of Dr Rippon."

EDWARD PEALE OF COMPTON.

EDWARD PEALE is in the list of the Divines, who met in the famous Assembly at Westminster. And, in the ordinance, which passed both Houses for calling an Assembly of Divines, in 1643, he was appointed one of their number. He is marked in my copy of Neal's list, as giving constant attendance. But I am not able at this time, to give any further account of him.

a See Mr Cawdrey's Writings, vol. i. p. 220.

ANDREW PERNE, A. M.

MINISTER OF WILBY, AND A MEMBER OF THE ASSEMBLY OF DIVINES AT WESTMINSTER.

ANDREW PERNE was born in the year 1596. He seems to have received his education in the University of Cambridge; for he was sometime fellow of Katherine-hall, in that University. Having finished his studies at the University, he, in course of time, became Minister of Wilby in Northamptonshire, where he continued a laborious, zealous, faithful, and successful, preacher, about twenty-seven years. In the year 1643, Mr Perne was chosen a Member of the Assembly of Divines at Westminster, and constantly attended during the whole session. Wood says, that "he was a frequent preacher before the members of the Long Parliament, that began at Westminster, in the year 1640, ran with those times, and published several sermons." And Brook also says, "He often preached before the Parliament, and several of his sermons were published." But I have not been able to ascertain how often he preached before the Parliament, nor what number of his sermons have been published. Nor have any of the above-mentioned authors given us particular information of more than one sermon which he preached before the House of Commons, of which the reader will find an account in its proper place. Upon close search, I have found that Mr Perne preached another time before the House of Commons, at the thanksgiving for the victory given to the forces under the command of Lord Fairfax at Selby in Yorkshire, April 23, 1644. But the sermon, which was preached from Exod. xxxiv. 6. is said not to be printed, at least at that time.

Upon his being called up to London to attend the Assembly, he gained a high reputation, and was offered several considerable preferments; but he refused all these, firmly resolving, with the will of Divine Providence, to return to his pastoral charge, to his affectionate and beloved people, at Wilby. In that place, by his awakening sermons, and very exemplary life and conversation, a most signal and comfortable reformation was, under the Divine blessing, speedily effected. His holy life was an excellent practical comment upon his pure doctrine. While he warmly urged the necessity of holiness upon other persons, he carefully practised it himself. He was a burning and shining light. His people revered and loved him as a father. Mr Ainsworth says, "He was full of spiritual warmth, filled with an holy indignation against sin, active in his work, and never more in his element than when he was in the pulpit." As his life was holy, so his death was happy. He blessed God that he was not afraid to die; nay, he earnestly desired to be gone; and often cried out, during his last sickness,—"When will that hour come? One assault more, and this earthen vessel will be broken, and I shall be with God."

He died Dec. 13, 1654, aged about sixty years. Mr Samuel Ainsworth, one of the silenced nonconformists, preached and published his funeral sermon. His remains were interred in the chancel of Wilby church; where, at the foot of the altar, is the following monumental inscription erected to his memory: *Here lieth interred, Mr Andrew Perne, a faithful servant of Jesus Christ, a zealous owner ever of God's cause in perilous times, a powerful and successful preacher of the Gospel, a great blessing to this town and country, where he lived twenty-seven years. He departed Dec.* 13, 1654.[a]

Mr Perne has a place in Burnham's Pious Memorials, and in Lives of the Puritans. I have seen only one sermon of his, which is entitled, "Gospel-Courage, or a Christian Resolution for God and his Truth; in a sermon

a Wood's Athenæ Oxon. vol. i. Fasti, col. 80. Neal's Puritans, vol. iv. Brook's Puritans, vol. iii. Cat. of the Preachers before Parliament.

preached from Micah iv. 5. before the honourable House of Commons, at Margaret's, Westminster, at a Publick Fast, the 31st of May, 1643." 4to. pp. 32. London, 1643.

JOHN PHILIPS.

JOHN PHILIPS is in the list of those eminent divines, who met in the famous Assembly at Westminster. His name is also in the ordinance of Parliament for calling an Assembly of learned and godly divines. In that ordinance, he is said to be, "John Philips of Wrentham." And, in my copy of Neal's list of those divines, he is marked as giving constant attendance in the Assembly. But I have not seen any of his writings, nor found any more account of him. Wood, in his Athenæ Oxon. 2d edit. London, 1721, mentions different persons of this name. One John Philipps, who was bishop of the Isle of Man, and who died in 1633, or about that time; another who wrote *A Summons to Repentance*, Lond. 1584; and one who wrote *The Way to Heaven*. The first was not our divine; and we have not evidence that any of them was.

BENJAMIN PICKERING.

BENJAMIN PICKERING was a member of the Assembly of Divines at Westminster. In the ordinance of Parliament for calling an Assembly of Divines, he is said to be, of East-Hoathly. He seems to have been pastor of that place, when he was called to sit in the Assembly of Divines. In the year 1644, when he was a member of the Assembly, we are informed, in the title-page of a Sermon, which he preached at that time before the House of Commons, that he was minister of God's Word at Buckstead in Sussex. He wrote his name Pikering.

Mr Pickering has published the above Sermon, which is entitled, "A Firebrand Pluckt out of the Burning," from Zech. iii. 2. 4to. pp. 28. London, 1645. And he has also published a very handsome Epistle, addressed to the honourable House of Commons, which is prefixed to that Sermon. In this epistle, he exhorts the honourable senators, to set up a faithful ministry, and to establish judgment and justice in the gates—to let their zeal for the Lord burn, setting up his worship and ordinances in purity. He says, "Be zealous for Christ's cause: delay not to establish his government and discipline with vigour. Proceed so in your reforming, that glory may dwell in our land; that mercy and truth, righteousness and peace may meet together, and kiss each other.—Continue in your integrity, and the Lord will continue a sun and shield to you.—Although Satan be at your right-hand, fear not, so long as our Mediator sits at the right-hand of God."

The following are some of his remarkable expressions and sayings, in his sermon. "It is the Lord's pleasure that the condition of his church many times should be such, as the prophet expresseth: *I beheld the earth, and, lo, it was without form and void; and the heavens, and they had no light*, Jer. iv. 23. Thus it was with God's people in the Babylonish captivity. Heaven and earth, church and commonwealth, were in confusion. The best undertakings meet with greatest discouragements.—The devil will still be hindering the acting hand, in the things of God. The devil hateth all divine order and pure ordinances, therefore he resists Joshua, in whom the priesthood and divine worship were restored.—Doctrine: God's people may be in the burning, but they shall certainly be rescued and perfectly delivered.—God's wisdom is best seen, when we are at our wit's end; and the Lord's power is most manifest, when we are at the extremity of misery; when we think and say, *we are cut off for our parts.*—Every sin makes us as ready to take fire, even as gun-powder: *let us therefore have grace, whereby we may serve God acceptably with reverence and godly fear: for our God is a consuming fire:* and this fire of the enemy is dreadful.—He has now drawn out his sword to avenge the quarrel of his Covenant, and the fire of his anger burns; but he may complain as of old, *The Founder melts in vain.*—When we are in the burning, look up to Jesus Christ.—In Christ we shall have safety. Labour for the Spirit of comfort; the refreshings of this Spirit, as living water, will cool the heat of the spent soul. Pray that the Lord would mitigate the flames—and labour to be constant—hold fast the name of Christ."—

From what our author has published to the world, he appears to have been furnished with considerable abilities, to have been pious and learned, and very courageous in the cause of truth.

SAMUEL DE LA PLACE.

SAMUEL DE LA PLACE was Minister of the French church, and a member of the Assembly of Divines at Westminster. His name is in the ordinance of the Parliament for calling an Assembly of learned and godly divines, in the year 1643; and it is also in the list of the divines who met in the Assembly at Westminster that year. And, he was one of the divines in that Assembly, who subscribed the proposition, "That Jesus Christ, as King of the Church, hath himself appointed a church-government distinct from the civil magistrate."—

I cannot give any farther account of Mr de la Place.

WILLIAM PRICE, B. D.

WILLIAM PRICE was one of the Assembly of Divines at Westminster. His name is both in the ordinance of the Parliament for calling the Assembly, and also in the list of those divines who met in it. In the ordinance of the Parliament, he is said to be, " Mr Price of Paul's Church in Covent-Garden." In the title-page of his sermon, in 1646, he is said to be " Pastor of Waltham-Abbey, and one of the Assembly of Divines." And we find, that in the year 1646, Mr Obadiah Sedgwick became preacher at Paul's, Covent-Garden. Mr Baillie considers Mr Price among the ablest divines in the Assembly, when speaking of his being against the institution of the ruling elder by divine right.[a] Mr Price subscribed the above-mentioned proposition, respecting Jesus Christ, as King of the Church.

Mr Price has published a Sermon, which is entitled, " Man's Delinquency attended by Divine Justice, intermixed with Mercy; displayed in a Sermon from Ezra ix. 6, 7, 8. to the House of Lords assembled in Parliament, in the Abbey-church, Westminster, Nov. 25, 1646. Fast." 4to. London, 1646. In that valuable sermon, Mr Price has the following choice sayings.—" We are ashamed of our glory, and *glory* in our *shame*.—When the soul-wounded publican durst not look up to heaven, heaven looked down to him." Speaking of sinning against clear light, he says, " Great knowledge greatens sins; for knowledge is like the unicorn's horn, that doth well in a wise and good man's hand, but ill on a beast's head." I have seen this sermon of Mr Price's both in England and in Scotland.

a Baillie's Letters, vol. i. p. 401.

NICHOLAS PROFFET.

NICHOLAS PROFFET was one of the Assembly of Divines at Westminster. His name is both in the ordinance of Parliament for calling that Assembly, and also in the list of those divines who met there. And, in Neal's list, he is marked as giving constant attendance during the session. He was sometime rector of Peter's in Marlborough, in the county of Wilts. He was in Marlborough, when he was appointed by the Parliament to sit in the Assembly of Divines at Westminster. In the year 1644, it is said, that he was then Minister of Edmonton, and one of the Assembly of Divines. Edmonton is a village of Middlesex, in the neighbourhood of London, and a convenient place for attending the Assembly.

Mr Proffet has published a very good and seasonable sermon, which is entitled, "England's Impenitence under Smiting, Causing Anger to Continue, and the Destroying hand of God to be stretched forth still;" a sermon preached from Isai. ix. 13. before the honourable House of Commons, at a Public Fast, Sept. 25, 1644. 4to. pp. 48. London, 1645. He was also the author of a very judicious Epistle, which was prefixed to this sermon, and addressed to the honourable House of Commons. 4to. pp. 4. Both this sermon and the epistle were again printed at Dumfries, in the year 1799, and dispersed through the south of Scotland, and in several parts of England and Ireland, and very highly esteemed by some persons. The author of these Memoirs has a number of the copies of this valuable sermon in hand, price 6d. He is sorry, upon reading the sermon, that he cannot give any farther account of Mr Nicholas Proffet.

WILLIAM RATHBAND, M. A.

WILLIAM RATHBAND was a Member of the Assembly of Divines at Westminster. I cannot find his name in the ordinance of Parliament for calling that Assembly. It is not in my copy; but it is found in the list of those Divines who convened in the Assembly at Westminster. In Mr Neal's list, he is said to be "Mr William Rathband, of High-gate;" and is marked as giving constant attendance. He seems to have been a superadded Divine. Beside those who were originally appointed to sit in the Assembly, in order to supply vacancies by death, desertion, or otherwise, the Parliament named other persons from time to time, who were called superadded Divines. —Mr Rathband preached before the Parliament from Jer. vii. 3, at their solemn fast, July 31, 1644; but the Sermon was not then printed. Messrs Simeon Ashe and William Rathband published "A Letter of many Ministers in Old England requesting the judgment of their Brethren in New England, concerning nine Propositions, &c." with a Preface, 4to. 1643. There were two eminent Divines of this name, in England, about that time, the father and the son. William Rathband, the father, was a Puritan Divine of great eminence in his day. He preached nineteen years at a Chapel in Lancashire, but afterward, being much persecuted for nonconformity, he removed into Northumberland. Having published a book against the Brownists, which Dr Stillingfleet quoted to prove that preaching, when prohibited by the established laws, was contrary to the doctrine of all the old Nonconformists; Mr William Rathband, his son, in a letter to Mr Baxter, assures him, that his father was not to be reckoned among those who held that sentiment, since he exercised his ministry, though contrary to law, for many years at a Chapel in Lancashire; and after he was silenced he preached in private, as he had opportunity, and the times would bear, of which I myself, says he, was sometimes a witness. Afterward, upon the invitation of a gentleman, he exercised his ministry at Belcham, in Northumberland, about a year; and from thence he removed to Ovingham, in the same county, where he preached about a year; till, being silenced there, he retired into a private family. He had two sons in the ministry, one of whom was a Puritan of considerable eminence; who, during the civil wars, and upon the reduction of York by the Parliament's forces, was constituted one of the four preachers maintained by the State in that city with honourable stipends. His other son, the above Mr William Rathband, was one of the silenced Nonconformists in 1662; and is said to have been one of the Assembly of Divines at Westminster, though Dr Calamy does not mention this, in his Account of him among the ejected or silenced Ministers. In the Account, he says, that Mr Rathband was ejected from Southhold by Burntwood, in the county of Essex, was M. A. brother to Mr Rathband sometime Preacher in the Minster of York. He had his education in Oxon. After many removes he settled at High-gate, where he continued till his death. In the Continuation of the Account, he says, "Mr Slater, who had been acquainted with him above fifty years, preached and published his funeral sermon. They two were of the same college, and under the same tutor. He died in October, 1695. As he is noted for the brother, so was he also the son of an old Nonconformist Minister, Mr William Rathband, who wrote against the Brownists.[a]

I cannot find any other nor further account of Mr Rathband.

a Calamy's Acc. vol. ii. Cont. vol. i. Brook's Puritans, vol. ii.

WILLIAM REYNER, B. D.

PASTOR OF EGGHAM IN SURREY, AND A MEMBER OF THE ASSEMBLY OF DIVINES AT WESTMINSTER.

WILLIAM REYNER received his education in the University of Cambridge. He had much success in his ministry, in his younger days, among the gentry. He was offered the Presidentship of Magdalen College in Oxford, or a Fellowship at Eaton, but he declined acceptance, because he had preached against Pluralities, and was firmly resolved to act according to his judgment, though his living was not worth above sixty pounds yearly. He was accounted an eminent divine, and accordingly he was chosen to be a Member of the Assembly of Divines at Westminster, and is said to have given constant attendance during the session. He was one of those who subscribed the proposition that "Jesus Christ, as King of the church, hath himself appointed a church-government distinct from the civil magistrate." He was Minister of Eggham, in the county of Surrey, near London, about forty-six years. He was cast out from that place, by the Act of Uniformity. He had no visible prospect of a future subsistence when he was ejected; and yet he lived cheerfully, and was never in want, under the unremitting care of Divine providence. And when he died he was worth little or nothing. He continued in the parish until his death in the year 1666, and left this world with a good reputation. He preached privately after his ejection, as far as his ability admitted, and was never disturbed. He was greatly afflicted with the stone for many years, though after he was silenced, he never had any acute pains. When he was dead, a stone was taken out of his bladder, weighing ten ounces, and measuring nine inches and a half, in the form of an heart. He was a man of general learning; and in particular an eminent Church Historian. He was intimate with Arch-bishop

Usher, and highly esteemed by him. The famous Nonconformist Divine, Mr Richard Wavel, who greatly exalted our Lord Jesus Christ, and the grace of God in him, in his preaching, was sent to live with Mr Reyner of Eggham in Surrey, and studied divinity under his direction, when he left the university of Oxford. Upon his being ready for the pulpit, Mr Reyner employed him to preach for him one part of the Lord's day; and marrying his wife's daughter, he assisted him constantly, as long as he continued to officiate in his church at Eggham.[a] Mr Wavel seems to have profited much, by being under such an instructor.

Mr Reyner has published "Babylon's Ruining Earthquake, and the Restoration of Zion;" a sermon from Hag. ii. 6, 7, before the honourable House of Commons, at Margaret's, Westminster, at their public fast, August 28th, 1644. 4to. pp. 60. London, 1644. Dr Calamy says that he printed nothing but this one sermon.

EDWARD REYNOLDS, D. D.

AN EMINENT ENGLISH DIVINE, AND A MEMBER OF THE ASSEMBLY OF DIVINES AT WESTMINSTER.

EDWARD REYNOLDS was born at Southampton, a sea-port town of Hampshire, in England, in the month of Nov. 1593. His father was Austin Reynolds, one of the customers of Southampton. The subject of this Memoir, being bred at the Free-school in that place, became postmaster of Merton-College, Oxford, in the year 1615, and Probationer-fellow in 1620. This place he obtained by his great knowledge of the Greek language in which he was eminently skilful. And here he was peculiarly distinguished as a good disputant and orator. After he had taken the degree of Master of Arts, he entered into the

a Calamy's Acc. vol. ii. p. 666. and Cont. vol. i. pp. 85, 86.

holy ministry, and became a very eminent preacher. He was sometime Preacher to the honourable Society of Lincoln's Inn, and Rector of Braynton in Northamptonshire. When the civil wars brake out in 1642, he espoused the cause of the Parliament, "having long before that time been Puritanically affected," as Wood says. In the year 1643, he was chosen one of the Assembly of Divines at Westminster, and is represented as giving constant attendance during the session. He was appointed one of the Select committee for the examination and approbation of those ministers who petitioned for sequestered livings. In 1645, he was chosen one of the Committee of accommodation.[a] He was a covenanter, a frequent preacher in London, and sometimes before the long Parliament, by whom he was appointed in 1646, one of the six ministers to go to Oxford, and preach the scholars into obedience to them. After this he was one of their Visitors in that University, was made Dean of Christ-Church, and Vice-chancellor of the University in 1648, when he proceeded Doctor of Divinity. He was also Vice-chancellor in 1649. But being ejected from his deanery in the latter end of the year 1650, for refusing to take the Engagement, he retired to his former charge for sometime He lived afterward mostly in London, and preached there, and became minister for sometime of Lawrence-jury. Afterward he struck in with General Monk, with a view to bring in the King, using his interest for that end in London, where he was much esteemed. Wood says that "in the city of London, he was the pride and glory of the Presbyterian party." He was of very great respectability among the Calvinists.

When the secluded Members were restored to Parliament they restored Dr Reynolds to his deanery of Christ-Church, on the 11th of March, 1659. And on the 26th of May, 1660, he, with Mr Edward Calamy, was made chaplain to the king, who was then at Canterbury, in order to his restoration. After this he preached several times before the King, and both Houses of Parliament,

a Neal's Puritans, vol. iii. chap. ii. and vi.

And in the end of June, being desired to quit his deanery, he was the next month elected, by virtue of the King's letter, Warden of Merton-College, Oxford. He now conformed, and was consecrated bishop of Norwich on the 6th of January following. Wood here observes, that, "after he had taken the covenant, and had preached against Episcopacy and the ceremonies of the Church of England, he was consecrated thereunto in Peter's church within the city of Westminster." He adds, that "it was verily thought by his contemporaries, that he would have never been given to change, had it not been to please a covetous and politic consort, who put him upon those things he did." Be that as it may, he became bishop of Norwich. The times were changed, and too many persons also changed with these. *It is a good thing that the heart be established with grace.* Wood says, that "Dr Reynolds was a person of excellent parts and endowments, of a very good wit, fancy and judgment, a great divine, and much esteemed by all parties for his preaching and florid style." Another person, who was well acquainted with him, says, "that he was a man of singular affability, meekness and humility, of great learning, a frequent preacher, and a constant resident."[a]

He died on the 28th of July, 1676, about the seventy-sixth year of his age. Neal says that "he was reckoned one of the most eloquent pulpit-men of his age, and a good old Puritan, who never concerned himself with the politics of the Court."

Dr Reynolds' Writings.—*The Vanity of the Creature,* Eccl. iv. 14, 4to.—*The Sinfulness of Sin, with the Use of the Law,* Rom. iv. 9. and vi. 12. and vii. 13.—*The Life of Christ:* or, *The Fellowship of the Saints with Him, in his Life, Sufferings, and Resurrection.* These three Treatises have been all bound together in one vol. 4to. Lond. 1631, and the fourth edit. pp. 535. Lond. 1642.—An Explication of the cx. Psalm, 4to. pp. 525. Lond. 1632. The second edit. 1635. The third edit.

a Wood's Athenæ Oxon, vol. ii.

1642.—*Meditations on the Holy Sacrament of the Lord's last Supper.* 4to. pp. 240. Lond. 1638. The 2d edit. 1647.—*Israel's Prayer in the time of Trouble, with God's gracious Answer thereunto*, in seven sermons on so many days of solemn humiliation, on the xivth chap. of Hos. 4to. Lond. 1645, and 1649. And the first sermon also, Lond. 1642.—*A Treatise of the Passions and Faculties of the Soul of Man.* 4to. about 500 pages, London, 1640, 1650, and 1656. All these pieces were collected into one folio volume and printed at London, 1658, pp. 1110, with the author's picture, and entitled, "The Works of Edward Reynolds, D. D."—Thirty of his sermons preached on several solemn occasions, between the year 1634, and that of his death, some of which had been different times printed, were reprinted in the second impression of his Works, Lond. 1679, large folio, very elegant. He wrote the English Annotations on Ecclesiastes, which are admirably done. He was also the author of the Epistolary Preface to Burlee's Correptory Correction, &c. of some Notes of T. Pierce of God's Decrees. He is also said to be the author of The Humble Proposals respecting the Engagement. 4to. London, 1650, one sheet. Probably he has written other things which I have not seen. His writings have been much esteemed, and he is very happy in his similitudes.

ARTHUR SALWEY.

PASTOR OF SEVERN-STOKE, AND A MEMBER OF THE ASSEMBLY OF DIVINES AT WESTMINSTER.

ARTHUR SALWEY was Pastor of Severn stoke, in the county of Worcester, in England. In the time of the civil war, he espoused the cause of the Parliament, and was a zealous Reformer. He was a warm friend to the interests of the Redeemer's kingdom, and of the reformation. In the year 1643, he was appointed one of the Assembly of Divines at Westminster. He is marked, in Mr Neal's list of those Divines, as giving constant attendance during the session.

He preached a sermon from 1 Kings xviii. 21, to the Honourable House of Commons, on the day of the monthly fast, 25th Oct. 1643, at Margaret's, Westminster. This sermon is entitled, "Halting Stigmatized." 4to. pp. 21. London, 1644. He has an Epistle Dedicatory to the Honourable House of Commons, which is prefixed to the sermon. In the application of that sermon, he says: "Honourable Senators, Hath there not been halting within your walls? Have not many of your members unworthily forsaken you, and miserably deserted the glorious cause of God? The Lord open their eyes and heal their backslidings."

He warmly exhorts to take up the profession of godliness upon good grounds, and for right ends. He adds, "Act in the strength of Jesus Christ. *I can do all things*, says the apostle, *through Christ who strengthens me.* Phil. iv. 13. Get your hearts warmed with the love of Jesus Christ, which the apostle calls a constraining love, 2 Cor. v. 14.—For love has a compulsive faculty. Reward draws, punishment drives; but love is most efficacious in persuading us unto the discharge of our duty. Lastly, fix your faith upon the promises, study Moses's opticks, eye Him who is invisible. Heb. xi. 27. And eye the threats also. Look upon that good which God promiseth, as the greatest good, and upon the evil which he threateneth, as the greatest evil. And Honourable Patriots, I beseech you suffer the word of exhortation. Let it be your chiefest care to follow God, in your personal holiness, and in promoting a National reformation. Follow him personally. It will be your greatest honour to be his servants.—You have an admirable pattern, the zealous prophet Elijah, a man of such transcendant zeal, that to heighten the expression thereof, some have said of him, that when he drew his mother's breasts, he was seen to suck in fire. I wish from my very soul, that a double portion of his spirit may be given unto you, that you may act in his power and spirit. Elijah opposed idolatry and oppression, so do ye. Down with Baal's altars, down with Baal's priests: do not, I beseech you, consent unto a toleration of Baal's worship in this kingdom upon any political consideration whatsoever. I have heard that you have already voted that you will never give your consent to the toleration of the Romish mass in this kingdom. I will take up the words of David's prayer, 1 Chron. xxix. 18. "*O Lord God of Abraham, Isaac, and of Israel, our fathers, keep this for ever in the imagination of the thoughts of your hearts.*" He faithfully reminds them of their solemn covenants, and of making the word of God their rule in the reformation of religion. Near the conclusion of the sermon, he says, "Shortly, I hope, a plat-form of worship, discipline, and government, will be presented unto you, by those whom you have employed for that purpose. I beseech you, bring all unto the touch-stone of the word. Believe it, Worthies, that form of government will be best for the state, which is most agreeable unto the word. It hath been often said by the bishops of the government of the Reformed churches, and they did commonly instance in Presbytery, that it was no friend to monarchy. But I am sure that Prelacy is no enemy unto *tyranny*. The Lord guide you in the managing hereof, that what you shall do herein, may tend unto the glory of God, and the good and peace of his church." The sermon is well composed for the time. I have seen this sermon in different parts of Scotland; but have not seen any more of the author's writings, which I lament.

HENRY SCUDDER, B. D.

PASTOR OF COLLINGBORN, AND A MEMBER OF THE ASSEMBLY OF DIVINES AT WESTMINSTER.

HENRY SCUDDER received his education in Christ's College, Cambridge. Dr Fuller has placed him among the learned writers of that College. He was afterward minister at Drayton in Oxfordshire. In that station, he was very highly esteemed on account of his singular and exemplary piety, his remarkable prudence, and his excellent ministerial labours. Mr William Whately, a man of distinguished eminence, being then at Banbury, Mr Robert Harris being placed at Hanwell, and Mr Scudder at Drayton, there were three eminently pious and learned neighbours, who were closely united, not only in judgment and affection, but also in affinity. Mr Harris married Mr Whately's sister, and Mr Scudder, his wife's sister. Those three eminent men met weekly for some time, and by turns translated and analyzed, each person his chapter of the Bible. Afterward, Mr Scudder became pastor of Collingburn dukes, in Wiltshire, a county of England. And, in the year 1643, he was chosen one of the Assembly of Divines at Westminster, and is said to have constantly attended. He was one of those divines who subscribed the proposition, "That Jesus Christ, as King of the church, has himself appointed a church-government distinct from the civil magistrate."

He was eminently distinguished as the author of a very excellent work, which is entitled, "The Christian's Daily Walk in Holy Security and Peace." This book contains familiar directions, clearly shewing how we should walk with God, in the whole course of our lives. It has passed through numerous editions, and is very highly esteemed, in the present day, among serious Christians. Dr Owen and Mr Richard Baxter have prefixed to it their recommendatory epistles.

Dr Owen says, "It is now above thirty years ago since I first perused the ensuing treatise. And although until upon this present occasion I never read it, nor to my knowledge saw it since; yet the impression it left upon me in the days of my youth has, to say no more, continued a grateful remembrance of it upon my mind. Being desired, upon this new edition, to give some testimony unto its worth and usefulness, I esteem myself obliged so to do, by the benefit which I had myself received from it." And upon informing us that he had then given it another perusal, he adds, "I shall only acquaint the reader, that I am so far from subducting my account, or making an abatement in an esteem thereof, that my respect unto it, and valuation of it, is greatly increased; wherein also I do rejoice, for reasons not here to be mentioned.—There is generally that soundness and gravity in the whole doctrine of the book, that weight of wisdom in the directions given for practice, that judgment in the resolution of doubts and objections, that breathing of a spirit of holiness, zeal, humility, and the fear of the Lord, in the whole; that I judge, and am satisfied therein, that it will be found of singular use, unto all such as in sincerity desire a compliance with the author's design."

Mr Baxter says, "I remember not any book which is written to be the daily companion of Christians, to guide them in the practice of a holy life, which I prefer before this: I am sure none of my own. For so sound is the doctrine of this book, and so prudent and spiritual, apt and savoury, and all so suited to our ordinary cases and conditions, that I heartily wish no family may be without it. And many a volume, good and useful, are now in religious people's hands, which I had rather were all unknown than this. And I think it more service to the souls of men, to call them to the notice and use of such a treasure, and to bring such old and excellent writings out of oblivion and the dust, than to encourage very many who overvalue their own, and to promote the multiplication of things common and undigested, to the burying of more excellent treatises in the heap."

This work was so very highly esteemed, that it was translated into High Dutch, by the eminently learned Mr Theodore Haak, who has translated the Dutch Annotations upon the Bible into English, and is said to have projected the first plan of the Royal Society in London.

Mr Scudder also wrote the Life of the celebrated Mr William Whately, which is prefixed to his Prototypes, or Examples out of the Book of Genesis, applied to our Instruction and Reformation, folio, London, 1640.[a]

a Wood's Athenæ Oxon, vol. i. p. 621. vol. ii. pp. 747, 846. 2d edit. and Brook's Puritans, vol. ii.

And our author was one of the preachers before the Parliament. One of his sermons, which was printed, is entitled, "God's Warning to England by the Voice of his Rod, delivered in a Sermon, preached at Margaret's, Westminster, before the Honourable House of Commons, at their Solemn Fast, Oct. 30, 1644." The text is Micah vi. 9. 4to. pp. 35. London, 1644. With a large epistle Dedicatory to the House of Commons prefixed. I have seen this sermon in different parts of Scotland, and also *The Christian's Daily Walk*, the 11th edition, 1674, recommended to all Professors by Dr Owen, and Mr Baxter. And I have seen the 12th edition of the Christian's Daily Walk, both in Scotland and England. London, 1761.

LAZARUS SEAMAN, D. D.

MINISTER OF ALLHALLOWS, BREAD-STREET, LONDON, MASTER OF PETER-HOUSE, CAMBRIDGE, AND ONE OF THE ASSEMBLY OF DIVINES AT WESTMINSTER.

LAZARUS SEAMAN was born in Leicester, the county-town and capital of Leicestershire, almost in the centre of England. He received his education in Emanuel-College, Cambridge; but as he came to the College, in mean circumstances, he was obliged soon to leave it and to teach School some time for his external support. Dr Calamy says, "that his learning sprang from himself." He seems to have been partly self-taught. He was some time Chaplain to the Earl of Northumberland. He applied himself closely to his studies, and made very great proficiency in different branches of learning. He is generally allowed to have been an eminently learned man. A sermon, which he preached at Martin's, Ludgate, was the mean, under Divine Providence, of procuring him that lecture. By his remarkable talents and industry, he soon gained a shining reputation, in the religious and learned world. And he came to be pastor of Allhallows, in Bread-street, London. He was presented, by Bishop Laud to Bread-street parish, in 1642, by order of Parliament; but Laud informed the Earl of Northumberland, whose chaplain Mr Seaman was, that out of respect to his Lordship, he had before he received that order designed him for that benefice.

In 1643, Mr Seaman was chosen one of the Assembly of Divines at Westminster, and is said to have constantly attended. He appeared very active in the Assembly, and was eminently skilful in managing controversies in divinity. Mr William Jenkyn, who was intimately acquainted with him, and who at his desire preached his funeral sermon, says; "He was a person of a *most deep, piercing*, and eagle-eyed judgment in all points of controversial divinity. He had few equals, if any superiors, in ability to decide and determine a dark and doubtful controversy. He could state a theological question with admirable clearness and acuteness, and knew how, in a controversy, to cleave, as we say, an hair. Nor was he less able to defend than to find out the truth." Dr Calamy says, that "he was a great Divine, thoroughly studied in the Original languages of the Holy Scriptures; always carrying about with him a small Plantin Bible, without points, for his ordinary use. He was well studied in the controversy of Church-government, which was the occasion of his being sent by the Parliament with their Commissioners, when they treated with King Charles I. in the Isle of Wight, where his Majesty took particular notice of the Doctor's singular ability in the debates about church-government, which were afterward printed in the Collection of his Majesty's works."

He was allowed to be a very able disputant. Mr Jenkyn says, "I had almost said, an invincible disputant." He adds; "His conquests were as many as his contentions (debates) with any adversaries of the truth; and so conspicuous were his abilities herein, that he sometimes disheartened opposers in their very entrance into the lists of disputation with him." Upon the invitation of an honourable lady, who was the head of a noble family, and who had been often solicited by the Romish priests to change her profession of religion, and become a Roman Catholic, he engaged two of the ablest priests they could select in a dispute, in the presence of both heads of the family for their satisfaction. He silenced these priests respecting *Transubstantiation*, which was the ground of the disputation, at that time, and was the instrument in preserving that whole family from a revolt, and in keeping them stedfast in the Protestant Religion. When the crafty seducers, who wished only to go over *where the hedge is lowest*, or like the Philistines, to fight when there are *no swords in Israel*, perceived the great abilities of their antagonist, they shamefully quitted the field, and never dared either to give or to take the stroke of a formed syllogism, according to Jenkyn. And those persons who were popishly inclined stood amazed, upon this occasion, in seeing the cowardliness of their champions.

In the year 1644, Mr Seaman was constituted Master of Peter-House, in the University of Cambridge, by the Earl of Manchester, upon having been first examined and approved by the Assembly of Divines at Westminster. The Earl of Manchester, in pursuance of an ordinance of Parliament, for regulating and reforming the University of Cambridge, came in person into the Chapel of Peter-House, on the 11th of April, 1644, and, by the authority to him committed, did, in that place, declare and publish Mr Lazarus Seaman to be constituted Master of the said Peter-House, in the room of Dr Cosins, late Master there, but now justly and lawfully ejected thence: requiring Mr Seaman, then present, to take upon him that office, putting him into the Master's seat, and delivering to him the statutes of the College, in token of his investiture, straitly charging the Fellows, &c. to acknowledge and yield obedience to him, as actually Master of the College, and sufficiently authorized to execute that office. Upon his admission, the Earl gave him an instrument under his hand and seal to the same effect; and he was required to make the following solemn declaration:

"I do solemnly and seriously promise, in the presence

of Almighty God, the Searcher of all hearts, that, during the time of my continuance in that charge, I shall faithfully labour to promote piety and learning in myself, the fellows, scholars, and students, who do or shall belong to the said College, agreeably to the late solemn national league and covenant by me sworn and subscribed, with respect to all the good and wholesome statutes of the said College, and of the University, correspondent to the said covenant; and by all means to procure the welfare, and perfect reformation both of that College and University, so far as to me appertains."

LAZARUS SEAMAN.

In this high and public station, he discovered his great abilities, learning and usefulness, and was beneficial to many persons. He acquitted himself very honourably. And he gained much reputation in the learned world, when he proceeded Doctor of Divinity. He took this degree by performing his exercises which were appointed by the statutes of the University; and did not obtain it by the favour of majesty, which some have accounted the fountain of honour, nor for money. He then displayed his abilities and erudition, in a peculiar manner, in polemical divinity. He asserted and maintained the Providence of God in disposing of political governments: and it is said, that he cast much light upon that subject, which was not well understood before that time, and but little studied. He defended his position with great ability and force of argument. He was generally allowed to be an excellent casuist, a good expositor of the Holy Scriptures, and both a very judicious and moving preacher. In his latter days, he much studied the prophetical parts of the Sacred Writings. He wrote some Notes on the Revelations, which he presented to Lord Warton; but it is said, that these were never printed.

He lost all his places at the Restoration, being ejected by the Act of Uniformity. He lived afterward a Nonconformist, mostly in Warwich-court, near Warwich-lane, in London, according to Wood. His patience, under very acute pains, in his last sickness, was truly admirable. In the midst of his tortures, he greatly admired free grace, justification by faith through the righteousness of Christ, and highly extolled the glorious Sovereign of the Universe, who is just in all his ways, and holy in all his works. Mr Jenkyn says, "I never admired his scholarship so much as I did his patience, the lesson in which he grew so perfect in the School of affliction."

He died in peace, Wood says, about the 9th of Sept. 1675, "much lamented by the Brethren in regard he was a learned man." Mr Jenkyn preached his funeral sermon from 2 Peter i. 15. on the 12th of Sept. 1675, in which he gives him a very high commendation. He says, that Dr Seaman was a *burning and shining light; an interpreter one of a thousand; a scribe instructed to the kingdom of heaven, like a man who is an householder, who bringeth out of his treasure things new and old.* I may justly say of him, That he was an *ocean of Theology*, and that he had so thoroughly digested the whole body of divinity, that he could upon all occasions discourse upon any point without labour. He was a living body of Divinity, *and his tongue as the pen of a ready writer*. He was a person of great stability and steadiness in the truth. I am confident that he valued one truth of Christ, above all the wealth of both the Indies.—He was deeply and tenderly sensible of the state of the church of Christ. He was ever very inquisitive how it fared with the people of God in foreign parts; and this not out of Athenian curiosity, but out of a public spirit of Christianity.—And he was as near to Germany, France, yea, to America, in his sympathy and resentments, as he was distant in place. —He was *ready to every good work*—Industrious and indefatigable in his *Calling*—Admirably prudent both in his speech and behaviour—And *an example of patience in suffering affliction.*

He left a very valuable Library, which is said to have been the first that was sold in England by auction, and brought seven hundred pounds. He has extant the following

---

Writings.—*Solomon's Choice*: or, *A Precedent for Kings and Princes, and all who are in Authority*; a sermon from 1 Kings iii. 9, before the Honourable House of Commons at Margaret's, Westminster, at their public Fast, Sept. 25th, 1644. 4to. pp. 47. Lond. 1644.—*The Head of the Church, the Judge of the World:* or, *The Doctrine of the Day of Judgment briefly Opened and Applied;* a sermon preached from Acts xvii. 30, 31, before the House of Peers, at Westminster, Fast, 27th Jan. 1646–47. London, 1647.—*A Vindication of the Judgment of the Reformed Churches, and Protestant Divines, from Misrepresentations concerning Ordination, and Laying on of Hands.* 4to. pp. 96. Lond. 1647. This was in Answer to Mr S. Simpson's Diatribe, of unordained persons preaching.—And a sermon before the Lord Mayor, against Divisions, April 7th, 1650.[a] Dr Seaman has also a Farewell Sermon from Heb. xiii. 20, 21, at his ejectment, at the close of which he observes, That the care of the Church is in the hands of Christ,—that all Providences respecting it, designed to exercise and to try it, must be borne with patience; approving what he orders, and doing whatever he commands; with a cheerful dependence upon the faithfulness of *the Great Shepherd of the Sheep, who being brought again from the dead,* lives for ever; and a firm reliance on God's Covenant.

OBADIAH SEDGWICK, B. D.

PASTOR OF COGGES-HALL IN ESSEX, AND A MEMBER OF THE ASSEMBLY OF DIVINES AT WESTMINSTER.

OBADIAH SEDGWICK was born in the parish of St. Peter in Marlborough, in Wiltshire, in England, in the year 1600. He received his grammatical education at or near the place of his birth. In the year 1616, he was sent to Queen's-College, Oxford; but not continuing

a Calamy's Account, vol. ii. pp. 16, 17. Cont. vol. i. p. 17. Wood's Athenæ Oxon. vol. ii. and Jenkyn's fun. sermon.

long there, he retired to Magdalen-hall, in the same University, where he took the degrees in Arts. Having finished his accademical studies, he entered into the ministerial office, and became Chaplain to Lord Horatio Vere, whom he accompanied to the Low Countries. After his return to his native country, he went again to Oxford, and, upon performing certain exercises, he was admitted to the reading of the sentences, in the latter end of the year 1629. He was tutor to Matthew Hale, who was afterward the much celebrated Lord Chief Justice. Leaving the University a second time, he became preacher at Mildred's, Bread-street, London; but was driven from his living and the people of his charge, by the merciless oppression and iron rod of the haughty prelates. In the year 1639, he became minister of Cogges-hall in Essex, where he continued two or three years. Upon the commencement of the civil wars, he returned to London, and to his ministry at Mildred's, and was often called to preach before the Parliament. In the year 1642, he became Chaplain to Colonel Hollis's regiment, in the Parliament's Army. In the following year, he was appointed one of the Licensers of the press for books of Divinity, and chosen one of the Assembly of Divines at Westminster, and he constantly attended.

He was a very zealous covenanter. Wood says, " that the Members of Parliament constituted him one of the *Assembly of Divines*, as being a covenanter to the purpose." The same writer observes, evidently with a very hostile design, " that while Mr Sedgwick preached at Mildred's, which was only to exasperate the people to rebel and confound Episcopacy, it was usual with him, especially in hot weather, to unbutton his doublet in the pulpit, that his breath might be the longer, and his voice more audible, to rail against the King's party, and those who were near him, whom he called *popish counsellors.*" The same author adds, " He was a great leader and abettor of the Reformation pretended to be carried on by the Presbyterians; whose peaceable maxims, like razors set with oil, cut the throat of majesty with a keen smoothness. This he did in an especial manner, in Sept. 1644, when he, with great concernment, told the people, several times, that *God was angry with the army for not cutting off delinquents.*"

It has also been said, that Mr Sedgwick was " a preacher of treason, rebellion, and nonsense," even in his sermons before the Parliament. But his sermons are extant, and how far he was guilty, every pious and judicious reader will easily judge. It has been the common lot of the faithful friends and servants of Christ to be loaded with calumnies and reproaches, since the commencement of Christianity. The malicious Jews *laid many and grievous complaints against Paul, which they could not prove; while he answered for himself, Neither against the law of the Jews, neither against the temple, nor yet against Cesar,* have I offended any thing at all, Acts xxv. 7, 8.

In the year 1646, Mr Sedgwick became preacher at Paul's, Covent-garden; where he was much followed, and is said to have been instrumental in the conversion of many souls. Wood says, " that there, as also sometimes in the country, he kept up the vigour of a Presbyterian ministry, which for divers years prospered according to his mind." In the year 1653, or 1654, he was, by the Parliament, appointed one of the *Tryers*, or examiners of ministers; and in the year following, he was constituted one of the assistant commissioners of London for ejecting ignorant and scandalous ministers and schoolmasters. He was a very zealous labourer in the Lord's vineyard, and exceedingly active in promoting the work of Reformation. Mr Sedgwick finding at length, that his health began to decline, he resigned his charge, and retired to Marlborough, his native place, where he died about the beginning of Jan. 1658, aged fifty-seven years, and his remains were interred in the chancel of Oglarn, St. Andrew, near Marlborough. He was esteemed a learned Divine, and an orthodox and admired preacher.[a]

His Writings.—1. *Military Discipline for a Christian Soldier.* Lond. 1639.—2. *Christ's Counsel to his Lan-*

a Wood's Athenæ Oxon, vol. ii. edit. 2. Brook's Puritans, vol. iii.

guishing Church of Sardis. Lond. 1640 —3. *England's Preservation*; a Sermon from Jer. iv. 3, before Commons, Fast, 25th May, 1642. Lond. 1642.—4. *Haman's Vanity*; a Sermon from Esther ix. 1, preached to the Honourable House of Commons, at their solemn thanksgiving, June 15th, 1643. 4to. pp. 32. Lond. 1643.—5. A Thanksgiving Sermon, 9th April 1644, from Psa. iii. 8. 4to. Lond. 1644. pp. 32.—6. *An Ark against a Deluge*; or, *Safety in Dangerous Times*; a Sermon from Heb. xi. 7, before the House of Commons, at their extraordinary Fast, Oct. 22d, 1644. 4to. pp. 31. Lond. 1644, and 1645.—7. *The Nature and Danger of Heresies*; a Sermon from Rev. xii. 15, 16, before Commons, Fast. 4to. pp. 44. Lond. 1647.—8. Speech in Guildhall, 1643.—9. The best and worst Malignant. 4to. 1648.—10. *Christ the Life, and Death the Gain*; a Sermon at the funeral of Rowl. Wilson, a Member of Parliament, from Phil. i. 21. 4to. Lond. 1650.—11. *The Doubting Christian Resolved*, Lond. 1653. There is a book of his entitled, *The Doubting Believer Resolved*. Lond. 1641, 12mo. but whether it is the same, or a different book, I cannot tell.—12. *Elisha's Lamentation upon the sudden translation of Elijah*, preached from 2 Kings ii. 12, at the funeral of Mr William Strong. 4to. Lond. 1654.—13. *The Humbled Sinner Resolved what he should do to be saved*: or, *Faith in the Lord Jesus Christ, the only way for sensible sinners, discovering the Quality, Object, Acts, Seat, Subject, inseparable Concomitants, and Degrees of Justifying Faith*. 4to. pp. 282. Lond. 1656.—14. *The Fountain opened, and the Water of Life flowing*, in several Sermons, from Isa. lv. 1, 2, 3. 4to. Lond. 1657.—15. *The Riches of Grace Displayed, in the Offer of Salvation to Poor Sinners*, in several Sermons from Rev. iii. 20. 2d edit. Lond. 1658.—16. *The Shepherd of Israel*: or, *God's Pastoral Care over his People*, on Psal. xxiii. *with the Doctrine of Providence practically handled*, on Mat. x. 29, 30, 31. 4to. Lond. 1658.—17. *Anatomy of Secret Sins*. 4to. Lond. 1660.—18. *The Parable of the Prodigal*. 4to. pp. 368. Lond. 1660.—19. *The Bowels of tender Mercy Sealed in the Everlasting Covenant*.

folio. pp. 734. Lond. 1661.—20. *Synopsis of Christianity.*—21. A Catechism.

I have seen Mr Sedgwick's Writings both in England and Scotland.

SIDRACH SIMPSON, B. D.

MINISTER OF THE GOSPEL, LONDON, AND ONE OF THE ASSEMBLY OF DIVINES AT WESTMINSTER.

SIDRACH SIMPSON received his education in the University of Cambridge. He afterward became a celebrated Preacher in London. His name has often been written Sydrach Simpson; but it was written Sidrach Simpson by himself, and so it is found both in Wood's Athenæ Oxon, and in the original list of those Divines who met at Westminster. He was appointed curate and lecturer of Margaret's Church, Fish-street; but his preaching soon gave offence to Arch-bishop Laud, who, in his metropolitical visitation, in the year 1635, convened him before him, with several other Divines, for breach of canons. Most of them having promised submission, they were dismissed. But by the intemperate superstition and bigotry of Laud, and the extreme violence with which he exacted conformity, many eminently pious and faithful Divines were driven out of their native country. Among those were Messrs Thomas Goodwin, Philip Nye, Jeremiah Burroughs, William Bridge, and Mr Simpson. They all retired to Holland, and were afterward denominated the five pillars of the Independent or Congregational party; and, in the Assembly of Divines, were distinguished by the name of the Dissenting Brethren.

Upon Mr Simpson's arrival in Holland, he went to Rotterdam; and seeing the comely order of the English church in that place, under the pastoral care of Mr Bridge, he expressed his desire to become a member; and, upon exhibiting the confession of his faith, he was received into their communion. But Mr Simpson, after some time, discovered certain things in that church, which did not meet with his approbation; and urged the utility and importance of prophesyings, that, after sermon on the Lord's-day, the people might express their doubts, and propose questions to the ministers, with a particular view to their better edification. This motion, however, in connection with some other things, produced a misunderstanding between Mr Bridge and Mr Simpson; which, at length, caused the latter even to separate himself from the church, and begin a new interest. This new society had a very small beginning, but afterward it considerably increased. Mr Joseph Symonds, another persecuted Puritan, succeeded him in the office of pastor to that church.

About the commencement of the civil war, Mr Simpson returned to England; and in the year 1643, he was chosen one of the Assembly of Divines at Westminster, and he is said to have constantly attended during the session. In all their debates, he conducted himself with great temper and moderation. He was one of the five Divines who published and presented to the House of Commons, "An Apologetical Narration submitted to the Honourable Houses of Parliament, in favour of the Independents. In the year 1645, he was appointed one of the Committee of Accommodation. In the year 1647, he united with his dissenting brethren in presenting their reasons to the Houses of Parliament, against some parts of the Presbyterian government. In the year 1650, he was appointed, by the Parliamentary Visitors, Master of Pembroke-hall, Cambridge, in the room of Mr Richard Vines, who was turned out for refusing the engagement. In 1654, he was chosen a Member of the Committee for drawing up a catalogue of fundamentals, to be presented to the Parliament. During the same year, he was constituted, by order of the Council, one of the commissioners for the approbation of public preachers; these commissioners were commonly distinguished by the name of *Tryers*. In the year 1655, he was appointed, by a commission from Cromwell, one of the new Visitors of the University of Cambridge. During the time of the Long Parliament, he gathered a congregation in London, upon the plan of the Independents, which assembled in Abchurch, near Cannon-street.

Mr Simpson was accounted a meek and quiet Divine of considerable learning, of great piety and devotion, and a celebrated preacher. Dr Grey calls him a celebrated preacher of *rebellious principles;* which is plain, he says, from the following passage in one of his sermons: "Reformation is liable to inhuman treacheries. Pharaoh's dealing was very treacherous. He bade the people go; gave them liberty by proclamation; and when he had got them at an advantage, he brought up an army to cut them off. The reforming of the church will meet with such kind of enemies." Mr Brook well observes here, "If the learned Doctor had not been in the habit of ascribing rebellion to the Puritan Divines, he would have found some difficulty in discovering *rebellious principles* from this passage. And so far from appearing *plain* from the passage, that he was a celebrated preacher of those principles, we think, it would puzzle all the learning of the two Universities of Oxford and Cambridge to make the discovery." Mr Edwards censures him for attempting to propagate his own sentiments respecting church discipline, liberty of conscience, and universal toleration.—In his last sickness, he laboured under spiritual darkness, and some melancholy apprehensions. In such circumstances, some of his friends and brethren assembled at his house, with a view to assist him by their prayers. Their labours were not in vain in the Lord; for in the evening, when they took their leave of him, he thanked them, and said, "He was now satisfied in his soul," and lifting up his hands toward heaven, cried out, "*He is come, He is come,*" and he died that night, in the year 1658.[a]

I have seen one sermon by Mr Simpson, which is entitled, "Reformation's Preservation; opened in a sermon preached from Isa. iv. 5, at Westminster, before the Honourable House of Commons, at their Solemn Fast, July 26th, 1643." 4to. pp. 30. London, 1643.

a Neal and Brook's Puritans, vol. iii.

PETER SMITH, D. D.

MINISTER OF THE GOSPEL AT BARKWAY, IN HARTFORDSHIRE, IN ENGLAND, AND ONE OF THE ASSEMBLY OF DIVINES AT WESTMINSTER.

PETER SMITH preached a Sermon from Psal. cvii. 6, before the Honourable House of Commons, at their Monthly Fast, May 29th, 1644. This Sermon was printed, 4to. pp. 46. London, 1644. From this Sermon, he clearly appears to have been furnished with considerable parts, to have been well informed, and no mean scholar. Many learned marginal notes are added to the Sermon. It is judicious, and faithfully applied. The author appears to have been well acquainted with the Greek and Hebrew languages. Dr Smith preached also before the Lords, but that Sermon was not printed. He was appointed one of the Select Committee for the examination and approbation of ministers who petitioned for sequestered livings. In the year 1645, he was chosen one of the Committee of Accommodation. And he was one of those Divines in the Assembly, who subscribed that proposition, "That Jesus Christ, as King of the church, has himself appointed a church-government distinct from the civil magistrate."[a]

WILLIAM SPURSTOWE, D. D.

MINISTER OF HAMPDEN, AND A MEMBER OF THE ASSEMBLY OF DIVINES AT WESTMINSTER.

WILLIAM SPURSTOWE, was the son and heir of William Spurstowe, citizen and merchant of London, but originally descended from the Spurstowes of Spur-

a Neal's Hist. vol. iii. chap. ii. vi. and vii.

stow in Cheshire, according to Wood. He received his education in Katherine-hall, Cambridge, of which he was sometime Fellow. Having finished his studies at the University, he entered into the ministerial office, and became minister of Hampden, in Buckinghamshire, in England. In the time of the civil war, he espoused the cause of the Parliament, and was made chaplain to the regiment of the celebrated Mr John Hampden, in the army under the command of the Earl of Essex.

In the year 1643, he was chosen one of the Assembly of Divines at Westminster, and is represented as constantly attending during the session. About that time, he became pastor of Hackney, near London, in the county of Middlesex. He was appointed by the Assembly one of the Select Committee for the examination and approbation of those ministers who petitioned for sequestered livings. Wood says, that he was "a grand Presbyterian." He preached some times before the Long Parliament. He was sometime Master of Katherine-hall in Cambridge; but was turned out of his mastership for refusing the engagement, and succeeded by the famous Dr Lightfoot. He proceeded Doctor of Divinity. He went with the Commissioners to the Treaty with King Charles at Newport, in the Isle of Wight, and was one of the Commissioners at the Savoy. He was ejected from Hackney, by the Act of Uniformity, 1662.

Being a sufferer for Nonconformity, he lived about Hackney, exercising his talents in private, as he had opportunity, until his death. He was preserved in the pestilential sickness; but died not long after, in Jan. or Feb. 1666. It is said, that his remains were interred at Hackney, Feb. 8th, 1666. He died in an advanced age.[a]

Dr Spurstowe was eminently distinguished by his great learning, humility, charity, and a cheerful conversation. He enjoyed a very peaceable disposition. Mr Baxter, in his own Life, frequently speaks of Dr Spurstowe, with

a Wood's Athenæ Oxon, vol. i. 2d edit. Calamy's Acc. and Cont. vol. ii. and Neal's Puritans.

very great respect. He mentions him among those "famous and excellent Divines who attended the Earl of Essex's army, being chaplain to Mr Hampden's regiment." And, it appears from the following circumstance which Mr Baxter records, that he was in the habit of particular intimacy with him. It being agreed by the ministers to draw up a Reply to a paper of the bishops, in answer to their exceptions against the Liturgy, he says, B. 1. p. 334, "This task they also imposed on me, and I went out of town, to Dr Spurstowe's house at Hackney for retirement; where in eight days I drew up a Reply to their Answer." And probably Dr Spurstowe was one of the *brethren*, who, he says, "read and consented to it."—There were some Alms Houses near the church of Hackney, that were his gift. And there was a stone before these houses which had this inscription: "William Spurstowe, D. D. Vicar of the parish of Hackney, out of his pious intention, ordered by his will these six Alms-Houses, for the habitation and dwelling of six poor widows of the said parish, of good life and conversation. And Henry Spurstowe, Esq. and merchant, and brother to the said Dr William Spurstowe, fulfilled his *will*. Erected and built, in the year 1666."

His Writings.—He was one of the authors of Smectymnuus, of which the reader may see an account, in the Life of Mr Calamy. Dr Spurstowe was also the author of the following Pieces: *England's Pattern and Duty in its Monthly Fasts;* a sermon preached from 1 Sam. vii. 6, to both Houses of Parliament, 21st July, 164[illegible], at an extraordinary fast. 4to. pp. 31. London, 1643.—*England's eminent Judgments caused by the abuse of God's eminent Mercies;* a sermon preached from Ezra ix. 13, 14, to the Right Honourable House of Lords, in the Abbey Church at Westminster, at the public thanksgiving, Nov. 5, 1644. 4to. pp. 31. London, 1644.—Fast sermon before the House of Commons, 24th June, 1646.—*The Magistrate's Dignity and Duty;* a sermon from Psal. lxxxii. 2. Oct. 30, 1653, before the Lord Mayor and Aldermen of the city of London. London, 1654.—

Death and the Grave no Bar to a Believer's Happiness; a sermon from Psal. xvii. 15, at the funeral of Lady Honor Vyner, July 10th, 1656. London, 1656.—A Funeral sermon for Mr William Taylor of Coleman-street, Sept. 12th, 1661.—*The Wells of Salvation Opened:* or, *A Treatise discovering the nature, preciousness, and usefulness, of the Gospel-Promises, and Rules for the right Application of them;* a small book. pp. 295. London, 1655, and the second edition, London, 1659.

This excellent Treatise contains the substance of several sermons. Edward Calamy's imprimatur is prefixed to it. In the Preface, the author says, "The Promises are the church's store-house, while it is on this side heaven, from whence believers in all ages may be filled with comfort, as every eye is with new light that beholds the sun. So that there is still a great opportunity for the ministers of God to put their sickle into this harvest; and an encouragement also to believers to take hold of all helps and advantages that may be afforded them for the clearing of their knowledge, and the quickening of their affections, in the daily use and application of the promises. And if to either, or both of these ends, this small Tract may in the least conduce, I shall seek no other recompence from thee than that I may have an interest in thy prayers, both for an encrease of grace, and of abilities, whereby I may be made more serviceable to the glory of his Name unto whom all ought to live."

A Practical Treatise of the excellency and right use of the Gospel-Promises. London, 1658.—*The Spiritual Chymist:* or, *Six Decads of Divine Meditations on several subjects;* a small book. pp. 260. London, 1666, and 1668.—*The Wiles of Satan;* in a Discourse on 2 Cor. ii. 11. Also a small piece.

EDMUND STAUNTON, D. D.

MINISTER OF THE GOSPEL AT KINGSTON UPON THAMES, PRESIDENT OF CORPUS CHRISTI COLLEGE, OXFORD, AND A MEMBER OF THE VENERABLE ASSEMBLY OF DIVINES AT WESTMINSTER.

EDMUND STAUNTON was born at Woburne in Bedfordshire, England, in the year 1600. He was descended from the ancient family of the Stauntons in Bedfordshire. His father, Sir Francis Staunton, had several sons, of whose education he was peculiarly careful, while he left them good temporal estates also. He reckoned, that *wisdom*, or *learning*, is good with an *inheritance*, Eccl. vii. 11. He accordingly trained up his children in learning, not only that it might be an ornament to them, but also that they might thereby be serviceable to the church or commonwealth. This Edmund, who was one of the youngest, when instructed in grammar learning, was sent early to Oxford University, and admitted into Corpus Christi College. Here he applied himself very closely to study, and made extraordinary proficiency in learning. And he obtained such applause, that while he was an under graduate, he was chosen a probationer fellow in that college before eighteen of his seniors.

When he was about eighteen years of age, he fell dangerously sick, and was much exhausted, and near unto death before his disease was understood; until a skilful physician found that it was a pleurisy, and ordered opening a vein. A surgeon was immediately sent for, but could not readily be found. At length the messenger brought him from a tavern, but he could not perform his work. He struck the patient's arm twice, but no blood came. In this mournful posture, the sottish swinish surgeon left his patient all night. When he had slept himself sober, he came the next morning very early, and knocked at the college gate. Upon this being opened, he ran immediately to Mr Staunton's chamber, and asked if he was yet alive. Upon finding him alive, he speedily opened a vein in his arm, which bled freely; and the patient, though half dead, soon recovered, and became healthy.—Here we may observe, that through the drunkenness of the surgeon, this celebrated person's life was in imminent danger.—This part of our narrative clearly discovers the very awful and dangerous consequences of the sin of drunkenness, with the sottish and swinish nature of that evil, which is full of deadly poison.

The subject of this Memoir was also another time as remarkably preserved from being drowned. Soon after he had commenced Bachelor of Arts, he went into the water alone to wash himself, and not being able to swim, he fell into a deep, where he could feel no bottom; but by the Providence of God he was remarkably delivered. He took hold of a little turf of grass by the side of the bank, by the means of which he climbed up, and was saved under God, and by his Providence.

These remarkable and merciful deliverances were preparatory to that good work of grace, which, about this time, the Autnor and Finisher of faith began in him. These dangerous circumstances wherein he was, with the wonderful deliverances from them, led him to serious thoughts with regard to his spiritual and eternal state, to close self examination and fervent prayer.

I shall give the account of this in his own words, as found with Mr Mayo, his Biographer, who says, that he had this account in a manuscript under his own hand. "About the year 1620, I had many sad and serious thoughts concerning my spiritual and eternal state. Then upon the advice of Dr Barcroft, I bought Brinsley's Watch, the second part; where the sins against the Commandments are set down in order, and I fell upon the work of examination; wherein this seems remarkable, that, reading over the several sins there mentioned, my heart (such was the blindness and deceitfulness of it) cried not guilty of any one of them: Whereupon I began to suspect my heart, and calling upon God to enlighten mine eyes, and discover my sins to me, and then reading them over again, I judged myself guilty, very guilty, even of most of the sins there set down and enumerated. After this I lay about two months under a spirit of bondage, being full of fears and inward trouble, so that many times I durst not close mine eyes in the night lest I should awake in hell. I thought every night the devil would come for me, and fetch me away; but anon, the Lord was graciously pleased to shine upon me, and this remarkable passage I shall never forget:—That, being one evening at prayer, all alone in the dark, I remember the chamber well in Corpus Christi College, and the corner of the chamber, I was very earnest with God for the manifestation of his love to my soul, and the assurance of pardon for my sins; and at length I brake out into these words, or words to this purpose: Lord, I will not go out of thy presence; I will not go off from my knees till thou speakest comfort to me;—whereupon I was immediately filled with a strong persuasion of the love of God to my soul, and with joys unspeakable and full of glory."

From this period, the study of the holy Scriptures was his peculiar delight; and he applied himself closely to the diligent reading of them, and to the study of divinity, and determined upon the work of the holy ministry. When he commenced Master of Arts, his father gave him the choice of the three learned professions, a Lawyer, a Physician, or a Preacher. The last of these was his choice. And he told his father, "that he had for some time past inclined his studies that way, and that he esteemed the turning of souls to righteousness to be the most desireable work in the world, and that it would have the greater reward hereafter, though the other callings were like to bring in more wealth and honour here." His affectionate father did make no opposition to his good design, but rather encouraged his pious resolution. He first preached on the Lord's day afternoon at Witney in Oxfordshire, about six months, and had here his first fruits unto Christ, as Paul had in Achaia, 1 Cor. xvi. 15, being successful in winning souls to him. Here his labours were so acceptable, that people flocked from all parts to hear him. This was not pleasant to the incumbent, who occupied the more time in reading prayers, that Mr Staunton might have the less time for preaching, and then left the church; but none followed his example except his clerk, whom he would not suffer to read the Psalm. Mr Staunton had preached some time from that text, *Buy the truth, and sell it not*, Prov. xxiii. 23.—Upon which the incumbent, when he met any coming into the church as he went out, would say, with a sneer, "What, are you going to buy the truth?" His continuance at Witney was very uncertain, and he had great opposition from the minister of the place; accordingly he removed, and became minister of Bushey in Hertfordshire. Here he had a welcome reception, especially from those who had any savour of religion. Here he preached and catechised on the Lord's day, and at other times, with great success; and many attended his ministry, not only the inhabitants of Bushey, but also those who dwelt at Watford, and other adjacent places. A respectable minister says, "That little time which Edmund Staunton spent in Bushey was not without good success—many persons, in my own hearing, having acknowledged his ministry to be the means of their conversion."

About this time, he married the daughter of one Mr Scudamore of Watford, by whom he had one daughter. But when he had been about two years in Bushey, Dr Seaton, of Kingston upon Thames, in Surrey, wishing to have this living, and either making or finding a flaw in his title, soon dispossessed him of it. Dr Seaton's Attorney, liking the ingenuity of Mr Staunton, proposed an exchange, to which both parties agreed. Mr Staunton preferred work to wages, and complied the more readily with this proposal, because his opportunities of service would be greater at Kingston. He reckoned his opportunities of doing good his greatest riches. But when Dr Seaton had obtained Bushey, he would not part with Kingston; but either Mr Staunton must be his Curate, or not go there. Mr Staunton related this to Dr Seaton's Attorney, who, abhorring such baseness, threatened to find a flaw in his title to Bushey.—And many of the inhabitants of Kingston, who greatly esteemed Mr Staunton's ministry, so worked the Doctor, that he soon resigned, and Mr Staunton took his place at Kingston upon Thames, in the county of Surrey. Here he continued about twenty years, endeavouring to fulfil the ministry which the Lord had given him. And being filled with zeal for the truth, he discharged the duties of his office with great diligence and faithfulness. He preached twice on the Lord's day, and catechised the younger and ignorant sort of people, teaching them also from house to house, though the town was large and populous. He also set up a weekly lecture, which was supplied by several eminent ministers in their turns. By these means, together with his holy and exemplary life, he was instrumental in working a general reformation in the town, both among magistrates and people. He was loved by all the godly, and feared by the wicked. The good seed then sown did spring up in the place long. And the reformation here was not wholly external; for when he left that place in the year 1648, there were thirty persons who gave him a paper, subscribed by themselves, in which they owned him as their spiritual father; and doubtless, many more could have added their names to the list.

He seems to have been very successful this way. When preaching once at Warborough, near Oxford, one person of the congregation was so affected with his first prayer, that he ran to his own house, (which was at a short distance) and told his wife, that she should make herself ready and come to church, for there was one in the pulpit who prayed like an angel, so as he never heard the like. The woman hastened away with her husband; and God so ordered, that this sermon proved a mean of her conversion, and she proved afterward a serious and eminent Christian.

As a preacher, he was very plain, affectionate, and practical. He found, by much and long experience, that a plain way of preaching was most effectual to the ends for which that ordinance was appointed; and therefore he constantly used it, even in the College and University. He could easily have appeared in another strain; but he preferred the work of his Master, and the advantage of immortal souls, unto every other consideration. And he was so affectionate, that he would not *only impart the gos-*

pel, but *also his very soul*, to his hearers. Some say, that the life of preaching lies in the application; and here, Mr Mayo says, he was indeed ever most lively. He was called the Searching Preacher.—This I have observed, says Mr Mayo, his Biographer, "That in every sermon, he would speak something still by way of trial and examination, ever and anon he would have his marks of distinction between the precious and the vile, the sincere person and the hypocrite." This story he tells himself, "That having suspicion of one man in his parish, who made a great profession of religion, and often thinking of him in his distinctions; that very person afterward came to him, and said, you will never leave distinguishing, till you distinguish me into hell." And he applied himself with all diligence to confirm his people in the truth, and to arm them against all false doctrines. He often said, that he was afraid to hear that rebuke from Christ another day, "Thou wicked and slothful servant." When he visited his friends, if they did not ask him to preach, he offered. And he would say, "Is there no work here for a preacher?"

Upon the death of his first wife, he married a second, by whom he had many sons and daughters. Ten of these were buried in one grave, in the parish church of Kingston, on whom he laid a fair stone, with this epitaph fairly engraven on it:

"Here lie the bodies of
Francis, Richard, Mary, Matthew, Mary, Richard,
Edmund, Edmund, Sarah, Richard:
Children,
whom the Lord graciously gave to
EDMUND STAUNTON, D. D.
Late Minister of Kingston-upon-Thames,
now President of C. C. C. in Oxford,
By MARY his Wife,
Daughter of Richard Balthrope, Esq.
Servant to the late Queen Elizabeth.

Ten children in one grave! a dreadful sight:
Seven sons, and daughters three, Job's number right.

Childhood and youth are vain, death reigns o'er all,
Even those who never sinn'd like Adam's fall.

But why o'er all? in the first man ev'ry one
Sinned and fell, not he himself alone.
Our hope's in Christ the second Adam; HE
Who saves the elect from sin and misery.

What's that to us poor children? 'tis our creed,
God is a God to the faithful and their seed.
Sleep on, dear children, never more to wake,
Till Christ doth raise you, and to glory take."

He left only one son living at his death.

In the year 1635, when the Book of Sports came out, he was suspended for not reading it, as many more were. He choosed rather to lose his place, than to give countenance to such an abominable practice. During his suspension, he took his degree of Doctor in Divinity at Oxford, which, he says, he did to put the greater honour upon his sufferings. His exercise was greatly applauded. But there were several Doctors in the University whose fingers itched to deal with him, because he was a Puritan; and a country minister, among whom was one, who was so miserably nonplust by Dr Staunton in the disputation, that the auditors hissed him, and called for a candle, that the Doctor might see his arguments. Doctor Staunton took particular notice of this, with thanksgiving, ascribing all the glory to God; and making use of that text, him "that honoureth me, I will honour." God gave him liberally in that hour what he should speak, to the confusion of his enemies. And at this time also, he preached in the University, from Mark viii. 36, when he was signally countenanced from heaven, and the sermon made very successful in doing good.

When the Assembly of Divines was called at Westminster, Dr Staunton was chosen to be a member of that venerable assembly; and he was much esteemed there. He was several times called upon to preach before the Parliament, and his sermons were ordered to be printed. He was also appointed one of the six morning-preachers in Westminster-abbey.

In the year 1648, when the Visitors appointed for the University of Oxford discharged Mr Newlin from the headship of Corpus Christi College, Dr Staunton was constituted President, and succeeded him. He continued here above twelve years, till he was ejected for nonconformity by the King's Commissioners, at the restoration, 1660.—While he was President of that College, his whole deportment was very exemplary. He first put in execution all the statutes, which were most conducive to the advancement of religion and learning, and was often present at lectures and other exercises to encourage the studious, and reprove the negligent. He set up a divinity-lecture every Lord's day, early, in the College-chapel, for exercising the senior students, and initiating them into the holy ministry. He constantly catechised the juniors publicly every Saturday, and preached once or twice every Lord's day, to the edification of many, beside his constant course in the University-church and College-chapel. And, in compassion to the souls of men, he often preached in the country, for which he rather sought opportunities than declined them. And one of the impropriations belonging to the College, about seven miles distant, having but a small stipend, before his time, not sufficient for the external subsistence of a minister, he first went himself, and afterward desired some of the senior Fellows to go over by course, and preach unto the people, which they readily complied with.—When the College affairs called him abroad into remote places, he was always ready to embrace every opportunity of doing good to the souls of mankind. If his business required his stay one day or two in any place, he seldom departed without preaching to the people.—He had a weekly meeting at his own lodgings for prayer and spiritual conference, consisting of college-members and others, wherein he bore a principal part; bringing forth out of his richly furnished store of experimental knowledge, *things both new and old.*—He was constantly present at the public worship in the chapel, morning and evening, to observe and reprove those who were remiss. And when he sat at meat in the College-hall, he always introduced wholesome discourse, tending to the instruction of those who were present. Spiritual discourse was his meat and drink: *His heart taught his mouth, and added learning to his lips.* When a portion of the holy Scriptures was read at dinner, which was the custom there at that time, that all might feed their souls while they were refreshing their bodies; and if there were any difficult places in it, he either propounded them to the Fellows who sat at table with him, for explanation, or performed the task himself. If the chapter read afforded ground for practical observations, it gave great pleasure to the godly to see and hear, how he applied *the great things of God's law*, and raised the mind to some heavenly contemplation. —He was very attentive to introduce such only into the College as discovered some signs of saving grace, or at least such as were docile, apt to learn, and inclinable to that which is good. Accordingly, when any shcolar's place became vacant, and many candidates appeared for it, he desired them, some time before the election, to attend him at his lodgings, where he examined them privately, and procured also testimonials concerning them, from such as knew them; and if, after examination, such a number of electors as was requisite could not agree upon one of them, when, in that case, the election devolved upon him, he always let piety have the honour to turn the scale, if there was an equality, or near it, in other respects. It gave him great pleasure to see parts, learning, and piety, grow together: and indeed they are a happy conjunction; especially in gospel ministers, whose work it is "to make manifest the savour of the knowledge of Christ in every place," 2 Cor. ii. 14. And in such, learning without grace, is like a ship without ballast; the least blast of applause is ready to drive him upon the quick-sands of pride, or upon the rocks of opposition to Christ and to his truth, to his own ruin. Dr Staunton's labour here was not in vain in the Lord: By means of his vigilant care, prudent government, and pious example, religion and learning flourished remarkably in this

College; and many who were educated under his care, became learned, pious, and useful men. Among these was Mr Joseph Allein, minister of the gospel at Taunton, in Somersetshire, and who was a great comfort to this holy man, while he continued in the College; and he was revived to hear, that he proved so eminently pious and useful in the church of God.

When he was discharged from the College, in 1660, he left Oxford, where he had sown much precious seed, and watered it well with his prayers and tears. His departure was very like that of Paul from Ephesus, Acts xx. And recommending himself unto divine Providence to fix the bounds of his habitation, he went first to Rickmansworth in Hertfordshire, where he was well received by persons of all ranks, as a minister of Jesus Christ. His chief design was to settle an able minister there; but his best endeavours were ineffectual. However he found the way to that pulpit himself;—but because the entrance was narrower than in some other places, he sought out a *wider door* and more *effectual.* He preached round about that country, and in the adjacent ones, though an old man, and somewhat infirm, *spending and being spent* in the service of his great Master, till the Uniformity Act imposed a general silence upon the Non-conformists, August 1662. After this he was not willing to be idle; for he observed a day of fasting almost every week, either in his own family, or that of some other godly minister or Christian friend. On such occasions, he endeavoured both to humble himself for his own sins, and on account of the abominations which prevailed in the midst of the land—See Ezek. ix. 4. And he discovered such a brokenness of spirit and dissolved soul, as those present could not readily forget. He then employed some hours in the word and in prayer often on these extraordinary occasions. His wife becoming infirm, he took apartments in a family at some distance, where he was very useful, so long as he lived there, as there was a church in that house. The savour of the knowledge of Christ, and the sense of the power of the world to come, were deeply impressed upon the minds of the inhabitants, during his abode with them. From thence he removed to another family near St. Alban's, in which town he was instrumental in correcting some extravagances. His frequent removals seem to have been designed with a view of doing more extensive service and good in the church of Christ. His last removal of this kind was to a place called Bovingden, a little village in Hertfordshire, famous in history, because of this eminent Divine living some time, and dying there. Here he had an offer of all accommodations gratis. He accepted the offer, but what he saved this way he expended in charity; particularly in the distribution of religious books in that village, and the adjacant places. He also gave some part in money to the poor. Here he attended daily to the duties of the family, and was very careful in the instruction of its members. He enjoyed much retirement in this place, an object which he loved dearly; and had he been born for himself alone, he would have chosen this always, as many worthy men have done, giving retirement the preference to the greatest preferments in church or state. But he had not so learned Christ. He often said, " Woe be to me if I preach not the gospel." He preached constantly. He was afraid that the Lord would come and find him idle. He often rode to St. Alban's, where he was useful to many; and once or twice in the year to London and Kingston. And when he could not preach in a church to many, he preached in a chamber to a few; like Paul, at Macedonia, who preached at the river side to a few hearers of the weaker sex, Acts xvi. 13.—Neither the place nor the hearers recommend our preaching in the sight of God. He was naturally of an exceeding good temper and disposition, gentle, affable, and courteous to all; and his natural temper being embellished with the grace of God, made him exceeding amiable, and very useful in all his conversation. His government of the College savoured much more of lenity and mildness, than of sharpness and severity; and yet he kept his College in very good order.

As a Christian, he was much given to self-examination, a duty which is now much neglected by many. He was very careful to ascertain his evidences for heaven; of which we shall give a specimen here to a believer on the Son of God: He had *the witness in himself*, 1 John v. 10, particularly effectual calling; which is accounted a good evidence for heaven, as appears from Rom. viii. 30. 2 Pet. i. 10. Change of company; choosing the society of the godly, and shunning the company of the wicked, Psal. i. 1. xxvi. 4, 5. cxix. 115. Acts ix. 26. Universal obedience to all God's commands, Psalm cxix. 6. cxxxix. 23, 24. Love to the godly as such, 1 John iii. 14. Sincerity; desiring more to approve his heart to God, than his ways to men: aiming more at God's manifestative glory than his own profit, or the applause of others, 2 Cor. i. 12. Kindly meltings of heart, and deep mournings for sin, upon a sense of God's free love in Christ Jesus, Zech. xii. 10. 2 Cor. vii. 9. 10. Zeal for God, and against sin, John ii. 17. 2 Cor. vii. 11. A love of, and an earnest longing for the appearing of Christ, 2 Tim. iv. 8. Heb. ix. 6. Rev. xxii. 20. And a careful sanctification of the Sabbath, Isa. lvi. 4, 5, and lviii. 13, 14. These evidences of being born again of water and of the Spirit, he says, he found in himself, through the gracious operation of the holy Spirit upon him, if his heart did not deceive him.

He kept a journal of God's favours toward him. This was peculiarly helpful to him in the exercise of grace, and in remembrance of the Divine goodness. We are very ready to forget the word which we hear, the sins which we commit, and the benefits which we receive. A journal or diary is very serviceable to keep us in mind of all these things; and a journal of our sins would soon make an awful catalogue, and might be very serviceable to set them in order before us on days of fasting, and on other occasions, that we might be hereby induced to apply unto the Saviour for pardon and purification.[a]

Dr Staunton gave himself to prayer, like David. Mr Mayo, his Biographer, says, " He was the most praying

a A very extraordinary journal of sins was found in the pocket of John Morris, who was executed at Chelmsford, in Essex, England, for burglary and robbery, as may be seen in the Cambridge Intelligencer, 25th August, 1798.

Christian that ever I was acquainted with." When he came to lodge at any friend's house, his custom was, after saluting such persons as came in his way, to retire to his chamber, and spend some time by himself, before that any friend could speak with him; and at night again, he shut up himself in his chamber a considerable time before any servant could be admitted. He often said to his godly friends, who came to visit him, "Come, might not we pray together before we part?" It might indeed be said, that prayer was his repast. He often wrestled with God as Jacob did.—He prayed in prayer, says Mr Mayo; and he generally wept when he made his supplication, both in fellowship with others, and in secret. Mr Mayo says, that he had the following passage under his own hand:—"The glory be God's; where I have shed one tear in prayer with others, I have, I think, (speaking within compass) shed two in secret betwixt God and mine own soul." He ordinarily performed this duty kneeling, even when he was almost overwhelmed by the multitude around him. He said, "The humblest gesture, as well as spirit, became the duty of prayer; and that he knew no way of wrestling with the Almighty, like that of lying at his feet, and prostrating ourselves before him.

He was a very strict observer of the Lord's day. Some have observed, that the sanctification of the Sabbath is one of the first things which a converted person makes conscience of, and that he is no true Christian who is careless with regard to this.—This eminent divine was very watchful over his thoughts, words, and actions, every day, but more especially on this holy day. It was very rare to hear him speak one idle word, or to see him do one unnecessary action, upon the Sabbath day. On account of his strictness in the observation of that day, he was like Joshua the high priest, and his fellows, *a man wondered at*, Zech. iii. 8, And he was also boldly censured for this by some. Mr Mayo says, that he spent some Sabbaths with him; but alas! he could not kept pace with him: He went from duty to duty, as bees do from one flower to another. From public duty to family duties; from family duty to closet duties, always finding much sweetness and comfort in them all. He used to say, "We must always be good husbands of time, especially of holy time: we must not spend that time, which is not our own, about our own things." He was accustomed to observe private fasts. He often passed whole days in prayer and humiliation, both by himself alone, and in conjunction with his family; especially before the administration of the sacrament of the Lord's supper, and when he found any corruption within beginning to prevail, or gain ground. He mentions one particular instance of spiritual pride, which he was greatly in danger of when a young preacher, and found much subdued by means of this humbling exercise. He set one day apart to make application unto God, with fasting, for strength against that sin; "and from that day forward he felt the neck and heart of it was broken," which is his own expression. And it was a common saying of his, "That spiritual pride is the special sin of young ministers." Fasting on such occasions, in this manner, was the ancient and commendable practice of the saints of the Most High; but alas! it is now almost become obsolete. See 2 Sam. xii. 16. Neh. i. 4 Esth. iv. 16. Dan. ix. 3. And yet the strong lusts of our deceitful and desperately wicked hearts will not be cast out, nor subdued otherwise. Our want of true humility is a great loss here. Dr Staunton's Biographer says, that "he was clothed all over with humility:" therefore he engaged more readily in this humble, and humbling exercise. Humiliation attends humility. He was very familiarly acquainted with the holy Scriptures; and, like Apollos the Jew, who was born at Alexandria, Acts xviii. 24, he was mighty in them, and made much use of them. If a good textuary is a good divine, he excelled in this. His memory was instead of a concordance. He could turn with great readiness to almost any text of the holy Scriptures, and he discovered great skill therein. He certainly might be called the Gospel Doctor, as Wickliffe was; because he was chiefly employed in the study of the holy Scriptures, and they were his principal delight. He delighted more in them than the maid in her ornaments, or the bride in her jewels. He carried along with him the New Testament, or the book of Psalms, always. He generally read a portion of the holy Scriptures first on the morning of each day, which was matter of meditation unto him all the day. And if any proper occasion offered in company, he raised useful observations therefrom, or proposed such practical questions, as were most conducive to the instruction and benefit of the hearers. In pursuing this plan, "his speech was always with grace, seasoned with salt," Col. iv. 6. As salt is a noble preservative from putrefaction, so was his gracious speech in company, from the errors and sins which prevail among mankind. As salt on meat draweth out, and drieth up noxious humours, and renders it more fit for digestion, and more wholesome for nourishment: so was his well-seasoned speech to the conversation of every company;—and as he well knew that salt must be rubbed in, and every vacuity filled with it, before it can produce its effects, so he delivered his gracious speeches with much animation and warmth, that they might properly affect the hearts of his hearers, under the divine blessing.[a] At night, when he thought of going to bed, he made search for some portion of the holy Scriptures, which was suited to his then present thoughts, and that was the subject of his meditation when awake. So great was his delight in the law of the Lord his God, that he made it the subject of his meditation both day and night. See Psalm i. 1, 2. He seldom wrote any letter, without adding three, four, or more texts of the holy Scriptures, as a postscript; and these were very pertinent to the occasion of his writing, the condition of the person to whom he wrote, or to the times, and providences of God. His Biographer says, that he received many letters from him, subscribed in this manner. And it was his custom when he visited any person, or met with any friend, to recommend some text of the holy Scriptures unto their consideration at parting. "Pray," he would say, "let me have one text of Scripture with you, and think of it when I am gone." He had much zeal for God and for his cause. He was fre-

a See Dr Staunton's Christian Conference, page 30.

quently employed in projecting how he might promote the honour and service of God in the world. And he was frequently heard saying to his friends, "Come, what shall we do for God this day? How shall we trade with our talents for the advancement of his glory?" In this, he much resembled the pious Divine, who was educated under his care, Mr Joseph Allein, concerning whom it is recorded, "That he never arose on the morning without some heavenly design of promoting God's glory and the good of souls." Dr Staunton also gave evidence of his eminent zeal for God in sharply reproving sin. Though he seldom sinned in being angry, yet he was often angry with sin, and reproved it. We shall give one instance, where many might be produced. Supping once at an inn, between Oxford and London, where many fellow-travellers did eat together, and one of these abounded in vain and profane discourse; he spake to him, and laboured to convince him of the evil of sin, and of the curse and wrath of God, which did hang over his head; and, afterward, he unfolded unto him the exceeding riches of God's grace to repenting sinners of mankind, and his readiness to receive them through Christ Jesus. Having pointed out the disease, he discovered also the remedy. Upon this the person became more silent; but what farther effect the reproof produced upon him, we are not informed by the narrative: however, the discovery of the riches of divine grace made upon this occasion, greatly affected a young scholar, who was present. It melted his very heart, under the divine blessing, and was a mean to deliver him from a spirit of bondage, under which he had been during some months.

Dr Staunton also excelled in generosity. He devised liberal things, and drew out his soul to the hungry. He was charitable to all men, especially to those who were of the household of faith. He gave liberally to the poor. And "blessed is he who considereth the poor." Psal. xli. 1. While others gathered and heaped up money, he dispersed and scattered his abroad, for the benefit of the poor and needy. His custom was, when he rode abroad, to put as much money into his pocket as he could spare for this purpose; and when he met with any indigent persons, he entered into conversation with them, and upon finding that they were proper objects of charity, he afforded them seasonable relief. In this particular, Dr Staunton's custom resembled that of Cimon, the son of Miltiades, the famous Athenian General, who was much renowned for his liberality as well as for his valour. Cornelius Nepos says, concerning Cimon, that "footmen always followed him with money, that if any one stood in need of his assistance, he might have what he should give him immediately, lest he should seem to deny him, by putting him off."[a] Such famous examples recal to our mind what is said, Job xxix. 12, 13, "I delivered the poor that cried, and the fatherless, and him who had none to help him. The blessing of him who was ready to perish came upon me: and I caused the widow's heart to sing for joy." And also, what is related concerning Cyprian, That he never sent away a widow empty. And he often said, "Let not that sleep in thy treasuries which may be a benefit to the poor." And, it is said, that Mr Fox never refused any one an alms, who asked for Christ's sake. Cornelius Nepos says, concerning Cimon, who is mentioned above, that he was possessed of the greatest liberality: "for he was a man of so great generosity, that when he had estates and gardens in many places, he never placed a keeper in them, for the sake of preserving the fruit, lest any should be hindered from enjoying what he possessed at pleasure.—Oftentimes, when he saw any one badly clothed, he gave him his own coat. His supper was so dressed for him every day, that he invited all whom he saw in the market-place, not invited elsewhere, which he omitted to do no day. His faithfulness was wanting to none, his service to none, his estate to none: he enriched many: he buried at his own expense, many poor people when dead, who had not left wherewith they might be buried."[b]—And all this may be properly applied to our Author, and much more; for he even excelled Cimon in liberality, as his advantages were far superior.

a Nep. Cim. 4.

b Nep. Cim. 2. 4.

He was always ready to give spiritual alms to the poor in spirit, who hungered and thirsted after righteousness, as well as temporal favours to those who were externally indigent. Mr Mayo, his Biographer, says, that "for purse-alms, and spiritual-alms together, I never knew his fellow." He often visited poor and needy families, or called for them as he passed by, and always left somewhat behind him for the benefit of both soul and body. God conferred upon him a competent estate; and by shewing pity to the poor, he did lend to the Lord, Prov. xix. 17, thus honouring him with his substance; accordingly he obliged many by his liberality, as Nepos says of Alcibiades.[a]

He also excelled in Christian conference. Both his dexterity and delight herein were great; and as there is a gift of prayer and of preaching, so without doubt there is a peculiar gift of Christian and godly conference. Our Author enjoyed this to a very great degree: His heart was generally inditing a good matter, and his tongue was like the pen of a ready writer. His lips fed many, and did drop as the honey-comb. He always endeavoured to make his discourse profitable to others; especially by turning their merry and idle talk into that which is serious and useful—and their worldly conversation into a heavenly conversation; which he could do very handsomely, without giving offence. As Cornelius Nepos says concerning Conon, the Athenian, that, when the affairs of his countrymen were in a bad condition, and he had heard that his native city was besieged, "he did not seek a place where he might live safely himself, but from whence he might be helpful to his countrymen."[b] So Dr Staunton always sought how far he might be helpful to his countrymen, especially by Christian conference. He warned the unruly, comforted the feeble-minded, and instructed the ignorant: even those whom others slighted, and did not reckon worthy of their notice, on account of their meanness and ignorance. He used to say, "That their souls were as precious as the souls of

a Nep. Alcib. 3. b Nep. Con. 2.

nobles." When he met with any person occasionally, either in the house or by the way, though a stranger, he immediately entered into conversation with such; and would ask what countryman he was, and where he was born—and, if he thought that he was born again: hereby taking occasion to explain the nature and necessity of regeneration, as Christ did, in his conference with Nicodemus, a ruler of the Jews, John iii. If he met with humbled and burthened souls, or such as were babes in Christ, he treated them suitably, and gently led them to the wells of salvation.

His patience and cheerfulness, under afflictions, were very remarkable. Mr Mayo says, That he was one of the greatest patterns of patience that the age produced: He was never seen out of humour, nor heard repining, though his troubles were considerable. His cheerfulness under his afflictions was admirable. He thereby much recommended the gospel of Christ, and real religion, unto others. He used to be somewhat merry and cheerful in company ordinarily, that he might the more recommend the ways of God, and the religion of Jesus to bystanders; and it is said that he sometimes had success this way. Suidas informs us, that Macarius, by his pleasant discourses on all occasions, drew many into the ways of God. Dr Staunton greatly lamented the unnatural hearts and divisions among Christians.

Upon the whole, what one said with regard to Mr Perkins, may be also applied to Dr Staunton:—"That as his preaching was a commentary on his text, so his practice was a comment on his preaching." And, here we have a shining example among the cloud of faithful and active witnesses, for the imitation of all mankind, in their different stations. Here grace or godliness, and fervour of spirit in serving the Lord, are clearly seen: Here religion and reason meet, and act in conjunction, for the glory of God, and the benefit of mankind; and these complete the man.—For, says an eminent writer, "Religion is as necessary as reason to complete a man: so that you are not men, but beasts, if you do not reverence God's authority, and live in subjection and obedience to him."[a] Let this great and venerable character; this distinguished ornament of his age and country; this divine, eminent for his ability, piety, diligence, and integrity, be often in our view.

The truly ornamental lives of the primitive Christians, and also of our Reformers in later times, were considerable means, in the hand of the divine Spirit, in producing the rapid and extensive spread of Christ's gospel, and advancing his spiritual kingdom among men. And, inattention to the *adorning the doctrine of God our Saviour in all things*, hath contributed much to reduce practical religion to its present mournful decayed state, where it hath been long professed. If the publication of such ornamental lives shall contribute now, in the divine Spirit, in any degree, to quicken and revive us, as in former times, our end is obtained, and God will be glorified, according to Mat. v. 16.

This eminent servant of Jesus Christ—this burning and shining light, was at last seized, all on one side, with the dead palsy, on the 8th of July, 1671. His speech much failed him, and he afterward spake little and seldom.—A friend coming to visit him, asked how he did. He answered in the words of the holy divinely inspired prophet, "In measure God debateth with me; and in the day of the east wind he stayeth his rough wind, Isa. xxvii. 8.—Some time after, he said to a friend who stood by him, "I neither fear death, nor desire life; but am willing to be at God's disposal." A remarkable and very comprehensive saying. Like David, "the man after God's own heart," 1 Sam. xiii. 14, confiding in the grace of God, under the pastoral care of the Lord Jesus Christ, the great Shepherd of the sheep, he *feared no evil, though walking through the valley of the shadow of death*, Psal. xxiii. 4. He saw the Almighty Reedeemer swallowing up death in victory, 1 Cor. xv. 54. The saying is also full of Christian resignation to the sovereign disposing will of Jehovah.

At another time, he expressed the following words,

a Wisheart's Theologia, vol. i. Serm. ix.

very audibly:—"I know that my Redeemer liveth." And soon after, he repeated Psalm xxxi. 5, in verse,

> "Into thine hands, I do commit,
> My sp'rit; for thou art HE,
> O thou Jehovah, God of truth,
> Who hast redeemed me."

While he had ability, he exhorted those around him, to make sure of heaven in the time of health; to keep their evidences fair and unblotted; to remember and keep holy the Sabbath day. He spake with all the fervour of a dying man, and acted like one who earnestly desired to be instrumental of doing good to souls even with his expiring breath, in his last moments. When he could not speak himself, he desired others to read the holy Scriptures to him; directing to the places which he most desired, which were generally the Psalms. He was either without any pain, or felt very little. In this respect, there was a striking resemblance between Dr Staunton's death, and that of the Rev James Beveridge, Minister of the Associate Congregation of Cambridge, State of New-York, North America.—Mr Beveridge sat up in the bed, and said, "I am a dying man;—I am dying fast;—but as to bodily pain, I am free of it. I feel no more of this than you do; nor is there a man in Barnet, (the place where he died) who is more at ease than I am."—Did you ever witness any thing similar to this? The resemblance in the deaths of these two eminent servants of Jesus Christ, was not less remarkable with regard to their use of, and their delight in, the holy Scriptures on their deathbed. Mr Beveridge was chiefly employed for three weeks immediately before his death, in the exercises of prayer and reading the holy Scriptures; and when he was unable to read himself, he desired others to read in his hearing, directing them to the particular passages, and very often made observations as they went along. And farther, Mr Beveridge, at his departure, with an audible voice, twice repeated that passage in the book of Job, xix. 25, 26, "For I know that my Redeemer liveth, &c."

a Christian Magazine, vol. iii. Feb. 4, 1799, Edinburgh.

On the 10th July, Dr Staunton was deprived of the use of speech: He lay four days seemingly in a very comfortable condition, lifting up his eyes and hands toward heaven, with a smiling and cheerful countenance. A little before his departure, when a minister prayed with him, he discovered much affection during the time of the prayer; and when prayer was ended, he took the minister by the hand, and held it fast, expressing his inward joy in God, and thanks to him, by outward signs. He died on the 14th of July, 1671, in the seventy-first year of his age.

His body was interred in the parish-church of Bovingden above-mentioned, under a fair stone, with an epitaph engraven upon it, made by the Rev. Dr Simon Ford, in Latin, English thus:—

"To the memory of
that learned and very pious man,
Edmund Staunton, D. D.
who resigned his soul
into the hands
of the Lord Jesus Christ,
with the greatest peace,
in the
71st year of his age,
on the 14th day of July,
in the year of our Lord 1671."

Mr Mayo says, "His modesty was such, that he never judged any thing he did worthy of the press; yet he consented that his Treatise of *Christian Conference* should be printed. And, having also by me a manuscript of his, entitled, "A Dialogue between a Minister and a Stranger," I thought good to print it with the aforesaid Treatise."

Dr Calamy says, that he published several Sermons preached before the Lord's and Commons;* and his printed Writings which I have seen are:—

* See his Life, by Mayo; Clark's Lives of Eminent Persons, London, 1683, and Wood's Athenæ, Oxon. vol. ii.

1. Rupes Israelis; the Rock of Israel; a Sermon preached from Deut. xxxii. 31, at Westminster, before the House of Commons, at their monthly fast, 24th April, 1644. 4to. London.

2. Phinehas's Zeal in Execution of Judgment: or a Divine Remedy for England's Misery; a Sermon preached from Psal. cvi. 30, before the House of Lords, in Westminster-Abbey, at their solemn monthly fast, 30th Oct. 1644. 4to. London, 1645.

3. A Sermon at Great Milton, from 1 Thess. iv. 14, 9th Dec. 1654, at the funeral of Mrs Elizabeth Wilkinson, late wife of Dr Henry Wilkinson, Principal of Magdalen-Hall, Oxford. Oxon. 1659. 4to.

4. His Treatise of Christian Conference. Lond. 1673.

5. A Dialogue or Discourse between a Minister and a Stranger, about Soul-affairs. London, 1673, and 1774. Both small pieces.

I suppose that he hath some other Sermons extant, which I have not yet seen. I have seen all the above pieces lately, in the county of Surrey, where he laboured many years, except the Oxford Sermon, and in different parts of Scotland. He has a Latin Poem, in Britannia Rediviva, 1660, upon King Charles' Return.

PETER STERRY, B. D.

PREACHER OF THE GOSPEL IN LONDON, AND ONE OF THE ASSEMBLY OF DIVINES AT WESTMINSTER.

PETER STERRY was born in the county of Surrey, in England. He received his education in Emanuel-College, Cambridge, where, in the year 1636, he was chosen Fellow; and he continued sometime Fellow of that College. Having finished his studies at the University, he entered into the holy ministry. During the national troubles and confusions, he appears to have been a very zealous and firm advocate in the cause of the Parliament,

In the year 1643, he was appointed one of the Assembly of Divines at Westminster, for the city of London; and he is said to have given constant attendance during the session. He sometimes preached at Whitehall, and before the Parliament, on which occasions he declared his sentiments with great freedom.—He was afterward one of Cromwell's Chaplains, and he is styled "a high-flown mystical divine." He is said indeed to have been deeply tinctured with mysticism. Mr Baxter observes, that he was intimate with the famous Sir Henry Vane, who was a principal leader in the House of Commons, and one of those singular characters that are seen but once in an age, and was thought to have been of his opinion in religious matters; and that "*vanity* and *sterility* were never more happily conjoined." Sir Henry Vane may, perhaps, be ranked in the first class of mystics; yet he possessed a genius far above the level of mankind; and he is said to have spoken like a philosopher upon every subject except religion. Mr Sterry is said to have imbibed his spirit, in religious matters. Sir Benjamin Rudyard said, respecting his obscurity in preaching, that he was "too high for this world, and too low for the other."[a] Mr Erbery includes him in the list of those divines who had the knowledge of Christ in the Spirit, and held forth Christ in the Spirit. He says, "Those men are nearest to Zion, yet are they not come into it. For as every prophet shall one day be ashamed of his vision; yea, prophecy itself shall fail; so it is manifest those men are of a dark and deeper speech than can be easily understood; therefore it is not Zion."

In the year 1654, Mr Sterry was appointed one of the Tryers of ministers. The approbation of public ministers had hitherto been reserved to the several Presbyteries in city and country; but the Protector observing some inconvenience in that method, and being unwilling to intrust the qualification of candidates all over England to a number of Presbyterians only, who might admit none but those of their own persuasion, he contrived a middle

a Sylvester's Life of Baxter, part i. p. 75.

way of joining the several parties together, and intrusting the work to certain commissioners of each denomination; men of as known abilities and integrity, he says, as any in the nation. This was done by an ordinance of Council, under the date of March 20th, 1654. Mr Sterry was one of those commissioners, who were commonly called Tryers. Among the commissioners were eight or nine Laymen, the rest were Ministers; all thirty-eight; of whom some were Presbyterians, others Independents, and two or three were Baptists. Any five were sufficient to approve; but no number under nine had power to reject a person as unqualified. In case of death, or removal of any of the commissioners, their numbers were to be filled up by the Protector, Oliver Cromwell, and his Council; or, by the Parliament, if sitting. But some of the Presbyterian divines declined to act in that affair, for want of better authority, and because they were not pleased with some of the company.[a]

It is said to be related by Ludlow, that when news arrived of Cromwell's death, Mr Sterry stood up, and desired those about him not to be troubled. "For, said he, this is good news: because, if he was of great use to the people of God when he was among us, now he will be much more so, being ascended to heaven to sit at the right hand of Jesus Christ,—there to intercede for us, and to be mindful of us on all occasions." One observes; "This, if true, was flattery or phrenzy in perfection."

Mr Sterry lived until after the restoration of King Charles II, when he is said to have held a conventicle in London. It has also been remarked, that he and one Sadler were the first who were observed to make a public profession of Platonism in the University of Cambridge.[b]

Mr Sterry is said to have been the author of several tracts. I have seen only the following sermons by him: *The Spirit's Conviction of Sin opened*, in a sermon from John xvi. 8, before the Honourable House of Commons, Fast, Nov. 26th, 1645. 4to. pp. 36. Lond. 1645, and

a Neal's Puritans, vol. iv. chap. iii. b Brook's Puritans, vol. iii.

1646.—And *The Clouds in which Christ Comes*; a sermon from Rev. i. 7, before the House of Commons, Fast, Oct. 27th, 1617. 4to pp. 56. London, 1648.

JOHN STRICKLAND, B. D.

PASTOR OF THE CHURCH AT EDMUND'S IN NEW SARUM, AND A MEMBER OF THE ASSEMBLY OF DIVINES AT WESTMINSTER.

JOHN STRICKLAND was born of, and descended from, an ancient and genteel family of his name in the county of Westmoreland in the north of England. He received his education in Queen's-College, Oxford, where he became a Butler, in the beginning of the year 1618, aged seventeen years. He took the degrees of Arts, and entered into the holy ministry. His first preferment was to be chaplain to the Earl of Hertford. In the month of May, in the year 1632, he was admitted Bachelor of Divinity; and in December that same year, Sir John Horner presented him to the Rectory of Middleton, or Pudimore Milton, in Somersetshire. Wood says that he was always Puritanically affected, which is very probable. Upon the commencement of the civil war, he espoused the cause of the Parliament, and preached frequently to the members, exciting them, as Wood says, "to proceed in their *blessed Cause*." He was chosen one of the Assembly of Divines at Westminster, and is said to have constantly attended. He seems to have been a superadded Divine. He was a Covenanter; and by his fervent zeal for the interests of the Redeemer's kingdom, he has incurred the great displeasure of the Royal party. Wood says, that "he prayed several times blasphemously." But Dr Calamy here observes, "He might as well have said he used to come into his pulpit naked, and without a rag of cloaths on; for the one is not more ridiculous to those who knew the man, than the other." Wood says, "that in 1645 or thereabout, he was made Minister of Peter's le poor in London, where he exercised his gifts against the King and his party, and was never wanting to excite the auditors to carry on the said *cause*." Afterward he became pastor of Edmund's Church in Salisbury. He was eminently distinguished for expounding the holy Scriptures, and for being an excellent Causist. About the year 1654, he was constituted an assistant to the commissioners of Wiltshire for ejecting ignorant and scandalous ministers and schoolmasters. On the fatal Bartholomew-day, he was turned out of Edmund's parish in New Sarum, by the Act of Uniformity, for his refusal to conform to the service, ceremonies and corruptions, of the church of England. He continued among his people, and preached to them as he had opportunity, and suffered many ways for his Nonconformity. Wood says he had been informed, that for keeping conventicles in, and near, Salisbury, he was several times imprisoned. The faithful servants of the Lord Jesus Christ have been oftentimes in prison.

He died in the month of October, in the year 1670. He was well in health and dead, in a very short time. He died on the evening of a Lord's day, after he had preached twice, from 2 Pet. i. 11, and administered the Lord's Supper. Finding himself disordered, he made this known to those persons who were about him, and then sat down in a chair and died. His remains were interred on the 25th of Oct. 1670, and accompanied to his grave by a numerous company of his friends, and Dr Calamy says, "His name is remembered with great respect to this day, at Sarum, where his body lies buried in St Edmund's church-yard." The Doctor also says, that Mr Strickland "was really a great Divine, and generally esteemed." He was accounted a most faithful preacher.[a]

Mr Strickland has published several sermons.—1. *God's Work of Mercy, in Zion's Misery*; a sermon preached from Isa. x. 20, before the honourable House of Com-

a Wood's Athenæ Oxon, vol. ii. Calamy's Account, vol. ii. p. 755. Cont. vol. ii. p. 865.

mons at Margaret's, Westminster, Dec. 27, 1643. 4to. pp. 33. London, 1644.—2. *A Discovery of Peace:* or, *The Thoughts of the Almighty for the ending of the People's Calamities*, &c. on Jer. xxix. 11. 4to. Lond. 1644.—3. *Immanuel:* or, *The Church Triumphing in God with us;* a sermon preached from Psal. xlvi. 7, before the Right Honourable House of Lords, in the Abbey of Westminster, at their public Thanksgiving, Nov. 5th, 1644. 4to. pp. 38. Lond. 1644.—4. *Mercy Rejoicing against Judgment:* or, *God Waiting to be Gracious to a sinful Nation;* a sermon preached from Isa. xxx. 18, before the Honourable House of Commons, in Margaret's, Westminster, Fast, Oct. 29th, 1645. 4to. pp. 28. London, 1645.

In his epistle Dedicatory to the House of Commons, he desires them to attend carefully to the public schools, to reform the Universities, and to plant the Northern counties of England, at Westmoreland, Cumberland, and Northumberland, with able ministers of the gospel; who, by preaching there, and travelling about, would communicate light to those who were living in darkness. Mr Strickland assisted Dr Chambers in writing his apology for the Ministers of the county of Wilts. And, perhaps, he has other writings extant, which I have not seen: but Dr Calamy says, that he did not know of any thing he has printed, beside his sermons before the Parliament.

FRANCIS TAYLOR, B. D.

PASTOR OF YALDING IN KENT, AND A MEMBER OF THE ASSEMBLY OF DIVINES AT WESTMINSTER.

FRANCIS TAYLOR, A. M. was sometime Rector of Chapham in the county of Surrey, near London. He was afterward pastor of Yalding in Kent. To one of those places he was presented by Archbishop Laud.

In the year 1643, he was chosen one of the Assembly of Divines at Westminster, and is said to have given constant attendance during the session. In that venerable Assembly, he was eminently distinguished by his great learning and moderation. He subscribed the Proposition, That "Jesus Christ, as King of the Church, hath himself appointed a Church-government distinct from the civil magistrate." He preached some times before the Parliament; but I have seen only two of these sermons, which are mentioned in their place. His eminent abilities and erudition were most richly displayed in his writings. He wrote the English Annotations upon the book of the Proverbs. He was most peculiarly distinguished for all kinds of Hebrew learning, and the knowledge of Jewish antiquities. He published several very learned and valuable works, and among these a translation of the Jerusalem Targum on the Pentateuch out of the Chaldee into Latin, which he dedicated to the learned Mr Gataker of Rotherhithe. This was accompanied with a Prefatory epistle of the eminently learned Mr Selden to our author. Mr Taylor maintained a learned correspondence with Boetius, Archbishop Usher, and the most celebrated scholars of his time. Among the letters to Archbishop Usher, which are still preserved, there is one from Mr Taylor, dated from Chapham, April, 1635, written in Latin.[a]

Our author removed from Yalding and became preacher in Christ's church in the city of Canterbury, where he appears to have died about the time of the Restoration. He left behind him the character of an able Critic, and of a most celebrated Divine. Mr Neal says, that "he was one of the most considerable Divines of the Assembly." Mr Edward Leigh says, that he was "a learned Linguist, and worthy Divine of the Assembly at Westminster."[b]

He had a son of the same name, who, though he lost the sight of both his eyes by the small-pox, while he was a student in Cambridge, became a minister of considerable learning, of genuine piety, and of great usefulness.

a Parr's Life of Usher. Folio. pp. 475, 476. b Leigh's Treatise of Religion and Learning. Book vi. chap. i.

Dr Calamy says, that "he had an enlightened mind, though a dark body." But he was ejected from Alphage-Church in Canterbury, for Nonconformity, in 1662; silenced and imprisoned. He was cheerful under all his afflictions. He has left behind him a small book of verses, which is entitled, "Grapes from Canaan; or, the Believer's present Taste of future Glory." In this little book may be read his own views and desires of the heavenly felicity, and also his laudable endeavours to recommend it unto his fellow-creatures.

The father, the subject of this Memoir, has left behind him several very valuable, learned, and pious, writings, to praise him in the gate, and to edify the church of Christ.

1. *Faith of the Church of England.* 4to. 1641.—2. *God's Covenant the Church's Plea;* a sermon preached from Psalm lxxiv. 20, before the Honourable House of Commons, at the Solemn Fast, in Margaret's Church at Westminster, Oct. 29th, 1645. 4to. pp. 29. London, 1645.—3. The Danger of Vows Neglected, and the Necessity of Reformation; a sermon preached from Gen. xxxv. 1, before the House of Lords, at a Solemn Fast, in the Abbey-Church, Westminster, May 27th, 1646. 4to. pp. 26. Lond. 1646.— 4. *God's Glory in Man's Happiness, God's Choice, and Man's Diligence, and on Justification,* are small Pieces bound together, 1654.— 5. An Exposition of the first nine chapters of the Proverbs, 2 vols. 4to. 1655.

Beside the Pieces mentioned in the Account of the Author's Life, he has written, *Opuscula Rabbinica.* 1654.— *Targum Prius et Posterius in Esteram.* 4to. pp. 107. Lond. 1655.—*Tractatus De Patribus: Rabbi Nathane Autore. In Linguam Latinam Translatus, Una cum notis marginalibus.* 4to. pp. 142. Lond. 1654.—*Capitula Patrum.* And Leigh, as above-mentioned, says, that he and Dr Boot wrote *Examen Præfationis Morini in Biblia Græca de Textus Ebraici Corruptione, et Græci Authoritate.* And probably he has other works.[a]

[a] Neal's Puritans, vol. iv. Brook's, vol. iii. Calamy's Acc. vol. ii.

THOMAS TEMPLE, D. D.

MINISTER OF BATTERSEA, AND ONE OF THE ASSEMBLY OF DIVINES AT WESTMINSTER.

THOMAS TEMPLE was brother to Sir John Temple, Master of the Rolls, and one of his Majesty's Privy Council in Ireland. He was M. A. and sometime Fellow of Trinity-College, Dublin. He afterward resided for some time in Lincoln-College, Oxford. Wood says, that he continued not long in Lincoln-College. He was settled first at Winwick in Northamptonshire, then at Battersea, in the county of Surrey. At this last place he was labouring in the year 1639, having Mr Samuel Wells for his assistant. Upon the commencement of the civil war, he espoused the cause of the Parliament.

In the year 1643, he was appointed one of the Licensers of the Press for Books of Divinity, and chosen to be one of the Assembly of Divines at Westminster; and he is said to have constantly attended during the session. He was appointed one of the Select Committee for the examination and approbation of those ministers who petitioned for sequestered livings. In the year 1645, he was chosen one of the Committee of Accommodation. In each of these public and important offices, he was eminently distinguished by his great learning and moderation. In the year 1648, he readily united with his brethren, the London ministers, in their declaration and protestation against the death of the King.

Wood says that he was "a forward preacher; and a frequent preacher before the members of the Long Parliament, and that he has certain sermons in print which he preached before the said members."[a] I have seen one of his sermons, which is entitled, *Christ's Government in and over his People*, from Psalm ii. 6, delivered before

a Wood's Athenæ Oxon, vol. i. Neal and Brook's Puritans, vol. iii.

the Honourable House of Commons, at their Public Fast, Oct. 26th, 1642. 4to. pp. 50. Lond. 1642. An excellent sermon. I have seen it in London, and in different parts of Scotland.—Dr Temple is said to have been a learned divine; but we have not been able to receive any more information respecting him, nor to say when he died.

CHRISTOPHER TESDALE, A. M.

PASTOR OF HUSBORNE-TARRANT, AND A MEMBER OF THE ASSEMBLY OF DIVINES AT WESTMINSTER.

CHRISTOPHER TESDALE seems to have been born at Abingdon, a market-town in Berkshire in England; for Wood says "that he was an Abingdon man born." He received his education in New-College, Oxford, where he proceeded Master of Arts, on the 10th of June, in the year 1618. He entered into the holy ministry, and became Pastor of Husborne-Tarrant, in the county of Southampton. At the commencement of the civil war, he espoused the cause of the Parliament; and in the year 1643, he was chosen a Member of the Assembly of Divines at Westminster, and is marked in Mr Neal's list as constantly attending during the session. He was also a preacher before the Long Parliament.

He has published *Hierusalem:* or, *A Vision of Peace;* a sermon preached from Psalm cxxii. 6, *Pray for the Peace of Jerusalem*, before the Honourable House of Commons, at their monthly Fast, at Margaret's in Westminster, Aug. 28th, 1644. 4to. pp. 30. Lond. 1644.[a] In his Epistle Dedicatory to the House of Commons, he says:

"Worthy Fathers of your country, It is said of the Ambassadors of the King of Persia, that coming to Athens, the metropolis of learning, in the time of the Seven Wise Men, they desired that each of them would deliver in his

a Wood's Athenæ Oxon, vol. i. 2d edit.

sentence that they might report unto their Master the Wisdom of Greece, which accordingly they did, only one of them was silent: which the Ambassadors observing, entreated him also to cast in his symbol with the rest. Tell your Prince, saith he, that there are of the Grecians who can hold their peace. Verily, it had been my wisdom to have altogether held my peace in such an audience, or having once spoken, to have proceeded no farther; but as this sermon, such as it is, came to the birth by your authority, so your command now is the midwifery to bring it forth:—I shall then be your remembrancer by restoring the loss of the ear to the eye. Words, we say, are wind, and unless they be taken upon the wing, even while they are flying, and brought to the press, they are gone and lost.—And now, ever honoured Patriots, that I have been God's remembrancer to you, I will be bold to be your remembrancer to God, that the Lord of Peace himself would give you peace always, and by all means, that he would let you see Jerusalem in prosperity, and peace upon Israel, and in recompence of all your work of faith, and labour of love, and patience of hope, he would fill you with length of honourable time here, and with a glorious eternity hereafter.

Your's in the Lord, the meanest and lowest of all my Master's servants,

CHRISTOPHER TESDALE.

In the above-mentioned sermon, he says: "The people were able to say, by their own happy experience, that our Saviour Christ taught as one having authority, and not as the Scribes and Pharisees, those dull Doctors of the Law, who were never able to keep Moses's chair warm, but cold sermons made bold sinners." And in p. 23, he says, "Surely God is about some great work, he intends some great blessing to the land; we trust he will bless our eyes with the happy sight of the King in his beauty, the Lord Jesus upon his glorious throne, with all his holy ordinances about him in their purity and power, that in his time the righteous may flourish, and abundance of peace as long as the moon endureth." And, speaking of fervent prayers with strong cries and tears at the Mercy-seat and the throne of Grace, he says: "A cold suitor begs his own denial; God will have us *Jacobs*, before we shall be *Israels.* "That which is soon gotten, is as soon forgotten.—Though God keep silence sometimes at our prayers, he will not hold his peace at our tears, Psalm xxxix. 12." In the application of the sermon, he makes a motion for a new association: "That zealous prayer, sound counsel, constant resolution, and speedy action, be firmly joined together."—In exhorting his hearers to strive together, as fellow-soldiers, with all their might, *for the Faith of the Gospel,* he says: "We must even compass Babylon, as the Israelites did Jericho, yet seven times more in one day, and shout against it with a great shout, before the walls will come down, and the angel cry, *Babylon is fallen, is fallen.*"

THOMAS THOROWGOOD, B. D.

RECTOR OF GRIMSTON, AND ONE OF THE ASSEMBLY OF DIVINES AT WESTMINSTER.

THOMAS THOROWGOOD received his education in the University of Cambridge, where he proceeded Master of Arts. He entered into the office of the holy ministry, and was afterward Bachelor of Divinity. On the 9th of July, in the year 1622, he, with several other Cambridge Scholars, was incorporated of the University of Oxford. Wood says, "that they were taken into the bosom of this University."—In the troublesome times of the civil war, Mr Thorowgood espoused the cause of the Parliament, and was called to preach before them, and chosen one of the Assembly of Divines at Westminster; and is represented as constantly attending. In the Ordinance of Parliament for calling an Assembly of Learned and Godly Divines in 1643, he is said to be "Thomas Thorowgood of Massingham," but in the year 1644, he is said to be Rector of Grimston, in the county of Norfolk.

He has published, *Moderation Justified, and the Lord's being at hand Improved;* a sermon preached from Phil. iv. 5, at Westminster, before the Honourable House of Commons, at their Solemn Fast, Dec. 25th, 1644. 4to. pp. 33. Lond. 1645.—*Jews in America:* or, *Probabilities that the Americans are of that Race.* With the Removal of some contrary reasonings, and earnest desires for effectual endeavours to make them Christian. 4to. pp. 139. Lond. 1650.

It has been said, that the American Indians have called themselves the children of Abraham, Isaac, and Israel. Mr Thorowgood grounds his conjectures on their own acknowledgment, their rites and customs, and their manner of speech, resembling those of the Jews, and the like.

ANTHONY TUCKNEY, D. D.

MINISTER OF BOSTON, MASTER OF EMANUEL AND ST. JOHNS'-COLLEGE, PROFESSOR OF DIVINITY, IN THE UNIVERSITY OF CAMBRIDGE, AND A MEMBER OF THE ASSEMRLY OF DIVINES AT WESTMINSTER.

ANTHONY TUCKNEY was the son of Mr Tuckney, Minister of Kirton, about three miles from Boston in Lincolnshire. He was born in Sept. 1599, and educated in Emanuel-College, Cambridge. When he had taken the degree of Master of Arts, he, for some time left the College, and became domestic chaplain to the Earl of Lincoln. But being afterward chosen Fellow of his College, he returned thither, and continued there till after his commencing Bachelor of Divinity. During that time, he was a most diligent and conscientious tutor. He trained up many pupils, who were afterward highly useful both in church and state; and who always retained a grateful remembrance of him. He left the University upon the invitation of the people of Boston, in his native country. Upon their solicitation, he became assistant to the celebrated Mr John Cotton, minister of Boston. He continued in that relation with Mr Cotton, until he removed to America. After Mr Cotton's removal to New England, in the year 1633, Mr Tuckney, who had for some time been Mr Cotton's assistant, became his successor in the pastoral office at Boston. He continued his ministry in that place during a sore visitation of Divine Providence by the pestilence; and he met with some disturbance from the Spiritual courts.

In the year 1643, he was called up to London by the Parliament, to sit in the Assembly of Divines at Westminster. He and Mr Coleman were chosen Members of that Assembly for the county of Lincoln. The times being very troublesome and dangerous, during the heat of the war, he took his whole family with him to London, and never returned to dwell in Boston. But, at the desire of the people, he retained his title to the place, until the year 1660, when King Charles the Second came in, and then he resigned it, and Dr Howe succeeded him. After he left the place, he received none of the profits. He was very highly esteemed in the Assembly, and is marked as constantly attending during the session. He was appointed one of the Committee for the examination and approbation of those ministers who petitioned for sequestered places. In 1645, he was chosen one of the Committee of Accommodation. He had a considerable hand in the Assembly's Confession of Faith, and Catechism. It is said, that many of the Answers in the Larger Catechism, and particularly the exquisite exposition of the Commandments, were his, and were continued for the most part in the very words which he brought in.

After he had been some time at London, he was settled minister of Michael-Quern, at the upper end of Cheapside, where he continued till 1648; with the exception, that after he became Master of Emanuel-College, which was in 1645, he spent some months in the year at Cambridge. In 1648, he removed to Cambridge with his family, and was that year Vice-Chancellor of the University. In the year 1653, when Dr Thomas Hill died, Dr Arrowsmith was chosen Master of Trinity-College, and Dr Tuckney was chosen Master of St. John's-College,

And he succeeded Dr Arrowsmith as Royal Professor. He was eminently courageous in opposing orders sent by the higher powers. He was a man of great humility; and yet few, if any, ever maintained their authority better than he did in the University when Vice-Chancellor, and in the College of which he was Master. Many gentlemen and ministers sent their sons to that Seminary of learning merely on his account, that they might have the benefit of his instruction.

After the Restoration of King Charles the Second, he was one of the Commissioners at the Savoy, but had no hope of any accommodation upon seeing how affairs were conducted. Before the time for the conferences was expired, he received a letter from the King, desiring him to resign both his Mastership and Professorship, which if he did, his Majesty, in consideration of his great pains and diligence in discharging the duties of his office, would oblige his successor to give him sufficient legal security, to pay him one hundred pounds yearly during his natural life. The Doctor thought that it would answer no good end to contend with the Court in that juncture, and that it would not be long that he could keep his places as things were then managed; and accordingly, upon receiving the King's letter, with another accompanying it from the Earl of Manchester, he resigned both his places. The annuity which was promised to him was punctually paid him, for several years, by Dr Gunning, who succeeded him. Wood, speaking of this annual allowance to Dr Tuckney, which was given by Dr Gunning, says, "Which act of his, being excellent and singular, is here remembered to his everlasting fame."

Dr Tuckney is classed among the Ministers, Masters of Colleges, &c. who were ejected or silenced after the Restoration, by, or before, the Act of Uniformity, in Dr Calamy's Account. Dr Tuckney, upon leaving the University of Cambridge, retired with his family to London, and lived in St. Mary-Axe, and continued there until the plague in 1665, preaching sometimes in his own house, and occasionally in the families of several friends.

In the time of the sickness he lived at Colwick-Hall

near Nottingham. There he was not long after troubled and confined; but it was in a gentleman's house, where he was treated very civilly, and within a few months discharged. After the Five-Mile-Act came out, he shifted about in several counties. He removed to Oundle in Northamptonshire, and from that place to Warmington, in the same county; and after the dreadful fire of London in 1666, in which his Library was burned, he removed to Stockerson, in Leicestershire; and thence to Tottenham, near London, and from that, in 1669, he removed to Spittle-yard, London, where he died in the month of Feb. 1670, in the seventy-first year of his age. And he has left behind him the character of an eminently pious and learned man, a genuine friend, an indefatigable student, a candid disputant, and an earnest promoter of truth and godliness. It was his custom to have a sermon preached in the chapel of Emanuel, and of St. John's College, the morning after every public commencement, by one who had been of the College. This laudable custom was carefully observed many years.

Dr Tuckney has several Writings, which praise him in the gate. He published some small Pieces himself: *The Balm of Gilead for the Wounds of England;* a sermon preached from Jer. viii. 22, at Westminster, before the Honourable House of Commons, at the Solemn Fast, Aug. 30th, 1643. 4to. pp. 43. Lond. 1643. This sermon was again printed in a small size, Lond. 1654.—*Death Disarmed; and the Grave Swallowed up in Victory;* a sermon preached from 1 Cor. xv. 55, at Mary's in Cambridge, Dec. 22d, 1653, at the funeral of Dr Thomas Hill, with an Account of his Life and Death, and two sermons more from the same text, preached afterward in the same place; small size, pp. 135. Lond. 1654.—*None but Christ;* a sermon from Acts iv. 12, preached at Mary's in Cambridge, on the Commencement Sabbath, July 4th, 1652; to which is annexed, An Inquiry after what hope may be had of the Salvation of Heathen, Jews, Infants, Idiots, &c. now under the Gospel. Small size, pp. 143. London, 1654.—*A Good*

Day Well Improved, in five sermons, from Acts ix. 31, and a sermon from 2 Tim. i. 13. 1656. And after his death, were published forty sermons of his upon several occasions, 4to. pp. 698. Lond. 1676. And his Prælectiones Theologicæ; Theological Lectures and Exercises, in the University, 4to. Amsterdam, 1679. In Latin. These Lectures, in which there is a very fine Dissertation against propogating religion by the sword, were refused a Licence in England, and therefore were printed in Holland.[a]

THOMAS VALENTINE, B. D.

MINISTER OF CHALFONT GILES, AND A MEMBER OF THE ASSEMBLY OF DIVINES AT WESTMINSTER.

THOMAS VALENTINE was a great sufferer for truth, in the cause of Nonconformity. He felt the shocking oppression and cruelty of the ruling prelates in England, in his time. In the year 1633, when the King, by the recommendation of Laud, republished the *Book of Sports*, for the encouragement of recreations and pastimes on the Lord's-day, he and his brethren felt the iron rod of their tyrannical oppressors. This profane book opened a flood-gate to every manner of licentiousness, and was the unhappy instrument of very great oppression to many eminently pious and learned divines, and to great numbers of his Majesty's best subjects. The ruling prelates, though not authorized by law, required the clergy to read that book publicly before the congregation. The Puritans refused to read it, and were suspended, and subjected to great sufferings, for their refusal. Dr Calamy informs us, that Mr Valentine was suspended by Sir John Lamb, Dean of the Arches, for not reading *the Book of*

a Calamy's Account, vol. ii. Cont. vol. i. Neal's Puritans, vols. iii. and iv.

Sports. And we are also told, that Mr Wroth and Mr Erbery from Wales, Mr James from Gloucestershire, and Mr Thomas Valentine, minister of Chalfont St. Giles, with many others, were brought from various parts of the country, and prosecuted in the High Commission.[a] Mr Valentine was afterward appointed one of the Assembly of Divines at Westminster, and is represented as constantly attending during the session. He has some sermons extant; which he preached before the Long Parliament. Dr Calamy says, that he was "a very popular and taking preacher." He was ejected from Chalfont St. Giles, in the county of Bucks, by the Act of Uniformity.[b]

His Writings.—A sermon from Zeph. iii. 8, before the House of Commons, at their Fast, Dec. 28th, 1642. 4to. Lond. 1643.—2, "A Charge against the Jews, and the Christian World, for not coming to Christ, who would have freely given them Eternal Life;" a sermon before the Peers, from John v. 40, at Westminster Fast, 26th May, 1647. Lond. 1647.—3. "Christ's Counsel to Poor and Naked Souls;" a sermon from Rev. iii. 18, before the Commons, Fast, 29th Sept. 1647. Lond. 1647.

From what Mr Valentine has published to the world, he appears to have been a very sweet evangelical preacher, and a divine of considerable talents and learning. I have seen his sermons in different parts of Scotland.

RICHARD VINES, A. M.

MINISTER OF THE GOSPEL AT WEDDINGTON, AND MASTER OF PEMBROKE-HALL, CAMBRIDGE.

RICHARD VINES was born at Blason, in the county of Leicester, in England, about the year 1600. He was

a Brook's Puritans, vol. i. Introduction, pp. 77, and 78.
b Calamy's Account, vol. ii.

educated in Magdalen College, Cambridge, where he continued a student some years, and commenced M. A. Dr Fuller, in his History of the University of Cambridge, says, "every year this House produced some eminent scholars, as living cheaper, and more private, freer from *town-temptations* by their remote situation." It produced an eminent scholar indeed, when it produced Mr Vines. Here he displayed much quickness of wit, and pregnancy of parts. And it was observable in him, that while these rendered him lively and acute, yet he was never wicked nor profane. He was not given to any extravagance in his youth. He studied hard, and made great proficiency. Having finished his courses at the University, he was chosen to be schoolmaster at Hinckley, a small town in Leicestershire, on the borders of the county toward Warwickshire. "A profession wherein many a good minister had been," says Dr Fuller. And Jacombe says, "I could instance in rare instruments of God's glory, in the church of Christ, who began with that employment; but Mr Vines is enough to himself, and may rather give than take credit from any."

From being schoolmaster at Hinckley, he was called to be minister of the gospel at Weddington, a private village, in Warwickshire. Here he laboured very diligently and faithfully; and his ministrations were attended by many from adjacent places. Caldcot, a small parish near Weddington, falling vacant, was given to him also. Beside, at the request of several friends, when preaching the gospel of Christ was a rare commodity, and much desired, he undertook a lecture at Nuneaton, a large market-town near him, in the county of Warwick, and about seven miles from Coventry. This lecture was much frequented, and carried on with great profit to the hearers, from whom he had high applause. Both ministers and private Christians travelled many miles to hear him. But, at the commencement of the civil war, in the year 1642, he was driven from his house and charge, and forced to take shelter in Coventry, with many others, a city in Warwickshire, situated ninety miles north-west of London. Here he was not idle; but set up a morning-lecture, with other ministers. And the inhabitants were so affected with his ministry, that they earnestly desired him to continue with them. And indeed "*it is a pity that great lights should burn out in little rooms,*" says Jacombe.

When the Parliament called an Assembly of Divines in 1643, he was nominated a Member of it, chosen to be one of their number for Warwickshire, and deputed to have a share in that great and important work performed by this Venerable Assembly. And Jacombe says, in his sermon at Mr Vines' death, "It was a mercy to the church of God that he was so, for how much service he did there in the matter of *church-government,* may safely be concealed, scarcely be expressed without offence." And Fuller, in his Worthies of England, says, he was "the champion of the party in the Assembly, therefore called their Luther." Upon his coming to London, he was chosen to preach some times before the House of Commons at their Solemn Fast; and was much esteemed for his sound judgment, masculine and nervous oratory. He had then a call to Clement's Danes, a very large and considerable parish, became minister there, and his preaching is said to have been highly beneficial to many souls, and several persons of quality were his constant hearers. Essex-house being in that parish, the Earl of Essex was his frequent hearer, and continued his true friend until his death. After some time, by the solicitation of the Earl of Essex, he resigned that place and removed to Walton in Hertfordshire. He afterward accepted an invitation to Lawrence Jewry, London; where his excellent talents were still employed in promoting the interests of the Redeemer's kingdom, and the salvation and happiness of his people. Many flocked to his ministry, and his labours were crowned with remarkable success. While pastor of Lawrence Jewry, he was chosen one of the weekly lecturers at Michael's, Cornhill. Upon the death of the Earl of Essex, the Parliament appointed a public funeral for him, which was attended with great solemnity in Peter's church, Westminster, when Mr Vines preached his funeral sermon to a very great audience, which was composed of persons of high distinction.

In the year 1644, Mr Vines was appointed Master of Pembroke-hall, Cambridge, by the Earl of Manchester; and, it is said, that he was a most industrious and useful man in his College, having both much learning, and the genuine spirit of government. It has been affirmed, that few persons were better qualified for that exalted station. There he earnestly promoted true religion and sound literature to the utmost of his power, and restored the college to a very flourishing condition, until, in the year 1649, he was turned out for refusing the engagement, which was a stone of stumbling and a rock of offence to many conscientious ministers in England, at that time.— He was appointed by the Parliament one of the Assistant Divines at the Treaty of Uxbridge. Whitlocke, speaking of this treaty, says, "that while Dr Steward and Dr Sheldon argued *very positively*, that the government by bishops was of *Divine Right;* Mr Vines and Mr Henderson argued *as positively*, but *more moderately*, to the contrary, and that the government of the church by Presbyteries was of *Divine Right*."[a]

Mr Vines was also chosen a member of the Committee of Accommodation, and was chairman at their meetings. On the subject of a general accommodation of all parties, he wrote an excellent letter to Mr Baxter, discovering his mild and accommodating spirit. In the year 1645, he was one of the Committee of learned Divines appointed by the Assembly to prepare the Confession of Faith. In 1648, he was appointed, by order of the Parliament, one of the Assistant Divines at the Treaty of the Isle of Wight; on which occasion he was greatly applauded by his own party, particularly for proving the sufficiency of Presbyterian Ordination. During the treaty, he had much converse and some disputation with the King. His Majesty highly valued him for his learning and ingenuity, and seldom spoke to him without touching his hat, which Mr Vines returned with most respectful language and gestures.

a Whitlocke's Mem. pp. 119, 123, 126, as with Brook.

When the King was under sentence of death, Mr Vines, Mr Calamy, and other ministers in London, presented their duty to his Majesty, with their humble desires to pray with him, and perform other services, if he would be pleased to accept them. The King returned them thanks for their kind offers and love to his soul, hoping that they and all other good subjects would, in their addresses to God, be mindful of him; but he declined the services which they offered, having chosen Dr Juxon, in whose abilities to administer comfort to him, he could confide.[a]—About the year 1653, Mr Vines was appointed, by order of the Parliament, one of the Divines to draw up the Fundamentals, which were to be presented to the House.

Messrs Ashe and Calamy, who were intimately acquainted with Mr Vines, say, that to their knowledge, he was a hearty Presbyterian. And Dr Fuller classes him among those Divines, who in their judgment favoured the Presbyterian discipline, or in process of time were brought over to embrace it.—He was a very solid, judicious, and orthodox divine. He was mighty in the Scriptures, and an interpreter one of a thousand. He was a great champion in controversy, and eminently distinguished for giving a mortal wound to error. In his powerful and spiritual ministry, he insisted very much upon the all-important doctrine of justification, which he had thoroughly studied; greatly debasing man and exalting the Lord Jesus Christ, and his finished righteousness. Toward the conclusion of his ministry, he discovered much earnestness, in driving man out of himself unto the Saviour; throwing down all false foundations of the hope of heaven, and warmly recommending the only sure foundation which Jehovah has laid in Zion. He seriously exhorted his hearers to study heart-holiness and a conversation becoming the gospel of Christ. And he knew well how to speak a word in season to wounded spirits.

After a very laborious and highly useful life, Mr Vines,

a Wood's, Athenae Oxon, vol. ii. 2d edit. p. 699.

at length, became the subject of painful bodily affliction. He had formerly a very strong constitution; but his strength soon began to abate after he was settled at Lawrence-Jewry. His infirmities rapidly increased. He was much afflicted with pains in his head, which greatly hurt his sight, that he could not see to read the largest print; nor could any glasses help him. But he would not cease from his public labours in the Lord's vineyard. He was firmly resolved both to spend and to be spent in the service of the church of Christ: like a candle which wastes itself, to give light unto others. His voice, at last, became very low. A few days before his death, when he was preaching at Gregory's church, a rude fellow cried aloud to him, "Lift up your voice, for I cannot hear you:" to whom Mr Vines replied, "Lift you up your ears, for I can speak no louder." The day before he died, he preached and administred the Lord's Supper; and about ten o'Clock the same evening, when going to bed, he was seized with a bleeding at the nose, and died quietly and comfortably between two and three o'clock the next morning, aged fifty-five years. His remains were interred, with great lamentation, in the church of Lawrence-Jewry, 7th Feb. 1655; when the celebrated Dr Thomas Jacombe preached his funeral sermon, giving him the following high commendation.—He was a burning and shining light in his day, possessing very excellent parts, even taller by the head than most of his brethren. He was an accomplished Scholar, a perfect Master of the Greek language, an excellent philologist, and an admirable orator. He was a ready and close disputant, and appeared to the admiration of many, in the Treaties of Uxbridge and the Isle of Wight. He wished to die praying or preaching. He had an undaunted spirit; and, like Luther, nothing would hinder him from a courageous and conscientious discharge of his duty.—Mr Newcomen calls him, "a most acute disputant, a very happy public speaker, and an eminent divine." He was accounted "the very prince of preachers, a thorough Calvinist, and a bold honest man, without pride and flattery." Dr Fuller styles him "an excellent preacher, and the very champion of the Assembly:" and adds, "that he was constant to his principles, yet moderate and charitable toward those who differed from him."[a] Many funeral poems and elegies were composed upon his death, both in Latin and in English. I have seen and read thirteen of these. Dr Jacombe says, that he was very averse to print any thing of his own. But Dr Fuller observes, that "many most able scholars have never publicly appeared in print: nor can their less learning be inferred from their more modesty."

Mr Vines was author of the following learned Writings, which have been printed.

1. *Caleb's Integrity in following the Lord fully;* a sermon from Numb. xiv. 24, before the Honourable House of Commons, at their Solemn Fast, Nov. 30th, 1642. Lond. 1642, and 1646.

2. *The Impostures of Seducing Teachers Discovered;* a sermon from Eph. iv. 14, 15, before the Lord Mayor and Court of Aldermen of the City of London, at their Anniversary meeting, April 23d, 1644. The 2d edit. Lond. 1656.

3. A sermon preached from Isa. lxiii. 8, before the Right Honourable, the Lord's and Commons, at Margaret's, Westminster, upon Thursday, July 18th, 1644, being the day of Public Thanksgiving for the great victory obtained near York. 4to. pp. 21. Lond. 1644, and 1646. At the conclusion of this sermon, he says, "Finally, let all men fortify their hearts against the evils which follow good success, that we be not made more loose in our Covenant than before; for we have reason to account this day to be the fruit of our entering and holding fast unto that. I say this day, which shews you the two nations formerly *two*, now made one in a covenant, in the field together, in a victory together, and in a pulpit to-

a Fuller's Worthies of England, fol. Lond. 1662. Ch. Hist. Cent. 17. Clark's Lives, Neal's Puritans, vol. iii. and iv. Jacombe's Fun. Ser. for Mr Vines.

gether, paying unto God his praises, and so let them be for ever, *one Judah yet ruling with God, and faithful with the saints.*"

4. *The Posture of David's Spirit, when he was in a Doubtful Condition;* a sermon from 2 Sam. xv. 25, 26, before the House of Commons, Oct. 22d, 1644. Fast, 4to. pp. 26. Lond. 1644.

5. *The Happiness of Israel;* a sermon from Deut. xxxiii. 29, before both Houses of Parliament, the Lord Mayor and Aldermen of the City of London being present, in Christ's Church, on a day of Solemn Thanksgiving, 12th March, 1645. The 2d edit. Lond. 1656.

6. *The Purifying of Unclean Hearts and Hands;* a sermon from James iv. 8, before the Honourable House of Commons, at their Solemn Fast, Jan. 28th, 1646. 4to. pp. 31. Lond. 1646.

7. Funeral Sermon for the Earl of Essex, from 2 Sam. iii. 38. Oct. 22d, 1646. Lond. 1646.

8. The Authors, Nature, and Danger, of Heresy; a sermon from 2 Pet. ii. 1, before the Commons, 4to. pp. 70. Lond. 1647.

9. *Obedience to Magistrates both Supreme and Subordinate,* in three sermons from 1 Pet. ii. 13—16, and Tit. iii. 1, preached upon the Anniversary election-day of three Lord Mayors successively, Sept. 29th, 1653, 1654, and 1655, at the Church of Lawrence-Jewry, London, 1656.

10. *The Corruption of Mind;* a sermon preached from 2 Cor. xi. 3, at Paul's, 24th June, 1655. Lond. 1656.

I have seen these twelve sermons, by Mr Vines, collected into one volume, in Scotland.

Mr Vines was also the author of *A Treatise of the Right Institution, Administration, and Receiving, of the Sacrament of the Lord's Supper;* delivered in twenty sermons at Lawrence-Jewry, London. Small 4to. pp. 376. Lond. 1657, 1660.—*Christ the Christian's only Gain,* 1661.—*God's Drawing and Man's Coming to Christ,* 1662.—*The Saint's Nearness to God,* a small piece, Lond. 1662. Dedicated by Wm. Drury to the

Countess Dowager of Exeter. It is said, that it was written upon request of an acquaintance.

Since writing the above, I have seen the third edition of Mr Vines's Treatise on the Sacrament of the Lord's Supper, London, 1677. And my Correspondent at London says, "a Bookseller told me that he had sold the single Funeral Sermon for the Earl of Essex, with a Head, by Vines, for 7s. and 6d. to be sent to Scotland."—A Funeral Sermon for Mr William Strong has been mentioned, in the list of Mr Vines's Writings, but I do not recollect to have seen it.

When Mr Vines was schoolmaster at Hinckley, he had for one of his pupils Mr John Cleivland, a noted Royalist and popular Poet in the reign of Charles I, who, it is said, "owed the heaving of his natural fancy, by the choicest elegancies in Greek and Latin, to Mr Vines."[a]

GEORGE WALKER, B. D.

PASTOR OF JOHN EVANGELIST'S, LONDON, AND A MEMBER OF THE ASSEMBLY OF DIVINES AT WESTMINSTER.

GEORGE WALKER was born at Hawkshead, a market-town, in Fourness, in Lancashire, a maritime county, in the North-west part of England, in the year 1581. He was descended from religious parents, who were highly beneficial unto him, in his early years, and peculiarly attentive to his education. It pleased the Lord to visit him, when he was a child, with the small-pox, and while those persons who attended him stood expecting his dissolution, he started out of a trance, with the following remarkable ejaculation, or fervent prayer, *Lord, take me not away till I have shewed forth thy praises.* This induced his parents, upon his recovery, to devote him in a solemn manner, to the important work of the holy ministry.—

a Brook's Puritans, vol. iii. under Vines.

With God all things are possible. That remarkable visitation with the small-pox seems to have proved a happy dispensation, under the divine blessing, to the subject of this Memoir, in great mercy laying the foundation of his spiritual health in his seemingly dangerous sickness. It is a happy sickness which terminates in the recovery of the soul to God. And the mercy which this unexpected recovery brought with it, was a rich equivalent for all the former sorrows of his relations and attendants. Both his religious parents and himself beautifully imitated the pious *gratitude* of that good *woman*, who, when recovered by *Jesus, immediately arose, and ministered to him, and to his followers.* Mat. viii. 14, 15. Those lives which are mercifully spared by the goodness of God, and that strength which is renewed by his almighty power, should be faithfully, affectionately, and solemnly, devoted to his most honourable service. Sparing our lives, healing our diseases, and renewing our strength, are certainly intended to fit us for action, that we may gratefully minister unto Christ, and unto those who are his, for his sake. Our religious youth, having been highly favoured with the pious instructions of his parents in very early life, found these instructions of peculiar advantage to him, while he was a stranger and pilgrim on the earth. In due time, he received a liberal education in St John's-College, in the University of Cambridge, where he applied with great assiduity to his studies, and his proficiency was very conspicuous in different parts of literature. He was esteemed an excellent logician, a good Oriental scholar, and an eminent divine. He proceeded B. D. in that College. Having finished his studies at the University, he went to London; and, in the year 1614, he became Rector of John the Evangelist, in Watling-street. In that place, he continued a faithful and labourious minister of the glorious gospel of the grace of God nearly forty years. He refused all other and higher preferments, though frequently offered him. He did not preach the gospel of Christ with a view to obtain preferment, but with the noble view of being an instrument in gaining precious and immortal souls to his glorious Redeemer. About the same time, he became chaplain to Dr Felton, bishop of Ely, who made choice of him on the very morning of his consecration. And the celebrated Dr Featly made choice of him as his second, in one of his disputations with Father Fisher, the famous Jesuit. Mr Walker was eminently distinguished by his very bold and successful opposition to popery, and he readily engaged several times in public disputations against its errors and superstitions, with some of the most subtle Jesuits. He boldly attacked that dreadful system of error and corruption, which is entirely contrary to the pure religion of the Bible, destructive to the souls of the human race, and inconsistent with both civil and religious liberty. He judiciously exposed the falsehoods of the Romish Church, and became very conspicuous as a zealous friend of the Reformation. On the last of May, in the year 1623, he had a public dispute with a popish priest of the name of Smith, before a very large assembly; and, by the consent of both parties, the account of it was afterward published, and entitled, "The Sum of a Disputation between Mr Walker, Pastor of St. John the Evangelist, and a Popish Priest, calling himself Mr Smith, but indeed Norris, printed 1623, 4to." Wood says that Norris was a Doctor of Divinity, and a publisher of several little popish pamphlets about the same time. In the following year, Mr Walker engaged with Fisher, the Jesuit, and thereupon published *Fisher's Folly Unfolded; or, The Vaunting Jesuit's Challenge Answered.* London, 1624. He had many encounters with Fisher, and several other persons, who were accounted the most able disputants of the Romish persuasion.

Mr Walker was a divine of genuine piety, and of very strict Sabbatarian principles. He frequently urged from the pulpit, with great energy, the necessity and propriety of an exact observance of the Lord's-day. The very little respect which is paid to the Lord's day, greatly contributes to increase that general inattention and indifference which evidently threaten to undermine the morals and religion of this country The observance of one day in seven, as a day of rest from business, and of engaging in religious exercises, is certainly one of the most ancient and venerable institutions which we have. Experience seems to have established a general idea of both its wisdom and utility. If mankind are capable of religion, as they certainly are, it appears to be of very great importance and utility to them, that there should be, at regular intervals, a cessation from labour, and opportunities of receiving religious instruction, and of having serious impressions made upon the mind. Mr Walker's very great regard for the Sabbath makes a conspicuous appearance in his writings. His sermons, which were afterward printed against the profanation of the Sabbath, and other evil practices and opinions, procured him much trouble, and two years' imprisonment. In the year 1635, having openly avowed his sentiments in one of his sermons, and warmly recommended the holy observance of the Sabbath, as opposed to a book which was published by Bishop White of Ely, and set forth by public authority, he was convened before Archbishop Laud, when he received canonical admonition. In the year 1638, he was prosecuted and severely censured in the Star-chamber. Having preached a sermon in his own church, with a view to prove *that it is a sin to obey the greatest monarch on earth, in those things which stand opposed to the commands of God*, he was committed twelve weeks to the custody of a pursuivant, to whom he paid fees to the amount of twenty pounds. Upon his prosecution, he was shut up ten weeks close prisoner in the Gatehouse, and at last compelled to enter into a bond of a *thousand* pounds, to confine himself prisoner in his brother's house at Cheswick, when his living was sequestered. He continued a prisoner about two years, but was afterward released by an order of the Parliament.

His case was laid before the House of Commons, in the year 1641, when it was resolved, "That his commitment from the Council-table for preaching a sermon, October 14, 1638, and his detainment twelve weeks for the same, is against the law and the liberty of the subject. That the prosecution of the said Walker in the Star chamber, for preaching the said sermon, and his close imprisonment thereupon for ten weeks in the Gatehouse, and the payment of twenty pounds fees, is against law and the liberty of the subject.—

That the five passages marked in the sermon, by Mr. Attorney and Sir John Banks, contain no crime, nor deserve any censure, nor he any punishment for them.—That the enforcing the said Walker to enter into the bond of one thousand pounds, for confinement in his brother's house at Cheswick, and his imprisonment there, is against law.—That the sequestration of the parsonage of the said Walker, by Sir John Lamb, was done without any warrant and against the law of the land.—That Walker ought to be restored to his parsonage, and the whole profits thereof, from the time of the said sequestration, and to have reparation for all such damages as he hath sustained by these several imprisonments, and his case transmitted to the lords."

After Mr Walker's release from confinement, he returned to his benefice and ministerial charge in Watling-Street, London, where he continued the rest of his days without further molestation. Laud, in the height of his pride, affirmed, and bade him assure himself of it, *That he should never come into a pulpit to preach any more.* But the proud persecuting prelate of Canterbury was once mistaken. Almighty God often controuls the wrath of wicked and unreasonable men, and when it rages like the sea in a storm, he says to it, *Hitherto shalt thou come, and no further. No weapon that is formed against thee shall prosper; and every tongue that shall rise against thee in judgment thou shalt condemn. This is the heritage of the servants of the Lord, and their righteousness is of me, saith the Lord. Yet if any man suffer as a Christian, let him not be ashamed; but let him glorify God on this behalf.* Mr Walker's persecutors could prove nothing against him, but a stedfast and consistent attachment to divine truth. May it ever be our constant care *to preserve consciences void of offence both toward God and toward man*, as he did. And may the unsearchable riches of divine grace always enable us *by well doing, to put to silence the ignorance of foolish men!*

In the year 1643, Mr Walker was chosen one of the Assembly of Divines at Westminster, where, by his munificent and generous behaviour, he gained a distinguished and shining reputation. He is marked in Mr Neal's list, as giving constant attendance. In the year following, he was appointed one of the Committee for the examination and ordination, by imposition of hands, of those persons who were judged qualified to be admitted into the sacred Ministry. The same year he was one of the witnesses against Archbishop Laud at his trial, when he deposed that the archbishop had endeavoured to introduce Arminianism and the popish superstitions into the church of England. He preached sometimes before the Parliament. Though Wood reproaches him with having preached, after the Long Parliament began, against the King and his followers, and having published several things, which before he was not permitted to do, he united with his brethren, the London ministers, in their protestation against the King's death, declaring that his majesty ought to have been released. He was a member of the first provincial assembly in London, and sometimes chosen moderator. He died in the year 1651, aged about seventy years, and his remains were interred in his own church in Watling-Street. Dr. Fuller says, "He was well skilled in the Oriental languages, and an excellent logician and divine. He was a man of a holy life, an humble spirit, and a liberal hand, who deserved well of Zion College library; and who, by his example and persuasion, advanced about a thousand pounds for the maintenance of preaching ministers in his native country. He ever wrote all his sermons, though making no other use of his notes in the pulpit, than keeping them in his pocket, being wont to say, that he thought he should be out if he had them not about him." Wood allows that he was a learned man, but a severe Puritan.[a]

a Wood's Athenæ, vol. i. 2 edit. Fuller's Worthies of England, 1662, folio. Brook's Puritans, vol. iii. Walker's Ser.

Mr Walker has published beside the two pieces which are mentioned in the account of his life, *Socinianism in the Fundamental Point of Justification Discovered and Confuted.* A small book, pp 355. London, 1641. An excellent work.—*The Doctrine of the Holy Weekly Sabbath*. 1641.—*The Manifold Wisdom of God;* in the divers dispensation of Grace by Jesus Christ. A small book, pp. 173. London, 1640, 1641.—*God made Visible in all his Works*, 1641.—A Sermon preached from Psalm lviii 9. before the House of Commons, Fast, 1644. 4to. pp. 53. London, 1645.

JOHN WALLIS, D. D.

AN EMINENT MATHEMATICIAN AND DIVINE, SOMETIME SAVILIAN PROFESSOR OF GEOMETRY, IN THE UNIVERSITY OF OXFORD, KEEPER OF THE ARCHIVES, MEMBER OF THE ROYAL SOCIETY OF LONDON, SOMETIME ONE OF THE SECRETARIES TO THE ASSEMBLY OF DIVINES AT WESTMINSTER, AND CHAPLAIN IN ORDINARY TO KING CHARLES THE SECOND.

JOHN WALLIS was born at Ashford, a large market town in the county of Kent, in England, on the 23d of Nov. 1616. His father was John Wallis, M. A. an eminently pious, learned, and orthodox divine, and minister of Ashford in Kent. His mother was Joanna, daughter of Henry and Sarah Chapman of Godmersham in Kent. His father died Nov. 30, 1622, when he was very young, and he was then and afterward under the tender care of his mother. She was peculiarly careful in the pious and prudent education of all her children; *bringing them up in the nurture and admonition of the Lord.*

In the year 1625, there was a great plague in London and many other places, and particularly in Ashford, which caused many of the inhabitants to remove for their safety. On this occasion, the subject of this Memoir was sent to Leygreen, near Tenterden, a market-town in

Kent, to receive his grammatical education. In that place, he was the scholar of Mr James Moffat, a Scotchman, for several years. By him he was well grounded in the technical part of grammar, so as to understand the rules, and the reason of these rules, with their application in such authors as are usually read in grammar-schools.

Our young scholar was always inclined from his very childhood, not only to learn rules by rote, but also to understand the true meaning and the reasons of these rules. The school at Leygreen at length broke up, when, for learning, he might have gone to the University; but he was thought too young; and therefore he was sent, toward the end of Dec. in the year 1630, to Felsted-school in Essex, which was at that time a school of good reputation, where he continued two years. By this time, he was well grounded in the Latin and Greek languages, having read several authors in both of these. He was always principally attentive to the grammar. And he had been accustomed in both schools to speak Latin, which rendered that language very familiar to him; and which he afterwards found highly advantageous. He had also learned so much Hebrew as that, by the help of his grammar and dictionary, he could proceed farther without a teacher. Afterward, in the University, he became very accurate in that language, especially in the grammatical part, the changes of points and seat of accents, and read over the Hebrew Bible, or the greater part of it, more than once. The knowledge of Hebrew is unquestionably essential to the knowledge of the Holy Scriptures. The want of that knowledge in Ministers of the Gospel is condemnable. While it is a disgrace to the order, it is a serious loss to the Christian community. —Our celebrated scholar pursued his studies, at all times, with great vigour, industry, and success. He was now also so far instructed in the rudiments of logic, music, and the French language. And during a vacation from school, when he was about a fortnight at home with his mother at Ashford, he learned the practical part of common Arithmetic from a younger brother of his, which was his first entry into mathematics, a science in which he afterward became very eminent.

In Dec. 1632, he was sent to the University of Cambridge, and there admitted in Emanuel-college, under the tuition of Mr Anthony Burgess, whom he himself says, was a pious, learned and able scholar, a good disputant, a good tutor, an eminent preacher, a sound and orthodox divine, and afterward minister of Sutton-Cofield, in Warwickshire. He there proceeded Bachelor of Arts at the beginning of the year 1637, and Master of Arts in 1640. His literature and talents appeared in a very respectable light. He was always reputed one of the best scholars of his rank.—In the year 1640, he entered into the holy ministry. He was ordained by Bishop Curle, who was then Bishop of Winchester. He was about a year chaplain to Sir Richard Darby, at Buttercrum, in York-shire. He afterward removed to the family of Lady Vere, widow of Lord Horatio Vere, with whom he continued about two years. While with her, he was sometimes in London, and sometimes at her house at Castle Hedingham in Essex. He was afterward, about a year, Fellow of Queen's College, Cambridge. But, when he married Susanna Clyde, of Northiam, in Essex, March 4th, 1644–5, he quitted that fellowship.

About the year 1644, he was chosen one of the Scribes or Secretaries to the Assembly of Divines at Westminster. He was not in the Assembly from the commencement of the session, nor is his name in the ordinance for calling that Assembly; but he came into it at the time above-mentioned, and was one of the Scribes or Secretaries. During his attendance on that Assembly, he was a minister in London, first in Fenchurch-street, and afterward in Ironmonger-lane; where he continued until his removal to Oxford. There he prosecuted his studies, till he at length attained to such proficiency, as to be reputed one of the first mathematicians of the age in which he lived. He had a most accurate judgment in all mathematical studies; and was successful to admiration in decyphering the most intricate writings; an argument of a most subtil searching wit and judgment. In a very great variety of cyphered letters, he discovered the mind of the writer, in spite of every method which art could devise to prevent it. Our author's own account of his first outset in this business, is as follows. "About the beginning of our civil wars, in the year 1642 or 1643, a chaplain of Sir William Waller shewed me one evening just as we were sitting down to supper at Lady Vere's, as a curiosity, an intercepted letter written in cypher, and it was, indeed, the first thing I had ever seen of the kind; and asked me, between jest and earnest, if I could make any thing of it, and was surprised when I told him, perhaps I might. It was about ten o'clock when we rose from supper, and I withdrew from my chamber to consider of it. By the number of different characters in it, there being not more than 22 or 23, I judged it could be no more than a new alphabet; and before I went to bed I found it out; which was my first attempt upon decyphering." He must have been endued with a ready turn for conjecture, because in several letters a figure or a character was used for whole words, and beside a great many nulls interspersed, which must have added very much to the difficulty of decyphering. He was often employed in that arduous work, and complained of being badly rewarded for his services.

When Academical studies were much interrupted by the civil wars in both the English Universities, the eminently learned men resorted to London, and there formed assemblies. Mr Wallis belonged to one of these, who met once a week, to discourse on philosophical subjects: and this society was the beginning of what was afterward incorporated under the name of the Royal Society. In 1649, he became Savilian Professor of Geometry at Oxford, where he passed agreeably the remainder of his days, in the cultivation of those sciences, which he much improved to the honour both of himself and of his country. He opened his lectures on the last day of October, with an inaugural speech in Latin, which was printed. On May 31st, in 1654, he took the degree of Doctor of Divinity. In 1658, he was chosen Keeper of the Archives of the University of Oxford. Upon the Restoration of King Charles II, he met with great respect; the King himself entertained a favourable opinion of him; he was therefore not only made one of the King's chaplains, but also confirmed in both his places of Savilian Professor and Keeper of the Archives. In 1661, he was appointed one of the Divines, who were empowered to review the Book of Common Prayer. He afterward complied with the terms of the act of Uniformity, and is said to have continued a steady conformist to the church of England till his death. He was one of the first members of the Royal Society, and kept a constant correspondence with it by letters and papers, many of which are published in the Transactions of that Society. Lord Brounker, Sir Isaac Newtown, Dr Burrow, Dr Wallis, Mr Gregory, Dr Halley, with other learned men of that day, were the respectable members, who, in the year 1668, formed the Royal Society in London.[a] William Brounker, Lord Viscount of Castle Lyons in Ireland, and first President of the Royal Society after its incorporation, was engaged in a literary correspondence on mathematical subjects with Dr Wallis.[b] And Dr Wallis addressed to the celebrated Mr Boyle his hypothesis on the flux and reflux of the sea, which was printed in the Philosophical Transactions. The wonderful memory of our learned author, who could extract the cube root by mere mental process to an hundred places of figures, is said to be well known in England. These operations required a seclusion of himself from the external impressions of light, sound, and muscular action. And we are informed that similar mental operations in the case of Mr Brindly, in extraordinary mechanical pursuits, required the same seclusion in the solitude of his bed.—Dr Wallis has attempted to prove that Gerbertus, Archbishop of Rheims, afterward Pope Silvester the II, had, before the year 1000, learned the art of Arithmetic as now practised with only nine characters, from the Saracens in Spain. Edward Bernard, a learned English astronomer and linguist, particularly eminent in Oriental literature, studied mathematics under Dr Wallis. We

a Monthly Review, vol iv. p. 582.
b Gen. Biogr. vol ii. under Brounker.

mention this, because the reputation of an illustrious man is augmented by that of his disciples.—Dr Wallis's depth of science and acuteness of intellect led him early to pronounce on speculation, the practicability of teaching the deaf to speak, and to verify his theory in the tuition of Mr Whally, a young gentleman of Northampton, deaf and dumb from his birth. Having fully succeeded in the first essay of his skill, he made a second with the son of Admiral Popham; and was afterward employed in instructing deaf and dumb pupils without teaching them to speak. He was also an eminent divine; and much employed in defence of the Trinity and of the Sabbath, He had a very clear apprehension in divine things, and could accurately distinguish truth from error.—He died, Oct. 28th, in 1703, in his 88th year, being 87 years, 3 months, and 5 days old; leaving behind him one son and two daughters, to lament the loss of a good father. His remains were interred in the chair of Mary's Church, in Oxford, where a handsome monument is erected to his memory.

The Monthly Reviewers, in reviewing Dr Wallis's Sermons, which were first published in the year 1791, give him the following character: they say that he was "a man of great ability, learning, worth, and celebrity, in his day; although, as it must happen, in the progress of years, to numbers who, like Dr Wallis, merit a favourable report, his memory has been too much disregarded.—Though Dr Wallis did not apply to this science, (mathematics) as a business, until he was upward of forty years of age, it presently appeared that he had a genius particularly fitted for the pursuit. He soon became eminent: of which he gave proof by the works that he published. He was allowed to be the first mathematician of the time in which he lived, next to Sir Isaac Newton. One *accidental* testimony of this, is his 'Commercium Epistolicum,' occasioned by a challenge given by Mr Fermate (a Frenchman,) to the English, Dutch, and French mathematicians (except those of Paris,) to answer a numerical question. The Doctor accomplished it with great applause, and received, among other commendations, in a letter addressed to Sir Kenelm Digby, the farther acknowledgement, 'Now must Holland yield to England, and Paris to Oxford.'

In connection, it is proper to mention his acuteness as a *decypherer;* in which art he was employed for several years, with great success, although for sometime with but inconsiderable emolument to himself. On the whole, Dr W. must be regarded as a man who stands high in the learned world. As a theologian, he ranked with those who at that time claimed the denomination of orthodox, and he appears to have been an adept in that kind of divinity: but, which is far more important, he also appears earnestly solicitous to advance the true interest of his hearers. Learned and skilful he certainly was; and we apprehend he acted conformably to the noble dictates of virtue, integrity and goodness."[a] This may be considered as a respectable testimony to Dr Wallis's professional character. We are told more particularly, that he had a vigorous constitution, a strong mind, calm, serene, and not easily ruffled or discomposed. He was reckoned the glory and ornament both of his country, and of the University. He had a clear apprehension, a solid and penetrating judgment. And he was a most strenuous and warm defender of the all-important doctrine of the Ever-blessed Trinity, and of the Sabbath-day. Memoirs of Dr Wallis, with a fine Portrait, were published in the Universal Magazine for March, 1802, vol. 110, London.

Dr Wallis's writings are numerous. In 1642, or 43, he published a book, which was entitled, *Truth Tried,* or Animadversions on Lord Brook's Treatise, called, *The Nature of Truth.* This, perhaps, might be thought a very learned work when it was written, though it may now be reckoned too scholastic, being written in the manner of the Peripatetic philosophy.—In 1650, he published some Animadversions on a book written by Mr Baxter, entitled, Aphorisms of Justification and of the Covenant.—About the year 1653, he published his *Tractus de Lo-*

a Monthly Review, Enlarged, vol. viii.

quela Grammatica Physicus, since many times reprinted: Or, *Grammatica Linguæ Anglicanæ, cum tractatu de Loquela seu sonorum formatione*, in 8vo In the piece *de Loquela*, he informs us, that he has philosophically considered the formation of all sounds used in articulate speech, as well of our own, as of any other language that he knew; by what organs, and in what position, each sound was formed; with the nice distinctions of each, which in some letters of the same organ are very subtile: so that by such organs, in such position, the breath issuing from the lungs will form such sounds, whether the person do or do not hear himself speak. Pursuing these reflections, he was led to think it possible, that a deaf person might be taught to speak, by being directed so to apply the organs of speech, as the sound of each letter required, which children learn by imitation and frequent attempts, rather than by art. Thus he undertook to teach some dumb persons to speak, with success.—

In the year 1653, was published, in Latin, his Grammar of the English tongue, for the use of Foreigners, in a manner entirely different from any thing of the kind, it is said, which has been before or since published. In this ingenious work, a remark is made which may be new to some of our readers; speaking of words which begin with or, as if, says he, these took their meaning from the cross—among other illustrations, he adds, Richard III, formerly King of England, was called, *Crouched-back*, not because his back was crooked, but because he wore on his back the form of the cross.—Of this valuable work, a new and handsome edition was printed, in 1765, at the expence of Mr Thomas Hollis, who was remarkable for appropriating a considerable part of his large estate to acts of *peculiar* benevolence, particularly to the patriotic purpose of reprinting scarce and valuable publications. Of his impressions of those, he usually gave away great numbers, especially to seminaries of learning, in most parts of the globe, as well as to private persons; and such presents were often clothed in the most elegant and expensive binding. He caused a fine portrait of Dr Wallis to be prefixed to his edition of a Latin Grammar, from a drawing by Cypriani, which print is well copied and placed as a frontispiece to the Doctor's sermons.

In 1655, Mr Thomas Hobbes having printed his Treatise *de Corpore Philosophico*, Dr Wallis, the same year, published a confutation of it in Latin, under the title of *Elenchus Geometriæ Hobbianae*, which was printed in Octavo at Oxford. This so provoked Mr Hobbes, that in 1656, he published it in English, with the addition of what he called, "Six Lessons to the Professors of Mathematics in Oxford," 4to. Upon this, Dr Wallis wrote an answer, in English. entitled, 'Due Correction for Mr Hobbes; or School Discipline for not saying his Lessons right, 1656.' To this Mr Hobbes replied in a pamphlet, entitled, Stigmai, or Marks of the Absurd Geometry, &c. of J. Wallis, 1657, 4to. This was immediately rejoined to by Dr W. in 'Hobbiani Puncti Dispunctio,' 1657; and here the controversy seems to have ended at this time. But in 1661, Mr Hobbes printed 'Examinatio,' &c. This caused Dr W. to publish the next year, 'Hobbius Heautontimoruminos,' in 8vo. addressed to Mr Boyle.— In 1657, he collected and published his mathematical works, in two parts, titled, 'Mathesis Universalis,' 4to. —In 1658, he published in 4to. at Oxford, 'Commercium Epistolicum de Questionibus Mathematicis.' He still continued to publish many useful mathematical works. In 1676, he gave an edition of Archimedes's Avenarius; and Dimensio Circuli. In 1682, he published from the Mss. Claudii Ptolemaei Opus Harmonicum, in Gr. with a Latin version and notes; to which he afterward added an Appendix.—He published several theological pieces. I have seen a quarto vol. of his theological discourses; containing 8 Letters and 3 sermons concerning the Blessed Trinity; *The Life of Faith*, in two sermons, to the University of Oxford; *God's Sovereignty and Justice*, in two sermons, before the Judges of Assize, from Gen. xviii. 25.—*The True Treasure*, two sermons from Mat. vi. 19, 20 21. *God's Deliverances of his People*; from 2 Cor. i. 10. Of Repentance; and Discourses concerning Melchizedek, Job, and the

Titles of the Psalms, &c. London, 1692. He also published two sermons, entitled, *The Necessity of Regeneration;* and *The Resurrection Asserted.*—He also wrote a Defence of the Sabbath, respecting which we find a Dissenter expressing himself to him as follows: "I have read over the first part of your Discourse upon the Christian Sabbath; and liked it so well that I was eager to get the second. In reading thereof I could not but admire the large measure of the understanding which the Lord out of his goodness has been pleased to bestow upon you above many other pious and learned men."—He also wrote 'A Defence of Infant-Baptism,' Oxford, 1697. —I have 'A Brief and Easy Explanation of the Shorter Catechism, which was presented by the Assembly of Divines at Westminster to both Houses of Parliament, by Dr Wallis. A small piece, the 8th edition, London, 1659. His pamphlets, letters, and books, on several subjects, are very numerous.

In 1697, the Curators of the press at Oxford thought it for the honour of the University, to collect all his works which had been printed separately, as well in English as in Latin, and to publish these together in Latin. They were accordingly published at Oxford, in 1699, in 3 vols. folio; and dedicated to King William.—A posthumous vol. of 13 sermons, with an ample account of Dr Wallis' life, was published at London, in 1791, in 8vo. from the author's original Mss. by his great grandson, Mr William Wallis, who had in possession some valuable Mss. and till lately a rich gold medal, which had been presented to Dr Wallis by the Elector of Brandenburgh, with an honourable inscription and a chain of gold of so great value as to produce from a refiner the sum of sixty-two pounds five shillings. In these sermons, the reader may see both the author's learning and piety; with the Calvinistic doctrines of the Reformation, and of the Holy Scriptures. They may indeed be accounted too *Puritanical* by some persons; but they will not be the less acceptable on that account to others. The style is plain, and the matter excellent.[a]

a Memoirs prefixed to these Sermons, and Universal Magazine, for March 1802, vol. cx.

JOHN WARD.

SEVERAL persons of this name were eminently pious, learned, and conscientious nonconformists, in England, about the time that our author lived. John Ward, who, in this place, comes under our consideration, was sometime Minister of the gospel, in Ipswich, the capital of Suffolk, in England. He was one of the Assembly of Divines at Westminster, superadded, and said to have constantly attended.

I have seen the following sermons, by this Mr Ward. —*God Judging Among the Gods:* a sermon from Psalm lxxxii. 1, before the Commons, Fast, 26th of March, 1645. London, 1645.—*The Good-Will of Him who Dwelt in the Bush;* or, *The Extraordinary Happiness of Living Under an Extraordinary Providence:* a sermon preached from Deut. xxxiii. 16, before the Lords, in the Abbey-Church, Westminster, Thanksgiving, 22d of July, 1645. London, 1645.

JOHN WHINCOP, D. D.

JOHN WHINCOP was a member of the Assembly of Divines at Westminster. His name is found in the ordinance of Parliament for calling an Assembly of learned and godly Divines; and he is said to be of St. Martin's in the Fields. In Neal's list, he is described, D. D. and as giving constant attendance during the session.

A John Whincop, D. D. said to be sometime Fellow of Trinity College, Cambridge, and about the year 1644, or 1645, Pastor of the Church of Clothall, in Hartfordshire, has two sermons extant, which I have now before me. 1. God's Call to Weeping and Mourning, from Isa. xxii. 12. preached to the House of Commons, at their solemn Fast, 4to. pp. 51. London, 1645.—2. Israel's Tears for Distressed Zion, from Psalm cxxxvii. 1, to the House of Lord's, at their solemn Fast, 4to. pp 47. London, 1645. Probably, though I cannot say certainly, this was the Dr Whincop, who was a Member of the Westminster Assembly. But be that as it may, I cannot give any farther account of any person of that name.

JEREMIAH WHITAKER, A. M.

PASTOR OF STRETTON, AND OF MARY MAGDALEN BERMONDSEY, IN SOUTHWARK, AND A MEMBER OF THE VENERABLE ASSEMBLY OF DIVINES AT WESTMINSTER.

JEREMIAH WHITAKER was born at Wakefield, in Yorkshire, in the year 1599. He was instructed in grammar-learning, at the place of his birth. His early piety was very remarkable. He appears to have been a young convert. The Lord, who hath *loved* his own chosen ones, *with an everlasting love*, seems to have *drawn him with loving-kindness*, in the days of his youth, Jer. xxxi. 3. As an evidence of this, while he was a boy at the school, he discovered strong and warm affections toward such as were religiously disposed. And Christ says, "By this shall all men know that ye are my disciples, if ye have love one to another," John xiii. 35. This is the livery of his family, the distinguishing character of his disciples.[a] See 1 John iii. 14. And, he often travelled eight or ten miles, in company with religious persons, to hear an awakening, soul-refreshing, and heart-searching sermon. He also joined with such persons in prayer, and other holy exercises and duties. And being very capable to take notes of sermons, he was peculiarly helpful to those private Christians, with whom he associated, in repeating what they had publicly heard. "Then they who feared the Lord spake often

a Henry, on the place.

one to another," Mal. iii. 16. And, here we may observe, that divine grace makes a very great change upon mankind-sinners, when they commence its subjects. Before, they are under the condemning and enslaving dominion of sin; being "by nature the children of wrath, even as others," Eph. ii 3. The grace of God doth not find mankind religious and godly; but it makes them so. As Seneca said concerning Plato, that philosophy did not find Plato noble, but made him so.[a] "By the grace of God I am what I am," 1 Cor. xv. 10. And here we may certainly say, in the language of Juvenal, great respect is due to youth of this description; and the church of Christ ought to be deeply concerned for their welfare.[b] Such are the hope of the church. Farther, with relation to our young Whitaker, while he was at the grammar-school, *there was found some good thing in him toward the Lord God of Israel*, 1 Kings xiv. 13. For on several occasions, he discovered a very strong propensity unto the office of the holy ministry. His father endeavoured earnestly, with repeated solicitations, to dissuade him from that choice; but could not prevail. And, the pious subject of this Memoir was so far from repenting of his choice, that both now, and afterward, he continued to magnify that office more and more. He often said, "I had much rather be a preacher of the gospel, than an emperor." And when he was, by a special designation of Divine providence, vested with that office, he esteemed it the most signal honour of his life to be employed therein. And, as the same objects of pursuit do not please all men; but some make choice of one employment, and others of another, according to their various inclinations:[c] So among different choices, this was his fixed and permanent choice. Accordingly, when a motion was once made to him, to be the head of a College in the University, he readily replied, "My heart doth more desire to be a constant preacher, than to be the Master of any College in the world."

a Sen. Epist. 44.
b Maxima debetur puero reverentia, Juv. 14, 47.
c Horace, Ode 1.

When he was sixteen years of age, being well instructed in grammar learning, he was sent to the University of Cambridge, and admitted into Sidney-College, where he had a liberal education, and proceeded in arts. He was soon held in high reputation for his excellent parts, and scholarship. And his name is enrolled among the learned writers of that College, by Dr Fuller, in his History of the University of Cambridge.[a] He commenced bachelor of arts, when he was twenty years of age. Afterward, he taught the free school in Okeham, the chief town in Rutlandshire, where he continued about seven years. Here he married the daughter of the Rev. and eminent William Peachy, minister at Okeham. By her he had four sons, and three daughters. He designed all his sons for the holy ministry, such was his regard for the service of Christ, his Lord and Master. And he lived to see two of them ordained to that office. One died while he was a student in Cambridge. He appointed the other one to be educated for that office. Being vested with that office which he so ardently desired, he entered upon a pastoral charge at Stretton, in the county of Rutland, where he continued a careful, faithful, and diligent minister of the gospel, about the space of thirteen years. He was now in his own element, like a fish in the water, or a bird in the air. Beside his pastoral employment, preaching twice every Lord's day at Stretton, he also constantly carried on a weekly lecture at Okeham; and supported some other institutions of that kind in the neighbourhood. —He set apart days for fasting and humiliation in secret and private often; and was very ready to join in such exercises, when called thereto, either in Rutlandshire, or in the adjacent countries. He was equally attentive to family duties, and the devotion of the closet, wherein he ardently sought communion with God. His ordinary course in his family was, to worship God, and to expound some part of the Holy Scriptures, twice every day. Beside, he read parts of God's word in secret; and he usually read all the epistles in the Greek Testament twice every

a Hist. page 154.

fortnight.[a] And when by extremity of pain and weakness, he could not read himself, he employed others to read to him. Hence he was *mighty in the Scriptures*, like Apollos, Acts xviii. 24. This course he earnestly commended to his eldest son, as an excellent mean, to make him both a ready and a profitable preacher.

While he lived in Rutlandshire, the book allowing sports on the Lord's day made its appearance. This he refused to read, although it was ardently pressed upon him, both by commands and threatenings. And afterward, when called to give in his answer relative to a contribution among ministers, to maintain a war against the Scots, he openly told the bishop, or his chancellor, that his conscience would not permit him to do it. This answer, given with zeal and courage, exposed him to the hazard of losing both his ministry and benefit, as the times then were. Upon this, one of his neighbours, pitying him and his family, through false compassion, payed the money required, and subscribed Mr Whitaker's name without his knowledge. This was long concealed from him; but when the deed was made known to him, he expressed his displeasure against it, with many complaints, and much grief of heart.

In the year 1643, he was nominated one of the Assembly of Divines at Westminster, on account of his eminent piety and learning. And he was accounted very useful and advantageous in that Assembly, by his brethren there, and acquaintances. Upon his coming to London, he was chosen and called to the pastoral charge of Mary Magdalen Bermondsey, a rectory in Southwark. In relation to the acceptance of this charge he consulted many godly and judicious ministers. And with their concurrence and approbation, he accepted it. He was now *in labours more abundant*, 2 Cor. xi. 23. Distinguished from many of his brethren, by more eminent services. He preached three or four sermons generally every week; two in Southwark, his own charge, one at

a Clarke's Lives of ten eminent Divines, London. 1662; and Ashe's Sermon at his funeral, page 57.

Westminster, and one at Christ-Church, London. And when he gave up his lecture at Christ-Church, he undertook another at Stepney. Beside, he was engaged in two lectures quarterly at Michael's Cornhill. And he preached monthly at the morning exercise, or else he assisted on the days of fasting in the conclusion of these exercises. Beside, he preached many occasional sermons, at the dispensation of the sacrament of the Lord's supper, and at funerals. Add to all this, his attending the work of the Assembly of Divines. In a word, he never withdrew from any opportunity of preaching, or serving the church of Christ otherwise, if he was in health. And though he preached so often, his sermons were not mean or empty; but solid and judicious. This narrative may call to our mind, Paul's commendation of Epaphroditus, his *brother, and companion in labour*, who, *for the work of Christ was nigh unto death, not regarding his life, to supply* the church's *lack of service*, Phil. ii. 25—30. And it calls upon all students of divinity, and ministers of the gospel, in a particular way, to be active and diligent in the work which Christ hath appointed them. "For Christ keeps no servants to be idle. Christ's servants receive their all from him; and our receiving from Christ is in order to our working for him.—The manifestation of the Spirit is given to every man to profit withal."[a] And the slothful servant is the wicked servant; whose *doom* is tremendous indeed, Mat. xxv. 26—30. "Whatever our particular snares in life may be, let us think of the *doom* of the *slothful servant*, to awaken our souls, and to deter us from every degree of unfaithfulness."[b] And let us imitate the diligence and faithfulness of this eminently laborious servant of Jesus Christ. "Setting before us excellent examples useth to spur us on to an imitation of them."[c]

Mr Whitaker was of the Presbyterian persuasion, and had a chief hand in composiong the Defence of the Gos-

a Henry on Mat. xxv. 14.
b Doddridge on Mat. xxv. 30. Improvement.
c Wishart's Theologia, vol. i. Disse. 7. Serm. 34.

pel Ministry, published in the year 1654, by the Provincial Synod of London. Dr Fuller ranks him among those, in the Assembly of Divines at Westminster, who in their judgment favoured the Presbyterian discipline, who *seemed to be pillars*, as on whose abilities the weight of the work mostly lay.[a] And Neal says, "No man was more beloved by the Presbyterian ministers of London than Mr Whitaker."[b] He refused the *engagement;* though he was thereby in danger of losing his lecture at Westminster. In these times of awful apostacy, confusion, and corruption, he discovered an undaunted courage, and much Christian magnanimity, both in public and private, in behalf of truth and holiness, against every prevailing evil, whether error or immorality. In his sermons preached at Westminster, from Eph. ii. 2, 3. concerning men's *walking according to the course of this world and fulfilling the lusts of the flesh;* and during the military despotism of Oliver Cromwell, he shewed much zeal for the glory of God, and warm attachment to his Lord and Master, Jesus Christ. When the stormy tempest seemed to blow harder and harder; and the faithful were in danger of suffering much *for righteousness' sake*, as he was riding with one of his intimate friends, past Tyburn, where many malefactors had been put to death, he stopped his horse, and expressed the following words with great affection: "Oh what a shame is it, that so many thousands should die for the satisfaction of their lusts, and so few be found willing to lay down their lives for Christ! Why should not we, in a good cause, and upon a good call, be ready to be hanged for Jesus Christ? It would be an everlasting honour: and it is a thousand times better to die for Christ, to be hanged, or to be burnt for Christ, than to die in our beds."

He much lamented the wars between England, Scotland, and Holland. He often told an intimate friend of his, that England's breach with Scotland, and the blood that was shed, together with the other sad consequences

a Church Hist. Cent. 17. Book 11. Sect. 9.
b Hist. Purit. vol. iv. Chap. 3.

thereof, had made such impression upon his heart, that the sorrow would never be removed until his death. And, the sufferings both in Holland and England, in the sea-fights, were an heavy burden upon his spirit.

With relation to his more particular character, as a Christian, the fruits, or graces of the Spirit, mentioned Gal. v. 22, 23. *love*, *joy*, *peace*, *long-suffering*, *gentleness*, *goodness*, *faith*, *meekness*, *and temperance*, all shined with remarkable lustre in him. And the Lord very graciously added humility, as a crown to all his other graces. This set a lustre on the whole. He was indeed *clothed with humility*. And we may say with regard to him, what Dr Fuller says, concerning Dr John Reynolds, in point of humility: "Admirable that the whole should be so "*low*, whose *several parts* were so *high*."[a] He conversed most familiarly with the poorest Christians, even with babes in Christ; and was very communicative, "like a tree loaden with fruit, bowing down its branches to all who desired to ease it of the burden thereof."[b] And few men of his estate, did so abound in works of charity. He often said, "It is a brave thing, when a man together with a full estate, hath a charitable heart." Sometimes upon special occasions, he gave away all the money that he had in the house. He frequently gave twenty shillings to a poor saint; and he had many experiences of God's gracious returns in such cases. By his last *will*, he gave twenty pounds to the godly poor of his own parish. And while he lived, he greatly abounded in kind and compassionate actions to the necessitous and afflicted saints around him. When he saw the Lord Jesus Christ *an hungered*, in his disciples and followers, or under any distress, he relieved as far as he could. And such charitable actions, comprehending all other fruits of faith, will be brought forth, and remembered with peculiar regard on the *day of judgment*, not at all as meritorious causes of salvation, but only as evident testimonies, proofs, and signs of true love to

a Fuller's Church Hist. Cent. 17. Book 10. Sect. 3.
b Fuller's Church Hist. as above.

God, of faith unfeigned, and of subjection to the Lord Jesus Christ in his offices of Mediator, Surety, Saviour, Redeemer, Prophet, Priest, and King. This is evident from Mat. xxv. 35—40.[a] That alms-deeds should be remembered with peculiar regard on the *day of judgment*, was an opinion which early prevailed among the Jews; as appears by the Chaldee paraphrase on Eccl. ix. 7. which bears a remarkable resemblance to these words of Christ, Mat. xxv. 35, &c. and might perhaps be an imitation of them.[b] And the saints in glory will be for ever reaping the harvest of these labours of love. Mr Whitaker's patience, and resignation to the sovereign will of God, were as remarkable, as his works of charity; but as these will come natively in course, in giving an account of his sickness and death, we shall pass them here.—He was an universal scholar, both in arts and languages; well acquainted both with the Fathers and Schoolmen. By much study, he had digested the whole body of divinity; was an acute and solid disputant, excellently versed in cases of conscience, and inferior to none in his acquaintance with the Holy Scriptures. Mr Calamy speaking of him says, "If I should enter upon his commendation, I might truly say what Nazianzen doth of his sister Gorgonia, that I have more cause to fear lest I should speak below, than above the truth; for he was a burning and a shining light in this our Israel. A messenger, and an interpreter one among a thousand; a Bezaleel in God's tabernacle; a true Nathaniel, who, by his integrity, humility, constancy, charity, publicness, and peaceableness of spirit, and by his diligence and faithfulness in preaching the gospel, made his life both amiable and desirable. I will say of him as it was said of Athanasius, that he was an adamant, and a load-stone. To all who conversed with him, he was a load-stone to draw their hearts to love him; but in the cause of God, and in reference to the truths of Christ, he was an unconquerable adamant. He was a Jeremiah, both in mourning for,

a See Dutch Annotations, and Dr Guise on the place.
b Dr Doddridge's Note on Mat. xxv. 40. Mede's Works.

and in witnessing against the sins of the times."[a]— And Dr Fuller says, he was "a solid divine, and a man made up of piety to God, pity to poor men, and patience in himself.—His liberality knew no bottom but an empty purse; so bountiful was he to all in want."[b] And Leigh, in his Treatise of Religious and Learned Men, says, "Jeremiah Whitaker, my worthy friend, a learned and pious divine of the Assembly, who was a man mighty in the Scriptures, of an humble melting spirit, laborious in his ministerial function, zealous for God's glory, and wonderfully patient in all the time of his heavy affliction."

He had much interest in the hearts of persons of great eminence, who filled places of power and trust in the nation, because of his plainness, and the power of godliness, which did shine very brightly in his conversation. He gained much authority and reputation among all with whom he conversed; whether in town or country.

By much study, and hard labour, he was afflicted with various bodily diseases from his youth. In the latter part of his time, he was several years much distressed with the painful distempers of the gout and stone. God corrects his people *because* he loves them, in order to *make them partakers* of his holiness, that they may learn his law, and *not be condemned with the world*, Rev. iii. 19. Heb. xii. 5—11. 1 Cor. xi. 32. And his sorest chastisements are fruits of his fatherly care. Though the means be grievous, yet they are healthful to the soul, and the end is glorious, 2 Cor. iv. 17. Diseases are God's servants, they come and go at his sovereign appointment, who can bring meat out of the eater, and sweetness out of the strong.

"Ye saints of God, fresh courage take,
And thank him for his grace;
Behind a frowning providence,
He hides a gracious face."[c]

a Calamy's Epistle prefixed to Mr Ashe's Sermon preached at Whitaker's Funeral.

b Fuller's Worthies of England.

c. Cowper.

Notwithstanding the frequent return of those tormenting pains, he attended upon his ministry both at home and abroad, while he was able to creep into the pulpit. And though oftentimes he went halting thither, and full of pain, yet he had no appearance of any distemper, while he was there. He sometimes went upon crutches unto his own congregation. Yea, once he adventured to preach at Michael's Cornhill, when he was scarce able to get into the pulpit, and his friends with much difficulty helped him out of the church homeward.[a] At other times, when his legs would not serve him, he rode to the church. And when he was by extreme pains taken off from his ministry, he told his intimate friends, that the pains which he felt were not so grieving to his spirit, as his inability for his work in the ministry. He often said, "If I could but preach, I should be much better." And he rejoiced with thankfulness, when in the times of weakness, he found himself not worse by preaching. He mentioned such experiences, as arguments to prevail with his friends, to comply with his preaching, when they endeavoured to dissuade him from it, as hurtful to his health. But about the beginning of November, the violent pain of the stone so increased, that he was confined to his bed or chamber, until his death, on the first of June. Many physicians in London, were consulted, and were very ready to serve him with their advice. They unanimously concluded, that his sharp pains proceeded originally from an ulcer in the kidneys, but immediately from an ulcer in the neck of the bladder, caused by a continual flux of ulcerous matter dropping down upon that part. And on account of the acuteness and quickness of the sense there, his pains were mostly in that place, though the fountain of them was from the kidneys. Several days of prayer and fasting were observed on his account. Mr Ashe says, "I never heard of any man so much prayed for, both in public and private. There was no particular case so frequently, so affectionately spread before God in most of the congregations about London as his."[b]

a Mr Ashe's Sermon at his Funeral, p. 54.
b Ashe's Sermon at his Funeral, p. 65, and Clarke's Lives.

During his heavy affliction, he had the sweet experience of very particular manifestations of divine love unto his soul; and much assurance of God's fatherly love in Christ. In his addresses unto God, he constantly claimed interest in him; *My God, and my Father.* "For it is the very essence of justifying faith, to attach itself to the Surety, and appropriate what is his as its own."[a] His confidence in the God of his salvation, his inward peace and joy, were the supports of his heart under all grinding pains. "My flesh and my heart faileth: *but* God is the strength of my heart, and my portion for ever," Psal. lxxiii. 26. And, he was confident that mercies were remarkably mingled with all his grievous distempers. Nor did he doubt of the sanctification of all his sharpest afflictions, through the grace of God. Accordingly in his supplications to his Maker, he often said: "Consider and save me, for I am thine. How long, Lord, how long shall I not be remembered? Yea, I am remembered, blessed be thy name. This is a fiery chariot, but it will carry me to heaven. Blessed be God who hath supported me hitherto. And he who hath delivered will deliver. Thou, Lord, never forgettest them who put their trust in thee." When the extremity of a paroxysm had passed over, the smiles always returned in his countenance, and he spake concerning the *tender mercies* of God, which are *over all his works*, Psal. cxlv. 9. and contemplated heaven, with great delight. And though he trembled when his pains began, he said with a very becoming confidence, "Now in the strength of the mighty God, I will undergo these pains. O, my God, underneath put thine *everlasting arms*, and strengthen me." See Deut. xxxiii. 27. Thus when cast down, he was not destroyed, when perplexed, he was not in despair, his heart being fixed, trusting in the Lord. He often told Mr Ashe, his bosom-friend, that notwithstanding all his rentings and roarings, from which he expected no deliverance but by death, he would not for a thousand worlds change estates with the greatest man on earth, living in sin. Wisdom's

a Christian Magazine, vol. vi. No. 62. p. 95.

ways are ways of pleasantness, and all her paths are peace, Prov. iii. 17. *Great peace have they who love thy law; and nothing shall offend them*, Psal. cxix. 165. He was far from charging God foolishly; but was all submission to his sovereign will, believing that he did all well. "The way God leads his people may be crooked and dark, but verily it is a right way. Our lot may be greatly variegated with prosperity and adversity: the sunshine and the shade may frequently succeed each other; but all is well, and shall be well. Our Father in heaven is the Author of the blessed texture in our lot. All our chastisements are in love, and will terminate in our eternal happiness. Behold, happy is the man whom the Lord correcteth."[a] And the kindness of his heavenly Father was such that Satan was never permitted to shake his confidence, nor dash his hopes. 'They who trust in the Lord shall be as mount Zion, which cannot be removed, but abideth for ever," Psal. cxxv. 1. And, he accounted the spiritual cordials, and divine supports, which he enjoyed liberally in his great distress, far superior to a deliverance from the gout, stone, and even death itself. He also viewed these extraordinary supernatural refreshments, as answers of the many prayers made to God in his behalf. And though it seemed good to his heavenly Father, to deny that ease and recovery much and earnestly begged, he granted what was better for him. And, his case was very like that of the apostle Paul, 2 Cor. xii. 7, 8, 9. Many have understood Paul's *thorn in the flesh* of *bodily pains:* and Mr Baxter, being himself subject to a Nephritick disorder, or disease in the reins, supposes it might be the *stone*, or *gravel.* Be that as it may, the case otherwise is exactly parallel. Very importunate petitions were presented in both cases, that the affliction might be removed, if it were the will of the Lord, or at least moderated in some considerable degree. And such prayers were not in vain; for, though the Hearer of prayer did not entirely and fully indulge the very earnest request, he said to these remarkable subjects

a Christian Magazine, vol. vi. No. 60. p. 76.

of his afflicting hand, in amazingly great condescension, *My grace is sufficient for thee*, to support thee under these acute pains, and bitter afflictions, though I permit them to continue, which I now choose to do.[a] Like Jonathan, he had and received his comfort at the end of a rod, that he might value it the more, and be more earnest and frequent in supplications to the God of his salvation. "In all our exigences, extremities, and complaints, let us apply to the Throne of Grace, and that blessed Redeemer, who intercedes before it, for proper assistance and relief. Nor let us be discouraged, though the *first*, or *second* address, should seem to be disregarded: The *third* or *fourth*, may be successful. And what, if we do not succeed to our wish in the *immediate* answer? Let it content us, that we may be assured by Christ of the *sufficiency of his grace*. In *our weakness* can he illustrate *his strength*. And, in that view too, may we *glory in our infirmities*."[b] Heavy afflictions, sanctified, greatly contribute to the vigorous exercise of grace.

Mr Whitaker's patience was so eminent under his heavy affliction, that he might be celebrated as a second Job. And many who saw him in the racking pains of his last sickness, so frequently reiterated, and so long continued, were persuaded that the Lord had put him into that furnace, and kept him there, to be a pattern of patience to posterity. He was patient to a wonderful degree, as Cornelius Nepos says concerning Epaminondas, the Theban.[c] In him we have a noble example of constancy and patience worthy of our most attentive consideration. Mr Ashe says indeed, he did roar many times till his throat was dry, but none ever heard him speak one word in the way of murmuring, or discontentment, on account of God's afflicting providence. He took up Job's complaint, Wherefore is light given to him who is in misery, and life unto the bitter in soul; which long for death, but it cometh not, and dig for it more than for hid treasures;

a See Doddridge on the place.

b Doddridge, as above, Improvement.

c C. Nep. Epam. Cap. 3.

which rejoice exceedingly, and are glad when they can find the grave?" Job iii. 20—22. But he always expressed the utmost submission to the sovereign will, and good pleasure of the Lord his God. He only discovered, that he felt, and was sensible when God touched him. "Insensibility of mind is so far from resignation, that it is one of the sorest judgments on earth, not to grieve when we are afflicted of the Lord."[a] When asked, how he did, he frequently answered: "The bush always burning, but not consumed. Though my pains be too great for the strength of nature, yet they are not above the supports of grace." Under the copious influences of the *Spirit of grace and of supplication*, in the abundant effusions of the soul, in holy divine expostulation and prayer, he expressed himself as follows: "O, my God, help! Father of mercies, pity! Do not contend for ever. Consider my frame that I am but dust. My God, who hath made heaven and earth, help me! Oh, give me patience, and inflict what thou wilt! If my patience was more, my pain would be less. Dear Saviour, where are thy bowels! Why dost thou make me an astonishment to myself and others? Why dost thou cover thyself with a thick cloud, that our prayers cannot pass? Blessed is the man who endureth temptation. Lord, this is a sad temptation; stand by me, and say, It is enough. Am I not thy servant? Consider, Lord, that I am thy servant. O, these bitter waters of Marah! Lord, drop sweet comfort into these bitter waters! O the blood of sprinkling! Lord, the blood of sprinkling! Lord, that blood which extinguisheth the fire of thine anger! O that it may allay my burning pains! I am in a fiery furnace. Lord, be with me, as thou wast with the three children, and bring me out refined from sin! When I have sailed through the ocean of these pains, and look back, I see that none of them can be wanting! I flee unto thee, O my God: hide me under the shadow of thy wings until these terrible storms be overpast." By an attentive consideration of these pious breathings of soul,

a Christian-Magazine, vol. vi. No. 60. pp. 73, 74.

we may see, that God in Christ is the believer's only refuge in adversity, unto whom he cries for help.[a] That the infinitely precious blood of the Lord Jesus Christ, our ever blessed Redeemer, is the only true cordial drop, which sweetens every affliction, in this life, however bitter. That this blood must be sprinkled upon us, and applied by the special appropriating acts of faith, under the influence of the divine, eternal Spirit of all grace, before we can enjoy the benefit of it. That the genuine children of God prefer deliverance from sin, to relief from trouble. And, that when affliction is sanctified unto us, we will see that it is all necessary, and that no single twig of the rod of any affliction could be wanting. Nor will such wish to have a single twig of the rod taken off.[b] The subject of this Memoir was ready to acknowledge with David, that God afflicted him in truth and faithfulness. In these sore afflictions, he clearly saw by faith the God of his salvation, and was taught to believe, that they were far from being against him, but did all work, in concurrence with other dispensations, for his real good and everlasting advantage, Rom. viii. 28. In them, he saw the Creator and Sovereign Lord of the universe, who giveth not account of any of his matters, doing with his creature as he pleased, *and fell down upon the ground, and worshipped* him, like Job, his companion in tribulation and patience, Job i. 20.[c] He revered Jehovah, the only-wise God, with his whole soul and heart; and uttered the most honourable expressions in his commendation, when in the fire, and upon the rack. Some love-breathings of his pious soul unto his God and Saviour follow: "Good Lord, keep me from dishonouring thy Name by impatience. Oh, who would not, even in burnings, have honourable thoughts of God! Who that knoweth thee would not fear thee, O Lord, love thee, and honour thee! Lord, thou givest me no cause to have any hard thought of thee! Blessed be God there is

a "Ergo te, rerum pater, invocavi,
Unum præsidium in malis." Buchanan, Psal. cxlii. 5.

b See Evangelical Magazine for Nov. 1797. London.

c See Christian Magazine, vol. vi. No. 60. p. 74. Edinburgh.

nothing of hell in all this! Blessed be his name for Jesus Christ, and the revelation of the everlasting gospel. Who knoweth the power of thy wrath? If it be so heavy upon thy servant here, how heavy shall it be to all those who shall endure it without mixture! Blessed be God for the peace of mine inward man, when my outward man is so full of trouble. This is a bitter cup, but it is of my Father's mixing, and shall I not drink it? Yes, Lord, through thy strength I will. This is my burden, and I will bear it." Upon any abatement of his pains, he was constantly employed in adoring and blessing the God of his salvation, whose way is in the sea, and his footsteps in the great waters. Upon such occasions, he used the following and similar expressions: "O, what a mercy is it that there is any mitigation, any intermission! Lord, make me thankful." And turning himself to such as were around him, he often addressed them with the same gracious spirit, as follows: "O, help me to be thankful! O, lift up a prayer for me, that I may be thankful! O, what a mercy is this! How much worse might this affliction have been! I might have been distracted, or laid roaring under disquiet and anguish of spirit." In the deeps of his affliction, he always added a mixture of cheerful acknowledgements of God's goodness, giving hearty thanks to him. And this is both most seemly, and also very conducive to the prosperity of the souls of the righteous.[a] And, as the Lord *our God punisheth us less than our iniquities deserve*, Ezra ix. 13. and makes the bitterest afflictions afford the most profitable instructions, there is ground of thanksgiving even for these. See Psal. xlix. 12. and cxix. 71. And "There is not any case incident to a Christian, but if he search thoroughly, there will be found some ground for thanksgiving and rejoicing, though not in himself, yet in God's dealing with him, either for mercies bestowed, or judgments not inflicted, Philip. ii. 27. for, while Paul commandeth them to exercise themselves, and chear up one another with giving of thanks, instead of foolish talking and jesting, he suppos-

a See Fergusson on Eph. v. 4.

eth there will be always reason of thanksgiving," Eph. v. 4.[a] It is surely of the Lord's mercies we are not consumed altogether. All is mercy on this side hell. Why then should a living man complain? Let him rather give thanks. —He often said to his bosom friend, Mr Ashe, "Brother, through mercy, I have not one repining thought against God." As another, who died under a very painful disease, used to say familiarly, "Joseph *may* complain, but he *dare not* repine."[b] This short speech made a very deep and sensible impression on Mr Ashe's heart; and moved his affections for him.

When the time of his dissolution drew nearer, his pains became more violent; but the grace of God, which was with him, still supported him, and so wonderfully succoured him, that his most violent pains never abated either his faith or his patience. The comfortable evidence which he still enjoyed of a saving interest in the Lord Jesus Christ, and the very delightful prospect of his soon joining the general assembly of the spirits of just men made perfect, beyond the reach of sin, pain, and death, brought his mind into a calm resignation to the sovereign disposing will of God. And animated with the cheering, and well-grounded hope of eternal happiness, built upon the sure foundation which God hath laid in Zion, his soul was often filled with longing desires, to be with the Lord Jesus Christ, attended with the greatest holy submission to the will of God. Like Paul, "having a desire to depart, and to be with Christ; which is far better," Phil. i. 23. He wished to be where his treasure and desires were; with Christ. The more the saints of God are pressed down to the earth by heavy afflictions, do they mount up to heaven in holy affections, when these troubles are sanctified to them. He rejoiced in the view of shaking himself from the dust, that his soul, like a bird set at liberty from its cage, might have full scope, and fly away in meditation, faith, and prayer, with joyful notes of praise to eternal glory. The following were some

a Fergusson as above.

b Evangelical Magazine for Nov. 1797. London.

of his expressions: "O, my God, break open the prison-door, and set my poor captive soul free: but enable me to wait willingly thy time. I desire to be dissolved. Never was any man more desirous of life, than I am of death. When will that time come, when I shall neither sin nor sorrow any more? When shall mortality put on immortality? When shall this earthly tabernacle be dissolved, that I may be clothed upon, with that house which is from heaven? Blessed are the dead which die in the Lord, for they rest from their labours; and follow the Lamb whithersoever he goeth."

"Lord, I am pain'd; but I resign
 To thy superior will:
'Tis grace, 'tis wisdom all divine,
 Appoints the pains I feel.
Dark are thy ways of providence,
 While those who love thee groan:
Thy reasons lie concealed from sense,
 Mysterious and unknown.
Yet nature may have leave to speak,
 And plead before her God,
Lest the o'er-burden'd heart should break
 Beneath thy heavy rod."[a]

Such as are of heavenly birth, being made truly wise unto salvation, who have their heart and their treasure in heaven, and are acquainted with real and substantial enjoyments, will look above this world, and all its fading allurements. They who are Christ's are dead to this world. *The world is crucified unto* them, and they *unto the world*, Gal. vi. 14. Such *have crucified the flesh with the affections and lusts*, Gal. v. 24. Accordingly, *forgetting those things which are behind, and reaching forth unto those things which are before*, they *press toward the mark for the prize of the high calling of God in Christ Jesus*, Phil. iii. 13, 14. Wearied here, they wish to leave this vale of tears, *looking for a city which hath*

a Watts' Remnants of Time, 5.

foundations, whose builder and maker is God, Heb. xi. 10. Where there is *neither sorrow, nor crying, neither shall there be any more pain: for the former things are passed away*, Rev. xxi. 4.

"The soul that would be truly wise,
And taste substantial joys,
Must rise above this giddy world,
And all its trifling toys.
Our treasure and our heart's with God,
We die to all on earth;
Our actions prove our words sincere,
And shew a heavenly birth.
Surmount, my soul, this earthly clod,
And the vain things of time;
Ascend yon bright etherial road,
And share the bliss divine.
Wearied, I turn my eyes around,
On all things here below;
And wish to quit this vale of tears,
And to my Saviour go.
Adieu, ye suns and rolling stars,
And all your radiant fires!
To nobler heights my spirit soars,
To fairer worlds aspires.
Away from all earth's dying things,
My soul impatient flies;
To view the glories of her God,
Beyond the azure skies.
Author and Guardian of my life,
Sweet source of light divine,
And, all endearing names in one,
My Saviour! I am thine.
What thanks I owe thee, and what love,
A boundless endless store,
Shall echo through the realms above,
When time shall be no more."[a]

a Evangelical Magazine, vol. v. No. 56. for Nov. 1797.

On the Sabbath seven-night before he died, his pains were very sharp. Notwithstanding, he employed the greatest part of the time of public worship in fervent prayer with those who attended him. His petitions then were mostly for the ministers of Christ, that he would accompany his ordinances, with his own power, and enable his ministers to speak unto the souls of the hearers. "If I forget thee, O Jerusalem, let my right hand forget her cunning. If I do not remember thee, let my tongue cleave to the roof of my mouth; If I prefer not Jerusalem above my chief joy," Psal. cxxxvii. 5, 6. His sharp pains were sent by the Lord for wise and holy purposes. They served to quicken him to the exercise of prayer, and every good work. The same salutary effects were produced in the pious Psalmist, by the increase of such as troubled him, Psal. iii. 1—4. The people of God have prayed most feelingly, fervently, and forcibly, when their afflictions were sharpest. See this exemplified in the case of the children of Israel, Judg. iii. 8—15. In that of Elisha, 2 Kings vi. 16—18. In Hezekiah, 2 Kings xix. 15, 16. In Jehoshaphat the king of Judah, when told, that there was a great multitude coming against him from beyond the sea on this side Syria, 2 Chron. xx. 2—13. See Isa. xxvi. 16. Hos. v. 15. Acts vii. 59. 60. And, Jonah slept securely when at ease in the ship, but *prayed fervently unto the Lord his God, by reason of his affliction, out of the fish's belly*, Jonah i. 5. and ii. 1, 2. Our hearts are like flint stones, they must be smitten before they will send forth these sparks of devotion. And sharp afflictions are in the hand of the Lord our God, like the file and whetstone: they serve to give a keen edge to our faith, love, prayer, and other religious exercises.—Heavy afflictions are to the souls of believers in Christ, enriched with the graces of the Holy Spirit, like weights unto clocks; they make them go. They influence the motion of such souls to Christ for grace and relief, Hos. v. 15. Psal. iii. 3—8. In the remarkable subject of this Memoir, the graces of God did all eminently shine forth, to the glory of their Author, at this time. As Abraham's faith, Job's patience, and Paul's courage, did shine most illustriously in the fire of affliction; so did the grace of God in Whitaker now. When the Lord designs to glorify himself by his graces in his people, he will readily find means to draw them forth, unto the view of others. And he may effect this, by sharp pains, often reiterated, as in the case now before us. Having lighted such candles, they must not be put under a bushel; but made to *give light to all who are in the house;* all who come where they are. As his pains increased, the heavenly graces became more odoriferous. Like aromatic spices, the more they are pounded, the sweeter they smell.—Such as were best acquainted with him reckoned, that it was disputable, whether he preached more by the heavenliness of his doctrine, or by the holiness of his life. But they conclude, that it is certain, he preached as effectually by his sickness and death, as by either his doctrine or his life.[a] He had such a tender feeling for his friends, that when his pains threatened to come with great violence he entreated them to withdraw from him, that they might not be distressed with his roarings. And, he often thanked God, that his compassionate friends were not under necessity to remain within the reach of his doleful lamentations.

At the near approach of death, his pains became so frequent, as to return every half-hour; and often every quarter; at last, twice or thrice in a quarter of an hour, which did soon exhaust his strength. The night before his death, Mr Ashe, who was his fidus Achates, faithful companion, and equally dear unto him as Jonathan was to David, upon hearing that he was not likely to live another day, went early in the morning to take his last farewell of him, *till the heavens be no more.* At this time, his bodily strength was very much abated. And, his friend finding that he could not speak without much difficulty, he spake the more unto him. He entered upon a conference with him in relation to the approach of his happy expected change. And, Mr Ashe's discourse on this occasion was very refreshing, through God's blessing,

a See Calamy's Preface to Ashe's Sermon at his Funeral.

unto his soul. "The Lord God hath given me the tongue of the learned, that I should know how to speak a word in season to *him who is weary*," Isa. xl. 4. "And a word spoken in due season, how good it is!" Prov. xv. 23. It is like *apples of gold in pictures of silver*, Prov. xxv. 11. Like sound sleep and refreshing rest to the weary; and as sweet water from the pure running stream to such as are parched with thirst.[a]—Mr Ashe minding him, that many of his friends intended to set apart that day in seeking the Lord by supplications in his behalf, desired him to say what in particular he would have them lay before the throne of grace. To this he replied, "Do not complain but bless God for me, and entreat him to open the prison-door." Here we see, that others also laboured in importunate prayers to God, for him, according to 2 Cor. i. 10, 11. Acts xii. 5—12. When one member suffers, all genuine members of the same one body participate in the sorrows thereof. It is only a Nero who can sit and sing while Rome burns. And this pious subject of divine chastisement desired that *thanks may be given by many on his behalf.* "As nothing can be more reasonable, than that mercies obtained by prayer, should be owned in praise."[b] And one well observes, "Our best mercies are, by the blessing of God, made to spring out of our bitterest trials. We will remember, with wonder, love, and praise, all the way the Lord led us through the wilderness, to prove us and try us, and to do us good in our latter end. Gratitude is a sister to humility of mind; and the more humble we are, the more thankful will we be at all times."[c]—And he still continued ardently to desire death. It is reported concerning Secundus, that he denominated death, "The wicked man's fear, and the godly man's wish." It was the ardent wish of this godly man. And viewing it disarmed of its sting, by the death of Christ, he considered it as the extinction of sin in him, a deliver-

a See Virg. Eccl. 5. 45, 46, 47.
b Doddridge on 2 Cor. i. 11.
c Christian Magazine, vol. vi. No. 59. Leumas.

ance from his enemies, a cessation from all his troubles, the quiet rest of his body, and the freedom of his soul; making way for his full and uninterrupted enjoyment of God in Christ, as his sure, enriching, satisfying and everlasting portion, through all eternity. And with such views, he as earnestly wished for death, as ever any Jew did for the jubilee; a year of rejoicing, celebrated every fiftieth year among the Jews, in commemoration of their deliverance out of Egypt. No stranger ever desired more to be at home, than he wished to be in his heavenly Father's house where there is *fulness of joy, and pleasures for evermore*, Psalm xvi. 11. And the continual conclusion of his prayers was, "Come quickly, Amen. Even so, come, Lord Jesus."—Mr Ashe, laying his hand upon Mr Whitaker's cold hand, covered with a clammy sweet, took his last farewell of him with a sore heart. Upon his departure, the last words, wherewith he addressed him were: "Brother, I thank you, I pray God bless you, and I bless God for you." That day of Mr Ashe's last interview with him was spent in supplications to God for him, at Peter's Cornhill, London. Here Mr Newcomen, quickened and assisted the prayers of his friends, in a sermon preached from John xi. 3. 4. insisting especially upon these words, *Lord, behold, he whom thou lovest is sick.* And Mr Jenkin endeavoured to moderate and regulate their sorrows, from Luke xxiii. 28.—*Weep not for me.* On this evening, he died, cheerfully resigning his soul into the hands of his gracious and merciful Redeemer, upon the first day of June, in the year 1654, about the fifty-fifth year of his age.

After his death, his body was opened, when both his kidneys were found full of ulcers, and one of them swelled to an extraordinary bigness, through the abundance of purulent matter in it; and on the neck of his bladder was found a stone, about an inch and an half long, and one inch broad, weighing above two ounces, when first taken out; and also an ulcer which was gangrened, judged to be the cause of his death. All other parts of his body were found upon examination firm and sound.[a] Hence learn, That the best of men may be subjected to the worst of diseases.

Here it may be asked; Why was a man of such distinguished piety subjected to endure so great a *fight of affliction*, and to encounter so many hardships?[b] Or, state the question in the words of Gideon unto the angel of the Lord, *Oh, my Lord, if the Lord be with us, why then is all this befallen us?* Judges vi. 13. To this we reply; There are many phænomena in those parts of the universe that come under our particular observation, the reasons and ends of which we cannot now understand. And, a great master of reasoning says, "The proper conduct in such a case, is to believe that there are most wise reasons for these things, though we do not now discern those reasons, and to argue from the uncontested characters of wisdom in things that we do know, that God most wise hath also acted with admirable wisdom in those things, the designs and ends of which we do not know. It would be wrong therefore to confine the measures of his wisdom precisely to what appeareth to our narrow apprehensions, in that part of his works which falleth under our immediate inspection. This was the great fault of the Epicureans, and other atheistical philosophers, who, judging by their own various views, urged several things as proofs of the want of wisdom and contrivance, which upon a fuller knowledge of God's works, furnish farther convincing proofs of the wisdom of the great Former of all things."[c] And though it may be difficult for us, who have very contracted views of the Divine administration, and see not afar off, to reconcile such an afflictive dispensation of Divine Providence, as this before us, with the goodness of God, and his everlasting love unto his chosen; yet we may be assured, that it is altogether consistent therewith. The certainty

a Ashe's Sermon at his Funeral, Clerk's Lives, and Burnham's Memorials.

b See Virg. Eccl. 1. 8, 9, 10, 11.

c Leland's View of Deistical Writers, vol. i. Letter 17. 5th edit. London.

hereof may appear, from the mode of reasoning above, and by the infallible testimony of Jehovah himself, Rom. viii. 28. "And we know that all things work together for good to them who love God, to them who are the called according to his purpose." The apostle having taken occasion to hint at many gospel-privileges enjoyed, here adds, that though our afflictions may lie heavy upon us, and though our burdens may be long continued, as in this case; yet *we* assuredly *know*, *that all things*, which occur in the course of Divine Providence, either in their present and immediate, or future and more remote consequences, do and shall *work together for* real and everlasting *good to them who* sincerely and affectionately *love* the Lord their *God*. It is plain from the whole context, that Providential events are meant, and included under this expression; and especially extraordinary afflictive dispensations of Divine Providence.[a] And since these shall most certainly *work together* for the real and everlasting *good* of God's chosen, they must incontestibly be altogether consistent with the goodness of God, and his love to such as are called according *to his purpose*. This is very beautifully set forth, in a well-known verse, from an illustrious pen, and a pious heart:

> "Good when he gives, supremely good,
> Nor less when he denies;
> Even crosses, from his sovereign hand,
> Are blessings in disguise!"

How comfortable and animating to the believer in Christ, is this enlivening thought, that all dispensations of Divine Providence whatever, prosperous, or adverse, even the most distressing and afflictive, shall assuredly be directed by the only wise God, and over-ruled by his almighty power, and infinite goodness, for the temporal, spiritual, and eternal good of his chosen! But what is the meaning of this glorious co-operation? With what or with whom, shall these work together? To this we

a Doddridge, Poole, Burkitt, Guyse.

reply; With God only wise, whose *kingdom ruleth over all*, who can bring good out of evil, light out of darkness, and make his people's cross their way to their crown; with God's blessing, which makes them effectual for the benefit of his people; with his word, ordinances, Spirit, grace, mercy, and loving-kindness; with the faith, hope, patience, and prayers of believers themselves; and with each other: The dispensations of Divine Providence ought not to be considered singly, or separately; especially such of them as are afflictive. Afflictions are God's physic. And, as in matter of physic, if some simples are used alone, they may prove hurtful, rather than effect a cure; but take them in composition, as made up by the direction of a skilful physician, and they prove an excellent medicine. Let us accordingly consider all the dispensations of Divine Providence *together*, in their connection, harmony, and effects; and thus we will see, that in the gracious issues of the sharpest afflictions, which the Lord allots any of his people in this world, he brings meat out of the eater and sweetness out of the strong. So, *the heads of the leviathan*, became meat *to such as inhabited the wilderness*, Psal. lxxiv. 14.[a] And with such views, the saints are found saying, "It is good for me that I have been afflicted," Psal. cxix. 71.—Dr Leland has an excellent observation on this subject, which I must subjoin here, for the benefit of the reader, and as a cautionary remark upon the whole. "It is highly reasonable, that when we meet with any phænomena, which we cannot reconcile with our ideas of the Divine goodness, we should conclude, that it is only for want of having the whole of things before us, and of considering them in their connection and harmony, that they appear to us with a disorderly aspect. And it is very just in such a case, to make use of any reasonable hypothesis, which tendeth to set the goodness of God in a fair and consistent light."[b]

His body was buried in the church of Mary Magdalen

a See Wisheart's Theologia, vol. i. Disse. 5. Sermon 20.
b Leland's View, as above.

Bermondsey, on the 6th of June, 1654. His funeral was attended by a very great multitude of eminently godly persons, both ministers and others of different ranks. Mr Calamy says, that it may be said of him, as it is said of Stephen, that "devout men carried Stephen to his burial, and made great lamentation over him." Many tears were shed on this occasion.

"What scenes of sorrow wake the soul to pain;
What floods of anguish cloud the sick'ning eye?
O, sons of Pity, pour the melting strain—
O, sons of Pity, heave the plaintive sigh!"[a]

I shall add here two passages from his last Will and Testament, the one expressive of the high estimation which he continued to have of the office of the holy ministry, until his departure from this world, and the other of the very low opinion, which he always had of himself. And these are given in his own words, and as written with his own hand. "For my son Jeremiah, my desire is, that he be bred a scholar, and that the Lord would spiritually incline his heart, freely to give up himself to the Lord, to serve him in the work of the ministry, which calling and employment, though now despised, I do esteem above all other in the world; and do commend it to all mine, that if the Lord bless them with sons, they would commend this calling to their posterity." Here we see one eminently pious and learned, who had well studied the controversies of the times in opposition to the holy ministry, giving his testimony in favour thereof, upon his death-bed, when about to give his account unto the Judge of all. And, this is certainly a strong testimony in behalf of the gospel-ministry. The other passage is: "I desire that at my funeral there may be no pomp; but that so poor a worthless wretch may be privately laid in the ground."

His Funeral Sermon was preached by Mr Ashe, who gave him a large and deserved encomium. And now the

a Scot's Chron.

reader may see, in this Memoir, one of Israel's sons passing through the flood, the tempestuous and stormy sea of affliction, under the Captain of Salvation; the only wise God his Saviour marching in triumph before him, and all his malicious enemies behind him sinking like lead into the mighty waters.

"Across the level bed of sand
The sons of Isra'l trod;
Behind them sunk the foe like lead,
Before them march'd their God."[a]

Many poems and elegies were composed on the occasion of his death, by several eminent divines, in and about London; as Jenkin, Jacombe, Robinson, Poole, Needler, Reynolds, and others. I shall subjoin one of these, which well deserves a place here.

On the death of my dear friend, Mr *Jeremiah Whitaker.*

"If death be but a servant sent, to call
The souls of saints to their original;
Dear saint, thine was a noble soul, to whom
Three messengers were sent to call thee home;
A stone, an ulcer, and a gangrene too,
Three deaths to hasten that which one should do!
'Twas not because thy soul was deeper set
Than ours, within its house of clay; nor yet
Because thou wert unwilling to depart
Thither, where long before had been thine heart.
They were not sent to hale, by violence,
A soul that ling'red when 'twas called hence.
God shew'd how welcome one death was to thee,
Who didst so meekly entertain all three.
Thus many deaths God's Isra'l did inclose,
The sea before, behind a sea of foes:

a Christian Magazine, vol. vi. No. 64. Viator.

On either side the jaws of mountains high:
No way from death, but unto death to fly.
Not to destroy them, but to let them see
The power of love, which then would set them free.
Thus Job's four messengers, which did relate
The doleful story of his ruin'd state:
And his three friends, who acted Satan's part,
(He on his flesh, and these upon his heart)
Who by disputing him into a curse,
Would make his spirit's torment far the worse,
Were, by God's wise disposal sent to show
The strength he on his champion would bestow.
Thus painters put dark grounds where they intend
To overlay with finest gold, and lend,
By deeper shadows, lustre to that face
On which they mean their choicest skill to place.
Thus workmen season much with sun and wind
Those greatest beams which must the building bind,
While smaller pieces, happ'ly, are put in
When they come bleeding from the wood, and green.
Oft, where is greatest grace, God's pleas'd to send
Great conflicts, those great graces to commend.
As the six finger'd giant's sword did bring
The more renown to little David's sling.
The vanquish'd lion, and the conquer'd bear,
Prepar'd that holy head a crown to wear.
The angel wrestled first, and then did bless,
And made the greater servant to the less.
Pain was too great for thee, God's grace for pain,
And made the greater serve the less again.
Thy pains serv'd thee for glory, and did fit
The head, on which a crown of life must sit.
This is God's method, to fetch joy from grief,
To turn our sorrows unto our relief:
To save by killing, and to bring to shore,
By the ship's planks, which was quite broke before.
And thus a barren womb first took the seed,
Which did six hundred thousand people breed.
That seed too must from knife and altar rise,
And be before a fire a sacrifice.

Great preacher of thy heavenly Father's will,
Thy tongue did many ears with manna fill.
Thy life out-preach'd thy tongue, O blessed strife!
Thy sickness the best sermon of thy life.
Before each doctrine must be prov'd anew
Thine end was one great proof that all was true.
Before thou preach'd by weeks, but now by hours,
Each minute taught thy mourning auditors;
Each patient groan, and each believing eye,
Was a new sermon in *brachygraphy.*[a]
When nature roars, without repining words;
Grace in the mouth, when in the bowels swords;
In midst of torments to triumph o'er hell;
To feel God's arrows, yet his praises tell;
Through thickest clouds to see the brighest light;
In blackest darkness to have clearest sight,
And with our Lord to cry, "My God, my God,"
Upon a cross, under the sharpest rod;
This is indeed to preach: this is to show
Faith's triumph over nature's greatest woe.
Then welcome fiery serpents, scorching sting,
Which did thee thus to the brazen serpent bring.
Then welcome whale, which, though it first devour,
Renders at last the prophet to the shore.
Well might'st thou bear the stone which death did throw,
Who had'st the *white stone*, the *new name* to show.
Well might'st thou be with such an ulcer calm,
Whose soul was heal'd before with Heaven's balm.
When spirits' wounds are cur'd, though nature groan,
An heart of flesh can heal a back of stone.
Let conscience have her feast, and let flesh roar,
This pain shall make the other's joy the more:
As many times those flowers most fragrant smell,
Which nearest to some noisome weeds do dwell.
Thus have you seen the forge most clearly glow,
On which the smith doth drops of water throw.
Keen frosts make fire the hotter, and deep night
Causeth celestial lamps to shine more bright,

a Brachygraphy is the art of writing in short-hand.

And by a dear antiperistasis,[a]
The child's distress sweetens the father's kiss.
A wounded body yields to a sound soul;
The joys of this do th' other's pains control.
As in the day that the sun-beams appear,
All other lesser stars do disappear.
When heaven shines, and divine love doth reign,
The soul is not at leisure to complain;
Internal joy his heart so well composes,
That they have judg'd their flames a bed of roses.
But what shall England do, from whence are lopt
Two of her richest acres, to heaven dropt?[b]
By loss of these two acres she's more poor,
Than if she'd lost an hundred lordships more.
'Twere a good purchase to gain these again,
By giving to the sea all Lincoln-fen.
Two little mines of gold do far surpass
Huge manors, where the whole vesture is but grass.
Learn we by them, what all men once will say,
One perch of heav'n's worth the whole globe of clay."

ED. REYNOLDS, D. D.

Writings of Jeremiah Whitaker.

1. *Christ the Settlement of Unsettled Times:* A Sermon from Hag. ii. 7. before the House of Commons, at their Public Fast, in Margaret's, Westminster, 25th Jan. 1642. 4to. pp. 61. London, 1642. With an Epistle to the House of Commons, of four pages.

2. *The Christian's Great Design on earth, is, To attain assurance for Heaven: Or, How in this life he may lay hold on Eternal Life:* Set forth in a Sermon preached from 1 Tim. vi. 17—19. before the Lord Mayor, the Court of Aldermen, and other citizens of London, at a solemn anniversary meeting, 8th April, 1645. 4to. pp. 47. London, 1645. With four pages of an Epistle Dedicatory.

a Antiperistasis is the action of opposite qualities; whereby that opposed becomes stronger.

b Gataker, and Whitaker; whose names seem to have been originally written Gatacre, and Whitacre. See Gataker's Life.

3. *The Christian's Hope Triumphing in these Glorious Truths;*—1. That Christ the ground of hope, is God, and not mere man; against the Arians, and other unbelievers.—2. That Christ is the true Messiah, against the unbelieving Jews.—3. That there is another life beside this, against the gross Atheist.—4. That the soul of man is immortal, and doth not sleep till the day of the resurrection, against the error of some seeming Semi-Atheists.—5. How the hope of heaven should be attained, while here on earth, against the carnal worldlings.—6. How this hope may be discerned where it is, and attained where it is not, for the comfort of every poor Christian: in a Sermon preached from 1 Cor. xv. 19. before the House of Lords, in the Abbey Church at Westminster, 28th May, 1645. Fast, 4to. pp. 52. London, 1645.

4. *The Danger of Greatness: Or, Uzziah's Exaltation and Destruction:* A Sermon from 2 Chron. xxvi. 15, 16. Preached before the Lords, Commons, and Assembly of Divines, 14th of Jan. 1645, being a special day of Humiliation set apart to seek God, for his direction in settling the great work of Church-Government. 4to. pp. 44. London, 1646.

These are all his writings that I have seen, making a small quarto volume.

HENRY WILKINSON, B. D.

PASTOR OF WADDESDON, AND A MEMBER OF THE ASSEMBLY OF DIVINES AT WESTMINSTER.

HENRY WILKINSON was born in the Vicarage of Halifax, in Yorkshire, England, on the 9th day of October, in the year 1566. He received his education in Merton-college, Oxford. He made his first entry into the University in 1581. He was related to Sir Henry Savile, by whose favour he was elected Probationer Fellow of the College. In the year 1586, he proceeded in

Arts, applied unto the study of Divinity, and after some time, he commenced Bachelor of Divinity; and in the year 1601, he became Pastor of Waddesdon in Buckinghamshire, where he continued in the laborious and faithful exercise of the holy ministry forty-six years. He married Sarah, the only daughter of Mr Arthur Wake, who is said to have been another zealous Puritan Divine, by whom he had six sons and three daughters. His wife was a woman of a very amiable character, and they lived together in a very becoming manner, more than fifty years. Mr Wilkinson was a man of considerable learning and piety, and being an old Puritan, as Wood says, he was elected one of the Assembly of Divines. It is certain, that he was chosen one of the Assembly of Divines at Westminster, in 1643, and that his name is in the list of those Divines who met in the Assembly at Westminster; but it is said that he spent the most part of his time among his parishioners, by whom he was exceedingly beloved and revered. He died at Waddesdon, on the 19th of March, 1647, aged eighty-one years. His mortal remains were laid in the chancel of his own church, where, against the south wall, was a monumental inscription erected, of which the following is a translation: "Henry Wilkinson, forty-six years the faithful pastor of this church, was born the ninth day of October, 1566, and died the 19th day of March, 1647. He married *Sarah*, the only daughter of *Arthur Wake* of *Sawey Forest*, in the county of Northampton, with whom he lived in holy concord fifty-three years, and by whom he had nine children, six sons and three daughters. The remains of the aforesaid Sarah Wilkinson who lived to the age of seventy years, were laid by the side of her husband, leaving us an example of a most upright and holy life, and a reputation scarcely to be exceeded. John Wilkinson, son of the above, who died Dec. 18, 1664, aged 61 years, was also interred near them."

Our Mr Wilkinson has written and published, "A Catechism for the Use of the Congregation of Waddesdon, which has been oftentimes printed. Mr Wood says, that the fourth impression came out at London, 1637. Our author has also published, "The Debt-Book; or, a Treatise upon Rom. xiii. 8, wherein is handled the civil debt of money or goods." London, 1625. Mr Wood here adds, "and other things which I have not yet seen."

The celebrated Dr Henry Wilkinson, who comes next in our list, and was Margaret Professor at Oxford, and ejected at the Restoration, was his son.[a]

HENRY WILKINSON, D. D.

MINISTER IN LONDON, MARGARET PROFESSOR IN THE UNIVERSITY OF OXFORD, AND A MEMBER OF THE ASSEMBLY OF DIVINES AT WESTMINSTER.

HENRY WILKINSON, son of the above-mentioned Henry Wilkinson, was born at Waddesdon, in Buckinghamshire, in England. He became a commoner of Magdalen-Hall, Oxford, in 1622, aged 13 years. There he made great proficiency in his studies, took the degrees in arts, became a noted tutor, master of the schools, and reader of divinity in his house. He entered into the holy ministry; and in the year 1638, he was admitted bachelor of divinity, and preached frequently in and near Oxford. He was a very celebrated preacher in Oxford about that time. He suffered for his conscientious freedom in preaching against the ceremonies and corruptions which then greatly prevailed. On the 6th of Sept. in 1640, he preached in his turn in Mary's Church, in Oxford, from Rev. iii. 16. *So then because thou art lukewarm, and neither cold nor hot, I will spue thee out of my mouth.* This sermon gave great offence to the royal party. Wood says, that it was "very bitter against some ceremonies of the church, very base also and fac-

a Wood's Athenæ Oxon. vol. ii. Neal and Brook's Puritans, vol. iii.

tious, and intended merely to make a party for the Scots." He was summoned the same day to make his recantation, in a form which was then prescribed for him; but he positively refused. Upon this refusal, he was suspended from all execution of his ministerial function within the University and its precincts, until he should make his recantation. He complained to the Long Parliament of the usage which he had received from the Vice-chancellor of the University. Upon this, a copy of the sermon was sent to the Committee of Religion in the House of Commons, with the exceptions against it, and was by them perused; but they finding nothing in it, which could make him liable to punishment, they released him from his suspension, and gave order that his sermon should be printed, which was accordingly done. Mr Wilkinson now *preached the kingdom of God, and taught those things which concern the Lord Jesus Christ, with all confidence, no man forbidding him.* He had undaunted courage to oppose all mankind, for the sake of what was right.—He was sometime Pastor of Faith's Under Paul's, in London; and was chosen one of the Assembly of Divines at Westminster, and is marked as giving constant attendance during the session. He preached several times before the members of Parliament, and became Pastor of Dunstan's in the East. He was appointed afterward to go to Oxford with the Parliamentary visitors, and was one of those visitors. He was made Senior Fellow of Magdalen-college, and canon of Christ-church. He commenced Doctor of Divinity, and at Cheynell's departure, he became Margaret Professor of the University. After the Restoration of Charles II. he was ejected, and thereupon retired to London, and lived a non-conformist. In the latter part of his life, he lived at Clapham in Surrey, near London, where he had an open meeting after the indulgence in 1671; and where he died, in the month of June, 1675.—Wood says, that he was a good scholar, always a close student, and an excellent preacher.

Under his name were published—A Sermon against Lukewarmness in Religion, from Rev. iii. 16. 4to. pp.

39. London, 1641.—*Babylon's Ruin, Jerusalem's Rising:* Fast Sermon from Zech. i. 18—21, before the House of Commons, 25 Oct. 1643. 4to. pp. 32. London, 1643, and 1644.—*The Gainful Cost:* Fast Sermon before the House of Lords, from 1 Chron. xxi. 24. Nov. 27, 1644. 4to. pp. 32. Lodon, 1644.—" Miranda, Stupenda; or, The Wonderful and Astonishing Mercies which the Lord hath Wrought for England, in Subduing and Captivating the Pride, Power and Policy of his Enemies:" Thanksgiving Sermon from Numb. xxiii. 23, before the House of Commons, 21 July 1646. London, 1646.—He has also a Sermon in the Morning Exercise at Cripple-gate, concerning our danger in things lawful. Another in the Supplement to it, of doing all things in the name of Christ. And a third in that against Popery; proving the Pope to be Antichrist, or the Man of Sin.[a]

THOMAS WILSON, A. M.

MINISTER OF THE GOSPEL AT OTHAM AND MAIDSTONE IN KENT, AND A MEMBER OF THE ASSEMBLY OF DIVINES AT WESTMINSTER.

THOMAS WILSON was born at Catterly in the county of Cumberland, in England, in the year 1601. His parents were sober and honest, had a competent estate, and were in good reputation among their neighbours. He was early sent to school, where his proficiency in learning was great; and even exceeded expectation. It is said, that he far excelled all his fellows. He had a sharp wit, a large memory, and was very bookish. He was sent to the university of Cambridge, before he was seventeen years of age, and admitted there into Christ's-college; where he was greatly admired for his indefatigable industry, and very great progress in useful learning,

[a] Wood's Athenæ Oxon. vol ii. 2 edit.

and where he proceeded in arts. *No day without doing something*, might have been written over the door of his study When engaged in academical learning, he did not neglect divinity, nor reading the Holy Scriptures. *From a child he knew the Holy Scriptures, which are able to make wise to salvation.* The Bible was exceedingly precious to him; and he read much in it. It is said, that, before he was bachelor of arts, he had read Fremellius and Junius on the whole Bible, three times over. His bodily constitution, which was strong and healthful, enabled him to apply unweariedly to his studies.

Upon his leaving the University, he taught school for about four years at Chartwood, in the county of Surrey, employing all his vacant hours in preparation for the holy ministry. Probably, he derived considerable benefit, in his studies, from the Rev. Mr Bristow, minister of Chartwood, where he was employed in teaching. Mr Bristow is said to have observed Mr Wilson's fitness for the work of the ministry, and to encourage him in going forward to that arduous work, though the want of him was a considerable loss to Mr Bristow and to his parish. Mr Wilson sometimes said, "That he knew no calling, except the ministry, wherein a man might be so serviceable to God, as in teaching youth." He entered into the holy ministry at Capel, in the same county, where he had been employed in teaching youth. There, by his judicious preaching, and holy example, he continued some time, directing the people in the way to eternal life. Though he received little or nothing for his labours, he was not the less faithful and diligent in promoting the welfare of their souls. He sought not theirs, but them, and was highly esteemed by the people, and by the godly ministers in the neighbourhood. He continued not long at Capel, but removed to Farlington, near Portsmouth, in Hampshire, where he laboured among very ignorant and heathenish people, eadeavouring, by the diligent use of means, to instruct and reform them. He soon removed again from that place to Teddington, near Kingston-upon-Thames, in the county of Surrey. In this situation, he continued several years, and his labours were crowned with remarkable success. He was made a blessing to many souls. During his abode at Teddington, he much desired to visit his native country, where his relations and friends lived. He was then about twenty-six years of age. That visit was highly beneficial to many persons. While he was in Cumberland, he was desired to preach in Penrith, a large market-town, in that county. In that place, for a long time, a considerable market for all kind of food had been attended every Lord's day, until nine of the clock in the morning. But Mr Wilson, having preached there two or three sermons, prevailed upon the ministers and other persons of the town to use means for the reformation of that abuse of the Lord's day. The means were crowned with success. A proclamation was made on the day of their weekly market, "That no person, for the time to come, should bring any *victuals* or *ware* whatsoever to be sold on the Lord's day, but that Saturday should be the time for the sale of their commodities." And it is said that for many years after, the people did forbear to sell any thing on the Lord's day, in that town. A due regard for the Lord's day, has generally been accounted a proper touch-stone of any person's religion, and a good evidence of the vigorous exercise of divine grace in the soul. Pious persons, in all ages and countries, have universally attended to the sanctification of the Sabbath-day. *In those days saw I in Judah some treading wine presses on the Sabbath, and bringing in sheaves, and lading asses; as also wine, grapes, and figs, and all burdens, which they brought into Jerasalem on the Sabbath-day: and I testified against them in the day wherein they sold victuals. There dwelt men of Tyre also therein, who brought fish, and all manner of ware, and sold on the Sabbath unto the children of Judah, and in Jerusalem. Then I contended with the nobles of Judah, and said unto them, What evil thing is this that ye do, and profane the Sabbath-day?—And some of my servants set I at the gates, that there should no burden be brought in on the Sabbath-day.—And I commanded the Levites, that they should cleanse themselves, and that they should come and keep the gates to sanctify the Sabbath-day*, Neh. xiii. 15, 16, 17—19—22.

Mr Wilson's next removal was to Otham near Maidstone, in the county of Kent. At Otham, he was made the instrument of awakening many careless sinners, of their conversion, and of building them up in faith and holiness. Multitudes flocked to attend his ministry from Maidstone and its vicinity; and, in a short time, the church was found too small to contain the people who assembled. The inhabitants of Maidstone were, at that time, badly accommodated with the ministry of the word. Alas! when the children asked *bread*, he who was their spiritual father, by profession and office, gave them *only stones*. Their souls were famished for want of wholesome spiritual food. Mr Wilson was a *faithful and wise steward, who gave every one his portion of meat, in due season*. He preached the terrors of the law to those persons, to whom terror belonged; and to such as came to him trembling, and crying out, *Sir, what shall I do to be saved?* he was a Barnabas, *a son of sweet consolation*. He beautifully displayed the unsearchable riches of divine grace, in the Lord Jesus Christ, unto sinners ready to perish. His doctrine was according to godliness; and his chief aim was to glorify God, and to win souls unto Christ. He neither sought to please the fancy, nor to gain the applause of his auditory, by *the enticing words of man's wisdom*. And, in obedience to the divine command, he preached the word, both *in season*, and *out of season;* not only twice on every Lord's-day, but also frequently on other days; and on different occasions, when partial and worldly men reckoned, that his preaching was unseasonable. His great popularity and usefulness soon awakened the envy of profane sinners, and also of several neighbouring ministers; but he constantly went on without dismay, trusting in the Lord, who, with the blessing which alone makes rich, crowned his labours with great success. He continued to be a very strict and zealous observer of the Lord's-day; always using means for checking the profanation of that day, and for promoting reformation.

Notwithstanding Mr Wilson's great labours and usefulness, he was at length silenced for refusing to read the profane Book of Sports. In the month of April, 1634, he was inhibited by Archbishop Laud's Vicar-general, from part of his public ministerial exercises. But, upon the publication of the Book of Sports, he refused to read it, when the Archbishop sent for him to Lambeth; and, April 29th, 1635, no less than *fourteen* charges were exhibited against him, to each of which he gave his answer, May 28th following, 1635. All these charges, together with Mr Wilson's answers, are too long for our insertion, in this place; but we shall here give the charge, with Mr Wilson's answer, respecting the Book of Sports.

Char. You refused to read the King's Declaration for Sports on Sundays, and spoke disdainfully to the Apparitor and Officer of the court.

Ans. I said unto the Apparitor. "Remember you to keep holy the Sabbath day;" and I said no more. I refused to read the Book, not out of contempt of any authority, but as being commanded by no law. The King's Majesty doth not in the Book command or appoint the minister to read it, nor it to be read, but published. Neither came it with, nor do I know of any seal to confirm it. And seeing there is no penalty threatened, nor authority given, that I know of, to any one to question those persons who refuse to read it, my refusal to read it was upon sufficient grounds of law and conscience; which, for the satisfaction of this high court, and to clear myself from contempt, I shall briefly express myself thus: His Majesty's express pleasure is, that the laws of the kingdom, and the canons of the church, be observed in all places of the kingdom; and, therefore, in Kent, and in Otham: but this book, as I conceive, is contrary to both. —It is contrary to the statute laws, Edward VI. Anno 5, Cap. iii. Caroli, Anno 1, Cap. 1, & Can. 13.—Our Church is against it. It is contrary to the ecclesiastical laws.—It is contrary to the Holy Scriptures, Exod. xx. 8. Isa. lviii. 13.—It is contrary to the councils.—It is contrary to divines, both ancient and modern; as Augustine, Chrysostom, Irenæus, Ignatius, Babington, Zanchy,

Junius, and Alsted.—And it is contrary to reason. Mr Wilson enlarges on these topics, in a very judicious manner.

It evidently appears, that Laud had laid the snare to catch Mr Wilson, chiefly for refusing to read the Book of Sports. And in this, that great oppressor of the Lord's heritage succeeded according to his wishes: for Mr Wilson's answers, in which he explicitly declared his refusal to read the Book, were no sooner given, than the proud archbishop haughtily replied, *I suspend you for ever from your office and benefice till you read it.* And this eminently pious and laborious servant of the Lord Jesus Christ continued suspended for about the space of four years. About the same time, he was committed to Maidstone jail for non-conformity, but how long he remained in that confinement, I cannot inform the reader. At the expiration of the above period, he was brought into the high commission court by means of the archbishop; and, to his great cost and trouble, was again prosecuted for the same crime.

While Mr Wilson remained under suspension, not being satisfied with the ministry of his successor at Otham, he removed to Maidstone, where he gave some private instructions among his friends, from whom he received some external support, both for himself and for his family. His malicious enemies, at the same time, traduced his character, and represented him as a favourer of division. With a view to wipe off that base reproach, he addressed a respectful letter to the parishioners of Otham, warmly exhorting them "to fear God and honour the King, and to walk in love toward each other; and not to nourish in themselves any dislike of government, or contempt of those whom the Lord had set over them." This letter, for the information and satisfaction of all persons, was publicly read to the congregation, by Dr Tuck, on the Lord's day, without the appointment of Mr Wilson. The news of this affair soon reached London, when Mr Wilson and Dr Tuck were cited to appear before the high commission court. Mr Wilson was charged in that court with having sent a scandalous and offensive letter to Otham, to nourish schism, and to confirm the people in the dislike of government. Upon that charge being presented against him, he readily acknowledged that he had written a letter to the people of Otham, but positively denied its bad tendency. He said, "I know that it was to exhort the people to fear God and the King, and not to meddle with those who are given to change; to walk in faith and love, and to call upon God: but I utterly deny all occasion of derogating from the church of England, or confirmation of any in the dislike of government, and protest against all aspersions and imputation of schism or scandal: neither did I direct any person to read it, nor intended or desired that it should be read in the church." And notwithstanding all that both Mr Wilson and Dr Tuck could allege in their own defence, they were obliged to continue their attendance on the court, for the space of three years, to their great cost and trouble. Dr Tuck's case was peculiarly distressing; for, on account of bodily infirmities, he was not able to ride, and under the necessity of making all his journies on foot, at the distance of more than thirty miles.

During Mr Wilson's suspension, a neighbouring minister, who eagerly wished to obtain his benefice, commenced a plea against him, with a view to eject him altogether out of Otham; but his patron made good his title, and so disappointed his adversary. In the year 1639, the Scots having entered England, and a Parliament being called, Laud took off Mr Wilson's suspension. But his troubles and sufferings were not then at an end, for, on Sep. 30th, in 1640, he was cited to appear before the archbishop's visitors at Feversham in Kent, together with other ministers in that county, to answer for not reading the prayer against the Scots. Upon the appearance of those ministers, Mr Edward Bright, being called first, was asked whether he had read that prayer; and when he said that he had not, the archdeacon immediately suspended him both from office and benefice, without admonition, or even giving him the least time for consideration. That tyranical court often proceeded in a very summary manner. Mr Wilson, who was a witness of this rash procedure, and now perceived that the service was to be much hotter than he had expected, was next called. When he was asked whether he had read the prayer against the Scots, he answered in the negative; adding, "because in the rubrick of the Common Prayer, it is enjoined that no prayer shall be publicly read, excepting those which are contained in the Book of Common Prayer, and that prayer against the Scots was not there." This very unexpected answer so puzzled and confounded the archdeacon that he did not know what to say. It cooled his fury, and caused him to proceed more deliberately with Mr Wilson than he had done with Mr Bright. He allowed him fourteen days for consideration, and then he was to deliver his answer at Canterbury; but whether he delivered any other answer, and what followed respecting that case, we are not able to inform the reader.

About the same time, a warrant was issued from the Lords of the private council, among whom were Archbishop Laud and the Bishop of London, to apprehend Mr Thomas Wilson of Otham, and to bring him before them. A pursuivant was sent with this warrant to bring Mr Wilson to London. We are not informed for what crime this prosecution was raised; but there is sufficient ground to conclude, that it was for the great sin of nonconformity. The pursuivant, having received his warrant, went without delay to Otham; and though he heard Mr Wilson preach, and was afterward in the same room with him, yet he escaped out of his hands. Mr Wilson, suspecting him as soon as he entered the room, retired and concealed himself, and so was delivered out of the snare. *Our soul is escaped as a bird out of the snare of the fowlers: the snare is broken, and we are escaped. Our help is in the name of Jehovah, who made heaven and earth.*—The zealous pursuivant was exceedingly enraged at his loss; but upon becoming a little cooler, he said, "that he had been a messenger to the council-table *thirty-six* years, and was never so served before."

Mr Wilson, having, in the goodness of Divine Providence, escaped that dangerous snare, withdrew from the furious storm until the meeting of the Long Parliament, when he went to London, and his case and petition were presented to the House of Commons. The House appointed a committee to take his case into consideration; and, Nov. 30th, 1640, Mr Rouse, who was one of that committee, reported to the house, "That Mr Wilson had been suspended four years from his living, worth sixty-pounds a-year, only for not reading the Book of Recreations on the Lord's day; that the archbishop himself had suspended him; and that for three years he had attended upon the high commission court." The House therefore resolved, That Mr Wilson had just cause of complaint; and that there was just cause for the House to afford him relief. Upon the presentation of his petition, Sir Edward Deering, who was one of the members for the county of Kent, said, Mr Wilson, your petitioner, is as orthodox in doctrine, as laborious in preaching, and as unblemished in life, as any minister we have. He is now separated from his flock, to both their griefs: for it is not with him as with many others, who are glad to set a pursuivant on work, that they may have an excuse to be out of the pulpit; it is his delight to preach." Sir Edward farther observes respecting Mr Wilson, "He is now a sufferer, as all good men are, under the general obloquy of a Puritan. The pursuivant watches his door, and divides him and his cure asunder, to both their griefs. About a week since, I went to Lambeth, to move that great bishop (too great indeed) to take this danger from off this minister, and to recall the pursuivant. And I did undertake for Mr Wilson, that he would answer his accusers, in any of the King's courts at Westminster. The bishop made me answer, 'I am sure that he will not be absent from his cure a twelvemonth together.'"

Upon the above resolution of the House of Commons, Mr Wilson was released from his troubles, and returned to his charge and labours at Otham. In the year 1643, he was chosen one of the Assembly of Divines at Westminster, and though at a considerable distance, he constantly attended, and also supplied his flock on the Lord's day. He was very much esteemed in the Assembly for his meek and humble deportment, and his grave and judicious discourses and counsels. Having continued some time at Otham, he removed to Maidstone, the county-town of Kent, where he remained until his death. Here his chief care was to promote the reformation of the church, and to administer the sacraments, according to his views of the word of God. In order to this end, he preached particularly upon the necessity of observing scriptural discipline, and the qualifications which were really necessary to the enjoyment of church-fellowship. Impressed deeply by the sense of duty, and very eager to dispense the divine light of the gospel of the Lord Jesus Christ, which burned with great ardour in his own breast, he disengaged himself from this world, and was entirely devoted to the interests of the Redeemer's kingdom. He met with considerable opposition at first, but by prudence and perseverance, *trusting in Jehovah, in whom there is everlasting strength*, things were brought to a favourable issue.

Mr Wilson laboured indefatigably in discharging the numerous duties of his office. He discharged the duties of the Lord's day, with exceedingly much pious zeal, and exemplary devotion. He commonly observed the following method: he continued his studies on Saturdays very late, often till about midnight, that he might be the better prepared for the important work of the Lord's day. He rose ordinarily by two or three o'clock on the Sabbath morning, and was much displeased with himself if he was at any time later. About seven he came out of his study, and called his family together, when he read and expounded a portion of the Holy Scriptures, requiring those persons who were present to give some account of the exposition; then sung some part of a psalm, and concluded with prayer. About nine o'clock he went to church, and entered upon public worship by singing part of a psalm commonly, then prayed for the divine blessing which makes rich, and expounded in the Old Testament, sometimes three, four, or more, verses, continuing about an hour, in that exercise; then, beside singing and prayer, he preached about an hour, and concluded. Then, going home, he constantly prayed with his family before dinner; and afterward, he spent some time with them in singing and other religious exercises. In the afternoon, he observed the same method in the public worship as in the morning; only his exposition was upon some part of the New Testament. Mr Wilson is said to have been an excellent expositor of the Holy Scriptures; and well acquainted with Junius, Tremellius, Piscator, Beza, Calvin, and several other commentators. It is said, that his expositions much resembled those of Mr Hutchison on the Gospel of John; but that he was fuller and larger than Mr Hutchison. The public services of the day being ended, Mr Wilson called his family together, when many neighbours attended, then they repeated the sermons and expositions, upon which he sung a psalm and concluded with prayer. After this he went to a friend's house in the town, where many attended, and engaged in the same exercises. He administered the Lord's Supper once a month; with much holy fervour: and, it is said, "that some of the communicants have thought themselves in the suburbs of heaven, when they joined with him in that ordinance, in which he commonly spent an hour and half."—He sanctified the Lord's day, by spending nine or ten hours in public and private worship, beside what time he spent in secret religious exercises. He also delivered weekly lectures, attended meetings for religious conference, and engaged in catechizing. He was a diligent labourer in the Lord's vineyard, and found his reward in the labour. When his friends attempted to dissuade him from such intense application, he was always deaf to their counsel, saying, "Would you have my Lord, when he comes, to find me idle?" He was persuaded that God makes no difference between an *idle* and an *evil* servant. We surely cannot but admire the benevolent exertions of this great and good man.

Mr Wilson was also very exact in setting a good example before all persons, and especially before his children and servants, knowing that inferiors are much influenced by the deportment of their superiors. What he preached, he practised all the week. *In all things, he shewed himself a pattern of good works.* He constantly exemplified his own wholesome instructions. He was a very strict observer of the Sabbath day, and eminently successful in promoting the due observation of it at Maidstone, as well as at other places. One of the judges noticing this at the assize, publicly declared, that, in all his circuit there was no town where the Lord's day was so strictly observed. All Mr Wilson's fervour was for some time exercised, in promoting the welfare of Maidstone. By his preaching and example, he excited those persons to engage in family worship who had formerly neglected it. They performed it both morning and evening. And, as they sung when they read the word of God and prayed, persons walking in the street, about nine and ten o'clock in the morning, might hear singing of Psalms in many families. This was a plentiful source of joy and gratitude to every mind which was seasoned with genuine piety. Mr Wilson was a man of a very courageous spirit, and feared no obstacles in the way of duty. Like the Roman Cato, he had "a resolution, a steadiness, and a composure of mind, not to be moved by flattery, nor to be shaken by threats." He feared God, and none else. He was like one of the celebrated ancients, who, when a threatening message of death was sent to him, desired the messenger to tell the Empress, *I fear nothing but sin.* Mr Wilson discovered much holy courage in reproving sin, and in appearing for the defence of the gospel. He was firmly persuaded, that the Lord would take special care of his own cause, whatever sufferings his servants might endure, therefore, when trials came upon them, he said, with Luther, "I had rather fall with Christ than reign with Cæsar." He lived much above this world. His treasure was in heaven, and his heart was there also; as appears from the following anecdote:—At the insurrection in 1648, the soldiers took from him a legacy of a hundred pounds left by a friend to his eldest daughter, though it was soon restored. But when the money was gone, upon being asked whether he was not much troubled, he replied, "No; I was no more troubled when I heard that the money was carried out of my house, than I was when I heard that it was brought into it." And upon being asked what frame of spirit he was in, when the town and county were in arms, and some base and profane wretches reproached him, when he was going out of the town, taking his horse by the bridle, and twice or thrice brought him back, crying aloud, *Wilson, Wilson, Where is your God now? Where is your God now?* He replied, " I then thought on that text, *My God is in Heaven, and hath done whatsoever he pleased.*" Psal. cxv. 3. With much patience, he beheld the frowns of the great, and heard the scoffs of the vulgar.

But Mr Wilson's eminent piety, humility, and integrity, did shine with peculiar lustre, in his affliction and death. When the Bridegroom came, he had his lamp trimmed, oil in his vessel, and his light burning. He was waiting for the coming of his Lord. And he endured his acute pains with great patience. He sometimes mourned, but he never murmured. He cheerfully submitted to the rod, in the hand of his heavenly Father. When lying upon his death-bed, he called his family around him. He desired his wife not to be discouraged, nor *to sorrow as those who have no hope;* but to trust in the Lord her God, in whom there is everlasting strength, and to continue in his service. He warmly exhorted his children to fear God, and directing his speech to his eldest daughter, he said, " Look to it, that you meet me not at the day of judgment in an unregenerate state." He commended all his children to the Lord, and left them in his hand. When Christian friends came to visit him, his mind seemed to collect new vigour, and he earnestly exhorted them to read the Holy Scriptures, to esteem highly and meditate much on the promises, to be holy in their conversation, and to attend divine ordinances with all diligence. He highly praised God, and spoke much of the preciousness of Christ, and said, that " one promise was more precious than a world." The prospect of his approaching death was very comfortable to him. To a pious lady of his acquaintance, who was leaving Maidstone, he pleasantly said, " What will you say, good Mrs Crisp, if I get the start of you, and get to heaven before you get to Dover." Another person saying, Sir, I think you are not far from your Father's house; he replied, "That is good news indeed, and is enough to make one leap for joy." To those who mourned over him, he said, "I bless God, who has suffered me to live so long to do him some service; and now I have finished the work appointed for me, that he is pleased to call me away so soon." He died in the exercise of faith and hope, commending his spirit into the hands of his dear Redeemer, on the Lord's day, toward the end of the year 1653, aged about fifty-two years. He had a strong constitution, a clear understanding, a quick invention, a sound judgment, a a tenacious memory, and was a good scholar, a hard student, well read both in ancient and modern authors, an excellent preacher, an eminent Christian, and *clothed with humility.* Mr Wilson was twice married, and by his second wife, he had eleven children, ten of whom were living at his death. Mr J. Wilson, ejected in 1662, is supposed to have been a son of his.

Our Mr Wilson was author of a sermon preached from Heb. xi. 30. before the House of Commons, at their solemn Fast, Sept. 28th, 1642. This sermon is entitled, "Jericho's Down-fall, 4to. pp. 48. London, 1643. I have not seen any more of Mr Wilson's writings. I have seen some Poems which were made upon his much lamented death. We rejoice at seeing the Muses twining garlands for the brow of such a man as Mr Wilson.[a]

a Life of Mr Wilson, printed in the year 1672, and Brook's Lives of the Puritans, vol. iii. London, 1813.

FRANCIS WOODCOCK, A. B.

MINISTER IN LONDON, AND ONE OF THE ASSEMBLY OF DIVINES AT WESTMINSTER.

FRANCIS WOODCOCK was born in the city of Chester, the capital of Cheshire, in England, in the year 1614. He received his education in Brazen-nose college, Oxford, where he took one degree in Arts. He entered into the holy ministry while he was at the University, and was episcopally ordained, soon after which he removed from that seat of learning, and had a charge of souls bestowed upon him. Wood says, that "he was always Puritanically affected;" which some persons will account no bad character. Accordingly, upon the commencement of the differences between the King and the Parliament, he readily espoused the cause of the latter, and was afterward chosen one of the Assembly of Divines at Westminster; and it is said, that he asiduously attended during the whole session. Being brought up to London, he was chosen Lecturer of Lawrence-Jewry, and frequently preached at Olaves in Southwark, to which he was afterward appointed minister by an ordinance of Parliament, which was dated July 10th, 1646. He took the Covenant with the rest of his brethren, and was chosen Proctor to the University of Cambridge. He preached several times before the House of Commons; and some of his sermons which he preached to that learned and respectable auditory have been published, and are still extant. He died in the midst of his days and of his usefulness. Wood says, that he died in 1651, or thereabout; but Mr Brook says, that he died in the year 1649, aged thirty-five years. His remains were interred in Olaves' church, Southwark. He was esteemed a good scholar, and an excellent preacher.[a]—Mr Woodcock died young: but Hooker said of

a Wood's Athenæ Oxon. vol. ii. Brook's Puritans, vol. iii.

that famous Prince, Edward the sixth, King of England, "That though he died young he lived long, for life is in *action.*" And the courtiers of Henry fourth, King of France, one day complimenting him upon the strength of his constitution, and telling him that he might live to be eighty years of age; he replied, "The number of our days is reckoned. I have often prayed to God for grace, but never for a long life. A man who has lived well, has always lived long enough, however early he may die."[a]

Mr Woodcock has written and published,—1. *The Two Witnesses;* in several Lectures at Lawrence-Jewry, London, on Rev. xi. 3, &c. with the great Question discussed, Whether the two Witnesses were slain or not? 4to. London, 1643.—This work was made public by an order from the Committee of the House of Commons, dated April 27, 1643. It was afterward reprinted.—2. *Christ's Warning-piece, Giving Notice to Every One to Watch and Keep Their Garments:* delivered in a Sermon at Margaret's, Westminster, before the Honourable House of Commons, at their solemn Fast, from Rev. xvi. 15. Oct. 30, 1644. 4to. pp. 32. London, 1644.—3. *Lex Talionis; or, God Paying Every Man in His Own Coin:* a Fast Sermon from 1 Sam. ii. 30. before the House of Commons, July 30th, 1645. 4to. London, 1645, and 1646.—4. *Joseph Paralelled by the Present Parliament, in His Sufferings and Advancement:* A Sermon preached from Gen. xlix. 23, 24, before the House of Commons, on their Solemn Day of Thanksgiving, Feb. 19th, 1645, or 1646. 4to. London, 1646.

"The universal friend, so formed to engage,
Was far too precious for this world and age.
Years were denied, for (such his worth and truth)
Kind Heaven has call'd him to eternal youth."

a Anecdotes of Distinguished Persons, vols. i. and iv.

THOMAS YOUNG, D.D.

MINISTER OF STOW-MARKET, AND A MEMBER OF THE ASSEMBLY OF DIVINES AT WESTMINSTER.

THOMAS YOUNG was an eminently learned and pious divine. Mr Brook says,—"This pious and learned divine was probably educated in the University of Cambridge. He was afterward preacher to the English merchants at Hamburgh; and, upon his return to his native country, he became vicar of Stow-market in Suffolk, in which situation he continued almost thirty years. He was a person of great learning, prudence, and piety, and discovered great fidelity and ability in the work of the ministry."—In the year 1643, he was chosen one of the Assembly of Divines at Westminster, and proved himself to be an eminently distinguished member of that illustrious body during the whole session. He was one of those who reasoned for the divine institution of the ruling elder, in that Assembly, and had an active hand in the Directory for reading of Scriptures, and singing of Psalms.[a] Upon being called to London, he was chosen pastor of Duke's-place in the city. In 1645, he was appointed one of the committee of accommodation; and about the same time he was chosen master of Jesus College, Cambridge, by the Earl of Manchester. In that eminent and public station, he displayed his great abilities, and was highly useful, until he was turned out of his place, in the year 1650, for refusing the engagement. Upon this he most probably retired to Stow-market, where he afterward died, in the year 1655, and his remains were interred in the church under a marble stone, with a monumental inscription.

a Baillie's Letters, vol. i. pp. 401, and 431.

Mr Baker says, that "he left behind him the character of a learned, wise, and pious man." Mr Leigh, in his Treatise of Religious and Learned Men, p. 369, styles him "a learned divine, one very well versed in the Fathers, and the Author of that excellent Treatise, entitled *Dies Dominica.*" He was also one of the authors of Smectymnuus.[b]—I have seen an excellent Sermon, both in England and Scotland, by Thomas Young, seemingly the same divine, entitled, "Hope's Encouragement pointed at, in a Sermon preached from Psalm xxxi. 24. in Margaret's, Westminster, before the Honourable House of Commons, at the Solemn Fast, Feb. 28th, 1643." 4to. pp. 38. London, 1644.

a Neal and Brook's Puritans, vol. iii.

SCOTTISH COMMISSIONERS.

We come now to those eminent Ministers, who were Commissioners from the Church of Scotland to the Assembly of Divines at Westminster. Fuller says; "As Livy calls the general meeting of Etolica, Pan-Etolium, this Assembly endeavoured to put on the face of Pan-Britanicum."[a] The English solicited the assistance of some of the Scottish Divines to join with those at Westminster, to settle an Uniformity of Religion and Church-government for the two Nations. The request was granted, and Messrs. Alexander Henderson, Robert Douglas, Samuel Rutherford, George Gillespie, and Robert Baillie, were by the General Assembly of the Church of Scotland appointed in August 18th, 1643, to go to London, as Commissioners to the Assembly of Divines at Westminster.[b]—Mr Douglas did not go to London, as all those who were appointed were not urged to go; but the other four went.—The writers of the Quarterly Review have very lately made a daring attempt, to consign the memory of our Presbyterian ancestors to contempt and oblivion. They have excommunicated from the pale of talent, literature, and common sense, all the Covenanters in a mass; and they endeavour to vindicate their unjust sentence, by a particular reference to two of our pious and eminently learned Commissioners, Messrs. Henderson and Gillespie. An able writer, who has completely rescued our respectable ancestors, and especially our Commissioners to the Westminster Assembly, from the foul aspersions of the Quarterly Reviewers, has made the following just remarks upon this part of their conduct. "They have not only gone wrong in their general statement, but through some strange infatuation, and as if to demonstrate their utter ignorance of fact, or their utter

a Fuller's Church Hist. B. 11. p. 199.
b Baillie's Letters, vol. i. pp. 349, 350, and 387.

contempt of decency, they have ventured to mention and to defame individuals, who, though every other "*brother of the covenant*" had been a mere niny, deserved nothing but esteem and reverence.—Why, it would not be in the least degree more absurd to assert, that England during the Commonwealth produced no great Poets, and then to quote Milton as an example."[c] We owe the tribute both of respect and of gratitude to the memory of those Commissioners;—of respect for their gifts, and of gratitude for their services. We proceed now to give some particular account of them.

ROBERT BAILLIE, D. D.

AN EMINENT PRESBYTERIAN DIVINE IN THE CHURCH OF SCOTLAND, IN THE SEVENTEENTH CENTURY, AND ONE OF THE COMMISSIONERS FROM THAT CHURCH TO THE ASSEMBLY OF DIVINES AT WESTMINSTER.

ROBERT BAILLIE was born in Glasgow, in the year 1599. His father, Mr Thomas Baillie, was a citizen of that place, and son to Baillie of Jerviston, who was a brother of the Family of Carphin, and a branch of the ancient Family of Lamington, all in the county of Lanerk. Baillie of Hoprig and Lamington was a branch of the Baliols, Lords of Galloway. Hoprig, by marrying the daughter of the famous Sir William Wallace, Regent of Scotland, obtained the estate of Lamington. Their second son was the first of the House of Carphin; of whom Jerviston, the predecessor of our author, according to Nisbet's Heraldry. His mother's name was Helen Gibson, of the stock of the Gibsons of Durie, several of whom were eminently distinguished by making a great figure in the Law. Our Robert Baillie received his education in the University of Glasgow, his native city,

c Edinburgh Christian Instructor, vol. vii. p. 406. A very valuable Publication, which justly claims the attention of the Public.

under the care and direction of Mr Sharp, who was then the head of that College. When at the University, he was a remarkable example of great literary diligence, giving always very close attention to his studies. Having taken his degrees in the arts, he turned his thoughts to the study of divinity, to which he applied with indefatigable industry. And having, about the year 1622, received orders from Archbishop Law, he was chosen a Regent of Philosophy in the University of Glasgow. While he was in that station, he had, for some years, the care of the education of Lord Montgomery, who, at length, carried him with him to Kilwinning; to which church he was presented by the Earl of Eglinton. There he lived in the strictest friendship with that noble family, and with his people; as he did also with his ordinary, the Archbishop of Glasgow, with whom he kept up an epistolary correspondence. In the year 1633, he declined, from a principle of modesty, an offer which was made to him of a church in Edinburgh. Being requested, in 1637, by the Archbishop of Glasgow, to preach a sermon before the General Assembly, in recommendation of the Book of Common-Prayer, and the Canon of the Church, then published and established by authority, he declined the service; and wrote a handsome letter to the Archbishop, assigning the reasons of his refusal. The letter is dated at Kilwinning, Aug. 19th, 1637, and is as follows:

"Please Your Lordship,

Your Lordship's letter of the 7th of this instant, I received the 13th, late, wherein I am desired to preach the last Wednesday of this instant, before the Assembly, and to frame my sermon to unite my hearers to the obedience and practice of the canon of our church and Service-book, published and established by authority. I am much obliged to your Lordship's estimation of my poor gifts, and do humbly thank your Lordship for intending to honour me with so great a service: but withal am sorry that my present disposition necessitates me to decline the charge.— The truth is, that as yet I have not studied the matters contained in that Book of our Canons and Common-prayer, only I have taken a slight view of them; whereby, for the present, my mind is no ways satisfied; yea, the little pleasure I have in these books, and the great displeasure I find the most part have, both of pastors and people wherever I come, conceived of them, have filled my mind with such a measure of grief, that I am scarcely able to preach to my own flock: but to preach in another congregation, and so famous a meeting, upon these matters, I am at this time utterly unable."'[a]

This spirited refusal greatly served to establish his reputation with the party who opposed Episcopacy in the Church of Scotland, at that time. At the commencement of the Reformation, he had his own difficulties from his education and his delicacy respecting the King's authority, in complying with some measures of the Covenanters; but after reasoning, reading and prayer, as he himself says, he came heartily into their measures. And being eminently distinguished by his peaceable and healing temper, his uncommon prudence, and solid judgment, he was much employed in the public and important affairs of the church from the year 1637. He was chosen and appointed, in the year 1638, by his own Presbytery of Irvine, a member of the very famous and memorable Assembly at Glasgow, which was a prelude to the civil war, and of which the reader may see a particular account in Mr Henderson's life. In that Assembly, Mr Baillie displayed great wisdom, zeal, and learning. He eminently appeared as one of the most able and zealous advocates for the Presbyterian cause. And he was peculiarly distinguished, by his strong opposition to Prelacy and Arminianism. He was also a member of all the following General Assemblies of the Church of Scotland, until the year 1653, excepting when he attended the Assembly of Divines at Westminster.

He was also one of those eminent ministers who attended the army of the Covenanters, as chaplain, in the years 1639, and 1640. He says, "I furnished to half a dozen

a Letters, vol. i. pp. 11, 12.

of good fellows, muskets and pikes, and to my boy a broad sword. I carried myself as the fashion was, a sword, and a couple of Dutch pistols at my saddle; but I promise for the offence of no man, excepting a robber in the way; for it was our part alone to pray and to preach for the encouragement of our countrymen, which I did most cheerfully to the utmost of my power.—Every company had, fleeing at the captain's tent-door, a brave new colour, stamped with the Scottish arms, and this motto, *For Christ's Crown and Covenant*, in golden letters."[a]—He adds: "Had you lent your ear in the morning, or especially at even, and heard in the tents the sound of some signing psalms, some praying, and some reading Scripture, ye would have been refreshed.—For myself, I never found my mind in better temper than it was all that time since I came from home, till my head was again homeward; for I was as a man who had taken my leave from the world, and was resolved to die in that service, without return. I found the favour of God shining upon me, and a sweet, meek, humble, yet strong and vehement spirit leading me all along; but I was no sooner on my way westward, after the conclusion of the peace, than my old security returned."[b]—Mr Baillie was present during the whole treaty with the King, which commenced at Kippon, and was concluded at London. And as one of the most able and zealous advocates for the Presbyterian cause, he was, in 1640, sent by the covenanting Lords of Scotland to London, to draw up an accusation against Laud, Archbishop of Canterbury. for attempting to obtrude unwelcome innovations upon the Church of Scotland. While he was in England upon that occasion, he wrote to the Presbytery of Irvine a large and regular account of the state of public affairs, and sent them, among other things, a particular Journal of the proceedings in the trial of the Earl of Strafford.[c] Not long after his return to his own country, in the year 1642, he was appointed Joint Professor of Divinity, with Mr David

a Letters, vol. i. pp. 174, 775, 176. b Vol. i. p. 178.
c Letters, vol. i. pp. 219—297.

Dickson, in the University of Glasgow. And his reputation was become so high, that he had before this received invitations from the other three Scottish Universities, all of which he refused. He continued in his Professorship till the Restoration; but his discharge of the duties of it was interrupted, for a considerable time, by his residence in England. As a divine eminently learned, and of approved orthodoxy, he was, in the year 1643, chosen one of the Commissioners from the Church of Scotland to the Assembly of Divines at Westminster. Though he did not distinguish himself by speaking much in the debates of that Assembly, he appears to have been very useful in it. He entirely concurred in the principles and views of its leading members; and gained great reputation by his writings. He wrote an account of the state of public affairs, and of the proceedings of the Assembly, while he was at London, which is very interesting. When he took his leave of the Assembly, the Prolocutor, in the name of the Assembly, gave him an honourable testimony, and thanks for his labours.[a] He remained there almost all the time that the Assembly was sitting; and returned to his own country in the latter end of the year 1646. When that Assembly rose, the English Parliament made him a handsome present of silver-plate, with an inscription, intimating that it was a token of their great respect to him, and to be viewed as an acknowledgement of his good services. It was long carefully preserved in the house of Carnbrae, in the county of Lanerk, an ancient seat of the Baillies.

Mr Baillie was an eminent confident of the Marquis of Argyle, of the Earls of Cassils, Eglinton, Lauderale and Loudon, of Lord Balmerino, Sir Archibald Johnston, Lord Warriston, and others of the chief managers among the Covenanters. He thereby obtained the most correct knowledge of the papers and most important transactions of those times, which he very carefully collected and preserved.

He was exceedingly averse to Episcopacy, but he was

a Letters, vol. ii. p. 252.

not deficient in loyality. The General Assembly of Scotland had so much confidence in his attachment to the House of Stuart, that, after the execution of King Charles I. in 1649, they appointed him one of the embassy from their body to Charles II. at the Hague, after he was proclaimed in Scotland. Upon that occasion Mr Baillie addressed the King in a loyal speech, expressing in the strongest terms his joy and that of his brethren in his succession to the throne, and their great abhorrence of the murder of his royal father. In his sentiments on this event, it appears, that the Presbyterian Divines of that period, both at home and abroad, very generally agreed.—Under Cromwell's usurpation, he joined with the party called *Resolutioners*, and wrote several of the papers on that side. He had a strong aversion to toleration, and availed himself of every opportunity in testifying against it. He seldom omits any oportunity of shewing his disapprobation of the doctrine of toleration, either in his Letters, or in his other writings.—After the Restoration of King Charles II. Mr Baillie, on the 23d of Jan. 1661, by the interest of the Earl of Lauderdale, with whom he was a great favourite, was made Principal of the University of Glasgow, upon the removal of Mr Patrick Gillespie, who had been patronised by Cromwell. It is said, by several writers, that Mr Baillie had the offer of a Bishopric, which he absolutely refused. This is highly probable.

He was very highly esteemed by some of the most eminent Biblical and classical scholars on the Continent in his time; as Spanheim, Salmasius, Rivet, Leusden, and Constantine L. Empereur. In his Letters, he writes as a man of great piety and intellect, and is found inquiring at his correspondent in Holland for the best and most recent publications on Hebrew, Syriac, and Arabic, literature, and even on mathematical science; all which shews at once the great variety and extent of his own attainments, and also his earnest desire to promote the interests of that academical institution with which he was intimately connected.—He was an excellent linguist. By his indefatigable industry, he acquired the knowledge of twelve or thirteen languages; and he could write a Latin style, which, in the opinion of learned men, might well become the Augustan age, and of which his *Opus Chronolo icum* is a decisive proof.—Mr Baillie was averse to funeral sermons, when he was in London. Speaking of Mr Pym's funeral, he says; "Marshall had a most eloquent and pertinent funeral sermon; which we would not hear; for funeral sermons we must have away."[a] He was twice married. By his first wife, Lilias Fleming, he had several children; and by his second wife, Principal Strang's daughter, he had one daughter, Margaret, who was married to Mr Walkingshaw of Barrowfield. Principal Baillie continued most firmly attached to the Presbyterian government, and in opposition to Prelacy, to the end of his life. As a proof of this, an eminent historian says; "I have it from an unquestionable hand, one of his scholars, who afterward was his successor, and waited on him a few weeks before his death, that he died a firm Presbyterian, and under a rooted aversion to Prelacy in this church. My author desired Mr Baillie's judgment of the courses which this church was so fast running into. His words to him were; 'Prelacy is now coming in like a *land-flood;* for my share, I have considered that controversy as far as I was able, and after all my inquiry I find it, (Prelacy) and am persuaded that it is inconsistent with Scripture, contrary to pure and primitive antiquity, and diametrically opposite to the true interest of those lands.'"[b] And during his last illness, when he was visited by the newly-made Archbishop of Glasgow, he is said to have addressed himself to him in the following words: "Mr Andrew, I will not call you my Lord. King Charles would have made me one of these Lords: but I do not find in the New Testament, that Christ has any Lords in his house." However, he treated the Archbishop very courteously. The coming in of Prelacy, like a *land-flood*, brake his heart, and had a strong tendency to hasten his dissolution. This is evident from two original letters under his own hand, to the Earl of Lauderale, the one dat-

a Letters, vol. i. p. 409. b Wodrow's Hist. vol. i. p. 128.

ed, June 16th, 1660, and the other April 18th, 1661, which are still preserved in Wodrow's History. His health failed him in the Spring of the year in 1662, and he died in the month of July that same year, aged 63 years.

The Author of the Appendix to Archbishop Spottiswoode's History, speaking of Principal Baillie, says respecting him; "Robert Baillie, Professor of Divinity, and afterward Principal, a learned and modest man; though he published some very violent writings, yet these flowed rather from the instigation of other persons than his own inclinations. He has left a great evidence of his diligence and learning in his *Opus Chronologicum.*"

And the celebrated Mr Wodrow, in his History of the Sufferings of the Church of Scotland, has given the following character of Principal Baillie. "Mr Robert Baillie may most justly be reckoned among the great men of this time, and was an honour to his country, for his profound and universal learning, his exact and solid judgement, that vast variety of languages which he understood, to the number of twelve or thirteen, and his writing a Latin style which might become the Augustan age. But I need not enlarge on his character; *his works do praise him in the gates.*"[a]

Mr Baillie's Writings are: *A Defence of the Reformation of the Church of Scotland*, against Mr Maxwell, Bishop of Ross.—*A Parallel between the Scottish Service-Book, and the Romish Missal, Breviary, &c.—Queries anent the Service-Book.—The Canterburian Self-Conviction.—Antidote to Arminianism.—A Treatise on Scottish Episcopacy.—Laudensisim.—Satan the Leader in chief to all who resist the Reparation of Zion.* A sermon preached from Zech. iii. 14. to the House of Commons, at their solemn Fast, Feb. 28th, 1644. 4to. London.—A sermon from Isa. lxiii. 17. before the Lords, July 30th, 1645. Fast, 4to. pp.

a Wodrow's Hist. vol. i. p. 128. Baillie's Life prefixed to his Letters, and Stevenson's Hist. Preface.

44 London, 1645.—*A Dissuasive from the Errors of the time*, especially of the Independents, 4to. pp. 252. London, 1645. A second part of the Dissuasive, 4to. pp. 179, and a long Preface, London, 1647.—*A Reply to the Modest Inquirer.—Opus Historicum and Chronologicum;* folio, B. 1. pp. 307. B. 2. pp. 151. with a frontispiece, printed at Amsterdam, 1668. It is written in classical and elegant Latin, and clearly proves that the author was a man of deep research and of very extensive knowledge. *Letters, and Journals*, in 2 vols. 8vo. vol. i. pp. 456. vol. ii. pp. 462. Edinburgh, 1775. The Journals contain a History of the General Assembly at Glasgow in 1638; an Account of the Earl of Strafford's Trial; of the General Assemblies, in 1641, and in 1643.

GEORGE GILLESPIE,

MINISTER OF EDINBURGH, AND ONE OF THE COMMISSIONERS FROM THE CHURCH OF SCOTLAND TO THE ASSEMBLY OF DIVINES AT WESTMINSTER.

GEORGE GILLESPIE was the son of Mr John Gillespie, who some time was minister of the Gospel at Kirkaldy, a royal burgh and market-town of Fifeshire, in Scotland. Wood says, that George Gillespie, the subject of this Memoir, was educated in the University of St Andrew's. He received a good classical education, and made very great proficiency in his studies. He was some time chaplain, in the Family of the Earl of Cassils, and waited on Lord Kennedy. He was also some time chaplain to the Viscount of Kenmure.—He was ordained minister of Wemyss, with the imposition of hands, by the Presbytery of Kirkcaldy, without the acknowledgement of the bishop. He was one of those illustrious reformers, who subscribed, as minister at Wemyss, the National Covenant which was agreed upon and sworn, in the year

1638.[a] Baillie, speaking of Mr George Gillespie, calls him "a youth who waited on Lord Kennedy," and says that he "was admitted to the Kirk of Weems, maugre St Andrew's beard, by the Presbytery." Our author adds, "this same youth is now given out also, by those who should know, for the author of the English Popish Ceremonies, whereof we all do marvel; for though he had gotten the papers, and help of the chief of that side; yet the composition would seem to be far above such an age: but if that book be truly of his making, I admire the man, though I mislike much of his matter; yea, I think, he may prove among the best wits of this isle.[b] Mr Baillie was a witness of the display of Mr Gillespie's abilities and learning, in the famous Assembly at Westminster. Stevenson says, that Mr Gillespie was the author of the anonymous piece above-mentioned; and that it was discharged by a proclamation, in the year 1637, as being of too corrosive a quality for the weak stomachs of the bishops.[c] In it the will-worship of Episcopacy is exposed. Mr Gillespie eminently appeared, at a very seasonable time, as one of the most able and zealous advocates for the Presbyterian cause. His literature and talents were highly respectable; and diligently employed in promoting the interests of the Redeemer's kingdom. He was a real friend to the work of Reformation; and strongly averse to Prelacy, to Erastianism, and to all corruption. At the venerable Assembly which convened at Glasgow, in 1638, he preached a very learned and judicious sermon, explaining these words, *The king's heart is in the hand of the Lord*, &c. This discourse did not altogether escape censure; for the Earl of Argyle thought that Mr Gillespie touched the royal prerogative too nearly, and very gravely admonished the Assembly to let authority alone, which all took in good part; and the moderator very prudently supported what Argyle had said, in a most judicious and beautiful speech.[d]

At the General Assembly which met at Edinburgh,

a Stevenson, vol. ii. pp. 292, & 326. b Baillie, vol. i. pp. 67, 68.
c History, vol. ii. p. 217. d Stevenson, vol. ii. p. 603.

1641, Mr Gillespie had a call from the town of Aberdeen to be their minister; but the Lord Commissioner and himself appeared in his cause, and managed it so well, that he was continued at Wemyss.[a] But in 1642. the General Assembly consented unto his transportation to the city of Edinburgh.[b] And he was one of those four eminent ministers, who were sent as Commissioners from the Church of Scotland, to the famous Assembly of Divines at Westminster, in the year 1643. He was but a young man when he went to that Assembly. There, however, he reasoned and conducted himself with all the skill and prudence of a veteran. Equally acute and learned, he commanded respectful attention when he spake. He even ventured to contend, with the eminently learned Selden and Lightfoot, who were at that time the great champions in the Erastian controversy, and truly formidable for their extraordinary acquaintance with Jewish antiquities and Rabinical learning.[c] Against those eminent opponents, Mr Gillespie laboured with success, in proving two courts among the Jews, from Deut. xvii. 12. respecting one going up from one court to another; that is, for appeals, as he strongly urged from hence: *The man who will do presumptuously, and will not hearken unto the priest who standeth to minister there before the Lord thy God, or unto the judge, even that man shall die:* Making the priest to hold one court, and the judge another.—And certainly to contend with such men on the field of controversy, required great store of erudition and much power of intellect. Mr Baillie, one of his colleagues in that Assembly, who had the best opportunity of being well acquainted with his abilities and learning, speaks of him as follows. "How many and how learned debates we had, in twelve or thirteen sessions, from nine to half-two, it were long to relate. None in all the company did reason more, and more pertinently, than Mr Gillespie. That is an excellent youth; my heart blesses God in his behalf." And when Acts xiv. 23. was pro-

a Stevenson, vol. iii. p. 979. Baillie, vol. i. pp. 306, 307.
b Stevenson, vol. iii. p. 1063.
c Lightfoot's Rem. Pref. pp. 12, 17. 18.

duced for a proof of the power which the apostles had of ordination, and after much debate, was going to be voiced, Baillie says; "Very learned and accute Mr Gillespie, a singular ornament of our Church, than whom not one in the whole Assembly speaks to better purpose, and with better acceptance by all the hearers, advertised, that the Greek word, of purpose by the Episcopal translators turned *ordaining*, was truly *chusing*, importing the people's suffrages in ellecting their officers. Hence arose a tough debate, that took up two whole sessions. Mr Henderson's overture ended the plea." And again, the same author says; "We get good help in our Assembly-debates of my Lord Wariston; but of none more than of that noble youth Mr Gillespie. I truly admire his faculty, and bless God, as for all my colleagues, so for him in that faculty with the first of the whole Assembly." And, in a letter to Mr Robert Blair, dated March 26th, 1644, the same writer says: Mr G. Gillespie, however I had a good opinion of his gifts, yet I profess he has much deceived me. Of a truth there is no man whose parts in a publick dispute, I do so admire. He has studied so accurately all the points which ever yet came to our Assembly, he has gotten so ready, so assured, so solid a way of publick debating, that though there are in the Assembly divers very excellent men, yet, in my poor judgement, there is not one who speaks more rationally, and to the point, than that brave youth has ever done; so that his absence would be prejudicial to our whole cause, and unpleasant to all here who wish it well.[a] And it has been said, that once when both the Parliament and the Assembly were convened, and a long studied discourse was made in favour of Erastianism, to which none seemed readily to offer any answer, that, Mr Gillespie, being urged by his brethren, the Scottish Commissioners, repeated the substance of the whole discourse, and refuted it, to the admiration of all persons who were present. And what struck them most was, that though it was common for the members to take notes of what

a Baillie, vol. i. pp. 407, 419, 431, and 451.

was spoken in the Assembly as helpful to their memory, and Mr Gillespie appeared to be so employed during the delivery of that speech to which he afterward made a reply, yet the persons who sat next him declared, that upon looking into his note book, they found nothing of that speech written, but in different places, *Lord, send light—Lord, give assistance—Lord, defend thine own cause.*

After his return to his own country from London, he was much employed in the public affairs of the Church of Scotland. And, having been eminently distinguished in the Assembly of Divines at Westminster for his erudition and zeal in the cause of truth, he was chosen Moderator of the General Assembly of the Church of Scotland, which convened at Edinburgh on the 12th of July, 1648. In this Assembly, several good acts were made in approbation and favour of the covenanted work of Reformation. And, in it, Mr Gillespie was nominated one of those ministers who should prosecute the Treaty of Uniformity in Religion with the English Parliament and their Assembly of Divines.[a] But in a short time after this, he was seized with sickness. Mr Rutherford, in a letter to him, when on his death-bed, dated St. Andrews, Sept. 27th, 1648, says: "I dare say nothing against his dispensation; I hope to follow quickly. The heirs who are not there before you, are posting with haste after you, and none shall take your lodging over your head. Be not heavy: the life of faith is now called for; doing was never reckoned in your accounts; though Christ in and by you hath done more than by twenty, yea, an hundred gray-haired and godly pastors. Believing now is your last. Look to that word, Gal. ii. 20.—Ye must leave the wife to a more choice Husband, and the children to a better Father. If ye leave any testimony to the Lord's work and covenant, against both malignants and sectaries, which I suppose may be needful, let it be under your hand, and subscribed before faithful witnesses."—Mr

a Stevenson, vol. iii. pp. 1260, 1281. Acts of General Assembly, edit. 1682.

Gillespie was always firmly attached to the work of Reformation, and left a faithful testimony in favour of it, and against all the prevailing evils of that time. He died toward the end of the year 1648; some say about the 17th of Dec. He was very little past the prime of life, and his death was greatly lamented. And the Public had such sense of his real worth, that first the Committee of Estates, and then the Parliament, ordered one thousand pounds sterling to be given to his widow and children; but through the troubles of the times that was not paid.[a]

Of Mr Gillespie's abilities, both natural and acquired, we have the most irrefragable proofs, in the testimony of his co-temporaries, and also in the excellent writings which he has left behind him. With the original languages of the Holy Scriptures he was intimately acquainted; his knowledge of antiquity was extensive and profound; and his talent, both for written argument and extemporary debate, has been generally allowed. We are much indebted to him, for that remarkable patience and ardour of research, which have enabled him to cast very great light on the deeply interesting subject of Church-government. In all his labours, he seems to have been truly active and zealous for the Lord God of Hosts, and to have been well directed in his zeal, by the Spirit of wisdom and of holiness.

Mr Gillespie has left behind him the following learned writings. Beside *The English Popish Ceremonies, obtruded upon the Church of Scotland*, above-mentioned, 4to. 1637, and 1660, said to be his; we have his *Assertion of the Government of the Church of Scotland*, published in 1641, in which he successfully combats the Independent Scheme.—A sermon preached from Ezek. xliii. 11. to the House of Commons, at their Solemn Fast, March 27th, 1644. 4to. pp. 42. London, 1644. A sermon from Mal. iii. 2. to the House of Peers, Fast, 27th of Aug. 1645. 4to. pp. 30. London, 1645.—*Aaron's Rod Blossoming*; Or, *The Divine Ordinance of*

a Stevenson, vol. iii. p. 1285.

Church-Government Vindicated. 4to. pp. 590. London, 1646.[a] In this elaborate work, the Erastian doctrine is clearly and triumphantly refuted. Mr Gillespie's Pieces on the Erastian controversy, in answer to Mr Coleman, are mentioned in Mr Coleman's Life. *Male Avilis*, by Mr Gillespie, 4to. pp. 56. Lond. 1646.—His Treatise of *Miscellany Questions* was printed at Edinburgh, 1649. 4to. pp. 281. And one of these Cases was selected, and printed again at Paisley, 1791, in a Collection.

ALEXANDER HENDERSON,

MINISTER OF EDINBURGH, AND ONE OF THE COMMISSIONERS FROM THE CHURCH OF SCOTLAND TO THE ASSEMBLY OF DIVINES AT WESTMINSTER.

THE memory of eminent men, who have performed services of great importance to their country, and who have filled conspicuous places with much reputation, ought to be greatly respected. In such respect is the memory of that illustrious statesman, the strenuous, yet temperate, Assertor of the liberties of his country, John Hampden, still held by his grateful countrymen, that, it is said, some years ago, one of his descendants being deficient in an account of public money, he was exonerated from the debt due to Government by an Act of Parliament, particularly expressing that it was for the services his illustrious relation had done to his country that this mark of favour was shown to him.[b] Certainly less honour ought not to be paid to the memory of this eminent Reformer, who is the subject of the following Memoir, and who cheerfully performed many remarkable services of very great importance to his country, and to the church of Christ. And, both his character, and the

a See Coleman's Life.

b Anecdotes of distinguished Persons, vol. iii. 3d edit. London.

particulars of his life, are highly interesting to us, who make a profession of adherence to Reformation-principles.

Alexander Henderson probably was born about the year 1583. But of his parents, of the place of his birth, or of the circumstances of the early part of his life, I have not been able to obtain any authentic information. Being intended for the service of the church, he was sent to the University of St. Andrew's, to complete his education, about the commencement of the 17th century. Here he was eminently distinguished by his rare abilities, and close application to his studies. And he soon became very conspicuous for his great proficiency in different branches of learning, which justly entitled him to respectful notice. And, after having finished the usual course of studies, and passed his degrees with applause, he was chosen teacher of a class of philosophy and rhetoric in the above-mentioned University.[a] He was one of the professors of St. Andrew's in the year 1611; for his name is affixed to a letter of thanks to the king, on occasion of his having founded a library in the College, by the Rector, Deans of Faculty, and other masters of the University of St. Andrew's, dated 4th May 1611.[b]

The Church of Scotland was in a very deplorable condition, about this time. The liberty of her Assemblies was greatly infringed; for the king claimed an absolute power over them, and arbitrarily changed both the time and place of meeting by his proclamations.[c] Ministers in the Church were commonly introduced to vote as bishops in the Parliament. And some of them were craftily nominated to the titles of bishoprics on the occasion.[d] The king reckoned, that equality among ministers could not agree with a monarchy; and that without bishops the three Estates in Parliament could not be firmly established; and therefore he very warmly and artfully urged the crea-

a Whitelocke's Memorials, p. 123.

b Wodrow's Mss. fol. No. 34. Advocates' Library, as with the Christian Magazine, vol. x. No. 112.

c Calderwood's Hist. Church of Scotland, page 435. Ann. 1600. p. 459. Ann. 1602. pp. 490, 491. Ann. 1605.

d Calderwood's Hist. p. 446.

tion of bishops.[a] And these creatures of his basely flattered him, in his crafty designs; and he conferred upon them preferment and worldly grandeur. And thus Episcopacy, closely attended with its numerous train of evils, was keenly obtruded upon the Church of Christ in Scotland, after she had deliberately, religiously, and very solemnly, cast off this heavy and insufferable yoke. And, that the way might be the more speedily prepared, and the gates the more easily and widely opened, for the entrance of Episcopacy, with its large train of ceremonies, and external splendour, into the city of the Lord, her most able ministers, and eminently faithful watchmen, were most shamefully and unjustly silenced, imprisoned, and either banished from the king's dominions, under the pain of death, as the six imprisoned in Blackness were, or forcibly driven into obscure and remote corners of the land, where only a small number could be profited by their ministry, and where they had no opportunity of effectually opposing the corrupt measures of the king and court. That renowned servant of the Lord Jesus Christ, most powerful preacher, and zealous and courageous opponent of Episcopacy, Mr Robert Bruce, was very unfairly excluded from his ministry in Edinburgh, and left in this condition, even at the time of the king's exaltation, and removal from Edinburgh to London. And, after Mr Bruce had been much harassed, and inhibited to preach, he was shut up in Inverness, a town in the north of Scotland, on the 27th Aug. 1605, where he remained four years, teached every Sabbath before noon, and every Wednesday.[b] And, these earnest Contenders *for the faith which was once delivered unto the saints*, Mr Andrew Melvil, and Mr John Davidson, were detained in confinement, at the king's removal to London, though the prison-doors were readily opened, on the way, as he proceeded in his journey, for the liberty of persons of a very different description.[c] And strong attempts were

a Calderwood, p. 428, &c.
b Calderwood's Hist. pp. 470—473, 495, 496.
c Calderwood, p. 478.

made to corrupt the seminaries of learning, by casting out sound teachers, and placing in their room, corrupt and time-serving men, who greatly encouraged the Court-measures. And, youth being put under the tuition of such teachers, the poison, which they industriously cast into the fountains, was very speedily disseminated through the whole land.

In this very dismal state of affairs, Mr Henderson, being then a young man of great abilities, eagerly desired preferment; and is said to have become a warm advocate for the new measures. Bishop Guthrie says, "This Mr Henderson had been in his youth very Episcopal, in token whereof, being a professor of philosophy in St. Andrew's, he did, at the laureation of his class, choose Archbishop Gladstanes for his patron, with a very flattering dedication, for the which he had the kirk of Leuchars given him shortly after."[a] Though the authority, it must be allowed, is not the very best, especially when Mr Henderson is brought to our view, yet there is reason to think that what the Bishop here says of him is not without foundation. Mr Henderson is said to have been very much inclined to Episcopacy in the early part of his life; and obtaining the parish of Leuchars through the patronage of Archbishop Gladstanes, his settlement there wes very unpopular. On the day of his ordination, such was the opposition of the people, that they firmly secured the church-doors, and the ministers who attended, together with the Presentee, were obliged to break in by the window. Mr Henderson not only was known to be a defender of those corruptions to which many of the people in Scotland were exceedingly averse; but it also appears that at the entrance into his ministry, he discovered little or no regard to the spiritual interests of the flock upon whom he had been obtruded. But he had not been long minister of Leuchars, when a most happy and important change was produced on the state of his mind. This remarkable change had a great influence upon the whole of his future conduct. About that time, the cele-

a Bishop Guthrie's Memoirs, p. 24.

brated Mr Robert Bruce, who had been banished from Edinburgh, had obtained liberty to return from Inverness, the place of his confinement. He improved his freedom in preaching the glorious Gospel of the Grace of God, as he had opportunity. Multitudes attended his ministry, particularly on fast-days and at communions. Mr Henderson, hearing of a communion in the neighbourhood, at which Mr Bruce was expected to assist, went secretly to the place, and took his seat in a dark corner of the church, where he would be most concealed. Mr Bruce entered the pulpit, and after a solemn pause, in his usual manner, which fixed Mr Henderson's attention upon him, he read, in due time, with his accustomed emphasis and deliberation, these words as his text, *Verily, verily, I say unto you, He that entereth not by the door into the sheep-fold, but climbeth up some other way, the same is a thief and a robber.* John x. i. Words most peculiarly descriptive of the character of an intruder, and so literally applicable to the manner in which Mr Henderson entered upon his ministry at Leuchars, went like *drawn swords* to his heart. He who carefully endeavoured to hide himself from the view of his fellow-creatures, soon found that he was under the eye of his Creator and Redeemer. He felt the powerful effects of the word of God, when the ministry of it is accompanied with the agency of the Holy Spirit. His conscience was deeply convicted, and he readily yielded to the irresistible force of divine truth. What he heard on this occasion, from that eminent servant of the Lord Jesus Christ, was by the divine blessing, the means of his conversion. And we are told, that ever after he retained a very great affection for his spiritual father, Mr Bruce, and often mentioned him with marks of the highest respect.[a]

Mr Henderson's change of mind was soon seen in his whole deportment. He now became a diligent and faithful labourer in the Lord's vineyard. He was peculiarly zealous and active in promoting the spiritual welfare

a Stevenson's Hist. p. 604.

of the people of his pastoral charge. He used his utmost endeavours to remove the offence which he had given, by the manner of his first entrance among them. It may not be amiss to hear his own address to his brethren, in the famous Assembly at Glasgow, upon this interesting subject, a considerable time after this period. "There are divers among us who have had no such warrant for our entry to the ministry, as were to be wished. Alas! how many of us have rather sought the kirk, than the kirk sought us! How many have rather gotten the kirk given to them, than they have been given to the kirk for the good thereof! And yet there must be a great difference put between those who have lived many years in an unlawful office without warrant of God, and therefore must be abominable in the sight of God, and those who in some respects have entered unlawfully, and with an ill conscience, and afterward have come to see the evil of this, and to do what in them lies to repair the injury. The one is like a marriage altogether unlawful, and null in itself: the other is like a marriage in some respects unlawful and inexpedient, but that may be mended by the diligence and fidelity of the parties in doing their duty afterwards: so should it be with us who entered lately into the calling of the ministry. If there were any faults or wrong steps in our entry, (as who of us are free?) acknowledge the Lord's calling of us, if we have since got a seal from Heaven of our ministry, and let us labour with diligence and faithfulness in our office."[a]

Mr Henderson now became a decided Presbyterian. He viewed the courses of the prevailing party in the Church of Scotland very differently from what he had formerly done, when he was guided by a worldly spirit, and by ambitious views. He very prudently, first fully satisfied himself by deliberate and minute inquiry, that Presbytery was more conformable to the Holy Scriptures, more favourable to the interests of practical religion, and more consistent with the liberties of the people, than that ecclesiastical system which had been lately introdu-

a Sermon before the Assembly at Glasgow, pp. 14, 15. 1638.

ced. Upon a candid and patient investigation of the existing controversy, he was firmly persuaded that Episcopacy was equally unauthorised by the word of God, and inconsistent with the reformed constitution of the Church of Scotland.[a] From that period, he was very active in opposing prelatical government, and in resisting those most imprudent and despotic measures by which the Court made a bold attempt to procure a general submsision to itself. And throughout the whole of the arduous conflict which he maintained, he was eminently distinguished by his ardent zeal, undaunted courage, dexterity in argument and debate, and peculiar skill in the management of the most difficult affairs. He was earnestly solicited to take an active and leading part, in the most important transactions of his time. And he always secured the confidence of his own party, and commanded the respect of his opponents. His conduct uniformly gave high satisfaction to the numerous and respectable body whose views he promoted, and they constantly turned their eye to him in cases of peculiar delicacy and moment.[b]

From the time that Episcopal government had first been obtruded upon the Church of Scotland, a scheme was contrived to render her worship also conformable to the English model. After different preparatory steps, an Assembly was suddenly convened at Perth, in the year 1618. To that Assembly the King invited by his letters, above thirty noblemen and gentlemen, who were sensible that it was his Majesty's earnest desire to have the form of worship in the Church of Scotland changed, and the many and various rites of the English Church introduced among the Scotch people, that the union of the two kingdoms might be the stronger. In this ecclesiastical assembly, by the most unbecoming influence, several superstitious innovations were authorised, and the five following articles admitted, which are commonly styled the Five Articles of Perth. These were, kneel-

a See the first of his Papers to the King at Newcastle.
b The Edinburgh Christian Instructor, vol. vii. pp. 406, 407.

ing at the sacrament of the Lord's supper; the celebration of five holy days, the nativity, passion, resurrection and ascension of our Lord Jesus Christ, and the descent of the Holy Spirit; private baptism; the private administration of the Lord's supper; and episcopal confirmation.[a] Among the faithful ministers of the Gospel, who had the courage to appear in opposition to these innovations, and to argue against them with great force of truth, we find the respectable name of *Mr Alexander Henderson of Leuchars.* It is very remarkable, that a proposal was made in that Assembly for the translation of Mr Henderson, and of his friend, Mr William Scot of Coupar, to Edinburgh. This proposal was seemingly made with the view of soothing the inhabitants of that city, and of procuring a more ready submission to the other acts of that Assembly. It is very probable that they had not any real design of settling those able advocates for the cause of truth and of nonconformity in that eminent station. Calderwood expressly says, that the bishops meant no such thing in earnest.[b] But the proposal clearly shows, that Mr Henderson was very highly esteemed, even at that early period, by the faithful part of the Church of Scotland, with whom he was then intimately connected.

In the month of Aug. 1619, Mr Henderson and two other ministers were called before the Court of High Commission in St. Andrew's, charged with composing and publishing a book, entitled *Perth Assembly*, proving the nullity of that Assembly, and with raising a contribution to defray the expence of printing the work. They appeared, and are said to have answered for themselves with such wisdom, that the bishops could gain no advantage against them, and were obliged to dismiss them with threatenings.[c]

When Mr Henderson enjoyed his beloved retirement, he spent a considerable part of his time in reading, and in those studies which were afterward highly useful to

a Stevenson's Hist. vol. i. p. 194.
b Hist. Church of Scotland, p. 713.
c Christian Magazine, vol. x. p. 221.

him in the public services of the church and of his country. And beside diligently discharging the pastoral duties in his own congregation, he met occasionally with his brethren at fasts and communions, when, by their sermons and conferences, they mutually encouraged each other in firmly adhering to the good old principles of the Church of Scotland; and joined in fervent prayer to Almighty God for deliverance from those evils under which they groaned. Mr Livingston mentions Mr Henderson as one of those eminently pious and able ministers with whom he became acquainted in attending such solemn occasions, between the years 1626 and 1630, the memory of whom, he says, is very precious and refreshing.[a] Mr Henderson was always indefatigable in his labours. And he was inflexible in his attachment to truth and rectitude of conduct. But in spite of the superiority of his talents, and of the purity of his intentions, he was very often harassed by calumnies and misrepresentations. Bishop Guthrie represents the tumult which was produced by the first reading of the Liturgy in Edinburgh, on the 23d of July, 1637, as the result of a previous consultation in the month of April, when he says Mr Alexander Henderson came from the brethren in Fife, and Mr David Dickson from those in the west, and, in concert with Lord Balmerino and Sir Thomas Hope, engaged certain matrons to put the first affront upon the Service-book.[b] But this story is at variance with the Official accounts, not only of the Town-council of Edinburgh, and of the Privy-council, but also of his Majesty, which expressly declare, that, upon the strictest inquiry, it appeared that the tumult was raised by the meaner people, without any influence, concert, or interference, of the better classes.[c] Mr Henderson had no hand in any such affairs, but publicly exposed their dangerous tendency.—On March 9th, 1637, we

a Life of Mr John Livingston, p. 12.

b Bishop Guthrie's Memoirs, pp. 23, 24.

c Large Declaration, pp. 23, 40. Burnet's Memoirs of D. Hamilton, p. 32.

find the eminently pious Mr Rutherford writing to him as follows: "As for your case, my reverend and dearest brother, ye are the talking of the north and south; and looked to so as if ye were all chrystal glass. Your motes and dust should soon be proclaimed, and trumpets blown at your slips; but I know that ye have laid help upon One who is mighty. Intrust not your comforts to men's airy and frothy applause, neither lay your down-castings on the tongues of sult-mockers and reproachers of godliness.—God has called you to Christ's side, and the wind is now in Christ's face in this land; and seeing ye are with Him, ye cannot expect the lee side or the sunny side of the brae: but I know that ye have resolved to take Christ upon any terms whatsoever."[a]—The Archbishop of St Andrew's, with a view to deter other persons, gave a charge to Mr Henderson, and to other two ministers, to purchase each of them two copies of the Liturgy, for the use of their parishes, within fifteen days, under the pain of rebellion. Mr Henderson went to Edinburgh, and, in the month of Aug. 1637, presented a petition to the Privy-council for himself and his brethren, stating their objections, and desiring a suspension of the charge Upon this petition, and others of a similar nature, being very Providentially presented about the same time, a favourable answer was obtained from the Council. And an account was transmitted to London respecting the people's great aversion to conformity. This step was of very great utility and importance, as it directed those persons in general who were aggrieved to a regular mode of obtaining redress. And we are informed, that the Privy-council having then testified their aversion to enforce the novations, did afterward, on different interesting occasions, befriend and promote the cause of the petitioners.[b] From that time, Mr Henderson was eminently distinguished by his great activity in all the measures of the petitioners; and his prudence and diligence contributed very much to bring those measures to

a Rutherford's Letters.

b Stevenson's Hist. vol. ii. p. 190. Baillie's Letters, vol. i. Letter ii. and Christ. Mag. vol. x. p. 225.

a comfortable conclusion. His worth was soon discovered, and he was frequently employed in the most important and delicate transactions of the times.

When the National Covenant was agreed upon and sworn, in the year 1638, our illustrious Reformer was called forth to act a very conspicuous part On the first of March, that year, the covenant was sworn with uplifted hands, and subscribed in the Grey-friars Church, Edinburgh, by thousands of the nobility, gentry, burgesses, ministers of the Gospel, and commons, assembled from almost all parts of Scotland; and copies of it being circulated throughout the kingdom, it was generally sworn with great alacrity. This memorable deed, of which it would be highly improper to forget the respectable authors, was prepared by Mr Henderson, and Archibald Johnston, afterward of Warringston, an advocate, in whom the supplicants chiefly confided; and revised by Balmerino, Loudon, and Rothes.[a] Mr Henderson, with those noblemen who have been mentioned, subscribed the covenant on that solemn occasion. The inhabitants of the kingdom were now divided into Covenanters and Non-covenanters. And some of the Covenanters had submitted to the Bishops, and conformed to the Articles of Perth, who were yet accounted orthodox preachers, and zealous opposers of Popery and Arminianism, as Messrs Robert Baillie, Henry Rollock, John Bell, Andrew and Robert Ramsay, who, upon the first appearance of the Service-book. joined with their brethren against the innovations. Others of the Covenanters would not conform to the Articles of Perth, among whom were Messrs Henderson, Dickson, Rutherford, Blair, Cant, and the two Livingstons.[b]—When the Marquis of Hamilton was sent by the King, to act as his high commissioner, with a view to suppress the Covenanters, who had several conferences with him without success, he at last told them that the Books of canons and liturgy should be discharged, on condition that the Covenanters would give up their

a Laing's Hist. Scotland, vol. i B. ii. p. 134. Stevenson, vol. ii. pp. 291, 292.
b Stevenson, vol. ii. pp. 294, 295.

covenant. This proposal exceedingly displeased all the Covenanters, and had a strong tendency to excite them unto greater vigilance and activity, in supporting and vindicating that most solemn deed. Upon this the celebrated Mr Henderson was again set to work, and the public were soon favoured with sufficient reasons why the Covenanters could not upon any terms give up their covenant, nor even pass from any part of it.—The King's commissioner afterward heard Mr Henderson preach, and conferred with him in private respecting the state of affairs, which had the desired effect of soothing the Covenanters into a belief of his affection to them.[a] It seems to have been about that time, that the city of Edinburgh fixed their eyes upon Mr Henderson, for one of their ministers. Among other articles of information sent up to the Scottish Bishops, who were then at London, by their friends in Scotland, was the following: "That the Council of Edinburgh have made choice of Mr Alexander Henderson to be helper to Mr Andrew Ramsay, and intend to admit him without advice or consent of the Bishops.[b]

In the month of July, 1638, the Tables at Edinburgh sent the Earls of Montrose and Kinghorn, and Lord Coupar, with Messrs Henderson, Dickson, and Cant, to the north country, with a view to use their influence in persuading the inhabitants to take the covenant, particularly those of Aberdeen, who, by means of their Doctors of divinity, of the university, and of the Marquis of Huntley, had hitherto declined to join with their brethren in other parts of the kingdom. Upon their arrival at Aberdeen, they were but coldly received. The Doctors presented unto them fourteen captious and ensnaring demands respecting the covenant, which they had drawn up with great care and art. Different papers passed between the Doctors and the deputed ministers of the Covenanters on this subject, which were published. Those papers of the latter are said to have been written

a Stevenson, vol. ii. pp 344—352

b Burnet's Memoirs of D. Hamilton, p. 41.

by Mr Henderson. The deputies, being otherwise engaged, and seeing no prospect of removing the prejudices of their opponents, desisted from the controversy. And after preaching in different places, and producing solid arguments for subscribing the covenant, and taking part in the work of reformation, and procuring the subscriptions of some hundreds in Aberdeen, and in other parts, they returned to their constituents.[a]

Mr Henderson was called to make a very public appearance in the much and justly celebrated Assembly which met at Glasgow, on the 21st November 1638. The petitioners continuing indefatigably diligent and being most firmly united, and very much animated in the defence of truth, the Court was obliged to grant their reasonable demands, by calling a General Assembly and a Parliament, that the national grievances might be duly considered and fairly redressed.

This very respectable Assembly convened in the High-church of Glasgow: and, beside a very great concourse of the people, all the nobility and gentry of any family or interest were present, either as members, assessors, or spectators. And, the multitudes assembled on this solemn occasion were so very great, that the members could scarcely obtain entrance, even by the assistance of the magistrates, with their town-guard, the noblemen, and gentlemen, and the High-commissioner himself in person, who, at first, sometimes made way for the members.[b] After solemn fasting, and a very good and pertinent sermon preached from Revelation i. 12, 13.—*I saw seven golden candlesticks; And in the midst of the seven candlesticks one like unto the Son of man, clothed with a garment down to the foot, and girt about the paps with a golden girdle*, by Mr John Bell, who did also constitute the Assembly in the name of the Lord Jesus Christ, the alone King and Head of his church, and moderate until another was chosen, the Assembly engaged in the

a Stevenson, vol. ii. pp. 372—375. Baillie, vol. i. pp. 72, 73.

b Hume's Hist. England, vol. vi. chap. liii. 1638. Baillie's Letters, vol. i. Let. x. pp. 96, 97. Stevenson's Hist. Church of Scotland, vol. ii. chap. iii. 1638.

choice of a Moderator.[a] But. at the same time, a declinature was presented from the Bishops, that is a protestation against the legality of the Assembly. And the Marquis of Hamilton. the King's Commissioner, warmly insisted that this should first be read. It was objected, that there was no Assembly without a Moderator, and therefore they ought necessarily to begin with his election. The High-commissioner seeing that he could not prevail, protested against the refusal to read the declinature before the choice of a Moderator, and ordered his protestation to be entered. Before the choice. the Royal commissioner entered another protest, that this choice should neither prejudice the King's prerogative, nor any law of the kingdom, nor bar the King from taking legal exceptions, either against the person elected, or the election itself At length, all objections against chusing a Moderator being overcome, Mr Alexander Henderson, as a minister eminently qualified to fill that exalted station in a proper manner, by his possessing great authority, much resolution, and uncommon prudence, was unanimously chosen Moderator of the Assembly, and most cheerfully called to the chair.[b] His distinguished conduct, in former times, clearly proved, that he could readily act in a very difficult situation. And, in the very critical state of affairs, when discussions of the greatest importance were expected, and a very great concourse of people assembled to witness these, he certainly was a very proper person to fill the Moderator's chair. Under the special care of Divine Providence, there are, at all times, such "innumerable gradations of ability. and endless varieties of study and inclination, *that* no employment can be vacant for want of a man qualified to discharge it."[c] This is particularly true, with reference unto the church of Christ, for which ample provision is always made. Mr Henderson, having solemnly consti-

a Baillie and Stevenson, as above.

b Rapin's Hist. England vol. ii. Book. 19. 1638. p. 306. See also, Baillie and Stevenson, as above.

c Rambler, vol. iv. No. 160.

tuted the Assembly, in the name of the Lord Jesus Christ, afterward addressed the members in a very beautiful and appropriate speech. He soon gained the good opinion and confidence of the members, especially of such of them who were not formerly much acquainted with him; and was honoured with marks of distinguished esteem. He behaved very respectfully unto all, and at the same time with that particular firmness and independence which became the President of a free Assembly. Mr Robert Baillie, who was a member of this venerable Assembly, and who wrote an history of it, says, speaking concerning the Moderator's prayers: "Among that man's other good parts, that was one, a faculty of grave, good, and zealous prayer, according to the matter in hand; which he exercised, without fagging, (fainting) to the last day of our meeting."[a]

The rare abilities, which strongly marked Mr Henderson's character, were particularly brought to the touch-stone, by the Royal commissioner's premature dissolution of this great Assembly, and the excommunication of the Bishops. And, bringing his rare abilities to the touch-stone, on these remarkable occasions, was like friction to the diamond: for their excellence was then sufficiently attested; they shined with additional lustre, and they excited new admiration.

Although the King had called this Assembly, he seemingly had no design to allow them fairly to proceed in the discussion of their business. A firm determination had been entered into, of utterly abolishing episcopacy;[b] which the nation now groaned under. and which many ardently wished deliverance from. But the King was evidently against the abolition of episcopacy; and so would not allow this Assembly to consider and redress grievances, but only to cause to be registered such concessions, flowing from himself, as he necessarily granted in present circumstances. And, it was very observable, that the King's commissioner did not formally consent to

a Baillie's Letters, Let. x. vol i. p. 101.
b Hume's Hist. vol. vi. chap. liii. 1638.

any part of the Assembly's procedure. It was his custom to give his voice rather by way of permission, than to say any thing that might imply his direct assent; for he seemingly resolved, to keep himself in all his words and deeds so free, that he might, when he would, disavow all that was done, or to be done, in that Assembly.[a] But the members considered themselves as a free Assembly, and were firmly resolved both to claim, and to exercise, that glorious liberty, and great authority, which the Lord Jesus Christ, as the King and Head of his church, had conferred upon them. The King's commissioner had formerly urged, that prior to the trial of commissions, the declinature of the Bishops should be read. But he was told, that the Assembly was not formed or fully constituted until the commissions of elections were examined, and the commissioners who were present, known to be duly authorised. This was an affair of great importance; for as the declinature contained reasons to shew that the election of the greatest part of the commissioners was null, it was easily seen, that these reasons would come too late, after the power of the commissioners should be allowed, and they admitted as members of the Assembly. When the Royal commissioner could not obtain his desire, he entered his protest. The declinature of the Bishops was at last read, at the repeated request of the Commissioner, wherein they pretended to prove the illegality of this Assembly; and also was answered very learnedly and solidly by the Assembly. The Assembly proceeding in course to vote themselves competent judges of the libels raised against them; when the Moderator stated the question, Whether this Assembly found themselves the judges of the Bishops, notwithstanding their declinature? the Royal commissioner interposed, and declared that if they pretended to assume a right to judge the Bishops, he could not give his consent, nor continue any longer with them. Upon this, he made a speech, the substance of which may be seen in Stevenson's History, and delivered the King's concessions to

a Baillie's Letters as above.

the clerk to be read and registered.[a] After the clerk had publicly read these concessions, the Moderator addressed the Royal commissioner in a very grave and well digested speech, which follows:

"It well becometh us, his Majesty's subjects convened in this honourable and reverend Assembly, with all thankfulness to receive so full a testimony of his Majesty's goodness, and not to undervalue the smallest crumbs of comfort that fall to us of his Majesty's liberality. With our hearts we do acknowledge before God, and with our mouths do we desire to testify to the world, how far we think ourselves obliged to our dread sovereign, wishing that the secret thoughts of our hearts, and the way wherein we have walked in time past were made manifest to him. It hath been the glory of the Reformed Churches, and we account it our glory in a special manner, to give unto kings and magistrates what belongs to their places: and, as we know the *fifth* command of the law to be a precept of the *second* table, so do we acknowledge it to be the first of that kind, and that, next unto piety toward God, we are obliged to loyalty and obedience to our king. There is nothing due to kings and princes in matters ecclesiastical, which, *I trust* shall be denied by this assembly to our King; for, beside authority and power in matters civil, to a Christian king belongeth, 1. Inspection over the affairs of the church. *And he ought not only diligently to watch over ecclesiastical persons, but also over ecclesiastical matters.* 2. The vindication of religion doth also belong to the King, for whom it is most proper, by his authority, to vindicate religion from contempt and all abuse, he being keeper also of the *first* table of the law. 3. The sanctions also are in his Majesty's hand, to confirm, by his royal authority, the constitutions of the kirk, and give them the strength of a law. 4. His Majesty also hath the power of correction: he both may and ought to compel kirk-men in the performance of the duties which

a Rapin's Hist. England, vol. ii. Book 19. 1638. Stevenson's Hist. vol ii. chap. iii.

God requires of them. 5. The coercive power also belongs to the prince, who hath power from God to restrain by his terror and authority, from what becometh not their places and callings. 6. The Christian magistrate hath power to convocate assemblies, when he finds the pressing affairs of the church calling for them; and in assemblies when they are convened, his power is great. 1. As he is a Christian, having the judgment of discretion in all matters debateable and controverted. 2. As he is king or magistrate, he must have the judgment of his eminent place and high vocation, to discern what concerns the spiritual welfare and salvation of his subjects. And, 3. as a magistrate singularly gifted with more than ordinary gifts of knowledge and authority. And we heartily acknowledge that your Grace, as his Majesty's High-commissioner, and representing his Royal person, hath an eminent place in this reverend and honourable Assembly, *first*, we hope as a good Christian, *next*, as his Majesty's High-commissioner; and *thirdly*, as one endued with singular gifts, and fitted in a special manner for this employment. Far be it from us to deny any thing that is due, either to those who are in supreme authority, or to such as are delegated by and subordinated to them. When Alexander the Great came to Jerusalem, he desired that his image might be set up in the temple. This the Jews did modestly refuse as inconsistent with the law, which was the law of God, but liberally offered what was in their power, and more honourable for the king, viz. That they would begin in the reckoning of time from his coming to Jerusalem, and would call all their first born sons by his name. What is ours, let it be given to Cæsar, but let God, by whom kings reign, have his own place. Let Christ Jesus, the King of kings, have his own prerogative, by whose grace our king reigneth, and we pray that he may reign long and prosperously over us."

This pathetic and judicious speech does honour both to the literary abilities, and to the good sense, of the author. It accurately discriminates between the power of the church-officer, and of the civil magistrate, respecting ecclesiastical affairs; and contains an explicit declaration that the Assembly were sincerely disposed to give unto their King and his Commissioner, all that honour and obedience which corresponded with the duty which they owed to Him who was King of kings and Lord of lords. It appears to me clearly expressive of *kings being nursing fathers* of the church, Isa. xlix. 23. Kings shall not only join themselves to the church of Christ; but they shall also use their power and authority for the increase and defence of it [a]—The speech is worthy of transmission to posterity; and may be of solid and lasting benefit to them The Royal commissioner received it with signs of pleasure, and of satisfaction; as appears by his following address to the Moderator, in way of reply: "Sir, You have spoken as becometh a good Christian, and a dutiful subject, and I am hopeful that you will conduct yourself with that deference which you owe to our Royal sovereign, all of whose commands will (I trust) be found agreeable to the commandments of God." The Moderator replied, that the Assembly being indicted by his Majesty, and consisting of such members, regularly authorised, as by the acts and practice in former times, had a right to represent the church, they considered themselves as a free Assembly; and he trusted that all things in it would be conducted conformable to the law of God and reason; that they would not advance one step but as clear light should chalk out the way before them, and that they would make it evidently appear to all men, that they were afraid to walk in another way; and that they were hopeful that their King, being such a lover of righteousness, needed only to have truth clearly pointed out before him, and, when this was done, that his Majesty would fall in love with it. Upon this, the Moderator again asked the members, If he should put the question, Whether or not the Assembly found themselves competent judges of the Bishops? But the Commissioner urged that this question should be deferred. The Moderator said, "Nay, with your Grace's permission, that cannot be; for it is fit to

[a] Dutch Annot. in loc.

be put only after the declinature hath been under consideration." The Commissioner repeated, that, in this case, he behoved to withdraw. Mr Henderson replied, "I wish the contrary from the bottom of my heart, and that your Grace would continue to favour us with your presence, without obstructing the work and freedom of the Assembly."—But the Commissioner plainly declared, after some other observations had been made, that he could not continue any longer, and urging the Moderator to conclude with prayer, without effect, he did, in his Majesty's name, dissolve the Assembly, prohibiting their further procedure.[a] He is said to have given these four principal reasons. 1. Lay-elders were introduced into the Assembly to vote there. 2. The ministers chosen commissioners, were elected by lay-elders, contrary to custom and practice. 3. The few commissioners chosen contrary to the instructions of the Tables, had been thrown out by mere cavils. 4. The cited Bishops were to be tried by persons who had already declared against them.[b] Seemingly, the Commissioner had the King's positive orders to dissolve the Assembly, if they should attempt to try the Bishops.[c] Mr Hume says, this measure was foreseen, and little regarded. The Court still continued to sit, and to finish their business.

Upon the Commissioner's departure, the Moderator deliverd the following animating speech to the Assembly. "All who are present know how this Assembly was indicted, and what power we allow to our Sovereign in matters ecclesiastic: But though we have acknowledged the power of Christian kings for convening Assemblies, and their power in them, yet that must not derogate from Christ's right, for he hath given warrant to convocate Assemblies, whether magistrates consent or not. Therefore, seeing we perceive his Grace, my lord Commissioner, to be zealous of his Royal master's commands, have not we as good reason to be zealous toward our

a Stevenson's Hist. vol. ii. chap. iii.
b Rapin's Hist. England, vol ii. Book 19. 1638.
c Rapin as above.

Lord, and to maintain the liberties and privileges of his kingdom? You all know that the work in hand hath had many difficulties, and yet hitherto the Lord hath helped and borne us through them all; therefore it becometh us not to be discouraged at our being deprived of human authority, but rather that ought to be a powerful motive to us to double our courage in answering the end for which we are convened."[a] Mr Henderson had the happy talent of suiting his expressions in his speeches to present circumstances; and thereby greatly encouraging the Assembly amid the difficulties which they had to encounter. Having delivered this speech, he desired that if any other of the reverend or honourable members pleased, they might speak a word for the encouragement of their brethren, as God should put it in their hearts. Upon this, Messrs. David Dickson, Henry Rollock, Andrew Cant, and Andrew Ramsay, of the clergy, Loudon of the nobility, Keir of the gentry, and Mr Robert Cunningham of the boroughs, delivered beautiful and pathetic speeches to the same purpose.[b] By these, both the other members, and many spectators, were greatly animated with a lively sense of present duty, and of the beauty of the Truth, as it is in Jesus. They were inspired with fresh courage. And the Moderator now put the question, Whether they would adhere to the protestation against the Royal commissioner's departure, and continue constituted until they finished their business? All, except about five, did, first with up-lifted hands, and afterward by a formal vote, declare their resolution to remain together until they finished the weighty business, which urgently demanded their consideration.[c] And, under the enlivening smiles and gracious influences of approving Heaven, this renowned Assembly proceeded in their most arduous work, with much success. They clearly displayed, on every occasion, great faithfulness, constancy, and consistency. Their measures amply proved, that they were certainly directed by unerring

a Stevenson's Hist. as above.
b Baillie and Stevenson.
c Christian Magazine, vol. x. No. 113. p. 265.

wisdom and goodness. And their difficulties only excited them unto the performance of their duty, and awakened their holy ardour. And the effects of perseverance, courage, and zeal, were clearly seen in their conduct.[a]

The last question of importance during that day was, Whether the Assembly do find themselves lawful and competent judges of the pretended Archbishops and Bishops of this kingdom, and of the complaint given in against them and their adherents, notwithstanding their declinature and protestation? Mr Stevenson says, that according to Mr Baillie, all voted affirmatively, but, according to the Journal, three or four voted in the negative.[b]

A proclamation was issued against the Assembly, and published with great solemnity, at the market-cross of Glasgow. But opposition in the course of duty, rather animated, than discouraged, the members of this venerable body. "Thus may all the opposition that we meet with in the course of our duty, animate, rather than overbear, our resolution in performing it!"[c]

At the opening of the next session, Mr Henderson again addressed the Assembly, and recommended gravity, quietness, and order, as in the sight of God; because they ought to have their judgments exercised concerning the matter in hand, and their minds elevated to God for light and direction. He added the following modest and beautiful remark: "Not that he assumed any thing to himself, but he was bold to direct them in that wherein he had the consent of their own minds."[d] This very seasonable recommendation was punctually observed, during the whole time of the sitting of this famous Assembly.

The Earl of Argyle returned to the Assembly this session, whose presence greatly encouraged them. And the Moderator earnestly entreated him, that, though he

a See Ferguson's Roman Republic, vol iii. chap. xxvii. p. 400. edit. Edin. 1799

b See Stevenson's Hist. vol. ii. p. 566 & Baillie's Letters. vol. i. p. 119.

c Doddridge's Fam. Expos. on Luke iv. 21. Improvement.

d Stevenson's Hist. vol. ii. p. 575.

was not a member of the Assembly, yet for the common interest which he had in the church, he would be pleased to countenance their meetings, and bear testimony to the rectitude of their proceedings; which he readily promised, and faithfully performed.[a] When Argyle desired an explanation of the *Confession of Faith* or *Covenant*, the Moderator said, "Although we do not compare the *Confession* of any reformed Church with the word of God, and are far from reckoning our *Confession* a rule of faith but only a form of *Confession*, yet we have great reason to account honourably of it. Other churches give a large testimony thereto, and it were a shame for us not to have the same good opinion of it; and, that we may have this it is necessary that we clearly understand the particular articles contained in the same, especially such as have been controverted. Ye all know what a great ado hath been made about this matter, some subscribing with an interpretation exclusive of the service book and canons, and others subscribing the short *Confession of Faith*, with the general bond lately urged by his Majesty, without the application made by the council to the sense in which it was originally sworn:" therefore he hoped that what should be now offered would administer light that should shine to others; but, because it would require a long time to hear and peruse all the acts and books necessary for clearing the *Confession*, he proposed that a committee might be named for that purpose, to which the Assembly readily agreed.[b]

When there was a near prospect of pronouncing sentence against some ministers who had been tried before their respective presbyteries, found guilty, and suspended, but remitted for an higher censure to the judgment of the Assembly, the Moderator delivered a grave and judicious discourse on the power of the church.[c] And, at the reading of the processes agninst the persons, he

a Baillie's Letters, vol. i. p. 119. Stevenson's Hist. vol. ii. pp. 575, 576.

b Stevenson's Hist. vol. ii. pp. 585, 586.

c See Stevenson's Hist. vol. ii. p. 597, &c.

justly observed, That they ought to be heard with a feeling sense of compassion toward the guilty persons, and also with joy that the Lord was putting forth his hand for the purging of his own house. When this respectable Assembly justly condemned six preceding corrupt Assemblies, the Moderator's observation was: "This Assembly have unanimously condemned these Assemblies, and I hope they shall be looked on as so many beacons, that we strike not again on such rocks."[a] And he exhorted that the several judicatures should now faithfully use that power which the Lord had freely committed to them. Before sentence was given against the Bishop of Galloway, the Moderator delivered a speech to the Assembly, to conciliate their minds to the step intended. In this he said; "The preaching of false doctrine and venomous poison of that kind, to seduce the people from their profession to popery and idolatry, must have a great censure. And this man's breach of the caveats, bringing in of the service-book, which you have already condemned for the great guilt involved in it, and declining this lawful Aseembly, abstracting from his personal faults, deserveth no less than excommunication.—It is known to you that the Church of Scotland have been in use to excommunicate papists and persons disobedient to the discipline of the church, from partaking of the holy communion; and seeing the Bishops are guilty in both these respects, why should not that high censure be inflicted on them? What a reverend father, Mr Andrew Melvil, said of Archbishop Adamson, *That the old serpent had so stung him with avarice, and he swelled so exorbitantly with pride, as threatened the destruction of the whole body if he were not cut off* doth evidently hold of the present pretended Bishops: and therefore, it seems necessary that the last mean be essayed. And let us solicit God to make his ordinance effectual for the destruction of the flesh that the spirit may be saved in the day of the Lord Jesus."[b]

a Stevenson, vol. ii. pp. 600, 610.
b Stevenson, vol. ii. p. 618, &c.

The Assembly, having finished the processes of the Bishops, agreed, at the close of their 19th Session, that the sentences which were passed against them should be publicly pronounced next day by the Moderator, in the presence of the Assembly, after a sermon preached by him suitable to the solemn occasion. He shewed great aversion to this arduous work; but all agreed that he should perform it. In vain he pleaded his fatigue, the multiplicity of affairs by which his attention was greatly perplexed, and the shortness of time for preparation; no excuse was admitted. Accordingly, at the time appointed, Mr Henderson preached before a very large auditory, from Psalm cx. 1. *The Lord said unto my Lord, Sit thou at my right hand, until I make thine enemies thy footstool.* Mr Baillie, who heard it, gives it the character of a good and learned sermon.[a] After delivering the sermon, he mentioned the Assembly's appointment, named the eight Bishops to be excommunicated, and afterward caused an abstract of the evidence against the Bishops to be publicly read by the clerk of the Assembly, for the satisfaction of the people, upon which he made some observations, shewing that they justly deserved the fearful sentence of excommunication. Upon this the Assembly's sentence against the Bishops was presented and heard; after which the Moderator desired the concurrence of the congregation of God's people in this solemn action, fully and accurately shewing their warrant for it, and the necessity of it, from the word of God, particularly, from Mat. xviii. 17, 18. 1 Cor. v. 1—6. 1 Tim. i. 20. He said, "Truly if the Lord had directed to another remedy for these men, the kirk of Scotland would have been glad to use it; but there is no other known mean to keep them from the condemnation of the devil, for the mortifying of their flesh, and saving of their souls, than this." After this, he most fervently and gravely called upon God by prayer: Prayer being ended, the Moderator pronounced the

a Baillie's Letters, vol. i. Let. x. p. 140. Stevenson, vol. ii. p. 638.

sentence of excommunication in these words: "*Since the eight persons before-mentioned have declared themselves strangers to the communion of saints, to be without hope of life eternal, and to be slaves of sin: Therefore we the people of God assembled together for this cause, and I as their mouth, In The Name of The Eternal God, and of his Son the Lord Jesus Christ, according to the direction of this Assembly, Do Excommunicate the said eight persons from the participation of the sacraments, from the communion of the visible church and from the prayers of the church, and so long as they continue obstinate, discharges you all, as ye would not be partakers of their vengeance, from keeping any religious fellowship with them; and thus give them over into the hands of the devil, assuring you in the name of the Lord Jesus, that except their repentance be evident, the fearful wrath and vengeance of the God of heaven shall overtake them even in this life, and after this world everlasting vengeance.*"[a]

He added, "Beloved, let us not think that this fearful sentence is merely the wind of man's voice; surely these unhappy men shall find the truth of it. It is true, a farther blindnes of mind, and hardness of heart, is one part of the execution of this sentence; but it may be that the Lord of heaven shall kythe some sensible judgment upon some of them, whereby they may be made spectacles of his wrath, except they repent."

At the same time, the Moderator intimated the Assembly's sentence of deposition, with reference to others.[b] The whole work was very awful and solemn. Mr Baillie, who was present, says, That the Moderator pronounced the sentences "in a very dreadful and grave manner."[c] And the whole Assembly must certainly be considered as "deeply affected, and filled with the mingling emotions of admiration, pity, and awe." And, Mr Henderson gave such a sample of his abilities, in this arduous work,

a The Bishops' Doom, pp. 28—38.
b The Bishops' Doom, pp. 40—42.
c Baillie's Letters, vol. i. p. 141.

that we may safely venture to consider him as fully equal to the task, that was imposed upon him. Whatever some may think with reference to these awful sentences of deposition and excommunication, persons of candour will undoubtedly find among the deposed and excommunicated, both characters and actions which deserved the severest censure. On the following day a petition from St Andrew's was presented to the Assembly, supplicating that Mr Alexander Henderson of Leuchars should be removed to that city. This was keenly opposed by the Commissioners from Edinburgh, who earnestly pleaded that he was already their elected minister. They also warmly urged their priviledge of transporting from any part of the kingdom. Mr Henderson himself was extremely averse to remove from his present charge, to any other place; and forcibly opposed his removal in the Assembly. He pleaded that he was too old a plant to take root in another soil. It is said, He was at that time fifty three years of age.[a] He also urged, that he might be more useful where he was, than in a more public station. And, if he was to be removed, his great love of retirement, which has, in all ages, closely adhered to intelligent and elevated minds, greatly inclined him to St Andrew's, rather than to Edinburgh. After a very warm contest between these two places, which continued some days, Mr Baillie says two or three, it carried by votes, much against Mr Henderson's inclination, that he should be translated to Edinburgh. Upon the Assembly's decision, he submitted, having obtained a promise that he should be allowed to remove unto a country charge, if his health should require it, or when the infirmities of old age should overtake him[b].

When the Assembly had finished their business, Mr Henderson addressed himself to them in a very judicious and appropriate speech of considerable length. A speech delivered on so remarkable an occasion was likely in sub-

a Christian Magazine, vol. x. No. 113. p. 266.

b Baillie's Letters, vol. i. p. 142. Stevenson's Hist. vol. ii. p. 642.

stance to be preserved; and may be seen in Stevenson's History.[a] In this able speech, he modestly apologised for his own infirmities in discharging the duties of his station; candidly acknowledged the admirable diligence, faithfulness, and zeal, of all ranks; reminded them gratefully to remember the wonderful goodness of Almighty God to Scotland, when the time of the promise drew near, that *the isles should wait for his law*, and in later times, when their adversaries were accounted the head, and they only the tail, and especially during the sitting of this famous Assembly. He reminded them of their wonderful and most glorious deliverance from the galling *yoke which neither they nor their fathers were able to bear.* "Now," said he, "we are freed of the service-book, which was a book of slavery indeed; of the book of canons which tied us in spiritual bondage; of the book of ordination, which was a yoke put on the neck of faithful ministers; of the high-commission, which was a guard to keep us all under that slavery; and of the civil places of church-men, which was the splendour of all these evils; and the Lord has led captivity captive, and made lords slaves. Seeing then that the Lord has granted us liberty, what should we do less than labour to be sensible of our liberty? We are like a man that has lain long in irons, who, after they are off, and he redeemed, feels not his liberty for a time, but the smart of them makes him apprehend that they are on him still: so it is with us; we do not yet feel our liberty, therefore, it were good for us to keep the bounds of our liberty wherewith Christ has made us free, and not to be entangled again with the yoke of bondage.—A courtier once degraded, doth scarcely ever regain his credit; and it doth especially hold true in spiritual things. I grant the Lord can miraculously give eyes to the blind, and raise the dead, as we are witnesses this day, having ourselves been brought back to him, after we had run far on in a course of defection: but take heed of a second defection; and rather endure the greatest extre-

a Stevenson's History, vol. ii. chap. iii. pp. 665—673.

mity than be entangled again with the yoke of bondage. I grant the cross is hard to look upon; but if we get strength from our Lord, it shall be an easy yoke. Remember the plague of Laodicea for lukewarmness, and beware of her sin; for ye know that the Lord threatens to spue them out of his mouth.—Concerning the nobles, barons, and burgesses, who have attended here, I must say, and may say it confidently from the Lord's word, *They who honour God, he will honour them.*—And, I dare not dissemble, that in a special manner my heart is toward these nobles, whose hearts the Lord hath moved to be chief instruments in this work. Ye know they, like the tops of the mountains, were first discovered in this deluge, which made the little vallies hope to be delivered from it also; and so it is come to pass. I remember to have read, that in the eastern countries, where they worship the sun, a multitude being assembled in the morning for that end, and striving who should first see their mistaken deity, a servant turned his face to the west, which all the rest accounted foolish, yet he obtained the first sight of the sun shining on the top of the western mountains. So truly he would have been thought a foolish man, who, a few years ago, would have looked for such things of our nobles as we now see; yet our Lord Jesus hath nobilitated them; so that contrary to their station, which is subject to manifold temptations, and the age of severals of them, which uses not to see much beauty or contentment in such affairs, they have taken part in our trials, and had a chief hand in all the conclusions which we have brought to pass, and their liberality hath abounded to many on this occasion. *The Sun of Righteousness* has been pleased to shine forth on these mountains, and long, long, may he shine on them, for the comfort of the hills, and refreshing of the vallies, may the blessing of God be on them and their families, and we trust it shall be seen to be so to the generations following." In this remarkable speech, Mr Henderson did not overlook the King; and warmly recommended a favourable construction of his opposition to them. He warmly expressed his high sense of the distinguished harmony which had conspicuously appeared among the ministers, while they had been assiduously employed in correcting the many errors and gross abuses which prevailed; and in *earnestly contending for the faith which was once delivered unto the saints.* He concluded this elaborate and well-digested speech, with gratefully acknowleging the very hospitable treatment which the members of this respectable Assembly had kindly received from the inhabitants of the city of Glasgow; and the particular countenance and aid afforded them by their chief magistrate. He justly subjoined, "The best recompence we can make them, is to pray for the blessing of God to them, and to give them a taste of our labours, by visiting their University, and any other thing that is in our power, without prejudice to the church of God; that so the kingdom of our Lord Jesus may be established among them, that the name of this city may from henceforth be, *Jehovah Shammah, The Lord is there.*" When Mr Henderson had ended his speech, he desired Mr David Dickson, Mr Andrew Ramsay, and some of the nobles, to supply what he had omitted. The two above named had discourses to the same purpose with the Moderator's speech. The Moderator judged, that the countenance given to this Assembly by the Earl of Argyle deserved respectful notice: he, therefore, mentioned him with approbation; and earnestly wished that his Lordship had sooner joined them; but he hoped God had reserved him for the best time, and that he would honour him here and hereafter. Upon this, Argyle delivered an extemporary speech. When Argyle had ended, the Moderator thanked him for his speech, supported it in a short discourse, and afterward concluded that very long and solemn Assembly with prayer, singing the cxxxiii Psalm, and pronouncing the apostolical blessing. Upon this, the Assembly rose in triumph. And Mr Henderson said, *We have now cast down the walls of Jericho, let him who rebuildeth them beware of the curse of Hiel the Bethelite.*[a]

a Stevenson, vol. ii. pp. 673—676.

And thus Episcopacy, the High Commission Court, the Articles of Perth, the Canons and the Liturgy, were abolished and declared unlawful: and the whole fabric, which James and Charles, in a long course of years, had been rearing with much care and policy, fell at once to the ground.[a] The church of Christ now gained a glorious victory; much resembling Cæsar's victory over Pharnaces, son of Mithradates, king of Pontus, whom Cæsar, in his war with Pompey, very quickly discomfited.[b] The trophies of Cæsar's victory over Pharnaces were distinguished by labels, containing the famous words, "I came, I saw, I vanquished."[c] When the members of this celebrated Assembly came to Glasgow, they saw a very formidable army of lordly Bishops, and their adherents, against them with the Marquis of Hamilton, the Archbishop of Canterbury, and the King himself, at their head. But by the special aid of the Lord their God, they obtained a complete victory over them all. *They came, They saw, They vanquished!*

Mr Henderson's elevated station, and his great activity, in this Assembly, fully exposed him to the violent resentment both of the Court and of the Bishops. And, from this, neither the strict propriety, nor the singular moderation, of his conduct, could protect him. It is said, that Dr Balcanqual, who had attended the Assembly, and agented the cause of the Bishops, seemed studiously to oppose himself to the Moderator; and on one occasion, during a debate, illiberally reminded him, that he, with others of his brethren, had once patronised those measures which he now so much reprobated. Mr Henderson prudently treated this reflection with dignified silence; and none of the members seemingly judged a reply necessary.[d] In the *Large Declaration*, drawn up by Dr Balcanqual, and published in the King's name, Mr Henderson is called "The prime and most rigid Covenanter

a Hume's Hist. England, vol. vi. chap. liii.

b Ainsworth's Lat. Dict. under Pharnaces.

c Ferguson's Roman Republic, vol. iv. chap. xxviii. The words in the original are, Veni, vidi, vici.

d Christian Magazine, vol. x. No. 113. p. 267.

in the kingdom."[a] Archbishop Laud, in a letter to the Marquis of Hamilton, says, that the only thing, in the full account sent him of the proceedings of this Assembly, which required an answer, was, "That Mr Alexander Henderson, who went all this while for a quiet and calm-spirited man, hath shewn himself a most violent and passionate man, and a Moderator without moderation." Nor was the Primate at any loss to account for this transformation of the lamb into the lion; for he adds, "Truly, my Lord, never did I see any man of that humour, (the Presbyterian,) but he was deep-dyed in some violence or other; and it would have been a wonder to me, if *Henderson* had held free."[b] But one very justly observes here, "The censures of men disappointed in the mad project of subjugating a whole nation under tyranny and superstition, will be regarded as praises by all good Christians and patriots."[c]

When the members of the above-mentioned General Assembly returned home, they carefully intimated their conclusions; and thereby the knowledge of what was done was both speedily and widely circulated. And as soon as it was known at Court, that the Assembly continued to sit after they were dissolved by the Royal Commissioner, and that the people greatly approved their conduct and conclusions, the King meditated revenge, and inconsiderately resolved to raise an army to reduce them unto obedience, thinking that their actions might justify his recourse to arms. While the inhabitants of Scotland were making preparations during the winter in 1639, for defending themselves against the hostile invasion from England, Mr Henderson's able pen was much employed in several publications, in vindication of their proceedings. By order of the Deputies, he drew up a paper, entitled, "The Remonstrance of the Nobility, Barons, Burgesses, Ministers, and Commons, within the Kingdom of Scotland, vindicating them and

a Large Decl. p. 237. as with the Christian Magazine.
b Burnet's Memoir of D. Hamilton, p. 109.
c Christian Magazine, as above.

their proceedings, from the crimes wherewith they are charged by the late proclamation in England, Feb. 27th 1639." This paper, after being revised and approved by the Deputies, was published and industriously circulated by their friends in England, and was very advantageous to their cause in that country. He also drew up "Instructions for defensive arms." The intention of this was, to give information and satisfaction to all among themselves, with reference unto the just and necessary defensive war into which they were forced. He did this, according to our information, somewhat against his inclination: and being hastily composed, and the subject delicate, he declined making it public by printing. But, though he would not allow it to go to the press, it was read from many pulpits, as the production of their best penman. And one Corbet, a deposed minister, who fled to Ireland, carried a copy with him, and published it with an answer, which contained little matter, but much spiteful venom, according to Mr Baillie, who flourished at that time.[a]

When the magnanimous appearance of the Scots, and the indifference which the English discovered in the cause, induced the King to listen unto overtures of peace, Mr Henderson was appointed one of the Commissioners from the Scottish army, to carry on the treaty of pacification, in the month of June, 1639.[b] This appointment clearly shows, that Mr Henderson was held in the highest veneration and esteem by his countrymen. He and Mr Archibald Johnstone declined going to the English camp with the rest of the Commissioners on the first day of the treaty; but, upon receiving information, that the King noticed their absence, they attended the next meeting on a following day. The King was much delighted with Mr Henderson's discourse.[c]—And during the whole treaty Mr Henderson eminently displayed his rare abilities, as on other remarkable occasions.

a Stevenson's Hist. vol. ii. chap iv. Baillie's Letters, vol. i. pp. 151, 152.
b Bishop Guthrie's Memoirs, p. 58.
c Baillie's Letters, vol. i. p. 180.

Bishop Burnet has observed, that it was strange to see Mr Henderson, who had most vigorously opposed the Bishops for meddling in civil affairs, made a Commissioner for this treaty, and employed in signing a paper so purely civil as that of the pacification was.[a] But an attentive consideration, and close comparison of the two cases, will very clearly shew, that this reflection is groundless. The present was evidently a very critical and an extraordinary conjuncture; and in extraordinary cases, extraordinary things may be done. All that was dear to the people was at stake; and certainly all their talents should then have been called forth and employed. Beside, religion was undoubtedly the chief ground of the quarrel, and, therefore, it's interests must have been deeply concerned in the termination thereof. And the articles of the pacification proceeded upon the King's declaration, engaging that all ecclesiastical affairs should be determined by the assemblies of the church; that General Assemblies should be called once a-year; that, as the King would not own their Assembly at Glasgow, so neither should they be urged to disown it; and that a full and free Assembly should be convened at Edinburgh on the 12th of August for the settlement of matters. When these things are candidly considered, the presence of a Minister of the Gospel, who could explain difficult things, and watch over the church's rights, may be easily vindicated.[b] And this reason is expressly assigned in the Act of the Committee of Parliament, empowering the Commissioners for a treaty of peace, in the year 1640. " And because many things may occur concerning the Church and her Assemblies, therefore, beside those of the Estates, we nominate and appoint, *Mr Alexander Henderson and Mr Archibald Johnstone*, whom we adjoin *for that effect*." But this is entirely different from Bishops sitting as lords of Parliament, or filling the highest offices of State, which, beside other

a Burnet's Memoirs of D. Hamilton.

b Bishop Guthrie's Memoirs, p. 58. Christian Magazine, vol. x. No. 114. p. 306.

evils, render it impossible for them to attend to the important duties of their ecclesiastical function.[a]

Mr Henderson was one of the fourteen chief persons among the Covenanters, who were required by an order from the King to go to his Court at Berwick, and meet him there, after the Scottish army was disbanded. Bishop Guthrie says, that the King's design in requiring the attendance of these fourteen Scottish Covenanters was, that he might consult with them concerning the way of his incoming, to hold the Assembly and Parliament in person.[b] Bishop Burnet says, The true reason of that message was, to try what fair treatment might do with the Scots.[c] But Sir James Balfour, lion king at arms, expressly says, that this was a trap laid for the chief of the Covenanters, by the advice of some corrupt counsellors; and that it was owing to a kind advertisement from some of their friends at Court, that they escaped the snare.[d] An alarm having speedily spread of a design against these persons, they were stopped, by the populace, when they were setting out on their journey to Berwick, at the Water-gate of Edinburgh. Their horses were taken from them, and they were obliged to return, and ordered to stay at home: nor was it judged prudent that they should afterward proceed on their journey. This measure greatly offended the King, who, without waiting the Assembly or Parliament, set out on his return to London, the 29th of July.[e]

At the opening of the General Assembly of the Church of Scotland, which met at Edinburgh upon Monday the 12th of August, 1639, Mr Henderson, the former Moderator, preached from Acts v. 33.—Toward the conclusion of his discourse, he addressed himself in very suitable exhortations both to the Earl of Traquaire, the Royal Commissioner, and to the members of the Assembly. To the Royal Commissioner he said, " We

a Christian Magazine, vol. x. as above.
b Guthrie's Memoirs, p. 61.
c Burnet's Memoirs of D. Hamilton, p. 148.
d Stevenson, vol. iii. pp. 762, 763.
e Stevenson.

beseech your Grace to see that Cæsar have his own, but let him not have what is due to God, by whom kings reign. God hath exalted your Grace to many high places within these few years, and is doing so more especially now: be thankful, and labour to exalt Christ's throne. Some are exalted like Haman, some like Mordecai; and I pray God that these eminent parts wherewith he hath endowed you may be used aright. When the Israelites came out of Egypt, they gave all the silver and gold they had carried thence for the building of the tabernacle. In like manner, your Grace must employ all your parts and endowments for building up the church of God in this land."

He addressed the members of the Assembly in the following manner: "Right Honourable, Worshipful and Reverend, constantly go on in your zeal. True zeal does not cool, but the longer it burns the more fervent will it grow. If it shall please God, that by your means the light of the Gospel shall be continued, and that you have the honour of being instruments of a blessed Reformation, it shall be useful and comfortable to yourselves and to your posterity. But let your zeal be always tempered with an holy moderation; for zeal is a good servant, but a bad master: like a ship that hath a full sail and no rudder. We have much need of Christian prudence, for ye know what advantages some have attempted to take of us this way. For this reason, let it be seen to the world, that Presbytery, the government we contend for in the church, can consist very well with monarchy in the state, and thereby we shall gain the favour of our King, and God shall get the glory."[a]

Mr Henderson's speeches and particular addresses, on such occasions, were of very great utility and importance unto the church. The Royal commissioner earnestly requested, at this time, that Mr Henderson, the former Moderator, should be continued in that station, out of respect to Mr Henderson's rare abilities, as he solemnly protested, but rather, as was suspected, to

a Stevenson's Hist. vol. iii. chap. ii. pp. 770, 771.

support the King's pretensions to the right of nominating their Moderator, and continuing him at pleasure. But the Assembly vigorously opposed this motion of the Commissioner, as too much favouring the practice of *the constant moderator*, which formerly had been employed for the introduction of Episcopacy: and no man discovered greater aversion to the motion than Mr Henderson himself.[a] Mr David Dickson, minister at Irvine, was, by a great majority, chosen Moderator. He is represented by Bishop Guthrie, as greatly inferior to Mr Henderson, in that station. And the Bishop says, that it had been worse with Mr Dickson, "were it not that Mr Henderson sat at his elbow as his coadjutor."[b] Whether this representation of Mr Dickson is just or not, it serves to show that Mr Henderson was very highly esteemed, even by the Episcopal party. Mr Dickson gave thanks, in the Assembly's name, to their last Moderaor, for the quick understanding, solid judgment, and great diligence, which he had displayed in that office, to the conviction even of his enemies.[c] And, when this Assembly condemned Episcopacy as unlawful, and contrary to the word of God;[d] and the Royal commissioner desired reasons of this condemnation, Mr Henderson, with the Moderator, and Mr Andrew Ramsay, shewed that Episcopacy is only an human institution, that it hath been destructive to the discipline of the church, and introductory to popery, superstition and idolatry.[e] A motion was made by Mr Henderson, concerning the expedience of drawing up a Confession, positively condemning the errors and immoralities charged on, and defended, or practised, by any ministers, and clearing the doctrine of the Church of Scotland, in opposition to them, that none might afterward pretend ignorance. The Synod of Dort adopted this method with the Arminians. Mr Henderson's motion, in imitation of that Synod, was unanimously approved, and a committee named for

a Stevenson, as above, p. 772.
b Bishop Guthrie's Memoirs, p. 62.
c Stevenson, vol. iii. p. 772.
d Guthrie's Memoirs as above.
e Stevenson, vol. iii. p. 777.

the purpose. But if they brought the matters referred to them, unto a conclusion, their report has not reached us.[a] Mr Henderson preached an excellent sermon, at the opening of the Parliament, at Edinburgh, concerning the utility and importance of magistracy, from 1 Tim. ii. 1, 2, 3, on the 31st of August, 1639.[b]

The Town-council of Edinburgh, who were the patrons and governors of the University of that city, having annually visited the College since the year 1614, the Rector was the more remiss in his office. The Council now resolved, that, instead of these periodical visitations of the College, they should annually chuse a Rector, whom they should direct, and ascertain the powers of his office, by articles framed for that end. Agreeably to this resolution, they chose Mr Alexander Henderson, one of the ministers of Edinburgh, Rector of the University, in the year 1640, ordaining a silver mace to be borne before him on all solemnities, and appointing certain members of the Town-council, ministers of Edinburgh, and professors in the College, his assessors. They drew up instructions, authorising him to superintend all matters respecting the College, whether connected with it's revenues, fabric, the education of youth, or the conduct of the *principal*, professors, and other members of the University, and their conformity to the regulations; with power to the Rector to admonish offenders, and in case of their obstinacy, to make report to the Council, and to judge and determine upon trifling disputes between the members among themselves. The custody of the matriculation-roll was also given to the Rector, and the students ordained to be matriculated in his presence, and that of the Principal, and of the Professors of the class, to which the students respectively belonged. He was also to be furnished with an inventory of the College-revenues, and donations in it's favour. The Rector continued to exercise his office, some years. But the troubles which distracted the nation, and the want

a Stevenson, vol. iii. pp. 789, 790.
b Stevenson, vol. iii. chap. iii. p. 807.

of regular records of this University, at that time, render it impracticable for us to ascertain when that office was discontinued, or how the College was governed for a considerable period of time.[a]

When the war was renewed with the Scots, and they were declared rebels, Mr Henderson was again called from his peaceful habitation. Each regiment was attended with a chaplain, one of the most eminent ministers in the bounds where they were raised, as Messrs Alexander Henderson, Robert Blair, John Livingston, Robert Baillie, Andrew Cant, George Gillespie, and others who were vested with Presbyterial authority, and were to perform every part of the ministerial function to them, proper in such circumstances.[b] In the beginning of August in 1640, the several regiments arrived at Dunse, where they were reviewed by their General: and the army marched into England on the 20th of August that year, with great courage and success. Notwithstanding these warlike measures, the Covenanters still preserved the most pathetic and the most submissive language. They declared that they entered England, with no other view, than to obtain access to the King's presence, and to lay their grievances and their humble petition at his royal feet. At Newburn upon Tyne, some miles above Newcastle, they were opposed by a detachment of 4,500 men under Conway, who seemed resolute to dispute with them the passage of the river. The Scots first entreated them, with great civility, not to stop them in their march to their gracious Sovereign; but the English would not listen to them. Upon this the Scottish army attacked the English with great bravery, killed several, and chased the rest from their ground, obtaining a signal victory over them, upon the 28th of August, in the year 1640. And such a panic seized the whole English army, that the forces at Newcastle fled immediately to Durham; and not yet thinking themselves safe, they deserted that town, and retreated into Yorkshire. Their

a Arnot's Hist. of Edinburgh, B. iii. chap. iii.

b Stevenson, vol. iii. chap v. p. 897. Livingston's Life, period iv.

consternation on this occasion is said to have been inexpressible.[a] And, in their flight, both officers and soldiers declared, that they would not fight to maintain the pride and power of the Bishops.

Quicquid delirant reges, plectuntur Achivi. HOR. Ep. 1, 2, 14.
'When doating Monarchs urge
Unsound resolves, their Subjects feel the scourge.' FRANCIS.

The Scots took possession of Newcastle; and though sufficiently elated with their victory, they preserved exact discipline, and persevered in their resolution of paying every thing, in order still to maintain the appearance of an amicable correspondence with England.[b] Mr Henderson, the eminent subject of these pages, preached in the Great Church of Newcastle, on the Sabbath day, to a large auditory.[c] This benevolent and enlightened Reformer had an enlarged capacity of action, and of usefulness: and his labours contributed essentially to the good of the Public, on many occasions. Public usefulness to others, when the Lord requires it, ought to be preferred to retirement, and to our own special pleasures; for it is more blessed to give, than to receive.[d] The nation was now universally and highly discontented. And, the great success of the Scottish army, and the very distressed condition in which the King was, obliged him to accede to proposals of peace a second time: and a treaty relative to this was agreed to, and commenced at Rippon in Yorkshire, which afterward was transferred to London.[e] Mr Henderson was appointed one of the Commissioners for this treaty.[f] The state of society both civil and religious requires, that some persons of distinguished abilities should be employed to consult what may be most advantaegous to the body. "It is not one of the least advantages derived from the division of labour which takes place in a refined state of society,

a Hume's History, vol. vi. chap. liii. Stevenson, vol. iii. pp. 916, 924. b Hume's History, vol. vi. chap. liii.

c Guthrie's Memoirs, p. 83. Baillie's Letters, vol. i. p. 204. Stevenson, vol. iii. p. 926. d Henry on Matt. xxviii. 7. vol. v.

e Hume's History, as above.

f Guthrie's Memoirs, p. 87. Stevenson, vol. iii.

that there is one class of men, whose occupation is *to think* for the benefit of the rest; and who, by the constant application of vigorous talents to the great object of public good, may produce effects which could never be expected from casual exertions."[a] On this remarkable occasion, the foundation was laid of that happy conjunction between Scotland and England, both in civil and religious affairs, which was afterward most solemnly ratified by oath. The Scottish Commissioners, agreeably to instructions received from their constituents, warmly urged unity in religion, and uniformity in church-government, as a special means for the preservation of peace between the two kingdoms. At the same time, they delivered to the English Commissioners, a paper, which is said to have been drawn up by Mr Henderson, stating very forcibly the grounds and reasons of what they urged, and condescending upon measures for carrying it into effect, which paper was transmitted to the English Parliament. This paper was of great importance, and is still preserved in MS.[b] And an abstract of it is given by Stevenson, vol. iii. p. 963. A favourable answer was given by the King and Parliament, to the above demand, intimating in general, their approbation of the affection which the Scottish subjects had expressed in their desire of having uniformity of church government in both nations; and that, as the Parliament had already taken into consideration the reformation of church-government, so they will proceed therein in due time, as shall best conduce to the glory of God, the peace of the church, and of both kingdoms.[c] This answer was ratified as one of the articles of the treaty.[d]

Mr Henderson was very laborious, while he was in London, attending the above-mentioned treaty, which was continued about nine months. The Scottish Commissioners found every advantage in conducting their

a Monthly Review Enlarged, vol. xxiii. p. 291.

b The Christian Magazine, vol. x. p. 308.

c Stevenson, vol. iii. pp. 965, 966.

d Articles of the Large Treaty, p. 25. Christian Magazine, as above.

treaty; yet it was not hastily concluded. They were lodged in the city, and had an intimate correspondence with the citizens, with the magistrates, and with the popular leaders in both Houses of Parliament. They warmly recommended the Religion of Jesus, and the Reformation for which they earnestly contended; and were the happy instruments of doing much good in that great metropolis. Antholine's church was assigned them for their public worship; and here their chaplains openly worshipped God in the Presbyterian form. Multitudes of all ranks attended this church: and there was a great revival of religion in London, at this time.[a] Mr Henderson now eminently distinguished himself, by employing all his influence and abilities, in promoting whatever was favourable to the amelioration of mankind, Beside taking his turn with the other eminent divines, who attended the Scottish Commissioners as chaplains, in Antholine's church, he and they were often employed in preaching for the London ministers, both on the Sabbath and on other days.[b] He prepared several useful tracts for the press. At the desire of the English ministers he wrote some very good reasons for the removal of Bishops out of the church, which were printed, in 1641. And Mr Baillie, in a letter to the Presbytery of Irvine, dated, London, Feb. 28th, 1641, says: "Think not that any of us live here to be idle. Mr Henderson has ready now a short treatise much called for, of our Church-discipline. Mr Gillespie has the Grounds of Presbyterian Government Well Asserted. Mr Blair, a Pertinent Answer to Bishop Hall's Remonstrance. All these are ready for the press."[c] The polishing of many important papers was committed to Mr Henderson: and he generally composed those respecting the Church.

While Mr Henderson was in London, he had a private conference with the King. The particular object

a Hume's History of England, vol. vi. chap. liv. 1640. And Stevenson, vol. iii. pp. 941—968, 969.

b Laing's History of Scotland, vol. i. p. 184. Stevenson, vol. iii. p. 968.

c Baillie's Letters, vol. i. pp. 236, 237, 245. See p. 233.

of this conference was, to procure some assistance for the Scottish Universities, from the rents formerly appropriated to the Bishops. He was well received, and had ground to expect that his request would be obtained.[a]—

Mr Henderson returned to Edinburgh toward the end of July in 1641. The General Assembly of the Church of Scotland had met at St Andrew's, on the 20th of July, according to the appointment of the former Assembly. But the Parliament, who were sitting in Edinburgh, sent Lord Cassils, witho thers, to the Assembly at St Andrew's, most earnestly entreating them to translate themselves to Edinburgh, for the convenience of those who were chosen members of both, before chusing a Moderator, or entering on any business of importance. Many most ardently desired, that Mr Henderson, who was not then returned from London, should act as Moderator of this meeting, and the members agreed that they should meet at Edinburgh on the 27th of July, and that the former Moderator should preside until that time. Mr Henderson had been elected a member of this Assembly; but, as it was uncertain that he could be present, his constituents had chosen Mr Andrew Fairful to supply his place, in case of his absence, and Mr Fairful had taken his seat at St Andrew's. Mr Fairful proposed to give his seat to Mr Henderson, upon his arrival. This was most keenly opposed by Mr Calderwood, though he was not a member, but only allowed by favour to sit in the Assembly. He warmly urged that Mr Henderson's commission could not now be received; and, in this, he was seconded by Mr Henderson himself. But, upon voting, Mr Henderson's commission was unanimously received, and sustained by the Assembly: and he was chosen to be their Moderator, under declaration, that neither that translation, without first chusing a new Moderator, nor election of one, whose place as a member was supplied before he came, should be drawn into a precedent. Mr Henderson earnestly deprecated the burden of moderating, at this time, but

a Baillie, vol. i. p. 242.

it was laid upon him, by a plurality of votes. Mr Calderwood still insisted upon the great irregularity of translating the Assembly without a permanent Moderator, and of choosing one to be Moderator who had no Commission. But though he spake both peevishly and unreasonably on this subject, Mr Henderson treated him most respectfully, on this occasion, bearing all with much patience. And prior to the dissolution of this meeting, Mr Henderson publicly said, he regretted, that Mr Calderwood, who had deserved well of this Church, had been so long neglected, and readily procured a recommendation of him by the Assembly, in consequence of which he was soon afterward admitted to the church of Pencaitland.[a]

Mr Henderson desired that some letters should be read, which he had brought from England, addressed to the Assembly. One of these was from several Ministers in London and it's vicinity, expressing their approbation of the proceedings in Scotland, in the work of Reformation, and their expectation that the Scottish discipline would soon be established in England. And they desired advice from the Assembly with reference to the opinions of some of their brethren, who were inclined to independency, and popular government in the church. The Assembly appointed Mr Henderson to write an answer to the brethren in England; which he did with accuracy.[b] Both letters may be seen in the printed Acts of this Assembly.

From the particular observations which Mr Henderson had made, during his late residence in London, and from the friendly intercourse which he enjoyed there, both with ministers and people, he clearly perceived that there would soon be a change in the English Church; and that there was a considerable prospect of their approaching to greater conformity with the Church of Scotland. This beautiful conformity was certainly an object of great utility and importance; and Mr Henderson most heartily concurred with his brethren in promoting it. As one of

a Baillie's Letters, vol. i. Let. xxx. Stevenson, vol. iii. chap. vi.
b Baillie, as above.

the late Commissioners for the above-mentioned treaty, he eminently distinguished himself by endeavouring to advance this conformity. Agreeably to this he prudently and seasonably moved, that the Assembly should take steps for drawing up a Confession of Faith, a Catechism, a Directory for all the parts of the public worship, and a Platform of government, in which the English and the Scots probably might afterward agree. This notable motion was unanimously approved; and the burden of that labour was laid on the mover; liberty being given him, at the same time, to abstain from preaching when he should find it necessary in attending to this very interesting business, and also of calling in the aid of such of his brethren as he pleased. He declined this very arduous task, but it was left upon him.[a] And, probably, this early appointment greatly contributed to prepare him for giving assistance in that useful and important work, when it was afterward undertaken by the famous Assembly at Westminster.[b]

While this Assembly were sitting, Mr Henderson petitioned for liberty to be translated from Edinburgh. He particularly urged that his voice was not sufficient for any church in the town; that he was always unhealthy there, and not so in any other place; that to keep him there was to kill him; and that, in the act for his transportation from Leuchars, there was an express clause, which allowed him the liberty that he now craved, when the public commotions were settled, if he found that he was unhealthful in that town. The Assembly were greatly perplexed by his insisting upon this petition. The inhabitants of Edinburgh were extremely averse to his removal. Beside the loss of that eminent man, they considered the transportation of any of their ministers by Assemblies, as a very dangerous precedent. And they offered to purchase an house and gardens for Mr Henderson, in an airy situation; and farther intimated for his encouragement, that he might cease from preaching

a Baillie's Letters, vol. i. Let. xxx. p. 304.
b Christian Magazine, vol. x. p. 310.

when he judged this necessary; and use his freedom in going to the country, at any time, when the state of his health required. They were the more averse to his removal, as a petition had been presented to the Assembly for his transportation to St Andrew's, to be Principal of the University there. He continued to insist for his liberty. Some reckoned that his great earnestness for a removal from Edinburgh arose from his displeasure at the keen speeches of some of the inhabitants against him, on account of his opposition to their humour for innovations; but he affirmed that his health was the sole ground of his petition; that if his health did not fail, he would continue at Edinburgh, even though liberty was now given him to remove; and that, if he did remove, he would not go to St Andrew's, but to some quiet country-charge. His earnest petition was at last granted, which much grieved many of the inhabitants of Edinburgh: but he either did not find his removal afterward necessary, or he was prevailed upon not to use that liberty which with much difficulty he now obtained.[a]

The King revisited Scotland, that he might be present in person at the Parliament, in his native kingdom, leaving both Houses of the English Parliament sitting at Westminster, in the month of August, 1641.[b] He was obliged now to cultivate the attachment of the Scottish nation for the support of his throne. He attended public worship, on the Sabbath-day, after his arrival at Edinburgh, and heard Mr Henderson preach, the forenoon, in the Abbey-Church, from Romans xi. 36 It is said, that he did not attend in the afternoon; but Mr Henderson having conversed with him relative to this, he afterward punctually attended the public worship. Mr Henderson waited on the King as his chaplain, and was appointed to provide preachers for his Majesty during the time that he was in Scotland, he having declared, that he would conform to their mode of worship while he was among them. And he attended regularly

a Baillie's Letters, vol. i. pp. 314, 315.
b Clarendon, vol. i. B. iii. p. 279.

family worship in the palace, morning and evening, as performed by his chaplain, in the Scottish form. And he exhibited no symptom of dissatisfaction with the want of a liturgy and the ceremonies. His whole deportment at this time, afforded some hope to his Scottish subjects, who were not thoroughly acquainted with his character, that he would not oppose, but encourage the work of Reformation. On the last day of the meeting of this Parliament, when great solemnity was observed, the King seated on his throne, and the Estates in their places, Mr Henderson began with prayer; and when the business was finished, he closed the meeting with a sermon. The revenues of the Bishoprics were divided at this time: and Mr Henderson now eminently exerted himself in favour of the Scottish Universities. And what belonged to the Bishopric of Edinburgh, and Priory, was, by his influence, though not without difficulty, procured for the University of that city. The emoluments of the Chapel royal, amounting to about 4000 merks yearly, were conferred upon Mr Henderson, as a recompense for his laborious and expensive services in the cause of the public. The King was, in general, very accommodating and favourable to the Scottish nation, in this visit, wishing to obtain their concurrence against the English Parliament. Argyle was created a Marquis; and the Lords Loudon and Lindsay, were raised to the dignity of Earls. And all parties were so well pleased, that when the King returned to England, it was said, "That he departed a contented King from a contented People."[a] But duplicity strongly marked the King's character, and the Scots were afraid to depend upon him, and, therefore, were obliged to join the English Parliament, and assist them in recovering their liberties and religion.

Mr Henderson was much employed in managing the correspondence with England respecting reformation, and religious uniformity during the year 1642. The English Parliament having agreed to abolish Episcopacy,

a Stevenson, vol. iii.—Acts of Assembly, edit. 1682. p. 129. Neal's Hist. Purit. vol. ii. chap. ix.

requested that some ministers should be sent from the Church of Scotland to assist in the Synod which they had resolved to convene. The Commission of the General Assembly of the Church of Scotland, being fully authorised by them, met, and nominated Commissioners, who were appointed that they might be ready to go to England as soon as it should be necessary. Mr Henderson was one of those, who came under this appointment, by the Committee. He was very averse to the appointment, protesting that in his former journey, he thought that he should have died before he arrived at London. But he could not be excused, and at last acquiesced, complaining, that several persons were very forward in imposing heavy burdens upon him, and afterward employed themselves in inventing or receiving calumnies, or reports, which were injurious to his character.—This journey was hindered for some time, by the confusions which attended the civil war.[a] Mr Henderson earnestly wished a reconciliation of the parties, upon honourable terms. Bishop Burnet says, That he joined with a number of leading men in an invitation to the Queen to come to Scotland, upon terms consistent with her safety and honour, with a view of promoting a mediation ; but the King rejected this proposition.[b] Mr Henderson afterward went in person to the King at Oxford, with the Commissioners from the State, who were sent to offer the mediation of the Scottish nation. But their aid was more desired than their intercession. Accordingly, their mission was unwelcome, and their reception unfavourable. Their powers were questioned, to interpose in the internal dissensions of England, as conservators of peace between the two kingdoms: and their importunate demand of religious uniformity did not relish. They were reviled and threatened by the royalists and recalled in disgust. At the first interview, the King endeavoured to convince Mr Henderson of the justice and necessity of his arms ; but when he found that Mr Hen-

a Baillie's Letters, vol. i. pp. 349, 350.
b Memoirs of D. Hamilton, p. 201.

derson was not so credulous as he expected, his behaviour toward him was entirely different, and frowns appeared in his countenance. Mr Henderson presented to the King, an humble Petition from the Commissioners of the General Assembly of the Church of Scotland, dated Jan. 4th 1643. And it is said, that Mr Henderson was the author of the Petition, which is very probable.[a] It contains a complaint of the insolence of Papists, and of others disaffected to the Reformation of Religion, supplicating the King to apply his royal authority, for disbanding their forces, and preventing their bloody projects;—for religious uniformity, an Assembly of Divines, the removal of the great mountain of Prelacy, and for promoting the glorious work of Reformation. The Petition may be seen in its original state, as given in by Mr Henderson, in Clarendon's History:[b] and also the King's answer to it, which was not favourable. While Mr Henderson remained at Oxford, some of the Doctors wished to engage him in controversy, respecting Church-government, but, judging that it was unbecoming his character, as a Representative of the Church of Scotland, to dispute with private individuals, and viewing them as disposed to cavil rather than to give or to receive information, he signified that his business was with the King. It is said, that a Popish Dr Taylor challenged Mr Henderson to a public dispute at Oxford; so insolent were Papists become through the Royal favour.[c] Clarendon is greatly offended at the distance, or, as he calls it, *the great insolence*, which Mr Henderson discovered at this time.[d] But upon his return to Edinburgh, he gave a full account of his proceedings with the King to the Commissioners of the Church, who expressed their entire satisfaction with his whole conduct, and their judgement was fully approved by the next Assembly, who readily pronounced his carriage to have been "faithful and wise."[e]

a Baillie, vol. i. pp. 358, 359.
b Book vi. vol. iii. pp. 175—180. 8vo. vol. ii. fol. p. 134, &c.
c Christian Magazine, vol. x. p. 313.
d Clarendon's Hist. vol. iii. p. 180. B. vi.
e Baillie, vol. i. p. 359. Christ. Mag. as above.

The Scots were greatly dissatisfied with the uncivil treatment which their Commissioners had received at Oxford, and being now fully convinced that the measures of the Royal party were highly dangerous to both countries, they soon afterward entered into a very close alliance with the English Parliament. Upon this, Mr Henderson was sent to London, where he spent the greater part of his remaining days on the earth.

The General Assembly of the Church of Scotland, which convened at Edinburgh, on the 2d of Aug. in the year 1643, was particularly distinguished by the presence of Commissioners from the English Parliament, and the formation of the famous Solemn League and Covenant. Keeping in view the deeply interesting business of that Assembly, their attention was again turned to Mr Henderson as Moderator, and he was the third time unanimously called to the chair. Mr Baillie says, "Our greatest consultation was for the Moderator. We foresaw great business was to be in hand; strangers were to be present; and the minds of many brethren were exasperated. Mr Henderson was the only man meet for the time."[a] Every thing was decently and properly conducted, in the presence of the English Commissioners; Sir William Armyn, Sir Henry Vane, younger, Mr Hatcher, and Mr Darley, with two Ministers of the Gospel, Mr Stephen Marshall, and Mr Philip Nye. After an appropriate introduction, said to have been drawn by Mr Marshall, and Sir Henry Vane, these delegates presented their commission from both Houses of the English Parliament, giving very ample power to the Earl of Rutland, Lord Grey, and these four above-mentioned, to treat with the Scottish Covenanters, and to the two Ministers, to assist in ecclesiastical affairs, according to their instructions given or to be given, or to any four of them. They also presented a declaration of both Houses to the General Assembly of the Church of Scotland, shewing their care of reforming religion, and their desire that some of the Scottish Di-

a Baillie, vol. i. p. 374.

vines should join with their Assembly of Divines for that end.[a] The Royalists were a furious and vindictive party, and very hostile to the liberties and religion of the nation. And when the royal arms were triumphant, the English Parliament implored the fraternal aid of the Scots, earnestly soliciting their immediate help. And with a view to unite the nations in a very close alliance in mutual reformation and defence, a Covenant was proposed. The English at first were for a civil League, and the Scots for a religious Covenant. Mr Henderson gave them a draught of a Covenant which he had composed. This at length obtained the assent of the three Committees, of the English Parliament, of the Convention of Estates, and of the General Assembly. Being adopted by them, it was immediately transmitted to the General Assembly and Convention. And being introduced into the Assembly by a very grave and appropriate speech from the Moderator, it was received with the highest applause, and adopted with tears of much joy. It was read distinctly the second time, by the Moderator. And, upon both ministers and ruling elders, in general, being asked, and having freely delivered their sentiments respecting it, the catalogue was read, and all readily and unanimously assented. On the afternoon, it passed the Convention of Estates, with the same cordial approbation, and it was appointed to be transmitted to the English Parliament for their approbation. The General Assembly of the Church of Scotland renewed the appointment of their Commission respecting the members who were to be sent from them to assist the Assembly of Divines sitting at Westminster: and Mr Henderson was appointed to set out immediately for London, with a view to obtain the ratification of the Solemn League and Covenant.

On the 30th of August, Mr Henderson sailed from Leith for London, in company with other Commissioners.[b] The Covenant having been approved by both Houses of the English Parliament, and by the Assembly

a Baillie, vol. i. p. 380. b Baillie, vol. i. pp. 380—390.

of Divines at Westminster, the members of the latter, with those of the House of Commons. convened in Margaret's Church, Westminster, upon the 25th of September; and having first solemnly sworn, afterward subscribed it. Immediately before they proceeded in that most important work, Mr Henderson delivered a very appropriate and encouraging speech to them, in which he very judiciously and warmly recommended the duty, as acceptable to God, and well pleasing in his sight—exemplified by the people of God, and by other reformed churches and kingdoms, both in former and later times,—as very necessary—and crowned with the most surprising success. The reader will find the speech at the conclusion of this work.

Mr Henderson acted a very conspicuous part in assisting the Assembly of Divines at Westminster, as a Commissioner from the Church of Scotland. His deportment was very grave, and highly becoming the dignity of his station; and great deference was paid to his opinions. He always discovered uprightness in his designs, and was indefatigable in the application of his talents. He honourably maintained a sway over men, who, in point of acuteness and erudition, have seldom been equalled. And when it became necessary to vindicate the principles of the Church of Scotland, and of the other Reformed Churches, from slanderous charges, he spoke with great facility, and most judiciously. His wisdom was seen in speaking with great propriety on the various subjects which were discussed. And his rare abilities were peculiarly displayed in reconciling contending interests, and in preserving harmony among the members of the Assembly, in the prosecution of that cause, which they had all solemnly sworn to promote. Several very striking instances of this kind occur in the History of the proceedings of that truly Venerable Assembly.[a] But he always most strenuously resisted every attempt which was made, with a view to introduce any principles which were opposite to those of the Church

a See Baillie's Letters, vol. i. pp. 401, 420.

of Scotland, and of other Reformed and Presbyterian Churches. Accordingly, he stated himself equally in opposition to the schemes of the Independents, and of a strong party in the House of Commons, who had imbibed Erastian principles, denying the Divine right of Church government, and wishing to subject the proceedings of Church judicatories to the controul and review of the Parliament.[a]—In the debates of the Assembly, there was often much heat. This was partly owing to their divesting their Prolocutor, or Moderator, of all power, as the House of Commons did their Speaker, and converting him into *a mere chair*, using the language of one who was a witness of their proceedings. Mr Henderson greatly lamented this evil, and on a fast-day, after the religious exercises were ended, he embraced the opportunity of bringing the members to a free and brotherly conference on the subject, in which having seen their fault, they resolved to guard against such excesses in time to come.[b] In the beginning of the year 1645, Mr Henderson was appointed to assist the Commissioners of the two Parliaments, in the treaty between them and the King, at Uxbridge. The Parliamentary Commissioners were instructed to demand the abolition of Episcopacy, and the ratification of the Presbyterian government. The King's Commissioners objected to the abolition of Episcopacy, upon which it was agreed to hear the Divines on both sides. Mr Henderson, in an elaborate speech, which Clarendon allows was not without eloquence, opened the cause, and took up that ground which offered fairest for bringing the controversy to a speedy conclusion. Waving the dispute respecting the lawfulness of Episcopacy, he said, " That the question was not, " Whether the government of the Church by Bishops was lawful, but whether it was so necessary that Christianity could not subsist without it ?" He argued that it was not ; and that the question could not be answered in the affirmative, without condemning all other

a Baillie, vol. ii. pp. 31, 68, 183, 194, 195.
b Christ. Mag. vol. x. p. 352.

Reformed Churches.—That the English Parliament had found Episcopacy a very inconvenient and corrupt government.—That the Hierarchy had been a public grievance from the Reformation downward.—That the Bishops had always encouraged Popery, and retained many superstitious rites and customs in their worship and government; and had lately brought in many innovations, and made a nearer approach to the Roman Communion, to the great scandal of the Protestant Churches of Germany, France, Scotland, and Holland.—That the Prelates had embroiled the British Island, and kindled the flame which raged through the three kingdoms.—That for these reasons the Parliament had resolved to change this inconvenient and mischievous government, and to set up another in it's room, more naturally formed for the advancement of piety.—And that this alteration was the best expedient to unite all Protestant Churches, and to extinguish the remains of Popery: nor could he conceive that His Majesty's conscience could be urged against this salutary change, seeing that he had agreed to the suppression of Prelacy in Scotland.

But the advocates for Episcopacy were fully determined not to hazard their cause upon such grounds as were plain to all, but endeavoured to involve the question, by introducing the dispute at large respecting Episcopal government. Dr Stewart, who was Commissioner for the King in religious affairs, enlarged upon the apostolical institution of Episcopacy, and endeavoured to prove, that without Bishops the sacerdotal character could not be conveyed, nor the sacraments administered to any significancy. Dr Stewart said, that the debate was too general, and desired that they should dispute syllogistically, as became scholars, to which Mr Henderson readily agreed. The dispute continued a considerable time; and though each party claimed the victory, as is common, yet, it was said by some auditors, who must be allowed not to have been prejudised in favour of Presbytery, that while Mr Henderson equalled the King's

Commissioners in learning, he surpassed them in modesty.[a]

The treaty was broken off without success, and Mr Henderson returned to London, and continued to assist the Assembly of Divines in their arduous work. This year, his health began visibly to decline. He suffered repeated attacks of the gravel, and other diseases which of course follow upon confinement and hard study.[b]

Toward the end of the year 1645, it was judged necessary that Mr Henderson, with some other persons, should go to Scotland, with a view to procure a better correspondence among the nobility and others; but he was detained by the weather, want of health, important business, and the importunity of friends in London.[c]

The King's affairs, which had been some time on the decline were entirely ruined, in the spring of 1646. Upon this, he cast himself into the Scottish army who retired with him to Newcastle. When he arrived there, he sent for Mr Henderson, who was his Chaplain, to come to him. The only measure which then promised a settlement to the nation, and the King's restoration to the actual exercise of his authority, was his taking the Covenant, and speedily consenting to the establishment of the Presbyterian Reformation in both kingdoms. Mr Henderson was judged the best qualified person to deal with the King respecting a compliance, and the removal of any difficulties with which his mind might be embarrassed. And notwithstanding his unfitness for the journey, he complied with the King's request, enforced by the advice and entreaties of his fellow-commissioners; clearly shewing his public spirit for the advancement of the interests of the Redeemer's kingdom, and for the good of his country. He arrived at Newcastle about the middle of the month of May. He received a kind welcome from his Majesty, but he soon perceived that he would not comply with the requisitions of his Parliaments. The

a Neal's Puritans, 1645. Whitelocke, pp. 123, 127. Clarendon. B. viii. Collier, vol. ii. p. 837.

b Baillie, vol. ii. p. 109. B. viii. c Baillie, vol. ii. pp. 170, 171.

King signified that he could not in conscience consent to the abolition of Episcopacy; and proposed that Mr Henderson should carry on a dispute with some Episcopal Divines, of whose names he gave him a list, in his presence. This Mr Henderson declined, as what he had no authority to undertake, and no reason to expect, when he complied with his Majesty's request in coming to Newcastle. Mr Henderson also added, "that such disputations had seldom any good effect, in ending controversies, and that, in the present instance; such a mode would be exceedingly prejudicial to his Majesty's affairs. All that I intended was a free, yet modest expression of my motives, and inducements, which drew my mind to the dislike of Episcopal government, wherein I was bred in the University." It was, therefore, agreed, that the King's scruples, should be discussed in a series of papers, which should pass privately between him and Mr Henderson. The papers are eight in number, five by his Majesty, and three by Mr Henderson; continued from some time in May, until the 16th of July. On that occasion, Mr Henderson gave the infatuated Monarch a very good advice, to leave off exciting learned men to dispute respecting the power or prerogative of Kings and Princes by which he had lost very much. The neglect of that advice cost him both his crown and his life. Perceiving that he obstinately adhered to opinions which were disowned by all the moderate Episcopalians, and maintained by those only who had acted as base incendiaries between the King and his Parliaments, Mr Henderson declined entering farther into a fruitless contest.

During the conference with the King, Mr Henderson's health, which was considerably impaired when he came to Newcastle, grew much worse. His constitution was now worn out with great labour and travel. His colleagues at London, greatly alarmed with the accounts which they received respecting him, wrote to him, earnestly entreating that he would be careful of himself, and not allow vexation on account of the King's obduracy to prey upon his spirits, and increase his disorder. Mr

Baillie, in a letter addressed to him, under the date of May 16, 1646, says, "If that man now go to tinkle on Bishops, and Delinquents, and such foolish toys, it seems he is mad. If he have the least grace and wisdom, he may, by God's mercy, presently end the miseries, wherein himself, and many more, are likely else to sink. Let me entreat you for one thing, when you have done your uttermost, if God is pleased to deny the success, not to vex yourself more than is meet. When we hear of your health and courage, it will refresh us." In another letter, dated Aug. 4, Mr Baillie writes to him as follows: "Your sickness has much grieved my heart. It is a part of my prayers to God, to restore you to health, and continue your service at this so necessary a time. We never had so much need of you as now. The King's madness has confounded us all. We know well the weight that lies on your heart." And in another letter, dated Aug. 13, 1646, he says: "Your weakness is much regretted here by many. To me it is one of the sad presages of the evils coming. If it be the Lord's will, it is my hearty prayer oft-times, that you might be lent to us yet for some time."

Mr Henderson, having now concluded that his disease was mortal, resolved to return to Scotland. But before he left Newcastle, he obtained an audience from the King, and having again reminded him of the very critical situation of his affairs, he took a final farewell of him, having faithfully discharged the duties of his commission, and of that employment which placed him about his Majesty's person, in the fulfilling of which he had enjoyed very little satisfaction. In dealing with the King, Mr Henderson only *failed* where he evidently could not *succeed*. He went to his native country by sea, and arrived at Edinburgh on the 11th of Aug. 1646, very sick and much exhausted. He continued so weak, that he was not able to speak much. But he enjoyed great peace of mind, and expressed himself, in what he was able to say, very much to the comfort of his brethren and Christian acquaintance who visited him. In a short confession of faith, which was afterward found among his papers, and written with his own hand, expressing, at the trying hour, his dying thoughts, among other mercies. he declares himself " most of all obliged to the grace and goodness of God, for calling him to believe the promises of the Gospel, and for exalting him to be a preacher of these to others, and to be a willing, though weak instrument, in this great and wonderful work of Reformation, which he earnestly beseecheth the Lord to bring to a happy conclusion." He rested from his labours, sickness, and sorrow, on the 19th of Aug. 1646. He died within eight days after his arrival in Scotland.[a] Mr Livingston, in his Characteristics, at the end of his Life, declares that he was present, and saw Mr Henderson die with great peace and comfort. Baillie says, " That he died as he lived, in great modesty, piety, and faith."[b]

His mortal remains were interred in Grayfriar's churchyard, Edinburgh. As he had no family of his own, his nephew, Mr George Henderson, performed the last kind office of humanity to his earthly part, and erected a monument over his grave with appropriate inscriptions, which testify that Mr Henderson was very highly esteemed by all classes. His life was much desired, and his death greatly lamented, both in Scotland and England. A London newspaper, Perfect Diurnal, No. 162, under the date of Aug. 31, 1646, says, " This day—the only news was by letters from the North, and first of all a sad lamentation for the death of Mr Henderson." After the Restoration, when all indignity was done to the work of Reformation, and to those persons who had been most active in promoting it, the Earl of Middleton, the King's Commissioner, procured an order of Parliament in July 1662, for erasing the inscriptions, and disfiguring his monument.[c] But at the Revolution, the monument was repaired, and the inscriptions replaced. It still stands entire on the south-west side of the Grey-

a Christ Mag vol. x. p. 394. Acts of Ass. ed. 1682. p. 421.

b Baillie's Letters, vol ii. p. 232.

c Woodrow's Hist. vol. i. p. 152. Ludlow's Detect. of Holingworth's Forgeries.

friar's church. It is a quadrangular pillar, with an urn at the top.

Mr Henderson having died soon after his conferences with the King at Newcastle, the Episcopalians industriously circulated the report, that he was not only vanquished, but also converted by his Royal antagonist. But this report had not the least shadow of foundation, and was very keenly contradicted by the concurring testimony of all who had access to be well acquainted with Mr Henderson's sentiments during that time. But this was not enough, for about two years after his death, a Declaration in Mr Henderson's name, the forgery of a Scots Episcopal Divine, was published, in which he was represented as expressing great contrition for acceding to the proceedings of the Presbyterians. Upon the appearance of that base pamphlet, the General Assembly of the Church of Scotland called and examined several persons, who were present with Mr Henderson during the conferences at Newcastle, and also during the time which elapsed from his return to Edinburgh till his death, who declared that he had continued to the last constant and unaltered in his sentiments; upon which the Assembly passed an act, declaring "the said pamphlet forged, scandalous, and false, and the author and contriver of the same void of charity and a good conscience, and a gross liar and calumniator, led by the spirit of the accuser of the brethren."[a] About the middle of the 18th century, this convicted forgery was credulously revived by Mr Ruddiman, who, notwithstanding his eminent learning, is well known to have had the weakest prejudices on the subject of Jacobitism and Episcopacy. This was triumphantly exposed by Mr Logan.[b]

When Mr Henderson had finished his academical studies at St Andrew's, he was chosen Professor of philosophy and rhetoric in that University. His talents and acquirements sufficiently recommended him to the office. Upon the change of his mind, he became a

a Acts of Assembly, p. 420, &c. edit. 1682.

b See Logan's second Letter to Ruddiman, 1799.

faithful Minister of the Gospel, and a decided Presbyterian. Educated in Episcopal sentiments, and having the fairest prospects of preferment in a rising hierarchy, he readily sacrificed his high expectations to the word of God, and to the deep convictions of his own conscience. He cheerfully espoused a cause, which, though honourable in the sight of God, was much despised and borne down by men who were high in place. He strongly resisted ecclesiastical oppression, and *earnestly contended for the faith which was once delivered unto the saints.* He was very highly esteemed by all ranks of the people, who were attached to the cause of Truth, and had much influence with both the Nobility and Clergy, even with the greatest and wisest men of the kingdom. He was called from his delightful retirement to the assistance of his dear countrymen, who groaned under the oppression of ambitious prelates, who were greatly supported by an arbitrary Court and corrupt Statesmen. "Though he sighed after his original solitude, and suffered from the fatigues and anxiety to which he was subjected, yet he did not relinquish his station, nor shrink from the difficult tasks imposed upon him, until his feeble and shattered constitution sunk under them, and he fell a martyr to the cause."[a]—Clarendon, with all his prejudices against Mr Henderson, cannot deny that he was eloquent though he is pleased to say, that he had more eloquence or rhetoric than logic.[b] Bishop Guthrie, in his Memoirs, p. 24, says; "Upon Mr Henderson all the ministry of that judgment depended; and no wonder, for in gravity, learning, wisdom, and state-policy, he far exceeded any of them." Pinkerton, in his Iconographia Scotica, calls him, "the Franklin of the Scottish commotions." And Grainger, a clergyman of the Church of England, gives the following character of him: "Mr Henderson, the chief of the Scottish Clergy in this reign, was learned, eloquent, polite, and perfectly versed in the knowledge of mankind. He was at the helm of

a Christian Magazine, vol. x. p. 398.
b Clarendon's History, B. viii.

affairs in the General Assemblies in Scotland, and was sent into England in the double capacity of a divine and plenipotentiary. He knew how to rouse the people to war, and to negotiate a peace. Whenever he preached, it was to a crowded audience, and when he pleaded or argued, he was regarded with mute attention."[a] And a very late writer, of great respectability, says: "Mr Henderson had talents and acquirements which fitted him for rising to eminence; that eminence he actually attained and preserved; and nothing but shameful ignorance or ruthless bigotry will deny him the praise of having been both a great and a good man."[b] It is certain, that he held a very conspicuous place, among our worthy Reformers, and was well known and highly respected for his judicious, faithful, and important services, in the cause of Christianity, which render the particulars of his Life deeply interesting to us. And to give such a name a distinguished place in the rolls of Biography, is a debt of gratitude which the public are bound to pay, in return for benefits received.

Mr Henderson having been much employed in public affairs, had little time to prepare works for the press. But the few sermons of his which were published, although hastily composed amid much business and many avocations, afford very favourable specimens of his talents, and clearly shew that in pulpit oratory he was inferior to none of his contemporaries. His compositions are distinguished by accurate thinking, appropriate illustration, and elegant simplicity of language,—and bear marks of a vigorous and well cultivated mind. These probably will be perused with great avidity by some persons at this present time, and may become an important record to posterity. Beside the pieces mentioned in his Life, I have seen the following sermons under his name, which are still extant.

1. A Sermon preached from Ezra vii. 23. to the Hon-

a Grainger's Biog. Hist. vol. i. p. 416, first edition.
b Edinburgh Christian Instructor, vol. vii. p. 408. 1813.

ourable House of Commons, at their solemn Fast, Wednesday, Dec. 27th, 1643. 4to. pp. 36. London, 1644. Mr Baillie calls it " A most gracious, wise, and learned Sermon."—2. A Sermon preached from Mat. xiv 31. before the Lords and Commons assembled in Parliament, in Margaret's Church, Westminster, 10th of July, 1644. Thanksgiving, 4to. pp. 24. London, 1644. and reprinted at Edinburgh in 1644. with a large Address prefixed to the Kirk and Kingdom of Scotland, his native country.—3. A Sermon preached from John xviii. 36, 37. before the House of Lords, in the Abbey Church, Westminster, solemn Fast, 28th of May, 1645. 4to. pp. 31. London, 1645. His Speech at taking the Covenant was printed both at London, and Edinburgh, in 1643, and several times afterward, with the Sermons at taking the Covenant.

SAMUEL RUTHERFORD,

PROFESSOR OF DIVINITY IN THE UNIVERSITY OF ST. ANDREW'S, AND ONE OF THE COMMISSIONERS FROM THE CHURCH OF SCOTLAND TO THE ASSEMBLY OF DIVINES AT WESTMINSTER.

SAMUEL RUTHERFORD is said to have been born of respectable parents, in the parish of Tongueland, near Kirkcudbright, in the south of Scotland. And it has also been said, that when he was a little boy, he narrowly escaped drowning in a well, from which he was delivered in a very remarkable manner; and that, this wonderful deliverance induced his father to dedicate him unto the service of his Lord and Saviour, expecting that he might probably become an eminent man. I have the account of these things only by tradition; but upon strict inquiry the authority seemed to be good, and therefore I have ventured to mention such circumstances, in the life of this learned and pious divine, wishing to be corrected, if the account is found not true. Be these particulars as they may, Mr Rutherford had a brother who was the Schoolmaster of Kirkcudbright, and being a non-conformist, he was summoned before the High-commission Court, and commanded to resign his charge immediately, and remove from Kirkcudbright.[a] The subject of this Memoir was much admired in early life, for the superior abilities which he possessed. He had a very good classical education and made great proficiency in his studies. And he soon gained such reputation in the learned world, that he was chosen a Professor in the University of Edinburgh, during the establishment of Episcopacy;[b] where it is said he received his education.

Afterward, he became Minister of the Gospel at Anwoth, in the Stewartry of Kirkcudbright, where he was indeed *a burning and shining light* some years. Whether Mr Rutherford, and other faithful ministers of that period, were ordained by Bishops, or by a Presbytery independent of Bishops? is a question which has been much agitated. Stevenson says; "All that we can assert concerning that matter, after the most inquisitive search, is, that until the beginning of the year 1628, some few preachers were suffered to enter the ministry without conformity, and of this number we suppose Mr Rutherford and Mr Douglas may be reckoned, because they were ordained before the door came to be more closely shut upon honest preachers."[c] In what year Mr Rutherford was settled at Anwoth, I cannot say; but there is one of his letters dated at Anwoth, June 6th, 1624, by which it may appear that he was there before that time. He laboured with very great diligence and zeal, in the Lord's vineyard, in that place.

In June, 1630, he was summoned before the High-commission Court; and though that diet was deserted, and the summons passed from for the time, he did not always escape. He was again summoned before the same Court, and accused by the Bishop of Galloway for non-conform-

a Stevenson, vol. i. p. 151.
b Edinburgh Christian Instructor, vol. vii. p. 411.
c Stevenson, vol. i. p. 70.

ity, particularly for preaching against Perth Articles, and writing a book, entitled, *Exercitationes apologeticæ pro divina gratia*, which did cut up Arminianism, and much vex the Episcopal clergy.[a] He appeared before the Court, but declined their jurisdiction, and refused to give the Bishops their titles. Lord Lorn favoured him to the utmost of his power; but the affair was carried against Mr Rutherford, and he was deprived upon the 27th of July, 1636, and discharged to exercise any part of his ministry within Scotland, under pain of rebellion, and ordered to confine himself, within six months, to Aberdeen, and its neighbourhood, during the King's pleasure. He yielded, and went to the place of his confinement.

The confinement in Aberdeen is one of the most interesting circumstances in the life of this eminently pious Christian, and faithful servant of Jesus Christ. And the manner in which he employed his time during that confinement, strongly marks his religious character, and is honourable to religion itself. From Aberdeen he wrote many of his truly excellent and religious letters, which eminently prove that very strong consolations are reserved for the people of God in their *persecutions for righteousness' sake;* and that they may count those very days of their confinement as the sweetest hours of their life, in a fair prison. We are told, that the confinement of M. de Voltaire in the Bastille was not prejudicial to his talents. He there composed several works, part of which he retained in his memory, and wrote the rest on the walls with a coal, or on the lead of the windows with the point of a pin.[b] Nor was Mr Rutherford's confinement in Aberdeen prejudicial to his talents, in the least degree, as clearly appears by his eminently pious letters, which were written there. He employed his talents in doing good; and his several epistles composed in that confinement, have been highly beneficial to many persons, and are still much admired by the pious mind.

Mr Rutherford seemingly enjoyed the particular ac-

a Stevenson, vol. i. pp. 148—150.
b Voltaire's Memoirs, English, Dublin, 1786, p. 26.

complishment of that exceedingly great and precious promise of Christ, *And, lo, I am with you alway, even unto the end of the world.* I am with you, to carry you comfortably and honourably through the manifold difficulties which ye may meet with in this present evil world. I am with you, to support you, and to plead your cause: with you in all your services, and in all your sufferings. When ye pass through the deep waters of affliction, and the violent fires of persecution, I shall most certainly be with you: both in the pulpit and in the prison; lo, I am with you.[a]

The weight of the chains, and the horrors of *the inner prison*, hindered not Paul and Silas from praying, and singing praises unto God at midnight, Acts xvi. 24, 25. They greatly rejoiced that God had *accounted them worthy*, conferring upon them the honour and the grace, to suffer for the cause and doctrine of Jesus Christ. See Acts v. 41. Nor could all the severities, cunningly contrived by the most malicious enemies, interrupt that soul-solacing, and sweet spiritual intercourse, which these notable prisoners enjoyed with their God and Saviour. In like manner, Mr Rutherford's confinement in Aberdeen hindered him not from praying, and singing praises unto the God of his salvation; while he much rejoiced that he was accounted worthy to suffer for Christ's sake, his renowned Lord, and Almighty Saviour. Nor could all the hardships to which he was subjected impair in the least degree, that most sweet spiritual intercourse which he now enjoyed with Heaven. His soul was richly stored with the truly comforting influences of divine grace, and with the sweet religious experiences, which mark the real Christian. *The Father of mercies, and the God of all comfort* most abundantly *comforted him in all his tribulations: For as the sufferings of Christ abounded in him, so his consolation also abounded by Christ;* as his admirable letters dated at Aberdeen sufficiently prove.

Mr Rutherford delighted exceedingly, in preaching the glorious gospel of the grace of God unto sinners who

a See Henry on Mat. xxviii. 20. vol. v.

were ready to perish; and, therefore, his silence on the Lord's day, under his confinement, was peculiarly distressing unto his well-disposed mind. He says, in a letter to Lady Kenmure, dated, Aberdeen, Nov. 22d, 1636; "my silence on the Lord's day keeps me from being exalted above measure.—I have wrestled long with this sad silence. I said, what aileth Christ at my service? And my soul has been at pleading with Christ; and at yea and nay: but I will yield to him, providing that my suffering may preach more than my tongue did; for I gave not Christ an inch, but for twice as good again. In a word, I am a fool, and he is God. I will hold my peace hereafter." In the same letter, he says; "My adversaries have sent me here to be feasted with love-banquets, with my Royal High, High, and Princely King Jesus. O how sweet are the sufferings of Christ, for Christ!—It were a sweet and honourable death, to die for the honour of that Royal and Princely King Jesus. This love is a mystery to the world. I would not have believed that there was so much in Christ as there is. Come and see, maketh Christ to be known in his excellency and glory."

Mr Rutherford was then the object of oppression and of persecution, and the victim of lawless power; but he enjoyed the consolations of the Gospel of Christ, in very great abundance, under all his sufferings. He suffered in a good cause; for the Truth of Christ. He was sufficiently armed; but his corrupt judges and persecutors were naked, and exposed to the terrible indignation of Almighty God.

"Thrice is he armed who hath his quarrel just,
And he but naked, tho' lock'd up in steel,
Whose conscience with injustice is corrupted."

Mr Rutherford continued in his confinement nearly two years, until he was informed that the Privy-council had received in a declinature against the High-commission, and then he adventured to return home unto Anwoth. This was a joyful event both to himself and to all persons who were concerned. Divine Providence having mercifully restored him to his flock, in the year 1638, he again laboured with great diligence among them. Many persons attended his ministry from all quarters, in that neighbourhood. The people had an ardent desire for the preaching of the glorious gospel of the grace of God, in purity and power, which was rarely to be found, at that time, in that country. But at Anwoth, the Lord God of salvation did make *waters to break out in the wilderness, and streams in the desert, to give drink unto his people, his chosen. The solitary place did then rejoice exceedingly, and blossom abundantly as the rose.*

Mr Rutherford attended the famous and venerable Assembly, which convened at Glasgow, on the 21st of Nov. 1638. He was one of the Commissioners from the Presbytery of Kirkcudbright to that Assembly. His name is still found standing in the roll of the members, as their minister at Anwoth. He gave them a satisfactory account of all his proceedings respecting his confinement at Aberdeen, and of the causes thereof. He was appointed by them one of the Select Committee for considering the Service-book, the Book of Canons and Ordination, and the High-commission Court, that posterity might well know what great and signal mercy the Lord God of salvation had shewed, in delivering his church from these. And also that the world might know, that the supplications against these books had been just, and that some monuments of their wickedness might be left to the succeeding generations.—Mr Rutherford was also appointed by that famous Assembly to be Professor of divinity, in the New College of St. Andrew's. He opposed his transportation to the utmost of his power; but his objections are said to have turned out rather to be reasons for his compliance with the call which was given to him. Yet in one thing the Assembly were obliged to yield unto him. He said, that the High-commission never did him a worse turn than to stop his mouth from preaching the gospel; that there was a woe to him if he preached not the gospel, and that he knew not who could go between him and that woe. And so he was allowed to be both colleague to the celebrated Mr Robert Blair, who was transported from Air to St. Andrew's, about that time, in preaching the glorious gospel of the grace of God, and also to be teacher of divinity. And, by means of his indefatigable labours, both in teaching in the schools, and preaching in the congregation, St. Andrew's was soon eminently distinguished for piety and learning. Under his care, a number of young men were trained up for the holy ministry, who came to be *burning and shining lights*, in the Church of Scotland.[a]

Mr Rutherford was also eminently distinguished for encouraging the people in the private duties of religion. In the year 1640, when a charge was brought before the General Assembly, at the instance of Mr Henry Guthrie, minister of Stirling, afterward bishop of Dunkeld, against private Society-meetings, which then prevailed in the land, on which much reasoning ensued, the one side allowing that a paper which had been before drawn up by Mr Henderson should be agreed unto respecting the order to be observed in these meetings; but Guthrie and his party opposed that motion. Mr Rutherford, who was before silent, cast in the following syllogism, and required them all to answer it: "What Scripture does warrant, an Assembly may not discharge; but private meetings for exercises of religion, Scripture warrants, Mal. iii. 16. James v. 16. These things could not be done in public meetings." The Earl of Seaforth, and Mr Guthrie, did not relish Mr Rutherford's logical syllogisms; and shewed that they were very averse to be troubled with any more of these It is said, that Seaforth chided Mr Rutherford; and then Guthrie with his party thought to have carried all their own way, and to obtain a dismission of all private meetings; but they met with opposition, and could only have an act passed respecting *the ordering of family-worship.* Mr Rutherford, in a treatise, has defended the lawfulness of these private religious meetings, in a very high degree.[b]

He was appointed one of the Committee for managing the negotiations between the Assembly at Edinburgh in

a Stevenson's Hist. vol ii. pp. 476, 583, 584, 586, 587, 660.

b Baillie, vol. i. pp. 196—200. Stevenson, vol. iii. p. 887, &c.

1643, and the English Commissioners, when the Solemn League and Covenant was formed [a]

As a divine eminently learned, and of approved orthodoxy, he was, in the year 1643, chosen one of the Commissioners from the Church of Scotland to the Assembly of the Divines at Westminster. He was highly useful in that famous Assembly, and distinguished himself by speaking to good purpose in their debates. Mr Baillie, speaking of the debates respecting the ruling elders, says; "Sundry times, Messrs Henderson, Rutherford, and Gillespie, all three, spoke exceedingly well." And again the same writer says; "Had not God sent Messrs Henderson, Rutherford, and Gillespie, among them, I see not that ever they could agree on any settled government."[b] Mr Rutherford and his brethren displayed the most ardent zeal and faithfulness, in that Assembly, especially in settling Church-government. And, Mr Rutherford, in particular, took his full share in the discussions which were carried on there, displaying much learning and knowledge even of the Rabbinical writings, and combating on some occasions the eminently learned Lightfoot with vigour and success [c] During his residence at London, he published his Lex Rex, and some other learned works against the Erastians, Anabaptists, Independents, and other Sectaries, greatly prevailing there at that time. Mr Baillie, speaking of this Assembly, says: "Mr Rutherford's other large book against the Independents is in the press, and will do good."[d] And, in a letter to Mr Robert Blair, dated March 26th, 1644, Mr Baillie calls Mr Rutherford "his sweet Colleague." He says further; "Thanks to God, never Colleagues had a greater harmony; for to this hour not the least difference between any of us, either State or Church Commissioners, in any thing.—Mr Samuel, for the great parts God has given him, and special acquaintance with the question in hand, is very necessary

a Stevenson, vol. iii. p. 1086.
b Baillie, vol. i. p. 401. vol. ii. p. 11.
c Lightfoot's Remarks, Preface, pp. 12—32.
d Baillie, vol. i. p. 414.

here; especially because of his book, which is daily enlarging, and it will not come off the press yet for some time It is very likely, whenever it comes out, it shall have some short affronting reply; and judge now if it be not necessary that he should not be here to answer for himself."[a] And Mr Flavel says, that Mr Rutherford appeared seasonably and successfully against the Familists in England. His own words are: "Our late Familists in England, of whom Henry Nichols was the chief leader, who decried the written word as a dead letter; and set up their own fond conceits and fancies under the notion of the Spirit; against whom, that heavenly and learned man, Mr Samuel Rutherford seasonably and successfully appeared."[b] And Mr Baillie, in a letter for Glasgow, July 14th, 1646, again says: "Mr Rutherford, Mr Gillespie, and your friend also, are all in the press again, for the defence of our Church and truth of God, against diverse enemies." And in a letter to Mr David Dickson, the same writer says: "Mr Rutherford's large piece against the Antinomians will in a few days come abroad." Oct. 1646. When the principal business of the famous Assembly at Westminster was nearly settled, Mr Rutherford, upon the 24th of Oct. 1647, moved, that it might be recorded in the books, that the Assembly had enjoyed the assisstance of the Commissioners of the Church of Scotland, during all the time that they had been debating and perfecting these four things mentioned in the Solemn League: Their composing a Directory for public worship, an Uniform Confession of Faith, a Form of Church government and Discipline, and a Public Catechism. Upon this, Mr Rutherford and the other Commissioners took their leave of the Assembly, and returned home. Upon that occasion, Mr Herle, who was then Prolocutor, arose, and in the name of the Assembly, thanked the honourable and reverend Commissioners for their assistance.[c]

a Baillie, vol. i. pp. 450, 451.
b Flavel's Works, Blow at the Root, Cause xiv.
c Stevenson, vol. iii. p. 1181.

Mr Rutherford's reputation was highly raised, by his writings in Latin against the Arminians and Jesuits. And he had a call to be Professor of Divinity and of the Hebrew tongue, in the newly erected University in Harderwych. Mr Spang, in a letter to his Cousin Mr Baillie, dated, March 19th, 1649, says: "Mr Samuel Rutherford is called to be Professor of divinity and the Hebrew tongue, in the newly erected University in Harderwych. You might be well advised at home what to do, if our kirk can want such a man in the great scarceness of such. It is not his English he writes that commendeth him, as his Latin Treatise against the Jesuits and Arminians."[a] And the motion was made in the General Assembly of the Church of Scotland, in 1649, for the transportation of Mr Rutherford to the University of Edinburgh; but Mr Baillie says, that this was thought absurd.[b] In that Assembly, Mr Rutherford gave his voice for the popular election of ministers. Mr Baillie, speaking of their great debate, says: "We had greatest debate for an act of election of ministers. Mr David Calderwood was peremptory, that according to the Second Book of Discipline, the election should be given to the Presbytery, with power to the major part of the people to dissent, upon reason to be judged of by the Presbytery. Mr Rutherford and Mr Wood were as peremptory to put the power and voices of election in the body of the people, contradistinct from their eldership; but the most of us were in Mr Gillespie's mind, in his Miscellanies, that the direction was the Presbytery's, the election the Session's, and the consent the people's."[c]

Mr Rutherford had an invitation to the Divinity-chair, in the University of Utrecht in Holland; an invitation, we mention it to his honour, which he patriotically declined to accept, only because he could not think of deserting his own country at that very critical period.

During the time of Cromwell's usurpation, he continu-

a Baillie, vol. ii. p. 327.
b Baillie, vol. ii. p. 342.
c Baillie, vol. ii. p. 339.

ed to labour with unabated zeal in his Master's service. He faithfully discharged his official duties, and testified against the boundless toleration, and the unscriptural tenets of the Sectaries which then greatly prevailed. When the unhappy difference commenced between those persons who were called the Protesters, and the Public Resolutioners, in 1650, and in 1651, Mr Rutherford joined the Protesters, and gave faithful warning against these Public Resolutions.[a]—The Testimony of some ministers, in the shires of Perth and Fife, for the whole of the covenanted work of Reformation, in Scotland, England, &c. was subscribed by Mr Rutherford, Oct. 1658.

King Charles II. upon his restoration, soon declared his displeasure with the Protesters, the opposers of the above mentioned Resolutions; and some of them were the first sufferers in the bloody and horrid persecution which followed. And, Mr Wodrow says, that "in a little time, the whole honest Presbyterian ministers were struck at, and sent to the furnace to unite them.[b]

On the 19th of Sept. 1660, a proclamation was published against that famous book, entitled, *Lex Rex*, which was written by our author, Mr Rutherford, and had been printed at London, in the year 1644, and *The Causes of God's Wrath*, supposed to be drawn up by Mr James Guthrie. Both the authors, and the printers and the dispersers of those books were accounted rebellious and seditious persons. The books were considered as containing many things injurious to the King, full of treasonable matter, and laying the foundation and seeds of rebellion, and the like. The copies were called in, and ordered to be delivered to Mr Robert Dalgleish, his Majesty's Solicitor, in less than a month; with a declaration, that all and every one who, after the 15th of October, shall have any copies of these books, shall not only be esteemed enemies to the King, but also be punished accordingly both in their persons and estates. The

a The reader who wishes to know the rise and nature of these Resolutions, may consult Wodrow's History, Introduction.

b Wodrow, vol. i. Introduction, p. 5.

books were burned at Edinburgh, by the hand of the hangman, on the 17th of October 1660. It was much easier to burn those books than to answer them.[a] It is a vain and senseless attempt, by an arbitrary and unrighteous act, to extinguish the light of truth and defraud posterity of due information. Genius and piety will thrive under all oppressors. Persecute the author, and you will enhance the value of his work. Tyrants and all persons who have imbibed their senseless and barbarous policy, have found this to be true By proscribing talents, the oppressors of the Lord's heritage have recorded their own eternal disgrace, and inadvertently given the writer a passport to immortality. Several copies of Lex Rex, which I have seen, are still preserved in good condition, in different parts of Scotland, and in London. And the sentiments which it contains cannot be destroyed by fire, nor by any despot in the universe. It is reported, that when King Charles saw Lex Rex, he said, That it would scarcely ever get an answer. Nor did it ever receive any answer, as far as I know; but men in power most keenly directed all their vengeance against it, by condemning and burning it. This pitiful and spiteful conduct served only to increase the reputation of the book, and was the occasion of it's being more generally sought and read. The fire is a conclusive, but not a convincing, argument, says a late writer. The truth is, that fire will certainly destroy any book; but it refutes no book. And burning is not a very good substitute for argument, though too many have applied to it, when they could not answer their opponents by fair reasoning.

The Parliament were to have had an indictment laid before them against Mr Rutherford, if his death had not prevented it. After Lex Rex had been burnt at the cross of Edinburgh and at the gate of the New College of St Andrew's, where he was Professor of divinity; they were pleased, when he was evidently dying, to cite him to appear before them at Edinburgh, to answer unto a charge of high treason. But he was called to appear be-

a Wodrow, vol. i. pp. 10, 16.

fore a higher tribunal, completely beyond their jurisdiction, where his Judge was his friend.[a]

When he was on his death-bed, he greatly lamented that he was hindered from bearing witness to the glorious work of Reformation since the year 1638, and giving his public testimony against the evil courses of the present time. But we are told that he was enabled to give a large and faithful testimony against the sinful courses of that time, which he subscribed about twelve days before his death, being full of joy and peace in believing.

During the time of his last sickness, he uttered many very savoury speeches, speaking much in commendation of the Lord Jesus Christ, and of his honourable service, especially when the time of his departure was near. Some of his last and dying expressions were: "I shall shine, I shall see Him as He is, and all the fair company with Him, and shall have my large share. It is not easy to be a Christian; but I have obtained the victory through Him who loved me, and Christ is holding forth his arms to embrace me. I have had my fears and faintings, like other sinful men to be carried creditably through; but as sure as ever he spake to me in his word, his Spirit witnessed to my heart, saying, Fear not, he had accepted my suffering, and the out-gate should not be matter of prayer, but of praise." He also said, "*Thy word was found, and I did eat it, and it was to me the joy and rejoicing of my heart.*" And a short time before his death, after some fainting, he said, "Now I feel, I believe, I enjoy, I rejoice." And turning to Mr Blair, who was present, he said; "I feed upon manna, I have angels' food, my eyes shall see my Redeemer, I know that He shall stand at the latter day on the earth, and I shall be caught up in the clouds to meet Him in the air." And afterward he said, "I sleep in Christ, and when I awake I shall be satisfied with his likeness. O for arms to embrace Him." And to a person speaking respecting his painfulness in the ministry, he cried out, "I disclaim all, the port I would be in at, is redemption and

a Wodrow, vol. i. pp. 77, 78.

forgiveness of sins through Christ's blood." We are informed that a gentleman who called on the Rev. J Newton in London, a short time before his death, mentioned to him how useful he had been by his writings: "I need none of these sweet-meats," said the good old man. Of the same mind was Mr Rutherford, who being full of the Holy Spirit, the Comforter, yea, as it were overcome with sensible enjoyment, he breathed out his soul into the hands of his God; and his last words were, *Glory, glory dwells in Emmanuel's land.* He died in the month of March 1661, the very day before the Act Rescissory was passed in the Parliament.[a]

Mr Wodrow gives his character as follows: "That bright shining light, Mr Samuel Rutherford, may very justly come in among the sufferers, during this session of Parliament. Certainly he was a martyr both in his own resolution, and in men's designs and determination. He is so well known to the learned and pious world, that I need say very little of him. Such who knew him best, were in a strait whether to admire him most for his sublime genius in the school, and peculiar exactness in mater of dispute and controversy, or his familiar condescensions in the pulpit, where he was one of the most moving and affectionate preachers in his time, or perhaps in any age of the church.—He seems to have outdone himself as well as every body else, in his admirable, and every way singular, Letters; which though jested upon by profane wits, because of some familiar expressions, yet will be owned by all who have any relish of piety, to contain such sublime flights of devotion, and to be fraughted with such massy thoughts, as loudly speak a soul united to Jesus Christ in the closest embraces, and must needs at once ravish and edify every serious reader." —And Mr Baillie in his Letters, says: "Mr Rutherford has an excellent gift both of preaching and of prayer, and, which helps all to the people's mind, fells all the fourteen bishops, and houghs the ceremonies."[b] And

a Wodrow as above, and Fleming, Fulfil. Scrip. vol. i. p. 359. Ed. 1801.

b Baillie, vol. i. p. 56.

Dr Cotton Mather, in his Student and Preacher, when mentioning Scottish writers, reckons Mr Rutherford among the champions for the doctrines of Grace. And an eminent late writer, speaking of Mr Rutherford, refers us to his Lex Rex, and to his posthumous work, entitled, Examen Arminianismi, as containing decisive proof of his erudition. Respecting the latter work, that writer adds: "It is spoken of by Nethenus, Voetius, and Essenus, theological Professors, at Utrecht, in terms of the highest commendation. And, indeed, on looking into it, any competent judge must at once be satisfied that it deserves all the praises which those divines have bestowed upon it. The Reviewers expressed a most favourable opinion of the "Refutation of Calvinism," and of course heaped upon its author all the laudatory epithets which reverence for a bishop could suggest. And yet we will venture to affirm, that, in point of knowledge of the subject discussed, fairness of statement, and conclusiveness of reasoning, the bishop of Lincoln's Refutation of Calvinism, is inferior by many degrees, to Mr Rutherford's Examen Arminianismi."[a] With Latin, Greek, and Hebrew, he was very familiar. And he employed these languages as means of procuring useful information to himself, and of communicating it to others. And it has been observed, that "even were he to be judged of by his faculty in making Latin verses, the judgment would be favourable; for we might produce verses of his composition, in which we could challenge the Quarterly Reviewers to detect one false quantity or one unclassical word."[b] He seems to have been much above the level of ordinary men. He had a liberal education, and his attainments were proportionate to his advantages. He was eminently distinguished for talent, learning, fervent piety, and indefatigable industry and zeal in his Royal Master's service.

a Edin. Christ. Instruc. vol. vii. p. 412.
b Edin. Christ. Instruc.

Mr Rutherford's writings are numerous.—1. Exercitationes Apologeticæ pro Divina Gratia, Contra Jesuitas et Arminianos. Amsterdam, 1636. This is a book of a small size, containing above 400 pages. A vindication of the orthodox doctrine of the divine decrees, of the efficacy of divine grace, and of man's free-will, against the Jesuits and Arminians. It is written in Latin.—2. A Peaceable and Temperate Plea for Paul's Presbytery in Scotland. 4to. pp. 326, London, 1642.—3. The True Right of Presbyteries. 4to. pp. 780, or thereabout, London, 1644. —4. Lex Rex. 4to. London, 1644, and again in 1648. pp. 467.—5. A Sermon preached from Dan. vi. 26, to the House of Commons, at their solemn Fast, Jan. 1644. 4to. pp. 64, London, 1644.—6. A Sermon preached from Luke viii. 22—25, to the House of Lords, in the Abbey Church, Westminster, 25th of June, 1645. 4to. London, 1645. These Sermons were also printed several times with his Trial and Triumph of Faith, and beside, reprinted, Edinburgh, 1709.—7. The Trial and Triumph of Faith, London, 1645; both in 4to. and in a small size; and London, 1652; and Edinburgh, 1721; and Glasgow, 1743. I do not recollect to have seen any more editions of this book, though it may perhaps have passed through more.—8. His Divine Right of Church-government and Excommunication. 4to. London, 1646.—9. Christ Dying, and Drawing Sinners to Himself. 4to. pp. 598, London, 1647: and Edinburgh, 1727: and Glasgow, 1803, in 8vo. pp. 730.—10. A Survey of the Spiritual Antichrist, in two parts. P. I. pp. 354. P. II. pp. 239. 4to. London, 1648.—11. A Free Disputation against Pretended Liberty of Conscience. 4to pp. 410, London, 1649.—12. Disputatio Scholastica De Divina Providentia. 4to. pp. 620. Edinburgh, 1649. This learned and elaborate book respecting Divine Providence, against Jesuits, Arminians, and Socinians, is written in Latin; and contains the substance of several Lectures delivered to the Students of Divinity in the University of St. Andrew's.—13. The Covenant of Grace Opened. 4to. pp. 368. Edinburgh, 1655.—14. A Survey of the Survey of that Sum of Church Discipline, by Mr Thomas Hooker; 4to. above 500 pages, London, 1658.—15. Influences of the Life of Grace. 4to. pp. 438. London, 1659.—16. His Religious Letters, which breathe a spirit of ardent and elevated piety, have been often printed. The first edition is said to have been printed, in the year 1664; but I have not seen a copy of that, nor of the 2d edit. I have seen a copy of the 3d edit. printed in the year 1675. An advertisement is prefixed to this edition, intimating that the Author had begun a large Commentary on Isaiah, and completed several chapters, when the troubles of the times and his last sickness seized him; but the manuscript could not be found after his death. The 4th edit. of his Letters was printed in 1692; of which I have seen several copies. The 5th edit. Edinburgh, 1724: and Edinburgh, 1738, said to be the 6th edit. of which I have seen 5 copies. These Letters were printed at Glasgow, 1765. This is said to be the 9th edit. and unto it is added, the Author's Testimony to the Covenanted work of Reformation, and some of his Dying words, with a large Preface and Postscript, which had been left out in some former editions. The 10th and 11th editions, Glasgow, 1783, and 1796: and the 12th edit. Aberdeen, 1802, price 5s. where a considerable number of those extraordinary Letters were first conceived and written. Beside the above-mentioned editions, I have seen copies of an edition, said to be the 6th, Edinburgh, printed by E. & J. Robertson, 1761, in 2 vols. Some of the editions which have been noticed are in 8vo. others in a lesser size, and are well known in this country. Some of those very valuable Letters have been printed separately, for the accommodation of poor persons; as that to his Parishioners, and the one to the Professors of Christ and of his Truth, in Ireland: Glasgow, 1771. We are informed, that Mr Rutherford's Letters were habitually read and greatly valued, by the late Rev. Mr Cecil, an English Episcopal Clergyman, eminently distinguished both for fervent piety and intellectual vigour.[a] And the Rev. Robert Traill, some time minister of the Gospel in London, in a letter to his wife, under his banishment, says—"Next unto your Bible, read some good godly books, as worthy Mr Rutherford's Letters, a book which has done much good to some souls, and will do good to more."[b]—17. Examen Arminianismi, formerly mentioned was reviewed and published by Nethenus, Professor of Divinity at Utrecht in Holland, and was printed there, in the year 1668. Mr Traill, already mentioned, when he retired to his father in Holland, 1667, was employed some time in assisting Nethenus, in the publication of this book of Mr Rutherford's —18. A Practical Discourse, on Mat. ix. 27—31, respecting the Power and Prevalence of Faith and Prayer; printed in the year 1713. Small piece. Several Sermons have been printed separately, under Mr Rutherford's name, beside those formerly mentioned; as the Lamb's Marriage, from Rev. xix. 7, &c. Glasgow, 1775.—Heavenly Salutations, with pleasant Conferences between Christ and his people, preached from Cant. ii. 14—17, at Anwoth, before the Communion, in 1630. Glasgow, 1778.—Glad Tidings to the People of God; or, Comfort afforded in views of Death, from Rev xxi. 4—8, preached in Kirkcudbright, at the Communion, May 10th, 1633. Glasgow, 1779.—The Cruel Watchmen. Glasgow, 1784.—Christ's Love to his Church, Cant. ii. 8—12. Glasgow, 1798. And a small collection of his Sermons, preached at Sacramental Occasions, was first published at Glasgow, 1802; of which I have dispersed some dozens, in the South of Scotland. I have also seen An Exhortation at a Communion, to a Scots Congregation in London, by Mr Rutherford. Second edition, Glasgow, 1804. Price Two-pence. I have seen all his above-mentioned Writings, in different parts of Scotland, except that on Church Discipline, which I saw in London, with a great part of his other Writings.

a Edin. Christ. Instruc. vol. vii. p. 411.
b Traill's Works, vol. iv. Glasgow, 1796.

ADONIRAM BYFIELD, A. M.

ONE OF THE SCRIBES TO THE ASSEMBLY OF DIVINES AT WESTMINSTER.

ADONIRAM BYFIELD received his education in Emanuel College, Cambridge. He came to be particularly known, in the year 1642, by being chosen chaplain to Sir Henry Calmly's regiment, in the army of the Parliament, under the Earl of Essex. In the following year, he was appointed Scribe to the Assembly of Divines at Westminster, being according to Wood, "a most zealous *Covenanter*."

Upon the first publication of the Directory, by order of the Parliament, the profits arising from the sale of it were bestowed upon Messrs Byfield and Roborough, who sold the copy, it is said, for several hundred pounds. In the year 1646, when the "Confession of Faith" was drawn up by the Assembly of Divines at Westminster, Messrs Byfield, Thomas Wilson, and Stanley Gower, were appointed as a Committee to collect proofs of the various articles from the Holy Scriptures; all of which, upon the examination of the Assembly, were inserted in the margin. And the year following, when the Confession of Faith was printed, Mr Byfield, by appointment of the House of Commons, delivered a copy to each member of the House with Scripture proofs, signed,

Charles Herle, Prolocutor,
Corn. Burgess, }
Herbert Palmer, } Assessors,
Henry Roborough, }
Adoniram Byfield, } Scribes.[a]

Mr Byfield was some time Rector of Fulham in the county of Middlesex; and after the wars, he became minister of Collingborn-Ducis, in Wiltshire. Upon his

a Neal's Puritans, vol. iii. chap. viii.

removal to the last mentioned place, he was appointed an assistant to the Commissioners in the county of Wilts for ejecting ignorant and scandalous ministers and schoolmasters.

Granger says, that Mr Byfield is one of those few writers, who have, by name, been stigmatised by Butler, in his Hudibras. This may be true, and he might be, as indeed he was, an eminently pious and useful Divine. He observes, that Mr Byfield was said to have been a broken apothecary; that he was of special note; and a very active zealot in the busy and boisterous reign of Charles I.; and then adds, that his portrait was published, "with a wind mill on his head, and the Devil blowing the sails." But the best of men and ministers have, in all ages and countries, suffered the vile reproaches of the world lying in wickedness.—*All who will live godly in Christ Jesus shall suffer persecution.* Such persons have frequently been accounted "the offscouring of all things."

Mr Byfield, with some other persons, assisted Dr Chambers in compiling his "Apology for the Ministers in Wiltshire." London, 1654. He died about the time of the restoration of Charles II. in 1660. Mr Isaac Knight, his successor at Fulham, and Mr Daniel Burgess, his successor at Collingborn, were both ejected Non-conformists in 1662.[b]

HENRY ROBOROUGH,

PASTOR OF LEONARD'S, EASTCHEAP, LONDON, AND SCRIBE OF THE ASSEMBLY OF DIVINES AT WESTMINSTER.

HENRY ROBOROUGH was chosen one of the Scribes to the Assembly of Divines at Westminster, and, about the same time, appointed Pastor of Leonard's, Eastcheap, London, which he held until his death. He was one of the Committee of Divines who were appointed

a Wood's Athenæ Oxon. vol. ii. Brook's Puritans, vol. iii.

to examine and ordain candidates for the holy ministry, by imposition of hands, in the year 1644. And he united with his brethren, the London ministers, in their declaration against the death of the King.—The profits of printing the Directory being given to him and Mr Byfield, the other Scribe of the Assembly, they are said to have sold the copy-right for several hundred pounds. Mr Roborough died in the year 1650, and was succeeded in his living by Mr Matthew Barker, one of the silenced Non-conformists, in 1662.[a]

I have only seen of Mr Henry Roborough's Writings, "The Doctrine of Justification Cleared and Vindicated from Arminian, Socinian, and Popish, Errors. Or, an Answer to Mr John Goodwin's Animadversions upon Mr George Walker's Defence of the true sense of Rom. iv. 3, 5. Together with an Examination of the said Mr John Goodwin's Treatise of Justification.—Wherein the Imputation of Faith in a proper sense is denied and confuted: and the Imputation of Christ's Righteousness is affirmed and proved." 4to.

APPENDIX.

WISHING to make the above work as complete as possible, the following additional information, respecting a few of those Eminent Divines who convened in the famous Assembly at Westminster, which has been received since the commencement of the work, is here subjoined.

After the Account of the birth of JOHN ARROWSMITH, who was born at Gateshead, near Newcastle-upon-Tyne, March 29, 1602, vol. i. p. 106, add; he received his education in St John's College, Cambridge, and was

a Neal and Brook's Puritans, vol. iii. Calamy's Cont. vol. ii. p. 743. Fuller's Church Hist. B. xi. p. 222.

afterward chosen Fellow of Kathrine-hall, in the same University. He was elected one of the University preachers, was beneficed at Lynn in Norfolk, afterward preacher at St Martin's, Ironmongers-lane, London, and chosen one of the Assembly of Divines. He is said to have constantly attended during the Session; and he united with several of his brethren in drawing up the Assembly's Catechism; and was one of the Divines approved by the Parliament to be consulted in Ecclesiastical matters. *Brook's Puritans*, vol. iii.—He died in Feb. 1659, aged 57 years.

Mr Ashe.—In addition to his Writings, I have seen another Sermon of his, entitled, *Self-surrender unto God Opened and Applied;* in a Sermon from 2 Chron. xxx. 8. before the House of Commons, at Westminster, Fast, Feb. 23, 1647. London, 1647.—It is said, that Mr Ashe has also a Sermon before the Parliament from Gen. xxii. 14. but I have not seen it.—

Mr Backhurst, or Bathurst.—I have now found that Mr Bathurst was appointed by the Assembly at Westminster, one of the select Committee for the examination and approbation of those ministers who petitioned for sequestered livings. *Neal's Puritans*, vol. iii. chap. ii.

Mr Oliver Bowles.—This venerable Divine was Fellow of Queen's College, Cambridge, where he most probably received his education. He was a man of great piety, an excellent Scholar, and a celebrated Tutor. The famous Dr Preston was one of his pupils. Upon his removal from the University, he became Rector of Sutton in Bedfordshire, about the beginning of the year 1607.—The Assembly at Westminster, of which he was a very useful member, having made a motion to the Parliament for a fast, previous to their entering upon business, Mr Bowles and Mr Newcomen were appointed to preach before both Houses and the Assembly, and the sermons were ordered to be published. *Brook's Puritans*, vol. iii.

Mr Bowles's work, entitled, *De Pastore Evangelico*, was published by his son, and dedicated to the Earl of Manchester. Dr Calamy calls this an excellent book; and adds that it was a book not suffered to creep out in the time of rampant episcopacy, not for any evil in it, but because some men do not care to be put upon too much work. Mr Bowles's son, Edward, who published this book, was one of the ministers in the city of York, and is classed among the ejected ministers. *Calamy's Account*, vol. ii. p. 779.—vol. i. p. 190.

William Carter.—W. Carter was born in the year 1605.—In 1654, he was appointed one of the Tryers of public preachers.—He was an excellent scholar, an admired preacher, and a man of most exemplary piety.—To his writings, add; he is said to have been author of a sermon entitled, *Israel's Peace with God Benjamin's Overthrow;* preached before the House of Commons, Fast, 1642. *Brook's Purit.* vol. iii.

Confession of Faith and other Pieces Composed by the Reverend and Venerable Assembly of Divines at Westminster.

The Confession of Faith, The Larger and Shorter Catechisms, The Form of Presbyterial Church-government, and of Ordination of Ministers, with The Directory for the Public Worship of God, all agreed upon by the Assembly of Divines at Westminster, with the assistance of the Commissioners from the Church of Scotland, and examined and approved by the General Assembly of that Church, are very valuable works. These excellent Compositions are the fruits of the combined and indefatigable labours, and of the long and learned debates, of the illustrious Divines who convened at Westminster, in the Seventeenth Century. In writing the Lives, particular attention has been paid to the diligence and activity of the respective members in the formation of the above-mentioned Pieces, as far as good information could be obtained. And it is evident, that the Scottish Commissioners signalized themselves, in settling the Presbyterial form of Church-government, as they did also in other performances.

The Confession of Faith, and the other Pieces, composed by this famous Assembly of Divines, have been highly beneficial to the Christian Church, and much commended by some eminent men. These have passed through a great number of editions. I once intended to have given a more particular Account of these Writings; but circumstances will not admit. My daily labour is beyond my ability; and the avocations from this work have been numerous. Of course, it has already been far too long delayed, in bringing it to a termination. Materials have been collected, with a view to give some Account of the editions, which the Westminster Confession of Faith, Catechisms, &c. have passed through; but this part of the work cannot now be performed. Some Account also of Mr Robert Douglas, a celebrated minister in his day, who was appointed by the General Assembly of the Church of Scotland, as a Commissioner to the Assembly of Divines at Westminster, was once intended; but this must be given up in like manner. I have given all the Account, in my power, of the Scottish Commissioners who attended that famous Assembly of Divines, who were Ministers.

CONCLUSION.

The Compiler of these Memoirs has laboured several years, all the time that he could spare from his other work, in endeavouring to give some Account of a considerable number of our illustrious Reformers, the men, whom the infinitely great and glorious Sovereign of the Universe raised up, and marked out to be, under Him, *the salt of the earth, and the lights of the world.*—The men, who were made the honoured instruments of the conversion of many sinners to God, and of the edification of many saints.—The men, whom Divine Providence employed, in fixing the wavering minds of many persons, among the unsettled multitude, who were *tossed to and fro, and carried about with every wind of doctrine; by the slight of men, and cunning craftiness, whereby they lie in wait to deceive.*—The men, who were taught and enabled, under the smiles and influences of approving Heaven, to display their talents, learning, piety, and zeal, *in earnestly contending for the faith, which was once delivered unto the saints.*—The men, who entirely devoted themselves to the honourable service of their Lord, in his vineyard, and uniformly sacrificed their own interest to that of their Redeemer's kingdom.—The men, who supported, with all their energy, the noble cause of divine Truth, under manifold privations and sufferings.—Men who, were not *ashamed of Christ, nor of his words, before an adulterous and sinful generation.*—And the men who did solemnly swear unto Jehovah, and cheerfully subscribe with their hand unto Him, and greatly *rejoiced at the oath.*

It may be observed here, that after the British Revolution, in 1688, the Westminster Confession of Faith was established, as the standard of orthodoxy, and the Presbyterian form of Church-government was also established, in all it's extent, in Scotland; but alas! the Covenants were over-looked or forgotten.[a] It is certainly matter of great lamentation, that these solemn deeds, which our noble ancestors very highly esteemed and rejoiced in, should be either over-looked or forgotten. It was one design of this publication, to keep these solemn deeds in remembrance, and excite mankind to turn there attention seriously to the Covenanted work of Reformation. But, alas! that glorious work seems, at this time, to occupy very little of our attention. The time, however, of favouring Zion will come; even the time which Jehovah himself has unalterably fixed. *For the vision is yet for an appointed time, but at the end it shall speak, and not lie: though it tarry, wait for it; because it will surely come, it will not tarry.*

Let us now hear the conclusion of the whole matter:

a Laing's Hist. Scot. vol. ii. B. x. p. 216. Anno 1690.

Fear God, and keep his commandments; for this is the whole (duty) of man. Let us attend carefully and strictly to both personal and family religion. Let us study *to do justly, and to love mercy, and to walk humbly with our God.* Let us *trust in the Lord for ever: for in the Lord Jehovah is everlasting strength.* Let us endeavour, through divine grace, in our station, to be *the salt of the earth, and the lights of the world;* to search the Holy Scriptures, bringing all to their test;—to *try the spirits whether they are of God;—to hold fast that which is good, contending earnestly for the faith once delivered to the saints; and to follow the Lamb whethersoever He goeth,* that we may be also *followers of them who through faith and paitience inherit the promises.*

And for the aid and encouragement of true Covenanters, and with a view to excite a laudable zeal for the glorious work of Reformation, two excellent Speeches which were delivered before subscribing the Covenant, at Margaret's Church, Westminster, on the 25th of Sep. 1643, are here subjoined at the end of this work, and as a conclusion to it. These Speeches were delivered by two eminent Divines, Messrs Nye and Henderson, and now follow.

An Exhortation made to the Honourable House of Commons, and Reverend Divines of the Assembly, by MR NYE, *before he read the Covenant.*

A GREAT and solemn work (Honourable and Reverend) this day is put into our hands, let us stir up and awaken our hearts unto it. We deal with God as well as with men, and with God in his greatness and excellency, for by him we swear; and at the same time we have to do with God and his goodness, who now reacheth out unto us a strong and seasonable arm of assistance. The goodness of God procuring succour and help to a sinful and afflicted people, (such are we) ought to be matter of fear and trembling even to all that hear of it, Jer. xxxiii. 9. We are to exalt and acknowledge him this day, who is fearful in praises, swear by that Name which is Holy and Reverend, enter into a Covenant and League that is never to be forgotten by us nor our posterity, and the fruit I hope of it shall be so great, as both we and they shall have cause to remember it with joy; and such an oath as for matter, persons, and other circumstances, the like hath not been in any age, or oath we read of in sacred or human stories, yet sufficiently warranted in both.

The parties engaging in this League, are three kingdoms, famous for the knowledge, and the acknowledgment of Christ above all the kingdoms in the world; to swear before such a presence, should mould the spirit of man into a great deal of reverence: what then to be engaged, to be incorporated, and that by sacred oath, with such an high and honourable fraternity? An oath is to be esteemed so much the more solemn, by how much greater the persons are that swear each to other: as in heaven when God swears to his Son, on earth, when kings swear each to other; so in this business, where kingdoms swear mutually.

And as the solemnity of an oath is to be measured by the persons swearing, so by the matter also that is to be sworn to. God would not swear to the covenant of works, he intended not to honour it so much, it was not to continue, it was not worthy of an oath of his; but to the covenant of grace, which is the gospel, he swears and repents not of it. God swears for the salvation of men, and of kingdoms: and if kingdoms swear, what subject of an oath becometh them better than the preservation and salvation of kingdoms, by establishing the kingdom of a Saviour amongst them, even our Lord and Saviour Jesus Christ, who is a Mediator and Saviour for nations as well as particular persons?

The end also is great and honourable, as either of the former. *Two is better than one*, saith he, who best knoweth what is best; and from whom alone every thing hath the goodness it hath. Association is of divine offspring; not only the being of creatures, but the putting of them together: the clustre as well as the grape is the work of God: consort and harmony amongst men, especially amongst saints, is very pleasing unto the Lord; if when but two or three agree and assent upon any thing on earth, it shall be confirmed in heaven: and for this, because they gather together in his Name, much more when two or three kingdoms shall meet and consent together *in his Name, and for his Name, that God may be one, and his Name one amongst them*, and his presence amidst them. That prayer of Christ seemeth to proceed from a feeling sense of his own blessedness, *Father, that they may be one, as thou in me*, &c. Unity amongst his churches and children must needs therefore be very acceptable unto him: for out of the more deep sense, desires are fetcht from within us, the more pleasing will be the answer of them unto us. Churches and kingdoms are near to God, his patience towards them, his compassions over them more than particular persons, sheweth it plainly. But kingdoms willingly engaging themselves for his kingdom, his Christ, his saints, the purity of religion, his worship and government, in all particulars, and in all humility sitting down at his feet to receive the law, and the rule from his mouth; what a price doth he set upon such? especially, when (as we this day) sensible of our infirmity, of an unfaithful heart not steady with our God, but apt to start from the cause, if we feel the knife or the fire; who bind ourselves with cords, as a sacrifice to the horns of the altar: we invocate the name of the great God, that his vows, yea, his curse may be upon us, if we do not this; yea, though we suffer for so doing, that is, if we endeavour not so far as the Lord shall assist us by his grace, to advance the kingdom of the Lord Jesus Christ here upon earth, and make *Jerusalem* once more the praise of the whole world notwithstanding all the contradictions of men.

What is this but the contents and matter of our oath? what do we covenant? what do we vow? is it not the preservation of religion, where it is reformed, and the reformation of religion, where it needs? is it not the reformation of three kingdoms, and a reformation universal, in doctrine, discipline, and worship, in whatsoever the word shall discover unto us? To practise, is a fruit of love;

to reform, a fruit of zeal; but so to reform, will be a token of great prudence and circumspection in each of these churches: and all this to be done according to God's word, the best rule, and according to the best reformed churches, the best interpreters of this rule. If *England* hath obtained to any greater perfection in so handling the word of righteousness, and truths, that are according to godliness, as to make men more godly, more righteous: and, if in the Churches of *Scotland* any more light and beauty in matters of order and discipline, by which their Assemblies are more orderly: or, if to any other Church, or person, it hath been given better to have learned Christ in any of his ways, than any of us, we shall humbly bow, and kiss their lips that can speak right words unto us, in this matter, and help us into the nearest uniformity with the word and mind of Christ in this great work of reformation.

Honourable and Reverend Brethren, there cannot be a more direct and effectual way to exhort and persuade the wise, and men of sad and serious spirits (and such are you to whom I am commanded to speak this day) than to let into their understandings the weight, and worth, and great importance of the work, they are persuaded unto. This oath is such, and in the matter and consequence of it, of such concernment, as I can truly say, it is worthy of us, yea, of all these kingdoms, yea, of all the kingdoms of the world; for it is swearing fealty and allegiance unto Christ, the King of kings; and a giving up of all these kingdoms which are in his inheritance, to be subdued more to his throne, and ruled more by his sceptre, upon whose shoulders the government is laid, and, *in the increase of whose government and peace there shall be no end*, Isa. ix. Yea, we find this very thing in the utmost accomplishment of it, to have been the oath of the greatest Angel that ever was, who setting his feet upon two of God's kingdoms, the one upon the sea, the other upon the earth, lifting up his hand to heaven, as you are to do this day, and so swearing, Rev. x. The effect of that oath you shall find to be this, that the kingdoms of the world become the kingdoms of the Lord and his Christ, and he shall reign for ever, Rev. xi. His oath was for the full and final accomplishment, this of yours for a gradual, yet a great performance towards it.

That which the apostles and primitive times did so much and so long pray for, though never long with much quietness enjoyed, that which our fathers in these latter times have fasted, prayed and mourned after, yet attained not; even the cause which many dear saints now with God, have furthered by extremest sufferings, poverty, imprisonment, banishment, death, even ever since the first dawning of Reformation: that and the very same is the very cause and work that we are come now, through the mercy of Jesus Christ, not only to pray for, but swear too. And surely it can be no other, but the result and answer of such prayers and tears of such sincerity and sufferings, that three kingdoms should be thus born, or rather new born in a day; that these kingdoms should be wrought about to so great an engagement, than which nothing is higher: for to this end, kings reign, kingdoms stand, and states are upheld.

It is a special grace and favour of God unto you Brethren, Reverend and Honourable, to vouchsafe you the opportunity, and to put into your hearts (as this day) to engage your lives and estates in matters so much concerning him and his glory. And if you should do no more but lay a foundation stone in this great work, and by so doing engage posterity after you to finish it, it were honour enough: but there may yet further use be made of you, who now are to take this oath: you are designed as chief master-builders and choice instruments for the effecting of this settled peace and reformation; which, if the Lord shall please to finish in your hands, a greater happiness on earth, nor a greater means to augment your glory and crown in heaven, you are not capable of. And this let me further add for your encouragement, of what extensive good and fruit in the success of it, this very oath may prove to be, we know not. God hath *set his covenant like the heavens*, not only for duration, but like also for extension. The heavens move and roll about, and so communicate their light, and heat, and virtue, to all places and parts of the earth; so doth the *Covenant* of God; so may this gift be given to other covenants that are framed to that pattern. How much this Solemn League and Oath may provoke other Reformed Churches to a further reformation of themselves; what light and heat it may communicate abroad to other parts of the world, it is only in Him to define to whom is given the *utmost ends of the earth for his inheritance*, and worketh by his exceeding great power, great things out of as small beginnings.

But however, this I am sure of, it is a way in all probability most likely to enable us to preserve and defend our religion against *our common enemies;* and possibly a more sure foundation this day will be laid for ruining popery and prelacy, the chief of them, than as yet we have been led into in any age.

For popery, it hath been a religion ever dexterous in fencing and mounting itself by association and joint strength. All sorts of professors amongst them are cast into fraternities and brother-hoods; and these orders carefully united by vow one with another and under some more general notion of common dependence. Such states also and kingdoms as they have thus made theirs, they endeavour to improve and secure by strict combinations and leagues each to other, witness of late years that *La Sainte ligue*, the holy league. It will not be unworthy your consideration, whether, seeing the preservation of popery hath been by leagues and covenant, God may not make a league or covenant to be the destruction of it. Nay, the very rise of popery seemeth to be after such a manner by kings, that is, kingdoms assenting and agreeing perhaps by some joint covenant (the text saith, *with one mind*, why not then with one mouth) to give their power and strength unto the Beast, and make war against the Lamb, Rev. xvii. where you read the Lamb shall overcome the Beast, and possibly with the same weapons: he is the Lord of lords, and King of kings, he can unite kings and kingdoms, and give them one mind also to destroy the whore, and be her utter ruin. And may not this day's work be a happy beginning of such a blessed expedition?

Prelacy another common enemy, that we covenant and swear against. What hath been, or what hath the strength of it been, but a subtile combination of clergy-men formed into a policy or body of their own invention, framing themselves into subordination and dependance one upon another; so that the interest of each is improved by all, and a great power by this means acquired to themselves, as by sad experience we have lately found. The joints and members of this body, you know were knit together by the sacred engagement of an oath, the oath of canonical obedience as they called it. You remember also with what cunning industry they endeavoured lately to make this oath and covenant more sure for themselves and their posterity, and intended a more public, solemn and universal engagement, than since popery this cause of theirs was ever maintained or supported by. And questionless, *Ireland* and *Scotland* also must at last have been brought into this holy league with *England*. But blessed be the Lord, and blessed be his good hand the Parliament, that from the indignation of their spirits against so horrid a yoke, have dashed out the very brains of this project, and are now this day present before the Lord to take and give possession of this blessed ordinance, even an oath and covenant as solemn and of as large extent as they intended theirs, uniting these three kingdoms into such a league and happy combination as will doubtless preserve us and our reformation against them, though their iniquity in the mysteries of it should still be working amongst us. *Come* therefore (I speak in the words of the Prophet) *let us join ourselves to the Lord*, and one to another, and each to all, *in a perpetual covenant that shall not be forgotten.*

We are now entering upon a work of the greatest moment and concernment to us, and to our posterity after us, that ever was undertaken by any of us, or any of our fore-fathers before us, or neighbouring nations about us; if the Lord shall bless this our beginning, it will be a happy day, and we shall be a happy people. An oath is a duty of the first commandment, and therefore of the highest and noblest order and rank of duties, therefore must come forth attended with choicest graces, especially with these two, humility, and fear.

Fear, not only of God, which ought to be in an eminent measure, Gen. xxxi. 53. *Jacob* sware by the fear of his father *Isaac*, as if he coveted to inherit his father's grace, as well as his father's God: but also, fear of an oath it being a dreadful duty, and hath this peculiar, it is established by the oath of God, *I have sworn, that unto me every tongue shall swear*, Isa. xlv. 23. It is made the very character of a saint, he fears an oath, Eccl. ix. 2.

Humility is another grace requisite. Set your hearts before God in an humble obedient frame; Deut. ix. *Thou shalt fear the Lord thy God, and serve him, and swear by his name.* The apostle Paul was sensible of this engagement, even in the very act of this duty, Rom. i. 9. *I call God to witness, whom I serve in my spirit;* although it be a work of the lips, yet the heart and the whole man must be interested if we expect this worship to be acceptable, Psal. cxix. 108. *Accept the free-will offering of my mouth, and teach me thy judgments.*

Also it must be done in the greatest simplicity and plainness of spirit, in respect of those with whom we covenant; we call God as a witness betwixt us who searcheth the heart: *with him is wisdom and strength, the deceived and deceiver is his*, Job xii. 19. He hath wisdom to discover, and strength to punish, if our hearts be not upright to our brethren in this matter. Let us be contented with this, that the words of our covenant be bands, it may not be so much as in the desire of our hearts that they should become snares, no not to the weakest and simplest person that joineth with us. On the whole work, make your address unto God, as *Jacob* did to his father *Isaac*, and let there be the like fear and jealousy over your spirits, Gen. xxvii. 12. *My father peradventure will feel me, and I shall seem to him as a deceiver, and I shall bring a curse upon me, and not a blessing.*

I take liberty with more earnestness to press this care upon you, because I have observed, oaths and covenants have been undertaken by us formerly, and by the command of authority, the fruit whereof, though great, yet not answered our expectation; the Lord surely hath been displeased with the slightness of our hearts in the work. I beseech you be more watchful, and stir up your hearts with more industry this day than ever before. As it is the last oath you are likely to take in this kind, so is it our last refuge, *tabula post naufragium.* If this help us not, we are likely to remain to our dying day, an unhappy people; but if otherwise, *you will indeed swear with all your hearts, and seek the Lord with your whole desire, God will be found, and give you rest round about,* 2 Chro. xv. 15.

And having sworn, and entered into this solemn engagement to God and man, make conscience to do accordingly, otherwise it is better thou shouldst not vow, Eccl. v. As is said of fasting, it is not the bowing down of the head for a day, so of this solemn swearing; it is not the lifting up of the hand for a day, but an honest and faithful endeavouring after the contents of this covenant all our days A truce-breaker is reckoned up amongst the vilest of Christians, 2 Tim. iii. 3. So a covenant-breaker is lifted up amongst the worst of Heathens, Rom. i. 31. But he that sweareth and changeth not, though he swear to his hurt, that is, he that will keep his Covenant and Oath, though the contents of it prove not for him, nay possibly against him, yet he will keep it for his oath's sake, such a one *shall have his habitation with the Most High, and dwell in his tabernacle,* Psal. xv. And as for you, Reverend Brethren, that are Ministers of the gospel, there is yet another obligation will lie upon you: let us look to ourselves, and make provision to walk answerable to this our Covenant for the gospel's sake; it will reflect a great asperation upon the truth of the gospel, if we should be false or unconstant in any word or purpose, though in a matter of less consequence, as you can easily, collect from that apology of *Paul,* 2 Cor. i. 17, 18, how much more in such a case as this is, if we should be found to purpose, nay more, to vow, and covenant, and swear, and all this *according unto the flesh, and with us there should be,* notwithstanding all these obligations, *yea, yea,* and *nay nay.*

That we may all who take the Covenant this day, be

constant, immoveble, and abound in this work of the Lord, that we may not start aside, or give back, or go on uncomfortably, there is a twofold grace or qualification to be laboured after.

1. We must get courage, spirits that are bold and resolute. It is said in *Haggai*, that *the Lord stirred up the spirit of Zerubbabel governor of Judah, and the spirit of Joshua the high priest, and the spirit of all the remnant of the people, and they came, and did work in the house of the Lord.* The work of God's house, reformation-work especially, is a stirring work: read stories, you find not any where, reformation made in any age, either in doctrine or discipline, without great stir and opposition. This was foretold by the same prophet, Chap. ii. ver. 7. the promise is, *He will fill his house with glory.* But what goeth before, ver. 6. *Yet once it is a little while and I will shake the heavens, and the earth and the sea, and the dry land, that is all nations,* as in the words following. This place is applied Heb. xii. to the removing Jewish rites, the moveables of God's house The like you find in the apostles' times, Acts xvii. the truth being preached, some believed, others did not: here beginneth the stir, ver. 6. Those that believed not, *took unto themselves certain lewd fellows of the baser sort, and gathered a company, and set all the city in an uproar;* and when they had done so, complained of the brethren to the rulers, as men that *turn the world upside down,* ver. 6. read also Acts xxi. 27, 30, 31. In such a work therefore, men had need be of stout, resolute, and composed spirits, that we may be able to go on in the main, and stir in the midst of such stirs, and not be amazed at any such doings. It may possibly happen, that even amongst yourselves, there will be outcries, Sir, you will undo all, saith one, you will put all into confusion, saith another; if you take this course, saith a third, we can expect nothing but blood: but a wise statesman, like an experienced seaman, knoweth the compass of his vessel, and though it heave, toss, and the passengers cry out about him, yet in the midst of all, he is himself, turneth not aside from his work, but steereth on his course. I beseech you, let

it be seriously considered, if you mean to do any such work in the house of God as this is; if you mean to pluck up what many years ago was planted, or to build up what so long ago was pulled down, and to go through with this work, and not be discouraged, you must beg of the Lord this excellent spirit, this resolute stirring spirit, otherwise you will be outspirited, and both you and your cause slighted and dishonoured.

2. On the other hand, we must labour for humility, prudence, gentleness, meekness. A man may be very zealous and resolute, and yet very meek and merciful: Jesus Christ was a Lion and yet a Lamb also; in one place he telleth them, he cometh to send *fire on the earth:* and in another place, rebuketh his disciples for their fiery spirits, Luke ix. 59. There was the like composition in *Moses*, and in *Paul;* and it is of great use, especially in this work of reformation. I have not observed any disputes carried on with more bitterness in men's writings, and with more unsanctified heat of spirit. yea, and by godly men too, than in controversies, about discipline, Church-government, ceremonies, and the like. Surely, to argue about government with such ungoverned passions, to argue for reformation with a spirit so unreformed, is very uncomely. Let us be zealous, as Christ was, to cast out all, to extirpate and root out every plant his heavenly Father hath not planted; and yet let us do it in an orderly way, and with the Spirit of Christ, whose servants we are. *The servant of the Lord must not strive, but be gentle to all men, apt to teach, patient, in meekness instructing those that oppose*, 2 Tim. ii. 24, 25. We solemnly engage this day our utmost endeavours for reformation; let us remember this, that too much heat, as well as too much coldness, may harden men in their ways, and hinder reformation.

Brethren, let us come to this blessed work with such a frame of heart, with such a mind for the present, with such resolutions for the time to come; let us not be wanting to the opportunity, God hath put into our hands this day; and then I can promise you, as the prophet, *consider this day and upwards, even from this day, that the foundation of the Lord's work is laid, consider it, from this day will I bless you, saith the Lord.* Nay, we have received as it were the first fruits of this promise; for as it is said of *some men's good works, they are manifest before hand,* 1 Tim. v. even so may be said of the good work of this day. it is manifest before hand. God hath as it were before hand testified his acceptance; while we were thinking and purposing this free-will offering, he was protecting and defending our army, causing our enemies, the enemies of this work to flee before us, and gave us a victory, not to be despised. Surely this Oath and Covenant shall be *Judah's* joy, the joy and comfort of this whole kingdom, yea, of all the three kingdoms.

Jesus Christ King of the saints govern us by his Spirit, strengthen us by his power, undertake for us according as he hath sworn, even *the oath which he sware to our father* Abraham, *that he would grant unto us, that we being delivered out of the hands of our enemies, might serve him without fear, in holiness and righteousness before him all the days of our life,* Luke i. Grant unto us also, that when this life is finished, and we gathered to our fathers, there may be a generation out of our loins to stand up in this cause, that his great, and reverend name may be exalted from one generation to another, until he himself shall come, and perfect all with his own wisdom: even so come Lord Jesus, come quickly, Amen.

A Speech delivered by Mr Alexander Henderson*, immediately before the taking of the Covenant by the House of Commons, and Assembly of Divines.*

ALTHOUGH the time be far spent, yet am I bold (Honourable, Reverend, and beloved in the Lord) to crave your patience a little. It were both sin and shame to us in this so acceptable a time in this day, which the Lord hath made, to be silent and to say nothing: if we should hold our peace, we could neither be answerable to God, whose cause and work is in hand, nor to this Church and kingdom, unto which we have made so large profession of duty, and owe much more; nor to our native kingdom, so abundant in affection towards you; nor to our own hearts, which exceedingly rejoice to see this day: we have greater reason than the leprous men sitting in a time of great extremity at the gate of *Samaria*, to say one to another, We do not well, this day is a day of good tidings, and we hold our peace; it is true the *Syrians* are not yet fled; but our hope is through God, that the work begun this day, being sincerely performed and faithfully pursued, shall put to flight, not only the *Syrians* and *Babylonians*, but all other enemies of the Church of God, of the king's honour, and of our liberty and peace.

For it is acceptable to God, and well pleasing in his sight, when his people come willingly in the day of his power (and how shall they not be willing in the day of his power?) to enter into a religious Covenant with him, and amongst themselves whatsoever be the condition of the people of God, whether in sorrow and humiliation before deliverance, or in rejoicing and thanksgiving after deliverance. This is it which the Lord waits for at their hands, which they have been used to perform, and with which he hath been so well pleased, that it hath been the fountain of many deliverances and blessings unto them. When a people beginneth to forget God, he lifteth up his hand against them and smiteth them: and when his people humbled before him, lift up their hands not only in supplication, but in Covenant before the most High God, he is pleased (such is his mercy and wonderful compassion) first, to lift up his hand unto them, saying, *I am the Lord your God*, as we have it three times in two verses of the twentieth of Ezekiel: and next he stretcheth out his hand against his enemies and theirs. It is the best work of faith, to join in Covenant with God, the best work of love and Christian communion to join in Covenant with the people of God; the best work of the best zeal, to join in Covenant for reformation, against the enemies of God and religion; the best work of true loyalty, to join in Covenant for the preservation of our kin and superiors; and the best proof of natural affection, (and to be without natural affection, is one of the great sins of the Gentiles) to join in Covenant for defence of our native country, liberties, and laws. Such, as from these necessary ends do with-draw, and are not willing to enter into Covenant, have reason to enter into their own hearts, and to look into their own faith, love, zeal, loyalty, and natural affection.

As it is acceptable to God, so have we for it the precedent and example, not only of the people of God of old, of the reformed Churches of *Germany*, and the Low Countries; but of our own noble and Christian progenitors in the time of the danger of religion, which is expressed in the Covenant itself. The defect was, they went not on throughly to enter in a solemn Covenant, an happiness reserved for this time; which had they done, the corruptions and calamities of these days might have been prevented. And if the Lord shall be pleased to move, loose, and enlarge the hearts of his people in His Majesty's dominions to take this Covenant, not in simulation, nor in lukewarmness, as those that are almost persuaded to be Christians, but as becometh the people of God, it shall be the prevention of many evils and miseries, and a mean of many and rich blessings, spiritual and temporal to ourselves, our little ones, and the posterity that shall come after us for many generations.

The near and neighbouring example of the Church and Kingdom of *Scotland*, is in this case worthy of our best observation: when the Prelates there, were grown by their rents and lordly dignities, by their exorbitant power over all sorts of his Majesty's subjects, ministers and others, by their places in Parliament, Council, College of Justice, Exchequer, and High Commission, to a monstrous dominion and greatness, and like giants, setting their one foot on the neck of the Church, and the other on the neck of the State, were become intolerably insolent. And when the people of God through their oppression in religion, liberties and laws, and what was dearest unto them, were brought so low that they choosed rather to die, than to live in such slavery, or to live in any other place, rather than in their own native country: then did the Lord say, *I have seen, I have seen the affliction of my people, and I have heard their groaning, and am come down to deliver them.* The beginnings were small, and contemptible in the eyes of the presumptuous enemies, such as used to be the beginnings of the greatest works of God; but were so seconded and continually followed by the undeniable evidences of Divine Providence, leading them forward from one step to another, that their mountain became strong in the end. No tongue can tell what motions filled the hearts, what tears were poured forth from the eyes, and what cries came from the mouths of many thousands in that land, when they found an unwonted flame warming their breasts, and perceived the power of God raising them from the dead, and creating for them a new world, wherein should dwell religion and righteousness. When they were destitute both of monies and munition, which next unto the spirit and arms of men, are the sinews of war, the Lord brought them forth out of his hid treasures, which was wonderful in their eyes, and matter of astonishment to their hearts; when they were many times at a pause in their deliberations, and brought to such perplexity, that they knew not what to choose or to do for prosecuting the work of God, only their eyes were towards him; not only the fears and furies, but the plots also and policies of the adversaries, opened the way unto them, their devices were turned upon their own heads, and served for the promoting of the work of God. The purity of their intentions elevated above base and earthly respects, and the constant peace of their hearts in the midst of many dangers, did bear them out against the malicious accusations and aspersions put upon their actions: all which, were sensible impressions of the good Providence of God, and legible characters of his work; which as the Church and Kingdom of *England* exercised at this time with greater difficulty than theirs, have in part already found; so shall the parallel be perfected to their greater comfort in the faithful pursuing of the work unto the end.

Necessity, which hath in it a kind of sovereignity, and is a law above all laws, and therefore is said to have no law, doth mightily press the Church and Kingdom of *Scot-*

land at this time. It is no small comfort unto them, that they have not been idle and at ease, but have used all good and lawful means of supplications, declarations and remonstrances to His Majesty, for quenching the combustion in this Kingdom: and after all these, that they sent Commissioners to His Majesty, humbly to mediate for a reconcilement and pacification: but the offer of their humble service was rejected from no other reason, but that they had no warrant nor capacity for such a mediation; and that the intermixture of the government of the Church of *England*, with the civil government of the Kingdom, was such a mystery as could not be understood by them. Although it be true, which was at that time often replied, that the eight demand of the treaty, and the answer given thereunto, concerning the uniformity of religion, was a sufficient ground of capacity; and the proceedings of the Houses of Parliament against Episcopal government, as a stumbling block hindering Reformation, and as a prejudice to the Civil State, was ground enough for their information. The Commissioners having returned from his Majesty without success, and the miseries of *Ireland*, the distresses of *England*, and the dangers and pressures of the Kingdom of *Scotland* growing to greater extremity; such as were intrusted with the public affairs of the Kingdom, were necessitate, according to the practice of former times, His Majesty having denied a Parliament, to call a Convention of the Estates, for considering of the present affairs, and for providing the best remedies: which immediately upon their meeting, by the special Providence of God, did receive information of diverse treacherous attempts of papists in all the three Kingdoms, as if they had been called for that effect. And by the same Providence, Commissioners were sent from both Houses of Parliament, to consider with the Estates of the Kingdom of *Scotland*, of such articles and propositions, as might make the conjunction betwixt the two nations, more beneficial and effectual for the securing of religion and liberty against papists and prelates with their adherents. Their consultations with the Commissioners of the General Assembly, did in the end bring forth a Covenant, as the only mean after all other have been essayed, for the deliverance of *England* and *Ireland* out of the depths of affliction, preservation of the Church an Kingdom of *Scotland* from the extremity of misery, and the safety of our native King and his kingdoms, from destruction and desolation. This is the manifold necessity, which nature, religion, loyalty and love hath laid upon them.

Nor is it unknown in this Honourable, Reverend and wise Audience, what errors and heresies in doctrine; what superstition and idolatry in worship, what usurpation and tyranny in government, what cruelty against the souls and bodies of the saints have been set on foot, exercised, and executed for many generations, and now of late by the Roman Church. All which we hope, through the blessing of God upon this work shall be brought to an end. Had the Pope at *Rome* the knowledge of what is doing this day in *England*, and were this Covenant written on the plaister of the wall over against him, where he sitteth *Belshazzar*-like in his sacrilegious pomp, it would make his heart to tremble, his countenance to change, his head and mitre to shake, his joints to loose, and all his cardinals and prelates to be astonished.

When the reformed Churches, which by their letters have been exciting us to Christian communion and sympathy in this time of the danger of religion and distress of the godly, shall hear of this blessed conjunction for uniformity in religion, according to the word of God and the defence thereof, it shall quicken their hearts against the heaviness of oppressing sorrows and fears; and be no other than a beginning of a jubilee and joyful deliverance unto them, from the antichristian yoke and tyranny.

Upon these and the like considerations, we are very confident, that the Church and Kingdom of *Scotland* will most cheerfully join in this Covenant; at the first motion whereof, their bowels were moved within them. And to give testimony of this our confidence, we who are Commissioners from the General Assembly, although we have no particular and express Commission for that end (not from want of willingness, but of foresight) offer to join our hearts and hands unto it, being assured, that the

Lord in his own time will, against all opposition, even against the gates of hell, crown it with a blessing from heaven. The word of God is for it, as you have been now resolved by the consent and testimony of a Reverend Assembly of so many godly, learned, and great *Divines.* In your own sense and experience, you will find, that although, while you are assaulted or exercised with worldly cares and fears, your thoughts may somewhat trouble and divert you; yet at other times, when upon seeking of God in private or public, as in the evening of a well spent Sabbath or day of fast and humiliation, your disposition is more spiritual and leaving the world behind you; you have found access unto God through *Jesus Christ;* the bent and inclinations of your hearts will be strongest to go through with this work. It is a good testimony that our designs and ways are agreeable to the will of God, if we affect them most when our hearts are furthest from the world, and our temper is most spiritual and heavenly, and least carnal and earthly. As the word of God, so the prayers of the people of God in all the reformed Churches are for us and on our side. It were more terrible than an army, to hear that there were any fervent supplications to God against us: blasphemies, curses, and horrid imprecations there be, proceeding from another spirit, and that is all. That Divine Providence also which hath maintained this cause, and supported his servants in a marvellous manner unto this day, and which this time past hath kept things in an equal balance and vicissitude of success, will, we trust from this day forth, through the weight of this Covenant, cast the balance and make religion and righteousness to prevail, to the glory of God, the honour of our King, the confusion of our common enemies, and the comfort and safety of the people of God: which may He grant, who is able to do above any thing that we can ask or think.

END OF VOL. II.

CONTENTS

OF VOLUME II.

SCOTTISH COMMISSIONERS.

SCRIBES.

APPENDIX.